Arresting Contagion

Arresting | Contagion

SCIENCE, POLICY, AND CONFLICTS OVER ANIMAL DISEASE CONTROL

Alan L. Olmstead | Paul W. Rhode

 Harvard University Press

Cambridge, Massachusetts
London, England   2015

Second printing

Library of Congress Cataloging-in-Publication Data

Olmstead, Alan L., author.
  Arresting contagion : science, policy, and conflicts over animal disease control / Alan
L. Olmstead and Paul W. Rhode.
      p. ; cm.
  Includes bibliographical references and index.
  ISBN 978-0-674-72877-6 (alk. paper)
  1. Communicable diseases in animals—United States—Prevention.   2. Livestock—
Diseases—United States—Prevention.   3. Animals—Diseases—United States—Prevention.
4. Animal health.   5. Food—Safety measures.   I. Rhode, Paul Webb, author.   II. Title.

  [DNLM: 1. United States. Bureau of Animal Industry. 2. Animal Diseases—history—
United States. 3. Disease Transmission, Infectious—prevention & control—United States.
4. Health Policy—history—United States. 5. History, 19th Century—United States.
6. History, 20th Century—United States. SF 623]

SF781.O46 2015
636.089'69—dc23   2014016723

To Marilyn, Dolores,
Edward, and Jason

Contents

Figures and Tables

Figures

Tables

Arresting | Contagion

1 An Enduring Struggle

AFTER A LONG BATTLE, victory. In October 2011, the Food and Agriculture Organization of the United Nations announced the global eradication of rinderpest, the most feared of all livestock diseases.[1] The systematic global eradication of a contagious disease had been declared only once before, with the conquest of smallpox in 1980. Rinderpest, a highly contagious viral disease, had long ravaged populations of cattle, water buffalo, sheep, goats, and other animals. It repeatedly battered Europe, likely killing over 200 million cattle in outbreaks in the eighteenth century. The reappearance of the "cattle plague" in Britain in 1865 spawned that nation's first systematic policies to combat animal diseases. The disease hit the horn of Africa in 1888 and spread south to the Cape Colony by 1896, contributing to one of the worst famines in that continent's history. Rinderpest was not to be trifled with: during World War II, a joint U.S. and Canadian biowarfare team selected rinderpest as its weapon of choice. In a secret laboratory on a St. Lawrence River island, scientists worked with the live virus to build offensive and defensive capabilities.[2]

The threat of rinderpest played a vital role in the birth of U.S. livestock disease policy: in December 1865, Congress temporarily prohibited the importation of cattle, and a short time later the Senate directed Commissioner of Agriculture Isaac Newton to investigate claims that the contagion had jumped the Atlantic. He determined that the reports were unfounded, but called for new laws to contain and destroy infected cattle within a "military cordon" should the disease ever strike.[3] Newton also recommended strengthening import controls and establishing quarantine stations. After the threat of rinderpest subsided, Congress lost interest in Newton's proposals.[4] The United States escaped the rinderpest epizootic, but other devastating livestock diseases did leap the nation's

1

ocean defenses. The spread of these new contagions along with the advance of diseases already enzootic in parts of the United States created serious health concerns.

Many present-day readers have likely never heard of rinderpest. The great cattle plague and other scourges that ravished livestock a century ago have passed from memory. Animal diseases still register in the public consciousness today, albeit more weakly, in the form of mad cow disease and other emerging risks. This book investigates the largely untold history of government interventions to combat livestock infections and contagions in the United States.[5]

Congress empowered a new agency in 1884 to fight livestock diseases. This move predated what is commonly considered the first significant federal thrust into economic regulation and also predated any sustained federal push to directly improve human health. The agency would make spectacular advances in both science and public policy. It is credited with creating the template for regional disease eradication that would be used around the world in fighting rinderpest and other animal and human diseases. This book shows how this agency evolved to overcome great obstacles, including ignorance, rampant disease denialism, constitutional impediments, knotty jurisdictional conflicts, and strong grassroots resistance. Its successes have led later generations to take these accomplishments for granted and to forget the scientific and political challenges that had to be overcome. Our story highlights how scientific advances interacted with public policy innovations to address serious animal and human health problems.[6]

Boundaries and Contagions

During the nineteenth century, the animal disease environment was growing worse in the United States. Contagious diseases were spreading unchecked in the country's livestock populations, sapping their health and productivity. Increasing specialization and trade among producers and improvements in transportation were making matters worse. Contagions paid no heed to political boundaries. Many states responded by enacting livestock sanitary laws and blocking interstate commerce.[7] This invariably incited charges that states were using health concerns as a ruse to protect their own producers from legitimate competition. Such charges were at times justifiable, but producers and their elected representatives in infected areas were also often in a state of denial. Furthermore, while the states bickered among themselves, many European nations restricted imports of U.S. livestock and livestock products. Clean states could not differentiate their products from those of infected states in international markets, so all suffered. For these and other reasons, state initiatives proved ineffective in the battle to control livestock contagions.

The increased threat of livestock diseases, coupled with the failure of state actions, increased the demand for federal intervention. At the same time, a small cadre of scientists defined the problem and created blueprints for action. These leaders emphasized that given the cumulative nature of contagions, interventions were more efficient before diseases became well established. Time was of the essence, but the political and legal institutions were slow to adapt. Step by step, Congress created a powerful national animal health bureaucracy, complete with authority to impose domestic and international quarantines, to advance scientific knowledge, and to conduct eradication campaigns within states. The federal courts increasingly upheld Congress's assertions of power over what had been the exclusive domain of the states. This was a contentious process, which repeatedly pitted powerful ideological, regional, and economic interests against one another. These battles over livestock health helped redefine American federalism and shape economic regulation in the United States. The scientists who directed the new institutions would have a major impact on enhancing agricultural productivity nationally and globally.

One Health

Much more than agricultural productivity was at stake. According to a recent estimate by the U.S. Centers for Disease Control and Prevention (CDC), approximately 60 percent of all infectious diseases affecting humans (and 75 percent of emerging infectious diseases) are shared by other vertebrate animals. Other authorities estimate that the percentages are even higher. These shared and transmissible diseases—zoonoses—include anthrax, brucellosis, cholera, Ebola, influenza, mad cow disease, malaria, plague, rabies, salmonellosis, trichinosis, tuberculosis, yellow fever, and hundreds of other killers.[8] The great fear of scientists who specialize in disease prevention is not *if* but *when* a new disease will emerge in animal populations and adapt to infect humans. Humans contract many zoonoses solely from other animal species. The most effective method of combating many zoonoses is to introduce more hygienic processing and distribution systems for animals and animal products, and to treat or cull the diseased animals. For these reasons, livestock sanitation policies, including those aimed at improving milk and meat hygiene, have had a significant impact on human health.

Animal health policies have contributed to preventing illnesses that otherwise might have killed hundreds of thousands of Americans in the first half of the twentieth century. There has been a close synergy between advances in animal and human medicine. Many scientific breakthroughs resulted from research that transcended traditional disciplinary boundaries.

The ethics and constraints governing animal health policies have differed from those governing human health. Most people care more about their own health than that of their animals, and most consider a human life more valuable than an animal's life. One might predict accordingly that human health would have advanced faster than animal health—but the reverse has often been the case. Law and custom have long prohibited using human bodies to conduct medical training and research, so much of what physicians learned in the past about human physiology was based on animal models. In addition, it has been easier to control livestock diseases because authorities can test and quarantine animals more indiscriminately, slaughter sick and suspect animals, and even depopulate entire districts.[9] But all such actions required a legal system that permitted the interruption of commerce, the confiscation of dangerous goods, and at times the payment of compensation. It also required leaders with a will to act. Studying changes in animal disease regimes sheds light on health policy more generally. Because disease control for livestock is less encumbered by the ethical constraints that apply to humans, the links between science, policy, and results are often sharper for livestock.

Societies have confronted fundamental problems with respect to animal and public health: contagious diseases create negative externalities that are often hard to address without collective action, the presence of a contagion harms the common interest, and arresting contagions is a public good. Whereas individuals have incentives to protect themselves and their loved ones, the incentives are weak to invest privately in protecting strangers. The result is an underinvestment in pre-cautions against the spread of contagions. The same logic applies to states vis-à-vis other states. In many institutional settings, a livestock owner has an incentive to conceal diseased animals in the hope of selling them or seeing them recover. In regions where a contagion is prevalent, the prospect of reinfection reduces the incentives for individuals to invest in cleaning up their own animal stocks. Unless one's neighbors cooperate, such investments would likely be wasted.

In the past, decentralized efforts almost always proved ineffective. Those seeking to address contagions turned to government, which could exercise police power. There are economies of scale and scope in disease control. It is generally more efficient for a central entity to police one large, all-encompassing border (be it a county, state, nation, or continent) than for each political entity within the larger area to regulate its own frontier. Solving coordination problems has proved difficult everywhere, so it is all the more remarkable that the United States, with its cultural traditions of voluntarism, localism, and pluralism, was a successful pioneer in con-trolling animal contagions.

Building a Federal Bureaucracy

By 1900, the United States had emerged as a world leader in control-ling contagious animal diseases, even though the nation was a laggard in human medicine and the biological sciences more generally. The prin-cipal organization that led the fight against livestock diseases was the Bureau of Animal Industry (BAI), which was created within the U.S. Department of Agriculture (USDA) in 1884. For its first two decades, the BAI was energetically directed by the veterinary scientist Daniel E. Salmon. By the early 1940s, the BAI had led campaigns that eradicated seven major animal diseases in the United States: contagious bovine pleuro-pneumonia (1892), fowl plague (1929), foot-and-mouth disease (1929), glanders (1934), bovine tuberculosis (1940), dourine fever (1942), and Texas fever (1943). Its eradication campaigns were complex, large-scale policy experiments. The scientists who led the global smallpox eradica-tion program acknowledged this precedent when they noted that the BAI's campaign against contagious bovine pleuropneumonia (CBPP) was the world's "first planned programme whose stated objective was eradication."[10]

The BAI represented a major institutional innovation. As pioneering historian of science A. Hunter Dupree noted, Congress "created whole at a single stroke a new type of scientific agency." The BAI had an explicit scientific research mission, and it was to be headed by a scientist.[11] It soon would become a leader in transferring medical knowledge from Europe to the United States, and in generating original research aimed at understanding and solving animal disease problems. It established the "first significant microbiological laboratory in the United States in 1884"— several years before the founding of a hygienic laboratory by the predecessor to the National Institutes of Health (NIH).[12] Early BAI breakthroughs included the discovery of the *Salmonella* bacterium (named after Daniel Salmon), the first use of an artificially heat-killed culture to make a vaccine, the observations that led to the typing of distinct tuberculosis bacteria, and the first proof that an arthropod vector (in this case a cattle tick) transmitted a microorganism that caused an infectious disease (Texas fever). This latter discovery sped advances in the understanding of other vector-borne diseases, including malaria, yellow fever, typhus, plague, and African sleeping sickness. Other early breakthroughs included the development of practical methods to eradicate cattle ticks, the discovery of the virus that caused hog cholera, and the identification of the hookworm parasite, which afflicted people in the Southern states. BAI scientists made numerous other advances in bacteriology, virology, immunology, parasitology, and other emerging disciplines.

The BAI's public policy innovations were as important as its research contributions. The science underlying its triumphs was readily available to animal health officials in other countries, but few nations were as successful as the United States in converting science into effective public policies to control animal contagions. Changes in legal interpretations and in administrative capabilities accompanied scientific progress as officials learned how to construct effective institutions. Disease control campaigns required building social capital. This involved creating coordinated surveillance systems dependent on farmers and local veterinarians to ring the alarm, gaining the trust and cooperation of state and local officials and farmers, educating stock owners about new and often alien scientific ideas, implementing incentive-compatible compensation schemes, organizing rural plebiscites, and much more. In designing programs, one size did not fit all; a process of trial and error was involved in tailoring policies to counter the specific disease threats and to ensure that the interventions actually worked in the field.[13]

The constitutional necessity to gain state support led to novel cooperative agreements that redefined the frontiers of American federalism by transferring police power from the states to the national government. These changes occurred earlier in animal health than in many other policy arenas. The BAI could deploy trained experts to hot spots and intervene with near-dictatorial power to nip problems in the bud. This policy of concentrating authority was dubbed the "one man principle." The BAI's quarantine system repeatedly blocked the entry of diseases into the United States. The United States and Canada both eventually adopted an "island-nation" mentality similar to that developed earlier in Britain. It was wiser to invest in eradicating existing diseases and to prevent their reintroduction than to employ more lax policies and coexist with diseases, as had been common in most European countries.[14]

Public Policy and Political Economy

Within the field of public economics, there are two contrasting views regarding economic regulation. One is the *public choice* school, whose adherents are generally critical of government regulations. In this view, rent-seeking interest groups and bureaucrats push interventions to limit competition, thereby creating inefficiencies. The polar view is the *public interest* school, whose followers advocate regulation to address market imperfections and business abuses. Both schools offer insights, but the merit of each argument in particular cases is often clouded by conflicting evidence. Assessing the motives of individuals and the effects of policies is apt to be controversial. The desires to protect special interests, redistribute wealth and power, and harm potential competitors are ever present, and all policy innovations have involved winners and losers. However, in the case of animal diseases, market failures were serious, and government-led research and collective action generated immense benefits for the nation and the world. To gain insight into why key participants behaved as they did, we investigate their correspondence and internal memos. These documents provide valuable clues regarding the participants' motives and actions. Our story shows how scientists, a shifting galaxy of competing special interests both in and outside the agricultural sector, and policy makers (themselves often scientists) interacted to convince successive

Congresses and state legislatures to enact increasingly tougher laws and provide funding to control diseases. USDA leaders and in particular those at the BAI took center stage in this process.

Recent transnational studies have examined the changing political coalitions and distributional dynamics that give rise to tax, subsidy, and tariff policies. These studies often treat "farmers" as a monolithic class. This depiction of a unified farm interest is generally at odds with the history of animal disease control. Disputes within the farm community were the rule rather than the exception. Income, scale, and ethnicity appear to have mattered in some cases, but geography was the far more visible dividing line separating groups in many policy debates. Important farmer organizations fought each other over animal disease control policies. However, once American animal health policies were in place, they earned the support of many of the former opponents—both conservative and liberal administrations endorsed the policies. The development of rural infrastructure and communications networks also appear to have been important determinants of the support for health policies.[15]

Origins of Economic Regulation

Our account paints a richer picture of the rise of federal regulation than hitherto told. Federal, state, and local governments have all been active participants in the American economy since the colonial period. After the Revolution, states built and ran transportation networks, chartered corporations (including banks), and regulated public health and morals. After the ratification of the Constitution, the federal government enacted tariffs, established a postal system, created a patent system, chartered a succession of national banks, acquired and distributed land, organized marine hospitals, regulated the fur trade, and implemented transportation improvements. The federal courts were the final arbitrators in defining economic rules under the Constitution. The federal government first regulated steamboat safety in 1838. Congress passed tougher regulations in 1852, and in 1871 it created the Steamboat Inspection Service.[16] Apart from times of war, many of the federal government's activities were, in Brian Balogh's evocative phrase, "out of sight."[17] The late nineteenth century saw a major increase in federal intervention in the economy with the establishment of agencies that could investigate the activities of private enterprises, set rules, and dictate business behavior. This represented a qualitative as well as a quantitative change in government involvement.

The standard historical view is that the rise of Big Government was a response to the prior rise of Big Business. Big Government represented, depending on one's point of view, an attempt to control the exercise of market power or to redistribute wealth.[18] This story typically begins in 1887 with the creation of the Interstate Commerce Commission (ICC), established to regulate railroads. The next steps were the passage of the Sherman Anti-Trust Act of 1890 and the Meat Inspection Act of 1891— America's first significant federal food safety legislation. This chronology overlooks the regulatory significance of the BAI. Created several years before the ICC, the BAI sought to solve coordination problems associated with combating infectious diseases and reopening foreign markets that had been closed ostensibly for sanitary reasons. The stakes were huge— during the late nineteenth century, the capital stock (valued at current dollars) invested in livestock and accoutrements exceeded that invested in railroads.[19] A laissez-faire regime relying on the tort system and local police powers could not protect life and property against animal contagions. The federal government intervened aggressively to provide pragmatic solutions to a set of very complex problems.

Our story is tied to a broader literature on the origins of federal food safety regulation.[20] The traditional accounts, influenced by the muckraking exposés of Upton Sinclair, viewed the federal government's intervention as nothing less than a triumph of good over evil, with the new federal laws and regulatory agencies acting in the public interest to protect health. Over the past few decades, with the rise of the Chicago public choice school, this view has lost favor. In its general form, the public choice argument is that powerful groups, pursuing a narrow interest, push for policy changes at the expense of the politically weak. Concentrated, well-organized interests generally prevail over more diffused interests. In some cases, these changes might result in gains to society as a whole, but such an outcome is unlikely. According to this now popular interpretation, public interest played little or no role either in explaining the origins of the food safety and livestock sanitary legislation or in determining the *ex post* effects of the legislation. Rent-seeking special interests lobbied for food safety and livestock sanitary regulation to limit competition. Virtually all claims of dangerous infectious animal diseases are viewed as pretexts for protectionism, anticompetitive legislation, and expanding bureaucracies. The only parasites recognized in this perspective are redistributive politicians and their backers. The claims made in the public choice literature echo the denials about the dangers of animal contagions and charges of rent seeking made by past opponents of government intervention. Many of those past critics could at least claim that the germ theory of disease was something new and unproven.

We know that contagious human diseases were rampant in the past. We know that human life expectancy has increased sharply in the United States since 1850, largely as a result of the fall in infectious disease mortality. The decrease in infectious disease mortality began long before the commercial appearance of sulfa drugs in the 1930s and antibiotics in the 1940s. The advance of knowledge about how diseases spread, public health investments in cleaner water and better waste disposal, and mandatory vaccination were all among a longer list of reasons for the decline in human diseases. Enlightened public policies also helped control animal diseases and improve animal health. The control of zoonotic diseases in animals played an important role in improving human health.

We also know that food-borne illnesses remain a major threat to human health today. Nontyphoidal *Salmonella* is extremely dangerous—between 1996 and 1999, there were about 1.4 million cases of this food-borne disease in the United States every year. More generally, the CDC estimated that between 2000 and 2007 food-borne illnesses caused 48 million illnesses, 128,000 hospitalizations, and about 3,000 deaths per year in the United States.[21] Many of these food-borne illnesses were traced to contaminated meat, poultry, and eggs.[22] Given the situation today when more is understood about the incidence of food-borne illnesses, when pathogen detection systems are in place, and when food-handling technologies are vastly improved, there is every reason to think that far more serious food-safety problems existed in the past. The lower incidence of animal contagions today is in large measure thanks to government-financed research, conducted by publicly employed scientists, along with intrusive government regulations.

A glaring flaw with some of the recent economic literature is the proposed alternative to preemptive regulation—namely, using the tort system to recover damages from contagious diseases.[23] Historically, the tort system provided little compensation to injured parties. The information costs of determining the individual responsible for infecting oneself or one's animals were prohibitively high. In addition, many victims could be affected by the same source, creating free-rider problems in establishing damage claims. Given the contagious nature of many diseases, trying to handle problems *ex post* increased the likelihood that diseases would spread to third parties.[24] In such cases, it is more efficient to prevent damages *ex ante* via regulation and control than to identity the sources of harm and correct them after the fact. It is much cheaper to arrest contagions in their early stages before they spread widely.

Contours and Themes

The expansion of federal powers to regulate disease in the late nineteenth century was a long and difficult process in which political and legal institutions haltingly responded to forces that were transforming both the domestic and international economies. Chapter 2 analyzes some of the key changes. The decades before the establishment of the BAI (in 1884) were an era of scientific discovery, which saw the growing acceptance of the germ theory of disease. A new cadre of European-trained veterinary scientists sought to transfer their knowledge into effective public policy in the United States. The chapter introduces several themes, including the interplay of science and public policy, the controversial constitutional issues at stake, the regional schisms, and the prevailing culture of denial that delayed the advent of animal disease control policies.

The BAI designed and implemented disease control and food safety policy in the United States. Its creation represented a landmark in the history of federal regulation and the rise of science policy. Chapter 3 examines the congressional debates stretching over a decade that led to the BAI's creation. This legislative history, coupled with subsequent policy initiatives, shows that the BAI Act of 1884 has a better claim to represent the birth of significant federal economic regulation than does the Interstate Commerce Act (ICA) of 1887. In addition, our analysis of the debates and voting patterns on the BAI bills sheds new light on congressional motives in passing the ICA.

Staunch opposition from Southerners and Northern stockyard interests significantly limited the BAI's original powers and staff. However, the need to expand the fledgling BAI's size and authority soon became evident. In the summer of 1884, CBPP erupted in the Midwest, and there would have been little hope of control if it had spread to the open range (Chapter 4). By 1886, the disease threatened to infect the nation's major distribution channels. Jurisdictional disputes between Chicago, the state of Illinois, and federal officials led to paralysis. The private sector was also divided and incapacitated. Fights broke out between meatpackers, urban livestock owners, stockyard interests, and others. It became clear to most that the BAI needed more powers, including the authority and wherewithal to pay indemnities (needed to gain cooperation from stock owners and state officials). Congress would soon grant additional powers and funding. The BAI's response to the CBPP crisis established precedents for later eradication efforts. State-federal agreements were hammered out that deputized BAI agents to exercise police powers within states. A new federalism was being born. In 1892, the Secretary of Agriculture declared CBPP eradicated from the United States. This was the first time that an established contagious disease had been eradicated on a continental scale.

This episode highlights many recurring patterns. Rifts between states disrupted trade; federal interventions generally promoted commerce. State and local officials generally lacked the scientific expertise to understand and handle the problems, and they were too beholden to local interests to make tough decisions. Contrary to popular assertions, local representatives were not more efficient managers than far-away federal bureaucrats when it came to arresting livestock contagions.

The success in eradicating CBPP along with subsequent animal disease control measures had an unexpected spillover for human health initiatives. In 1906, the American Association for the Advancement of Science formed the Committee of One Hundred, chaired by Yale economist Irving Fisher, to crusade for more aggressive federal public health policies. Its founders took inspiration from the successes in controlling livestock contagions: they advocated the "creation of a National Department of Health, which should spread throughout the country a knowledge of effective ways of stamping out disease, as the Department of Agriculture has done in the case of cattle."[25]

Our story deals in large part with the legal changes that led to the development of a national market in the United States. Individual states frequently banned the movement of livestock from other states. An 1878 U.S. Supreme Court ruling on a Texas fever case changed the legal landscape by seriously restricting the ability of states to limit trade on health grounds. This case added to the pressure for federal intervention (Chapter 2). Gradually the courts responded to new scientific findings to allow state restrictions of Southern cattle. By the late 1880s, Southern cattle interests were once again bucking against myriad state prohibitions. It was in this setting that in 1889 the federal government segregated the U.S. cattle market, relegating Southern stock to special pens and separate railroad cars over much of the year. These policies curbed the spread of the disease outside the South, but did little to improve productivity within the South. Chapter 5 analyzes the successful attempts to understand Texas fever and limit its spread to Northern cattle.

States also erected quarantines to block the spread of many other diseases, including cattle and sheep scab, foot-and-mouth disease, hog cholera, and bovine tuberculosis (Chapters 5, 6, 7, and 10, respectively). At first, federal interventions attempted to give more order and specificity to what otherwise were less-targeted state barriers to trade. An important element in maintaining or restoring trade was convincing threatened parties that competent and independent monitors were at work. During disease outbreaks, the testaments of state and local officials and of industry executives had no currency, but in general the assurances of top BAI and USDA leaders carried considerable weight. The BAI could offer a valuable seal of approval that the states could not.

There was a wide range of disease-control policy options, and the methods chosen typically depended on a disease's infectious characteristics and on the economic damage it might inflict. Foot-and-mouth disease (FMD) was so contagious that it called for far more draconian interventions than for either CBPP or Texas fever. FMD repeatedly struck the United States; during the worst outbreak (1914–1916), it infected cattle in twenty-two states and the District of Columbia. This was a potential tipping point for the livestock industry, and only "heroic" policies saved the country from the plight of nations such as Argentina, where FMD became enzootic. Authorities in the United States made the utilitarian calculation to sacrifice the few to protect the many. Not everyone agreed, but the grim business of culling infected and exposed animals went forward. Recurrent FMD outbreaks in the first two decades of the twentieth century revealed that efficient control of the contagion required an extensive surveillance system, a plan of action, preapproved funding to handle emergencies, teams of trained responders, and a clearly defined chain of command built into state-federal cooperative arrangements. When confronted with FMD, many interests who originally had opposed a powerful federal authority changed their tune. The broad support for controlling FMD led Congress to allocate more funding and authority to the BAI. By the mid-1910s, the institutions of disease control and eradication were maturing. Chapter 6 details this little-known story.

FMD never became enzootic in the United States. It was relatively easy to identify, it was highly contagious, and it required immediate action. This made stamping out the preferred policy. With compensation, such policies were politically acceptable to most—especially in light of the fact that trade would be cut off if the disease was not controlled. Other diseases, such as hog cholera and Texas fever, were initially too enigmatic and too widespread to make eradication a feasible policy option. In bad years, hog cholera killed nearly all the swine in hard-hit regions, and over 10 percent of the total American swine population. As with Texas fever, BAI scientists made fundamental discoveries that would unravel the mysteries of this disease. Chapter 7 analyzes how this quest led to important advances in immunology, and the discoveries of the *Salmonella* bacterium and the hog cholera virus. These advances depended on European ideas, techniques, and equipment, but were also in part a product of mission-directed BAI research projects. The march of science was marked by missteps and vitriolic disputes among researchers. This was especially evident in the case of hog cholera. Such divisions in scientific opinion delayed effective public policy.

The public policy story of hog cholera ranges over a broad front dealing with the discoveries by BAI scientists, the emergence and regulation of the new biologics industry, and the transfer of scientific advances to the farm. Hog cholera represents a case where policy makers long opted against collective action. Individual farmers and their private veterinarians could limit the disease's impact with a succession of vaccines—all of which created serious negative externalities.

Chapters 8, 9, and 10 deal directly with the links between animal and human health. Once again we see the interactions of science and public policy, the effect of widespread denialism, the crushing impact of disease threats on domestic and international trade, the failure of state and local interventions, and the eventual success of new federal regulations. Trichinosis outbreaks caused panic in Europe in the mid-nineteenth century (Chapter 8). When American pork products were implicated, most European nations rapidly erected import barriers, igniting a two-decade-long trade war. In this case, most Americans, including the leaders of the BAI, cried foul. Much later, researchers at the USDA and what would become the NIH discovered the ugly truth: trichinosis among Americans was much more prevalent than earlier claimed. By the early 1940s, several NIH studies had showed that one of six Americans had at some time in their lives been infected by the disease. Other research showed that dangerous numbers of trichinae often survived the curing methods employed by U.S. packers. We next reexamine the political economy of early meat inspection legislation. Deniers—including meatpackers, congressmen, and more recently public choice scholars—have all claimed that there were no significant health problems and no need for federal meat inspection. We disagree. Chapters 8 and 9 make our case.

In the late nineteenth century, milk was the conduit for scores of deadly diseases. By 1940, milk hygiene was approaching the sanitary conditions that are common in the twenty-first century. Chapter 10 begins the discussion of why and how this change occurred, with an emphasis on the efforts to understand and control the spread of bovine tuberculosis (BTB) in cattle and humans. Circa 1900, BTB was likely killing about 10,000 Americans a year. In that age of discovery and control, scientists working for the BAI and state universities made key advances in both understanding and detecting the disease. However, the diagnostic test was controversial; many farmers thought that the procedure spread the disease, caused abortions in cows, and harmed humans. They cited the eminent scientist Robert Koch's position in a raging dispute with other researchers over the dangers of BTB to humans. The great Koch was proved wrong, but his discredited ideas lingered on for decades. State and local efforts to control BTB increased after 1900, with the unintended consequence of encouraging farmers to sell their suspect and infected animals. Middlemen facilitated this nefarious trade: one prominent Chicago-area cattle dealer, James Dorsey, knowingly shipped diseased cattle that infected at least 10,000 dairy herds in the

United States, Canada, and Mexico. His actions exposed tens of thousands of families to tuberculosis. This case brought home the flaws in relying on the tort system to control the problem and proved a catalyst for stronger government intervention. By 1914, at least a dozen states had closed their borders to Illinois livestock. Only federal intervention helped reopen trade.

For CBPP and FMD, eradication came with the initial federal attempts to control eruptions. But for many other diseases, eradication could be entertained only after firmer scientific and political foundations were established. In the case of Texas fever, the age of federal eradication policy began in 1906 (Chapter 11). The ensuing state-federal campaign established a model for large-area vector eradication employed around the world. Texas fever eradication was a part of a broader movement. At this time, livestock in roughly three-fourths of the territory of the United States was under federal lockdown to prevent the spread of parasitic diseases. Hostilities festered, and violence was common; opponents murdered agents and dynamited dipping vats.

The history of these campaigns shows how strongly held views about states' rights changed with economic conditions. Once an area was cleansed, its leaders generally became defenders of federal intervention because they did not want their constituents' farms reinfected. This political dynamic was a common feature of most control and eradication programs. For this reason, the BAI often started programs with velvet gloves and became more authoritarian as political support increased. This was certainly the case with BTB eradication (Chapter 12), which began in 1917. The BTB campaign was the BAI's most ambitious and controversial endeavor, and it involved an unprecedented peacetime use of police power. Success required developing and adjusting incentive programs to gain farmer cooperation. By 1940, this program and parallel programs of mandatory pasteurization were preventing roughly 25,000 deaths a year in the United States from BTB infections.[26]

BTB eradication also paid huge dividends by increasing agricultural productivity. This was true for other programs. In every case for which we could assemble data, our conservative estimates of the benefits to the agricultural sector of disease eradication exceeded the costs by at least ten to one. As with BTB, the spillovers to human health and to advancing science added significantly to the net benefits.

The age of hog cholera eradication began in earnest only in 1961, when the federal government abandoned its policy of coexisting with the disease. A prolonged quarantine and slaughter campaign achieved success by 1977. Chapter 13 tells this story. Changes in the disease environment mandated the new policy. The threat from two new diseases dramatically increased the risks of misidentifying diseases in the early stages of a contagion, which could have had catastrophic consequences. Suddenly powerful producer interests, which had previously opposed stringent measures, now lobbied for eradication. This required mandating changes to long-standing feeding practices, which had the additional benefit of significantly reducing the incidence of trichinosis. We close in Chapter 14 by providing perspective on past achievements in light of current challenges.

This is a story of achievements that are now largely taken for granted.[27] Rather than tell a highly streamlined or sweeping account, we delve into the nitty-gritty, recounting more of the bloody details than some readers might desire. The outcomes were neither inevitable nor predetermined. Contingencies abounded. We do not argue the policies pursued were the only options available or always the best. One can with hindsight perceive alternative paths and argue that one not followed would have been better. Sometimes the alternatives were clearly seen at the time, but often they were not. We attempt to explain how the conflicts played out and how the choices were made. We describe the ego-driven, trial-and-error process of scientific discovery. The generation of knowledge was chaotic and controversial, and many deserving researchers did not get the credit they merited. "Bad" advice often received attention because it came from persons of authority or served the interests of the powerful. We note the missteps of the actors, including those recognized by other contemporaries. The proponents of change often worked together, but on many occasions they were divided among themselves. Sometimes the proponents exceeded their authority, and sometimes they went easy to avoid creating food panics. Just as the proponents of new sanitation policies were not always correct, the opponents were not always wrong. Opponents often acted from an understandable desire to be left alone to manage their own affairs. But it is important to recognize that they were often obstructing changes that promoted the general welfare. Some denied the existence of obvious problems because the proposed policy solutions, or even the mere admission that all was not right, ran counter to their own interests or ideology. Many past denials were exposed at the time as preposterous. There is no reason to treat them uncritically now. One of the most compelling parts of our story is how the opponents of animal and public health initiatives shifted their views over time to become leading supporters.

Arresting Contagion chronicles large-scale government interventions that successfully eliminated major diseases and created models later used worldwide. The overwhelming message is one of progress.

2 Livestock Disease Environment and Industry Dynamics

IN THE NINETEENTH CENTURY, animal diseases were a mystery. A wide range of illnesses had similar symptoms, making it nearly impossible for livestock owners to distinguish among diseases. Maladies were commonly called by generic names such as the plague, the scourge, or the murrain, an archaic term meaning death. Frequently, reports misidentified diseases. As examples, alleged attacks of rinderpest in New York in 1868 and of foot-and-mouth disease in Kansas in 1884 caused panics but were later revealed to be less serious afflictions. Farmers also believed in the existence of ailments that veterinarians do not now recognize.

Controversy raged over the origins of specific diseases. Was the malady contagious, hereditary, environmental, or of spontaneous origin? If it was contagious, how did it spread? If the disease was due to the environment, was it caused by climate, poor air, filthy surroundings, or a poisonous plant? Did the disease affect humans? Answering such questions proved difficult. The prevalence of certain diseases varied with the climate, living conditions, and the susceptibility of the livestock. Some correlates of disease—such as bad sanitation, overcrowding, or poor diet—were consistent with multiple causal explanations. A disease's virulence and course could also vary, leading to dramatically different symptoms and diagnoses. Some diseases had long incubation periods and thus could be spread by apparently healthy animals. At times, the most visible symptoms were caused by secondary infections, adding to the confusion.

For diseases such as Texas fever, the involvement of parasites and the development of partial immunity due to previous infections greatly intensified the difficulty of explaining why some animals died and others

survived in apparent good health. Gradually, scientists revealed the secrets of specific diseases, and often their findings were so revolutionary
that it was difficult to convince other scientists, let alone the public, of
their veracity. In other instances, the folk wisdom of livestock owners
who had observed certain diseases up close proved nearer to the mark
than the pronouncements of the world's leading experts. Deciphering
the mysteries of animal diseases was a major achievement that had enormous productivity benefits for farmers and positive spillovers for consumers and human health.

Germ Theory of Disease

The discovery and gradual acceptance of the germ theory of disease
was one of the major scientific advances of the nineteenth century. The
theory revolutionized the understanding of human and animal health,
and gave rise to the scientific fields of bacteriology, immunology, microbiology, virology, and others. Table 2.1 provides a capsule timeline. The
German Robert Koch (1843–1910) and the Frenchman Louis Pasteur
(1822–1895) were among the eminent scientists who advanced the germ
theory of disease, and both conducted extensive research on animal
health. Koch was trained as a physician, but he made fundamental contributions to the understanding of anthrax, tuberculosis, cholera, and
other zoonoses. Pasteur was trained as a chemist and made seminal advances in the understanding and development of vaccines for anthrax,
cholera, and rabies. Many other prominent scientists also merged the
study of animal health with human medicine.[1]

By the last half of the nineteenth century, Germany, France, and
Britain all had rich medical and veterinary traditions, with research
and training academies superior to any found in the United States. The
first dedicated veterinary college in Europe, the Lyon Veterinary Institute, opened in 1762 with the goal of finding a cure for rinderpest; the
second, the Royal Veterinary School of Alfort, opened four years later.
Students trained at these pioneering institutions would spearhead the
creation of similar institutions across Europe. By 1830, there were at
least twenty-five veterinary schools in Europe. In contrast, formal scientific veterinary training in the United States did not begin until 1868,
when Cornell University established an undergraduate veterinary program. Cornell's program was directed by James Law, a distinguished

Table 2.1 Selected advances in the germ theory of disease to 1900

1670s	Anton van Leeuwenhoek invented the microscope.
1798	Edward Jenner popularized the use of cowpox material to confer resistance to smallpox.
1854	John Snow amassed evidence that cholera was water-borne, advancing epidemiology.
1860s	Joseph Lister conducted surgery using antiseptics.
1865	Louis Pasteur showed microorganisms causes wine spoilage.
1876	Robert Koch found bacterial cause of anthrax.
1880	Pasteur showed artificially attenuated chicken cholera can be used as a vaccine.
1882	Koch identified the tubercle bacillus.
1884	Charles Chamberland developed porcelain filters, facilitating the discovery of viruses.
1893	Theobald Smith, Cooper Curtice, and Frederick Kilborne offered first proof of arthropod vector transmission of disease (Texas fever).
1898	Friedrich Loeffler and Paul Frosch discovered foot-and-mouth disease virus—the second virus and first vertebrate virus.
1900	Walter Reed and others discovered yellow fever virus and transmission cycle—the first human virus.

Source: For a more thorough treatment, see Frederick A. Murphy, *The Foundations of Virology: Discovers and Discoveries, Inventors and Inventions, Developers and Technologies,* rev. ed. (West Conshohocken, PA: Infinity, 2014), www.utmb.edu/virusimages/; Robert P. Gaynes, *Germ Theory: Medical Pioneers in Infectious Diseases* (Washington, DC: ASM Press, 2011), pp. 63–71, 104–07, 148–52, 159–61, 163–66, 177–79, 183–86, 219–21.

Doctor of Veterinary Medicine (DVM) trained at the Edinburgh Veterinary College. Law was a leader of a small cadre of veterinary scientists who would play a major role in shaping American animal disease policies. In 1876, Cornell granted Daniel E. Salmon the first DVM degree awarded in the United States.[2] The U.S. Department of Agriculture (USDA) hired Salmon to oversee its fledgling Veterinary Division in 1883. With the creation of the Bureau of Animal Industry (BAI) the next year, he was appointed as the agency's first chief.

Scientific breakthroughs were changing how many people perceived diseases. Among most scientists, theories of contagion gained sway over those based strictly on sanitary conditions, but the public debate raged for decades. New discoveries about the causes of diseases, their transmission mechanisms, and their dangers and economic consequences were lowering the cost of control efforts and helping to build a consensus in favor of more vigorous regulation. A few veterinary leaders envisioned federal policies that went beyond containing and controlling local disease outbreaks: they believed in the possibility of totally eradicating established diseases. The BAI, using methods grounded firmly in scientific theories of contagion, would play a leading role in developing these new ideas and disseminating them to a skeptical public.

Worsening Animal Disease Environment

At the same time that scientists were gaining a better understanding of diseases in the late nineteenth century, a number of animal diseases were spreading in the United States and Western Europe, some at alarming rates.[3] Economic progress brought in its wake forces that contributed to the spread of diseases. Higher incomes led to more trade in animals. Innovations in rail and ocean transportation promoted the movement of livestock over greater distances and reduced the time in transit relative to the incubation periods of diseases. In addition, the increasing concentration of animals in dairies and stockyards as well as the growing attention to herd improvement led to more intermingling of animals, which promoted the spread of diseases. The increasing distance between producers and consumers eroded the effectiveness of state and local regulations, and intensified uncertainties over animal health and food safety. In response to these changing conditions, national governments on both sides of the Atlantic erected new sanitary trade barriers.

The equines of the United States suffered greatly from the worsening health environment in the 1860s and 1870s. As was common with armed conflicts, the American Civil War spread diseases, most notably glanders, among horses and mules. Glanders, also known as farcy, is an incurable zoonotic bacterial disease that is easily communicated via contaminated water or food. The malady attacks an animal's respiratory tract, often leading to rapid death. Glanders is thought to have entered North America in the late eighteenth century, and imports of British stock in the antebellum era increased its prevalence. By the eve of the Civil War, the disease was well established in the middle states on the eastern seaboard. During the war, the contagion exacted a heavy toll on the concentrated populations of horses and mules.[4] The disease remained widespread in the postbellum period.

Other afflictions struck North American equines. The most alarming outbreak was the "Great Epizootic," a debilitating influenza that erupted near Toronto, Canada, in 1872. The disease spread rapidly, initially along railroad routes, eventually reaching thirty-three of thirty-seven U.S. states, Mexico, the Caribbean, and Central America. Northeastern cities were especially hard hit. Thousands of urban animals—working on streetcar lines, hauling freight, and providing livery services—died; many more were temporarily incapacitated. In an era reliant on draft power, the influenza brought daily life to a halt. A small blaze in a Boston warehouse turned into the city's Great Fire of 1872 when the fire department's horses were too weak to pull its engines. James Law estimated that the illness affected over 80 percent and killed 1 to 2 percent of all U.S. equines.[5]

The disease environment for swine was also worsening. As Chapter 7 details, a mysterious epizootic known as "hog cholera" raged through the North American swine population between 1856 and 1858. Farmers from Illinois to Massachusetts to Virginia all reported heavy loses. Again, concentrated animal populations were especially susceptible: over 10,000 hogs died when the cholera struck one Indiana distillery. Contemporaries debated the malady's geographical origin and relationship to other diseases. The disease (or complex of diseases) displayed a wide array of symptoms of varying severity in swine. The public was terrified by reports that it had infected and killed humans. Reports of the spread of hog cholera in North America, coupled with a greater awareness of the parasitic disease trichinosis, alarmed Europeans. These sanitary fears, combined with the desire to protect their domestic producers, led European governments to block imports from the United States.

The late 1850s also witnessed the eruption of a new and still mysterious disease among Southern cattle. The disease, known to contemporaries as "black tongue," first appeared in Florida in 1858. Newspapers across the South tracked its spread, reporting that black tongue was ravishing local cattle and deer. Although the disease was concentrated in the Old South, outbreaks stuck as far west as Texas and as far north as Ohio. Anxiety increased with accounts of humans dying after consuming contaminated beef and milk. Butchers and public officials in Jacksonville, Florida, and Columbia, South Carolina, restricted beef sales. "In Montgomery [Alabama], the citizens have refused to eat beef and it is not offered in that market," and in New Orleans there was "quite a panic," and "most of the families of that city have abandoned the use of fresh beef."[6] This was a major regional epizootic that apparently subsided on its own. We do not know the modern name of the black tongue disease of the 1850s, but the repeated statements that it afflicted humans and other nonruminant animals should be treated with skepticism. Scores of other diseases threatened livestock, but two cattle diseases—Texas fever and contagious bovine pleuropneumonia (CBPP)—dominated the debates leading to federal intervention.[7]

Texas Fever

From colonial times, cattle owners in Northern and border states faced the annual invasion of a disease that later would be known as Texas fever. This tick-borne blood disease was enzootic in the American South and Mexico. Mortality rates often approached 100 percent among infected Northern cattle. The first symptoms included high fever and weakness, and death could follow within a few weeks. The disease was an enigma: Southern cattle remained in apparent good health while Northern animals perished. Northern stock did not need to come into direct contact with Southern cattle—merely visiting the same trails, pastures, or enclosures that had been occupied by Southern cattle in the previous weeks led to infections. Paradoxically, Southern cattle that moved north during the cold season did not spread the disease. In 1868, the British medical journal the *Lancet* described Texas fever as "a very subtle and terribly fatal disease."[8]

A disease with symptoms suggestive of Texas fever struck cattle in Georgia, Virginia, and the Carolinas in the mid-eighteenth century. In the 1790s, an outbreak ravished cattle in South Carolina, prompting North Carolina to prohibit driving cattle from the south into the state during the warm months. In 1796, the disease appeared in Lancaster County, Pennsylvania, after the arrival of a herd from South Carolina. This episode sparked James Mease, an astute Philadelphia physician, to study the disease. Over the next three decades, he provided an accurate description of the fever's symptoms and incidence.[9] Little of substance would be added to Mease's insights until the 1880s.

Cattle drives from Texas intensified conflicts over the fever in the late antebellum period. Missouri was the first state in the line of fire. In

1853, about one-half of the local cattle along a Missouri trail died following the passing of Texas herds. Missouri ranchers subsequently imposed "shotgun" quarantines to block the drives. As new cattle trails opened further west, vigilantes in Kansas, Colorado, and the Texas Panhandle also attacked drovers. These were violent times. " 'Talk to a Missourian about moderation, when a drove of Texas cattle is coming and he will call you a fool, while he coolly loads his gun and joins his neighbors; and they intend no scare, either. They mean to kill, do kill, and will keep killing.' "[10] In part to avoid such problems, many Texans took to shipping their animals to Illinois by riverboat. This resulted in more serious outbreaks in the Northern states because the animals shipped by boat remained tick infested whereas those driven over land for long distances tended to drop their ticks by the time they arrived. Although observers at the time noted the upsurge in Northern outbreaks, the role of ticks was not yet recognized.

The Civil War temporarily put a halt to the problem, but the resumption of cattle drives in 1866 led to new outbreaks of Texas fever. In 1868, "the disease spread from Kansas to the New England States," inflicting "immense losses." Responding to the widespread concerns of Northern livestock interests, Governor Richard Oglesby of Illinois convened a meeting in Springfield in December 1868, which was attended by representatives from twelve states and Ontario. "The convention recommended the enactment of stringent laws to prevent the transit of Texas or Cherokee cattle through their respective States between the first of March and the first of November, and to make their owners responsible for damages caused by the introduction of such cattle."[11]

In the late 1860s and the 1870s, Kansas, Missouri, Iowa, and Illinois all passed tough quarantine laws aimed at Texan, Mexican, and "Indian" cattle. Most other Northern and border states prohibited the introduction of diseased animals.[12] Although many states passed legislation, the laws were not systematically enforced because of conflicting interests. Moreover, the limited understanding of how the disease was transmitted made successful prosecution nearly impossible. Efforts to control Texas fever were particularly divisive. Cattlemen in the Northern and border states clamored for protection while Southerners asserted their constitutional right to engage in interstate commerce and steadfastly denied that their animals were the cause of any problems.

State attempts to control the entry of Southern cattle ran afoul of the federal courts. During the late nineteenth century, the courts were deeply involved in a process that historian Richard Bensel has called the "political construction of the national market," in which they were defining the authority of the states and the federal government in interstate commerce. The most important decision restricting state power to control animal diseases was *Hannibal and St. Joseph Railroad Co. v. Husen* (95 U.S. 465, 1878), in which the Supreme Court struck down an 1872 Missouri statute that prohibited any Texan, Indian, or Mexican cattle from entering Missouri between March and November.[13] The Court reasoned that the law did not provide for inspections to distinguish between safe and dangerous cattle, nor did it offer any means of determining whether diseases were actually present in the sending area. Such blanket inference with interstate transportation went "beyond what is absolutely necessary for self protection." The decision had wide-ranging implications for the authority of states to control animal diseases, intensifying demands for federal intervention. The spread of other diseases added to the pressure.

Contagious Bovine Pleuropneumonia

CBPP represented another grave, mysterious, and growing danger. This disease, also known as the lung plague, was highly destructive to cattle and was hard to control because of its long incubation period. James Law noted that "the lung plague strikes slyly, hides its tracks, and, creeping into the stables unseen, it diffuses its poison, infects, benumbs, and paralyzes the lungs without the body appearing to suffer, and it only manifests itself by outward symptoms when all is lost."[14] Dairy operators could limit losses and hide the presence of disease by slaughtering cows for beef as symptoms intensified. The apparent health of infected animals in the early stages of the disease made it difficult for veterinarians to convince farmers and public officials that there was even a problem.

Given that CBPP can hide in asymptomatic animals, the early history of the disease must be treated with some skepticism. The standard accounts maintain that it first entered the United States in 1843, when Peter Dunn, a New York dairyman, purchased an infected "ship's cow" off a vessel from England. The disease spread to nearby herds, and it soon became enzootic in the New York City area. In 1847, CBPP appeared on the farm of Thomas Richardson in New Jersey. Quick action, including Richardson's voluntary slaughter of his entire herd, temporarily arrested the contagion in that state. But CBPP was reintroduced from New York, and it subsequently spread into Pennsylvania, Delaware, Maryland, Virginia, and the District of Columbia. Further north, CBPP broke out in a dairy herd in Belmont, Massachusetts, in 1859 and rapidly spread. In April 1860, the Massachusetts legislature established a board of commissioners with powers to quarantine, kill, and dispose of infected and exposed animals. Within the first year, officials destroyed over 900 cattle, but the disease continued to spread. After six years of a vigorous quarantine-slaughter program, which included state-funded compensation payments, Massachusetts succeeded in extirpating CBPP (or so it was thought).[15] Connecticut suffered repeated invasions from both New York and Massachusetts, but each time the state employed a strict quarantine-slaughter program that purportedly kept the disease at bay.[16]

In August 1877, CBPP erupted in a dairy herd near Clinton, New Jersey. Officials dragged their feet and belatedly enacted emergency measures in March 1879. The law gave the governor considerable discretion, including the powers to quarantine farms and stockyards, to inspect shipments into the state, and to order the destruction of animals. But the state's response was too slow: the contagion had already spread through the northern part of the state.[17]

Outbreaks also cropped up near Philadelphia and New York City. CBPP was particularly prevalent among cattle crammed into industrial-scale distillery feedlots and swill dairies. On Long Island, CBPP infected the large stables of the Gaff-Fleischman distillery (in present-day Queens). New York State sprang into action under an 1878 law, placing former Civil War General Marsena Patrick in charge of its quarantine and eradication campaign. New Jersey, New York, and Pennsylvania initially sought to cooperate to eradicate the disease, without much to show for the effort.[18] Overcoming coordination problems in the face of conflicting reports and interests was a difficult challenge. CBPP also hit dairy herds near Washington, D.C., and reinfected Connecticut. In response to reports that the disease had entered the Union Stock Yards in Chicago, the U.S. Department of Agriculture (USDA) dispatched the U.S. Inspector of Cattle, Dr. H. J. Detmers, to investigate. After a thorough review, Detmers declared that the outbreak was a "false alarm." But rumors continued to circulate, damaging consumer confidence at home and abroad. Chicago stockyard dealers and meatpackers were furious that Detmers had not reached his conclusion earlier, and for years to come they would blame him and the USDA for causing this stain on their reputations.[19]

The disjointed and weak actions of individual states were doomed in the face of a persistent contagion like CBPP. The New Jersey law, which allowed for partial compensation to livestock owners, was repealed in March 1880 because of its high cost. In practice, the animals were never killed "unless by consent of the owner or by agreement with him as to the price." The legislature transferred authority to the underfunded State Board of Health, and the contagion spread into southern New Jersey. The State Board of Agriculture concluded in 1880 that it is "vain to battle with such a disease by half measures."[20]

A culture of denial was ever present. The practice of dismissing disease threats was particularly common among Southern cattle owners, drovers, and Northern stockyard interests. Deniers argued that contagious livestock diseases either did not exist or were not dangerous. In their view, animals raised on pure feed in the open air could not spread diseases. The deniers saw the animal health officials as bungling "horse doctors" who exploited their "expertise" to gain office and power. The deniers further asserted that the germ theory of disease was novel and unproven, that its advocates raised unwarranted suspicions about healthy animals, and that their hasty and inept misdiagnoses touched off health scares and created the pretext for trade restrictions. In their view, disease control was a "racket" that destroyed commerce and wealth. In opposing control measures, many stock owners and meatpackers went beyond debating science or specific policies to deny the very possibility of contagions in the face of clear evidence to the contrary.[21]

Despite the prevailing philosophy of laissez-faire and rampant disease denialism, there were many attempts to gain federal intervention. In 1865, Congress authorized the Secretary of the Treasury to prohibit the import of foreign cattle unless the president certified that the sending area was disease free, although the actual certification was a hit-or-miss process that generally fell on U.S. consuls. In 1869, Commissioner of Agriculture Horace Capron became the first of several USDA leaders to ask Congress to establish a veterinary office to help control diseases, but Congress failed to act.[22] The twin threats of CBPP and Texas fever prompted J. R. Dodge of the USDA to argue in 1871 that "either the general Government should enact a law providing for the suppression of contagious diseases of farm stock and for the regulation of the transportation and movement of farm animals, or the State governments should be induced to act simultaneously and harmoniously on the subject."[23] The federal government continued to ignore the problem and, try as they might, the states proved ineffective. In 1878, Commissioner of Agriculture William G. LeDuc advised Congress that the CBPP problem required federal attention—but again nothing of consequence happened.

European embargoes on U.S. livestock and meats prompted congressional pressure on both LeDuc, and the Secretary of the Treasury, John Sherman, to investigate CBPP in 1880.[24] Sherman issued a well-publicized report in February 1880 that concluded that the "disease now exists only in the eastern parts of New York, in New Jersey, Pennsylvania, and perhaps in parts of Maryland, Virginia, and the District of Columbia." Sherman recommended that Congress establish a strong federal veterinary sanitary commission. "State and municipal regulation are not to be relied upon to prevent the importation and spread of the disease, or to effect its extirpation." Congress waited until March 1881 to establish a three-person Cattle Commission within the Treasury Department and until May 1883 to create a Veterinary Division within the USDA. However, neither body had any powers beyond investigation.[25]

The long period of congressional inaction in the face of the CBPP threat reflected the novelty of federal intervention in a domain traditionally reserved to the states. Even the strongest proponents of national action asserted that the federal government should limit its interventions to addressing problems that generated significant externalities. In an 1878 communication to Congress, James Law opined that government interference to control animal diseases was "altogether uncalled for, excepting in the case of such maladies as are communicable by contagion or otherwise from animal to animal, or from animal to man, and vice versa." Such contagious and communicable diseases were "a source of danger to the entire country." He likened the CBPP situation in the United States to being "asleep over a smouldering volcano." Law clearly distinguished between diseases with and without spillover effects: he saw no call to intervene with "non-transmissible" diseases that "extend no further than the stock of the individual owner, and in no sense endanger that of his neighbor," or the country as a whole.[26] In an 1879 letter that circulated among policy makers, Law strongly opposed adopting only half-measures such as quarantines and health inspections to address contagions, demanding instead actions that "will strike at the root and exterminate the pestilential growth."[27]

Changing Market Structure and Diseases

During the two decades following the Civil War, technological and organizational changes were remaking the American livestock industry. These changes contributed to increases in the frequency and geographic scale of disease problems. Trade in purebred stock boomed; the number of animals imported for breeding purposes soared from an annual average of 5,400 in 1873–1877 to over 56,000 in 1883–1887. Through the efforts of commercial breeders, newly founded purebred associations, and progressive farmers, the "blood" of these animals was disseminating rapidly.[28] These changes brought unintended consequences, as the increased movement of breeding stock spread diseases. Improvements also fostered greater divisions within the farm sector; farmers with high-value dairy and beef cattle developed different interests than other farmers. Intraindustry conflicts arose in part because stock in high-input production systems faced a higher probability of exposure and often was less resistant to diseases than stock in low-input systems.

Cattle production moved westward as the slaughter of buffalo and subjugation of indigenous populations opened the plains and mountain regions to ranchers. Texas sent hundreds of thousands of cattle annually to the Northern ranges and Midwestern markets. The number of longhorns driven out of Texas increased from an annual average of less than 125,000 in 1866–1868 to over 450,000 in 1871–1873. It then declined to roughly 275,000 in 1882–1884. The drop-off was in part due to the increased movement of cattle by rail and boat. The stock of cattle (including dairy cows) in the United States increased from about 31 million in 1870 to 47 million by 1883. In the latter year, there were 18 million cattle in the West—9 million in Texas alone. By comparison, circa 1880 there were about 6 million cattle in Great Britain and 62 million in all of Western Europe.[29] An economic boom in the early 1880s attracted large flows of capital from Eastern U.S. and British investors to cattle ranches in Texas and the Great Plains. As a part of the new geographical specialization, farmers in Iowa, Illinois, and Missouri developed profitable businesses in fattening cattle from the Western range and calves from the East. These new trade patterns increased the danger of spreading Western diseases (such as scab and Texas fever) into the Midwest and Eastern diseases (such as CBPP and foot-and-mouth disease) across the entire continent.

Similar forces were transforming the American sheep and swine industries. The U.S. sheep flock increased from 36 million in 1870 to 51 million by 1883—this was more than twice the sheep stock of Great Britain and about one-half of the total stock in Western Europe. As with cattle, it was common for Western ranchers to ship sheep to Midwestern farms for fattening. The U.S. swine population increased from 37 million in 1870 to 46 million by 1883. This population dwarfed those of its trading partners. Germany was the leading Western European producer with about 9 million swine; all of Western Europe had only 28 million. A large fraction of U.S. hog products were destined for foreign markets. America's growing exports would make U.S. swine a target of European protectionists.[30]

Professional drovers were still a key segment of the livestock industry in early 1880s, but their importance declined as railroads pushed railheads closer to the sources of supply. The mileage of railroad track west of the Mississippi River increased from roughly 3,000 in 1865 to 50,000 by 1884; most of the increase occurred after 1877.[31] Freight trains could carry cattle farther in thirty minutes than they could be herded in a day. Sheep and hogs were even slower a-hoof, and thus trains had a relatively greater impact on their mobility. The developments facilitated the spread of diseases. The new distribution system brought livestock from different regions into close contact at transit depots, feedlots, and stockyards, creating new avenues for contagion.

The unprecedented concentrations of animals around Chicago and other transportation hubs added to the danger. The Union Stock Yards, established just south of Chicago by a consortium of railroads in 1865, emerged as the largest livestock depot in the world. Circa 1883, the vast facility comprised 360 acres of land and 40 miles of railroad track, with a capacity for yarding 20,000 cattle, 5,000 sheep, and 150,000 hogs at a given time. Throughput was the key to the company's success. In 1882 and 1883, the company received, on average, 1.7 million cattle, 700,000 sheep, and 5.7 million hogs each year. A growing share of the livestock received by Western stockyards went to nearby packers, who shipped dressed and processed meats to distant markets.[32]

The meat processing and packing industry underwent an organizational revolution most closely associated with rise of the giant Chicago packers such as Philip D. Armour, Nelson Morris, and G. F. Swift. The introduction of refrigeration technologies to ships, railroads, and packing houses created new trade possibilities in dressed meat. Achieving greater capacity utilization of specialized facilities and reducing waste in the handling of byproducts were also central to the giant packers' success. The transformation was spectacular. In 1880, the tonnage of dressed beef shipped east from Chicago was less than 8 percent of the tonnage of live cattle shipments. In 1885, the tonnages were virtually equal.[33] Exports of animals and animal products reached new heights. Many of these changes affected the disease environment and food safety concerns. Meat butchered at a location distant from the place of consumption raised suspicions, even if unwarranted, because such products bypassed the municipal health authorities that oversaw local butchers. All of these structural changes in the livestock industry created new opportunities and tensions that spurred the demands for government intervention—in some cases, to address market failures including health concerns, and in others to redistribute rents.

Foreign Trade Restrictions

As we noted earlier, events in Europe enhanced the drive for more vigorous federal intervention in the United States. The international trade in animals and animal products was big business: live animals and animal products accounted for almost one-fifth of American merchandise exports in the late 1870s.[34] As Table 2.2 shows, at this time European governments began restricting the importation of U.S. livestock. On 18 December 1878, the British threatened to restrict imports of American cattle unless they were accompanied by government-issued certificates of health. Responding without clear authority, Treasury Secretary Sherman instituted a voluntary inspection program whereby customs officials would employ state veterinarians to certify the health of

Table 2.2   European restrictions affecting U.S. trade in animals and meat
products

Britain

1866   European cattle largely excluded under Cattle Diseases Prevention
Act of February 20.

1878   Cattle Disease Act tightened standards on European cattle.

1879   Due to contagious bovine pleuropneumonia (CBPP) fears, U.S.
cattle subject to port slaughter after March.

1880   Publication of health concerns about U.S. hogs led to trade reductions but no formal regulations.

1881   British Consul George Crump made unflattering remarks about
hog cholera in the United States.

1884   Diseases of Animals Act banned inland traffic of all live imported
cattle (except those from Canada).

1892   Canadian cattle subject to port slaughter.

1896   Diseases of Animals Act ended all live animal imports.

1904   The *Lancet* published exposés criticizing unsanitary standards at
U.S. meat processors.

France

1881   Ban of U.S. pork in February.

1883   Ban of U.S. pork dropped in November but reinstated in December.

1892   Ban of U.S. pork lifted in January.

1894   Exclusion of U.S. cattle for fears of Texas fever and CBPP.

Germany

1880   Ban of imports of U.S. ground pork and sausage.

1883   Ban extended to U.S. bacon, ham, and all forms of pork.

1891   Ban rescinded in September.

1894   Ban of imports of live cattle and fresh beef from U.S. due to fears of
Texas fever and CBPP.

1900   National meat inspection established; canned meat and sausage
prohibited.

1902   Meat cured with borax and other chemicals prohibited.

Austria-Hungary

1879   Ban of U.S. pork in Hungary.

1881   Ban extended to remainder of Austro-Hungarian Empire.

1891   Ban lifted.

Italy

1879   Ban of U.S. pork, later extended to all foreign pork.

1891   Ban lifted.

Denmark

1881   Ban of U.S. pork considered in order to maintain access to German
market.

(*continued*)

Table 2.2   (continued)

1883	Ban of U.S. pork adopted to maintain access to German market.
1891	Ban of U.S. pork lifted.
1894	Exclusion of U.S. cattle for fears of Texas fever and CBPP.

Spain

1880	Suspension of U.S. pork imports 28 February, but ban revoked July 10 subject to microscopic inspection of imports.
1892	Ban lifted in May.

Portugal

1879	Ban all products made from U.S. swine.

Source: Suellen Hoy and Walter Nugent, "Public Health or Protectionism? The German-American Pork War, 1880–1891," *Bulletin of the History of Medicine* 63, no. 2 (1989): 198–224; James H. Cassedy, "Applied Microscopy and American Pork Diplomacy: Charles Wardell Stiles in Germany 1898–1899," *Isis* 62, no. 1 (1971): 5–20; John L. Gignilliat, "Pigs, Politics, and Protection: The European Boycott of American Pork, 1879–1891," *Agricultural History* 35, no. 1 (1961): 3–12; Justin Kastner, Douglas Powell, Terry Crowley, and Karen Huff, "Scientific Conviction amidst Scientific Controversy in the Transatlantic Livestock and Meat Trade," *Endeavour* 29, no. 2 (2005): 78–83; William David Zimmerman, "Live Cattle Export Trade between United States and Great Britain, 1868–1885," *Agricultural History* 36, no. 1 (1962): 46–52; Richard Perren, "The North American Beef and Cattle Trade with Great Britain, 1870–1914," *Economic History Review* 24, no. 3 (1971): 430–44; Houck, *Bureau of Animal Industry*; Kastner, "Sanitary Related."

Note: There were also restrictions on pork in Greece, Turkey, and Romania, as discussed elsewhere.

animals destined for England. When this proved inadequate, he issued a compulsory inspection order on 1 February 1879. However, Sherman's initiatives were too little, too late.

The European market began to close. On 10 February 1879, the Privy Council of the United Kingdom decided that starting on March 3 all U.S. cattle would have to be slaughtered at the port of entry.[35] This was a major blow that meant that British dealers could no longer fatten U.S. cattle, which had suffered during the long railroad and ocean trips, before marketing them to butchers. The price of U.S. steers in England immediately fell by about $10 per head relative to the price of comparable animals from Canada, which entered without restrictions. The differential represented over 10 percent of the average value of the typical animal shipped. To maintain its privileged access to British markets, Canada tightened its own controls on U.S. imports and transshipments.

Great Britain added restrictions on sheep and mutton imports from the United States in 1879, asserting the presence of foot-and-mouth disease. In 1880, Germany banned cattle shipments from the United States, citing health concerns.[36]

An international pork trade war also erupted in 1879. Porkophobia gripped Europe, with widespread reports that U.S. pork was infested with trichinae and carried hog cholera. By the end of 1880, most European nations restricted or prohibited U.S. pork imports, ostensibly on sanitary grounds. The European embargoes hit hard, as the data on export values of animal products in Figure 2.1 reveal. Britain, which was by far the largest importer of U.S. pork, lifted its ban after a few months, but most continental countries maintained their embargoes for a decade.

The trade barriers were not a one-sided affair. Since 1866, the U.S. Treasury had regulated animal imports, and in many years it had banned all imports to prevent the introduction of foreign diseases. To facilitate

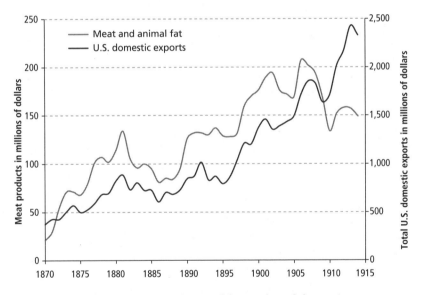

Figure 2.1. Value of U.S. meat and animal fats and total domestic exports, 1870–1914. *Notes:* "Meat and animal fats" combines Ee578 "animal fats" (first available in 1882) with Ee580 "meat products" (which is called "meat and products" in 1881 and before and called "meats" from 1882 on). Years ending June 30. *Source:* Compiled from Carter et al., *Historical Statistics,* vol. 5, series Ee446, Ee578, Ee580, pp. 520–22, 546–49.

the livestock improvement boom, the Treasury allowed purebred animals, accompanied by health certificates, to be imported from Great Britain and Ireland after 16 March 1876. But upon learning of an outbreak of CBPP in England (and in retaliation for new British restrictions of U.S. trade), Secretary Sherman closed Atlantic ports to all English cattle on 26 February 1879.[37] This interrupted a booming trade in breeding stock. On 19 July 1879, the Treasury revoked its total ban on imports, provided that all cattle from any part of Europe were quarantined under control of customs officers for not less than ninety days. Based on an Act of 3 March 1883, the Treasury established a system of port stations to quarantine imported cattle. The oversight and enforcement of the quarantine system was transferred to the USDA in August 1884.[38]

The Constitutional Setting

The struggles to control specific livestock diseases took place in an institutional setting that tightly constrained federal intervention and limited state powers. The constitutional challenge was to define the powers of the two levels of government in order to deal with new and growing disease problems. Until the 1878 *Husen* decision, state powers over disease control were far more akin to those of independent nations than is the situation today. Both Secretary Sherman's 1879 quarantines and the subsequent 1883 law, which established port inspection, represented controversial extensions of federal powers. In the last decades of the nineteenth century, the legislative battles to control livestock diseases typically pitted states' rights Southern Democrats against activist Northern Republicans. But the North-South split was not hard and fast on all issues, and before the Civil War Southerners often spearheaded calls for federal intervention to control human diseases.

Article 1, Section 8, of the U.S. Constitution explicitly granted to Congress the power "to regulate Commerce with foreign nations and among the several States," and Article I, Section 10, declared that "No State shall, without the Consent of the Congress, lay any Imposts or Duties on Imports or Exports, except what may be absolutely necessary for executing it's [sic] inspection Laws." Federal courts generally included measures that regulated diseased animals within the broad police powers reserved for state and local governments. For example, in 1824, Chief Justice John Marshall ruled in *Gibbons v. Odgen* (22 U.S. 1) that navigation was a part of interstate commerce and therefore was subject to exclusively federal regulation. But he added that "inspection laws, quarantine laws, and health laws of every description" were among the "immense mass of legislation" that was "not surrendered to the general government" and "which can be most advantageously exercised by the States themselves." States retained the power to limit trade to protect the public health and morals of their inhabitants, but restrictions were vulnerable to legal challenges if they discriminated against outsiders.[39]

In almost every state, ownership of animals with contagious diseases was illegal, and, if discovered, the animals were subjected to immediate destruction with compensation, if any, to be settled later. The courts generally upheld state authority to exercise broad police powers against these public nuisances and to impose strict quarantines and inspection regulations to prevent the importation of diseased stock (so long as the laws treated outsiders fairly). An important example was *Lawton v. Steele* (152 U.S. 136, decided 6 March 1894), in which the Supreme Court affirmed that state police power "is universally conceded to include everything essential to the public safety, health and morals, and to justify the destruction or abatement, by summary proceedings, of whatever may be a public nuisance [including] . . . the slaughter of diseased cattle; the destruction of decayed or unwholesome food."[40] In practice, however, state and local governments failed to enforce measures to control livestock diseases. Officials often lacked an understanding of diseases, gave low weight to the damage contagions might cause to other communities, and found it difficult to stand up to powerful local livestock owners.

The flip side of the states' rights and responsibilities were the limits on federal quarantine authority. The strength of congressional sentiment against federal intervention is evident in the debates over actions to control human diseases. In 1796, Congress passed its first quarantine legislation, which directed federal agents to aid state and local officials if requested. However, provisions to locate federal quarantine stations in ports were viewed as an intrusion on states' rights and were struck from the legislation during debate. Philadelphia and New York City officials, who already had local quarantine stations, resisted federal interference. Some of the most vocal support for federal quarantine legislation came from Maryland and South Carolina. Representative William L. Smith (Federalist-S.C.) succinctly explained the need to expand federal power.

Epidemic diseases, once imported, "affect the United States at large. They do not merely affect the city where first imported, but they obstruct the commerce of all others; they not only embarrassed the commerce but injured the revenues of the United States."[41] Concerned about the links between health and trade, Congress established the Marine Hospital Service (MHS) in 1798 to provide medical relief to merchant seamen. The MHS for roughly its first seven decades was tarnished by political patronage, graft, and inefficiency. In 1799, Congress passed legislation authorizing federal revenue officials to assist the states in their quarantine measures.[42] This law served as the basis of federal policy for much of the nineteenth century.

Several calls for federal legislation to deal with human diseases in the pre-Civil War era came to naught.[43] In 1866, the same year that the Treasury Department began port inspection of livestock, there were renewed demands for a uniform national quarantine system for humans and internal federal sanitary cordons to protect against cholera. Senator Henry Anthony (R-R.I.), among others, objected to the further expansion of federal power, noting that "I would rather have the cholera than such a proposition as this." Even with Southern pro-states' rights Democrats "conspicuously absent" from Congress at that time, Northern opposition was sufficient to block the measure.[44]

Yellow fever outbreaks in the South in 1873 and 1876 intensified calls for federal intervention. An Act passed on 29 April 1878 empowered the supervising surgeon of the MHS and the Secretary of the Treasury to assist states and localities in upholding their quarantines, but federal agents were explicitly forbidden from interfering with state laws. State-federal cooperation was a key feature—state and municipal agents, upon request, could be deputized as officers of the U.S. government on quarantine matters. Before the 1878 Act went into effect, an even more severe yellow fever epidemic hit the Mississippi valley. Officials estimated that the "Great Fever" took 20,000 lives and cost over $100 million. Trade and normal civic discourse collapsed, as states and cities quarantined New Orleans and other afflicted localities. As was common with livestock diseases, public authorities in the infected areas often hid or minimized the problem. Citizens (including those exposed) fled when the disease appeared or when governments threatened to restrict movement, contributing to the further spread of yellow fever.[45]

In spite of the catastrophe, the federal response was muted. President Rutherford B. Hayes urged Congress to create a "national sanitary administration" to protect ports and supervise internal commerce during epidemics. Several Southerners introduced bills to expand federal powers to protect public health.[46] Representative Vannoy Manning (D-Miss.) argued that if state and local officials failed to guard an area, federal officers should fill the gap. Interventionists reasoned that yellow fever destroyed commerce, that the general government had the power to regulate commerce, and therefore that the federal government could regulate yellow fever. This opinion was far from unanimous. Representative John Reagan (D-Tex.) rejected the idea that the commerce clause empowered the federal government to aid the states to prevent the interstate transmission of diseases. Once again, the more effective proposals were whittled away.[47]

After several months of debate, Congress established the National Board of Health (NBH) on 3 March 1879 as an independent public health agency. On 2 June 1879, Congress empowered the NBH to impose national quarantines where local rules were lacking.[48] The Board conducted investigations but accomplished little. In 1883, Congress transferred the limited federal quarantine authority back to the Board's jealous rival, the MHS.[49]

It was against this backdrop that a parallel debate raged over the federal government's role in controlling livestock diseases. In 1873, Congress had passed a law prohibiting the continuous confinement of livestock while in interstate transit for more than 28 hours. This legislation represented a significant extension of federal powers because it provided for federal regulation of railroads and for U.S. marshals to prosecute violators in federal courts.[50] Congress revisited livestock-related transit regulations several times in the 1870s. Senate bill 206, debated on 26 and 27 May 1879 offers an example. It continued the twenty-eight-hour unloading mandate and authorized the Commissioner of Agriculture to employ inspectors at ports to certify that animals destined for export were free of infectious and contagious diseases.[51] This latter provision sought to allay British concerns about CBPP and would be a regular feature of subsequent bills. The debate, which occupied over twenty pages in the *Congressional Record*, featured leading opponents Samuel Maxey (D-Tex.) and Daniel Voorhees (D-Ind.) decrying the expansion of the federal bureaucracy and the arbitrary powers granted to inspectors. Voorhees asserted that these political appointees would have the "power at any port to destroy the sale of any merchant's cattle," which would open the doors to "constant bribery and corruption." Voorhees and his Senate allies succeeded in killing the bill.[52]

The debates on human and animal health sometimes occurred in Congress on the same days and covered the same constitutional terrain. The link between human and animal health legislation was an underlying concern, with all the participants recognizing that the legal issues affecting one branch of health could affect the other.[53] Both debates, and the resulting legislative acts, were influenced by the same rapidly evolving scientific and technological environments.

However, the geographical alliances in the two sets of debates were dramatically different. As we detail in Chapter 3, the division over the creation of the BAI was to a large extent between Northerners and Southerners: almost all Republicans eventually favored livestock health legislation, almost all Southerners opposed it, and Northern and border-state Democrats were split. Representatives from inland areas in both the North and South tended to strongly favor federal intervention to regulate human health; those from cities located in harm's way up the Mississippi from New Orleans were especially vocal proponents. In the South, opposition came from coastal port cities.[54] These positions were not hard and fast. On many occasions, Southerners wavered in their ideological adherence to a narrow interpretation of the commerce clause when they perceived federal intervention to be in their interests.

Conclusion

The livestock business witnessed revolutionary changes in the decades following the Civil War. Improved transportation, the adoption of specialized breeds, expansion into new areas, marketing innovations, and the growth of large-scale processing plants all transformed business opportunities. Simultaneously, the disease environment was growing worse: between 1865 and 1884, the United States suffered outbreaks of numerous animal diseases—hog cholera, equine influenza, glanders, Texas fever, CBPP, foot-and-mouth disease, and many more. Advances in scientific knowledge and the rise of professional veterinary medicine could not halt the spread of diseases, but they increasingly offered hope of reducing some threats. However, effective policies would require collective action, and this was blocked by the prevailing interpretation of the Constitution's limitations on federal powers to regulate trade and health. Constitutional interpretations changed, but slowly. The efficiency and distributional issues at stake were huge.

Texas fever and CBPP dominated the early congressional debates over livestock sanitation. State and local attempts to control both diseases proved costly and ineffective. Areas cleared of CBPP were reinfected by animals from neighboring states; without a comprehensive eradication campaign, the expenditures were largely wasted. Private control was not possible because livestock owners hid and spread the diseases. For both diseases, deniers rejected new scientific findings and opposed government regulations. The Supreme Court's 1878 *Husen* decision undermined state regulatory powers. The problem was compounded when European countries, beginning with Britain in 1879, restricted U.S. access to their markets, citing animal and human health concerns. In this environment, the movement to create a federal agency to control animal diseases gained momentum.

3 The Battle to Create the Bureau of Animal Industry

THE MEMBERS of the 48th Congress were treated to a spectacle. The political theater was aimed at calling the bluff of departing Representative James Singleton (D-Ill.), who had offered $1,000 for proof that contagious bovine pleuropneumonia (CBPP) existed anywhere in the United States. On 12 January 1884, at the Commissioner of Agriculture's request, Daniel Salmon butchered three local cows, all of which had shown clear signs of CBPP. Representative James "Tama" Wilson (R-Iowa) then gathered the animals' diseased lungs into a bucket and prominently displayed the evidence in the Capitol building.[1] Such was the drama leading up to the passage of one of the most important but underappreciated pieces of agricultural and food safety legislation in American history: the organic legislation (23 Stat. 31) establishing the Bureau of Animal Industry (BAI) signed 29 May 1884.

Most accounts date the first significant exercise of federal power to regulate domestic commerce to the Interstate Commerce Act (ICA) of 1887. The problem with this chronology is that the BAI was established several years earlier, and it helped pave the way for subsequent regulatory initiatives. Many of the interest groups (e.g., railroads, farmers, and shippers) and many of the key players in the BAI debate (most importantly, Representative John Reagan of Texas) would lock horns in the ICA debate. The BAI debate was much more than a preliminary scrimmage for the main event. The BAI and ICA dealt with similar issues concerning public intervention in the operation of private enterprises, the division of authority between the state and federal governments, and the constitutionality and consequences of empowering independent bureau-

42

cracies. Both acts aimed to regulate large and technologically dynamic industries that affected citizens in every state of the Union, and in both cases, a Supreme Court decision limiting the power of state governments to regulate interstate commerce intensified the demands for federal action.

The BAI bill (HR 3967) stands apart—way apart. Political scientists Gary Cox and Mathew McCubbins have devoted decades to making sense of the federal legislative process.[2] They concluded that the Speaker of the House of Representatives would not allow significant bills that were expected to gain the approval of the Senate and president to come to a floor vote unless a majority of the party in power in the House supported the bill. (This is now known as the Hastert rule.) Out of the thousands of bills that Cox and McCubbins analyzed, the 1884 legislation to establish the BAI was unique. HR 3967 was the *only* significant bill passed between the end of Reconstruction (1877) and the 1960s in which a majority of the party in power opposed the bill. Even at the time, the participants in the debate recognized that something unusual was going on.

Two diseases discussed in Chapter 2—CBPP and Texas fever—were at the heart of the BAI legislative struggle. There was growing grassroots support in the North for federal action to control both diseases. It was understandable that most Southerners opposed Texas fever legislation, which would interfere with their exports. The congressional debate reflected these North-South tensions, and also pitted legislators ideologically comfortable with creating a powerful new federal bureaucracy against lawmakers who wanted to limit federal power. The latter charged that claims about the dangers of CBPP and Texas fever were overblown and that the proposed laws represented a dangerous and unconstitutional infringement of individual and state rights. However, as we shall see, although ideological posturing dominated the debates, in many cases legislators changed their constitutional positions to defend their constituents perceived self-interests.

Chester Arthur's signature on the BAI bill in May 1884 marked the end of a legislative battle that had lasted six years. The bill's critics from the majority Democratic Party repeatedly chided its sponsor, William H. Hatch (D-Mo.), for advancing a Republican bill.[3] Congressman William Eaton (D-Conn.) charged that "this is the most mischievous bill that I have seen . . . it is in utter violation of the Constitution of the United

States," and that its title ought to be "a bill to abrogate and annul the Constitution of the United States and deprive the States of the rights which belong to them." The debate in the Senate was no less discordant, with Senator Richard Coke (D-Tex.) charging that this "monstrous" bill would turn all of the nation's livestock over to the Commissioner of Agriculture who "is to be judge, jury, and executioner."[4]

This chapter analyzes the legislative battles that took place over the formation of the BAI. Supporters had to overcome widespread disease denialism and entrenched hostility to creating an administrative agency with such broad scope. The BAI represented an experiment in a new form of federal bureaucracy—one headed by a professional director with the power to gather data, conduct scientific research, and work with the states to fight diseases. Its creation represented an important step in the rise of the federal administrative state, in the growth of American scientific infrastructure, and in the development of modern economic regulation in the United States.

The Preliminary Skirmishes

As discussed in Chapter 2, by the late 1870s, several forces were intensifying the calls for a federal bureaucracy to regulate animal health. Particularly galling to U.S. cattle interests were British moves to restrict live cattle imports because of CBPP. Many American officials and cattlemen asserted that these restrictions were unjustified non-tariff barriers to trade. However, Cornell University's James Law sided with the Europeans. He riled cattle interests when he scoffed at their idea of allowing an exception for cattle from disease-free areas in the West by correctly pointing out that the stock could easily contract the disease in transit. Law called for much deeper reforms.[5] Massachusetts and Connecticut (as well as some regions of Europe) had employed stamping out policies and strict quarantines to extirpate CBPP locally. These successes convinced Law and a few of his veterinary colleagues that the United States should attempt to purge the disease completely.[6] They feared that the disastrous experiences in Australia and South Africa, where CBPP had killed millions of cattle, would be repeated in the United States.[7] If the disease ever became established on the open range of North America, it would have been nearly impossible to stamp out. Problems with Texas fever, along with the Supreme Court's 1878 *Husen* decision, reinforced the demand for federal action.

In 1880, several bills were reported to the House and Senate dealing with the suppression of CBPP and other contagious and infectious diseases. By February 1881, bills that explicitly called for the establishment of a "bureau of animal industry" had reached the floor in both houses.[8] On 18 February 1881, the debate on Senate bill 2097 began to heat up. The bill would have established a Bureau of Animal Industry within the Department of Agriculture with a chief, two senior assistants, and agents in every state and territory. It authorized the Commissioner of Agriculture to set rules and regulations as he deemed necessary for the suppression of contagious diseases and empowered the Secretary of the Treasury to set rules dealing with the interstate and international shipment of animals. It further granted the president the power to pay indemnities and to quarantine infected states that did not cooperate with the commissioner.[9]

Opponents charged that the bill would create a bureaucracy filled with patronage positions, bestow dictatorial powers on the executive branch, and usurp the powers of the states and Congress. Some of the strongest remarks were directed at the clause stating that "the Secretary of the Treasury shall establish such regulations concerning the exportation and transportation of live stock as the results of such investigations may require." Senator Roscoe Conkling (R-N.Y.) questioned whether Congress had ever bestowed such power on one official who was to be guided only by his own judgment. Senator Samuel Maxey (D-Tex.) regarded "the whole bill as a war with the theory of our Government, as centralizing of power here, as depriving the States of their reserved rights." John Ingalls (R-Kans.) damned the measure as "the worst bill that I ever read upon any subject," naming it "a legislative devil-fish." Opponents such as Senator John McPherson (D-N.J.) also questioned the danger of CBPP, viewing it as a relatively benign irritant that was unlikely to affect well-tended animals. McPherson and others would long advance a miasmic view of disease despite the growing evidence to the contrary. On 21 February 1881, the Senate bill was tabled. However, at least three other bills dealing with animal disease control were working their ways through the committee process, so the issue was not going to disappear.[10]

Throughout the debates, there was clear recognition that the Supreme Court's 1878 *Husen* decision put the onus on Congress to craft regulations on commerce and health. Reflecting the novelty of granting the executive branch broad regulatory powers, there were questions concerning which part of the federal government should control animal diseases. Should these powers be placed with the Department of Agriculture, the Department of the Treasury, the Department of the Interior, or the new National Board of Health? There was concern about the administrative mechanisms of any new bureau. Common questions included how much rule-making detail should be specified by Congress and how much should be left to the executive branch, how many staff to authorize, and where the BAI agents would be allowed operate. There was strong opposition to compensating owners for condemned animals.[11]

When the Senate BAI bill stalled, Edward H. Rollins (R-N.H.) amended an appropriations bill to authorize the Department of the Treasury to inspect and certify animals free of CBPP for export and to study animal diseases. In July 1881, Secretary of the Treasury John Windom established the Treasury Cattle Commission, appointing as commissioners James Law, J. H. Saunders, the Chicago publisher of the *Breeder's Gazette,* and E. F. Thayer, a Massachusetts physician. The commissioners did not pull any punches. Over the next three years, they made numerous recommendations for stronger state and federal actions, including internal quarantines to contain CBPP and to restrict the movement of cattle from areas infected with Texas fever. At the behest of the commission, Illinois enacted legislation in November 1881 to prohibit the importation of cattle from Eastern states infected with CBPP. Several other Western states and territories followed suit.[12] From 1881 on, the Wyoming Stock Growers Association (WSGA), a powerful organization closely tied to the Wyoming territorial government, employed a veterinary staff at the major stockyards of the Plains to inspect Eastern cattle for CBPP before they were shipped west.[13]

On 16 December 1881, Representative William Hatch introduced a new bill (HR 896) "for the establishment of a bureau of animal industry to prevent the exportation of diseased cattle and the spread of infectious or contagious diseases among domestic animals." On 19 June 1882, the House took up debate under special rules barring any amendments. This bill was similar in many ways to the earlier Senate version, but it called for a smaller budget and limited the Commissioner of Agriculture's power to quarantine and slaughter animals to the territory of the District of Columbia. Again, reflecting the unfamiliar territory of creating a federal regulatory agency, Congress focused on minutiae such as the salaries of clerks and per diem payments.[14]

Although CBPP was the only disease explicitly mentioned in the bill, Texas fever proved a major bone of contention. Texas congressmen led the opposition. Representative Roger Mills declared that the bill would establish a "tribunal with authority to condemn our cattle and drive them from Northern markets." In spite of this opposition, the bill passed on a voice vote. The road was rougher in the Senate, and, after a brief debate in late August of 1882, the bill was tabled in a close vote, killing it for that session. Senator Coke maintained that legislation addressing Texas fever was not needed because Texans knew better than to "drive their cattle at a time when this disease can be communicated."[15] Texans would continue to minimize, and in many cases flat out deny, the existence of a Texas fever problem for decades.[16]

The next substantive step occurred in November 1883, when USDA Commissioner George B. Loring organized a meeting in Chicago with leading Western cattle-raisers. A major concern was that the growing practice of sending Eastern stock west for fattening and breeding would carry CBPP into the Midwest and beyond. Daniel Salmon used the occasion to lash out against the deniers, who were attempting to "cover up" contagious diseases with "white-washing reports" and other deceptions.[17] At Loring's prompting, the cattlemen began an organized push for federal legislation to stamp out CBPP. President Arthur responded. In his annual message, he urged congressional action to control CBPP and other contagious livestock diseases.[18] It was against this backdrop that Representative Wilson displayed his pail of diseased lungs in the Capitol.

In the 48th Congress, the Democrats controlled the House of Representatives and the Republicans controlled the Senate. This split contrasted with the 47th Congress, where the Republicans were in charge of both chambers, and with the 46th Congress where the Democrats controlled both. Table 3.1 charts the changing composition of the House of Representatives and the Senate over the relevant sessions of Congress. The Republican loss of the House seemingly should have made the passage of a BAI bill unlikely, but there was a shift within the Democratic Party. The source of the new Democrat majority in the House came primarily from a surge of members from the West; Southerners constituted a minority of the caucus for the first time since 1876.[19]

Table 3.1 Composition of Congress, 1879–1897

Years	Congress	House			Senate			President
		Republicans	Democrats	Other	Republicans	Democrats	Other	
1879–1881	46	130	**149**	14	33	**42**	1	Republican
1881–1883	47	**147**	135	11	**37**	37	2	Republican
1883–1885	48	118	**197**	10	**38**	36	2	Republican
1885–1887	49	140	**183**	2	**43**	34	0	Democrat
1887–1889	50	152	**169**	4	**39**	37	0	Democrat
1889–1891	51	**166**	159	0	**39**	37	0	Republican
1891–1893	52	88	**235**	9	**47**	39	2	Republican
1893–1895	53	127	**218**	11	38	**44**	3	Democrat
1895–1897	54	**244**	105	7	**43**	39	6	Democrat

Source: Susan B. Carter et al., *Historical Statistics,* vol. 5, series Eb293–308, pp. 200–1.
Note: Majority party in bold.

The Entering Wedge

In January 1884, Representative Hatch introduced a bill (HR 3967) that would eventually pass, albeit with major amendments and after months of acrimonious debate filling over 150 pages of the *Congressional Record*.[20] The new bill had many working parts. (a) It proposed the creation of a bureau within the USDA to collect information on livestock and contagious animal diseases. (b) It specified four employees—a chief, a clerk, and two "competent agents"—and set their rates of pay. (c) It authorized the Commissioner of Agriculture to set rules for disease suppression and to certify the rules of the various states and territories. (d) It provided for the compensation for the owners of diseased animals and stipulated that if a state cooperated with the federal program, the state and the federal government would equally split all expenses of the eradication programs. (e) If a state did not cooperate, Section 4 authorized the president to quarantine the state (or part of the state). (f) The commissioner was instructed to inspect animals intended for export and report to the Secretary of the Treasury who was "to take such steps and adopt such measures . . . as he may deem necessary" to ensure the health of the livestock exported. (g) The bill prohibited railroads, ship companies, corporations, and individuals from *knowingly* transporting animals with contagious diseases across state lines and established penalties for violators. The bill appropriated $250,000 to finance these varied operations. As in previous bills, CBPP was the only disease explicitly mentioned, but the proposed legislation would have applied to all contagious diseases.[21]

By 1884, the battle lines were drawn. The bill made it through the Democratic-controlled Agricultural Committee, chaired by Hatch, but faced opposition from most House Democrats. Hatch stressed the grassroots support for the bill, including an extensive list of endorsements by state officials, cattle breeders, scientific experts, and agricultural organizations such as the Grange.[22] For the supporters, the Commerce Clause (Article 1, Section 8, Clause 3) of the U.S. Constitution provided ample grounds for federal intervention. If that were not enough, Congress also had the duty to provide for the "General Welfare." In line with this activist philosophy, Representative Reuben Ellwood (R-Ill.) noted that "the great central thought of the Constitution of the United States is the promotion of the good of the whole people."[23]

Texans again led the opposition. They were joined by Bourbon (conservative, probusiness) Democrats who feared an expanded federal bureaucracy employing Republican placemen, by strict constructionists from both parties and regions, and by those apprehensive about the concentration and abuse of power. Opponents saw the attempt to regulate CBPP as an "entering wedge" that would set a broad precedent for federal intervention. They were right.[24]

Scientific opinion played an important role in the eventual outcome. Hatch led off his introductory remarks in the House debate by reading a lengthy document prepared by Daniel Salmon that described the dangers the nation faced from livestock diseases and the hope that science offered. A proponent of the germ theory of disease, Salmon noted that science was discovering the "cause of these plagues, which has been an impenetrable mystery during all the past ages. . . . The infinitely small organisms which are able to produce such terrible havoc in our flocks and herds . . . are at last being brought under subjection." Salmon also explicitly warned of the spillovers on human health.[25] The bill's advocates were typically receptive to scientific arguments and understood that contagious diseases ignored state borders. They saw a dynamic world filled with both dangers and opportunities for improvement, but progress required social investments.

Most opponents viewed the issues in an entirely different light. "Veterinary surgeons" such as Salmon and Law were "horse doctors," who were harming the nation's commerce by spreading rumors and frightening consumers to create government jobs for their ilk. For many, the "cure"—expanding bureaucratic power—was worse than the disease. Others continued to deny that disease threats were serious. In the words of Senator William Sewell (R-N.J.), CBPP would always be around like "chicken-pox in children."[26]

Hatch countered that to prevent CBPP from jumping the Allegheny Mountains the nation needed a draconian policy with "the destruction of the animals that may be diseased and of such stables or barns as it may be thought expedient." Every state would have to develop its own disease control bureaucracy and carry a heavy share of the burden. It was the duty of the federal government to help coordinate the state efforts by setting standards and providing expertise and money. Woe to a state that chose not to cooperate, because it faced a federal quarantine.

Hatch noted, "I would erect a Chinese wall around it; . . . high enough and broad enough to hem the disease in. . . . I would make that wall a wall of fire if it were necessary." Violators of the regulations would be prosecuted in federal courts, making it harder for local cronies to allow offenders to walk free. Hatch held up the examples of Great Britain and her dependents, which "have lost $500,000,000" because of CBPP, as a grim picture of America's future should Congress fail to act.[27]

The Texans were incensed by Hatch's rhetoric and by the recent call from the Treasury Cattle Commission to impose a seasonal quarantine on Texas cattle.[28] Representative Samuel Lanham proclaimed that the bill was part of a conspiracy to destroy the great cattle industry of Texas. Echoing earlier debates, Lanham decried "the lodgment of extraordinary power and authority in the hands of a few," and complained that quarantines would be based on the findings of a "horse-doctor" and that railroads would be compelled to refuse to transport cattle because of "imaginary *contagia*." John Reagan charged that the bill trampled on the Constitution by usurping police powers reserved to the states, and Representative Orlando Potter (D-N.Y.) condemned the bill because "it invades the domestic life, the domestic concerns of the States, and it undertakes by a system of espionage to enter our cattle-yards, our very domestic homes, upon our farms, and to regulate them by a corps of officials sent from the central capital of the United States."[29]

Reagan's persistent opposition to the many BAI bills bears special attention because of his leadership role in passing the Interstate Commerce Act (ICA). In their analysis of the buildup to the ICA, Keith Poole and Howard Rosenthal note that Reagan had been promoting "his railroad regulation bill" in the House since 1878. They assert that "Reagan did not believe federal regulation to be constitutional until the *Munn v. Illinois* decision of 1 March 1877. Reagan was evidently influenced by the Court's reasoning that 'when private property is devoted to a public use it is subject to public regulation.' This declaration of the Court about the nature and function of railroad property coupled with the unquestioned authority of Congress over interstate commerce evidently changed Reagan's mind."[30] Poole and Rosenthal show that "Confederacy and Border congressmen overwhelmingly favored regulation of the railroads."[31] The South was "the root of the proregulation coalition." This interpretation aids their larger argument that the economic self-interest of a congressman's constituency was of relatively minor importance compared to more deep-seated philosophical values, party loyalty, and North-South location.

There is a conundrum. In both the BAI and ICC legislation, the constitutional debates struggled with defining the boundaries of congressional authority to regulate railroads. In both cases, key court decisions—*Husen* (1878) regarding the animal quarantines, and *Wabash* (1886) regarding the interstate railroad rates—struck down state attempts to regulate commerce, thereby putting more pressure on the federal government to act. However, Reagan's emphatic stance that Congress lacked the constitutional authority to regulate the interstate shipment of animals while simultaneously upholding that Congress had the constitutional right to regulate railroad rates suggests that philosophical principles took a back seat to economic interests. Furthermore, in the BAI debates, Southerners generally spearheaded the antiregulatory forces in the name of defending states' rights.

Contemporaries recognized the contradictions. On February 6, Representative William Hepburn (R-Iowa)—who would author an act in 1906 empowering the ICC to set maximum railroad rates—questioned the consistency of Reagan's positions. Hepburn expressed "wonderment" that Reagan could "find broad warrant in the Constitution . . . to lay his hand upon the entire transportation of this country . . . to secure his ideas of economy of transportation and cheapness of rates," but when the question of livestock disease control came up, he would see "the bugaboo of State rights looming up before him and can find himself shriven of all power to help the people."[32]

Hepburn later pointed out the contradictions of other Southerners who had advocated the creation of the National Board of Health (NBH) in 1879 and then opposed the BAI bill. The NBH bill had set a precedent (Chapter 2). Hepburn observed that the federal "power was not confined by the law to ports of entry, but extended to every city and village of this country. . . . If the bill under consideration is unconstitutional, so was the [NBH] act of 1879." In both the NBH and the BAI debates, Congress struggled with establishing a bureaucracy to work with the states to establish quarantines and fight diseases. The debates regarding science and policy were similar, and the substance of the constitutional disputes was nearly identical.[33]

One of the prevailing states' rights arguments was that the national government possessed authority only at the state line, and that federal facilities located within a state's boundaries were subject to the state's jurisdiction. This contention attracted the ire of the BAI bill's supporters. Representative John Anderson (R-Kans.) inquired about the width of a state line. If a cow was straddling a state line, "with her tail and body in Kansas, say, while her neck, head, and horns, are sticking over into Missouri . . . , you might possibly find a point the hundred-thousandth part of an inch wide just above the State line into which you might constitutionally put a knife and kill that part of the cow. But you would have no right to kill either part of the cow which was sticking over." Anderson argued that the states' rights doctrine made it impossible for the federal government to arrest contagions.[34]

For the bill's supporters, the states' rights argument advanced contradictory positions, which guaranteed inaction. The Texans denied that the federal government had the power to regulate the trade of animals while simultaneously applauding the *Husen* decision that forbade the states from imposing effective quarantines. Representative Jonathan Rowell (R-Ill.) spoke to this issue, noting that "after thousands of cattle had died" from Texas fever, his state had passed a law to make importers liable for civil damages. But "the courts held that we had not the authority." "When a State undertakes to make a law to protect itself the courts come in and tell them that is the business of the United States. When the United States attempts to pass a law and protect the people against the inroads of disease, some sensitive gentleman says you are trenching upon the rights of the States." The frustration with the *Husen* decision, and the inability to obtain compensation for the damage caused by Texas fever repeatedly boiled over during the debates. Hatch clearly linked potential scientific advances with policy. He accused the Texas delegation of opposing the bill because they feared research: "Science may find out how the Texas or Spanish fever is communicated." Without this proven link, it would be difficult to quarantine Texas cattle or ever win a court judgment against their owners.[35]

Hatch emphasized that the bill specified that only the states would police and destroy diseased animals. The federal government would provide oversight and "aid the States" by providing one-half of the eradication cost. Hatch failed to mention what would happen if a state chose not cooperate—but his opponents did this for him. Representative James Broadhead (D-Mo.) maintained that the law would give BAI agents the power to "enter upon a man's farm, inspect his cattle, determine that some of them are diseased, and have them taken out and shot."[36]

Many representatives were clearly concerned with the quarantine provisions in Section 4, and they struggled to find a way to limit this authority. On 27 February 1884, the House amended the bill by a vote of 115 to 64 requiring the president to gain the assent of a state's governor before imposing a quarantine. An attempt to kill the bill ended in a 114 to 114 tie; on a recount, the motion lost by a vote of 114 to 118. Thus, the movement to create a BAI had barely survived. Henry Muldrow (D-Miss.) then moved to limit the entire bill to CBPP by striking out clauses that referred to other "contagious, infectious and communicable diseases." This was hotly contested and ultimately rejected by a vote of 56 to 124.[37]

The final House consideration of HR 3967 took place on 28 February 1884. The first order of business was an amendment to delete Section 4 on quarantine powers from the bill. This passed by a roll-call vote of 155 to 116. An attempt by Samuel Randall (D-Pa.) to kill the bill by recommitting it to the Agricultural Committee then failed by seven votes—138 to 145. This was followed by a vote on the weakened bill which passed 155 to 127. The Democrats split 52 to 122. Many congressmen who had been critical of the early drafts voted in favor of final passage.[38] These legislators presumably found merit in the federal government helping to control contagious animal diseases but were not willing to grant strong powers to the executive branch. A few others who preferred a more aggressive approach voted against the weakened bill.

A House Divided

The *Chicago Tribune* noted, "The passage of the bill is rather remarkable. Only one-fourth of the Democratic membership, and the Democrats have a seventy majority, voted for the bill. . . . The Northwestern Democrats voted almost solidly for the bill, while the Southern Democrats, with seven exceptions, voted against it." The *New York Times* noted in the lead-up to the final vote: "The Democrats have indulged in some acrimonious flings at their own demoralized party. . . . The Republicans must win the largest share of the credit for helping the measure to a favorable conclusion."[39]

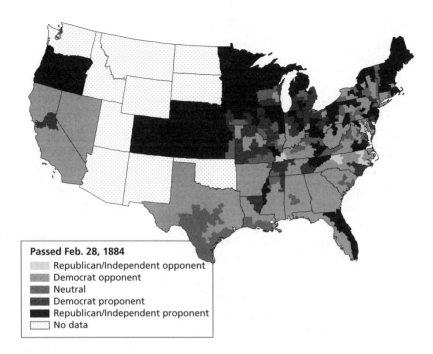

Figure 3.1. A House divided over the Bureau of Animal Industry.
Source: Compiled from *Congressional Record,* 28 February 1884, p. 1466.

Why then did House Speaker John G. Carlisle (D-Ky.) allow the bill to go to a vote? Recall, by Cox and McCubbins's accounting, the BAI bill was the only instance in the century after the end of Reconstruction in which a significant bill opposed by the majority of the party in power passed in the House. Figure 3.1 maps the final House votes on 28 February 1884 on HR 3967 by congressional district. The map shows the support for and opposition to a strong BAI broken down by party affiliation (proponents voting yea). The core of support for the Bureau in New England and the upper Midwest is evident, as is the core of opposition in the South. But to understand why the bill passed, it is important to consider the divisions within the Democratic caucus. Among all 174 Democrats voting on final passage, 52 voted yea. Among the 40 Eastern Democrats, only 4 supported the bill. Among the 73 Southerners, only 8 supported it, and 4 of these came from the border South. But among the 61 Western Democrats, 40 voted yea. They represented a region threatened by both CBPP and Texas fever. This Western Democrat block, which had more than doubled in strength in the previous election, combined with a virtually unanimous Republican minority to pass the measure.[40]

A coalition of Southern and Eastern Democrats voting to oppose reform measures favored by Western Democrats is also notable because it conflicts with now-standard interpretations of prevailing sectional alliances. In *Roots of Reform,* political scientist Elizabeth Sanders argued that politically mobilized farmers drove the movement for federal regulation in the late nineteenth century. Her picture of the populist alliance includes both Southern and Western agrarians.[41] In this case, Western legislators supported the 1884 BAI Act whereas Southern legislators opposed it.

Perhaps Speaker Carlisle allowed a floor vote on the BAI bill just for show because he expected it to die in the Senate, as had similar bills in earlier sessions of Congress. The success in the House certainly mobilized strong interest groups seeking to defeat the bill in the Senate. Although they failed to achieve this objective, opponents successfully lobbied to remove the provisions most offensive to the Southern Democrats. A look at some of the major outside protagonists helps explain the conflicting pressures on Congress as the bill moved forward.

Organized Opposition

Among the most vigorous opponents of the reforms were the Chicago stock-dealers, who handled cattle from the Western and Southern ranges and were concerned that a new livestock sanitary bureaucracy would cut into their Texas business and incite animal-health scares.[42] Harvey Goodall, publisher of the *Drovers Journal,* along with the packer-stockyard magnates Nelson Morris and Samuel Allerton led the drive to "Kill the Bill." To coordinate their efforts, the dealers organized the Chicago Live Stock Exchange beginning in February 1884—the Exchange would be a fixture in the livestock trade well into the twentieth century. The dealers asserted that the existence of livestock contagions (in the West, at least) was a myth that was being perpetuated by "unscrupulous office-seekers" whose "sensational reports have damaged the export trade." Representatives of fifty-eight stockyard brokers signed a petition to Congress against passage. The *Chicago Tribune* would later charge that the stockyard men "would rather see contagious cattle diseases spread throughout the length and breadth of the country than lose the smallest part of their business."[43]

Fights flared up within the livestock industry. J. H. Saunders of the *Breeder's Gazette* launched a strong defense of the bill and attacked the stockyard interests for their stance. A new coalition of Midwestern and mountain cattle-raisers joined the fray, protesting against "the petty, selfish, and short-sighted opposition of the cattle-brokers and freight-agents." Thomas Sturgis, Secretary of the Wyoming Stock Growers Association, also vocally supported the bill; the WSGA eventually threatened to blacklist the dealers who had signed the petition.[44] As these battles raged between the concentrated stockyard interests and the more diffuse Northern cattle-owner interests, some Chicago commission men broke ranks. Despite the counterattack, the Live Stock Exchange dispatched a delegation, headed by its president Elmer Washburn, to Washington to lobby against the BAI bill. Chicago Republican politico Emery Storrs led the charge.[45]

Passage in the Senate

The Senate took up debate of HR 3967 on 12 March 1884, with the chair of the Committee on Agriculture and Forestry, Warner Miller (R-N.Y.) shepherding the bill. His committee had made many changes, which would later be voted on as amendments to the House version. Most importantly, the committee had reintroduced the quarantine provision of the old Section 4, and made the federal government assume all the eradication costs. The debate on "the Pleuro-pneumonia bill" again centered on Texas fever. Numerous senators weighed in, with Coke of Texas charging that the bill would "hand over to the custody of the Commissioner of Agriculture and the Secretary of the Treasury" all of the South's cattle industry. Coke asserted that Texas cattle "are in a perfectly natural and normal condition of health. . . . The people need no assistance from the Government." He feared that "no foreign country will take them [Southern cattle] when denounced as infected with disease."[46]

Disease outbreaks repeatedly affected animal health legislation and policy. An example occurred during the Senate debate on the BAI bill, when an outbreak in Kansas initially (and mistakenly) diagnosed as foot-and-mouth disease (FMD) interrupted the proceedings. On 3 March 1884, Kansas Governor G. W. Glick alerted Commissioner Loring of the outbreak, asking if he could send "a competent veterinary surgeon? No one here can advise what to do." The USDA rushed veterinarian M. R. Trumbower to the scene, and he confirmed the local diagnosis of FMD on March 10. With several states on the verge of quarantining Kansas, Governor Glick called a special session of the state legislature, which quickly passed bills by nearly unanimous votes to grant unprecedented powers to the executive branch. State officials pleaded for federal help.[47]

The highly contagious nature of FMD added to the urgency and likely changed many minds in favor of federal action. On 13 March 1884, Senator Preston Plumb (R-Kans.) introduced S 75, which called for an appropriation of $25,000 to help his state stamp out the disease. The debate on the FMD bill, which occupied thirty-three pages in the *Congressional Record,* showed that even when faced with an imminent threat to the nation's livestock industry, many rejected federal involvement. With reports that FMD had spread to Illinois, Iowa, and Missouri, the bill was amended to include all states. There were close parallels with the BAI debate. Plumb and his allies raised the specter of FMD engulfing the continent as it had done in Europe and elsewhere. If FMD spread to the open range, it would be impossible to contain. Plumb argued that federal involvement was needed to counter the inclination of farmers in infected states to hide the disease and try to ship their cattle to clean areas: "The very moment the disease is well defined in any locality the men ship the cattle off." Only federal officials could credibly guarantee that a disease had been eradicated and that cattle and beef were safe— nobody would believe reports issued by state officials. The threat of foreign quarantines against all cattle shipments made the outbreak a national problem.[48]

The FMD scare was a wake-up call for Kansas Senator Ingalls. He had branded the 1881 BAI bill a "devil-fish" and opposed similar legislation in 1882 and 1883, but in March 1884 Ingalls was an ardent supporter of the FMD bill. He declared that "the doctrine of State rights and State sovereignty dies hard, but I think it is moribund and in the course of time will eventually be buried." Whereas in 1881 the principle of states' rights had been sacred for the senator, it was now an "exploded, abandoned, and defunct interpretation of the Constitution."[49]

Not all opponents were swayed. Some suspected that the whole crisis was overblown or even concocted to aid in the passage of the BAI

Act. Many argued that the individual states were capable of controlling the problem. Thomas Bayard (D-Del.) pounded on the moral hazard problem, noting that government compensation for diseased animals would encourage farmers to lower their guard and aid in the spread of contagions. Both sides clearly recognized that the FMD bill bore on the BAI debate.[50] Following several amendments, including one increasing the appropriation to $50,000, the FMD bill passed the Senate by a vote of 29 to 14 on March 17 and was sent to the House.

Chicago Live Stock Exchange lobbyist Emery Storrs was among those dismissing the FMD outbreak as a ruse. On March 25, Storrs formally presented his brief against the BAI bill. He denounced the measure as "highly inimical" to the nation's livestock interests and charged that proponents of the BAI bill fabricated disease scares "to demonstrate the necessarily of creating a bureau." He concluded, "To make this bill a law is to declare to all the world that our cattle are thus diseased," ruining "our export trade." He further added that "to defeat the bill is to declare . . . American cattle are affected with no infectious or contagious diseases." In place of the BAI bill, Storrs drafted a substitute to create yet another investigative commission.[51]

On April 23, the Senate returned to debate the pleuropneumonia bill. Recognizing their weak position, the BAI's supporters immediately offered a substitute bill that was similar to that passed in the House without the offending quarantine provisions. Coke again went on the attack, repeatedly noting that Texas fever "is not a disease" and that the concern over CBPP was a giant hoax because it did not exist. Senator McPherson proclaimed that CBPP "could not exist in New Jersey for an hour under our laws." This was decades after the disease had been confirmed in his home state.[52] The substitute bill went nowhere.

New participants rehashed old arguments as the debate continued for four more days.[53] A series of amendments significantly limited the power and jurisdiction of the proposed bureau. Senator Coke secured a crucial amendment declaring that "Texas fever shall not be considered a contagious, infectious, or communicable disease . . . as to cattle being transported by rail to market for slaughter, when the same are unloaded only to be fed and watered in lots on the way thereto." Other changes cut the agency's budget from $200,000 to $150,000, explicitly prohibited the Commissioner of Agriculture from paying indemnities, and removed the House's stipulation that the federal and state governments equally share eradication costs.[54] The Senate passed the amended bill by a vote of 34 to 9 on April 29 and sent it to conference committee. The Republicans supported final passage 24 to 0; Northern Democrats split 4 yeas, 2 nays, and Southern Democrats voted 6 yeas, 7 nays.

Analyzing roll call votes helps explain why the BAI bill passed in 1884. Tracking the votes of individual senators shows rising support among Republicans. Twelve Republican senators, who had voted to table and thus kill the BAI bill on 3 August 1882, voted yes on the final bill on 29 April 1884. Although Ingalls did not vote on final passage, he also likely had changed sides. He voted with supporters on two early votes; every other senator who did so also voted for final passage. No Democratic opponent in 1882 switched to support the bill in 1884, although two who were absent in the 1882 did vote for passage in 1884, and two who were in favor of the 1882 bill voted against the 1884 bill. Seven Democrats voted in support of the measure in both years, and only the two Texas senators (Coke and Maxey) voted nay both times. Although most Southerners opposed the measure, both of Mississippi's senators, L. Q. C. Lamar and James George, voted for the final bill as did Wilkinson Call of Florida and Augustus Garland of Arkansas.

Final Passage

The private correspondence and briefings of the principal lobbyists for the opposing interest groups offer a rare behind-the-scenes glimpse that helps explain the bill's passage. G. W. Simpson, head of the Bay State Live Stock Company, supported strong BAI legislation. On 10 May 1884, he wrote another supporter, WSGA Secretary Sturgis, about his efforts on behalf of the BAI bill. Simpson had been fearful that "the decided stand" taken by some die-hard supporters in Congress "might result in our not getting any bill" passed in that session. He consulted with opposing lobbyist Emery Storrs and detected that the WSGA's threatened blacklist was undermining the Chicago dealers' united front. According to Simpson, Storrs considered it "in the interest of his clients to have an amicable agreement by which the Chicago men could perhaps secure some Wyoming shipments which they are at present very liable to lose." With the bill moving forward, Storrs "has met with a defeat." Simpson concluded that "if we secure a bill with an appropriation, it can be amended from time to time, so that within a few years . . . we shall have what the interests of the stock-growers require, and . . . the people who now so strongly oppose it will be very glad to acknowledge that it is a great benefit to all."[55]

On May 22, Storrs briefed the Chicago Live Stock Exchange about his lobbying against the BAI bill as originally drafted. His report differed in tone and thrust from Simpson's account without contradicting it directly. Storrs gloated over securing the Texas fever exemption and restricting the number of Bureau employees to neuter its threat to the Texas cattle trade. He claimed credit for convincing Simpson that pushing for a Texas fever quarantine was "an unwise course," one that had to be sacrificed to secure the passage of the CBPP legislation. Storrs exulted that the amended bill was "the most profitable piece of legislation that livestock men ever had" because the exemption "cut off all possibility of interference with the transportation of Texas cattle even by State legislation."[56] With the changes, Storrs threw his support behind the Senate bill.

The many amendments made the bill acceptable to Storrs, but it was now unpopular with the staunchest House supporters of a BAI. In addition, many authorities, such as James Law, also found the weakened legislation wanting.[57] It appeared that defections would kill HR 3967. On May 7, the House voted by a large majority to non-concur in the hope that its conference committee members might claw back some of what had been lost, but to no avail. The House finally accepted the Senate version on 24 May 1884 without a recorded vote, and President Arthur signed it into law on May 29.[58]

Conclusion

The history of the BAI bill is special. It was the only significant legislation passed between the end of Reconstruction (1877) and the 1960s that was opposed by a majority of the party in power in the House. Its passage involved a rupture of the coalition of Western and Southern agrarians seeking reform, as each group pursued its own interests. The BAI legislation was also unusual because of its content. A comparison of the congressional debates and legislation on livestock health with those on creating institutions to confront human contagions highlights the significance of the step Congress took in 1884. In the passage of the BAI bill, Congress created a bureaucracy with powers that vastly exceeded those previously entrusted to other health-related and regulatory agencies. The BAI was a new type of scientific agency. It pioneered microbiological research in the United States and was at the forefront of the application of science to public policy. The law called for a strong leader—a chief as opposed to a committee chair—and specified that the chief be a scientist. It empowered the chief to gather information, conduct research, and report on disease control. Furthermore, Congress placed the BAI within a strong existing department, immediately affording it political connections and support. The new BAI took over the duties of the Treasury Cattle Commission and the USDA's recently formed Veterinary Division. In August 1884, it assumed control of port inspection and quarantine from the Department of the Treasury. It had an independent base of support in the private sector and among state livestock and health officials.[59]

Americans celebrate many important agricultural legislative initiatives such as the Morrill Land-Grant College Act (1862), the Hatch Experiment Station Act (1887), and the Smith-Lever Extension Act (1914), but these took years, even decades, to realize their potential. The BAI was different. It was born in a crisis. When the BAI Act was signed in May 1884, many proponents recognized its limitations but saw it as a "first step in the right direction."[60] They understood that the agency's powers could be strengthened in future appropriation hearings. Daniel Salmon and his small staff settled into their new jobs in the summer of 1884, but their honeymoon proved short. Within weeks, the nightmare long dreaded came true—CBPP erupted in the Midwest. Facing the crisis, the Bureau, Congress, and the states struggled to adjust in order to arrest the contagion. The response challenged deep-seated social, political, and legal attitudes—it required collective action to solve national and global problems.

4 The BAI in Action

Establishing the Area Eradication Model

ON 26 SEPTEMBER 1892, Secretary of Agriculture Jeremiah Rusk officially declared that "the United States is free from the disease known as contagious pleuro-pneumonia."[1] This achievement was all the more impressive because just eight years earlier the disease had breached the Appalachians and threatened to become permanently established on the open range. Never before had an established contagious disease been purged on a continental scale. In eradicating contagious bovine pleuro-pneumonia (CBPP), the newly created Bureau of Animal Industry (BAI) established a successful model for "area eradication." This was a valuable legacy that would pay rich dividends. Indeed, modern researchers working to eradicate smallpox credited the BAI's CBPP campaign with creating "the precedent and mechanisms" for "area-wide eradication programs."[2] The victory over CBPP increased the BAI's political legitimacy and gave its leaders the confidence to undertake even greater challenges.

The Bureau's success against CBPP was not merely another example of the inexorable march of science. There were no fundamental breakthroughs in understanding the disease, and there were no new wonder drugs. Rather, the story of this achievement is primarily an account of how a nation forged new legal and institutional arrangements to address serious problems. After a rocky start, the campaign gained momentum. Infected states strengthened their own animal health bureaucracies and enacted laws to facilitate state-federal cooperation. Most governors signed agreements that granted the U.S. Commissioner of Agriculture power to declare quarantines *within* their states, to send federal agents onto private property, to slaughter infected and exposed animals, and to destroy buildings and materials. Even bestowing such powers to state officials was a contentious issue; to grant them to federal agents required a major change in legal and political opinion. Some state legislatures debated for years before proceeding. The prospect of other states and the federal government quarantining holdouts helped ensure compliance. In early 1886, Commissioner of Agriculture Norman J. Colman proclaimed that "the heroic treatment, the one man power, is necessary" to stamp out CBPP. By 1887, Colman (and his designate, BAI Chief Daniel Salmon) had acquired such power. The traditional balance of state versus federal powers shifted significantly.[3] A new federalism was being forged.

Many in the cattle business had long denied that CBPP existed or dismissed it as a minor irritant. Contrary to such claims, the disease was in fact a grave and growing danger. Modern studies show that the mortality rate was between 10 and 70 percent among infected cattle. Confined cattle, such as valuable dairy and breeding stock, were at a higher risk than range cattle. Infected animals exhibited symptoms— elevated temperatures, difficulty breathing, reduced milk production, and a frequent painful cough—similar to other diseases, making diagnosis difficult without post-mortem inspections. The incubation period lasted from two weeks to six months, and asymptomatic animals could spread the contagion, making control difficult. CBPP was indeed a major threat.[4]

Baptism by Fire

In summer of 1884, CBPP broke out of its eastern confines, hitting Ohio, Illinois, and Kentucky. The specter that CBPP would become enzootic on the open range seemed imminent. On 15 July 1884, M. R. Trumbower, a BAI veterinarian, confirmed a case of CBPP on C. A. Keefer's farm near Sterling, Illinois. Trumbower initially had diagnosed the animal as suffering from tuberculosis, which added to the confusion. The BAI traced the contagion to infected Jerseys that had been shipped from Maryland to Ohio in November 1883; one of these cows was subsequently forwarded to Illinois (see Figure 4.1). The BAI soon interdicted shipments from infected herds destined for Tennessee, Nebraska, and North Carolina, along with a large shipment scheduled to pass through Chicago.[5] The existing protocols for destroying animals were exceedingly cumbersome: to dispose of ten Jerseys, Illinois State Veterinarian N. H. Paaren had to locate the justice of the peace, who had to commis-

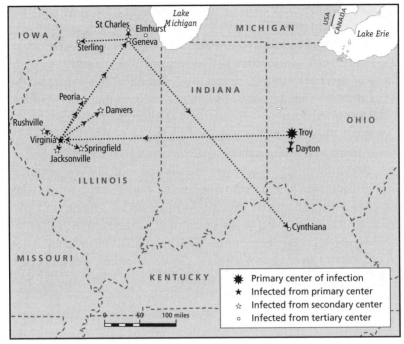

Figure 4.1. Tracing the spread of contagious bovine pleuropneumonia, 1884. *Source:* U.S. Bureau of Animal Industry, *Report for 1884*, insert between pp. 16 and 17.

sion three disinterested appraisers. They in turn had to gain access to and appraise the cattle, after which the town magistrate had to sign and return the appraisal documents before Paaren could begin his work.[6] Clearly mass cullings would require more streamlined procedures.

On 20 August 1884, the U.S. Commissioner of Agriculture, George Loring, requested that Jersey owners who had recently received new stock cease all shipments. He also reminded cattle owners and railroad companies that it was now a federal crime to knowingly ship diseased animals across state lines. Finally, he requested the "cordial co-operation of State authorities." Loring could do little more. The limitations of the 1884 Act—the requirement to gain state cooperation in the midst of an emergency, the cap of the number of BAI employees at twenty, and the small budget—were all too evident. To focus resources on the Midwestern hotspots, BAI director Daniel Salmon had to suspend operations in several Eastern states.[7]

Disease-deniers went into full battle mode. The *Drovers Journal,* voice of the stockyard interests, insisted that the outbreak was an enormous fraud perpetrated by the "Pleuro-pneumonia racket" who sought offices and funds. The Chicago Live Stock Exchange also got into the act. In late September 1884, its president, Elmer Washburn, demanded that the BAI essentially stop its work and conduct a several-month experiment to determine whether the disease that was affecting cattle was actually contagious. He offered pens and animals for the research. Salmon refused. There were well-established protocols to diagnose CBPP, and he feared that the disease might spread from the trial site. His resources were already stretched to their limit, and he did not want to divert any of his staff to meeting what he considered an "idiotic and inexcusable" demand.[8] The doubts and denials persisted. As the *Farmers' Review* lamented, even though the existence of CBPP in the Midwest had "been proved beyond all chance of denial . . . many stop their ears and cry 'it is not so!' . . . Because the fact is not agreeable therefore the fact does not exist."[9]

Delays ensued. In many states, officials who wished to cooperate were hamstrung by legal constraints; in others, officials were downright hostile. In the summer of 1884, BAI audits of suspect cattle shipped from Illinois led to the discovery of CBPP in a herd owned by H. D. Frisbie and J. K. Lake, nationally known livestock traders based in Cynthiana, Kentucky. Events soon went awry. On 1 August 1884, Salmon requested that Kentucky Governor J. Proctor Knott immediately quarantine the animals, but Knott dragged his feet. After personally inspecting the herd in September, Salmon concluded the sick animals "were handled so recklessly that many others were infected; the plague notoriously existed in the herd of Messrs. Frisbie & Lake for month after month."[10]

Kentucky had no livestock sanitary bureau, no budget for animal disease control, and no emergency powers to condemn or even to quarantine the diseased animals. Suggestions to call a special session of the legislature went nowhere, and private efforts by "the stockmen of the State . . . to raise enough money to purchase and slaughter all the cattle belonging to Messrs. Frisbie and Lake" collapsed. The prospect of receiving private payments for their whole herd apparently encouraged Frisbie and Lake to postpone separating their diseased animals from their healthy stock. The attempt to employ a Coasian-style solution may have made a bad situation even worse. On September 24, Knott finally acted, asserting that the common law gave him all the police powers needed. He instructed local justices of the peace to enact quarantines and reminded owners of diseased animals that they could be held liable for damage to other herds. But Knott's proclamation achieved little; BAI bungling would magnify the problems. Concerned with the absence of an effective state quarantine, Salmon hired a private veterinarian, D. A. Woodroffe, on 3 December 1884 "to keep supervision of the cattle about Cynthiana, and to inform the Department of any violation of the law." Instead of containing the problem, Woodroffe inexplicably issued "a certificate of good health" for a lot of 146 cattle that Frisbie and Lake wanted to ship to Texas.[11]

Thus, in 1885 the fledgling BAI rang in the New Year facing a mounting crisis. On January 3, Commissioner Loring warned Texas Governor John Ireland that the animals were en route and requested that he bar their entry. Salmon then followed the cattle to Austin, where he received a hostile reception. Under Texas statutes, the governor was powerless to act. The state legislature was in session and could have passed legislation to address the emergency, but it too did nothing. State authorities and the local press remained antagonistic to the BAI, asserting that nothing was wrong with Frisbie's stock even as the imported cattle were dying at an alarming rate. Subsequent inspections found no signs of CBPP—Texas fever was the probable cause of the premature deaths. Texas had dodged a bullet, in spite of the inaction of state officials.[12]

The contagion continued in Kentucky, engulfing a wide region by the close of 1885. The Kentucky legislature subsequently empowered the State Board of Health to quarantine the Cynthiana area but refused to authorize cooperation with the BAI. This meant that the federal government could not reimburse the state for expenses. The systematic slaughter of diseased and exposed cattle did not begin until 15 March 1886—roughly twenty months after the alarm first sounded. Before this date, individual owners had culled some exposed animals, and in two cases armed farmers took matters into their own hands by slaughtering their neighbors' herds. On 25 February 1886, Governor Knott vetoed legislation that would have given the Board of Health blanket powers to control the disease on the grounds that it improperly delegated legislative authority.[13] The search for an appropriate legal means to combat the disease continued for many years.

The legal and administrative barriers that hampered the Bureau's containment efforts in 1884–1885 had been anticipated in the debates leading to its creation, but opponents had succeeded in stripping significant powers from the bill that eventually passed.[14] When the CBPP crisis hit, many politicians, including incoming Commissioner of Agriculture Colman, changed their views about the disease and what constituted appropriate remedies. As a result, powers previously deemed unacceptable were inserted into later appropriation acts. The Agricultural Appropriations Act of 30 June 1886 maintained the Bureau's budget at $100,000, removed the restriction on the number of employees, and allowed the BAI to purchase diseased animals to prevent the spread of CBPP across state lines. This later provision was essentially a mechanism to compensate the owners of infected stock.[15] Although there were many precedents for compensation in other nations and in several states, it rubbed many people the wrong way to pay stock owners to destroy a public nuisance.[16]

With the new powers in place, Commissioner Colman issued a revised set of rules and regulations for dealing with CBPP in August 1886. He requested that the governors sign a cooperative agreement that specified procedures to purchase and destroy affected stock and that gave federal officials powers to operate within a participating state. This represented an important step in the evolution of what would later be termed "coercive federalism." A number of states acted quickly in response to Colman's initiative, but many, including Illinois, resisted.

The Chicago Fiasco

The CBPP situation took a turn for the worse in September 1886 when the disease was discovered near Chicago.[17] Given the proximity to the stockyards and large packinghouses, this outbreak was national news. On September 12, the Illinois State Veterinarian John Casewell diagnosed CBPP in a Jersey cow owned by John Carne Jr. of the Ridgeland region (about eight miles west of downtown Chicago). Two days later, Casewell quarantined Carne's property and began tracing the past movement of the first sick cow. Carne had purchased the cow from a dealer named Silas Palmer, who had acquired it at the Union Stock Yards and had subsequently kept the animal on a farm owned by Ira Harvey on the outskirts of Chicago. This farm served as a pasture for numerous dairies; much as on a public commons, the stock intermingled freely. By September 18, state investigators had discovered five cases of CBPP on the Harvey property. Before going to the stockyards, the Palmer cow had been housed in the Phoenix Distillery. Investigators soon discovered that the Phoenix and Chicago's other distilleries were disease breeding grounds (see Figure 4.2 for the centrality of these distilleries). On September 19, Casewell extended the state quarantine to the Chicago Alcohol Works and to the Phoenix, Empire, and Lynch-Shufeldt distilleries.[18]

Dairymen and livestock owners contracted with these distilleries to feed their stock on grain byproducts. This was a big business, and several thousand cattle and pigs were crowded into the facilities. To make matters worse, the dairymen frequently shifted their cows among the distilleries and other feeding areas such as the Harvey farm. In this disease-friendly environment, investigators discovered that a lung plague had been afflicting cattle since 1884, when CBPP first hit the state. Many dairymen had been aware that their animals were falling sick, but they had hidden the problem by selling their cows to local butchers soon after milk production fell. Milk and meat from these animals were routinely sold for human consumption.[19]

On September 19, roughly 3,000 bovines were under state quarantine at the four distilleries in the heart of Chicago, and all were suspected of carrying CBPP. The fear of all fears was that the disease would infect the Union Stock Yards and spread from there across North America. The BAI leapt into action. With much fanfare, Daniel Salmon traveled to Chicago and immediately began an inspection tour of the quarantined areas on September 22. Among the participants in Salmon's tour were John Sherman and Elmer Washburn from the Union Stock Yards. At the Phoenix Distillery, the veterinarians killed and dissected four cows, all of which proved infected. Similar events played out at the Lynch-Shufeldt Distillery. Hiram McChesney of the Illinois Board of Live Stock Commissioners boasted that "if I had my own way, I would kill all the cattle." Such a slaughter would have caused losses valued at the time between $100,000 and $250,000. The question of who would pay for the clean-up and what should be done with the contaminated

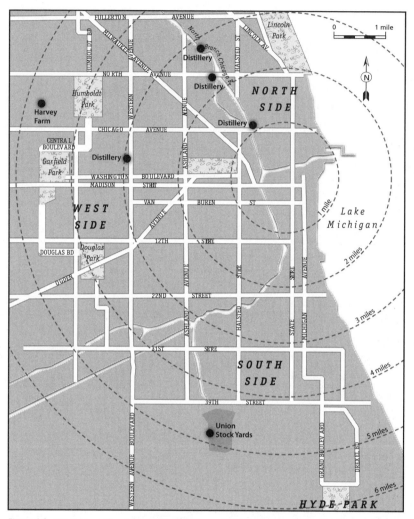

Figure 4.2. Mapping the "mess" in Chicago, 1886. *Source:* Compiled by authors.

buildings and the carcasses of the exposed and infected animals became the issue of the day.[20]

Illinois had long struggled to bolster its defenses against livestock diseases, but when the Chicago outbreak hit, the state's institutions and leaders proved woefully inadequate. As of 1 July 1885, Illinois statutes directed state officials to investigate contagious diseases, to impose quarantines, and to slaughter diseased and exposed animals. State officials could pay fair market value for condemned animals shown to be sound, but were explicitly prohibited from providing compensation "for such animals as are already diseased at the time of slaughter." The laws also failed to authorize cooperation with federal authorities. These policies created stumbling blocks because by mid-1886 the BAI could purchase diseased animals but would not do so without state cooperation. As a result, an important policy tool was left unused.[21] To make matters worse, there was at most $10,000 in the state's coffers to pay for the exposed animals. There was little immediate prospect for additional funding because the General Assembly was not in session. In addition, there was no contingency plan in place.

Pushed and pulled by competing special interests, state and local officials wavered and reversed course repeatedly. There was much talk but little action, and the mess got worse as stakeholders turned on each other. Representatives of the stockyards and large packers feared that the reputation of the Chicago beef industry would be damaged. Reflecting this position, John Sherman opined that that the sale of any meat from the quarantined animals would cause " 'ruination of the meat trade altogether.' " These objections slowed the initial momentum to slaughter the animals quickly.[22] Distillers and dairymen emphatically denied that CBPP infected the herds. At the same time, they also argued that if the disease did exist, it was far more widespread than announced, so it was unfair to single out the Cook County businesses. Public health enforcement mechanisms broke down almost immediately. When Oscar De-Wolf, Chicago's Commissioner of Health, asked police to quarantine milk from the suspect distilleries, Chicago's finest refused.[23]

On September 23, Governor Oglesby and the state livestock commissioners decided to slaughter the 3,000 cattle under quarantine. The *Chicago Tribune* lauded the decision to "Stamp It Out" in an editorial that dismissed the legal and constitutional niceties: "Let the Live-Stock Commissioners go ahead, then, with the killing, unhampered by any construction of statutory law if they are sure of their facts. If necessary the Governor can and should convene the Legislature in extra session. There will be no excuse for it if the scourge is not thoroughly and swiftly stamped out." Reflecting on the position of the stockyard and packing industries, the *Tribune* continued: "The beef interest of Chicago is afraid

that if any of the exposed cattle are dressed . . . there will be a preju-
dice against Chicago beef which would involve a much greater loss
than the first cost of all the cattle in all the distillery sheds of the city.
There is great force in this argument in favor of the nonuse of any of
the cattle . . . [but none] against the stamping out the terrible pest by
slaughter."[24]

Strapped for cash, the Illinois livestock commission sought "a beef or
cattle dealer" to buy and destroy all of the animals in return for a pledge
of future reimbursement. On September 26, the local wholesale butcher
firm of Miller & Armour—headed by Thomas Armour (not associated
with the packing giant Philip Armour)—offered to buy the apparently
healthy cattle. The plan called for the cattle to be slaughtered under the
watch of a veterinarian who would direct all tainted carcasses to the
rendering tank and allow the good meat onto the local market. The BAI's
Salmon purportedly agreed to the slaughter of the "good carcasses." This
news was well received by dairymen and distillers, but generated howls
of protest from the Union Stock Yards interests and Western cattle associations. In response, USDA Commissioner Colman declared it was
"crazy to think that the department will permit any of these cattle to be
sold."[25] In the meantime, Governor Oglesby and his lieutenants wavered on their decision to slaughter the distillery cattle. Newspapers pil-
loried the state officials for neglecting their civic duty amid reports that
dairymen were evading the quarantine and selling bovines from infected herds to local butchers.[26]

At the end of September, Oglesby finally agreed to Colman's August
1886 rules and regulations to cooperate with the USDA. But Oglesby
made " 'certain erasures, interlineations, and alterations' " before sign-
ing.[27] From the outset, Illinois officials ignored the conditions of the
agreement. Oglesby also refused to call for an extra session of the legislature to secure more authority and funding. Throughout October, federal authorities unsuccessfully pressed for the slaughter of the quarantined cows. The Illinois livestock commissioners and BAI leaders fought
incessantly over lines of communication, the command structure, and
the division of expenses. The milk situation added to the evidence that of
regulatory failure.

The continued marketing of the milk from the distillery herds sparked
a public furor. Existing Chicago ordinances, which prohibited the sale of
swill milk, had not been enforced for several years. The presence of

CBPP further raised food safety concerns. The milkmen and some veterinarians asserted that the milk from sick cows was safe; others, including many public health officials, disagreed. The crusading *Tribune* added its voice with headlines such as "Milk of Diseased Cows: It Is Sold in Chicago to North Side Families Every Day." The paper quoted a veterinarian stationed at the Phoenix Distillery that he would not allow his family to drink the milk, even " 'if we were starving.' " As the pressure mounted, Health Commissioner DeWolf gave notice on October 8 that he would prohibit the swill-milk trade as of October 12. After a fiery debate and a divided vote, the City Council backed DeWolf.[28] The milkmen now threatened to stop paying the distillers for feed; the distillers, in turn, threatened to stop feeding the animals. Chicago faced the specter of 3,000 bovines starving to death. The owner of one of the city's largest dairy herds, Simon Ryan, obtained a temporary injunction against the ban. Ryan sold milk only to wholesalers, and thus escaped direct pressure from consumers. After further hearings, the judge allowed the city's ban to stand, noting that selling swill milk is "a crime against society." Enforcing the ban proved problematic, as indicated by the arrests of several "milk smugglers," and exposés on smugglers "dodging" and "bribing" guards at the distillery sheds.[29]

Chicago Cattle Interests and CBPP

The adamant opposition of the stockyard interests and most giant packers to butchering the distillery cattle reflected their concern with maintaining a quality reputation. This reputation had a collective dimension: demand for all livestock and meat from Chicago was affected. In response to the crisis, the stockyard management introduced stringent measures to isolate their facilities and animals from the outbreak. Nevertheless, several cases of suspect animals passing through the yards subsequently came to light.[30] At no point did the stockyard interests agree to bear any of the costs of destroying other people's property. As we show in Chapters 8 and 9, when the costs associated with higher health standards fell directly on them, the large packers often behaved like the dairymen and distillers: they denied that any problems existed, opposed and sought to evade corrective regulations, demanded that someone else pay, and unmercifully attacked those exposing unsanitary practices.[31] The mess in Chicago did force the city's beef interests to face up to the CBPP problem.

The packer and stockyard magnate Nelson Morris was among the fiercest early deniers of CBPP. He blamed the 1879 British trade closure on the hesitation of inspector H. J. Detmers to declare the Union Stock Yards clean (see Chapter 2). Morris asserted that the "lung plague excitement" in the mid-1880s was fanned by veterinarians to gain business. The distillery mess left Morris between a rock and a hard place. He had stocked 380 cattle in the Phoenix sheds shortly before the outbreak. Although he was apparently aware of the disease scare, Morris chose to bear the risk. Many animals were soon succumbing to CBPP. Confronted with this cold reality, Morris hired a French veterinarian to inoculate the remainder in the hope of obtaining their eventual release from quarantine. The USDA frowned upon the inoculation because it kept the disease alive in the population, imposing serious costs on others. Inoculation rules had been one of the sticking points between Oglesby and Colman, and Oglesby had negotiated an exception to weaken the USDA's inoculation guidelines. Nevertheless the USDA imposed stringent rules that required quarantining with a lock and chain on *every* animal, strict record keeping, movement of the animals only for immediate slaughter, and a post-mortem report on each animal.[32]

Others associated with the Chicago Live Stock Exchange also did an about-face. After witnessing the autopsy of one steer afflicted with CBPP, Samuel Allerton "came away convinced. A great change of opinion followed."[33] Elmer Washburn, the head of the Exchange, also became a convert. He had lobbied Congress to defeat the BAI bill in March 1884 and six months later, in the midst of CBPP outbreak in Illinois, had advocated a wait-and-see policy. Two years later, after he toured the distilleries with Daniel Salmon in late September 1886, Washburn agreed that the animals should be condemned, although he doubted that they suffered from a contagious disease. On 16 November 1886, Washburn spoke before the Chicago meeting of Consolidated Cattle-Growers Association on the "Necessary Legislation to Get Rid of Contagious Cattle Diseases." Without acknowledging his past denials, Washburn now called for a powerful new commission with unilateral authority to quarantine any place or state, to destroy all animals infected or exposed to contagious diseases, and to destroy contaminated buildings. Washburn wanted his proposed commission, operating in place of the BAI, to be amply funded to meet any emergency, hire the most skilled veterinarians, and compensate the owners of destroyed animals at generous rates to encourage cooperation. He further sought federal penalties for obstructing or assaulting commission officials. Washburn had crossed the Rubicon regarding the seriousness of the disease threat and now demanded a federal agency with greatly enhanced powers—much like those he had helped gut from the early BAI proposals.[34]

In mid-November, the paralysis in Illinois began to ease. On 17 November 1886, the State Board of Live Stock Commissioners appointed three appraisers to assign values for the animals to be slaughtered, and the next day officials began destroying both diseased and exposed animals. However, the state program proceeded slowly, and the commissioners granted numerous exceptions, allowing the movement of cattle. The already serious state-federal row intensified, with Salmon publicly condemning the state's sloppy management. On 31 December 1886, Commissioner Colman issued a harsh critique, accusing Oglesby and the state commissioners of endangering the public with their delays, and charging that they violated the cooperative agreement by allowing the distilleries to restock their contaminated stables. Governor Oglesby retorted that the federal plan would have cost the state over $150,000 and undercut public support. But many in Chicago sided with Colman and demanded "heroic measures." The *Chicago Tribune* chided the Union Stock Yards interests, the members of the General Assembly, the State Live Stock Commissioners, and especially Oglesby for "pitiful incompetence." It also came to light that the state had sold the meat from the condemned animals.[35]

In January 1887, the Illinois legislature convened in a regular session, but it struggled to address the Chicago crisis, now four months old. The lack of legislative action is of special interest because in 1885, before the crisis hit Cook County, the General Assembly had passed a resolution by acclamation imploring the President of the United States to quarantine states with CBPP "or which refuse to take the proper steps for suppressing contagious disease."[36] At that time, Oglesby had been quick to slap strict quarantines on infected states, including Colman's home state of Missouri. The contradictions ran deeper. Recall from Chapter 2 that the same Richard Oglesby convened a conference in 1868 to demand strong national legislation to block the shipment of Southern cattle. It was much easier to point fingers at others than to deal with the problem when it struck home.

Expanding Federal Power

The failure to snuff out CBPP in Chicago had a major impact on the national debate over the BAI's powers. Eradicating the disease was, in the words of the *Breeder's Gazette*, like the mythical cleaning of the "stables of Augeas," a "Herculean undertaking," beyond the powers of those currently in charge. In December 1886, President Grover Cleveland requested that Congress grant stronger authority to remedy the CBPP problem so far as "the limits of a constitutional delegation of power to the General Government will permit." In the same month, the Consolidated Cattle-Growers Association, in league with the *Breeder's Gazette*, proposed creating a temporary three-member presidential cattle commission with a budget of $1 million and emergency powers to rid the country of CBPP. The original BAI "has proven a failure" due to its "state cooperation clause." Many early BAI advocates, along with converts such as Washburn, now sought a much more powerful agency to combat the lung plague. Other cattle interests, including Texans, preferred keeping the Bureau as it was.[37]

In early 1887, Senator Warner Miller (R-N.Y.) introduced a bill that called for a temporary commission as a supplement to rather than a complete replacement for the BAI. After several days of prickly debate and a series of unfriendly amendments, the Senate passed Miller's bill on 28 February 1887. Upon receiving it in the House, William Hatch noted that the debate would last for weeks, extending long after the close of the 49th Congress. As an alternative, the conference committee amended the 1887 Agricultural Appropriations bill to enhance the BAI's power and budget. The Appropriations Act of 3 March 1887 increased the Bureau's budget fivefold to $500,000 and made $100,000 available immediately; as a result, in 1888 the BAI's appropriation accounted for one-half of the USDA's total budget. The commissioner could spend these funds as he saw fit to prevent the spread of CBPP. The Act also authorized the purchase of both infected and exposed animals, allowed the Bureau to hire any number of staff, and enhanced its powers to enforce interstate quarantines. Specifically, the commissioner could issue quarantines as he deemed necessary to prevent the spread of CBPP "from one State to another."[38]

Raising the Bar: Eradication

With the expanded funding and power, Commissioner Colman shifted the BAI's goals from preventing the interstate spread of CBPP to eradicating the disease in the United States.[39] He promptly issued a new set of rules and regulations that went into effect on 15 April 1887. These dealt principally with CBPP, but they applied to "all contagious, infectious, and communicable diseases of domestic animals" that the BAI chief believed might spread across state lines. These rules vastly expanded the BAI's powers by granting the chief (and BAI inspectors) the authority, as "deemed necessary," to establish temporary quarantines and impose sanitary measures to prevent the spread of the disease. Upon receiving confirmation of a disease's existence, the commissioner could quarantine that *locality*—that is, the BAI could work within a state's borders. The chief could order the disinfection of buildings, farms, stockyards, and so on. The chief could order the slaughter of animals as he deemed necessary. He could also regulate (including quarantining equipment and yards) transportation companies that operated in more than one state or connected to interstate transportation companies. Violators of the commissioner's policies could be prosecuted in federal courts. The commissioner understood that BAI officials had no constitutional authority to exercise police powers within states, but he never explicitly mentioned state co-operation. To deal with this problem, Rule 12 stated that should the chief find it impossible to enforce the rules and regulations in any state, the commissioner could quarantine the entire state, shutting down the "exportation of animals of the kind diseased."[40] The message was clear: cooperate or else.

On 15 April 1887, Colman sent a letter to all governors asking them to accept his revised rules and regulations. He provided a form letter for the governors to sign:

_____ 188_,

I, _____, governor of the State of ____, and chief executive officer thereof, do hereby acknowledge the receipt of the rules and regulations certified to by the Commissioner of Agriculture of the United States, as having been prepared by him April 15, 1887, in pursuance of the authority of section 3 of an act of Congress approved May 29, 1884, establishing the Bureau of Animal Industry, and further acknowledge the receipt of the invitation to the executive authority of the State of ____ to co-operate in the enforcement of the provisions of said act, and of said rules and regulations.

And on behalf of the State of ____, and by virtue of my authority as the chief executive officer thereof, I do hereby accept the rules and regulations prepared by the Commissioner of Agriculture, April 15, 1887, for the suppression and extirpation of contagious diseases of animals, and agree that the executive authority of the State of ____ will co-operate with the Bureau of Animal Industry in carrying out the provisions of the act of May 29, 1884, to the full extent of its authority; and that I will direct the sheriffs and other peace officers of the State to render all necessary aid and assistance to the inspectors of the Bureau of Animal Industry in the performance of the duties imposed upon them by said rules and regulations.

————————,

Governor of the State of ____ [41]

The new conditions were much stronger than previous arrangements. "The governors of thirty-four States and Territories at once accepted these rules and regulations and agreed to co-operate with the Department."[42] Many governors no doubt desired more effective state-federal cooperation, but even those with qualms had to have been influenced by the threat that other states and the federal government could enact quarantines. The whole process smacked of the "one man principle"—the authoritarian concentration of power—that had so alarmed the Bureau's congressional opponents. A governor's acceptance gave the Commissioner of Agriculture the *carte blanche* power to declare and enforce quarantines within his state. Acceptance committed state and local police to aid and protect federal agents; the failure to do so could trigger the intervention of federal marshals and a statewide federal quarantine.[43]

To assist states to pass effective (and uniform) disease control legislation that would explicitly allow state officials to cooperate with the federal government, the BAI also supplied wording for draft legislation. Five states (New Hampshire, Massachusetts, Rhode Island, New York,

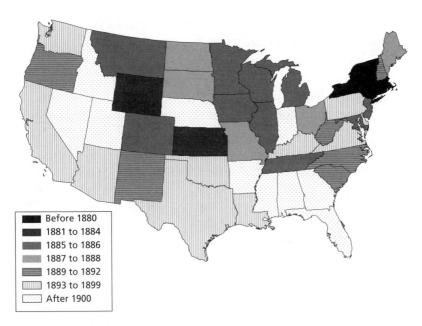

Figure 4.3. Adoption of state livestock sanitary offices. *Source:* Compiled from Marshall, "Presidential Address," pp. 84–85.

and Virginia) promptly adopted the template as law, and many other states worked out compromises acceptable to the USDA.[44] All the early adopting states harbored CBPP. The power of both the state and federal agencies was expanding dramatically, and cooperative agreements linking state and federal policies were becoming commonplace. Figure 4.3 maps the dates of establishment of livestock bureaucracies in the states and territories between 1860 and 1910.[45] Four states, all in the Northeast, created livestock sanitary boards or offices of state veterinarians before 1880. Two more, including Wyoming and Kansas, did so during the 1881–1884 period. Ten states, mostly in the upper Midwest, created such bureaucracies during 1885 and 1886. Five more states followed suit during 1887 and 1888. Most of those that adopted bureaucracies after 1888 were in areas not infected with CBPP in the South and West.

Dropping the Hammer on Chicago

Armed with new powers, Colman sent Salmon back to Illinois to try again to reach an understanding with state officials.[46] The Illinois legislature had been struggling to revise its laws to deal with infectious livestock diseases since it reconvened in January 1887. On March 19, Salmon met with Oglesby and members of the Board of Live Stock Commissioners to mend their differences and to map out a joint campaign. They agreed to merge the state and federal eradication efforts, with the USDA compensating owners for the slaughter of both infected and exposed cattle.

Faced with the increased threat of a federal quarantine, the state legislature passed a law on April 20 explicitly authorizing the Illinois cattle commissioners to cooperate with U.S. officials to suppress contagious livestock diseases. Oglesby immediately signed the bill, but he still refused to accept Colman's revised agreement. Salmon swiftly dispatched James Law to command of the BAI's Illinois operations. On April 22, Oglesby quarantined a small part of Cook County, but Law and Salmon deemed this step inadequate. In early May, by Salmon's account the state put " 'the whole matter in the hands of the department [USDA].' "[47]

It was time to drop the hammer. On May 24, Commissioner Colman shut down cattle traffic in Cook County. In this same order, Colman also quarantined six counties in New York, and four in Maryland. This edict represented a significant expansion in the application of federal police powers within state boundaries. Colman's quarantine did not include cattle moving through Chicago via the Union Stock Yards after the stockyard managers had agreed to prohibit the entry of any cattle from infected areas, but many states were not satisfied with this exception and erected their own quarantines that included the yards. As of the end of September 1886, the governors of Iowa, Wisconsin, Colorado, Nebraska, and Kansas had barred the entry of cattle from Illinois (and in some cases other states) on account of CBPP. Many other states and territories soon followed.[48]

Despite the ongoing crisis, the Illinois legislature dallied until the waning hours of the session. On 15 June 1887, it passed a bill that explicitly required the governor to accept the USDA's rules and regulations. It also explicitly authorized BAI agents to enter property to inspect, quarantine, and condemn infected and suspect animals. It mandated that all sheriffs and peace officers assist federal agents and specified that federal agents "shall have the same powers and protection as peace officers while engaged in the discharge of their duties." The bill called for stiff fines and prison terms for anyone who violated the quarantines or other regulations, and it stipulated that the federal government would pay all expenses associated with the eradication of CBPP. Oglesby refused to sign the bill because it conveyed almost unlimited power to the federal government and limited the state's ability to restrain any abuse of authority that might occur. To avoid the threatened blanket federal quarantine, Oglesby let the law take effect automatically on June 28.[49] It was preferable to let the federal government quarantine the infected districts than to shut down the entire livestock trade of Illinois, including the stockyards.

Most observers have missed the significance of the BAI's extension of federal power into state affairs. One year after the dust up in Illinois, British statesman and traveler James Bryce published his widely cited treatise *American Commonwealth* in which he asserted that the national government and state governments acted separately, wholly "within their respective spheres." The system operated like "a great factory wherein two sets of machinery are at work . . . each set doing its own work without touching or hampering the other." In further characterizing what was later called the "dual federalism regime," Bryce observed that the national government could not coerce a state.[50] In the summer of 1887, Governor Oglesby surely would have begged to differ.

Under the new arrangements, the BAI finally began to gain the upper hand in the fight against CBPP. James Law's arrival in Chicago marked a major turning point. As an experienced outside expert, Law helped heal the strained relationship between state and federal officials. The State Board of Live Stock Commissioners appointed several of Law's lieutenants as assistant state veterinarians, giving them powers under state law. They went block-by-block to tag and register animals. When the agents discovered a diseased animal, protocol called for the slaughter for the entire herd. In one case, Law summarily ordered the slaughter of 300 animals exposed to a single infected cow. In 1887, the BAI's agents inspected 7,411 herds and conducted 7,267 post-mortem examinations in Cook County. Only 350 of these examinations proved positive. A disinfection team cleansed 677 stables. With these actions, Law eradicated CBPP from Chicago by December 1887. To play it safe, the USDA did not lift the quarantine on Cook County until April 1888. By this date, the federal expenditure totaled $80,000. The territory west of the Allegheny Mountains was again free of the disease.[51]

Reflecting on the Chicago outbreak, Daniel Salmon itemized a number of lessons. The existence of the contagion in even one locale in the

United States could endanger the entire country. CBPP (and other diseases that could be transmitted by asymptomatic carriers) could spread widely before discovered, which called for better monitoring. New outbreaks would lead to trade disruptions, and quarantines would have "disastrous" economic consequences beyond the infected area. An emergency was not the best time to seek "new and radical legislation:" rather, an effective response demanded that the accommodating legal frameworks and professional organizations be established in advance. To this end, it was essential for the federal government to cooperate with state and business leaders. These conditions were not met in Illinois where an "exceeding hostile" environment inhibited disease control. Business hostility and official indecision "engendered doubt, and doubt led to delay, and delay enabled the owners of infected herds to dispose of their animals" into commercial channels. To prevent such behavior, officials needed to promptly implement strong control measures. The work should be directed by veterinarians with professional expertise rather than by businessmen with practical knowledge. Local businessmen lacked diagnostic expertise, and they became "uncertain, hesitating, and wavering" when their economic interests were at stake. Most fundamentally, Salmon concluded, the "quickest, the most thorough, the most radical method of stamping out pleuro-pneumonia is not only the best, but the cheapest."[52]

Eradication in the East

Eliminating CBPP from the Midwest was not enough. The problem would have to be attacked in the Eastern states where it had long resided. As more states brought their laws into conformity with federal guidelines and strengthened their own livestock control agencies, it became easier for government officials to identify, isolate, and destroy infected and exposed animals.[53] The success in Chicago and the larger budget allowed the BAI to dramatically increase the national scope of its CBPP campaign 1887 and 1888, with work in Virginia, Pennsylvania, Maryland, Massachusetts, New Jersey, New York, and the District of Columbia. In fiscal year 1889–1890, the Bureau inspected more than 283,000 cattle, reexamined some 200,000, and conducted 50,000 post-mortem examinations. In all, fewer than 1,000 diseased animals were discovered. Table 4.1 provides a sense of the progress of the CBPP campaign, showing its buildup in 1887, peak in 1888, and final mopping-up operations in 1892.

Table 4.1 Progress of the Bureau of Animal Industry campaign against contagious bovine pleuropneumonia

Activity	1887	1888	1889	1890	1891	1892	Total	Percentage
Cattle inspected								
New York	25,122	99,726	149,396	150,474	136,111	49,925	610,754	38.0
New Jersey	16,461	72,095	76,001	60,659	68,262	128,017	421,495	26.2
Pennsylvania		72,565	24,003	24,388	55,533	66,487	242,976	15.1
Maryland	57,868	60,312	79,606	108,376	—	—	306,162	19.1
Illinois	24,059	285	—	—	—	—	24,344	1.5
Total U.S.	123,510	304,983	329,006	343,897	259,906	244,429	1,605,731	
Percentage	7.7	19.0	20.5	21.4	16.2	15.2		
Infected and exposed cattle purchased for destruction								
New York	1,002	4,772	3,872	2,411	309	0	12,366	54.8
New Jersey	211	1,447	830	286	275	262	3,311	14.7
Pennsylvania	0	194	11	0	0	0	205	0.9
Maryland	3,006	1,495	383	20	0	0	4,904	21.7
Virginia	0	102	0	0	0	0	102	0.5
Illinois	1,547	130	0	0	0	0	1,677	7.4
Total U.S.	5,766	8,140	5,096	2,717	584	262	22,565	
Percentage	25.6	36.1	22.6	12.0	2.6	1.2		

Source: USDA, Yearbook of Agriculture, 1892, pp. 86–88; U.S. BAI, Reports for 1891 and 1892, pp. 72–73.

As in Illinois, officials in other states wrestled with enacting state-federal cooperative agreements to transfer cherished state prerogatives to a federal agency. Pennsylvania finally accepted the BAI's terms in 1888: the ensuing tough quarantine and slaughter measures swept CBPP from the state by 1889. The success in Illinois was achieved rapidly compared with the efforts required in the more established CBPP hotbeds of Maryland, New York, and New Jersey. Federal officials became more aggressive in the last reservoirs of the contagion; this practice would become a feature of later eradication programs. On 1 December 1887, Salmon transferred James Law from Illinois to New York, where he assumed command of all federal activities in the state. Law immediately initiated a program to register and tag every bovine in the five quarantined counties in the New York City region.[54]

New York Governor David H. Hill's "Cattle Quarantine Proclamation" of 14 May 1888 demonstrates the close interaction of state and federal police powers. Hill's five-county quarantine placed all cattle under lockdown—no animal could be moved, sold, or slaughtered without a BAI permit. Railroads and shipping companies were forbidden to transport cattle without a BAI permit. Cattle from outside the quarantine area could pass through to ports, but they needed a special permit to be shipped. Hill granted BAI agents the power to inspect all cattle and condemn those infected or exposed to CBPP, with the USDA compensating the owners. Butchers could slaughter cattle only in the presence of a BAI agent. BAI personnel were granted free access "to all places infected or suspected to be infected with lung plague." Sheriffs were ordered to assist and protect BAI employees. Hill appointed James Law and his BAI deputies to carry out the edicts. Law exercised one-man power because he was simultaneously the lead BAI official and the state veterinarian. In early 1889, he ordered the destruction of dilapidated stables suspected of harboring the contagion, forbid communal grazing, and summarily killed hundreds of animals found off their owners' lands. In addition, Law arrested cattle owners who violated the quarantine regulations. Law's imposition of the stringent USDA orders did not always go smoothly: his task force had to disperse a large mob of armed Long Island dairy farmers and deal with persistent opposition mounted by the local cattle associations.[55]

The last infected animal in New York was discovered in April 1891, and the last case in New Jersey was found in March 1892.[56] On 26 September 1892, USDA Secretary Rusk officially declared the United States free of CBPP. About five years after Colman's eradication decision, and at a cost to the federal government of only $1.5 million, the BAI, working with the infected states, had achieved a spectacular success.

To offer perspective, the total federal expenditure compared quite favorably to the Bureau's estimate that American farmers had been losing about $1 million annually due to the lower price paid for U.S. cattle in the British market alone.[57] This represented only a small fraction of the potential total losses from the disease. According to USDA estimates, CBPP killed about 20 percent of the bovines exposed and significantly reduced the productivity of the survivors. Eradication eliminated the threatened losses to the U.S. cattle population, valued at some $977 million in 1892. Without gauging the costs borne by the affected states and farmers, a rigorous cost-benefit analysis is not possible; however, in any reasonable scenario concerning the unchecked spread of the disease, the benefits of the eradication campaign well exceeded its costs.[58] This conclusion is reinforced by the experiences in other countries highlighted in the next section.

In his insider history of the BAI, U. G. Houck expressed his enthusiasm for the BAI's achievement:

> The United States was the first of the large nations of the world . . . which, having been extensively infected with contagious pleuro-pneumonia, was able to extirpate it completely. When it is considered that there were grave doubts entertained of the possibility of eradicating pleuropneumonia, that the States were not prepared to cooperate effectively, that serious opposition was met on almost every hand, and that other countries had labored a much longer time and made greater expenditures of money without success, the favorable outcome must be regarded as a great achievement for the new Bureau of Animal Industry. It accomplished the first great thing it undertook, the paramount purpose for which it was created.[59]

The campaign helped forge innovative guidelines for state-federal cooperative agreements and led many states to strengthen their legal and administrative structures. The powers and size of the Bureau expanded rapidly as more members of Congress saw the need for heroic measures. In 1884, the agency was limited to twenty employees (plus four enumerated staff); by 1888, the *Annual Report* listed 279 employees, a force was augmented by a large number of state employees who were put under the BAI's command.[60] When the BAI first addressed the CBPP problem, confusion reigned. By the end of the campaign, the protocols for identifying and extirpating the disease were well defined.

In 1890, Secretary Rusk sketched the main features of the U.S. policy in correspondence with a member of the British Parliament. Later, James Law would set to paper the elements of the area eradication model:

- Identify the area for treatment.
- Prevent the entry and egress of all cattle.
- Prevent all movement of cattle from herd to herd within the area and prohibit the pasturage of cattle on public highways and on unfenced lands.
- Immediately condemn and slaughter cattle found in violation of these rules.
- Enumerate and tag all bovines.
- Conduct a necropsy of every animal slaughtered or dying casually.
- Hold the owner criminally liable for every animal that goes missing or is slaughtered without a post-mortem examination.
- Appraise and slaughter (with necropsies) all cattle in exposed and suspect herds.
- Indemnify the owners for least two-thirds of the sound market value for all except the advanced cases and animals recently introduced.
- Disinfect all infected premises and equipment at public expense.
- Condemn and safely dispose of all feed, straw, and manure.
- Close fields for three months and allow restocking only from sound districts.
- Strictly supervise and control herds for up to six months.[61]

Implementing and enforcing these rules required a substantial force of inspectors with broad authority. These protocols would be adapted to combat other diseases around the world. The success of this model gave leaders in the veterinary community the confidence to confront even larger challenges.

International Comparisons

Comparing the American experience with what transpired in Great Britain and Australia provides a better appreciation of the BAI's accomplishment. By 1842, CBPP had become prevalent in the London area, having arrived recently from Holland and Ireland. The disease spread across Britain and was especially severe in dairy herds near urban centers. Despite the magnitude of the problem, national legislation did not address CBPP until 1867, when Parliament prohibited taking infected animals to markets or fairs. Ironically, the rinderpest epizootic, which killed hundreds of thousands of cattle in Britain between 1865 and 1867, did more to suppress CBPP than any government policies to that date. In a series of measures enacted over the next decade, Parliament and the Privy Council authorized local action. However, local policies were poorly enforced and ineffectual—cattle could easily be moved among jurisdictions. Finally, in 1890, Britain adopted a national eradication program, which stamped out CBPP in 1898. British leaders were keenly aware of the organization and progress of the U.S. campaign.[62]

As in the United States, responsibility for CBPP control in Australia had long rested with the states. CBPP hit Melbourne in 1858, and within a few years had spread to herds as far as a thousand miles to the north. By 1900, it was "deeply entrenched" throughout the continent, with cattle on the open range acting as a reservoir. The early governmental responses were too little, too late. Quarantines, along with the slaughter of sick and suspect animals with compensation for owners, led to temporary eradication in the southern colonies. By the first decades of the twentieth century, Victoria, New South Wales, and South Australia protected their valuable dairy herds with expensive cordons. Circa 1940, New South Wales and Victoria required entering cattle (not intended for immediate slaughter) to be detained in quarantine for 180 days. Despite these precautions, the disease repeatedly reinfected cleansed areas. The Australian government finally embarked on a national eradication campaign in 1961. Aided by improved vaccines and diagnostic methods, veterinarians systematically cleared one area after another. In 1973, Australia was officially declared free of CBPP. This was eight decades after the success in the United States. The Australian story, as well of those of South Africa, Argentina, and many other countries, reinforces our assertion that the United States was very fortunate.[63] The first fifty years of spasmodic and largely ineffectual state-level efforts in the United States were not vastly different from the policies that failed in Australia. The BAI's campaign came in the nick of time to prevent CBPP from spreading onto the open range. An ounce of prevention was worth a pound of cure.

Placing the BAI in Context

Our account of the origins and early expansion of the BAI sheds light on several broader themes in American political and economic development. American constitutional and economic historians have pondered the federal government's emergence as a regulator of economic activity. This discussion often dates the first significant federal economic regulatory initiative to the creation of the Interstate Commerce Commission (ICC) in 1887. Reflecting this view, the eminent legal historian Harry Scheiber notes that the Interstate Commerce Act represented "the first Congressional railroad regulatory law" and "the beginning of federal-level government-by-commission and of a federal administrative law." Many others also start their analysis with the ICC.[64]

The ICC bill was signed on 3 February 1887, and the commissioners did not receive their first complaint until 17 April 1887.[65] By this latter date, the BAI had been in business for almost three years, and Congress had twice greatly expanded its budget and powers. Boots were on the ground as BAI agents entered private property, killed stock, and destroyed facilities. The BAI was forging new state-federal agreements that radically changed jurisdictional boundaries, dictating livestock export and import policies, and managing quarantine stations. Congress had set general guidelines; the details of actual policies were being created and revised by USDA and BAI administrators. BAI health regulations directly affected railroad companies, which were held liable for enforcing its orders. As a result of BAI policies, federal and state government inspectors descended on railroads, stockyards, and ports to demand compliance with new sanitary rules. In April 1887, BAI Chief Daniel Salmon was vested with the unprecedented peacetime authority to take over state police powers. The ICC never once exercised such broad powers during the nineteenth century.

Indeed, the history of the BAI confounds many other standard accounts of the evolution of federalism in the United States. One popular account describes the relationships between the national and state governments as transitioning through a succession of regimes. In the earliest regime, labeled "dual federalism," federal and state governments acted in separate and exclusive spheres of jurisdiction. The beginning of this regime is dated, by various scholars, to the adoption of the Constitution in 1789 or to the Jacksonian period in the 1830s. In the second regime, labeled "cooperative federalism," the national government is said to have worked with the states to carry out mutually desired purposes. Examples include federal funding for agricultural extension, highway construction, and maternal-and-infant health programs with requirements for state matching. The transition to this regime is commonly dated between the mid-1910s and the 1930s.[66] In the third regime, sometimes labeled "regulatory" or "coercive federalism," the federal government mandated minimum standards that the state governments had to meet or exceed. This regime is dated to the mid-1960s or 1970s, with examples including the Water Quality Act of 1965 and Air Quality Act of 1967. BAI policies—exemplified by the choice that Governor Oglesby faced between deputizing BAI agents to carry out USDA policies within Illinois or seeing his state's interstate cattle trade shut down—suggest the need to scrap this neat periodization—and, in particular, to re-date the dawn of coercive federalism from the 1960s to the 1880s. The BAI's activities made the federal government far more visible and intrusive than political historians such as Brian Balogh have suggested.[67]

There were other political and regulatory innovations that have gone unnoticed. Scheiber dates "a new dimension" to the federal system to an "increase in intergovernmental collaboration and genuine sharing of functions" to the Carey Act of 1894, which gave federal grants to states for irrigation. This act "also instituted a policy of requiring states to submit comprehensive plans for approval by federal officials." Scheiber further dates the rise of intergovernmental cooperation in the deployment of police powers to the Lacey Act of 1900, which regulated interstate shipment of wild game. He places the inauguration of federal grants in aid to 1902 and of matching-fund requirements to 1911. Scheiber notes that the integral functioning of the federal system depended on the emergence of "functional bureaucracies."[68] Kimberly Johnson has recently argued that the shift to the "new federalism" of continuing grants-in-aid began earlier, with the Hatch Experiment Station Act of 1887.[69] In fact, the BAI was aggressively engaging in such cooperative activities by

1886 in its fight against CBPP. The federal interventions that accompanied the BAI's CBPP campaign were far more intrusive and extensive than the programs Scheiber and Johnson have identified.

Anyone interested in understanding the development of the American administrative state would do well to begin with Daniel Carpenter's magisterial analysis. Carpenter properly highlights the role of bureaucratic-entrepreneurs in building independent constituencies, fostering professional networks, and expanding agency power in the late nineteenth and early twentieth centuries. The successful middle-level administrators came to set agendas, draft legislation, generate valuable information, and secure stable funding. Bureaucrats gained autonomy only when their agencies established broad-based legitimacy, which made it costly for Congress rein in their initiatives. Carpenter focuses on the USDA (as well as the military and the postal service). He correctly emphasizes the USDA's scientific preeminence within the United States at the dawn of the twentieth century. He primarily analyzes the activities of Harvey Wiley (Bureau of Chemistry), Seaman Knapp (Extension), Gifford Pinchot (Bureau of Forestry), and Beverly Galloway (Bureau of Plant Industry). But inexplicably Carpenter largely passed over Daniel Salmon and the BAI, one of the USDA's oldest, largest, and most successful bureaus. Including the BAI would reinforce many of Carpenter's main insights, but doing so would require pushing back the timing of key scientific and administrative break points to an earlier date.[70]

Political scientist Stephen Skowronek describes the evolution of America's modern political system between the 1870s and 1920, emphasizing that the federal bureaucracy gained power relative to political parties and the courts. He sees a break in these developments in 1900. In the earlier period, the national administrative state expanded only in a "patchwork" manner; after 1900, federal bureaucracies became broadly accepted and emerged as "the centerpiece of a new governmental order." Skowronek focused on civil service reform, railroad regulation, and the reorganization of the army, but neglected animal and human health initiatives. Accounting for the BAI's power and activities strengthens his analysis of the state-building process, but again would require an earlier transition date.[71]

Another influential body of scholarship also identifies a significant break in the political system around 1900. According to Richard L.

McCormick, the era from "the 1830s to the early 1900s" represented the "Party Period" in American politics, during which the "government's most pervasive role was that of promoting development by distributing resources and privileges to individuals and groups." By this account, the national and state governments "gave away" land, corporate charters, and tariff protection, but did little to regulate or restrict economic activity. Serious administrative tasks were too "difficult to accomplish for nineteenth-century governments. . . . Not until early in the twentieth century did social and economic developments permanently enlarge governmental responsibilities by strengthening both regulation and administration."[72] The distributional nature of party politics during the period made it difficult to adopt policies imposing high direct costs of losers. The BAI's interventions to eradicate CBPP were clearly very early in this chronology, and they involved far more aggressive measures—restrictions (through quarantines), takings (through the destruction of property with incomplete compensation), and setting specific policies for common carriers—than the "Party Period" image conjures.

Public choice economists have also failed to grasp the revolutionary significance of the BAI in explaining the growth of the federal government. Robert Higgs's analysis of the rise of Big Government in the United States shows that government agencies, power, and budgets expand in response to crises, most commonly wars and depressions. By Higgs's account, when the emergency subsided, government's role did not fully retreat, but instead was permanently ratcheted up. This is consistent with our account (albeit with a different class of crises) of the BAI experience. Higgs argues that the general ratcheting up of government budgets and power was inefficient and occurred because of the connivances of rent-seeking bureaucrats, politicians, and special interests. These actors were at work in the BAI case, but as we have indicated, efficiency issues drove the debate leading to its creation. Once in place, it developed a constituency. Both the opponents to federal intervention and those who desired stronger policies failed in their attempts to abolish the Bureau. As we show in the following chapters, contrary to Higgs's general depiction, the growth of the BAI had a positive impact on the economy. The primary reason for the BAI's growth after CBPP's eradication was the increasing recognition of other disease problems and the accompanying market failures that required collective action. The campaign against CBPP changed the position of key groups—especially the Chicago livestock interests—from opponents to supporters of aggressive federal disease control policies. There would still be opposition from the Chicago interests on other issues, but time after time the resistance would wane as the benefits of regulation became evident. The growth of BAI occurred during a period when Higgs believes that "government did little of much consequence or expense."[73] This generalization clearly needs to be revised.

Conclusion

A statement attributed to Benjamin Franklin asserts: "By failing to prepare, you are preparing to fail." The United States was not prepared to deal with CBPP in 1884, and the leaders of its new livestock disease bureaucracy struggled to meet the challenge. The experience taught many lessons that would help prepare the response to future problems. Eruptions of contagious diseases induced confusion and fear. For the unprepared, an outbreak led to paralysis and fighting over authority and the distribution of costs. Absurd denials were common, local officials and business leaders often proposed a wait-and-see strategy, and the owners of suspect stock frequently scrambled to hide or sell their animals before regulators could investigate and impose quarantines. These outcomes accompanied CBPP crises wherever they hit—be it in Kentucky, Illinois, or New York. In addition to the now nameless farmers, the deniers and obstructionists included the captains of industry, cattle barons, and prominent politicians.

Before CBPP was eradicated in 1892, the infected states would all undergo similar trauma, with quarantines and federal-state veterinary forces entering private property to inspect and condemn cattle. Most of these states accepted federally drafted cooperative agreements, and many revised their legal codes to strengthen their livestock sanitation bureaucracies and to facilitate interagency cooperation. Some resisted ceding authority to the federal government until they were threatened with total quarantine of their state. Most states in the South and Far West escaped the CBPP crisis. As a result, they had to confront the difficult political challenges associated with drafting new livestock sanitation laws when the USDA turned its attention to Texas fever, scab in sheep and cattle, and other diseases that affected those regions. Federal officials worked hard to build alliances, trust, and legal and government institutions; these efforts paid dividends for subsequent campaigns.

Crises can create the impetus for change—but not always. In most times and most places, disease outbreaks just created misery. The scientific knowledge did not exist, the powers of the government were not sufficient, or the political leadership was lacking to overcome market failures and opposition. What transpired in the United States with the stamping out of CBPP between 1884 and 1892 was both unusual and path setting.

5 Bad Blood

Deciphering Texas Fever and Confining Its Spread

MARTIN W. PHILIPS was an agricultural innovator and a prolific writer on Southern farming. His Log Hall Plantation in Hinds County, Mississippi, was akin to an early experiment station. In late January 1840, Philips introduced "a lot of Durham cattle"—improved Shorthorn stock. In mid-May, his slaves finished building a new barn. But on June 6, Philips found several of his "Durham cattle sick, discharges of bloody urine, drooping, no disposition to eat." Day after day, the afflicted animals succumbed to a disease that "I cannot name." The symptoms point to what would become known as Texas fever. "The sickness in the lot of Durham cattle is astonishing and truly very discouraging. . . . I cannot attribute it to any bad management." The deaths continued. Then, on June 19, Philips wrote that the surviving "Durham cattle, though very poor, eat very hearty, and appear to be doing well. I fear to hope they are safe." All attempts at cures came to naught; the improved stock imported by his neighbors suffered similar fates—"during the first summer, almost nine-tenths of them die of disease."[1]

In the antebellum period, Northerners often derided the poor quality of Southern cattle, attributing the animals' inferiority to indifferent treatment or outright abuse. Southerners, in this popular view, lacked an improving spirit.[2] However, there is another explanation—many Southern cattle were infested with blood-sucking ticks and infected with communicable blood diseases carried by the ticks. Together, the ticks and infections stunted the cattle's growth, diminished their strength as draft animals, and reduced the milk flow in cows.[3] In addition, the disease made it extremely risky to introduce improved breeding stock into the

South. Only scrubby native or acclimated cattle thrived. No amount of care could have prevented the harm done by Texas fever. The individual initiatives of improvers such as Philips were doomed. Collective action would be needed. This would require significant advances in knowledge and coercive government programs to convert the new information into effective policy. Thus, for many Southerners adopting a low-input cattle management system represented a rational response to local environmental conditions and to their animals' inherently poor health.

Texas fever is a common term for the parasitic blood disease babesiosis, which is carried by ticks that feed on cattle. The disease has had many other names, including tick fever, Spanish fever, Texas cattle fever, Southern cattle fever, splenetic fever, bloody murrain, and bovine piroplasmosis. In the United States, two distinct ticks served as vectors, passing a protozoan parasite *(Babesia bigemina)* into the bitten cattle's bloodstream that destroys red blood corpuscles.[4] Babesiosis often coexisted with another major veterinary scourge, anaplasmosis, a bacterial infection of the blood, which was also transmitted by ticks, albeit other species. Cattle diagnosed with "Texas fever" could in reality have been suffering from either or both diseases, adding to the confusion. Tick eradication policies (Chapter 11) reduced both infections as well as the direct parasitic load caused by ticks. The chapter appendix offers more information on the ticks, the diseases they caused, and the evolving terminology.

In the early stages of Texas fever, the symptoms include a high fever, weakness, constipation, and reduced milk production. As the disease advances, the spleen and liver become enlarged, and the animal loses weight; death can occur within a few days to several weeks. Animals that recover suffer prolonged morbidity and are more susceptible to other diseases and stresses. Calves infected with the disease typically suffer milder cases and quickly recover. These animals usually acquired a limited immunity to the more serious complications if regularly exposed; however, the death rate often exceeded 90 percent for cattle first exposed as yearlings and adults.[5]

The inadequate understanding of Texas fever delayed the creation of a federal bureaucracy and control policies. As a sop to Southern cattle owners and Northern traders, the 1884 organic legislation establishing the Bureau of Animal Industry (BAI) explicitly excluded Texas fever from consideration as a contagious or infectious disease for cattle being

transported by rail for immediate slaughter. Texans and their stockyard
allies feared that the new BAI might someday restrict their cattle trade.
Their concern was well founded. For all the uncertainty and Southern
resistance, in 1889, just five years after the BAI's creation, the Secretary
of Agriculture quarantined Southern cattle. By this date, most endangered states already restricted the entry of Southern cattle. The federal
actions coordinated, standardized, and managed the problem far more
effectively than the hodgepodge of state initiatives. This chapter examines the events that led to the quarantining of Southern cattle and the
revolutionary advances by BAI scientists that unlocked the mysteries of
the disease. The analysis adds to our understanding of the legal basis for
the growth in the federal government's authority over livestock diseases
and intrastate and interstate trade. Chapter 11 examines the contentious program that eradicated Texas fever from the United States.

Our account relates to two separate historical literatures. One, reflected in the work of economic historians Terry Anderson, Peter J. Hill,
and David Galenson, offers a public choice account of the cattle trade on
the Western range. Their work focuses mainly on the early efforts to
quarantine Southern cattle.[6] The other, best exemplified by the writings
of Claire Strom, focuses on the social and cultural history of the Southern yeomen who adopted a low-input cattle-raising regime and fought
the later eradication efforts.[7] Despite different philosophical priors and
methodologies, these literatures present surprisingly similar interpretations of Texas fever policies: both see the control programs as heavy-
handed, top-down attempts to benefit the powerful at the expense of
others, and both emphasize redistribution rather than efficiency. Both
downplay the damage caused by Texas fever. Strom argues that many
Southern farmers perceived the costs of tick eradication as far outweigh-
ing the benefits. The public choice literature goes further by treating
state and federal tick policies as counterproductive rent-seeking activities. This depiction dovetails seamlessly with the broader public choice
perspective on the origin of government policies to regulate food safety
and infectious animal diseases, namely, that there were no significant
problems that justified government interference. We disagree.

The Mysteries of Texas Fever

Until the early 1890s, when BAI scientists revealed the role of ticks
in transmitting the disease, Texas fever's etiology baffled observers. The

disease somehow spread from Southern cattle to Northern cattle. Direct physical contact was not required for transmission; it was sufficient that the Northern animals entered pastures, trails, stockyards, or railroad cars previously occupied by Southern animals. Stock imported into the South commonly fell ill and soon died. Cattle raised in the South were to all appearances healthy, if somewhat stunted. In the North, the disease was seasonal (because the ticks could not survive prolonged freezes). Texas fever could wreak havoc in the Northern states during the warmer months, but not in the winter. Numerous hypotheses abounded into the 1890s. Perhaps cattle transmitted the disease via their saliva, urine, manure, or a fungus on their hooves; perhaps it was related to anthrax or some other known disease. Northerners were quick to associate their cattle's malaise with the arrival of Southern cattle, but because these animals appeared healthy, Southerners maintained that their stock and the ticks they carried posed no danger. The Texans and their allies persisted with their denial even as evidence to the contrary mounted.[8]

Early Spanish colonizers likely introduced Texas fever into North America. It spread northward, with probable outbreaks in Georgia, Virginia, and the Carolinas in the mid-eighteenth century. Historians have interpreted the passage of several early cattle control laws as signs of the disease's presence. In 1744, South Carolina passed legislation to control the movement of sick cattle. In 1762, Virginia considered restricting the entry of cattle from further south, and two years later North Carolina quarantined cattle driven from South Carolina. In the 1790s, a disease resembling Texas fever killed a large number of cattle in South Carolina, prompting North Carolina to pass a statute in 1795 that prohibited driving cattle into the state " 'between April 1 and November 1 from either South Carolina or Georgia.' " Clearly, by the end of the eighteenth century, many observers understood the seasonal characteristics of the disease. Throughout the early nineteenth century, Southern legislatures enacted laws against the introduction of such "distempered" cattle.[9]

The USDA's efforts to understand Texas fever predated the formation of the BAI. Outbreaks in the North following the renewal of Texas cattle drives after 1865 generated intense interest in the disease (Chapter 2). The Commissioner of Agriculture's 1868 *Annual Report* devoted several pages to "Spanish fever." In 1868, the recently established USDA also commissioned the eminent British scientist John Gamgee to study the disease. For the most part, Gamgee's report of 1869 accurately described the disease's pathology, but he dismissed the hypothesis that ticks spread the disease as an "absurdity." This was one of many instances when scientific expertise proved less reliable that the folk wisdom of practical farmers.[10] Historian of science A. Hunter Dupree opines that "in light of later discoveries," Gamgee's mistakes showed "the young department to very poor advantage," reflecting in part its early "inability to organize a long-term intensive research effort."[11] This would change.

In 1879, Daniel Salmon began to study how Texas fever was transmitted. The following year, he too dismissed the tick theory as wishful thinking. Salmon turned his attention to ascertaining the geographical area of permanent year-round infection in hopes of unlocking the disease's mysteries.[12] This research led to the delineation of a roughly 200-mile Texas-fever line from the Atlantic seaboard westward in 1883. Gamgee's and Salmon's investigations were among the first of many federally backed studies. The BAI's research eventually would generate breakthroughs that yielded extraordinary payoffs.

Setting the Stage for Federal Intervention

From the late 1850s on, many border and Northern states attempted to restrict the movement of Southern cattle during the warm months.[13] Enforcement of these laws was often lax, in part because the interests of local livestock owners frequently conflicted with those of drovers, railroads, and other businesses that profited from the cattle trade. In one famous example in the late 1860s, Joseph McCoy established a cattle shipping point at Abilene, Kansas, after inducing Governor Samuel Crawford to limit the enforcement of state's quarantine and after promising local livestock owners indemnities for harm from Texas fever. However, within five years, the trailing business wore out its welcome and was forced further west, in large part because of the uncompensated damages imposed on local farmers.[14]

In a revisionist account of the end of the Chisholm Trail in the 1880s, economic historian David Galenson has attributed its demise to the rational response of ranchers to changing market conditions rather than to the erection of state quarantine barriers. He claims such laws were uniformly ineffective and evaded, and that they were primarily motivated "by a desire of the northern ranchers to keep Texas cattle away from the already over-supplied northern cattle markets." Echoing the arguments of nineteenth-century proponents of the Texas trade, Galenson also asserts that the danger of Texas fever was seriously overstated.[15]

The U.S. Supreme Court's 1878 *Railroad Co. v. Husen* decision (see Chapter 2) scuttled existing state initiatives when it declared that Missouri's blanket state-level quarantine represented an unconstitutional infringement on Congress' authority to regulate interstate trade. The sweeping coverage of the Missouri law influenced the Court. The limited understanding of how the disease was transmitted made it nearly impossible to prove that Southern cattle caused the problem.[16]

As more was learned about Texas fever, federal and state courts became increasingly tolerant of states' policing the interstate movement of livestock from regions harboring communicable diseases. The evolving situation in Kansas is of special interest because it illustrates the influence of other diseases on Texas fever policy. In the early 1880s, the fever hit Kansas hard. The losses in 1884 alone were estimated between $250,000 and $500,000. The internal divisions over Texas fever that previously had delayed state action were swept aside in early 1884, when outbreaks of ergotism (caused by a grain fungus) were mistakenly identified as foot-and-mouth disease. Kansas faced an economic calamity as other states and countries scrambled to erect quarantines. In response, Governor George W. Glick convened a special session of the Kansas legislature, which enacted sweeping revisions to the state's livestock laws. The legislation authorized closer cooperation with federal officials, strengthened the state's power to quarantine and destroy animals, and created a new bureaucracy—including a Live-Stock Sanitary Commission and a State Veterinary Surgeon.[17] As a part of this initiative, Governor Glick issued an executive order to quarantine cattle with Texas fever. In the 1885 session, the legislature outlawed driving cattle from below the 34th parallel through any part of the state from the March 1 to December 1. These measures had an immediate impact. The Joint Committee of the State Legislature tasked with reviewing the new laws reported that in 1885 "for the first time in the history of the State a season has passed in which that disease has not ravaged our herds." The new laws protecting against Texas fever had given "universal satisfaction." In 1886, the reported losses to Texas fever fell to less than one-tenth of the 1884 level; the few outbreaks that did occur were traced to six herds illegally driven into the state. By the close of 1885, at least ten

Midwest and Great Plains states and territories had laws and quarantines in place restricting the entry of cattle from Texas and Indian Territory during the warm months.[18]

"They profess great fear of Texan fever, though what they really do fear is Texan competition" opined the British business journal the *Statist* in 1886.[19] More recently, Anderson and Hill have interpreted these laws as rent-seeking edicts. They further argue (as did Galenson) that state and federal legislation was a direct response to the admonitions of cattlemen in Wyoming and Montana.[20] But Ernest Osgood, one of their key sources, raises serious doubts that ranchers in the Montana or Wyoming Territories had sufficient political clout in Washington, D.C., let alone in other state capitals, to drive events. Osgood maintained that the Wyoming cattle raisers " 'are too far off to be heeded by Congress.' "[21] The call for protection came directly after the opening of fast rail links to transport cattle north had led to serious outbreaks of Texas fever in Nebraska and Wyoming in 1884. This suggests that the threat of the disease was serious. Osgood also details why local and state actions were inefficient: "It was obviously more effective to establish a quarantine over the area where the disease had broken out, than it was for all the rest of the country through its separate state and territorial governments to set up barriers against the admission of cattle from the infected area."[22] Many interests besides Northern ranchers were searching for a solution to the Texas fever problem.

In November 1884, the National Cattle and Horse Growers Association petitioned Congress to devote federal land to a National Cattle Trail extending from the Red River to the Canadian border. The permanent six-mile wide trail, crossing through either Kansas or Colorado, would effectively circumvent their state quarantine laws. The Kansas legislature objected. But the Texans, who so staunchly defended states' rights, had few qualms about trampling on the sovereignty of other states. When Texas congressman James Miller introduced his National Trail bill in early 1885, a coalition of Northern cattle interests and Texas railroads lobbied to kill the measure in committee. In the next Congress, Texans again introduced legislation to establish a national trail. In promoting the measure, John Reagan persisted in denying the disease threat; a report from his House Commerce Committee argued "splenetic fever, if it exists at all, is confined to cattle on the low lands adjacent to the Gulf and South Atlantic Coasts." The bill, which would have created a two-mile-wide path through Colorado, failed to pass. The national livestock highway never won federal recognition.[23]

Some Texans began to express a preference for a single set of national regulations. As early as 1884, the editor of the *Galveston Daily News* opined that the cattle trade would "be much less liable to harassment and injury under sanitary regulations . . . administered by the general government, than it would if they were left to state governments in sympathy with local cattle interests."[24] In 1888, the North Texas Cattle Raisers' Association had called for the General Government to enact and enforce uniform stock laws, and the *Texas Live-Stock Journal* declared that " 'Texas cattle are tired of driving against quarantines,' " and " 'all quarantine matters should be in the hands of the Federal authorities and in their hands only.' "[25] But many Texans remained highly antagonistic to the new federal livestock sanitation bureaucracy.

Segregating Southern Cattle in Transit

During the House debates over the creation of the BAI, William Hatch had called for building a "Chinese wall" around areas infected with livestock diseases.[26] Salmon was already laying the groundwork for such protective measures with detailed surveys to ascertain the area of year-round infection. The initial Texas fever line stretched from the Atlantic seaboard through Virginia in 1883. The BAI extended the line to the Mississippi River in 1884, to the Rio Grande River in 1885, and to the Pacific Coast in 1895.[27] The early lines were at first purely informational, but they would soon provide the foundation for federal and state policies to quarantine the South and to segregate Southern cattle in transit.

The idea of requiring separate facilities for Southern cattle in transit dated back to at least 1877. After the 1884 outbreaks of Texas fever, the BAI requested that railroads segregate Southern cattle and disinfect the railcars with quicklime. USDA Commissioner George Loring acknowledged that the BAI had neither the "power to enforce such regulations, nor even men to supervise the work."[28] In February 1885, the National Cattle and Horse Growers' Association called for railroad companies to segregate Southern cattle. The association's leaders hoped that a unified railroad policy would lead to an "abrogation of the present conflicting state quarantine laws."[29]

As an example of state actions, Ohio quarantined cattle from districts infected with contagious diseases in October 1885. It established a number of burdensome requirements, including a certificate of good health signed by a BAI inspector or the State Veterinarian. The order further prohibited railroads from unloading cattle from Texas and the Gulf states from May 1 to November 1 unless the company provided separate yards and thoroughly disinfected the pens and cars before allowing other cattle to use them. Cattle brought in illegally were to be held in quarantine indefinitely at the owner's expense.[30] Between 1886 and 1888, Illinois adopted similar policies as part of initiatives led by Illinois Governor Richard Oglesby. His actions highlight the machinations common to many politicians, both Northern and Southern, over the control of livestock diseases. As we saw in Chapter 2, in 1868 he had called for tough national Texas fever policies and engineered a multistate campaign to bar the movement of Southern cattle. At the same time as he was erecting barriers to protect his state's farmers from Texas fever in the 1880s, he was fighting the efforts of other states and the BAI to deal with contagious bovine pleuropneumonia in Illinois (Chapter 4). The problems with enforcement at the state level and with voluntary railroad compliance came to light in 1889, when Illinois officials discovered that many shippers had altered waybills to indicate that the cattle were from safe areas. It was very costly for every state to independently check the veracity of shipping documents.[31]

Experiments conducted at the Union Stock Yards in Chicago in the summer of 1888 added to the pressure to segregate Southern cattle. In an investigation sponsored by the Chicago Live Stock Exchange, Illinois State Veterinarian John Casewell placed five healthy Northern cattle into pens recently occupied by ticky Southern cattle to test the tick theory. All five soon fell violently ill and four died. The press broadcast the results, and the stockyard management, led by Elmer Washburn, pledged to segregate Southern stock. Illinois authorities required that local railroads maintain separate facilities and disinfect cars used for Southern cattle.[32] Because the stockyard and railroad executives did not follow through with sufficient diligence, the problems continued.

This and other research conducted in the 1880s did have an impact on legal opinion, inducing jurists to chip away at the *Husen* restraints on the states' regulatory powers. A major turning point came with the U.S.

Supreme Court ruling in *P. C. Kimmish v. John J. Ball* (129 U.S. 217, decided 28 January 1889) dealing with an 1873 Iowa law (as amended in 1885) regulating "Texas cattle." Writing for the Court, Stephen J. Field affirmed the constitutionality of the statute that established liability for damages caused by "Texas cattle" running at large. Field presumed that cattle from Texas and surrounding "malarial" areas likely carried the disease. Citing the BAI *Annual Reports* for 1884 and 1885, he noted "that cattle coming from those sections of the country during the spring and summer months are often infected with a contagious and dangerous fever is a notorious fact." "Scientists are not agreed as to the causes of the malady, and it is not important to our decision which of the many theories advanced by them is correct."

On 3 July 1889, the new Secretary of Agriculture, Jeremiah Rusk, declared Texas fever "a contagious and infectious disease." Rusk concluded that the annual spread of Texas fever could be "easily prevented by providing separate pens for the susceptible and dangerous cattle, and by promptly cleaning the infected cars." Rusk's original order did not apply to the entire South. It demanded that railroad and transportation companies establish separate channels of distribution for cattle from parts of Arkansas, the Indian Territory, and Texas during the dangerous season. It also required that railroads disinfect cars and premises that had been occupied by cattle from these areas.[33]

The response in Texas to Rusk's order was surprisingly muted, with little commentary in the state's leading newspapers. The main complaint was an objection to the Rusk's usage of "Texas fever" rather than "splenetic fever."[34] The timing of Rusk's order and the response in the Texans were revealing of the political dynamics of the day. In 1889, pro-regulation Republicans controlled the presidency and both houses of Congress for the first time since 1875, so any substantive complaints by the Texas congressional delegation would have failed. Moreover, the Texans could have faced even stronger sanctions. Rusk concluded his order with a threat: "A rigid compliance with the . . . regulations will . . . render it unnecessary to adopt a more stringent regulation, such as the absolute prohibition of the movement of Texas cattle except for slaughter during the time of year that this disease is fatal."[35] The legal basis for Rusk's actual quarantine order regarding cattle shipped by rail was suspect, but there were no challenges in the courts. The Texas fever exemption in the 1884 BAI Act was specific: it permitted the shipment of exposed and suspect animals across state lines if intended for immediate slaughter. Emery Storrs had indeed represented the interests of his packinghouse and stockyard backers well. How Rusk could regulate the conditions of shipment was unclear. This represents one of many examples where the Bureau's *de facto* exercise of power exceeded its *de jure* authority. BAI officials would later request Congress make these quarantine powers explicit.

With the arrival of cold weather, Rusk rescinded the order effective 1 November 1889; but on 24 February 1890, he reinstated the restrictions effective 15 March to 1 December 1890. He also expanded the quarantine area to include most of Texas. On 5 February 1891, Rusk issued an even tougher federal quarantine order, which restricted shipments from the entire area south of the quarantine line (see Figure 5.1). Less than two years after the initial quarantine order of July 1889, the BAI had cordoned Southern cattle behind a roughly 2,000 mile legal barrier and established a system of internal inspection stations.[36] In 1891, BAI leaders still viewed their regulatory powers to be inadequate and requested that Congress enact legislation to compel railroads to comply with orders to clean and disinfect cars.[37]

Livestock interests, even those that normally downplayed disease threats, lauded Rusk's Texas fever measures. In September 1890, Chicago packer Nelson Morris congratulated Rusk "for the great success you have made in preventing Texas fever from spreading this year, as I have been for the last thirty five years in Chicago daily in contact with all cattle raisers and cattle traders, and I have never seem them as happy before, and their whole happiness comes from your taking a hold in due time, and preventing the great wrong of spreading Texas Fever for the profit of few, and to the injury of millions."[38] Morris was not the only critic to change his tune; industry officials vocally urged Rusk's successor to continue his aggressive Texas fever policies.[39]

The new regulations led to a marked fall in the incidence of Texas fever in the North. By the end of 1892, the decrease in losses due to Texas fever aboard ships bound for foreign ports netted a savings in insurance premiums of nearly $2 million, or roughly $5 per animal exported. This amounted to about 6 percent of an animal's value upon arrival in Europe. The scale of the quarantine and segregation effort was impressive. In 1892 alone, the Bureau's agents inspected over 90,000 railroad cars containing

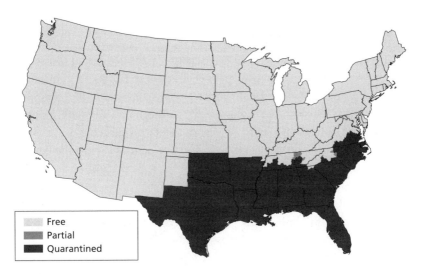

Figure 5.1. Area quarantined for Texas fever, 1891. *Source:* U.S. Bureau of Animal Industry, *Reports for 1891 and 1892*, pp. 25–26.

2.5 million Southern cattle. These cars were marked, and the animals were segregated from susceptible cattle at watering stations and transfer points. Agents also supervised the disinfecting of the cars and certified hundreds of thousands of cattle driven from tick-free areas in Texas for grazing in the North.[40] Rusk's policy proved popular with stockyards interests, although some lobbied to make operational adjustments.

By 1892, many Texans were becoming resigned to the new state of affairs. The *Texas Live-Stock Journal* reported that "'Texas can much better afford to have a few [clean] counties quarantined than to take any chances of ever again communicating Texas fever to Northern cattle. Under the circumstances Secretary Rusk has given the State all that could be reasonably asked for.'"[41] Cattlemen had good reason to rethink their stance because it was becoming costly to spread the disease. As an example, in 1894 a Kansas court awarded $47,000 to a group of farmers who had sued a Kansas City merchant for importing infected cattle from Texas.[42] In this rare case where the source of damages could be identified, the tort system contributed to the solution. Many more court cases and federal legislation would effectively reposition the quarantine powers of the federal government relative to those of the states.

Defining Quarantine Powers

The legal setting governing state-federal jurisdictions and quarantine powers shifted dramatically with changes in the party controlling the White House and the Department of Agriculture. In 1890, Republican Secretary Rusk asked Congress for authority to regulate diseases within state boundaries, with or without a state's agreement. Congress responded with a significant revision from previous years in the Appropriations Act for the fiscal year 1891 (Act of 14 July 1890, 26 Stat. 282). The new language authorized the Secretary of Agriculture to use the BAI's budget as "he may deem necessary or expedient, and in such matter as he may think best, to prevent the spread of pleuro-pneumonia *and other diseases of animals,* and for this purpose, . . . and to expend any part of this sum in the purchase and destruction of diseased or exposed animals and to quarantine the same . . . to prevent the spread of pleuro-pneumonia, *or other diseases of animals,* from one State into another" [italics added]. Rusk and many in Congress interpreted the act as authorizing the secretary to unilaterally quarantine *sections* of states to prevent animal diseases from spreading between states.

In 1891, Rusk established a federal quarantine line that ran through Texas, Arkansas, Tennessee, and Oklahoma Territory. Lines running through states remained in force through 1895, but in February 1896, USDA Secretary J. Sterling Morton (who had taken office in 1893) shifted the line to the state borders. The conservative Nebraska Democrat maintained that the BAI had no powers to operate within a state without the explicit cooperation of that state. He required that the states enact laws allowing such cooperation and that the states enforce the quarantines. In the case of Texas, Morton asserted that the state had not enforced BAI quarantine rules.[43]

Morton's stance induced heated protests in Congress. Senator George Vest (D-Mo.), who was a leading congressional voice on livestock matters (see Chapter 9), railed against Morton. Given market conditions in the mid-1890s, Missouri farmers wanted access to healthy young feeders from Texas to fatten on their surplus corn. They were also concerned that all of Missouri might be placed under quarantine if Texas fever broke out in its southern counties. Vest recounted the language and intent of the 1891 Appropriations Act and charged Morton with failing to exercise his duties. Senator James Berry (D-Ark.) agreed, arguing that Morton's new regulations were costing farmers in northern Arkansas $2 to $3 on every animal shipped out of the state. Morton held firm that there had been no legal authority for the policies he had inherited from Rusk.[44]

The courts repeatedly weighed in on the twin issues of the boundaries of federal authority within states and of the power of states to regulate interstate trade. This latter matter was complicated by situations where the authority of the federal government was superior to that of the states, but where Congress had failed to enact explicit legislation. Did the "silence of Congress" mean that commerce was to be free from all regulation—the so-called dormant power interpretation—or that states were free to enact their own regulations policing public health and safety? Many of these cases dealt with diseases other than Texas fever.

In an 1891 *American Law Review* article, William H. Cowles surveyed the long-standing and confusing problem of determining "the relation of State quarantine laws to the Federal constitution." Tracing the line separating the police powers of the states from those of the federal government was extremely difficult. "The Supreme Court has uniformly declined the task of locating it as a whole, and has contented itself with determining the position of the single point in the line which is necessary for the decision of each case as presented. Nor does the court yet think it safe to connect the points that have been fixed and thus complete the line."[45]

The U.S. Supreme Court repeatedly affirmed that states could impose reasonable health measures affecting interstate livestock trade. In *Missouri, Kansas & Texas Railroad Co. v. Haber* (169 U.S. 613, decided 14 March 1898), the Court upheld a Kansas statute making cattle importers civilly liable for the damages due to Texas fever. "While the states were invited to co-operate with the general government in the execution and enforcement of the [1884 BAI] act, whatever power they had to protect their domestic cattle against such disease was left untouched and unimpaired."[46] In *Rasmussen v. Idaho* (181 U.S. 198, decided 22 April 1901), the Court affirmed the right of Idaho to quarantine sheep from areas in Utah and Nevada where its inspector found the disease scab to be prevalent. The law was judged "a purely quarantine act"—the restrictions were based on investigations and subject to review. Unlike *Husen*, they did not constitute an "absolute prohibition of the introduction of sheep."[47] As a further demonstration of how the BAI's expertise affected legal outcomes, the earlier Idaho Supreme Court decision *Idaho v. Rasmussen* (7 Idaho 1, 59 Pac 733, decided 23 January 1900) quoted extensively from the recently published research by Daniel Salmon and Charles Wardell Stiles on scab. Legal interpretations were responding to scientific advances.[48]

The U.S. Supreme Court was also supportive of the exercise of state police powers in *Reid v. Colorado* (187 U.S. 137, decided 1 December 1902). It upheld an 1885 Colorado law requiring a certificate of health for Southern cattle issued by the state's own inspectors. In 1901, E. H. Reid attempted to ship cattle from Texas to Wyoming by way of Denver. At the point of origin, a BAI agent had certified the cattle free of Texas fever, and Reid refused further inspection by Colorado officials. The Court acknowledged that the federal government, when it chose to act, had authority to regulate interstate commerce. But when creating the BAI in 1884, Congress did not intend "to override the power of the states to care for the safety of the property of their peoples." It did not give the BAI "authority to go into a state and without its assent take charge of the work suppressing or extirpating contagious, infectious, or communicable diseases," nor did it give the BAI's agents authority "to inspect cattle within the limits of a state, and give a certificate that should be of superior authority in that or other states." Thus, a BAI certificate did not prohibit or trump state inspections. The Court further reaffirmed that in 1884 Congress had only made it an offense to *knowingly* transport across state lines livestock that were *actually affected* with a contagious or infectious disease. Thus, the standard BAI policy of quarantining entire states or counties within states to limit the interstate movement of both infected and potentially exposed livestock was suddenly on weak footing.

An emergency stemming from an eruption of foot-and-mouth disease in 1902, coupled with the several court decisions (especially *Reid*), led Congress to expand the BAI's quarantine powers in 1903 and again in 1905. We analyze these changes in our discussion of foot-and-mouth disease (Chapter 6). In order to understand Texas fever policy it is sufficient to know that by 3 March 1905, the agency could quarantine any portion of a state as opposed to the entire state, and could fine railroads if they failed to disinfect their property. Congress also significantly eased the burden of proof for federal prosecutions. To establish guilt, the government had to demonstrate only that the shipper had moved stock across a publicly posted quarantine line, not that the offender knew the animals were diseased. The new law also protected BAI agents from hostile acts.[49]

In *Illinois Central Railroad Co. v. McKendree* (203 U.S. 514, decided 17 December 1906), the U.S. Supreme Court ruled that the USDA had overstepped its authority when it had established quarantine lines within state boundaries.[50] The reaction of stockyard interests attests to their support for the existing quarantine regime. Upon learning of the *McKendree* decision, M. P. Buel, a commission agent at the Chicago stockyard, wrote the Secretary of Agriculture that it would be a "calamity" if the Texas fever quarantine "is to be destroyed, by the ruling of the Court." In turn, the USDA rewrote its rules so as to require cooperating states to prevent the movement of livestock between quarantined and free areas within their borders.[51] A review of orders issued in 1907 showed how this worked. A state had to petition the Secretary of Agriculture demonstrating that it had the laws, personnel, and resolve to enforce a quarantine governing a part of the state. If convinced, the secretary would accept the state's internal line as the federal line and issue a federal quarantine on the portion of the state infected. But the federal quarantine restricted only the movement of livestock out of the quarantine zone into another state or territory. If the state failed to live up to its obligations to enforce the intrastate movement, the secretary could rescind his acceptance and move the federal line to the state border, effectively quarantining the entire state.

Research Breakthroughs

The imposition of quarantines and the segregation of Southern cattle in transit made it easier for the Northern cattle trade to coexist with Texas fever, but the South would remain in a low-level equilibrium as long as most of its territory was infected. Before officials could seriously contemplate fighting Texas fever where it was enzootic, researchers needed to unlock the secrets of the disease's etiology. Recall that the federal government had commissioned Gamgee (1868) and Salmon (1879) to study Texas fever. Scientists employed by several state governments were also at work. One of Salmon's first acts as Chief of the BAI was to hire Theobald Smith, effective 1 July 1884, to work in the Bureau's pioneering microbiological laboratory. Even as the fledgling BAI confronted the contagious bovine pleuropneumonia emergency, Salmon invested vital resources in Texas fever research. In 1885, he assigned Frederick L. Kilborne to investigate the possibility that ticks played a role in spreading the disease. Salmon directed Smith to work on Texas fever in September 1886, and after February 1889 Smith worked on little else. In 1888, Cooper Curtice began field studies on tick biology. Salmon's team was aggressively pursuing a laymen's theory that most reputable scientists (including Gamgee and Salmon himself) had previously ridiculed.[52] Smith, Kilborne, and Curtice produced epochal results.

In the summer of 1888, Smith discovered that red corpuscles were destroyed in blood drawn from infected cattle, but he did not establish a link to ticks until August 1889. The date is important because this discovery came after Secretary Rusk had issued his first quarantine order. Experiments headed by Kilborne in mid-1889 showed that cattle fell ill if exposed to ticks, but not by other means (except by inoculations of blood from infected cattle). Smith also showed that ticks carried the disease internally from one generation to the next, indicating that infected cattle were not necessary as a reservoir to spread the disease. By late 1892, Smith concluded that "it is highly probable that the ticks are the only agents which carry Texas fever to Northern pastures." In 1893, Smith and Kilborne provided the final pieces of the puzzle by linking Texas fever to a protozoan. They further established conclusively that the parasite was carried by ticks.[53]

There is controversy over the assignment of credit for Texas fever discoveries. Smith's initial draft of the 1893 publication did not include Kilborne as a coauthor. Salmon, in his capacity as laboratory director, added Kilborne's name. Smith considered this an injustice, as do his bibliographers Claude Dolman and Richard Wolfe. Calvin Schwabe, an expert on history of the veterinary sciences, disagreed. Schwabe had enormous respect for Smith, but emphasized the collaborative nature of the BAI research and the important contributions of Kilborne and Curtice.[54] Such conflicts over credit highlight how the pursuit of glory drove scientific research then, much as it does today.

The BAI's discovery represented a fundamental scientific breakthrough. Texas fever was the first disease caused by a microorganism shown to be transmitted by an arthropod vector, in this case solely by cattle ticks. Until that time, the only known means of transmitting infectious agents were contact with infected hosts (direct touch contact or indirect contact via infected secretions), with contaminated inanimate objects (fomites), or through vehicles such as water, air, or food. Transmission by vectors was new. The BAI discovery sped medical advances in understanding other vector-borne diseases, including malaria, plague, yellow fever, typhus, African sleeping sickness, and Rocky Mountain spotted fever.[55] By 1893, the scientific foundation needed to make tick eradication possible had been laid, but many more advances would be required before the BAI could seriously consider embarking on this course.

The early history of the BAI points to the need to revise the standard portrayal of the development of organized biological research in the United States. Almost all accounts celebrate Joseph Kinyoun's establishment in August 1887 of a bacteriological laboratory in the Marine Hospital Service (MHS) in the port of New York as setting a precedent. Victoria Harden notes that, unlike in Europe, there was no organized research tradition in the United States, and that in the same year that the MHS laboratory was created "the Lawrence Experiment Station was established in Massachusetts; the hygienic laboratory in Ann Arbor, Michigan, was set up during the winter of 1887–88; and the first municipal public health laboratory was founded in 1888 in Providence, Rhode Island." The MHS laboratory received legal recognition four years later when it was mentioned in a congressional act of 1891. According to Harden "very little original research was performed . . . in these early years of its existence." Not until legislation passed in 1901 and 1902 was MHS's Hygienic Laboratory significantly expanded and put on a more solid footing.[56] By comparison, Salmon established a bacteriological laboratory (and an experiment station) in 1883 while he was in the USDA's Veterinary Division. This pioneering laboratory was absorbed by the BAI in 1884. By the time the MHS facility was truly up and running, the BAI's scientists had made discoveries that changed the world.[57]

The BAI's laboratory was at the cutting edge of scientific inquiry within the American agricultural research establishment. As Charles Rosenberg observes, the Hatch Act of 1887 chartered the federal-state cooperative experiment station system, but over the early decades of operation its researchers were largely bogged down with mundane tasks such as testing the chemical composition of commercial fertilizers and running field trials of existing seed varieties. A focus on "original investigations" did not begin until sometime after the passage of the Adams Act of 1906.[58] By comparison, BAI science got off to a rapid start. There were important consequences for the course of state-federal relations: as federal scientific institutions developed, the gap between most states and the federal government in knowledge, expertise, and resources widened significantly. This increased the states' dependence on the BAI.

Conclusion

By the late 1890s, it became possible to conceive of eradicating Texas fever by eliminating its tick vector. The research conducted by Curtice, Kilborne, and Smith at the BAI in the late 1880s and the early 1890s led to revolutionary breakthroughs, which had broad implications for the medical sciences. Long after the scientific verdict that Texas cattle were a menace to Northern stock was in, many Southern leaders remained in a state of denial. A stream of subsequent discoveries, most of which sprung from public research enterprises, made it possible to consider eradicating cattle ticks from the United States. However, scientific advances were only one step in the story. Stronger legislation and changing judicial opinion on fundamental constitutional principles allowed the federal government to quarantine most of the South and segregate Southern cattle in transit to markets. Federal action reduced the plethora of state embargos, but some states continued to restrict the cattle trade. Rent seeking certainly played a role—economic and regional special interests were at work. Some sought to block competition just as others sought to preserve their "right" to trade even at the risk of damage to other people's property. However, the overwhelming story was one of building efficient institutions to counter serious market failures associated with a communicable disease.

Eradication would have to wait for Congress to demand, and the courts to accept, collective action and federal intervention on a massive scale across the South. Eradication would also have to wait for cracks in the normally solid Southern alliance opposing federal intervention. A softening of Southern attitudes resulted in part from the devastation caused by the boll weevil after 1892. Southerners now looked north for help; they wanted federal money, extension services, and research to combat the weevil. Southerners also searched for alternatives to cotton production. Among these alternatives were dairying and raising higher-quality beef cattle. Another key change was the creation of a permanent organization of state livestock regulatory officials. After several years of off-and-on collaboration, officials from seven mid-continent states assembled at Fort Worth, Texas, in September 1897 to form the Interstate Association of Live Stock Sanitary Boards. (The body expanded into the U.S. Live Stock Sanitary Association and later the Animal Health Association.) The organization's chief early mission was taking coordinated action to control Texas fever.[59]

The struggle to develop new institutions and redefine state-federal relationships to fight other animal diseases had a direct bearing on the subsequent campaign to eradicate Texas fever (analyzed in Chapter 11). The quarantines that isolated the South and the area-based vector-eradication program that would eventually push the offending cattle ticks out of one county after another were a part of a much larger set of measures, which cordoned off roughly one-half the land mass of the contiguous United States (for diseases other than Texas fever) and led to the mandated slaughter of millions of animals.

APPENDIX: Ticks and the Tick Fever

The terminology of the protozoa, the ticks, and the diseases has changed over time. When BAI researchers Theobald Smith and Frederick L. Kilborne first identified the protozoan infecting cattle, they named it *Pyrosoma bigeminum*.[60] Later, scientists recognized that two species renamed *Babesia* (*Babesia bigemina* and *Babesia bovis*) might be associated with Texas fever. More recently, researchers have reclassified *Boophilus* as a subgenus of *Rhipicephalus* (and thus have relabeled the ticks *R. microplus* and *R. annulatus*), but to be consistent with our historical sources we employ the traditional names. With the advent of DNA-tracing technologies, researchers have found many species within the genera *Anaplasma* and *Babesia*. Most of the pre-1990s research done on both *Anaplasma* and *Babesia* relied on serology. The pre-DNA methodology did not enable researchers to differentiate species within those genera. Thus, there is little sense as to whether the researchers were dealing either disease singly or with mixed infections.

Anaplasmosis is a rickettsial infection caused by any of several *Anaplasma* species. This intercellular bacterial infection was originally thought to be a type of babesiosis. The findings of recent decades bear on the issue of acquired immunity, because immunity to one species or disease would not protect against another.[61]

Two tick species, *Boophilus annulatus* and *Boophilus microplus,* transmit *Babesia* to cattle. In the United States, *B. annulatus* was the most common culprit, with a larger and more northerly range. *B. microplus* required a hotter, more humid climate and typically ranged within 100 miles of the Gulf of Mexico.[62] It would prove harder to eradicate. Other tick species transmit *Anaplasma.* Smith and Kilborne saw both *Babesia* and *Anaplasma* and concluded that they were forms of the same disease. Working in Africa, Arnold Theiler differentiated the two diseases in 1910, but it was not until the mid-1920s that anaplasmosis was identified as a serious problem in the United States.

These developments highlight that the search for an understanding of what we now know as tick-borne diseases was a worldwide enterprise that attracted some of the best minds of the day. Notably, the eminent Romanian scientist Victor Babes had observed red corpuscle problems in local cattle at about the same time as Smith. The modern name *Babesia* recognizes the contributions of Babes. Working on African ticks, Robert Koch discovered in 1906 the infective agent that caused the disease within both the bodies of ticks and in their eggs, thus providing further evidence that the offspring of infected ticks were themselves carriers.[63]

6 Contagions and Crises

Foot-and-Mouth Disease

ON 19 FEBRUARY 2001, foot-and-mouth disease (FMD) was discovered at a slaughterhouse near London, England. Authorities responded with draconian measures, including the immediate slaughter of infected and suspect livestock, a ban on movement of animals within the country, and a suspension of British exports of livestock products. The army mobilized to help cull over 6 million animals. In spite of these measures, pockets of FMD soon appeared in Western Europe. Spain, France, Belgium, the Netherlands, Ireland, and Germany adopted their own eradication policies. Everyday life was disrupted. In Britain, officials closed national parks and cancelled horse races, dog shows, and football matches. In Ireland, authorities even cancelled St. Patrick's Day parades. The mass destruction of suspect animals, including entire lines of pedigree stock, led to loud condemnations. The livestock, transportation, and tourism sectors all suffered significant economic losses.[1] In September 2001, after costly cleanup efforts, France, the Netherlands, and Ireland regained the coveted Office International des Epizooties (OIE) certification as a "FMD free country where vaccination is not practiced." The United Kingdom did not reacquire this status until January 2002.[2]

The severity of the government's actions provoked widespread criticism. Reviewing the episode from a science-and-technology-studies perspective, Abigail Woods traced the roots of the "slaughter-only" policy back to late Victorian Britain and explored why alternatives such as vaccination were taken off the table.[3] The U.K. response to a 2007 outbreak (caused by releases from a vaccine plant) was more rapid and more restrained. The responses of authorities in other countries to recent FMD

115

outbreaks also have been very aggressive. Between November 2010 and March 2011, the South Korean government culled over 3.4 million animals (mostly swine and cattle); authorities drew international condemnation when in their haste they buried 1.4 million pigs alive. The government mobilized over 175,000 personnel, imposed tight travel restrictions, and vaccinated several million animals. When the Koreans ran out of vaccine, the United States sent 2.5 million doses. What prompted this massive response? As of 13 May 2012, authorities had only discovered 153 confirmed cases of FMD. The contagion also attacked other Asian countries.[4]

FMD is a highly communicable viral disease of cloven-footed animals. The disease holds a special place in the history of medicine. In 1898, the Germans Paul Frosch and Friedrich Loeffler discovered the FMD virus. This was the first discovery of a vertebrate virus, and the first time that scientists correctly interpreted that the causative agent was a small particle different from a bacterium. Some prominent scientists thus date the origins of virology to Frosch and Loeffler's work (see Table 2.1).[5]

Cattle, hogs, sheep, goats, buffalo, deer, and many other animals (including humans) are susceptible to FMD. Infected animals develop blisters on the mouth and on the tissue above the hoof and between the toes—hence the name "foot-and-mouth disease." Symptoms include an elevated temperature, lameness, rapid weight loss, spontaneous abortion, sterility, lesions on newborn calves, and reduced milk production. Modern pasteurization procedures will kill the virus, but FMD-infected cows often develop chronic mastitis, which makes their milk unfit for human consumption.[6]

The virus is readily transmitted by wind, fluids, utensils, untreated milk, uncooked meat, and hides. Dogs, rats, and birds can serve as vectors. Humans leaving infected areas carry the virus on their clothing, shoes, tools, and vehicles. In addition, the virus can survive for several months to infect animals brought in to restock farms.[7] Unlike many infectious diseases, FMD can attack the same animal repeatedly. Recovery from FMD generates immunity to the infecting virus serotype but little protection against the other serotypes. This lack of immunity makes controlling the disease particularly difficult.

FMD is not a killer in the league with rinderpest, pleuropneumonia, Texas fever, and anthrax. The death rates for infected cattle typically hover between 1 and 5 percent, but they are much higher for calves and young pigs. Virulent strains of FMD, such as those that afflicted Europe between 1918 and 1921, can cause 30 to 50 percent mortality rates in cattle. The disease also has serious morbidity effects for surviving animals, reducing productivity by 20 to 30 percent. In addition to these physical effects, FMD leads to commercial losses due to trade closures.

The United States and Canada have generally followed Britain's historical policy of stamping out FMD as soon as it is discovered, lest it gain a foothold. This has involved border and port inspection facilities, imposition of strict quarantines, tracking of possible exposures, immediate slaughter of infected and suspect animals, safe disposal of the carcasses (by burial or cremation), and disinfection of the exposed premises. Imposing these measures has necessitated centralized planning. Because most infected animals recover and pose little direct threat to human health, owners have an incentive to conceal the disease, even though this puts their neighbors at risk. As a result, animal health officials are particularly aggressive in dealing with FMD crises. To gain cooperation, officials generally offer full compensation for all infected and exposed animals.

Early American Outbreaks

The United States has dodged the bullet several times. FMD first appeared in North America in 1870.[8] The disease likely entered Canada in August; by mid-November, it hit the stockyards in Albany, New York. It soon spread into Massachusetts, Rhode Island, Connecticut, New Hampshire, and possibly Maine. Infected stock contaminated roads, stables, railroad cars, and stockyards, including the Brighton yards (near Boston), resulting in "many thousands of cases, in scores of different towns." The region's most prominent veterinarian, James Law, provided guidance to policy makers and farmers. State and local officials responded vigorously with quarantines. With the good fortune of a harsh winter (which limited traffic), private, municipal, and coordinated state actions stamped out the epizootic without direct federal intervention.[9]

Minor outbreaks hit New York City in January 1881 and Portland, Maine, in February 1884. In both cases, authorities discovered the disease at or near ports, and stamped it out. There were also several false scares, such as when the 1884 outbreak of ergotism in Kansas was misdiagnosed as FMD (Chapter 3). These experiences contributed to the drive to intensify federal port and border inspections and quarantines. In 1884, the USDA took over active operation for the port quarantine stations from the Treasury Department. The new regulatory regime required that importers obtain forms from American consular agents in the sending regions attesting that the animals came from disease-free zones. Upon arrival, the animals were inspected and placed in quarantine.[10]

The next documented outbreak originated from an unexpected source. In November 1902, cases were discovered in Massachusetts, Rhode Island, New Hampshire, and Vermont. The disease most likely had originated in August on Owen Clark's farm in Chelsea, Massachusetts. Clark had rented calves to the New England Vaccine Company, which used them to propagate vaccines. The calves were likely infected by contaminated vaccines, apparently of Japanese origin. Infections in other isolated herds were also traced to this same company.[11] Tainted vaccines would prove a persistent problem, which eventually led to early federal pharmaceutical regulations.

During this episode, the Bureau of Animal Industry (BAI) established the policies that would guide its future efforts. John R. Mohler, then the head of the BAI's Pathological Division, assumed charge of the preliminary investigation and conducted inoculation tests that confirmed FMD.[12] On 27 November 1902, Secretary of Agriculture James Wilson quarantined Connecticut, Rhode Island, Massachusetts, and Vermont. He also closed the port of Boston to livestock exports. The BAI rushed resources into the infected area, and Bureau Chief Daniel Salmon arrived on December 1 to personally command federal forces. Wilson's orders were to act aggressively, to spare no pain or expense to stamp FMD out as quickly as possible. USDA agents began to slaughter all infected animals and to disinfect the contaminated areas. Officials initiated farm-to-farm searches after discovering that some farmers had deliberately concealed infected herds. To promote cooperation, the Bureau advocated fully compensating farmers for the appraised value of the animals as if they had been in good health. Using an emergency congressional appropriation of $500,000, the federal government paid 70 percent of the appraised value, leaving the remainder for the states. The BAI declared victory in June 1903, but only after the slaughter of 4,461 animals.[13] What at the time seemed like draconian policies were relatively trivial compared to those later employed in Britain, South Korea, and elsewhere.

Legislative Responses

The 1902–1903 FMD outbreak, in combination with other developments, exposed weaknesses in the BAI's legal authority. Recall that in the 1902 *Reid v. Colorado* decision (Chapter 5), the Supreme Court ruled that in 1884 Congress had made it an offense only to *knowingly* transport across state lines livestock that were *actually infected* with a contagious or infectious disease. Thus, the policy of quarantining entire states or counties within states to limit the interstate movement of infected livestock was acceptable, but the standard policy of quarantining exposed animals that might be infected was suddenly on weak footing. The Court further ruled that Congress did not intend for federal certificates of health to trump reasonable requirements imposed by state authorities.

It also came to light that Congress had never properly transferred the powers that it had originally conferred in the 1884 organic legislation to the Secretary of the Treasury over to the Secretary of Agriculture when the Cabinet post was created in 1889.[14] Faced with an emergency that threatened to shut down much of the BAI's regulatory apparatus in the midst of a FMD crisis, Congress passed and President Theodore Roosevelt signed the Cattle Contagious Disease Act of 2 February 1903.[15] The Act properly empowered the Secretary of Agriculture and addressed the problems highlighted in the 1902 *Reid v. Colorado* case by giving force to BAI certificates of health. Once a BAI official had certified livestock as free of disease, the animals could be shipped in interstate commerce and exported without further inspections or fees. This represented an important step in fostering a national market. The 1903 Act confirmed the USDA's power to establish quarantines even within state boundaries. In addition, the USDA was given power to seize, quarantine, and dispose of any hay, straw, animal products, or similar materials that might spread contagious diseases through international and interstate commerce.[16] In March 1903, the USDA used these powers to issue new regulations to prevent the spread of Texas fever, scabies in sheep and cattle, and hog cholera.

Legal challenges soon gutted the 1903 law, threatening ongoing control efforts. In separate decisions, courts ruled that the 1903 Act granted authority to prohibit shipment only of infected animals, not exposed animals, and that only parties who *knowingly* violated federal orders could be held accountable. As things stood, the federal government could not compel a shipper "to submit his cattle to inspection before shipment in order to form an intelligent opinion as to whether or not they are in fact diseased." Yet another decision declared the 1903 Act unconstitutional because it improperly delegated to the secretary the legislative powers to define and impose criminal penalties.[17]

Once again, the livestock industry faced an emergency. On 1 March 1905, President Roosevelt wrote Congress urging haste in drafting new legislation. He warned that lower court decisions working their way up to the Supreme Court might soon make it impossible for the federal government to control livestock diseases. In addition, he warned that each state would implement its own controls, creating a morass of laws with drastic consequences for domestic and foreign commerce. Congress responded two days later with stronger and more precisely written legislation. The Cattle Contagious Disease Act of 3 March 1905 expanded the secretary's power by authorizing him "to quarantine any State or Territory . . . , *or any portion* of any State or Territory . . . affected with any communicable disease."[18] The law covered all transportation modes used in interstate commerce including driving on foot. In addition, the law allowed the BAI to fine railroads that failed to disinfect cars properly. It explicitly authorized the regulation of infected and exposed animals, and it specified criminal penalties, thereby addressing the objections regarding an improper delegation of powers. The Act further specified criminal and civil penalties for "every person who forcefully assaults, resists, opposes, prevents, impedes, or interferes" with BAI officers or employees while they were executing their official duties. This provision was included because "during the past year two vicious, deadly, and unprovoked assaults have been made upon inspectors."[19] The 1906 McKendree decision (Chapter 5) necessitated policy changes to allow the BAI to enforce quarantine within states. Given the highly contagious nature of FMD, states were typically anxious to cooperate.

1908: A Serious Test and an Unexpected Spillover

Animal health officials were next tested in the fall of 1908. On October 26, two carloads of cattle infected with FMD were shipped from the stockyards at East Buffalo, New York, to central Pennsylvania. The disease was first suspected by Danville, Pennsylvania, farmer Jacob Shultz, who compared his cattle's symptoms to those described in a BAI publication. By November 8, state authorities confirmed the FMD diagnosis. Pennsylvania State Veterinarian Leonard Pearson immediately quarantined the Shultz farm, and requested the BAI's assistance. Over the next few days, Pearson quarantined several nearby farms where Pennsylvania officials discovered the infection. His edicts prohibited any movement of animals, and required people and equipment to be disinfected before crossing the quarantine lines. The Bureau's second chief, A. D. Melvin, rushed with his associates to Danville to investigate. On November 12, the Secretary of Agriculture declared a federal quarantine for four Pennsylvania counties, but FMD soon erupted in eleven other Pennsylvania counties, in five New York counties, and, by the end of the month, in one Maryland and two Michigan counties. The ports of New York, Philadelphia, and Baltimore were closed to the cattle trade. By November 27, the four states were under federal quarantines.[20]

The states carried a large share of the burden. Pennsylvania had passed legislation in 1895 that granted state officials the discretionary power to shut down infected farms, as Pearson repeatedly did in early November. The 1895 legislation also empowered the State Livestock Sanitary Board to issue blanket quarantines. On November 13, the day after the first federal quarantine, the Board issued a parallel order. In addition, the Board authorized its secretary to appoint BAI employees as state agents. This gave federal employees the power to interdict intrastate trade, enter farms and destroy property, and carry out other functions reserved to the states under the Constitution. The Board's swift actions followed protocols that had been hammered out in earlier crises.[21]

The *Breeder's Gazette* described the relentless state-federal campaign. "The pole-ax and the torch pursue their merciless work. All infected and exposed animals are killed, and all buildings in which they were quartered are burned. Full valuation is allowed and the Federal government pays two-thirds and the state one-third of this valuation." Over five months, officials slaughtered 2,025 cattle, 1,329 hogs, 275 sheep, and 7 goats worth about $90,000. At the height of this campaign, the BAI had 572 employees in the field, including 159 veterinarians. In total, the Bureau's staff made over 108,000 farm visits and inspected and reinspected nearly 1.6 million animals. Congress passed a special appropriation of $300,000 to suppress the epizootic. The four infected states reported expenditures totaling roughly $226,000. These outlays do not account for the losses from the extended trade disruptions. Although many farmers undoubtedly objected to the aggressive policies, America's most influential livestock journal applauded "celerity and efficiency of the government's intervention." The BAI "has again proved its ability to serve promptly and well the great interests under its jurisdiction."[22] As with the earlier CBPP campaign, the BAI's successes created political support for yet stronger interventions.

Subsequent investigations traced the 1908 FMD eruption to calves in the Detroit area that had been used to propagate smallpox vaccine. The vaccine was contaminated with the foot-and-mouth virus. The contaminated human vaccine was then tracked to a Philadelphia firm that had imported the vaccine from Japan in 1902. This was the second time in six years that foreign vaccines had caused a FMD outbreak. These revelations had a lasting effect on public health policy. Surgeon General Walter Wyman issued a recall of smallpox vaccine and required that henceforth the manufacturers of vaccines intended for human use test their products for contamination from infectious diseases, including the FMD virus.[23] The BAI's tracking system and investigative work were paying dividends for human health.

The Great 1914–1916 Epizootic

America's most severe FMD outbreak began in 1914. The disease got out of hand due to delays in diagnosing it and because it had spread undetected in areas where livestock commonly transited through the Chicago stockyards. On August 23, a veterinarian from Niles, Michigan, notified Dr. William T. Graham, the Michigan State Veterinarian, of local cattle with suspicious symptoms. It was not until September 3 that Graham and E. P. Schaffter, a BAI veterinarian, actually investigated. Schaffter misdiagnosed the ailment as a less serious disease, necrotic stomatitis. A month later, Schaffter reinspected the infected farms and again failed to positively identify FMD, but as a precaution he sent samples drawn from the infected animals to the BAI laboratory in Maryland. Inexplicably, the tests proved negative. When the Bureau Chief A. D. Melvin finally learned of Schaffter's inconclusive diagnoses on October 10, he immediately dispatched the BAI's chief pathologist, Adolph Eichhorn, to Michigan. Based on clinical observation, Eichhorn concluded the malady was in fact FMD; on October 15, John R. Mohler arrived in Niles and confirmed Eichhorn's diagnosis. Nearly six weeks had elapsed since the BAI was first contacted.[24]

On October 19, the USDA quarantined four Michigan and Indiana counties and began depopulating infected herds. Melvin strained to find experienced veterinarians to meet the emergency and had to hire mostly green hands. He drastically curtailed meat inspection and contracted with private practitioners; altogether, over 2,000 veterinarians participated. Over the next few weeks, reports of possible FMD outbreaks flowed in from across the Midwest. On October 27, the BAI received news from Blissfield, Michigan, that three steers that had just passed through Chicago were sick. The BAI now focused attention on Chicago.[25]

The National Dairy Show had opened there on October 22—the barns adjacent to the Union Stock Yards housed over 700 of the most valuable breeding bovines in the country. These animals were scheduled to leave on October 31. At the behest of the BAI, on October 29, the Illinois State Veterinarian, O. E. Dyson, ordered that these animals be held in their pens for a few extra days. Two days later the USDA quarantined the Union Stock Yards. On November 1, a show cow exhibited FMD symptoms; two days later, animals elsewhere in the yards were falling ill. The Union Stock Yards and the prized show cattle were infected. Around the same time, FMD appeared in the heart of Chicago's milkshed. On November 2, the USDA quarantined all of Illinois, Michigan, Indiana, and Pennsylvania. However, it was too late—most of the states in the Midwest and North Atlantic regions were soon infected.[26]

The October 31 decision to quarantine the Union Stock Yards underscores the gravity of the crisis. The Yards had been in continuous operation since 1865, and this unprecedented move effectively shut down the trade in livestock over a large part of the United States.[27] At first, livestock could be received but only for immediate slaughter. Then, on November 6, Illinois Governor Edward Dunne ordered the "Stockyards and Packingtown" operations entirely closed for ten days. During the shutdown, hundreds of stockyard workers engaged in a massive cleanup operation, removing rubbish, disinfecting the pens and chutes, fumigating the

Exchange buildings, and killing some 15,000 pigeons. The Yards became a "Spotless Town." On November 16, they began again accepting stock for immediate slaughter. When the yards reopened on November 29, the facility was segregated into a sector handling animals from FMD-free areas and one receiving stock from quarantined areas.[28]

The change in posture of the Chicago stockyard interests concerning animal diseases was evident. Three decades before, they had tried to kill the BAI bill and had obstructed the Bureau's fight against contagious bovine pleuropneumonia (CBPP). They had previously urged moving slowly, dismissed sound evidence and reasoned investigation as rumor-mongering, demonized professional veterinarians, and railed against the cost of a new bureaucracy. During the 1914 FMD epizootic, the Chicago interests welcomed swift and decisive action to combat the outbreak, advocated full compensation to the owners of condemned cattle, and harshly criticized stock owners who held back the eradication efforts. They wanted more, not less government regulation. Their major complaint was that the BAI did not act sooner and spend even more money. Telling headlines in the *Drovers Journal* read "Countrywide Censure of Dr. Melvin for Saving Bureau Funds" and "Houston Denies Economy Charge," referring to Melvin's boss, Secretary of Agriculture David Houston. It would be hard to imagine a fuller reversal of position.[29]

At the peak of the crisis in 1915, twenty-two states and Washington, D.C., fell under BAI quarantines. FMD had thoroughly infected herds in several states and gained scores of toeholds over a vast area stretching from southern Canada to Virginia and Kentucky, and from the Atlantic to Pacific states. Figure 6.1 shows the enormous range of the 1914–1916 outbreak. To provide perspective, the area of just two states near the epizootic's epicenter—Illinois and Indiana—roughly equals that of the entire United Kingdom. The contagion erupted with unprecedented speed. In addition to the normal paths of contamination via contact with infected animals, feed, railroad cars, and the like, veterinarians unwittingly spread the virus by inoculating swine with FMD contaminated hog cholera serum. This was at least the third instance where contaminated serums and vaccines had contributed to the spread of FMD.[30]

Following previously established guidelines, BAI and state officials immediately locked down infected and suspect properties (often posting armed guards) and began culling animals. Most states passed enabling

Figure 6.1. Area quarantined for foot-and-mouth disease, 1914–1916.
Source: Mohler, "Outbreak of 1914," p. 2.

legislation giving BAI agents broad powers. For a state to have resisted would have led to the cutting off of federal aid and the imposition of even harsher quarantines by other states and the federal government.

Culling stock and disinfecting property were massive undertakings. Animals targeted for destruction were usually appraised in the presence of the farmer by two knowledgeable cattlemen, one representing the state and the other the federal government. The government hired locals to dig burial trenches. The animals were herded into the trenches, shot, and then typically covered with lime. Next, a disinfectant crew began its work. This required spraying ceilings; scrubbing posts, walls, and floors; safely disposing of manure and hay; and bathing dogs, cats, and poultry in a cresol solution. Agents then inspected all animals and premises in an area up to three miles from the infected sites. Officials also inspected creameries and stockyards, closing and disinfecting contaminated establishments. Investigators traced the past movements of cattle, people, and materials in an effort to determine the source of local outbreaks to identify contaminated areas including rail cars and public pens, and to help target new quarantines. The BAI enlisted some of America's most renowned scientists, including Simon Flexner, the director of the Rockefeller Institute for Medical Research, to advise on the case. The press was rightfully critical of the initial misdiagnosis the diseased but generally applauded the BAI's eradication efforts.[31]

Educational events informed local farmers about the nature of the disease and the need for its eradication, but the owners of infected farms were not invited for fear they would carry the virus on their shoes and clothing. In spite of these efforts, many farmers resisted the government's quarantines and culling programs by hiding animals, obtaining restraining orders, and requesting special exemptions. The most prominent holdout was Grace Durand, the wealthy owner of a large herd of purebred Guernsey cows near Chicago. In early September 1915, after confirming a FMD outbreak at Durand's Crab Tree dairy farm, authorities placed the estate in Lake Forest (north of Chicago) under quarantine and ordered the animals destroyed. A person of means and connections, Durand retained legal counsel and gained a stay of execution. A Christian Scientist, she was unconvinced by the diagnosis of the state veterinarians and applied her own unconventional cures. As the standoff endured, so did the trade restriction on Illinois cattle shipments. To expedite the animals' slaughter, the Chicago Live Stock Exchange offered to buy the herd at premium prices. Durand, who called the cows her "pets," refused. After the Illinois Supreme Court overturned the injunction, Durand armed herself and her staff, threatening "to shoot the first person who attempts to harm any of my cattle." On November 9, the Lake County sheriff, on orders of the Illinois governor, entered her Crab Tree estate with a large posse of deputies and veterinarians, locked Durand in her home, and slayed her stock.[32]

Authorities had made an exception to their general eradication policy for the highly valuable breeding stock at the National Dairy Show. When FMD broke out, these prized animals "were confined to brick buildings where it was possible to maintain a stricter quarantine than could be maintained on farms." Most young calves died, and several animals developed serious secondary infections, but most survived and were released from quarantine on 31 May 1915. U. G. Houck concluded that "the expense connected with the care and maintaining the quarantine of this herd under the most favorable conditions was so great that it exceeded several times the average value of farm cattle and showed conclusively that it would not pay to attempt to save farm animals under ordinary farm conditions."[33] Although the USDA tried to put a positive spin on the decision to spare the show cattle as saving the nation's premier dairy breeding stock, most officials probably regretted the clemency. Illinois State Veterinarian Dyson noted that to avoid an injunction he placed the show herd in isolation. As a result, every owner of an infected herd "wanted to know why his cattle were not treated the same as the dairy herd in Chicago. . . . I don't think that we ever succeeded in a single instance in making a satisfactory explanation." Veterinary officials from other states were also frustrated with the politically powerful owners of the show cattle receiving special treatment.[34]

The cleanup campaign in response to this outbreak dwarfed previous efforts. Between October 1914 and May 1916, authorities slaughtered over 172,000 animals, including over 77,000 cattle. Illinois was hardest hit, accounting for about 46 percent of all the animals culled. Together, the federal government and the affected states spent roughly $9 million, with about $6 million going to reimburse farmers. The last outbreak was suppressed in Wisconsin in May 1916, and the last quarantines were lifted in June 1916. The United States and Canada had come perilously close to having FMD become entrenched for many decades. Without the lessons learned in the earlier FMD and CBPP campaigns, it is unlikely that the BAI and state authorities would have had the political and scientific infrastructure needed for success in place.

Following the 1914–1916 episode, the BAI expanded its surveillance system, placing "experienced veterinarians at public stockyards especially assigned to making careful inspections of livestock" for the disease.[35] Congress responded by expanding the BAI's budget with precommitted emergency funding that would be available immediately to meet future crises. The BAI started planning for future outbreaks, strengthening its relations with the states. By 1917, all forty-eight states had signed onto the Bureau's detailed FMD plans specifying notification, tracking, quarantine, culling, and cleanup procedures.

Planning Pays: Texas and California

These preparations proved valuable when FMD hit Texas and California in 1924. On 25 September 1924, reports reached Washington, D.C., of a possible outbreak in Texas. Two days later, veterinarians confirmed FMD on the farm of W. S. Jacobs in Harris County, near Houston. The best guess is that the virus arrived in Texas aboard a ship from South America. The Secretary of Agriculture immediately quarantined all of Harris and Galveston Counties, and parts of two other counties. Within a few days the BAI had a force of experienced veterinarians, headed by the veteran FMD fighter Marion Imes, on station. On October 1, Texas Governor Pat Neff transferred total control of the state taskforce to the USDA in order to create a unified command. Thus, within six days of the first word that there might be a problem, a sizeable taskforce with a well-defined chain of command was on the ground and running.[36]

The teamwork was impressive. In addition to local officers, the Texas Rangers provided security, manned guard posts, and rode patrol to prevent the movement of animals or people. The Texas Livestock Sanitary Commission, the State Veterinarian, the United States Biological Survey, and the Texas and Southwestern Cattle Raisers Association also provided men and resources. County extension agents joined the force, and Texas railroads participated by helping to enforce the quarantine. When threatened with FMD, Texas cattlemen of 1920s embraced the "one man principle," conveying summary powers to federal officers.[37] Within thirty days, the disease was eradicated. The rapidity of the victory belies the seriousness of the situation because, given a few weeks, range animals could have infected a far greater area. The Bureau addressed the problem of roaming animals by purchasing and killing all cloven-footed animals (including those in enclosed pastures) within a wide radius of the known infection sites. Carcasses were buried or incinerated and properties disinfected. In addition, riders set fire to the range.[38]

On 26 July 1925, FMD appeared again in a herd owned by W. S. Jacobs. A BAI inspector confirmed the disease the next day. Within days, the same general plan kicked into gear. Over the next several months, new hot spots emerged. An outbreak on August 25 on the northern side of the Houston ship channel was particularly alarming because this area "bordered an immense open-range country in which disease-control operations would be very difficult." In response, the BAI fenced the area and culled all susceptible animals in the enclosure. In the open range, Texas Rangers flushed animals out of thickets, wooded areas, and ravines to be appraised and slaughtered. The Rangers camped out within the infected territory and left only after being disinfected when the job was done.

On 4 September 1925, the disease appeared in Galveston County. Contrary to legal precedent, "local interests" were able to obtain injunctions delaying eradication. Even with such challenges, the last infected animals in this flare up were culled by October 2. Altogether about 31,000 animals (mostly cattle) were slaughtered in the two Texas outbreaks. Throughout the outbreak, the BAI was in charge, giving detailed instructions on monitoring, eradication, cleanup, and disposal.[39]

California also suffered two FMD attacks during the 1920s. On 17 February 1924, a local veterinarian discovered FMD in a dairy herd in West Berkeley; other infected herds soon came to light. The BAI immediately launched an investigation, and tests quickly confirmed FMD. State officials deployed armed guards to seal off the infected farms and close local roads. G. H. Hecke, the California Director of Agriculture, quarantined all livestock in Alameda County on February 22. The virus probably had been smoldering in neighboring counties for over a month after arriving at the nearby Mare Island Navy Yard from Asia in a ship's garbage—the nation's port defenses would repeatedly be breached by the sloppy treatment of garbage. By the end of February, the USDA had quarantined nine northern California counties. With a detailed plan at the ready, the BAI quickly mobilized experts from across the country, and established an emergency field headquarters in Oakland. To help stem the spread, the Bureau notified sanitary officials around the world to be on high alert.[40]

Eradication in the San Francisco Bay Area progressed rapidly. Within a month of the disease's discovery, veterinarians had depopulated all the infected herds and disinfected contaminated farms. But on March 22, FMD was discovered in Merced County, over 100 miles southeast of Berkeley. Merced, Madera, Mariposa, and Stanislaus Counties were quarantined on March 24. The work was complicated because of the rough and remote terrain. The situation deteriorated with the discovery of infected animals in Los Angeles and San Francisco in late March, and in Kern, San Bernardino, Orange, Tulare, Tuolumne, and Fresno Counties by the middle of May. The disease eventually spread to sixteen counties, and all or parts of twenty-three California counties were quarantined. At one time, the BAI had 204 agents in the field (plus many laborers, private veterinarians, and staff drawn from the meat inspection service). The state also supplied a large taskforce.[41] Officials destroyed more than

Figure 6.2. Culling cattle near Merced, California, 1924. *Source:* Merced County Historical Society.

100,000 animals by the end of August 1924. Figure 6.2 shows agents wearing rubberized coats culling cattle. Such grim scenes were a common sight in FMD eradication zones. Another nasty situation arose when BAI agents discovered FMD in California's deer population. In the Stanislaus National Forest, officials dispatched more than 200 hunters. Strychnine-laced salt licks dotted the countryside. In all, over 22,000 deer were destroyed; about 10 percent showed FMD lesions.[42]

California's trade and tourism suffered. Soon after the crisis began, thirty-six states, Hawaii, and several foreign nations slapped embargoes on California products, including livestock, poultry, and their products, straw, grain, and grasses, fruit (including dried and canned fruit), vegetables, nursery stock, packing materials, and other biological products. The rules lacked coherence and sometimes were unreasonable, reflecting both unfounded fears and, in some cases, attempts to limit competition. It became impossible for railroads to keep up with the rapidly changing mishmash of state restrictions.

Oregon and Arizona imposed especially severe measures. Arizona blocked roads and stranded travelers. At the Yuma Crossing, guards turned fire hoses on a crowd of 800 who tried to rush the barriers. Transcontinental travelers were forced to travel east via the Salt Lake City route. Even after travel bans were relaxed, Arizona and Oregon still demanded that automobiles and goods be disinfected. Arizona also fumigated trains and disinfected all eastbound tourists. In one case, the traffic delays at the border purportedly contributed to a baby's death. Within California, FMD disrupted regular life, leading to the cancellation of civic events and the closure of national forests, parks, camping facilities, trails, and fishing and hunting areas. Counties free of the disease locked out their neighbors. Communities dispatched armed guards to close roads and disinfected vehicles and people. Figure 6.3 shows a disinfection station near Merced. Los Angeles county supervisors authorized the hiring of 600 extra deputy sheriffs and inspectors to police their territory.[43]

A great concern was that embargoes would block the interstate shipment of the state's approaching spring and summer fruit and vegetable crops. A series of conferences in March and April 1924 led to a set of standardized regulations for the signatories. The rules allowed for the shipment of fruit, vegetables, nursery stock, and other enumerated products from uninfected areas if they were closely monitored and certified. In spite of the refusal of Arizona, Nevada, Oregon, and Washington to sign the accord, roughly 1 million certified shipments left the state before FMD was eradicated. Authorities disinfected over 21,000 railroad cars.[44]

The 1924 outbreak exposed a major defect in California's ability to respond to animal diseases. Between March and May, Congress appropriated $6 million to fight the California epizootic, but the federal government demanded that the state pay 50 percent of the compensation for destroyed animals and property. However, the state's constitution

Figure 6.3. Disinfecting automobiles and people near Merced, California, 1924. *Source:* Merced County Historical Society.

was interpreted to prohibit compensating the owners of condemned animals for their losses. Based on their earlier experiences in controlling CBPP and FMD outbreaks, most Eastern states found providing indemnities to yield benefits well worth the costs and adjusted their laws accordingly. California had escaped these earlier epizootics and thus had never modified its legal institutions. To compound the problem, California had approved the USDA's 1917 template for FMD eradication but had neglected to empower state officials to cull suspect animals. USDA operating procedures demanded the slaughter of all susceptible animals that might have been exposed.

There was no quick solution to these financial and legal binds. The legislature was on recess, and, for political reasons unrelated to the emergency, Governor Friend Richardson refused to call a special session. Officials skirted the legal issue by asserting the right to slaughter healthy animals under the state's power to protect health. To address the financial impasse, Richardson appealed to the State Bankers' Association for a loan of $600,000 to pay the state's share of indemnity payments. Given the prospect of catastrophic losses to the state's livestock and a continua-

tion of the ruinous trade embargoes, the bankers "patriotically" choose
to advance a sizable sum, although there was no binding provision to
repay them.[45] California's anemic infrastructure remained a work in
progress, which would haunt the state in future eradication campaigns.

A second, albeit far less serious, episode hit the Golden State in January 1929, when FMD was discovered among swine near Montebello in
Los Angeles County. Once again, authorities traced the outbreak to infected garbage from a ship. Early discovery, a timely, well-planned reaction, and perhaps considerable luck quelled the outbreak. Within two
months, the quarantines were lifted.[46] Most accounts assert that this
1929 episode was the last FMD outbreak in the United States, but there
is some doubt. The controversy centered on whether a 1932 contagion in
Southern California was FMD or a new disease, vesicular exanthema
of swine. In any case, authorities slaughtered nearly 120,000 animals
in 1932.[47]

The California outbreak in 1924 and a Mexican outbreak in 1926
spurred interest in a binational sanitary convention to fight FMD in
North America. In January 1930, the United States and Mexico ratified
a treaty banning the entry of cattle from countries where FMD existed.
U.S. negotiators hoped to ensure a southern buffer zone to block the
virus. The Smoot-Hawley Tariff Act, ratified in June 1930, further
strengthened U.S. FMD protections. The Act made it a penal offense to
import domesticated ruminants, swine, and most fresh, chilled, or fro-
zen meats from any country infected by FMD or rinderpest. Mexico
carried out an aggressive slaughter, quarantine, and area vaccination
program that eradicated FMD in 1954. Strict trade barriers have kept
North America free of the disease since that time.[48]

Comparative Perspectives

In opting for an eradication strategy, the USDA was influenced by its
success in eradicating CBPP in 1892 and by the record in Great Britain.
FMD had repeatedly entered Britain in the second half of the nineteenth century; each time the government stamped it out. FMD was
enzootic in many regions of continental Europe. Many countries did
not seriously commit to eradicating the disease until after World War II,
after better vaccines became available. Vaccination was not an option in
the United States in the early twentieth century. Today, policy makers

in FMD-free nations hit with a new outbreak regard vaccination as a last ditch option to be employed only if stamping-out policies prove too expensive and the disease threatens to become established.

Vaccination has many disadvantages. Vaccines are expensive and need to be administered every four to six months. Much like vaccines to combat human influenza, FMD vaccines must be targeted at specific strains, and there is uncertainty as to which strain may be on the horizon. In the past, there was a danger that vaccines were not properly inactivated, and thus they might spread the infection. Finally, a nation that turned to vaccination would lose its privileged trade status. Because it is difficult for tests to "distinguish between animals and meat that have had the disease and those that have been vaccinated," countries that vaccinate must wait two years (instead of one year) following the last clinical case to regain FMD-free status.[49]

The different policies in large part reflected the different realities dictated by history and geography. In Britain and the United States, the disease had not gained a foothold, and eradication, thought costly, was both feasible and economically sensible. Once FMD was eradicated, a national inspection and quarantine system at ports and borders could block reentry. For much of continental Europe, FMD was so widespread that eradication would have been extremely costly. Norway, Sweden, Holland, and Denmark were among the exceptions. BAI officials closely tracked FMD in other nations to help muster political support for the efforts to block its entry.[50]

U.S. FMD eradication policies were always controversial. Farmers whose livestock were not exposed typically demanded strong policies, whereas many farmers with infected or exposed animals called for moderation. However, in light of the culling of 6 million animals in the United Kingdom during the 2001–2002 outbreak and of several million animals in South Korea in 2011, American officials have been relatively lenient. Britain's continuous kill policy called for culling all livestock within a three-kilometer radius of a confirmed FMD incident. Official data indicate that 4.9 million sheep, 0.7 million cattle, and 0.4 million pigs were culled (critics of British policy claim far larger numbers). Based on the animal population in the United Kingdom in 2000, officials culled 11.6 percent of the nation's sheep, 6.3 percent of the cattle, and 6.2 percent of the pigs.[51] By comparison, U.S. officials quarantined entire states or infected regions, shutting down all traffic in animals. In 1914, policy called for locking down and monitoring all animals within a radius of one-mile (about 1.6 kilometers) of confirmed cases, but in general only infected or directly exposed animals were killed. During America's worst episode (1914–1916), only 172,000 animals were culled.

Was It Worth It?

Agricultural economists have generated numerous estimates of the costs and benefits of measures to control hypothetical outbreaks of FMD in the United States.[52] The outbreak in the United Kingdom, along with the heightened concerns with bioterrorism, has increased the interest in understanding the ramifications of possible future outbreaks. According to Dustin Pendell and colleagues, even a modest outbreak (by historical standards) limited to a fourteen-county region in southwest Kansas could be expected to lead to losses in excess of $200 million. Javier Ekboir's analysis of the impact of a serious FMD outbreak in California suggests that the eradication costs and trade losses could easily exceed the total annual value of the state's entire annual livestock output (including all dairy products).[53] The losses are so large in part because the affected localities could suffer drops in tourism and trade.[54] Another set of estimates from the 1970s suggests a benefit-to-cost ratio of roughly 120 to 1 for the prevention policies then in place.[55]

Rather than speculate about the future, we provide a rough estimate of the costs and benefits of the BAI's policies for controlling FMD in the period up to the last certified outbreak in 1929. Between 1900 and 1929, the BAI spent between $12,000 and $73,000 a year on quarantine and inspection operations at America's ports to reduce the likelihood of exotic diseases gaining a foothold in the United States. Adjusting the stream of annual expenditures for port operations for price changes and compounding annual data by 3 percent a year yields a total expenditure in 1929 prices of $3,864,056 for port operations. The quarantine services targeted a plethora of diseases, and FMD prevention represented a "minor part of the inspection" process. We allocated of all port costs to FMD; this generates an upper-bound estimate of the policy costs.[56] Next, we reckoned all the state and federal expenditures during the eradication campaigns of 1902, 1908, 1914, 1924, 1925, and 1929. We also price adjusted and compounded these costs, yielding a 1929 value of $36.4 million.

The compounded real cost in 1929 of all FMD control operations sums to $40.2 million.

In 1930, the stock of livestock most affected by FMD was valued at $4,376 million, with cattle making up $3,304 million. To assess the benefits of prevention and eradication expenditures on the livestock industry, one needs to know how much the value of the stock of cattle, swine, sheep, and goats would have depreciated if the disease had spread throughout the United States in the absence of controls. We assume that the 1930 livestock values reflected the discounted value of future production. We can offer a range of benefit-cost estimates based on different assumptions of the depreciation caused by FMD. If FMD caused a 10 percent deprecation to the value of the 1930 livestock population, the control policies would have generated $10.88 in benefits for every dollar expended. The relationship is linear: a 40 percent depreciation implies benefits of $43.50 for every dollar spent. The depreciation ratio would depend on many factors, including the severity of the infection, but it would have been well above 10 percent. Most mature animals survive a FMD outbreak, but the survivor's productivity is reduced by about 25 percent.[57] Accounting for trade losses and the high death rate among young animals would add significantly to the costs, perhaps taking the total loss to 40 percent or more of the value of susceptible livestock. This higher estimate is in rough accordance with the BAI's earlier assessments. Whatever the final accounting, there can be little doubt that the USDA's FMD policies had a highly favorable benefit-to-cost ratio.[58]

Another way to answer the question of whether the control measures were "worth it" is to compare the number of animals sacrificed with the number saved. The U.S. campaigns to control FMD in the early twentieth century involved the slaughter of 173,000 head of cattle, 110,000 swine, and 43,000 sheep and goats. FMD was feared more for its morbidity effects (and its impact of trade) than for its mortality effects. But it does kill. Consider the estimated immediate deaths resulting from an uncontrolled outbreak. Drawing parameters from McCauley and colleagues, a baseline uncontrolled FMD epizootic would infect 70 percent of all susceptible animals, killing 6 percent of infected calves, 1 percent of older cattle, 80 percent of piglets, 2 percent of older swine, 60 percent of lambs and goat kids, 2 percent of other sheep and goats, and 10 percent of cloven-hoofed wildlife. Had such an outbreak struck the United States in 1925, the death toll would have exceeded 1.1 million head of cattle, 15.5 million swine, 7.0 million sheep and goats, and millions of deer, among other animals. The losses would have continued after the disease had become enzootic. In the absence of control measures, the death toll would have been enormous.[59]

Conclusion

Unlike CBPP, Texas fever, and hog cholera (Chapters 4, 5, and 7), FMD never became firmly established in the United States. In the late nineteenth century, most of the world lived with FMD. America's good fortune was a result of geographic isolation, luck, and determination—namely, a resolve to stamp out eruptions without delay through draconian internal quarantine-slaughter-and-disinfection efforts. Successful control was neither easy nor assured. Indeed, during the great 1914–1916 epizootic, the disease entered twenty-two states and led to a quarantine of the Union Stock Yards in Chicago. The recent epizootics in Britain in 2001 and South Korea in 2010 offer vivid reminders of the panic, mass cullings, disruptions to travel and trade, bureaucratic missteps, and public backlashes that can accompany FMD outbreaks.

The BAI's strategy for combating FMD differed significantly from its work on Texas fever. Unlike Texas fever, an FMD outbreak always represented a crisis. Once in motion, the BAI's major initiative against Texas fever was to methodically push the quarantine line southward across a broad front. The fight against FMD was more akin to the response to CBPP, with veterinarians rushing to control hot spots when they unexpectedly erupted.

Successfully combating FMD required major institutional innovations, which would subsequently facilitate the control of other animal diseases. These included extensive surveillance-and-containment systems, well-established cooperative relations with state authorities, a cadre of trained experts with protocols ready to respond to crises, and regular appropriations from Congress even in the absence of ongoing outbreaks to facilitate rapid responses to emergencies. The threat of FMD, along with the BAI's repeated success in stamping it out, created political support for federal livestock sanitary institutions, even in the heart of Texas.

7 The Hog Cholera Puzzle

Controversy and Discovery

IN 1897, Marion Dorset arrived at his new posting in Sidney, Iowa. From his hotel window he could see the glow of fires in the surrounding countryside—local farmers were burning swine carcasses. Such fires were a regular occurrence in Midwestern prairies during the late summer and fall, when hog cholera typically peaked. The Bureau of Animal Industry (BAI) had just dispatched Dorset to Iowa to combat this dreaded killer.[1]

Hog cholera is a severe viral infection, which before the advent of effective treatment accounted for up to 90 percent of all U.S. hog deaths from diseases. Hog cholera is highly contagious, and the periodic outbreaks often wiped out entire herds. In 1886–87, 1896, and 1913, the national death toll exceeded 10 percent of all U.S. swine. Hog cholera (also called classical swine fever and other names) presented variable symptoms and was frequently accompanied by serious secondary infections. These variable manifestations made the disease difficult to understand, much less to control. In the hectic years after the BAI's founding, its leaders became embroiled in a nasty dispute over hog cholera as rival scientists advanced conflicting claims about its causes and potential cures. For almost two decades, most researchers pursued the false course that Daniel Salmon first set in 1884–85 based on the erroneous conclusion that the disease was bacterial.

The major breakthrough came in 1903, when Dorset and his BAI colleague Emil Alexander de Schweinitz discovered the hog cholera virus. With this knowledge, they devised vaccines that reduced the damage caused by the disease. However, there were drawbacks. The vaccines contained live virus, which meant that their deployment reduced the risk of catastrophic outbreaks, but at the same time guaranteed that the disease would remain present. In part because of the availability of vaccines, the USDA chose not to stamp out hog cholera as it had done with contagious bovine pleuropneumonia (CBPP) in the nineteenth century and many other major diseases in the first half of the twentieth century.

Origins

The early history of hog cholera is shrouded in uncertainty, with some authorities maintaining that it was of European origin and others asserting that it emerged *de novo* in the United States.[2] The date of the first U.S. occurrence is disputed, but most accounts assert that it first struck in southern Ohio in 1833. The disease likely gained its moniker "hog cholera" in the mid-1850s.[3] Much of what has been written about the disease's early history comes from USDA reports published in the late 1870s and the 1880s, which compiled over one thousand responses from local correspondents. The responders referenced many early outbreaks. As examples, a correspondent from Muskingum County, Ohio, stated that hog cholera had erupted in his area in 1833; and the correspondent for Harrison County, Indiana, noted that in 1840 the disease swept along the Wabash River valley. Based on these retrospective (and sometimes secondhand) accounts, USDA researchers placed the first outbreak in Ohio in 1833. They concluded that there were about ten outbreaks from 1833 to 1845, ninety-three from 1846 to 1855, 293 in the 1856 to 1865 period, and roughly 200 per decade thereafter.[4]

We are skeptical of this account. Nobody claiming that there were outbreaks in the 1830s or early 1840s has offered any contemporary evidence. The early Patent Office and USDA publications are silent on this issue as are the early reports of the state agricultural societies of Ohio and Indiana. A widely referenced article in the *Prairie Farmer* (1853) describes the recent deaths of hundreds of hogs at a Carrollton, Kentucky, distillery and alludes to a bad outbreak in the mid-1830s, but there are no specifics. In a similar fashion, O. H. V. Stalheim asserts that hog cholera epizootics killed one-half of all the pigs in Kentucky and Tennessee in the 1840s, but he provides no evidence.[5]

Our research suggests that if hog cholera (whatever its name) existed at all in North America before the 1850s, it was a minor problem. In fact, we have not found *any* contemporary newspaper reports about swine calamities for the 1830s and 1840s. Newspapers published near the epi-center of the purported 1833 Muskingum County outbreak do not men-tion an epizootic, despite the fact that that these papers contained stories dealing with local hogs and reports on the 1832–1833 human cholera outbreak in the Ohio River valley. The lack of mention of a rash of swine deaths in the Midwestern agricultural press of the day further fuels our skepticism.[6]

However, there is no doubt that hog cholera repeatedly struck in the 1850s, so America's most serious swine killer was likely an emerging disease at mid-century. From 1856 through 1858, the disease swept across the Midwest and Northeast, often killing the entire population of infected herds. In 1856, a distillery in Indiana reported losing 11,000 hogs. Farm-ers in Illinois, Kentucky, Indiana, Ohio, New York, New Jersey, Massachu-setts, Pennsylvania, Maryland, and Virginia all recorded heavy losses. In 1857, the number of hogs packed in the West fell by 34 percent from the previous year. Although other factors may have contributed to the decline, hog cholera played a prominent role. Whatever its origins, by the late 1850s the disease had become established in the Midwest, Northeast, and Upper South. Its emergence and spread represents a clear case of the stock-raising environment in the United States taking a decided turn for the worse.[7]

Human Health Concerns

By the 1870s, hog cholera had spread to all swine-raising regions of the country. There seemed little prospect of controlling the disease, let alone of finding a cure or eradicating it completely. Hog cholera is not transmittable to humans, but in the nineteenth century there were many alarming reports to the contrary. As an example, in 1858 the *Prairie Farmer* opined, "In several sections of the West this epidemic is committing great ravages among porkers; in some places it is estimated that two-thirds of the hogs have already been destroyed; the worst complaints are from the American Bottom [the confluence of the Missouri, Illinois, and Mis-sissippi rivers], where not only the swine but also the people are suffer-ing from disease." Such concerns continued. In 1886, news accounts noted that George Wilson of Muncie, Indiana, died after tending swine with hog cholera. "Attending physicians claim the disease is similar to hog cholera, and that it may become epidemic. Wilson was sick for only four hours and died in the most agonizing pain. The entire southern portion of the county is horror-stricken, and many farmers are anxious to sell their farms and go west. It is reported that many farmers have left their homes and will not return until the question of epidemic is decided in this case."[8]

Europeans were also terrified that hog cholera could infect humans. As a sign of the disease's importance, many renowned British scientists, including the pioneering physician William Budd, addressed this question. Budd had earlier gained notoriety when he established the etiology of typhoid fever, much as John Snow and John Simon had done for cholera. Budd tentatively concluded that that the new swine disease, which he dubbed "pig typhoid," was not zoonotic, but his widely publicized speculations likely increased the terror.[9]

Reports that U.S. meatpackers processed the carcasses of swine that had died from hog cholera raised alarms. Even after states required that the carcasses of afflicted hogs be promptly buried or burned, the meat and lard from such animals found their way into the market. The evidence is indirect but persuasive. As an example, in 1901 there was an active market in dead hogs in Sioux City, Iowa. "One buyer bought 92,000 pounds of dead hogs in two days. Another said he paid out an average of $1,000 a day for the previous two weeks for dead hogs at his plant."[10] Given that a high percentage of swine that died from hog cholera harbored secondary infections that were perilous to humans, there was in fact a genuine health problem.

The spread of hog cholera had international repercussions for U.S. producers. When the disease hit Britain in 1862, there was a reasonable presumption that it had come from the United States. In 1879, the Privy Council adopted stern measures in an attempt to stamp out the disease; these included a mandate that all swine imported from the United States be slaughtered at the docks as cattle were. In spite of these measures, the United Kingdom would not wipe out hog cholera until 1967. In the early 1880s, most of continental Europe restricted imports of U.S. swine and pork products. Trichinosis was the primary health concern (see Chapter 8), but hog cholera was also a serious issue. The two diseases were often lumped together in European criticisms of American sanitary standards. As an example, in 1881 George Crump, the assistant

British consul in Philadelphia, coupled his charge that American pork was crawling with trichinae with the erroneous claim that in the previous year over 700,000 Illinois hogs had succumbed to hog cholera. Enraged replies from American farming and commercial interests along with those from Secretaries of State William Evarts and James G. Blaine never fully repaired the damage. Two years later, fresh reports circulated in Europe that that the products of diseased hogs were being shipped from Chicago stockyards to France. American officials protested that this was a "perversion of facts," but again consumer confidence and trade undoubtedly suffered. Given the lax inspection standards of the day, it is likely that products from diseased swine did in fact enter international commerce.[11] Of course, Europeans were not the only parties concerned. Many U.S. states enacted quarantines when neighboring regions experienced hog cholera eruptions, but, these were not very effective.[12]

Early Investigations

Hog cholera long baffled farmers and researchers because of its wide array of symptoms, which depended on the virulence of the strain and the susceptibility of the hosts. In the 1850s, George Sutton of Aurora, Indiana, performed controlled tests in which he exposed healthy pigs to diseased animals and to contaminated fields. He closely observed hundreds of sick swine and reported several pages of symptoms that combined in a perplexing variety of ways.[13] Later researchers reported that the incubation period was usually three to eight days, but it could be more or less. The more virulent strains came on rapidly, causing an acute illness followed by death within two or three weeks. Young pigs often died shortly after being exposed. In some cases, hogs might languish for over a month with mild symptoms before falling mortally ill. Sick animals often became feverish and listless and would cease eating. Diarrhea was common (as in human cholera), but so was constipation. Eye infections, muscle tremors, and skin lesions, especially purple hemorrhagic areas on the abdomen, were common but not universal symptoms.[14] Mild or "chronic" strains with low death rates could provide a continual source of infections. Individual swine varied greatly in their natural susceptibility to the virus. Animals that survived an attack obtained lifetime immunity but were likely to be stunted.

Swine afflicted with hog cholera were so weakened that they became very susceptible to serious secondary infections. These had their own confusing array of symptoms, which were often misinterpreted as symptoms of hog cholera.[15] Unrelated diseases were also sometimes confused with hog cholera. Most notably, the European hog disease swine erysipelas, known as *rouget* in France, produced a fever and red spots on the skin, much as hog cholera did. There were many false starts before researchers disentangled these many problems.

In 1878, Congress appropriated $10,000 for a study of animal diseases. Commissioner of Agriculture William G. De Luc appointed a nine-man commission of veterinarians, which included H. J. Detmers, James Law, and Daniel Salmon, to study swine ailments. The commissioners individually conducted experiments on hog cholera, but they failed to make much headway.[16] Detmers's 1879 report did accurately note that hog cholera was a major problem in the Midwest. This provided ammunition for European officials when erecting trade barriers against U.S. pork in the early 1880s.[17] Meatpacking and stockyard interests long held a grudge against Detmers, and his assessment contributed to their hostility to veterinarians and independent scientific inquiry. They correctly perceived that open discussion of animal contagions in the United States might harm their reputations at home and aboard.[18]

Seeking to address such health concerns, President Chester Arthur created an expert commission in February 1883 to study swine production and processing conditions in the United States. The body was headed by the current USDA Commissioner George Loring and included Daniel Salmon of the USDA's Veterinary Division and E. W. Blatchford of the Chicago Board of Trade. The Pork Commission surveyed numerous packers, shippers, and railroad officials about their practices.[19] The response from John T. Steward, a packer from Council Bluffs, Iowa, represented the common practice of denying the existence of any problems: the hogs from his region "are as absolutely free from disease as an animal like the swine can be. The air water & climate are perfect in their conditions for health & all hogs are fed on corn or maize." The packers knew well "that their own interests are conserved best by making the interests of the consumers their own" and most understood "that the sale of unsound meat . . . would return like a boomerang to injure them." Steward's maintenance of the sanitary (rather than contagion) theory of disease reflected an entrenched view in the livestock industry. Overcoming this belief would be a major challenge for health officials.

Swine diseases did not figure nearly as prominently as cattle diseases in the congressional debates that led up to the creation of the BAI. Swine producers lagged behind cattlemen in lobbying for national legislation. The National Swine Breeders' Association was formed in November 1883. Its leaders petitioned for state quarantines to prevent the spread of hog cholera, but at the time they did seek not federal action.[20] In early 1884, Congress considered federal meat inspection in the hope of reopening foreign pork markets, but nothing came of those deliberations. Given the state of veterinary knowledge, there was more to be gained by acting collectively to combat cattle diseases than swine diseases. Hog owners had to rely on individual measures such as folk remedies and patent medicines.

As the BAI began to pay more attention to hog cholera, its incidence and impact came into sharper view. Figure 7.1 shows the estimated rates of death from hog cholera in the United States from 1884 to 1940. Large outbreaks in 1886–1887 and 1897 led to the death of about 13 percent of the U.S. swine population: in 1914, about 12 percent died.[21] Observers speculated that major outbreaks occurred with periodicity of 10 to 15 years because the disease tended to wipe out the most susceptible animals, leaving a population of survivors that was relatively im-

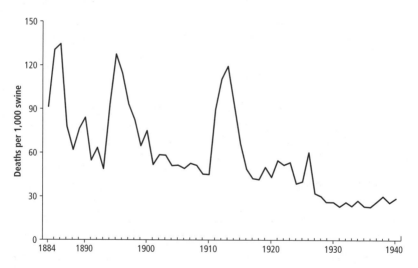

Figure 7.1. Swine deaths due to hog cholera, 1884–1940. *Source:* U.S. Department of Agriculture, *Yearbook of Agriculture, 1942*, p. 674.

mune. The impact in hard-hit areas was devastating. In 1884, newspapers reported that the "scourge" had appeared in two-thirds of Nebraska's counties. "Sarpy County fares the worst, the total loss in that county being 70,000. No hogs are left in the county."[22]

BAI Research and Scientific Rancor

In 1884, Salmon directed Theobald Smith to initiate the Bureau's research on swine diseases. Their early joint work investigated the modes of transmission, the efficacy of various disinfectants, symptoms and post-mortem appearances, preventives and cures, and possible relations to human illnesses. To explore the possibility that hog cholera was the same as the European disease *rouget*, Salmon and Smith obtained *rouget* vaccine, recently developed in Louis Pasteur's laboratory. In 1885, they demonstrated that Pasteur's vaccine provided no protection against hog cholera, suggesting two distinct diseases. In the same year, Smith working under Salmon's direction isolated a bacterium from infected swine that they dubbed the "hog cholera bacilli" or *bacterium suis*. Smith and Salmon had made a revolutionary advance in bacteriology as the first to identify a member of the large genus of disease-causing bacteria that would later be named *Salmonella* in honor of the BAI chief. The specific type identified in 1885 was renamed *Salmonella choleraesuis*.[23]

With this discovery, Salmon triumphantly announced that the Bureau had found the cause of hog cholera. Excitement mounted in February 1886 when Salmon and Smith reported that injections of sterilized cultures of a bacterium immunized pigeons against exposure to the live organism. This experiment represented another scientific milestone: the first use of killed (as opposed to attenuated) cultures to make vaccines.[24] Salmon and Smith grasped the broader implications for combating "all bacterial plagues of man and animals in which one attack confers immunity from the effects of that particular virus in the future." Indeed, this breakthrough helped set the course for developing immunizations against whooping cough, typhoid fever, anthrax, and other diseases.[25] Based on research conducted by Detmers and Smith, Salmon announced that "there are really two diseases of swine, both of which are widely distributed and both communicable, which have not heretofore been distinguished from each other." He asserted that one, "swine-plague," was caused by a "micrococcus" and the other, "hog cholera," was caused by the bacterium that his BAI team had found.[26] This shift in nomenclature added to the general confusion.

However, there was a huge problem. Although swine exposed to the bacteria usually became ill, the attenuated cultures made from the bacteria did not protect against hog cholera in most animals thought to be infected with the disease. Later investigations would reveal that Smith and Salmon had in fact identified the organism causing *necrotic enteritis* in swine, a secondary infection that frequently accompanied hog cholera.[27] But it was not the agent causing hog cholera. This agent, as it turns out, was a "filterable" virus, a type of microbe that was not understood in the early days of bacteriology and that could not be seen under a microscope. It would pass through filters used to eliminate the bacteria. In 1891, Smith observed that the hog cholera bacillus was not present in all hog cholera cases. He did not know it, but this was because some of the sick swine were free of secondary *Salmonella* infections. He noted similar inconsistencies in the presence of the so-called swine plague organism. However, the erroneous beliefs as to the root causes of hog cholera and swine plague were so entrenched that Smith's observations failed to stimulate a search for other causal agents.[28] The first virus of vertebrates would not be discovered until 1898. For nearly two decades, researchers would try to perfect hog cholera vaccines without success because they were defending against the bacterium not the virus. This basic misunderstanding led to conflicting results and created an atmosphere for intense scientific turmoil.

Several leading scientists advanced hog cholera claims that were at odds with those coming out of the BAI.[29] The most vitriolic of these disputes involved Frank Billings of the University of Nebraska.[30] Billings was a prominent figure of the day; he was the first American to receive a veterinary degree from a German university, and he later studied under the renowned German pathologist Rudolf Virchow. There was also a personal aspect to the controversy; in 1886, Salmon had rejected Billings for an appointment with the BAI. Billings charged that Salmon was an incompetent bureaucrat who headed the " 'Bureau of Animal Idleness.' " In 1887, he attacked the BAI findings of two separate swine diseases. He further claimed to have developed and successfully tested preventive inoculations; Salmon considered Billings's claim to be humbug.[31] It is not surprising that rival researchers staked out strong positions concerning hog cholera and related maladies, or that intense controversies ensued in the battle for scientific reputations and research budgets. But the degree of animosity in this conflict not only left many observers confused, it also eroded support for the BAI.[32]

The controversy raged so intensely that USDA Commissioner Norman Colman felt compelled, in December 1888, to appoint an external Board of Inquiry to investigate the swine epizootics and the BAI's policies. When the commission's report, issued in August 1889, sided with Salmon, the critics charged that it was merely a "whitewash."[33] The BAI gained stature when William Welch of Johns Hopkins published the results of his two-year investigation of hog cholera. While differing on some points, Welch was in "essential harmony" with the BAI's findings. He was also extremely critical of Billings's claims and methodology.[34] Salmon would not let go at that: as late as 1892, he characterized Billings's cures as "failures" with "no practical value."[35] Salmon was correct— but so were many of the critics of his own efforts.

A New Path

The ultimate breakthrough would come from BAI researchers with different training and perspectives from Salmon and Smith. In 1890, Salmon hired Dr. E. A. de Schweinitz to head the new Biochemic Laboratory, and in 1894 added Marion Dorset to the staff.[36] Both were chemists. Working together, they continued along the path that Salmon and Smith had set, developing mixed-sera in an attempt to protect against both hog cholera and swine plague. In 1897, Salmon dispatched Dorset to Sidney, Iowa, to head the first field experiments with a new serum. None of the pigs that Dorset vaccinated in the early trials survived exposure to hog cholera. Gradually, the Iowa team refined their doses and procedures. Over the next several years of trials, treated swine died at one-third of the rate of untreated populations. The high death rates among some inoculated herds and unexplained irregularities in their trials prompted de Schweinitz and Dorset to search for a causal agent other than the "hog cholera bacillus."[37]

In 1903, with the aid of ceramic filters obtained from the Pasteur laboratory, they created a filtrate that was free of the bacteria. When injected into susceptible pigs, the filtrate produced hog cholera. This was a eureka moment. Dorset and de Schweinitz correctly concluded that hog cholera was caused by a "filterable virus" and "that the hog cholera and swine plague organisms were only secondary invaders." These findings were so unexpected that the first reports were cautiously guarded. Their research did not occur in isolation. De Schweinitz had studied in Europe, and both the Americans were aware of formative developments in virology. The hog cholera discovery was only five years after the identification of the first vertebrate virus (which caused foot-and-mouth disease), and some in the scientific world resisted the concept that such tiny agents could cause disease. Further, in light of the past controversies, the work of two unknown chemists overturning the findings of the world's leading bacteriologists needed confirmation.[38] Salmon was one of the first to accept the new findings, even though they exposed the errors of his work with Smith.

Determining the cause of hog cholera opened the possibility of developing a vaccine. Dorset returned to Iowa in 1905 to head the BAI's hog cholera research project.[39] Researchers first attempted to produce serum from pigs that had survived hog cholera, but this provided little protection. Success came when Dorset made serum from the blood of hyperimmune swine, those with especially strong defenses. He created hyperimmunity by repeatedly injecting an immune hog with ever larger doses of virulent blood. As with his virus research, Dorset's work on hyperimmunity was a venture into a relatively new scientific domain. Wilhelm Kolle and George Turner had first succeeded in creating hyperimmune animals for serum production while working on rinderpest in South Africa in 1896–1897.[40] The entire field of immunology was new and rapidly expanding. Louis Pasteur had developed his chicken cholera vaccine in 1879–1880, an anthrax vaccine in 1881, and a rabies vaccine in 1885 (with Emile Roux). These vaccines involved artificially weakening the infective agents. The original vaccines and methods were improved upon many times.[41]

Before Dorset's live serum would be of practical value, myriad details needed to be worked out in laboratory and field tests. Researchers had to determine the proper dosages and procedures to create hyperimmunity and devise ways to manufacture the serum. In 1906, experiments showed that to impart long-lasting immunity it was necessary to inject swine with protective sera and simultaneously expose them to live virus, typically by separate injections of virulent blood.[42] In 1907, the BAI's W. B. Niles began "practical" tests of hyperimmune serum on about 2,000 swine near Ames, Iowa. When hog cholera subsequently swept through the area, none of the treated swine in the test herds died compared with 68 percent of the controls. After more than 20 years, BAI researchers finally had developed an effective method to control hog cholera.[43] The vaccine technology would still have to be perfected, and there was considerable discussion concerning the production and distribution of vaccines as well. This latter issue would embroil the BAI in a long controversy over the proper function of government within the economy.

Public-Private Boundaries

Government involvement in the biological materials industry was a response to a long history of abuses. Since hog cholera first appeared, the farm press, veterinarians, government officials, and purveyors of various elixirs had bombarded farmers with panaceas. Farmers themselves also were the purveyors of many nostrums. Recommendations to break off a tooth, cut off the ears, bleed the animal, feed it cooked corn, starve it, or administer any number of chemicals—sulfur, alum, saltpeter, turpentine—all had advocates. Many desperate farmers paid charlatans for bogus or even harmful tonics and serums.[44] These problems led to calls for the government to provide better information about commercial remedies and to regulate the production and distribution of such materials.

Defining the proper role for the BAI proved difficult, all the more so because the Bureau was involved in providing two different public goods: scientific research and control of contagious diseases. When the government prepared and distributed materials, even of its own creation, controversies inevitably erupted. Private businesses argued that the government manufacture and distribution of biological materials represented unfair competition, eroding profit opportunities for their investments in research, production, and marketing. Starting in 1898, the drug maker Parke, Davis & Co. of Detroit, Michigan, protested against large expenditures by the BAI for hog cholera research. Especially objectionable was "the Government's going into the manufacture of medicines, be it for hog cholera or anything else." The firm recognized a place for a BAI, but held that its activities should be purely experimental. "When, if ever, they find a remedy for an animal disease their work should cease," and the scientific knowledge should be transferred to the drug makers and the general public.[45] In early 1899, Senator James McMillan (R-Mich.) joined the protest against the USDA invading "the province of legitimate manufacturers" by supplying hog cholera serum. Without reckoning with any potential spillovers in health-related goods, McMillan asserted that the Department "should no more distribute serum than it should distribute pitch-forks." Secretary James Wilson replied, perhaps with more truth than he realized, that the USDA's hog cholera serum was still experimental.[46] This exchange occurred roughly five years before Dorset and de Schweinitz discovered the hog cholera virus, when the government and privately produced serums were relatively worthless.

Such complaints were not limited to hog cholera medicines. The archival records of the BAI document other flare-ups, most notably regarding the blackleg vaccine that the BAI perfected in 1897 and distributed freely in large quantities thereafter. Blackleg is a highly fatal bacterial disease of cattle and sheep. It was the most serious livestock disease in large areas of the United States circa 1900.[47] In 1904, Parke-Davis enlisted U.S. Representative Alfred Lucking (D-Mich.) to lobby the USDA against providing its blackleg vaccine to the New Zealand Agricultural Department in "unjust competition with our home manufacturers." In reply, Secretary Wilson noted that the USDA had a general policy of cooperating "with the Agricultural Departments and other scientific organizations of other countries" to engage reciprocal exchanges "to advance agriculture in the United States by giving information of progress in all parts of the world."[48]

Parke-Davis and Lucking also complained that the BAI was freely supplying blackleg vaccine to American stockmen. In Lucking's view, engaging in such activities to the "injury of manufacturing interests" was "contrary to the fundamental principles of our Government." Lucking went a step farther in his criticism of the government provision of blackleg vaccine: it "would be fully as justifiable . . . to supply small-pox vaccine to eradicate small-pox or quinine to eradicate malarial difficulties in different sections of the country." The "present course of the Bureau is indefensible, unless it is right for the Government to assume the position of 'the Great Father' to the people."[49] Many conservatives shared this view, opposing government activism in preventing the spread of contagions. For example, J. Sterling Morton, Wilson's predecessor at the USDA, also saw "no more reason why the government should supply the [blackleg] vaccine for cattle than it should freely furnish the virus to vaccinate mankind against small pox."[50]

Secretary Wilson's view differed sharply. He retorted to Lucking that Congress intended the BAI to both "make experiments" and "do executive work in stamping out" animal diseases. The blackleg vaccine remained experimental because it was an open question "whether the continued use of the vaccine will cause the disease to gradually disappear." Wilson continued that "if at any time Congress desires to limit or prohibit the work with reference to any disease and to preserve such diseases in order that the manufacturers of remedies may have a clear field, and the stock raisers be compelled for all time to purchase these remedies, I am sure the Department will not go counter to the expressed instructions of the legislative body." Until Congress explicitly restricted the work repressing diseases, the USDA would not let the "question of injury to the manufacturers of medicines" stand in its way.[51] Playing to his constituency, Wilson urged the nation's farmers to write to their representatives about whether the USDA should continue to distribute free vaccines. The response was overwhelmingly positive.[52] The BAI had produced and distributed over 47 million doses of blackleg vaccine by 1922, when Congress ended the program.[53]

For Dorset's hog cholera serum, the USDA opted for a different approach. The complicated production process and the potential that demand would exceed the BAI's supply capabilities led to a more decentralized regime. The USDA patented the serum production process and made this knowledge freely available to American citizens. The next step was to educate professionals and the public on the new technology. By July 1909, representatives from fifteen states had visited Ames, Iowa, and roughly a dozen states had begun producing serum.[54] By the end of 1912, thirty states were distributing serum, some of which was purchased from private companies that were rapidly expanding production.[55]

The decentralized production regime created serious problems as careless suppliers sold impotent and contaminated serums. These faulty products made the hog cholera problem worse and eroded public confidence in Dorset's remedy. Early experiences with dangerous and worthless products led to the passage of Virus-Serum-Toxin Act on 4 March

1913, which granted the USDA authority to license and regulate the production and trade of animal "biological products" entering interstate trade. The act supplemented a law of 1 July 1902 that regulated the sale and interstate trade of human biological products. The USDA's regulation of this industry would attract considerable criticism for being too lax because of repeated problems with substandard products.[56]

Living with the Disease

In the aftermath of the major 1912–1913 hog cholera outbreak, many congressmen from swine-producing areas pressed for more action. It riled many legislators that federal expenditures to prevent the spread of the boll weevil across the South, which was the bastion of opposition to federal intervention, exceeded by a large multiple those devoted to preventing swine diseases. Bowing to pressure, Congress made a regular appropriation of $75,000 to the BAI for the 1914 fiscal year and a special appropriation of another $450,000 for the 1915 fiscal year to conduct investigations and demonstrations in cooperation with the newly formed agricultural extension service. In addition, the BAI received $25,000 to inspect the production of serum as mandated by the Virus-Serum-Toxin Act of 1913.[57]

The initial hog cholera control program involved many of the staples of modern disease-fighting efforts. A first step was to experiment with models of control. Two or three veterinarians were dispatched to selected counties to gain the cooperation of the state and local governments, canvass area farmers, treat all infected and exposed herds, and disinfect farms. The goal of these feasibility studies was to determine whether the disease could be controlled or stamped out, and to create goodwill for broader efforts.[58] Experimental work began in late 1913 in three counties in Indiana, Iowa, and Missouri, and by the summer of 1914 it had expanded to fourteen counties in twelve states. In the process, researchers conducted experiments to fine-tune the procedures. The selected counties subsequently fared much better during outbreaks than nearby counties that received no intervention.[59] Education and outreach were an important element of the hog cholera program. In public demonstrations, BAI officials exposed swine to the virus and injected some with hog cholera serum. Spectators could visit the exhibition daily to watch the results unfold over the next several weeks. Such demonstrations were widely followed in the agricultural press, and by all accounts many farmers took notice.

The use of hog cholera inoculation was voluntary, and far from universal. The percentage of U.S. swine vaccinated only increased from about 20 percent in 1926 to about 37 percent in 1960. Most farmers chose to accept the risk of their animals contracting hog cholera rather than bear the expense of the serum-virus treatment. In the early years of the serum-virus regime, treatment costs for those farmers using the vaccine equaled about 20 percent of their net profit.[60]

From 1916 on, the BAI was active across the hog belt. By 1919, the project had expanded sufficiently to justify the creation of a new Division of Hog-Cholera Control within the BAI. The division's officials created and distributed literature, investigated farms, held local meetings and demonstrations, and trained private veterinarians. By 1919, the program operated in thirty-four states, with a dedicated force of roughly 175 BAI veterinarians in the field. Improved systems for tracking shipments and stockyard surveillance were put in place, and local veterinarians helped provide an early warning network. The scale of the enterprise was impressive: in fiscal year 1919, BAI agents conducted over 53,000 post-mortem examinations, organized 2,743 meetings with an attendance of nearly 79,000, and interviewed and advised over 325,000 farmers.[61] After 1919, the number of outbreaks declined, and, apart from a 1927 surge, mortality remained low. The hog sector was learning to live with cholera.

Conclusion

The early fight against hog cholera illustrates the close interaction of science and public policy along with the international exchange of ideas. Policy could not advance without an understanding of the disease and the tools to help control it. Many general scientific advances related to hog cholera drew on a rapidly developing global body of knowledge. Salmon, Smith, and Billings all developed and tested vaccines, but they benefited from methods developed by Pasteur and others. The 1898 discovery of the foot-and-mouth disease virus in Germany pointed de Schweinitz and Dorset in a new direction, and the ceramic filters and techniques they used came directly from Pasteur's laboratory. The development of hyperimmune donor swine was a direct spinoff from similar work done to combat rinderpest by English and German nationals associated with the Robert Koch Institute working in South Africa. The international flow of knowledge had another dimension as well: most leading hog cholera researchers in the United States had studied at European universities or were themselves European emigrants. Many of Europe's most eminent scientists also worked to solve the mysteries of swine diseases. Their successes and failures influenced the direction of research in the United States.

The hog cholera research program represented a classic example of the government providing a public good. Much of the research that led to an understanding of hog cholera was itself a product of public policy supported by both Democrats and Republicans. Knowledge advanced policy, and policy promoted knowledge. The highly focused research on hog cholera at the BAI led to new laboratory techniques and fundamental, and often quite unexpected, advances in bacteriology, virology, and immunology. These discoveries pushed forward both the understanding and the treatment of other animal and human diseases. Smith and Salmon's discovery of *Salmonella,* their success in using killed cultures to immunize animals, Dorset's improvements in hyperimmunity techniques, and de Schweinitz and Dorset's discovery of a virus as the cause of hog cholera head a long list of achievements.

The fact that a high percentage of the key hog cholera breakthroughs emerged from BAI laboratories and field stations provides yet another accreditation of the research infrastructure that Salmon created. Although Salmon and Smith had made a serious error in misidentifying the hog cholera bacilli as the root cause of the viral disease, there was enough independence within the BAI research system to allow two intellectual outsiders—researchers trained as chemists rather than as bacteriologists—to pursue a contrarian course of study. The widely publicized rancor among scientists did erode public confidence at times, but disagreements were part of the discovery process. The major story was that by 1920 scientists and policy makers had made huge strides in understanding hog cholera.

In the case of hog cholera, states policed trade, and the federal and state governments regulated the biologics industry. Nevertheless, the decision to coexist with hog cholera differed markedly from the coercive collective eradication programs used to fight other major animal diseases. The new serum technology was a double-edged sword—it offered protection, but employing it spread live virus across the landscape. The hog cholera technology was not as effective as the vaccines deployed against anthrax, rabies, or blackleg. Rather than affording herd immunity by sharply reducing the likelihood of contact for free riders, the technology had the opposite effect. Farmers who eschewed treating their animals now faced added risks of loss when shipping swine, using stockyards, and participating in fairs. The use of vaccines set the nation on a course that would not change until 1961, when the United States launched a hog cholera eradication campaign, the subject of Chapter 13.

8 Trichinosis, Trade, and Food Safety

LIBBIE BACON started a new job in June 1891 on the south side of Chicago. The press and officials from several foreign governments were out in force to observe her performance. She was one of an elite group of educated "young women attired in slight summer gowns with prettily poised heads" peering "through shinning microscopes at pieces of pork at the Stock-Yards."[1] She was on the frontline of a new Bureau of Animal Industry (BAI) program designed to help reopen European markets to American packers and farmers. Her job required meticulous care and attention. Lives were at stake. Bacon was looking for trichinae. Figure 8.1 shows trichinoscopists at work in Chicago circa 1900.

Trichinosis played a prominent role in the origins of food safety regulation in the United States and Europe, and in the prolonged diplomatic squabbles over the sanitary standards of American meat exports. Trichinosis is a parasitic zoonosis that affects humans and numerous other mammals. Trichinae are small roundworms, which, in their larval stage, reside in tissues. Humans usually acquire the disease by consuming uncooked or undercooked pork infected with trichinae. Trichinae are among the many parasites, including tapeworms and flukes, that humans can contract from meat. Trichinosis exhibits a wide range of symptoms and mimics scores of other diseases; it is a "chameleon of diseases" and was rarely properly diagnosed.[2] In U.S. public health circles, concerns about the disease peaked in the 1940s when researchers estimated that 16.2 percent of the population—one out of six Americans—had been infected by the parasite. Even this shocking finding likely underestimated the extent of the problem.[3]

Scientific advances brought trichinosis to the forefront of public attention in the nineteenth century. In 1835, London medical student

156

Figure 8.1. Trichinoscopy in Chicago, circa 1900. *Source:* National Agricultural Library, Special Collection, History of the Parasite Institute, m col 223, Box 1 (no folder no.), "Trichinosis Inspection Lab, Chicago, Illinois, 1898–1905."

James Paget first observed trichina larvae in human tissue. Trichinosis was added to the list of human diseases in 1860 when the German physician Friedrich von Zenker discovered trichina larvae in the tissue of a woman who had died from what had been misdiagnosed as typhoid fever. Europe and the United States suffered numerous frightful epidemics. Germany was the hardest hit due to the national penchant for consuming raw and undercooked pork. Between 1860 and 1890, there were 14,817 cases recorded in Germany—the mortality rate typically ranged between 5 to 10 percent. One of the worst episodes occurred in Hedersleden in 1865 when 337 people became ill and 101 died. As with Dr. Zenker's patient, most victims were misdiagnosed—often with typhoid fever, cholera, arthritis, or influenza.[4]

International Condemnation and American Policy

As U.S. pork exports surged in the late 1870s, Europeans became increasingly alarmed about the quantity of the commodity flows and the purity of the products. Porkophobia soon gripped Europe. Scientists contributed to the food scare. In June 1878, Richard Heschl, noted professor of anatomy at the University of Vienna, asserted that up to one-fifth of American hams contained trichinae. In September 1879, Dr. Ludwig von Grose delivered his findings on the high prevalence of trichinae in U.S. pork to the International Medical Congress in Amsterdam.[5] Exposés published across Europe claimed that the infection rates of American pork were frequently 100 times that of the European product. "A 'genuine panic' broke out in France" during 1880 and 1881, after trichinae were discovered in bacon strips imported from New York.[6] American packers and scientists disputed these claims, steadfastly maintaining that salting and curing killed all trichinae. Such statements did little to repair the damage—European protectionists had ample cover to embargo American pork.

An international pork trade war erupted beginning in 1879, when Italy, Portugal, Greece, and Hungary banned American pork. On 25 June 1880, German Chancellor Bismarck, citing sanitary justifications, prohibited the importation of ground pork and sausage from the United States. This move came in the wake of a general rise in German tariffs in 1879. On 18 February 1881, at the behest of his minister of agriculture and commerce, the president of the French Republic issued a decree barring the unloading of U.S. salted pork, ostensibly to protect consumers.[7] On February 19, the *London Times* printed warnings from the acting British consul in Philadelphia, George Crump, who asserted that hog cholera was rampant and trichinae in swine was on the rise. The implication for many was that packers were processing diseased and dead animals. This, coupled with his livid description of worms "being scraped and squeezed from the pores" of a stricken farmer were translated and reprinted across the Continent, sometimes with considerable embellishment. American diplomats, including Secretary of State James G. Blaine, immediately charged that Crump was mixing up different swine diseases and creating a wholly unwarranted food scare. The British government stood behind Crump's report, and protectionists everywhere had more "evidence" to support banning American pork.[8]

By early 1881, most European nations had restricted or prohibited American pork imports. This was not a trivial matter because in fiscal year 1880 hog products accounted for nearly 12 percent of all American merchandise exports—only exceeded by the values of breadstuffs exports and cotton exports. Roughly 90 percent of U.S. pork exports were shipped to Europe, with Britain receiving nearly 60 percent of the trans-Atlantic trade; Germany was a distant second, taking about 10 percent. The European pork embargoes hit hard. French imports of salt pork products from the United States fell from over 70 million pounds in 1880 to about 460,000 pounds in 1882. Exports to Germany fell from about 43 million pounds in 1881 to around 4.5 million pounds in 1882. Britain lifted its ban after a few months, but many consumers sharply curtailed their purchases of American pork.[9]

In 1880, Germany had exempted whole hams and sides of bacon because these products could be visually inspected for trichinae; lard was also permitted because it was heat processed. Opponents of the U.S. pork trade soon sought complete exclusion. An intense debate over a total ban of all U.S. pork products raged in both the Reichstag and the Bundesrath for several months, beginning in December 1882. On 25 February 1883, the Bundesrath adopted a resolution prohibiting all U.S. pork imports. On March 6, the Emperor enacted a total ban, except for lard.[10]

In early 1883, President Chester Arthur created his Pork Commission to study production and processing conditions (see Chapter 7). German officials refused his invitation to cooperate in the investigation on the grounds that American animal health conditions were a domestic U.S. matter and that Germany's sanitary standards, which were imposed uniformly on domestic and foreign products, were its own domestic matter. The European policies outraged American farmers and packers, who petitioned the federal government for relief. In addition to official protests, leading packers, including Philip Armour and Nelson Morris, traveled repeatedly to Europe to assure officials and consumers that their goods were wholesome and to reestablish their trade.[11]

Most American politicians and animal health officials interpreted the embargoes on U.S. livestock and meat, and especially those on pork, as thinly veiled protectionist measures. Europeans were by no means united in supporting the condemnation of American pork, with urban and labor interests tending to oppose the bans while farming interests typically supported them. Leading scientists, including Rudolf Virchow, sided with the U.S. position. Virchow was keenly aware that trichinosis was a serious problem, but he asserted that American pork represented no greater threat than the domestic German product.[12]

Governments have numerous reasons for imposing sanitary trade closures. One is to benefit domestic producers (at the expense of domestic consumers) by providing protection from outside competition.[13] Other reasons, however, include aiding domestic consumers by preventing exposure to diseased products and helping domestic producers by preventing the introduction of productivity-sapping diseases or by sustaining demand in spite of negative shocks arising from food scares or trade closures in other markets. Governments also impose sanitary restrictions for reasons unrelated to livestock markets themselves. The commercial treaties of the nineteenth and early twentieth centuries often supplemented their general most-favored-nation clauses with exemptions for targeted sanitary prohibitions. Restrictions thus serve as bargaining chips in more general negotiations. Determining whether motives behind specific trade closures were sanitary, protectionist, or related to a larger sovereignty/trade bargaining strategy is no easy task.[14]

Although protectionism played a major role in motivating European policies, the fear of disease was ever present. The British press regularly fanned the flames of the trichinosis fires. As one of many examples, the *Lancet* reported in December 1882 on numerous outbreaks in the United States. The journal's correspondent charged that after microscopists found trichinae in a high percentage of the hogs examined in Chicago, there were no further investigations. Rather, the "common policy of all interested in the exportation of pork from the United States is to deny that trichinae exist in American hogs." On the Continent, the spread of microscopic inspection of pork clearly points to genuine health concerns.[15] Following the publication in 1860 of Virchow's influential treatise on trichinosis in Germany, many localities passed regulations requiring microscopic inspection of pork at the time of slaughter. This was long before U.S. meat or large-scale packers represented a serious competitive threat to German farmers. In 1875, Prussia made pork inspection compulsory, and circa 1890 there were about 25,000 inspectors armed with microscopes on the job. In the 1890s, German spending on pork inspection probably exceeded the entire USDA budget.[16]

France, for dietary reasons, experienced fewer trichinosis outbreaks than Germany. Nevertheless, official scientific commissions regularly assessed the scope of the problem and the efficacy of American curing methods throughout the late 1870s and the 1880s. French scientific opinion vacillated on the extent of the danger. Some French scientists were concerned that allowing the entry of infected meats from the United States and infected animals from Germany and Belgium would cause the worms to multiply in the French swine population, thus endangering human health in the future. The prominent zoologist Paul Bert emphasized that although most epidemics die out and life returns to normal, if trichinosis was introduced, it would become established as it had in Germany.[17]

The BAI devoted considerable effort both to documenting the extent of the disease in American swine and to defending American trade interests. In 1885, BAI Chief Daniel Salmon reported that only 2.1 percent of the nearly 300,000 microscopic examinations of American pork found trichinae. However, given that one contaminated hog could conceivably infect hundreds of people, this was not a particularly comforting finding. American officials maintained that the U.S. infection rate was comparable with many areas of Europe. In 1885, Salmon rejected the data on European swine infection rates, charging that many Prussian inspectors were "utterly incompetent," and that their equipment and methodology were often flawed. "An examination in 1877 showed that many of the microscopes were useless, that the glasses used were too dirty to permit the examination, and that some of the inspectors were incapable of detecting the parasite." By contrast, Salmon boasted that well-trained U.S. microscopists "would not overlook a single case."[18]

Almost all American pork exports were salted or cured. American packers and public officials assured the world that these processes killed the trichinae. Several American politicians got into the act. Chester Arthur, for example, attested to the safety of American hog products in his 1883 Annual Message to Congress. In 1884, Secretary of State Frederick T. Frelinghuysen erroneously asserted that a few days of even a slight salting "suffices to reduce the severity of the symptoms below a fatal state."[19] When French scientists questioned the safety of U.S. curing methods, the Americans cried protectionism.

From the beginning of the embargoes, many exporters lobbied for a U.S. government microscopic inspection program. As early as December 1881, Levi Morton, the American ambassador to France, noted that establishing federal inspection of salted meat for exports would likely

reopen the French market. The Chicago Board of Trade called for inspection in 1883. Most meatpackers initially opposed federal inspection,
but Philip Armour broke ranks and sided with inspection advocates.
Proponents asserted that anything less than a rigorous and honest inspection system would not have credibility in Europe.[20]

The leading policy alternative to inspection was an intensified trade
war, but this was controversial and potentially costly. In 1883 and 1884
the Western press, livestock associations, and major packers pushed
hard for retaliatory actions. On 15 January 1884, Senator John Logan
(R-Ill.) introduced a bill empowering the president to retaliate against
foreign products of an "unhealthy character." In reply, Senators George
Vest (D-Mo.), John Ingalls (R-Kans.) and Samuel Maxey (D-Tex.) advocated creating an inspection system. More detailed investigations were
under way. The President's Pork Commission, headed by George Loring,
reported on 29 February 1884 that there were no legitimate bases for
the restrictions, but nonetheless recommended microscopic inspection
of pork intended for export. On 24 March 1884, the Senate Committee
on Foreign Relations released a report that recommended combining
inspection with the threat of U.S. retaliation. At roughly the same time,
Emery Storrs, lobbying for Swift, Allerton, and other Chicago packers,
testified before the House Commerce Committee in favor of federal inspection of meat products intended for export. His proposal, crafted
with Chairman John Reagan (D-Tex.), called for packer-financed voluntary *non-microscopic* inspection.[21]

Neither President Arthur nor his successor Grover Cleveland pursued
retaliatory policies, and Congress did not institute federal inspection
during their terms. As we shall discuss in the Chapter 9, the first federal
meat inspection bill was not enacted until 1890 (and it proved ineffective). The delay was not for want of trying. In 1886 and 1888, the Senate
passed bills introduced by George Edmunds (R-Vt.) that established meat
inspection and prohibited the importation of adulterated articles of food
and drink, but in both sessions the bills died in the House.[22]

With the election of Benjamin Harrison in 1888, both retaliation
and inspection were up for consideration. At this time, contemporaries
reckoned that the restrictions on pork exports were costing American
trade $50 million annually.[23] On 30 August 1890, Harrison signed legis-
lation authorizing the inspection of salted pork and bacon intended for

export; on 3 March 1891, he approved additional legislation authorizing federal inspection of hogs before slaughter and of pork products after slaughter but before salting. The implementation of the USDA regulations included microscopic inspection of pork for export. Inspection, which began in June 1891 in major Chicago plants, was witnessed by representatives of several countries sent to certify the procedures.

The 30 August 1890 Act also added the threat of retaliation. It authorized the president to exclude products from any nation unfairly discriminating against American products. Soon Congress gave the president more bargaining chips: the McKinley Tariff Act of 1 October 1890, as part of its system of reciprocity, empowered the president to reimpose a tariff on German and French sugar beginning in 1892. French wine was also on the table. Federal inspection coupled with credible threats got the desired results. Extensive negotiations ensued between the United States and Germany. President Harrison entered the fray, demanding a change in German policy. The replacement of Bismarck by Leo von Caprivi as German Chancellor also contributed to the new political environment. In the "Saratoga Agreement" of August 1891, the two nations agreed on a *quid pro quo* to exchange the suspension of the McKinley tariff on German sugar for access to German markets for U.S. pork certified free of trichinae by USDA inspectors. On 3 September 1891, more than a decade after it had been imposed, Germany lifted its ban on U.S. pork. On 5 December, 1891, French ports reopened for fully cured U.S. pork. The new procedures required a USDA inspection certificate and French inspection at the port of arrival. But this was only a partial victory for American interests, because the French replaced the pork embargo with a high tariff. Several other nations also followed Germany's lead and opened their markets to U.S. pork products by the end of 1891.[24]

The trade story, as it is often told, ends here, but the pork war continued to simmer. Inspectors in Bremen, Germany, discovered trichinae-infested meat in one of the first shipments to arrive after the resumption of trade. The American consul confirmed the problem. Further investigations indicated that the shipping documents were likely fraudulent and that the meat had never been inspected. Moreover, instances of diseased meat that had been inspected and of meat accompanied by counterfeit certificates continued to appear. This led many German localities to refuse to honor American inspection certificates and to insist on reinspecting the meat locally. American officials complained that the reinspections—with their accompanying delays, fees, and taxes—represented a serious restraint on trade, but the German imperial government responded that localities had the right to impose health standards. In August 1892, the Prussian minister of health sent a circular to provincial health officers recommending they reinspect American hams and sides before allowing them to be sold to consumers. By 1894, eleven German states prescribed inspection of foreign pork. This was no longer just a local affair.[25]

An examination of the broader context of German-American economic relations bolsters the case that protectionism and trade retaliation were important explanations for the ongoing pork dispute. In August 1894, the Cleveland administration reimposed a duty on raw sugar—the hopes of the Saratoga Agreement had all but vanished. Binational relations worsened in October 1894 when Germany banned both cattle and fresh beef imports from the United States. The Germans justified this move on sanitary grounds after the arrival of two shipments of American cattle supposedly suffering from Texas fever. The ban rested on weak scientific footing. It is unlikely that German veterinarians had much direct experience with Texas fever, and their diagnoses essentially misapplied Theobald Smith and Frederick Kilborne's recent findings (Chapter 5). Citing the outdated research of Frank Billings, they relied on the "bacterial" theory of the disease. The German position could initially be dismissed as a case of faulty science leading a cautious government to protect its home industry, but the ban dragged on. American counterarguments received little sympathy.[26] The German cattle and beef policies shed considerable light on the motivation for the more important pork restrictions and the subsequent obstructions employing reinspections.

Doubts grew within the BAI about the value of microscopic inspection, but because of potential trade losses, abandoning inspection was not a serious option. It was in this context that the Department of State dispatched Charles Wardell Stiles to Berlin in the spring of 1898 to investigate trichinosis outbreaks and meat inspection in Germany and neighboring countries. The young BAI zoologist spent over a year and a half on the assignment. He deduced in his 1901 report that 53 percent of all reported German human trichinosis cases and 41 percent of the deaths between 1881 and 1898 "appear to have been due to faults in the German inspection system." Stiles argued that universal U.S. inspection was not economically justified because he maintained that few Americans contracted trichinosis. "Our methods of curing and cooking" were superior to spending $3 to 4 million a year on a system that gives consumers a false sense of security and perpetuates "that exceedingly unhygienic German custom of eating raw or rare pork." Stiles reckoned that American pork was far safer than German pork.[27]

In June 1900, Germany passed new strict meat inspection legislation banning the importation of sausage, canned meat, or meat with preservatives; cured or dressed meats could enter only in large pieces. This legislation reflected the power of agrarian interests in the ongoing rural-urban power struggle. In this case, agrarians received trade restrictions in exchange for their votes to expand the German navy. In 1906, the United States did an about-face and abolished the microscopic inspection of pork destined for export. The BAI's studies showed that too many infected animals slipped through the inspections, and that in some cases the parasites were discovered only after twenty or more samples were examined. But microscopic inspection made a comeback. In April 1912, President William Taft requested a supplementary appropriation of $1 million to reintroduce microscopic inspection of pork intended for meat products ordinarily consumed without cooking. Taft's move was in response to renewed alarm over the safety of the U.S. products. Several Swiss citizens had died after "eating American meat which was infested with trichinae," prompting the Swiss minister to demand reparations. The USDA added to the adverse publicity when it increased its domestic warnings about the dangers of eating uncooked pork.[28]

Most Americans historian have sided with the official U.S. interpretation, downplaying the legitimacy of sanitary issues and interpreting the European embargoes as thinly veiled protectionist measures. As we have seen, protectionism surely played a role, but so did the fear of disease and distrust of American assurances. Costly systems of microscopic inspection in Germany were initiated before U.S. pork exports threatened German farmers, offering evidence of genuine health concerns.[29] Subsequent events would prove these fears justified.

Reassessing the Trichinosis Problem

The historical accounts of the pork trade war have missed much of the story. Whatever the motives of the Europeans who railed against U.S. imports, there is little doubt that American pork products were far more dangerous than American packers and government officials claimed. The health threats were very real. The USDA implicitly recognized this but concluded that it was sufficient to warn consumers to thoroughly cook pork products. Practitioners, and subsequently scholars, have tended to adopt a specific cultural stance, attributing the health problems associated with trichinosis to the failure of consumers to cook pork properly.[30] This division is part of an ongoing dispute over the attribution of responsibility for controlling food-borne diseases. As an example, in recent years, when an outbreak of *Salmonella* in humans was attributed to a specific packer, the company response typically noted that its products were safe if properly handled. As we shall discuss in Chapters 10 and 12, American policy makers chose both to clean up milk by addressing animal health and dairy sanitation (the rough equivalent to cleaning up feeding operations and packinghouses) and to push for pasteurization (analogous to telling consumers to cook their meats). Trichinosis policy was akin to pasteurization in that salting, curing, and the like aimed to clean up as well as preserve the product. Swine policies devoted little attention to farm practices.

New research, aided by new methods and technologies, increased the detection rate of trichina larvae in humans, in some cases by over three times. In the 1930s and 1940s, a research team headed by Willard H. Wright at the U.S. National Institute of Health (NIH) found that, circa 1940, roughly one out of six Americans had been infected with trichinae, and that there were roughly 1 to 2 million new infections every year. These studies probably missed many live trichinae; later technological advances nearly doubled the detection rates. Wright's findings were consistent with expected demographic exposure patterns. As examples, Americans of German and Italian extraction were nearly twice as likely to harbor trichinae as the overall population, whereas in the Jewish population, which was less likely to consume pork, there was almost no evidence of past infections.[31] Studies also showed that Americans of German extraction were far more likely to be infected than their cousins in the home country and that Americans in general were more likely to be infected than Europeans.[32]

The new understanding of the frequency and seriousness of the malady was widely publicized in Berton Roueché's celebrated 1950 *New Yorker* article "A Pig from Jersey."[33] Roueché traced the skillful detective work of physicians at the New York City Health Department in the diagnosis and discovery of the source of a fatal 1942 trichinosis outbreak in the local German American community. The culprit was the New Jersey swine of the article's title. The animal had been served as a roast and as sausage at a *Schachtfest* held at the New York Labor Temple. Among those afflicted were sausage-makers who had sampled minuscule portions of raw pork in the seasoning process. Nor was this New York outbreak an isolated case—informed observers held that the United States led the world in trichinosis.[34]

It is unknown how many people were sickened or killed by meat-borne diseases such as trichinosis. Early estimates of overall food poisoning rates suggest that problems were minor. In 1938 for the entire United States, the Public Health Service listed only seventy reported outbreaks, 2,247 individual cases, and twenty-five deaths due to illnesses conveyed by foods other than milk and milk products.[35] In light of the current estimates from Centers for Disease Control and Prevention (Chapter 1), such low numbers are simply not credible.[36] The more scientists learned and the more doctors tested for foodborne diseases, the more they found. The illnesses and deaths in the United States from trichinosis were orders of magnitude higher than what was first thought.

By drawing on the medical literature linking the presence of trichinae with physical symptoms, we can provide a rough range of estimates of the number of clinical cases and deaths.[37] Circa 1940, conventional wisdom suggested that every year about 300 to 500 people suffered bouts of trichinosis, and twenty to thirty people died. A reevaluation, based on a cautious reading of the NIH research, suggests instead that there were at least 40,000 clinical illnesses and over 200 deaths per year; the actual numbers may have been much larger.[38] This was the view of Maurice C. Hall, who oversaw the early NIH trichinosis project as chief of the agency's Division of Zoology. In 1937, he noted that "there are possibly several thousand deaths annually." He further emphasized that very few of the clinical cases were ever diagnosed as trichinosis.[39] Most of these illnesses either went unreported or were recorded as influenza, typhoid fever, food poisoning, rheumatism, or other afflictions.

Hall's disdain for officials who had minimized the problems was palpable: "Fifty years ago competent authorities concluded . . . that trichinosis was a minor public health problem in the United States, and this fiction, once established, had maintained itself . . . for a half century. . . . There was an export trade involved, and . . . a desire to make facts fit the needs of that export trade played a role in the minds of observers who did not lack the mental qualifications to draw sound conclusions from adequate data, provided that they had an unprejudiced status in the matter."[40] Other research buttresses Hall's conclusion. In 1920, USDA scientists noted that past guarantees that American curing processes rendered the pork safe had "no apparent basis except the opinions of the writers that made them," and that several common curing methods yielded meat infested with dangerous levels of live trichinae. Seemingly small variations in the curing process could mean total failure in destroying trichinae. In addition, "few ham processors exactly follow . . . the prescribed methods." Packer incompetence and ignorance yielded sporadic results, and even large packers such as Armour experienced curing breakdowns. Researchers continued to find live trichinae in American hams well into the second half of the twentieth century.[41]

Agricultural Policy and Trichinosis

Public health studies show that by 1966–1970 the trichinae infection rate in the American population had fallen dramatically.[42] We know why. In line with the One Health perspective, the decline in the incidence of trichinosis in people was due primarily to policies that attacked the disease in swine. The Federal Meat-Inspection Service (FMS) did play a supporting role. Extensive tests conducted in the late 1930s showed that pork (intended to be eaten without cooking) cured under FMS guidelines in inspected plants was free of live trichinae whereas about 5 percent of samples from non-FMS plants were contaminated. Some of this difference could have been due to farmers directing suspect hogs to non-FMS plants, but the evidence points to the conclusion that inspection and standards helped reduce the incidence of human exposure.[43] In any case, a federal stamp did offer a valuable certificate of quality.

However, government regulations designed to clean up swine-feeding practices were the major force behind the declining incidence of human infections. By the 1880s, research showed that garbage-fed swine had significantly higher infection rates than animals raised on pasture and grain. The decrease in the prevalence of trichinosis in American hogs before the 1950s was due primarily to the gradual decline in the practice of feeding swine offal containing raw hog scraps, which in turn was largely due to the changing location and economics of hog-raising.[44] These changes cut the cycle of reinfection.

Public health leaders had long advocated restrictions on feeding uncooked garbage to swine, but they were stymied by farmer and packer opposition. During World War I, authorities in both the United States and Canada actually urged the increased feeding of garbage to swine as a conservation/food production measure.[45] Pioneering public health advocate Charles V. Chapin enlisted in the garbage-feeding campaign. In his early work as a health official in Providence, Rhode Island, Chapin had opposed feeding the city's refuse to swine as "unsanitary." But he came to believe such concerns were "esthetic" and "pseudo-scientific" prejudices, associated with the outmoded "filth theory of disease." In 1917, Chapin flatly denied that garbage-fed hogs were more likely than grain-fed hogs to carry trichinae or other contagious diseases and confidently asserted proper cooking of the pork would eliminate any health hazards. Faced with a pending food shortage, Chapin proclaimed that "the wolf is at the door!" and America could not afford to let its urban garbage go to waste.[46]

Wartime shortages brought similar pressures to bear even earlier in Canada. But in 1916, Canadian authorities did an about face, prohibiting the feeding of raw garbage to swine and heavily regulating the feeding of cooked garbage. Such steps would not be taken in the United States for roughly forty years. In 1952, Brock Chisholm, director general of the World Health Organization, singled out the United States for its lax trichinosis policies. "There is no other well-developed country which allows trichinosis among its hogs as this country does, affecting the health literally of millions of people all the time."[47]

Coincidentally, U.S. hog feeding policies began to change due in large part to the spread of vesicular exanthema, an acute and extremely infectious viral disease of swine (see Chapter 13). Vesicular exanthema was easily confused with foot-and-mouth disease and other very serious afflictions. Unlike trichinosis, vesicular exanthema represented a serious financial threat to hog farmers; but like trichinosis, the new disease spread via infected garbage. Many farmers shifted their stance and began to demand government controls to restrict the feeding of uncooked garbage to swine. Most states and the USDA responded, and within a decade feeding raw garbage to swine was a rarity. As a result, the prevalence of trichina larvae in swine and pork products plummeted.[48] Human health also improved.

Conclusion

The history of U.S. trichinosis policy is first-and-foremost a story of industry and government denialism in the face of tremendous international trade pressures. In Europe, widespread fears that American pork was infested led to demands for trade barriers. European agricultural interests no doubt exploited the scare in their push to limit competition from the large and growing American swine industry. The resulting embargoes hit one of America's largest export sectors, causing an international uproar that involved several U.S. presidents and secretaries of state. In Chapter 9, we note that during the controversies leading up to the meat inspection acts of 1891 and 1906, American packers generally condemned federal veterinarians as alarmists, who in their quest for employment and power damaged consumer confidence with fraudulent sanitary concerns. However, during the long trichinosis controversy, the federal animal health bureaucracy almost always stood with the packers in asserting that trichinosis was not a problem. The prominent zoologist Maurice Hall would later assert that government officials misinterpreted or denied evidence that trichinosis was far more serious than they let on to protect U.S. trade interests. In addition, BAI Chief Daniel Salmon long opposed microscopic inspection—this was hardly consistent with the charges that he was primarily interested in enlarging his agency's budget.

The new evidence on the prevalence of trichinosis in swine and humans, along with recognition of the deficiencies of early testing procedures, casts a new light on the European-American pork trade wars and on food safety in the United States. The embargoes, while imposed in part for domestic political motives, were indeed justified on health grounds. Meatpackers were marketing dangerous pork products. Producers and U.S. government regulators sanctimoniously espoused the safety of the packers' methods and products in spite of evidence produced by European scientists to the contrary. It was easier for the packers to slander their detractors than to clean up their business practices.

Most scholars dealing with the history of the pork wars have failed to consult the subsequent medical literature.[49] Just as an understanding of the past can inform the present, the present can inform our understanding of the past. However, for all the government's failings, it was government scientists employed by the USDA and the NIH who conducted most of the research that eventually defined the extent of the trichinosis problem. The meatpackers made little investment to advance such public goods.

The real policy failure was the unwillingness to attack the problem at its source by changing swine-feeding practices in order to clean up the swine population. The USDA bowed to farmers and meatpackers who opposed regulation. Once the USDA and the Public Health Service regulated feeding garbage to swine in the 1950s, trichinae counts in both swine and humans plummeted. The policy change was driven by the switch in farmer and meatpacker interests due to the spread of vesicular exanthema—a disease that represented a financial threat to the meat industry. Concerns for human health had little effect on policy. The One Health advocates can rightly point to the rapid fall in human trichinosis cases as yet another example of the spillovers of controlling of livestock diseases on human health. These findings bear on our analysis of the political economy of meat inspection in the next chapter. There is little reason to suspect that same packers who so willfully denied food safety problems in their pork trade were above reproach more generally.

9 The Benevolence of the Butcher

The Creation of Federal Meat Inspection

"IN ARMOUR'S ESTABLISHMENT I saw with my own eyes the doctoring of hams that were so putrefied that I could not force myself to remain near them. The hams were on a working table, and a man with a foot pump, which worked on the principle of a gigantic hypodermic needle, filled them with a chemical which killed the odor." A former meat inspector testified that 90 percent of the cattle condemned for lumpy jaw were "passed for human food." A former Swift & Co. salesman reported that the company's cheaper grades of sausage "are preserved with . . . a combination of borax and some embalming material." These statements represent a small taste of the "affidavits and documents" that Upton Sinclair provided to the *New York Times* during the height of the 1906 congressional debate on meat inspection to bolster the claims in his recent best-seller *The Jungle* (1906).[1]

There is little wonder that the public was alarmed. President Theodore Roosevelt and his congressional allies were pitted in a battle against the Chicago meatpackers to clean up the meat supply. The passage of the Federal Meat Inspection Act of 1906 represented a victory for consumers. In 2006, the USDA celebrated the centennial of this act as the birth of federal food safety legislation.[2] This *public interest* story, of using regulation to address market imperfections, represents one of several potted histories of the origins of meat inspection in the United States.

A second potted history builds on the *public choice* critique, which emphasizes *rent seeking* and *regulatory capture*. There are many variants, but the proponents dismiss the existence of any serious livestock disease or meat sanitation issues and deny that there were any significant mar-

172

ket failures. By these accounts, federal inspection dates to the Meat Inspection Act of 1891. The development of refrigerated railcars and cold storage facilities, along with the rise of giant packing firms, triggered a restructuring of the American meat trade. The ensuing competition undercut local butchers who, in a ploy to turn consumers against the "Meat Trust" and to obtain government protection, accused the large packers of selling tainted products. Cattle raisers, threatened by the monopsony power of the large packers and a trade downturn, also demanded restrictive legislation. The 1891 Act grew out of these interindustry rivalries. In the regulatory capture literature, claims that the legislation was enacted at the urging of small-scale butchers and farmers coexist with assertions that the Act reflected the interests of large packers.[3] Gabriel Kolko, an early advocate of the regulatory capture hypothesis, argued that both the 1891 and 1906 Meat Inspection Acts were written primarily at the request of the giant packers to help open export markets.[4] By this reckoning, the 1906 debate involving congressional leaders and Theodore Roosevelt focused on peripheral issues such as who should pay for inspection, and that otherwise there were never any fundamental differences on the core principles. Some have argued that federal regulation was unnecessary because the Chicago packers maintained state-of-the-art sanitary practices out of self-interest.[5] For those who fell short, market pressures would identify and correct any serious problems.

This regulatory capture story is further darkened by the rent-seeking federal bureaucrats who sought to expand their budgets and power. This account maintains that the leaders of the Bureau of Animal Industry (BAI) persistently lobbied Congress to expand its inspection domain even though they "admitted" that livestock diseases were a minor problem in the United States compared to conditions that prevailed in Europe and that the Chicago packers had stringent sanitary procedures.[6] This latter charge is consistent with a further thesis that the zealous federal bureaucrats were aided by muckraking journalists who inflamed public-health concerns to gain attention for themselves and increase print sales.[7]

In reference to the work of George Stigler, Ronald Coase, Richard Posner, Sam Peltzman, and others, Andrei Shleifer concluded that "the Chicago critique of public interest regulation theory is one of the finest moments of twentieth-century economics." For public choice adherents, the political economy of early meatpacking regulation seamlessly fits into the broader public choice critique. This is significant because, as Gary Libecap notes, the 1891 Meat Inspection Act (together with Interstate Commence Act of 1887 and the Sherman Act of 1890) represented "a significant break from what had previously been considered an appropriate role for the federal government." Shleifer pondered the Chicago school's failure to explain why consumers "are generally happy with most regulations that protect us."[8] Our examination of the origins of federal meat inspection, when coupled with our analysis of trichinosis in Chapter 8 and of milk hygiene in Chapters 10 and 12, helps explain why consumers embraced meat inspection. Government policies addressed serious health threats and market failures, making for a safer world.

Rethinking the Issues

There is no question that meat can and does transmit diseases to humans. As we noted in Chapter 1, the Centers for Disease Control and Prevention (CDC) estimated that, circa 2010, Americans suffered 48 million bouts of food-borne illnesses annually, a large but undetermined number of which resulted from contaminated meat, poultry, and eggs.[9] Common meat-borne diseases include salmonellosis, *Escherichia coli* poisoning, listeriosis, cryptosporidiosis, campylobacteriosis, botulism, actinomycosis, and staphylococcal infections. In the past, trichinosis and tuberculosis were also serious threats. Before reliable refrigeration, many of the problems resulting from tainted meat were likely worse, and the ability of consumers to take precautions was weaker. So the issue is not whether meat spreads disease, but whether meatpackers (and in particular the large packers) took reasonable steps to mitigate the dangers, and whether well-functioning markets produced sufficiently clear signals to guarantee a reasonable level of consumer safety.[10]

At the time of the debates on the early meat inspection acts, knowledgeable scientists would have ridiculed the notion that meat-borne diseases posed few if any threats to humans. The leading German veterinarian Robert Ostertag dealt with scores of diseases, including most of those we have mentioned, in the 1904 edition of his *Handbook of Meat Inspection*.[11] In previous chapters, we alluded to the many food scares both at home and aboard about the hygienic purity of American meat. Consumers were concerned about whether the product was unhealthy or unwholesome, whether it would spread disease, or whether it was otherwise disgusting. They were also concerned that producers, especially distant large packers, used chemicals to hide problems. A sick animal did not have to be a health threat to make consuming its meat highly undesirable—beyond rationally calculated risks, the elemental forces of disgust and repugnance against consuming the flesh of diseased animals came into play.[12] Nor were concerns about meat hygiene novel to the nineteenth century—in fact, they date to antiquity.

This chapter explores the state of meat hygiene and quality control before federal intervention, the character of the debates, political alliances, and actual problems leading up to the major federal inspection laws, the rollout and operation of inspection services, the shifting attitudes and policies of the major meatpackers on hygiene and inspection, the international calls for inspection, and the extent of the real health problems associated with meat. A major question we will address is whether the private markets were doing an adequate job of dealing with problems of meat safety, given the scientific knowledge of the day.

Inspection before 1890

Regulation of the meat trade in the United States was not new. Municipal regulation of butchering dates back to early restrictions of the urban meat trade to public market spaces.[13] But municipal meat inspection was generally hit or miss. After a two-year investigation (1888–89) of "Dressed Beef," Senator George Vest (D-Mo.) concluded that the local inspection standards were often criminally negligent.[14] Countering Vest's charges, the representatives of the Chicago stockyards and packinghouses insisted that their "rigid inspection" system guaranteed food safety.

Based on the available information, Chicago's inspection system was comparable to the systems in many cities and was more thorough than those in some. Press accounts tout a surveillance system with many layers of protection.[15] One layer was provided by the state of Illinois. Since 1872, the state's Humane Society kept one inspector at the Union Stock Yards to ensure the animals were fed and watered and to prevent cruel treatment. In late 1888, the State Livestock Board added two inspectors to separate out cattle suspected of having the disease lumpy jaw; once a week, the state veterinarian visited to make condemnation decisions. This represented the totality of the state presence. A second layer was provided by the Chicago Department of Health. It typically maintained three inspectors at the Union Stock Yards. The chief inspector, Matthew Lamb, was stationed at the large arches at the main entrance to the Stock Yards; the other two officers worked in the yard's many divisions and other entrances. All were "practical butchers." They conducted ante-mortem inspections looking for crippled and visibly diseased animals, and in cases of doubt, performed immediate post-mortem inspections. However, there does not appear to have been any examinations of the animals' internal organs—a process that, at the time, veterinarians deemed essential for detecting many serious diseases dangerous to hu-mans. After completing their tasks in the yards, the city inspectors "gen-erally go through the slaughter-houses in the afternoon."[16] There was more conflict than cooperation between the state and city inspectors, so the whole of the inspection effort was less than the sum of the parts.[17]

Figure 9.1 offers a view of a small segment of the Union Stock Yards and packinghouses. The photograph is from 1905, but it captures earlier conditions as well. The inspectors in the 1880s had a vast domain. Dur-ing the 1888–1890 period, the Chicago stockyards received on average 6.2 million hogs and 3.0 million cattle annually. Its producers packed 4.4 million hogs and 2.3 million cattle annually. The city inspectors, headed by Matthew Lamb, condemned and sent to the rendering tanks, on average, about 1,500 hogs and 790 cattle per year, a rate on the order of 2.5 per 10,000 animals.[18]

The packers provided a third layer of inspection. Almost every pack-ing company stationed an inspector at its scales to judge the condition of animals to be purchased. As Chicago Health Commissioner Oscar De-Wolf exuded in 1888, "Armour pays three men $5,000 a year to inspect cattle for him. They are experts, and no cattle pass into his slaughter-house unless they are first-class."[19] DeWolf deputized a small number of the large packers' employees as "special inspectors." They wore city badges and exercised municipal police power to pass meat as fit for con-sumption and condemn carcasses. Until late 1889, the "special inspec-tors" were not at all accountable to the city. Thereafter, DeWolf's succes-sor Shawn Wickersham required that they file reports with the city and made them subject to the mayor's dismissal, but they continued in the packers' pay. News stories indicate that Armour had four such inspectors, Swift five, and Morris three, but the reports do not say whether any of these deputies were the same people as the inspectors at the packing-house scales.[20]

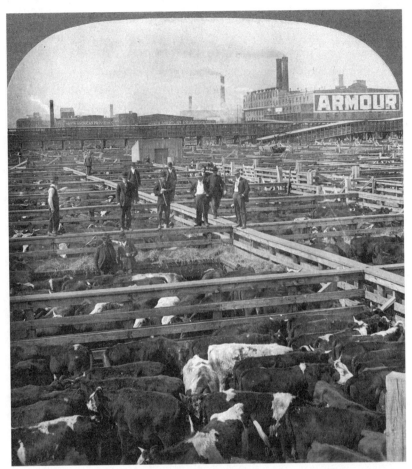

Figure 9.1. A small section of the Union Stock Yards and Packingtown, 1905. *Source:* Library of Congress, "A Busy Morning in the Great Union Stockyards, Chicago," www.loc.gov/pictures/resource/cph.3b43425/.

The press accounts describe a final layer of surveillance operating within the packinghouses. It was not a staff of trained hygienic specialists, but rather the throngs of tourists who stopped by Packingtown. As one denizen put it, "There are hundreds of visitors from all over the world at the house every day, who follow every step of the operation, from the time a steer is driven into the shambles until his carcass is swung up in the refrigerating-room. If the animal were diseased or the meat spoiled, don't you suppose some of these visitors would notice it?"[21] Whether having guided tours of lay people dressed in street clothes tramping through food processing areas prevented more health problems than it caused is an open question.[22]

Although the Chicago packers and their stockyard allies repeatedly assured the public that they upheld the highest hygienic standards, they do not appear to have employed any professional veterinarians to that end. The Chicago Live Stock Exchange did sponsor public inspection of swine, but only to address conflicts over dockage and shrinkage, not sanitary concerns. In fact, the inspectors at the scales were called "shrinkers," and there is no evidence they were medically trained.[23] Opposition to veterinarians was widespread in the trade. Amid suggestions in 1884 that federal inspection of pork might be valuable in reopening markets, Nelson Morris opined that he was "greatly opposed to the employment of veterinarians as inspectors" because they think that in order to keep their jobs "they must find and report disease, whether there is a disease or not."[24] In late 1885, the Chicago livestock trade celebrated the removal of N. H. Paaren, the activist Illinois State Veterinarian, from office.[25] At a meeting of the Chicago Live Stock Exchange (CLSE) held in early October 1886 to draft a response to the local contagious bovine pleuropneumonia (CBPP) outbreak, one member asserted, "We have no use for veterinarians. They have only damaged our business," and another stated they had caused "enough trouble" and "ought to be suppressed." At the behest of a committee that included Nelson Morris's son Edward, the CLSE adopted a resolution denying that CBPP existed in Chicago.[26] Philip Armour was also indifferent or disdainful of contemporary veterinary and medical science. In late 1889, during the Senate "Dressed Beef" hearings, Preston Plumb (R-Kans.) asked Armour whether CBPP had ever been present in the United States. "I am not an expert and would not care to discuss that question," Armour replied, then volunteered that "the best experts claim that we have not had it here."[27] This exchange took place over five years after CBPP had been confirmed in the West and nearly a half-century after the initial discovery of the disease in North America.

The summary picture of the inspection in Chicago before 1890 was that the highly publicized multilayer program involved a small number of "practical" men who visually examined live animals. Until 1888, only three outside city inspectors and one Humane Society representative were regularly on site in the stockyards—the city staff also made cursory passes through the packinghouses. The packers' own small teams were managed by industrial barons who were hostile to veterinary science. The last layer of defense relied on tourists. By way of comparison, in 1895 the BAI would maintain an inspection task force in Chicago of over 220 trained employees under the supervision of professional veterinarians.[28]

The Push for State and Local Regulation

Although public health officials had long advocated for more rigorous action at the state and local levels, a major impetus came from the opponents of the large packers in the late 1880s.[29] Many butchers, threatened by rapidly expanding supplies of dressed beef, sought to inflame consumers' fears about meat slaughtered far away. In March 1886, these butchers, under the leadership of Thomas Armour (a Chicago butcher who was no relation to the large packer), formed the Butchers' National Protective Association (BNPA). Over the next several years, the Association charged that the Chicago packers attained a competitive advantage by selling the meat of diseased or dead animals, which were preserved with chemicals to appear wholesome. In November 1888, the BNPA held a meeting in St. Louis with the International Cattle Range Association in conjunction with Senator Vest's investigation. The two associations reached common ground on a policy recommendation that states require "on the hoof" inspection of live animals near the place of consumption. Such state laws would have effectively ended the national dressed beef trade. In March 1889, the governor of Kansas convened an "Anti-Beef Trust" conference of legislators from cattle-producing states which drafted a model state inspection bill. Almost everyone saw the on-the-hoof campaign for what it was—an attempt to gain anticompetitive protection in the guise of public health.[30] Legislation following the butchers' designs was passed in Colorado, Indiana, Kansas, Minnesota, New Mexico, and Virginia. Many other states considered similar bills, and the butchers' charges against the Chicago packers circulated in foreign markets as well.[31]

Armour & Co. challenged the state inspection laws. The firm sent agents (including Henry E. Barber and William Rebman) with dressed beef in tow to select states to create test cases. Armour's lawyers won

immediate victories in state and federal courts.[32] Their efforts culmi-
nated in the U.S. Supreme Court decision of *Minnesota v. Barber* (36 U.S.
313, decided 19 May 1890), striking down the state's inspection law for
unconstitutionally discriminating against meat that was "entirely sound,
healthy, and fit for human food, taken from animals slaughtered in other
states."[33] Armour won another major legal victory in *Brimmer v. Rebman*
(138 U.S. 78, decided 19 January 1891), which invalidated the Virginia
inspection law. Writing for the majority in both cases, Justice John Marshall Harlan reaffirmed that a state may protect its citizens against unwholesome meats but not discriminate against the products and industries
of other states. According to the *Chicago Tribune*, the large packers' fight
was against barriers to interstate trade, not against inspection to promote
public health: "The Chicago dressed beef firms will welcome such inspection under Federal authority."[34] By January 1890, Senator Vest came to
doubt that state initiatives were a constitutionally viable way to combat
the power of the large packers. Vest had previously opposed federal antitrust legislation but now considered the proposed Sherman Act as the
second-best alternative.[35] Vest clearly saw meat inspection and antitrust
policies as substitutes.

In addition to lobbying for on-the-hoof inspection, the BNPA also
pursued direct action. They focused on an emerging disease, *actinomycosis*, commonly known as "lumpy jaw." This malady was at the center
of many intraindustry conflicts and disputes between packers and government officials although it has not received any attention in the
modern literature on the origins of meat inspection. The disease was
caused by a bacterial infection that led to large abscesses, typically near
the animal's mouth and throat. As its popular name implies, the afflicted
cattle developed pronounced, painful lumps in their jawbones. Many
experts, including James Law, considered it to be highly contagious
among animals and dangerous to humans. The press and politicians
(including Senator Vest) referred to the lump as a "cancerous tumor,"
heightening consumer fear.[36] Figure 9.2 shows contemporary images of
bovine and human disease victims. The BNPA played on these fears: its
agents purchased lumpy-jaw cattle in the West and paraded the hideously
deformed animals through the streets of Eastern cities as examples of
the big packers' meat supply.[37] The leaders of the BNPA knew what they
were doing.

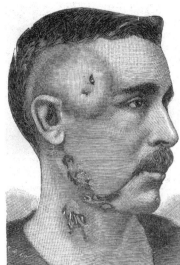

Figure 9.2. Images of bovine and human actinomycosis cases, circa 1890. *Source:* Illinois, *Annual Report of Board of Live Stock Commissioners, Fiscal Year Ending October 31, 1892,* facing pp. 12, 18.

In response to the bad publicity, officials in the Illinois meatpacking centers moved to clean up the trade. In October 1888, the ever-evolving Chicago Live Stock Exchange took charge of disposing of infected animals at the Union Stock Yards, and the Illinois legislature expanded the powers of the State Board of Live Stock Commissioners to control tuberculous and lumpy-jaw cattle. The packers' response to lumpy jaw represented one of many instances in which they begrudgingly adopted hygienic measures in response to exposés of shoddy practices. Appearances were important. In fact, the packers paid more attention to lumpy jaw, which had highly visible manifestations, than to bovine tuberculosis (BTB). Both were contagious and zoonotic diseases; but actinomycosis subsequently proved to be a limited threat to humans, whereas BTB was a killer. The efforts of the Illinois State Board of Live Stock Commissioners to control lumpy jaw in Illinois ran afoul of the Chicago Board of Health, which wanted even tougher enforcement and claimed exclusive jurisdiction over sanitary policies in the Windy City.[38] A controversy raged for several decades about whether dealers were systematically

dumping lumpy-jaw cattle into the city's meat supply after removing
the visibly infected parts—as, in fact, was their standard practice.

Passage of the 1890 and 1891 Meat Inspection Acts

Proposals for federal inspection predated the lobbying efforts of the
BNPA by several years. As noted in Chapter 8, a number of bills to inspect pork intended for export were introduced in Congress during the
Arthur and (first) Cleveland administrations, but they made little head-
way. President Harrison's USDA Secretary, Jeremiah Rusk, renewed the
push for federal meat inspection. In November 1889, Rusk called for
"national inspection of cattle at the time of slaughter" to guarantee that
meat products were "untainted by disease." Rusk had a larger purpose in
mind—he saw inspection as a part of an integrated monitoring system,
which would "enable the national authorities to promptly discover any
cattle-disease centers" so that the USDA could "take immediate steps for
its control and eradication."[39] At this early date, Rusk envisioned a trace-
back system that would become a cornerstone of modern livestock disease control. But he was also interested in addressing narrow economic
problems to yield short-term political dividends. Rusk asserted that the
propaganda of the BNPA in their fight for state on-the-hoof inspection
had harmed the reputation of American meat in Europe and lowered
U.S. livestock values. "The stories circulated on this side of the Atlantic
soon spread to the other, where they were assisted along by parties interested in introducing dressed beef from the Argentine and other Re-
publics into foreign countries. These false statements impugning the
wholesomeness of our meats have been a burden on our exporters."[40]
Instituting national meat inspection was "essential to the revival and
extension of our foreign meat trade."[41]

The early meat inspection acts came out of the 51st Congress (March
1889 to March 1891). This was an active legislative body that passed a
number of landmark laws. Republicans controlled both houses of Congress and the presidency for the first time since March 1875. The speaker
of the house, Thomas "Czar" Reed, was noted for driving Congress hard.
According to the veteran Maine Republican, "The danger in a free country is not that power will be exercised too freely, but that it will be exercised too sparingly."[42] On 29 January 1890, Reed changed the House
rules to eliminate the "disappearing quorum," a procedure that had allowed the minority to block action. The 51st Congress not only passed

much of the interventionist GOP agenda, they also allocated money so liberally that it became known as the "Billion Dollar Congress." The leading Democratic voices on agricultural issues still had a say, but the Republicans were in charge and on the move. The 51st Congress considered a number of bills concerning food and food safety, including the Conger Compound Lard bill, the Paddock Pure Food Act, and three important meat and livestock inspection bills. Table 9.1 outlines the major federal livestock and meat legislation passed in the United States between 1873 and 1906.

Senator George Edmunds (R-Vt.) introduced the first bill (S 2594) at the direct request of the Secretaries of Agriculture, State, and Treasury to deal with the ongoing trade war. As amended, this bill was destined to become America's first federal meat inspection law. The Senate debated the Edmunds bill several times between 26 February and 5 April 1890, when it passed without a vote count.[43] Numerous packers, including the Chicago producers, had opposed the initial version of the bill because it centralized inspection at Atlantic ports, made it compulsory, and imposed specific health-oriented provisions.[44] After the language was amended, several packers flipped to support the bill, but others remained opposed. Senator Preston Plumb (R-Kans.) noted on 5 April 1890 that prominent packers had testified that "they did not want this inspection on any account at all . . . ; they did not want the Government to interfere with their business." Some "had built up a special trade" based on "personal reputation" and "did not want it understood that all American food was good."[45]

The debate in the House, which began on 20 August 1890, reopened long-standing schisms.[46] In addition to pork products, the bill called for the inspection of *live* animals for export. This provision was a red flag for the Texas delegation. Joseph Sayers (D-Tex.) objected that it granted the Secretary of Agriculture "extraordinary powers" over the cattle trade, but he was willing to overlook this if the bill were amended to exempt Texas fever, as in the 1884 BAI Act. But the tide had swung against the Texans. The House overwhelmingly rejected the Sayers amendment and passed the bill by a 107 to 15 vote on August 20. The Senate rapidly accepted the House version, and President Harrison signed it into law on 30 August 1890.[47]

The final version of the Edmunds bill was aimed exclusively at the foreign market. It covered only exported live animals and salted pork

Table 9.1 Federal livestock and meat inspection laws and regulations

---

Acts passed in 1873 and 1906

Prevent cruelty to animals in transit requiring railroads to unload, feed, and water stock every 28 hours.

Regulations of 1889 (and revised in subsequent years)

BAI inspected Southern cattle in transit, and required separate cars and pens as well as disinfection of facilities.

Regulation of 1890

Americans inspected U.S. cattle in Great Britain upon arrival to determine health conditions.

Act of 30 August 1890 (26 Stat. 414)

Inspection of salted pork and bacon intended for export (regulations issued 12 September 1890).

Inspection of cattle for export (regulations issued 13 October 1890).

Inspection of cattle, sheep, and swine imported into United States (13 October 1890).

Act 3 March 1891 (26 Stat. 1089, 1090)

Inspection of vessels (regulations issued 6 June 1891).

Inspection of livestock (ante-mortem) and their products (post-mortem) for cattle, sheep, and swine destined for international and interstate trade (regulations issued 25 March 1891; inspections began 12 May 1891).

Microscopic inspection of pork for export (began 22 June 1891).

Meat Inspection Division organized within BAI (1 April 1891)

Presidential Order (effective 1 July 1894)

Placed BAI employees, including meat inspectors, under classified service.

Appropriation Act of 2 March 1895 (28 Stat. 727, 731, 732)

BAI authorized to prevent the use of condemned carcasses for export or interstate traffic.

Inspection extended to interstate cattle trade.

Meat Inspection Act of 30 June 1906 (34 Stat. 679)

BAI gained authority to eliminate diseased animals and unwholesome products from the meat supply, to regulate sanitary conditions at the processing facilities, and to prevent the use of harmful ingredients or false or misleading labeling.

In plants producing for interstate or international trade, animals were subject to pre-slaughter inspection and their carcasses and parts to post-slaughter examination.

Source: U.S. Bureau of Animal Industry (BAI), *Reports for 1889–1890,* pp. 69–78; *Reports for 1891–92,* pp. 25–40, 89–93; *Reports for 1893–94,* pp. 14–22, 26–28; *Reports for 1895–96,* pp. 7–10, 13–26; *Report for 1897,* pp. 33–41; *Report for 1899,* pp. 9–16; Houck, *Bureau of Animal Industry,* pp. 255–77; Mohler, "History and Present Status," pp. xv–xxxv; USDA, *Yearbook of Agriculture, 1917,* pp. 77–97; USDA, *The Twenty-Eight Hour Law and the Animal Quarantine Laws Annotated* (Washington, DC: U.S. Government Printing Office, 1915), pp. 7–8.

and bacon destined for export. It also included a club to assist the president in his negotiations over foreign embargoes, authorizing him to exclude any product of any nation that unjustly prohibited the importation of any U.S. product. But European statesmen did not flinch. Their major objections were that there were no provisions for either ante-mortem inspection or post-mortem inspection before curing.[48] In light of the European stance, no pork packer or exporter ever requested USDA inspection. Stronger measures were needed if the United States was going to regain its lucrative meat export trade.

On 1 May 1890, Vest introduced legislation to inspect cattle and beef products for export (S 3719).[49] Following the Supreme Court's *Minnesota v. Barber* decision on May 19, the Senate Agriculture Committee, led by Algernon Paddock (R-Nebr.), rewrote Vest's bill to also cover interstate commerce. The amended bill mandated ante-mortem inspection of all cattle and hogs *intended* for interstate shipment, and post-mortem inspection of their carcasses. It specifically called for the destruction without compensation of any condemned animals, carcasses, or meat products. It further prohibited the interstate shippers from accepting carcasses or meat that had not been inspected.[50] During the Senate debates in June, Preston Plumb, a supporter of the amended bill, noted that jurisdictional squabbles between Illinois state officials and Chicago health authorities had threatened public health. The federal government needed "to certify that what comes out of those places is fit for food." He observed that the packinghouse operations were continuous, and that requiring both ante-mortem and post-mortem inspection would "secure greater vigilance"— what one examination missed, the other might catch. Both Texas Senators were antagonistic. John Reagan (D-Tex.) inquired about the salaries of the inspectors, raising concerns over a growing federal bureaucracy. Richard Coke (D-Tex.), citing a recent U.S. Supreme Court ruling (*Coe v. Errol,* 116 U.S. 517, decided 25 January 1886) that regulation had to be based on the *actual* journey, argued that the meat-inspection bill would regulate *intended* commerce and was therefore unconstitutional. Others, including Northern Republicans, echoed these concerns. Sensing a gathering tempest, Vest requested that his original bill, which dealt only with the export trade, be considered instead. He wanted to avoid "this maze of constitutional construction." Plumb agreed to jettison the domestic provisions, and Vest's original bill passed on June 11. Vest's bill then went to the House, where it languished.[51]

The third important bill introduced in 1890 was the Paddock bill (S 4155). The bill, which included inspection of the interstate trade, had much in common with Paddock's proposed amendments to Vest's bill. The Senate considered the bill on September 18, passing a slightly amended version with none of the previous acrimonious debate and no recorded vote. The House Commerce Committee reported the Paddock bill to the House on 9 December 1890 at the beginning of the second session of the 51st Congress.[52] This was a lame-duck session that followed the Republicans' defeat in the midterm elections; any hope of an inspection bill would vanish once the Democrats took control.

Henry Stockbridge (R-Md.), who carried the bill, emphasized it was "Pure Food" legislation—public health was paramount in his report. In this vein, he cited a study by Olaf Schwartzkopf, the state veterinarian of Minnesota, that explicitly listed the diseases that meat could spread to humans. Schwartzkopf argued that the "general public can have no sufficient knowledge of these facts. . . . Individual self protection seems impossible; consequently it falls upon the government." Stockbridge emphasized that after the *Barber* ruling, federal legislation appeared to be the only recourse.[53] Thus, as with the creation of the BAI and the Interstate Commerce Commission, a Supreme Court decision tilted the case in favor of federal intervention.

The House considered the Paddock bill on 13 December 1890. Samuel Lanham (D-Tex.) protested that the bill conferred "extraordinary and unusual power" to the USDA and gave its inspectors "ipse dixit" power "to decide what is diseased meat and what cattle and hogs are fit for human consumption." Roger Mills (D-Tex.) attacked the bill as a "monstrous" measure that gave the federal government "absolute control" of the interstate meat trade. Its sponsors assumed "the people themselves are not sufficiently well informed as to what they want to buy, or to eat, or what are fit articles for food without the permission of the Government." Mills asserted that the condemnation and slaughter of animals without compensation to the owner ran afoul of the Takings Clause of the Constitution. He fumed, "Let us abandon at once the whole theory on which the Government has been framed and give the President . . . the power to control even the appetites of the people, as well as the products of their labor and their liberties." Even William Hatch (D-Mo.) called the bill an "extreme measure" that would not pass the House. He suggested that the Agriculture Committee be allowed to re-craft the bill. This suggestion won agreement.[54]

As with the 1884 BAI bill, it fell to the Democrat Hatch to advance what was essentially a Republican bill. Hatch's substitute measure was debated on the floor on March 2.[55] The revised "Paddock" bill contained language drawn from the sidelined Vest bill regarding cattle and beef exports, added a new Section 3 mandating ante-mortem inspection of cattle, sheep, and swine "subject to interstate commerce," and allowed for post-mortem inspection when the Secretary of Agriculture "deems necessary and expedient." There would be no appeal of the USDA's findings. The federal inspector would stamp carcasses judged fit for consumption. Animals or carcasses judged unsound or diseased would be barred from interstate trade. The inspector could not condemn and order destroyed rejected animals or carcasses but instead had to return the property to its owner for disposition under the local sanitation laws. In the ensuing debate, Hatch countered numerous objections, primarily from Texans. He denied that the bill interfered with state police powers and chided his opponents for questioning the expense and the delegation of powers just as they had done in 1884. The debate did address coverage of small versus large plants, but chiefly with an eye to economizing on government expenditures.[56]

The impending end to the lame-duck session added a sense of urgency to the proceedings. The measure came to a vote on 2 March 1891. This was the first roll-call vote directly concerning a meat-inspection measure—the outcome was 163 yeas, 70 nays, with 96 not voting. The Republicans approved the measure almost unanimously, voting 135 to 1. Southern Democrats overwhelmingly disapproved (7 yeas, 39 nays) as did Northeastern Democrats (4 yeas, 16 nays). Western Democrats were mildly favorable (16 yeas, 14 nays). The Union-Labor representative provided the remaining yes vote. Not only was the tenor of the debate on the 1891 Meat Inspection Act—with its arguments over the constitutional limits of federal action and the growth of the federal bureaucracy— similar to that over the 1884 BAI bill, but the division of House votes for the two measures also were remarkably similar (see Chapter 3). Later in the day on March 2, the Senate concurred with the House amendment, but without recording a roll call. President Harrison signed the bill on 3 March 1891.[57]

This account of the 1890 and 1891 Acts does not conform to the public choice rendition. Three bills were debated within a short period, and two passed. The 1890 Edmunds bill was clearly aimed at opening foreign markets. The main opposition came from legislators who feared that any growth in federal power would infringe on the ability to ship tick-infested cattle out of the South. It was introduced at the behest of the Secretaries of Agriculture, State, and Treasury; many packers opposed the early drafts, and some never came on board. The resulting bill was too weak to have the desired effect. The original Vest bill had also been meant to increase access to foreign markets. After the *Barber* decision, the bill was rewritten to cover domestic trade, but those amendments were very divisive and soon scrapped. The 1891 Paddock bill, as amended by Hatch, was considered in the final days of the lame-duck session.[58] Butchers, meatpackers (including those outside Chicago), railroad executives, and all stock growers had a stake in the outcome, and these interests all offered testimony before the Vest committee. But in the actual congressional debate, the opposition focused primarily on constitutional principles. The one vote that was recorded reflected familiar party and sectional divisions, with Southerners advancing a narrow interpretation of the Constitution. These Southern representatives had little direct stake in the conflict between small butchers and large packers that dominates the public choice critique. Meat safety and consumer interests figured crucially in the debate. The frequent claim that the large packers needed the bill to ward off state on-the-hoof legislation misses the fact that the Supreme Court had already resolved this issue.

Operation of Federal Meat Inspection

The rollout of inspection services initially focused almost exclusively on beef and pork intended for Europe. Inspection for interstate trade was not mandatory. Abattoirs applied for inspection services to the BAI. The Bureau, given the limited resources provided by Congress, could not satisfy all the requests. The first federal inspections started on May 12 at the Eastman & Co. plant in New York City (but only for the company's exports). The first microscopic inspection for trichinae in pork began 22 June 1891 at the Chicago plant of Nelson Morris.[59] For cattle, inspection at the time of slaughter commenced in May 1891; for calves and sheep, in fiscal year 1892; and for swine not intended for export, in fiscal year 1894.

Figure 9.3 charts the growth in the meat trade and meat inspection. The bottom lines in both panels trace the rise of federal inspection for cattle and swine from 1891 to 1914. To provide perspective, we include the USDA's retrospective estimates of all cattle and hogs slaughtered annually (the top lines in each panel), and of the total wholesale slaughter for interstate and international markets (the middle lines in the figure). The bottom two lines merge after the 1906 Meat Inspection Act required federal inspection of all interstate trade. Meat destined for interstate and international trade accounted for the bulk of the industry's expansion between 1880 and 1914. For cattle, this trade made up about one-quarter of the output in 1880 and well over one-half by 1914. The lower lines in both panels illustrate that most of the growth of federal meat inspection up to 1914 occurred under the 1891 Act (rather than its more celebrated successor). In 1894, federal inspection covered roughly 43 percent of total cattle slaughtered in the United States and 76 percent of the wholesale slaughter destined for interstate and international markets. It covered 23 percent of all swine and 52 percent of those subject to wholesale slaughter for interstate and international markets.

The 1891 Act was judged a great success because most European nations soon reopened their markets to imported pork that passed the USDA's microscopic inspections. Germany removed its ban on American pork products on 3 September 1891. Denmark, Italy, France, Austria, and the other continental importers rapidly followed (see Table 2.2 of Chapter 2). Philip Armour, Nelson Morris, and Gustavus Swift all congratulated Secretary Rusk.[60] The increased access to continental markets and higher hog prices in the United States generated considerable favorable publicity for Rusk as he toured the country opening inspection stations.[61]

A closer look at Chicago illustrates how the new inspection system operated and how the burdens of condemnation shifted as the animals passed through the stockyards into the packinghouses.[62] Ante-mortem inspection occurred at the scales of the Union Stock Yards. At this point, the animals still belonged to the sellers, who bore any losses from condemnations. The animals changed ownership when they passed through the packers' gates. Those packers who were engaged in international trade requested post-mortem inspection, conducted in their plants. The packers had to bear the losses from these condemnations. The extent of the potential losses depended on policy. Consumer advocates pressured

A. Cattle slaughtered annually, 1869–1914

B. Swine slaughtered annually, 1869–1914

Figure 9.3. Federal meat inspection: (A) cattle and (B) swine. *Source:* The total slaughter series are based on calendar-year estimates of animals slaughtered annually from 1869 to 1914, appearing in Frederick Strauss and Louis H. Bean, "Gross Farm Income and Indices of Farm Production and Prices in the United States, 1869–1937," USDA, *Technical Bulletin*, no. 703 (Washington, DC: U.S. Government Printing Office, 1940), pp. 110, 119. The interstate and international series are based on calendar-year estimates for "federally inspected" (including the "estimated equivalent" for the period before 1907) covering 1880–1914 that appear in U.S. Department of Agriculture, *Yearbook of Agriculture, 1933,* pp. 596, 605. Fiscal-year data on actual (as opposed to "equivalent") post-mortem federal inspections of swine for the period before 1907 period appear in Houck, *Bureau of Animal Industry,* p. 272. The interstate and international series are derived by converting the actual fiscal-year inspection counts to a calendar basis using the seasonal distribution of activity reported in U.S. Department of Agriculture (USDA), "Monthly Slaughter under Federal Inspection," in *Livestock, Meats, and Wool Market Statistics and Related Data, 1942* (Washington, DC: USDA, 1943), pp. 28, 31.

the USDA to condemn the entire carcasses of diseased animals whereas producers lobbied to only trim diseased parts. In Illinois, a fight broke out almost immediately between BAI officials and the State Board of Live Stock Commissioners over the treatment of cattle infected with lumpy jaw and BTB. The Bureau sided with cattle growers and packers, requiring only the trimming of diseased parts. Such disputes over standards erupted regularly.[63]

J. Sterling Morton and the Packers

The entire federal meat-inspection program faced a severe trial when J. Sterling Morton took over as the USDA secretary in March 1893. A fiscal conservative and strict constitutional constructionist, Cleveland's appointee believed that Rusk's USDA was "too paternalistic" and sought to cut the department's budget by 25 percent.[64] Morton called BAI the "Bureau of Animal Indolence" and considered replacing Daniel Salmon as chief with Frank Billings, a fellow Nebraskan.[65] Morton labeled meat inspection "not only useless, but a highly expensive amusement" performed by Rusk's army of Republican placeholders. In June 1893, rumors that Morton planned to eliminate all meat inspection began to circulate. The reports generated a strong backlash, including threats from Germany to shutter their markets to U.S. imports again.[66]

Morton sharply changed tack in September 1893. To protect U.S. citizens, he issued an order extending the visual inspection to live hogs intended for interstate commerce. At the same time, he limited the expensive microscopic inspections to pork products intended for export to countries that specifically required the service. Morton justified expanding inspection because he had discovered that some packers were diverting condemned carcasses into the American market.[67] As the *St. Louis Republic* put it, " 'Uncle Sam paid for the protection of the foreign stomach while his own was a receptacle for all the refuse.' "[68] The 1891 law required that condemned carcasses be removed from federally inspected plants and be disposed of according to state law, if any existed. In practice, there was considerable arbitraging of regulatory jurisdictions, and even within regulated plants there were reports of irregularities.

In April 1894, the secretary received a tip from his son, Joy Morton, that a Chicago packinghouse belonging to Nelson Morris had been systematically removing condemned meat from the rendering tanks and butchering downer cattle after the USDA inspectors had left for the night. The meat was sold locally and distributed more broadly as canned products. Joy Morton, who resided in Chicago, considered the packer's behavior an "outrage," adding that "they would sell Rat Meat, if they could work it off on the public." Joy was no rabble-rouser, publicity seeker, disgruntled employee, or gentile outsider, but a conservative businessman involved in the salt trade who had customers in the packing industry and would later found the Morton Salt Company. He requested to remain anonymous because "I do not care to make an enemy of this House unnecessarily, as they buy more or less Salt of us."[69]

In mid-May 1894, Secretary Morton went public with the allegations that an unnamed large Chicago packer was selling condemned meat and sent BAI inspector William S. Devoe to investigate.[70] Although Devoe's final report has been lost (or officially declared so), surviving BAI documents do include eyewitness testimony that on 1 February 1894, Morris Co. foreman Patrick Walsh ordered worker J. Donaski "to drop into the tanks through the hole in the top, which he did by means of a rope and tackle and the assistance of other employees, and take out carcasses of meat which had been condemned and tanked by order of the Government Inspectors. . . . These carcasses [were] taken out and removed to the cutting room and cut up for the local trade." The same operation was performed on March 3 and several other occasions.[71]

In June 1894, Secretary Morton sent a warning to John F. Hopkins, Chicago's mayor, that "a large part of the beef and pork condemned by the [BAI] inspectors . . . at Chicago is sold to local dealers, put upon the market in your city, and . . . consumed in the houses of your citizens. This is an endangerment of the public health." But it was not within the existing authority of BAI to stop this trade; only local cooperation "can prevent the sale of the diseased meat."[72]

The Chicago packers decried Morton's accusations as "ridiculous," even laughable because "the big packers have too much business sagacity to embark in a business that if discovered would mean ruin."[73] The tanks were closely watched by the inspectors and once filled were "immediately subjected to a jet of steam," destroying the value of the meat. Nelson Morris further asserted the "practices alleged are impossible" because neither retail butchers nor anyone else would ever buy the carcasses. In early 1895, when the reports were picked up by the British press and discussed in Parliament, a representative of a large packer "intimated that the author of the story had been identified as a discharged employé of a Stock Yards concern."[74] Devoe later testified under oath that he had received confirming, if inconclusive, evidence from both discharged and active employees. Nothing directly implicated the company's managers in the practices, but both Inspector Devoe and Secretary Morton were satisfied the complaints had foundation. The packers continued to dismiss their critics and issue blanket denials.[75]

Although he knew better than to believe the packers' public statements, Morton was in a bind. If he broadcast specific evidence of wrongdoing or took such cases to court, he would inflict grave harm on the entire livestock industry. Instead, he resorted to moral suasion. On 21 July 1894, Morton wrote privately to Nelson Morris that based on the BAI's investigation he found the charges creditable and demanded that Morris unequivocally order his employees to send all condemned meat to the fertilizer tanks. The secretary pointed out that consumer confidence "in the honor of the packers as a guarantee of their protection against diseased meats" was already weak and that releasing legal affidavits would cause a panic that would harm the meat industry and farmers as well as do "immense injury" to Morris's own business.[76] Because the reputation of the entire industry was at stake, the Morris firm escaped direct public sanctions for its misdeeds.

The Morris affair was not an isolated case. In March 1895, Morton privately chastised officials at Swift & Co. for evading USDA regulations and exporting pork to Germany that had not passed microscopic inspection. Swift had been duping German officials by attaching regular USDA stamps. Morton noted that if the Germans examined this pork microscopically, they would likely "find such a large proportion of pieces affected with trichinosis, that it would not only discredit the inspection of this Department, but would probably be disastrous to the export trade of this country." He further expressed surprise "that a firm of your standing would do a thing of this kind" and noted that "I have heretofore gone on the theory that the packers . . . would do everything in their power to see that the regulations were entirely complied with." Morton then threatened stronger "supervision" if the firm did not do its part to protect trade and health. During this episode, Morton vented his frustration to his son that the packers "desire all the benefits of inspection with none of the disadvantages."[77]

A decade before the publication of *The Jungle,* Morton's departmental letter-book was filled with charges of abuse every bit as revolting as those found by Sinclair. Morton accused U.S. packers of removing and misusing BAI inspection tags, of butchering and selling condemned meat, of creating secret supply chains for diseased hogs, of fraudulently labeling cans of tainted meat as being federally inspected, of knowingly violating international sanitary agreements, and more. Many of these accusations were in private letters that Morton sent to the packers, in which he often pleaded for more responsible behavior.[78] The accounts are specific with names, dates, and places, and they make clear that there were systematic patterns of deceitful behavior, not just occasional accidental lapses in judgment.

As a conservative, Morton struggled with the propriety of intervening in the affairs of the meatpackers. He wrote to his son Joy that "it seems to me that among the constitutional and proper functions of the Government of the United States, is the preservation of the lives of its citizens, and I know of no more direct or better method of conserving human life than preventing the consumption of unhealthy food by the masses of the people."[79] In letters to several packers (including Armour), the secretary rejected the claim that the inspection law had been passed for strictly commercial rather than sanitary reasons. Packers large and small repeatedly pestered Morton to allow them to sell in the domestic market trichinae-infested pork that had failed microscopic inspection for export; Morton repeatedly rejected these overtures.[80] He sought to toughen inspection by increasing the professionalism and vigilance of the staff and by adopting better technologies (tags, labels, and tank locks) to secure the condemned meat.

In response to lobbying by Secretary Morton, Congress granted the USDA powers to penalize those transporting condemned carcasses across state lines in the 1896 Agricultural Appropriation Act (passed on 2 March 1895). Congress was still unwilling to empower the USDA to confiscate and destroy tainted meat, but under Morton's new regulations (effective 1 July 1895), inspectors were to stamp "Condemned" directly on unfit meat and log its disposition.[81] In addition, the BAI stretched its *de facto* clout beyond what was explicitly authorized *de jure*. It threatened to remove its inspectors if a plant did not destroy the condemned meat. For this threat to work, its services had to have been adding value. Five years after passage of the 1891 Act, Congress still had not appropriated sufficient funds to hire inspectors for all the plants requesting federal coverage. Morton advocated raising funds by charging the meatpackers for inspection, as it was a valuable service that gave the recipients a competitive advantage over packers without government inspectors. But opponents, offering the long-standing rebuttal that no one would trust inspectors in the pay of packers, won the day. The scarcity of government-funded inspection services enhanced the incentives of participating packers to comply with BAI demands to tank condemned carcasses and parts.[82] In spite of the budgetary limitations, by 1897, inspection covered most of the beef, pork, and meat products shipped to Europe, along with "a large amount of the meat intended for interstate commerce."[83] Between 1893 and 1897, the number of cities served more than doubled, and the number of plants more than tripled.

Despite his hostility to federal meat inspection when he entered office, Morton significantly expanded the service to cover much of the domestic supply. Morton's actions bear on a much larger story. He and his boss, President Cleveland, are often lauded as champions of small government.[84] Not only do such accounts fail to take note of Morton's about-face on meat inspection, but they are oblivious to the fact that during Cleveland's first term he allowed his Commissioner of Agriculture Norman J. Colman to take over the police powers of states to regulate livestock diseases (Chapter 4).

There is good reason why many scholars have misinterpreted the BAI's actions and the need for meat inspection: the USDA leadership led them astray. Leaders such Morton and Salmon maintained a Janus face—one public and one private. Publicly they wanted to open foreign markets and protect U.S. farming and business interests, so they repeatedly testified to the hygienic soundness of American meat. At the same time, they lobbied for greater powers and funding for meat inspection. Privately, they knew that there remained serious health dangers, but they largely refrained from exposing them for fear of causing food panics.

Scholars also have been misled by the meatpacking and stockyard magnets about the vigor of their private actions to address sanitary concerns. Adopting by-laws similar to those authorizing the Chicago Board of Trade's inspection of grain, the Chicago Live Stock Exchange pledged

in 1884 to enforce "rigid inspection" to prevent the sale of unhealthy and
unfit meat. At times in the 1880s, CLSE leaders also announced their
intention to hire a "competent" and independent veterinary surgeon. We
have seen no evidence that the Exchange actually followed through on
these measures during the 1880s. The stockyard's own spokesmen do
not mention such CLSE personnel or activities in their press statements
regarding the inspection system.[85] In the mid-1890s, the Exchange did
begin to cooperate more fully with the state of Illinois to increase inspection at the yards. The reasons that a leading industry journal offered for this alliance are revealing: "The trade in diseased cattle had
become so well organized, the opportunities . . . were so great and the
financial rewards . . . so large that the state found itself unable . . . to
cope with the situation. . . . The evil had become so widespread" that it
generated bad publicity and threatened the entire trade. In response,
the CLSE agreed to fund stronger government interventions to rein in
unscrupulous actors.[86]

Constitutional Challenges to Federal Inspection

As with other legislation passed in the 1880s and 1890s that expanded
federal regulation of business, meat inspection faced important court
challenges.[87] On 28 February 1898, John H. Rogers, a federal district judge
in Fort Smith, Arkansas, ruled the 1891 Act unconstitutional in the *United
States v. Harry Boyer*. The case involved the indictment of Harry E. Boyer,
a foreman at the Jacob Dold Packing Company in Kansas City, for attempting to bribe federal inspectors. Rogers ruled that Boyer had not
committed a crime because the animals and meat in question had not
yet entered interstate commerce so the inspections were invalid.[88] Rogers reasoned, in keeping with the *U.S. v. E.C. Knight* decision (156 U.S. 1,
decided 21 January 1895), that although the products of the packinghouse were destined for interstate and international commerce, the
slaughtering and packing itself was conducted entirely within one state.
Congress thus had no authority to regulate.[89] Because the criminal
defendant was declared not guilty, the government could not appeal
the case.

President McKinley's USDA Secretary, James Wilson, had received
prior notice of the bombshell ruling.[90] Fearing that it would damage
exports, he announced on 1 March 1898 that he would ignore Rogers's

verdict and "administer the law just as if no decision had been rendered."[91] Again, the BAI was operating in a legal gray area. Its chief, Salmon, offered a solution to the enforcement problem: "Should . . . the proprietors of the packing houses . . . refuse to permit our inspectors to do their work as heretofore, we shall, when shipments reach the state boundaries, simply refuse to give a certificate of inspection."[92] Here was a clear statement of how the BAI used it power to regulate interstate commerce to affect intrastate activities.

The reactions to the Rogers decision offer a litmus test of packer support for the existing legislation as of that date. The representatives of the leading packing companies and retail butchers stated that they regretted the ruling, chiefly owing to its potentially adverse effect in Europe. The *Butchers' Advocate* editorialized that "it would be a sad blow to this industry if the present system of inspection were discontinued." A representative from Armour & Co. made a more nuanced statement: "The packers themselves do not seek the inspection. We know our meats are good, but the inspection acts as a guarantee by the government that they contain no disease."[93]

Farm and stockyard representatives were outraged by Rogers's ruling. As the *Drovers Journal* asserted, "Everybody is well pleased with Federal inspection, even the packers and dealers in meat, for it gives their goods the stamp of approval that makes them acceptable in every country on the globe. If such inspection is not legal the sooner it is made so the better."[94] The *Ohio Farmer* fumed: "Perhaps, in a hundred years from now, the authority and jurisdiction of the government will be enlarged so that these obstructions to general laws for the good of the people . . . will be removed. Instead of 44 different systems of law, we should have one. . . . Half the states have no pure food laws, while in the other half they are conflicting. . . . No state in the Union maintains an effective meat inspection law and consumers of meats are left to the mercy of men who would spread contagion broadcast if they could enrich themselves."[95] Whatever their concerns with federal intervention had been in 1890 and 1891, most participants in the meat trade now endorsed the inspection system because they recognized that uniform national standards promoted commerce.

Rogers's claims about interstate commerce were addressed indirectly in the Supreme Court decision in *Swift & Co. v. United States* (196 U.S. 375, decided 30 January 1905). The case arose after Theodore Roosevelt's trust-busters sought to apply the Sherman Anti-Trust Act to price-fixing activities among meatpackers. Lawyers for Swift argued that the commerce involved was strictly local. The Court unanimously disagreed. As Justice Oliver W. Holmes wrote, "When cattle are sent for sale from a place in one State with the expectation that they will end their transit, after purchase in another, and when in effect they do so with only the interruption necessary to find a purchaser at the stockyards, and when this is a constantly recurring course, it constitutes interstate commerce." Because the cattle were part of the "stream of commerce," the efforts by Swift and others to fix their prices restrained interstate commerce and were subject to the Sherman Act.[96] Such reasoning would render Rogers's objection to federal meat inspection moot.

The Court's redefinition of the "stream of commerce" helped lower the barriers to federal regulation of interstate commerce. Congress had the exclusive authority to regulate interstate commerce, but under the *E. C. Knight* ruling could not do so with manufacturing activities within any state. The states could exercise their police powers only within their borders in ways that did not impinge on interstate commerce (with prescribed exceptions). This division of authority had created a regulatory void, which the packers had long exploited. In the on-the-hoof inspection cases, the packers had argued that state laws were unconstitutional inferences with interstate commerce, but in *Swift* they argued that the Sherman Anti-Trust Act did not apply because their business was conducted within state boundaries. The threads of antitrust policy and meat-inspection history became further entangled when Theodore Roosevelt's attempts to bust the "Meat Trust" were frustrated after a lower court threw out evidence garnered from the packers' voluntary testimony to the Bureau of Corporations. Roosevelt's anger over this setback was shaped by his experiences in the Spanish-American War and in turn later shaped his response to the publication of Upton Sinclair's *The Jungle*.

The Embalmed Beef Scandal

A decade of controversy surrounding trichinosis, frequent reports of butchers and packers processing diseased animals, and the lags in expansion of federal inspection put the public on edge.[97] During the summer of 1898, the press reported that tainted beef was distributed to the troops fighting in the Spanish-American War. In September 1898, President McKinley appointed a commission, headed by General Grenville M. Dodge, to investigate the health conditions of soldiers, including the "embalmed beef scandal."[98] The real fireworks began in December 1898, when Major General Nelson A. Miles charged that over 300 tons of poorly preserved refrigerated beef had sickened his troops, killing several men. In response, McKinley empaneled a new "beef inquiry court," whose members toured the large packinghouses in Chicago and took testimony from at least eighty Army officers.[99] The officers generally condemned the refrigerated and canned beef as miserable food that often made their troops sick; it was common for their men to throw the meat away and go hungry.[100] Many others, including Rough Rider Theodore Roosevelt, supported these charges.

The press had a field day with the hearings, as charges and counter charges dragged on into 1899. It is probable that some beef tins were not properly sealed and that the "refrigerated" beef spoiled in the hot climate. Apparently a small shipment of fresh beef also had been treated with preservatives by a New York meat dealer, Alexander B. Powell. The whole sordid affair left a strong impression: the poet Carl Sandburg, who had served in the war, would later relate that the canned beef "*was* embalmed" and was more noxious than "a properly embalmed cadaver."[101]

The controversy evoked a strong response from USDA Secretary Wilson. As a member of the U.S. House of Representatives from Iowa in early 1884, he had been a leading advocate for the creation of the BAI (see Chapter 3). After losing his House seat, Wilson became an official with the Consolidated Cattle Growers Association, and he had petitioned Congress for national meat inspection in the mid-1880s. In 1891, he became the director of the Experiment Station at Iowa State College. He was by no means a disease denier, but in the face of the embalmed beef scandal, Secretary Wilson leapt to the defense of the livestock interests. He saw the inflammatory charges of General Miles as another threat to export markets. As he wrote in a private letter to his brother, West W. Wilson, a commission merchant at the Union Stock Yards in Chicago, he felt it was his duty to "stand between the producers and packers, and the mischief now being done" by Miles. With President McKinley's approval, Wilson was "doing everything I can possible do to take care of and encourage and defend the agricultural interests of the country, as well as the packers."[102] Wilson ordered Harvey W. Wiley of the USDA's Bureau of Chemistry to conduct a special investigation, and he trumpeted Wiley's subsequent findings that the U.S. meat supply was free of dangerous chemicals.

However, like Morton before him, Wilson was being duplicitous. He knew that the embalmed beef charges contained more truth than he or anyone in the administration would publicly reveal. As he wrote his brother, "Our Commissary Department got into some of its advertisements for bids for meat last summer something along the line of requiring meat to keep 72 hours in the tropics [which] . . . resulted in experimentation being conducted more or less by people throughout the country, but whether by the packers or not, I do not know. . . . We do know that doctored quarters of meat did get to both Santiago and Porto Rico and we think we know who sent them."[103] (Wilson does not reveal who this was; it may have been the aforementioned Alexander Powell.) Wilson and the Board of Inquiry were also less than forthcoming: when the 1894 Devoe inquiry came under a new bout of press scrutiny—they claimed the files of this investigation had been lost.[104]

Both the Dodge Commission and the Board of Inquiry largely absolved the meat industry of charges of wrongdoing.[105] However, the embalmed meat scandal created considerable distrust of both the government and the large packers. Upton Sinclair would soon reignite the public's concern. At the time of the war with Spain, the USDA had no control over meat processing or the use of chemicals. That would change.

The Jungle and the 1906 Act

In early 1905, the London-based medical journal the *Lancet* published a series of articles that were highly critical of the Chicago packers.[106] The table was set for Upton Sinclair's *The Jungle* to become an international sensation following its publication by Doubleday in February 1906. The BAI reacted to the public outcry by imposing tougher standards. On February 8, A. D. Melvin, who had recently replaced Salmon as Chief of the BAI, instructed his inspectors to tighten sanitary standards; on February 14, Secretary Wilson sent an order requiring all federally regulated packing plants to improve hygienic conditions.

Everyone, including Melvin, understood that the BAI had no power to enforce the new order, but rather had to rely on moral suasion and the threat of withdrawing inspectors. Melvin was loath to do the latter because he feared that the firms would put more carcasses from diseased animals into interstate trade.[107] To rebut the slanderous attacks by "professional agitators," J. O. Armour published several articles in the *Saturday Evening Post* in March 1906, which he then collected and published as a single volume. Armour emphasized that his company did not send even *"one atom of any condemned animal or carcass"* into the food chain. As for government inspection, he noted that any "attempt to evade it would be, from a purely commercial viewpoint, suicidal. *No packer can do an interstate or export business without government inspection."*[108] Such statements did little to quell the public outrage.

Theodore Roosevelt was revolted by Sinclair's depictions of the unsanitary conditions in the packinghouses. With an eye to public opinion, he ordered the USDA to investigate the sanitary conditions in the Chicago plants and the efficacy of the federal inspection service. In mid-February, Secretary Wilson dispatched a team consisting of two BAI division chiefs and the department's solicitor. Events were moving fast. In mid-March, Frank Doubleday provided Roosevelt with advance copies of three articles by credible observers intended for release in the May edition of the *World's Work* under a banner headline for the trilogy "Selling Diseased Meat." Because Upton Sinclair was a socialist novelist, his portrayal might have been dismissed for political reasons; but the authors of the forthcoming articles included a former Chicago meat inspector, a physician, and a lawyer that the publisher Doubleday had previously detailed to confirm the general nature of Sinclair's account. All three articles damned the quality of federal inspection. The new charges cast an even larger shadow over the USDA's ability to provide an impartial assessment.

To obtain independent counsel, Roosevelt directed two outsiders, the new Commissioner of Labor Charles P. Neill and a trusted lawyer James B. Reynolds, to investigate and report to him directly. At about this time, Senator Albert Beveridge (R-Ind.) began to draft aggressive meat-inspection legislation. He and Roosevelt soon joined forces.[109] The USDA team visited eighteen federally inspected enterprises and four locally inspected Chicago plants in mid-March. Its report of 5 April 1906 defended federal inspection and criticized both the muckrakers and the meatpackers. They stated that Sinclair and the *Lancet* had grossly exaggerated the problems; for example, the claim that thousands of rats raced upon piles of meat was among several "willful and deliberate misrepresentations of fact." Nevertheless, they did find serious sanitary problems, including water dripping from the ceilings onto sausages and meat falling on the floor at one large plant. Many plants had inadequate and unsanitary toilet facilities and filthy equipment and work areas. Worse yet, many of the work areas were in disrepair and made of permeable materials that were impossible to sanitize properly.[110]

The report also recommended changes to strengthen the inspection laws. Post-mortem inspection should be mandatory. Once meat had passed inspection, the USDA needed to retain the power to condemn it if it subsequently became tainted. The USDA should have the power to compel the destruction of condemned animals and meats, and to forbid interstate shippers from accepting carcasses and food products that had not passed federal inspection. Upon receiving the report, Melvin issued several orders in April and May, even though he still lacked the legal authority to enforce compliance. Among his orders were requirements that the packers cease throwing and mixing meats on the floors, and that they install lavatories and sinks. The USDA, however, needed new legislation to give these regulations legal standing.

Melvin's actions were not all one sided. In the midst of the turmoil, the marketing of meat from cattle infected with lumpy jaw regained the spotlight. Chicago's health commissioner had recently tightened the Windy City's standards, but in May he reversed course under pressure from USDA officials.[111]

The Neill-Reynolds study was still in the works, and all indications were that its findings would be even more scathing than the internal USDA report. The big packers were suffering a public relations disaster. They repeatedly lobbied Roosevelt and his representatives, promising to voluntarily make the necessary improvements in sanitary conditions if he would bury the report. In the meantime, the Beveridge measure passed the Senate on May 25 as an amendment to the Agricultural Appropriation Bill without debate or dissent. It mandated federal inspection of all meat and meat products entering interstate or international commerce. This provision would have closed loopholes but not dramatically changed existing practice (see Table 9.1), but the Beveridge Amendment also proposed extending federal regulation into entirely new areas by empowering the Secretary of Agriculture to set and enforce sanitary rules and oversee all aspects of production. It further mandated that canned products be dated and that the cost of inspection be shifted to the packers. Particularly threatening to the packers was a provision that prevented them from challenging the rulings of the secretary in the courts.[112] The packers and their close political allies argued the Beveridge Amendment gave federal authorities unwarranted and unconstitutional powers over their manufacturing operations, including the power to shut plants down.[113] These were not peripheral issues as Kolko maintained.

While publicly supporting regulation, the major packers fought to gut the Beveridge bill. They orchestrated a petition campaign from stockmen condemning the Senate bill and pressuring the president to withhold the Neill-Reynolds report. Theodore Roosevelt initially did suppress the report to avoid collateral damage to the entire meat trade. He also hoped that the threat of release would convince House leaders, most specifically James Wadsworth (R-N.Y.) of the Agricultural Committee, to accept the Beveridge Amendment. To improve his position, Roosevelt privately communicated to Wadsworth that the Neill-Reynolds findings were "hideous," and he insisted that conditions "must be remedied at once."[114] One of the findings that greatly disturbed the righteous president was that packers were labeling prepared products such as canned ham as "Inspected and passed by the United States Government" when in fact "no government inspector had ever seen any part of the process of the making or the canning" and "in some cases there was very little of 'ham' or even of pork in the cans."[115] Such deceitful practices did not sit well with the champion of the "Square Deal."

By late May, the packers' allies in the House, led by Wadsworth, had drafted substitute legislation. It required the government to pay for inspection, did not mandate that meat cans be dated, and allowed some interstate shipment of meats not federally inspected. It further allowed the packers to appeal the USDA's rulings in the courts. In Roosevelt's view, this latter provision would have permitted the packers to engage in judicial shopping and "put on the judge, who had no knowledge of the conditions, the burden of stating whether or not the Secretary [of Agriculture] was right." Roosevelt felt this would eviscerate any meaningful reform. The House bill represented what the packers really meant when they said they favored meat inspection.[116]

To rally support for the tougher standards, Roosevelt released the Neill-Reynolds report on 4 June 1906. His hand had been forced: Upton Sinclair had already leaked the main findings of the report to an eager press. The findings were indeed disgusting: floors, tables, and equipment where the meat was prepared were filthy and rarely cleaned; meat intended for canning and for sausages was strewn on the floors; employees spit, and in some cases, urinated in work areas; all sort of rubbish, including splinters, rope, and pigskin, went into the potted ham; and cans containing moldy meat were being livened up by reheating then given fresh labels and sold. Criticisms also focused on the wooden work surfaces and walls, which were rotting and waterlogged—one of the major points of contention in 1906 was that federal inspectors had no legal authority over the conditions within the plants. The packers wanted it to stay that way. On June 8, Theodore Roosevelt made public the observations of "a most competent and trustworthy witness in Chicago," Mary McDowell. This local settlement worker, who had toured several plants in late May, noted it was "miraculous" how fast Morris, Armour, Swift, and Libby were cleaning up their operations. "The haste toward reform would have been amusing had it not been so nearly tragic."[117] Apparently not all was well in the large plants before the investigations.

In the hearings on the House bill, the large packers' representative, Thomas E. Wilson, asserted that "any practical recommendations would be welcomed and adopted," but the packers were opposed to "a bill that will put our business in the hands of theorists, chemists, sociologists, etc." Wilson argued that the cost of inspection (estimated at 5 to 8 cents per bovine and about 2 cents per hog and sheep) would put them at a competitive disadvantage relative to intrastate packers who were not subject to federal inspection.[118] The competitive pressures that supposedly forced the big packers to take hygienic measures to ensure their high-quality reputations also, they claimed, inhibited them from bearing the costs of inspection. Wilson further emphasized that the bad publicity resulting from *The Jungle* and the follow-up investigations had harmed consumer confidence and devastated sales.[119]

The compromise bill, which passed on June 30, required continuous surveillance of processing and both ante-mortem and post-mortem inspection of all meats in interstate commerce. The 1906 Act explicitly empowered the USDA to withdraw inspection at plants that did not destroy condemned animals or carcasses. The compromise bill eliminated the Senate provision on dating cans and the requirement that packers pay inspection fees. The key issue of whether the packers could appeal to the courts was left in limbo.[120] Despite sharp criticisms of the final bill by the press and pure food advocates, federal meat inspectors emerged from the battle with greater powers and greater funding.

The debate leading to the 1906 Act echoed the debates that had led to the founding of the BAI and those over the 1890 and 1891 Acts, with the same constitutional themes appearing in each. The earlier two inspection acts, as passed, were clearly aimed at advancing American meat exports, but the most heated congressional debates in the 1890s centered on attempts to extend coverage to regulate interstate trade to protect American consumers. These provisions aimed at the domestic market were gutted. Southern Democrats opposed all three bills. As health concerns grew over time, they became more important in the lead up to the 1906 legislation and in its implementation. All three Acts (but especially those of 1891 and 1906) were entwined in the broader antitrust conflicts of the era. There were also major contrasts with past episodes. As we have detailed, a succession of BAI and USDA leaders had felt constrained to publicize poor sanitary conditions in the meat industry for fear of creating food scares that might destroy foreign and domestic markets.[121] Theodore Roosevelt held a similar view, and he initially struggled to reach a compromise that would avoid excessive collateral damage. But packer resistance to both meaningful inspection and to antitrust policy, coupled with the pressure created by the muckraking press and Roosevelt's personal revulsion with the existing hygienic conditions, pushed him to intensify his public demands for stronger legislation. Theodore Roosevelt was a political animal of a different breed.

Post-1906 Legislation and Inspection Trends

The 1906 Act was a landmark achievement that would be copied by Canada and other nations. Changes in regulations came largely through a succession of revised administrative orders issued by the Secretary of Agriculture rather than via legislative action. Meat industry leaders formed the American Meat Packers Association in late 1906 to help firms adapt to the new regime. And in May 1907, the BAI began to publish monthly "Service Announcements," which included lists of convictions for violating meat inspection laws. Bringing the physical capital stock up to sanitary standards was a major task. The new standards demanded the use of impermeable materials in work surfaces, floors, and walls to make them easier to disinfect, better drainage and water systems, the separation of activities to reduce the chance of contamination, and hygienic toilet facilities.[122] Attaining compliance was a slow process that required extensive structural modifications and phasing out old facilities. The USDA gave priority to ensuring the cleanliness of rooms, equipment, and handling processes. In 1906, very few establishments had facilities and equipment that would meet the basic hygiene requirements in place by the early 1920s. Legislative changes extended the inspection to meat imports in 1913 and to horsemeat in 1919.

The 1906 legislation inaugurated major increases in the meat-inspection budget, the size of the workforce, and in the number of cities and facilities covered. The largest amount spent on inspection prior to the 1906 Act was $800,000; the new legislation provided for a permanent annual budget of $3 million. The number of USDA employees assigned to meat inspection rose from 760 in 1906 to 2,230 in 1908. Over this same period, the number of establishments covered increased from 163 (in 58 cities) to 787 (in 211 cities).[123] Figure 9.4 shows that 1906 was clearly a watershed in federal meat inspection coverage, with the number of plants in the system increasing about five times by 1910.

State and local inspection continued to vary across locales, and in general they provided only weak coverage of products not entering interstate or international commerce. Whereas the BAI meat inspection service advanced high standards and attracted professional veterinarians, most state and municipal inspectors were poorly educated and motivated.[124] In some areas, local inspectors were butchers without any formal training in identifying diseases. There was also a fundamental difference in the effectiveness of the political pressure put on state and local versus federal agents, which swayed regulatory outcomes. State and local politicians, dependent on the support of local business interests, often were slow to act. Even when laws and procedures were in place, politicians often pressured their administrative subordinates to ignore problems and go easy on violators. After joining the civil service in 1894, federal meat inspectors were much less likely to be influenced by cronyism and political pressure.[125] New inspectors and assistant inspectors had to be graduates of veterinary colleges and pass a civil service examination. Only three out of over thirty test-takers passed the first exam. One of these three was then weeded out on other merit grounds. An extensive survey circa 1940 of municipal inspection in North America showed that the inspectors were typically poorly trained and stretched thin, with one inspector for every eighty-five plants.[126] Clearly, federal inspection was an improvement, but just as clearly there were still major gaps in coverage.

The passage of the 1906 Act did not end the controversies over federal meat inspection. Consumer advocates such as Caroline Bartlett Crane, a Unitarian minister from Kalamazoo, Michigan, and a crusading member of the Women's Health Protective Association, kept up the pressure. In congressional testimony, speaking appearances before public health groups, and articles in popular magazines, Crane complained that BAI officials were too cozy with the large packers and that the inspectors let too much flesh from diseased animals into the meat supply

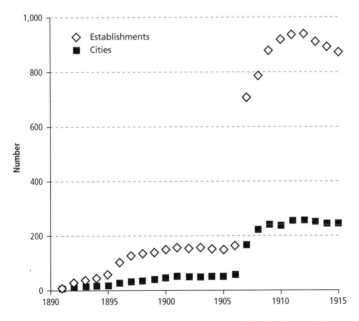

Figure 9.4. Number of establishments and cities with federal meat inspection, fiscal year 1891–1915. *Source:* U.S. Bureau of Animal Industry, *Report for 1911*, p. 40; U.S. Department of Agriculture, *Yearbook of Agriculture, 1915*, p. 538.

and did not sufficiently ensure the destruction of condemned carcasses. Albert Leffingwell, former president of the American Humane Association, was also a frequent critic of the federal inspection system.[127] But these charges caused only a ripple compared with those triggered by *The Jungle.*

Attitudes of the Packers

There are claims that the large packers supported federal inspection and counterclaims that they opposed it. In early 1890, packers from Chicago, St. Louis, and elsewhere opposed the early drafts of the Edmunds legislation, but switched to supporting it after the bill had been revised to their liking. In December 1890, the *Chicago Tribune* asserted that the large packers desired the "Inter-State Meat Inspection Act."[128] Philip Armour opined in reference to the Paddock bill: "We are in favor of inspection. This bill seems to meet the case fairly well, and there is no objection to it on our part."[129] The *Tribune* added in March 1891 that the bill, as amended, is "entirely satisfactory" to the packers. This is all consistent with Gabriel Kolko's assertion that the large packers favored federal inspection, especially if they did not have to pick up the tab.[130]

Armour's biographers wrote, "The first Federal meat-inspection act [of 1890] . . . served to calm the fears of the prejudiced. Although the act was passed largely at the behest of the packers to overcome the political pressure of domestic meat producers in Europe, it became one of the strongest means of attaining virtually complete control of the American market." They also assert that the "federal inspection of meats became the best advertising the packers enjoyed."[131]

The packers repeatedly straddled the fence on federal regulation. *National Provisioner,* the leading trade journal, suggests the packers' position changed rapidly in late May and early June 1906 as negotiations with Roosevelt collapsed. As late as May 26, the *Provisioner* reported that the packers did not oppose the Beveridge bill. An Armour spokesman noted, "Let the federal government control the sanitary and hygienic features of the packinghouse, if by so doing all question as to the wholesomeness of our products is removed."[132] The Neill-Reynolds report was still under wraps, and the packers were in a conciliatory mood.

By June 2, after a breakdown in negotiations, the *Provisioner* was in full attack mode: "President and 'Yellow' Fiction Writer Combine in Underhanded Effort to Destroy American Packinghouse Trade." Neill was a "labor agitator," Reynolds was "a bestirrer of social unrest," and both were "too effeminate to witness the letting of blood." Roosevelt was a modern-day "Nero" and a "criminal." The packers claimed that they had supported the Beveridge amendment, but the bill, which was the work of "theorists, and those whose object it was to strangle the meat trade," had been "rushed" through the Senate and was only now getting "proper" attention in the House.[133] The packers brought in "two scientific experts who made a two days' tour of the Chicago plants." The two University of Illinois professors were generally impressed with the sanitary conditions and offered recommendations overlapping with the USDA report from April. The *Provisioner* rebutted the Neill-Reynolds report at length, often stretching the limits of credulity. In response to the charge that meat was thrown onto the floor, it claimed that "these floors are really immense work 'tables,'" kept "scrupulously" clean.[134]

The packers' attacks on Neill and Reynolds went largely unanswered in light of Roosevelt's concern with forging a compromise that would not further damage American exports. However, in private exchanges Neill left no doubt that he held fast to his convictions. On 13 June 1906, Neill wrote former Commissioner of Labor Carroll Wright that "we simply told what we saw, told it straight, and stuck by it." A few days later, he noted to his brother that he had taken a grilling at the hands of the packers' allies in the House but that he that gotten "the best of it." While being accosted by an unnamed detractor during a break in the hearings, Neill threatened to present further evidence. After he had read one of his many documents to the critic, "the gentleman gasped, looked startled, and held a hurried conference with some of his colleagues—and the hearing was then adjourned."[135]

Following the passage of the 1906 Act, the *Provisioner* claimed that the industry now had the bill it had advocated all along. The leading packers, according to this new spin, had long been begging for more inspectors, making post-slaughter inspection mandatory, examining products intended for interstate commerce at every stage of the production process, and giving the Secretary of Agriculture the power to make rules governing sanitation and the construction of their buildings. They also professed to have wanted the stipulations forbidding the transportation or offering for transportation across state lines of any meat-foods not federally inspected.[136] The historical record offers little evidence to support these claims.

So the packers both supported and opposed legislation, depending on its makeup. From the mid-1880s through the 1906 debacle, they wanted to avoid any health- or sanitation-related controversy that might damage their image and sales. The large packers absolutely hated negative publicity. The correspondence between the large packers and the USDA is replete with requests to hush up problems. As one example, in November 1891, Nelson Morris wrote to USDA Secretary Rusk complaining about actions of Illinois Commissioner Hiram McChesney to suppress lumpy jaw cattle in the state's meat supply. Morris saw the hand of Liverpool-based investors in an Argentine meat canning firm behind the wave of negative news stories. Morris hoped Rusk would "benefit this industry in future [sic] as you have in the past and keep everything out of the newspapers."[137] It is not clear how Rusk responded, but he too blamed those hoping to expand the Anglo-Argentine beef trade with a disinformation campaign against American dressed meat.

The desire of the large packers to control public information was not limited to combating false reporting. When J. Sterling Morton replaced Rusk in the spring of 1893 and patronage positions in the inspection service opened up, he solicited the opinions of Llewellyn James of the Armour Packing Co. in Kansas City. James argued that one of the key job requirements of the chief microscopist was "to keep the young ladies under him from talking too much . . . it is very undesirable to have the public informed through newspapers and other channels as to just the amount of trichina that is found."[138] This factual information, James felt, should remain a secret.

Even when confronted with clear evidence of significant sanitation failings, the packers' first impulses were to discredit their critics and issue blanket denials. This policy of shooting the messenger typified their responses to the veterinarians who discovered the existence of livestock diseases in the mid-1880s—and their responses to claims of health deficiencies in 1890 and 1894, during the Spanish-American War, during the debate on the 1906 Act, in the hearings on the use of chemical preservatives, and over the long controversy dealing with the dangers from trichinosis.

The attitudes and behavior of the Chicago packers did change over time. The passing of old guard and the growth of scientific knowledge contributed to the shift, but so did the inspection system forced upon them. Due to large losses from tuberculosis in cattle and hogs, the packers eventually led the charge for federal and state intervention to eradicate the disease on farms. In 1916, the packers formed a sanitary committee and hired an animal science professor, Howard R. Smith, as their point-man to push for tuberculosis eradication. Smith noted that, before the 1906 Act, the "superficial system" of post-mortem inspection failed to "give complete information as to the prevalence of the disease." He applauded Theodore Roosevelt for appointing a committee of eminent scientists to design more exacting regulations. By his account, the law was primarily a public health measure, but it also enforced record keeping and gave "a true picture" of the prevalence of diseases. In 1917, "enough cattle and hogs were condemned for tuberculosis to fill a stock train twenty-two miles long." The carcasses were rendered into inedible grease and fertilizer.[139] For industry leaders such as Thomas Wilson, the way forward lay in aggressively addressing rather than denying health concerns.

Food Safety before 1906

A hallmark of the public choice literature is to downplay—in many cases deny outright—food safety concerns.[140] By this account, in the absence of problems, rent-seeking bureaucrats clamored for inspection to enlarge their domains. Although there are many unsupported assertions that the large packers had strong quality controls in place, the public choice case rests on theory rather than fact. The packers had huge investments in firm-specific capital that would depreciate in value with a loss of consumer confidence. In the public choice view, packer self-interest thus guaranteed a fastidious attention to hygiene. In addition, consumers were well-served by local butchers and wholesalers, who would lose customers if they did not maintain quality. These market forces ensured that there were no major health hazards.[141] These conceptual notions all make some sense, but so does the argument that there were serious information problems that contributed to unscrupulous behavior. Consumers often could not distinguish between wholesome and unwholesome meats (especially in sausages). Neither consumers nor local butchers could determine whether a dressed carcass came from a diseased animal. Should someone fall ill, it was very difficult to pinpoint the cause. Epidemiologists, let alone individual consumers, would be hard pressed to identify disease organisms or trace them to their source.

As we noted earlier in the chapter, for all the claims of exemplary sanitary conditions, the public choice literature offers little explicit evidence as to how the packers self-policed beyond opening their plants for public tours. It may be that the large packers had higher hygienic standards than their smaller brethren, but no evidence has been proffered that the large packers had medically competent inspectors, let alone about how such inspectors were hired, trained, and supervised. There is no commentary about how the packers updated their practices given new information, or that they supported sanitary research. Running directly contrary to the assertions of high standards and good practices was the litany of documented accounts of butchers, packers big and small, and dealers (in the United States and Europe) trading in sick animals and tainted meat.[142]

Competitive forces may have helped promote hygienic conditions as the public choice literature maintains, but competition also had undesirable consequences. The 1905 BAI report noted that it "is inconceivable" that the plants without trained inspectors could detect most of the animals infected with diseases most dangerous to humans. Due to inadequate enforcement and the absence of legislation prohibiting common carriers from accepting uninspected meats, the plants operating outside the federal system were still shipping uninspected products in interstate and international commerce. These plants had a competitive advantage over inspected facilities. Uninspected abattoirs could put infected carcasses on the market on the same terms as healthy ones. The system of partial inspection thus encouraged "others to operate without it."[143] This claim of a race to the bottom might be dismissed as the self-serving reasoning of bureaucrats angling for a larger regulatory realm and budget, except for the fact that the large Chicago packers repeatedly made precisely the same argument.[144]

A comparison of the extent of meat condemnation before and after the introduction of federal inspection offers a sense of whether the packers were doing an adequate job of dealing with dangerous meat. Under the "rigid system" of local inspection at the Union Stock Yards in the late 1880s, city inspectors condemned as unfit for food roughly 0.025 percent of the hogs and cattle transiting through the facility. Federal inspection greatly tightened standards. In fiscal year 1905 (on the eve of the debates over the 1906 Act), USDA inspectors condemned 26 million pounds of pork, including 0.8 million pounds due to trichinosis. Daniel Salmon reported that "about 3 per cent of the hogs coming to some of our largest abattoirs are affected with tuberculosis," about half of which were so rotten that inspectors ordered the carcasses condemned. About 1 percent of federally inspected cattle were either excluded during ante-mortem inspections at the stockyards or condemned in the abattoirs. Although tuberculosis and hog cholera were the most common cause of condemnation, inspectors discovered numerous other more dangerous diseases such as enteritis, peritonitis, and septicemia. In total, during fiscal year 1905, inspectors found and destroyed 21,555 carcasses contaminated with "acute septic diseases that" are "extremely dangerous" to human health.[145] The 1906 law authorized federal inspection of meat after the post-mortem examination. This proved to be a valuable extension: in 1919, inspectors condemned 17 million pounds of meat and meat products that had become tainted during processing, storage, or shipping.[146]

The BAI's officials were at the cutting-edge of applying science-based regulation to meat inspection. Many of the scientist-public health entrepreneurs who would define the inspection program were among the most respected researchers of their era. After the passage of the 1906 Act, Secretary Wilson appointed a blue ribbon scientific commission to advise in crafting the new sanitary standards. The commission was headed by Professor William C. Welch, a noted pathologist and the founder of the Johns Hopkins University's School of Hygiene and Public Health.[147] The guidelines that governed the day-to-day operations on the shop floor reflected the scientific knowledge of the day and paid heed to the costs and benefits of particular actions.

The BAI conducted research and published numerous studies on meat inspection and livestock diseases. Some of these are still judged as outstanding scientific achievements. As one example, in 1898, Charles Wardell Stiles, the BAI's chief zoologist, who would later make fundamental advances in controlling the hookworm (see Chapter 8), wrote a sophisticated guide for inspectors to help identify parasitic diseases of meat. Stiles analyzed hundreds of flukes and tapeworms. Tapeworms that caused beef and pork "measles" represented serious threats to humans, so proper abattoir procedures were essential for their control. The *Butchers' Advocate* lauded Stiles's manual for providing new and valuable information. Without Stiles's work and without properly trained inspectors, packers were unlikely to have identified many of these problems.[148] Industry leaders would later credit the BAI's scientific and technical knowledge with advancing meat sanitation.

A Comparative Perspective

Across Europe, a common story unfolded that had many parallels with what transpired in the United States. Exposés detailed the butchering of sick and dead animals and shined a light on the filthy conditions in slaughterhouses and local butcher shops. At the same time, scientific advances increased the general awareness of meat-borne diseases and fueled demands for more effective legislation. As examples, between 1883 and 1901, at least fourteen international medical and veterinary conferences contributed to the debate on the dangers of tuberculous meat.[149] At the time, European farmers and meat traders were generally in a state of disease denial and opposed effective regulations.

Between 1889 and 1901, at least ten countries toughened their laws. Within Europe, two polar inspection regimes emerged: the strict German regime and the lax British regime. In Germany, inspection was initially governed by states and municipalities. Many toughened their standards in the second half of the nineteenth century. As an example, in 1868 Prussia passed a law, which Ostertag credited with laying the foundation for "scientific meat control," to promote public slaughterhouses and inspection for cysts. The passage of tougher inspection in Berlin in 1883 led to a dramatic drop in the incidence of tapeworm-related diseases in humans. An 1879 imperial law aimed at preventing the trade in tainted meat represented a weak first step toward national legislation. The Imperial Act of June 1900 (which went fully into effect in April 1903) laid the groundwork for uniform meat inspection throughout the German Empire. It called for ante- and post-mortem inspections. This and subsequent legislation established guidelines for the hygienic design of slaughterhouses and stockyards and for the inspection in stockyards, which would be among the major features of the 1906 Federal Meat Inspection Act in the United States. The Germans faced a serious problem with BTB, with roughly 25 to 40 percent of all German cattle infected. To have condemned all infected animals would have caused sharp increases in the price of meat. The German solution (one followed in many countries) was to establish a separate market in meat from animals infected with tuberculosis. Special shops, termed *freibanks,* restricted sales to final users (that is, no restaurants, hotels, etc.) and informed the buyers of the dangers. Only meat that could not be rendered safe by cooking or pickling was destroyed.[150]

Britain was the most open market in Europe and the major buyer of U.S. meats and livestock. American packers justifiably complained that U.S. meat-inspection laws were far stricter than those in Britain, where regulations depended on local institutions and funding. Urban reformers tried without success to clean up the meat and milk supplies. Their failure reflected the power of the farmer and butcher lobbies. In the nineteenth and early twentieth centuries, Parliament passed numerous acts granting local authorities the power to regulate local meat markets to protect public health and abate nuisances, but because of the measures' failure to provide funding and enforcement, little if any of this legislation was very effective. In London, city officials seized more than 400 tons of contaminated meat between 1861 and 1865, but it is probable that more than that amount had escaped detection and reached consumers. In 1879, "80 per cent of the portions of meat sold in London were said to have been from tubercular animals." Across England, medical officials filed similar reports.[151]

This was also true in Scotland, which has its own history of meat inspection. In 1857, the noted veterinarian John Gamgee (see Chapter 5) reckoned that most of the cows slaughtered for human consumption in the Edinburgh area had been diseased or had actually died from diseases before slaughter. At this time, the Edinburgh Police Act prohibited butchering meat " 'of any animal which may appear to have died of, or been killed in consequence of disease.' " However, the city had only two inspectors to enforce its law. Scottish cattle traders readily avoided urban inspection. Cows that died in Edinburgh were carted to an outlying village, where they were dressed, and the meat was returned to the city for sale. When city inspectors ventured outside their jurisdiction to monitor this traffic, many dead and diseased animals were directed to other markets. A much publicized 1889 Glasgow court case, involving the confiscation of tuberculous meat, attracted the testimony of prominent scientists. When the judge ruled against the butchers, meat trade and farmer representatives pressured their political allies for relief, and the Board of Agriculture refused to confirm the Glasgow ruling. Brief parliamentary hearings pushed by meat interests to whitewash the dangers did little to defuse the uproar. Two royal commissions appointed in the 1890s to investigate the dangers of tuberculosis in the food supply did little. Public health advocates, leading medical and veterinary journals, and newspapers railed that the government's stalling endangered the public. Local standards continued to vary significantly, enabling farmers and traders to direct suspect animals intended for slaughter to locales with weak inspection.[152] The official history of British meat inspection credits the Slaughterhouse Act of 1958 as the first effective national legislation, but even after this date international observers were derisive of British standards.[153]

The shortcomings of England, and to a lesser extent of Scotland, included too few inspectors, the inadequate training of inspectors, the use of former butchers (who had a tendency to side with their former associates) as inspectors, the existence of thousands of small and largely unregulated slaughterhouses, and the absence of coordinated ante- and post-mortem inspection. Local control encouraged the movement of suspect animals and meat to areas with lax inspection. These failings were in large part due to the persistent opposition of farmers and meat traders, who as a group belittled the mounting scientific evidence of serious health hazards. These were precisely the types of problems that existed in the United States, with its fragmented system of poorly managed local and state systems coexisting with the more rigorous federal system. The debates in Britain heated up during the same period in which the push for federal meat inspection in the United States intensified, but in Britain the special interests were able to delay and weaken inspection longer than in the United States. Britain's status as a meat importer meant that it was not susceptible to the types of pressure that it exerted on the United States and other exporting nations. The British story offers considerable evidence of the failure of market forces to regulate meat quality.

Conclusion

The introduction of meat inspection in the United States was a part of a broader international movement. Most European nations, along with the major exporters such as Canada, Australia, New Zealand, and

Argentina, also strengthened and centralized their meat inspection systems. All were influenced by a growing scientific understanding of diseases and by a heightened public awareness that market forces were failing to adequately protect human health. Asymmetric information, free riding, and the unscrupulous behavior by farmers, butchers, packers, and middlemen were not problems unique to any one nation. All major exporting nations implemented meat inspection to provide a seal of approval that would be recognized by foreign governments and consumers. The interindustry rivalries in the United States between the giant meatpackers and local butchers resulted in considerable political controversy, but these domestic disputes cannot explain the more widespread international push for regulation.

Once federal meat inspection was in place in the United States, it became a real lifesaver. Inspection reduced the quantity of meat carrying pathogens that entered the human food chain. In addition, it provided the foundation for an effective surveillance system that aided in detecting and tracking outbreaks of livestock diseases. We agree with the proposition that because the major meatpackers had brand-name reputations to protect, they had *more* incentive than small operators to provide wholesome products. But, as J. Sterling Morton could attest, it does not follow that the giant packers were beyond reproach—far from it. Certainly, the much touted multilayer system of inspection in place in the Chicago stockyards in the 1880s was woefully inadequate. Many large packers at that time opposed having scientifically trained veterinarians near their plants, and many packers made statements suggesting that they did not understand or subscribe to the fundamental principles of disease control. All segments of the livestock industry—growers, dairymen, shippers, and packers—selectively denied major health threats. All fought investigating health problems and enacting effective regulations because they feared exposure might threaten consumer confidence and trade. On multiple occasions, the large packers scrambled to redress serious, long-standing problems, but only after they had been exposed in the press.

The push for early meat inspection offers perspective on the prolonged controversies surrounding the Federal Safety and Inspection Service's introduction of Hazard Analysis and Critical Control Points (HACCP) standards in 1996. The new rules employed stronger scientific

criteria and focused on key points in the production process. They required processors to upgrade equipment and facilities to reduce cross-
contamination, and improve data collection to enhance trace-back capabilities. The HACCP rules raised overhead costs, eliciting howls especially
from small producers. The early meat inspection systems were far more
contentious than the HACCP changes. The goal was to apply science,
albeit a far more primitive science, to limit the spread of pathogens. It
strove for efficiency by focusing inspectors at key check points and by
concentrating on larger plants. The surveillance system in the twentieth
century would prove critical in identifying the extent of diseases and
building political support for control policies.[154]

The findings in this chapter on meat safety dovetail with our results
on trichinosis in Chapter 8. Government officials often overlooked problems to protect markets. There were serious health issues that the major
packers were aware of and ignored. Market forces did a poor job of ensuring high standards. Outside pressure and government inspection
and research helped improve sanitary conditions. Our analysis of BTB
and the milk supply in Chapters 10 and 12 highlights the complexities of
the political economy of regulation and food safety. After long denying
disease problems, the large packers pushed hard for aggressive federal
policies to regulate the dairy industry to control BTB on the farm. The
packers' position on BTB evolved due to the rapid spread of the disease
in cattle and swine and the resulting financial losses they suffered from
condemnations by federal inspectors.

10 Bovine Tuberculosis and the Milk Problem

IN 1919, the Child Welfare Committee of the League of Women Voters launched its campaign for the Sheppard-Towner bill. The law, enacted in November 1921, provided federal matching funds for states to promote investments in child and maternal health. The budget of the Bureau of Animal Industry (BAI) figured prominently in the League's messaging.[1] Advocates sought to shame Congress for spending fifteen times more on preserving the health of young domestic animals than on children, treating the "lamb in the fold" as more precious than "the baby in the crib." BAI spending had long aroused the envy of those seeking similar investments in human health. Lobbying on behalf of the Committee of One Hundred in 1909, Yale economist Irving Fisher demanded that the federal government "remove the reproach that more pains are now taken to protect the health of farm cattle than of human beings."[2] From the One Health perspective, attempts to separate efforts to control human and animal diseases were misguided. The history of bovine tuberculosis (BTB) policy illustrates the complementarity of human and animal health investments.

BTB plays a special role in our story because of its direct impact on human health, its importance in the development of human medical science, and the scale and complexity of the organizational efforts needed to combat the disease in livestock and humans. In 1900, tuberculosis (TB) was the leading cause of death in the United States, taking roughly 148,000 human lives. This was about one out of every nine deaths.[3] Countless more suffered and were permanently crippled. The financial toll of the disease was staggering. Irving Fisher estimated that the total loss to the United States from tuberculosis in 1906 "exceeds $1,100,000,000 per annum. Should this annual cost continue indefinitely, it means a total capitalized loss of $22,000,000,000."[4]

Although the precise fraction is unknown, it is likely that at least 10 percent of these TB sufferers had contracted the bovine form of the disease, most likely from cattle, cattle products, or swine infected by cattle (see the appendix to this chapter). A series of breakthroughs, highlighted by Robert Koch's discovery of the tubercle bacillus in 1882, advanced the understanding of tuberculosis. By 1910, there was a consensus that the bovine strain of tuberculosis (*Mycobacterium bovis*) was distinct from the human strain (*Mycobacterium tuberculosis*). There was also mounting evidence that the bovine strain of the bacteria could be passed between animals and humans, and that it could produce symptoms clinically indistinguishable from the human strain.[5] This evidence, although still controversial within the scientific community, led to local requirements to screen dairy cows for the disease and to proposals to institute a comprehensive test-and-slaughter campaign to eradicate BTB in the United States. Closely coupled with the testing program was the controversial drive to mandate milk pasteurization. Commercially pasteurized milk, which was virtually nonexistent in 1895, composed about 98 percent of the milk supply in major cities by 1936.[6] Both of these initiatives required overcoming the problem of collective action. The eradication program entailed one of the most aggressive uses of police power in the peacetime history of the United States.

Until the development of the tuberculin test in the early 1890s, veterinarians identified the disease in only about one in ten infected live animals and in only about one-half of all tuberculous carcasses in postmortem examinations at slaughterhouses. The disease's deceiving appearances created confusion and contributed to farmer resistance to BTB control measures. Some of the world's most prominent TB researchers argued that the destruction of whole herds, including prized purebreds, was often arbitrary and inefficient, and many farmers complained that the program's administration was heavy handed. For all the controversy, the success of the eradication program, coupled with the spread of milk pasteurization, prevented roughly 25,600 TB deaths per year in the United States circa 1940. The international spinoffs of this achievement were enormous; the BAI created a precedent that would subsequently guide BTB eradication efforts around the world (see Chapter 12).

BTB in Cattle

BTB is an insidious disease because most infected cattle appear normal, yet many of these apparently healthy animals are capable of spreading the disease.[7] As the disease progresses, infected cattle display symptoms similar to those exhibited by humans suffering from TB. It can take years for cattle to develop tuberculous lesions in organs, tissues, and bones. Infected animals have difficulty gaining or maintaining weight, and they lose strength; cows suffer significant declines in milk production and fecundity.[8] Eventually, tuberculous cattle might show external signs of lesions, have coughing attacks (if the disease settles in the lungs), become lethargic, and die prematurely. The disease spreads among cattle through inhalation of airborne agents and via contact with contaminated feed, milk, straw, water, sputum, and feces.

Infection rates were far higher among penned cattle than in free-range animals. The prevalence of BTB also increased with the animal's age. Older stock obviously had a longer period of exposure to contract the bacteria and more time to develop full-blown, highly contagious cases. As a result, BTB was much more common in the proximity of major cities, in dairy herds, in purebred stock, and more generally in the "advanced" agricultural regions of the country. Attempts to improve livestock herds by importing purebred cattle often increased the incidence of the disease. The "backward" nature of the cattle industry in the Southern states helps explain that region's relatively low BTB rates.[9]

The inability to detect the disease in its early but infectious stages made its control nigh impossible. In 1890, Koch's search for a vaccine led to his development of tuberculin—originally, a broth of veal flesh planted with live tubercle bacilli, which after aging was heated and filtered to kill and remove the infectious agent. Although tuberculin proved ineffective as a vaccine, it became an important diagnostic tool, making it possible to detect BTB in animals without visible symptoms.[10] Early applications of the tuberculin test showed that the extent of the infection was far more widespread than had been suspected. Even the most prized and apparently healthy animals harbored the disease: thirty-five out of the forty dairy cows tested on Queen Victoria's Windsor estate reacted positively.[11]

In 1892, Leonard Pearson, who recently had been studying bacteriology under Koch, introduced tuberculin testing to the United States.[12] Shortly after, H. L. Russell of the University of Wisconsin returned from training in Koch's laboratory with tuberculin. When he tested the university's herd, 26 out of 30 animals reacted. Disbelievers were won over when post-mortem examinations confirmed the results.[13] The earliest form of the tuberculin test involved injecting the substance beneath the animal's skin (the subcutaneous test) and checking for signs of a fever. This procedure required many hours of a veterinarian's time and a large quantity of expensive tuberculin. To obtain an accurate result, the veterinarian had to take the animal's temperature, typically three to four times at two-hour intervals, before the injection to establish a baseline reading. Then, beginning about six hours after the injection, the veterinarian again took temperature readings every two to three hours, continuing the process for up to twenty-four hours. Surviving test charts show that to test a herd the veterinarian had to be on site for about thirty-six hours, inspecting each animal from ten to fifteen times. Figure 10.1 shows part of the record of sixty-two animals tested on the farm of Max Freed in Bellevue, Washington. The veterinarian began his baseline temperature tests at 10:00 AM on 16 January 1914, injected the tuberculin at about 8:00 PM, and began the last round of testing at 2:00 PM the following day.[14]

A far cheaper approach, suited to mass testing, became the standard practice in 1920. Employing the new (intradermic) process, the tester injected a few drops of tuberculin into the animal—usually in a flap in the tail—and then returned to reexamine the animal visually two to three days later. If the site of the intradermic injection showed significant signs of swelling, the animal was labeled a reactor. This procedure represented an important labor-saving technological advance. A veterinarian could test three herds in a day—a job that had previously taken a week.[15] Testing was not an exact science. Under either procedure, detecting a "reaction" was a judgment call. Both false positives and false negatives occurred, with some of the false negatives due to recent exposure to tuberculin that "produces a tolerance . . . lasting for about six weeks." Thus, the standard testing protocols required that the subject animal had not been tested in the previous sixty to ninety days.[16]

The fact that tuberculin provided an extended immunity to further reactions had important consequences for its use and abuse. Using privately administered tests, it was possible for livestock owners to detect the disease in their cattle and then sell the reactors to unknowing buyers. Even if the buyers tested the animals, they would appear to be clean. It would take two to three months for the retest to become accurate, and by this time a few sick animals could have infected whole herds. The discovery of the diagnostic technology actually made the operation of markets worse. It widened the information asymmetries inherent in the livestock market, where sellers were typically far better informed than buyers about the characteristics of their animals. "Plugging the test" by recent exposure to tuberculin was a serious problem.[17]

Based on a sampling of tuberculin tests and slaughterhouse inspections, the prevailing wisdom circa 1915 was that 10 percent of the nation's dairy cattle and 1 to 2 percent of all range cattle were infected with BTB. The aggregate rate was approximately 5 percent in 1915, up from 3.5 percent eight years earlier. Tuberculous meat represented a growing health concern, and it accounted for about two-thirds of the beef carcasses condemned during the early decades of federal inspection.[18] Nevertheless, the U.S. cattle infection rate was significantly below those prevailing in Europe, where between 25 and 80 percent of the cattle were tuberculous.[19] The European situation offers a stark picture of how the incidence of the disease might have increased in the United States if left unchecked. Before the start of the U.S. eradication program, the national infection rate was rising at an alarming pace. The proportion of slaughtered cattle retained (that is, those showing visual signs of TB lesions) by federal meat inspectors rose from 1 percent in 1908 to about 2.5 percent in 1917. Of the roughly 220,000 carcasses retained in fiscal year 1917, about 46,000 were so rotten that they were condemned and sent to the rendering tanks to be used for fertilizer, and another 3,000 were boiled to be used in sausage or pet food. The remainder were trimmed of the obvious lesions and declared fit for human consumption. Extrapolating the BTB condemnation rate, and allowing for the disease's spread in the absence of eradication, would suggest several hundred thousand condemnations in 1960. In actuality, there were 282.[20]

The Impact of BTB on Humans

BTB had a zoonotic character that distinguished it from contagious bovine pleuropneumonia (CBPP) and many other diseases that the BAI

RECORD OF TUBERCULIN TEST.

Date: January 16, 1914. Date: January 17, 1914.

No. of Animal	Breed or Markings	Sex	Age	Weight Sep. 20	Amount Injected	Date and Time of Injection	Temperatures before Injection	Temperatures after Injection	Maximum Before Injection	Maximum After Injection	Local Lesions and Decision
1	Holstein		382		4 c.c.	July			102.4	102.2	Healthy
2	"		383		"	"			101.9	102.2	"
3	"		356		"	"			102.5	103.6	Diseased
4	"		425		"	"			103.5	105.6	"
5	"		326		"	"			101.5	101.6	Healthy
6	whitish sion, 0.? ray		340		"	"			100.9	100.9	"
7	Holstein, horned		—		"	"			101.6	101.6	"
8	"		351		"	"			102.7	102.6	"
9	"		395		"	"			101.5	101.6	"
10	"		393		"	"			101.2	101.3	"
11	"		409		"	"			121.1	106.5	Diseased
12	"		358		"	"			101.4	101.4	Healthy
13	"		401		"	"			101.5	101.0	"
14	"		353		"	"			101.5	101.3	"
15	"		385		"	"			102.1	102.1	"
16	the temp up back		—		"	"			101.7	101.8	Suspicious
17	Holstein		372		"	"			101.8	103.6	Healthy
18	"		379		"	"			101.8	102.5	"
19	"		416		"	"			100.7	100.8	"
20	"		374		"	"			101.5	100.5	"
21	"		348		"	"			101.1	105.3	Diseased
22	"		377		"	"			101.9	105.7	Diseased
23	the stab being shall ye not may		424		"	"			101.1	102.1	"
24	Holstein		—		"	"			102.2	102.7	"
25	Holstein		421		"	"			101.3	101.6	"

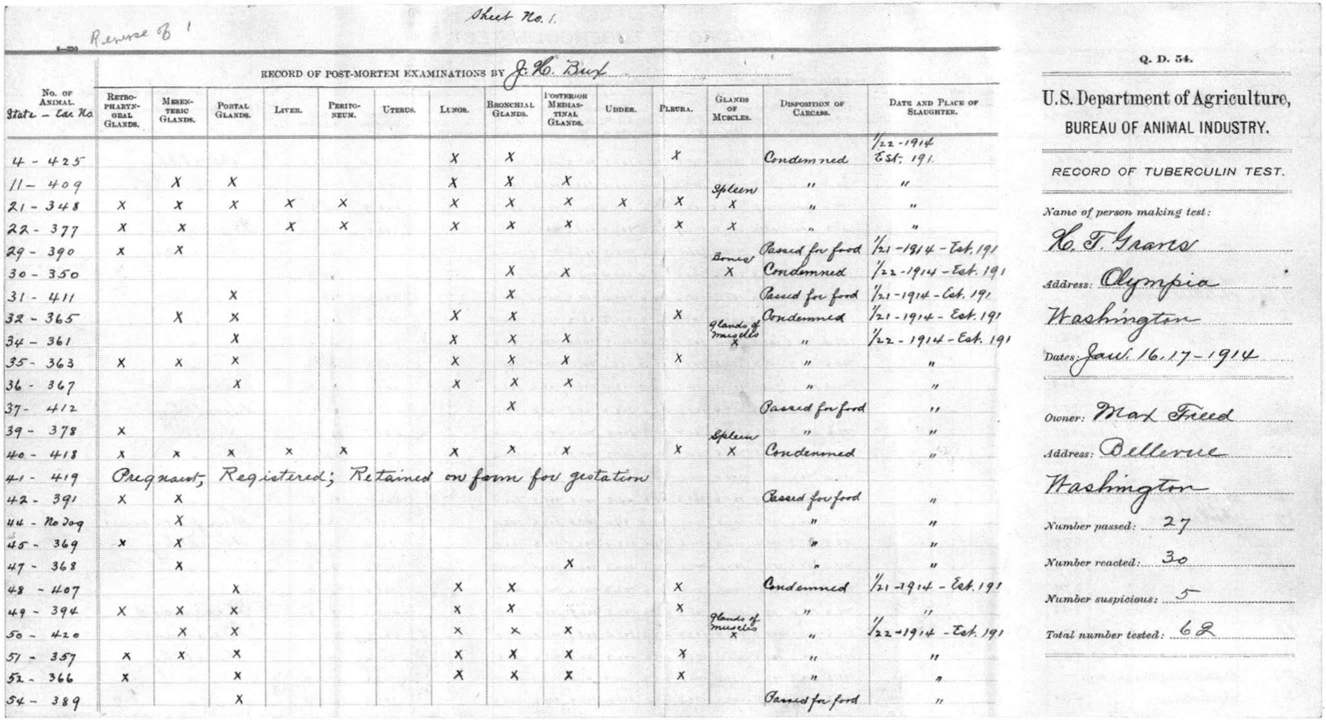

Reverse of 1

Sheet No. 1.

RECORD OF POST-MORTEM EXAMINATIONS BY J. H. Buf

No. of Animal. State – Ear No.	Retro-pharyngeal Glands.	Mesenteric Glands.	Portal Glands.	Liver.	Peritoneum.	Uterus.	Lungs.	Bronchial Glands.	Posterior Mediastinal Glands.	Udder.	Pleura.	Glands of Muscles.	Disposition of Carcass.	Date and Place of Slaughter.
4 - 425							X	X			X		Condemned	1/22-1914 Est. 191
11 - 409		X	X				X	X	X				"	"
21 - 348	X	X	X	X	X		X	X	X	X	X	Spleen X	"	"
22 - 377	X	X		X	X		X	X	X		X	X	"	"
29 - 390	X	X											Passed for food	1/21-1914 - Est. 191
30 - 350								X	X			Bones X	Condemned	1/22-1914 - Est. 191
31 - 411			X					X					Passed for food	1/21-1914 - Est. 191
32 - 365		X	X				X	X			X		Condemned	1/21-1914 - Est. 191
34 - 361			X				X	X	X			Glands of muscles X	"	1/22 - 1914 - Est. 191
35 - 363	X	X	X				X	X	X		X		"	"
36 - 367			X				X	X	X				"	"
37 - 412								X					Passed for food	"
39 - 378	X												"	"
40 - 418	X	X	X	X	X		X	X	X		X	Spleen X	Condemned	"
41 - 419	Pregnant; Registered; Retained on farm for gestation													
42 - 391	X	X											Passed for food	"
44 - No Tag		X											"	"
45 - 369	X	X											"	"
47 - 368		X							X				"	"
48 - 407			X				X	X			X		Condemned	1/21-1914 - Est. 191
49 - 394	X	X	X				X	X			X		"	"
50 - 420		X	X				X	X	X			Glands of muscles X	"	1/22-1914 - Est. 191
51 - 357	X	X	X				X	X	X		X		"	"
52 - 366	X		X				X	X	X		X		"	"
54 - 389			X										Passed for food	"

Q. D. 54.

U.S. Department of Agriculture,
BUREAU OF ANIMAL INDUSTRY.

RECORD OF TUBERCULIN TEST.

Name of person making test: H. T. Graves

Address: Olympia Washington

Dates: Jan. 16.17 - 1914

Owner: Max Freed

Address: Bellevue Washington

Number passed: 27

Number reacted: 30

Number suspicious: 5

Total number tested: 62

Figure 10.1. Tuberculin test results in Bellevue, Washington, January 16–17, 1914. *Source:* Dr. Jens Madsen (Bureau of Animal Industry inspector) to A. D. Melvin, 30 January 1914, and charts, Entry 3, Box 340, U.S. BAI Records.

confronted. The quest to understand the linkage between tuberculosis in animals and humans was a slow process marked by many heresies and trips down blind alleys. In 1898, Theobald Smith (by this time, a professor at Harvard University) identified differences in the bovine and human strains. In 1901, Koch seriously misinterpreted Smith's findings and proclaimed that BTB posed little threat to humans and, indeed, that exposure provided children with immunity against the human form. Koch's declarations helped galvanize the opposition to BTB eradication efforts. In 1901, the *Breeder's Gazette* offered a sense of the rage, noting that for years "half-baked scientists and zealots" with tuberculin squirt guns have been "beating tom-toms and brandishing the pole-axe, crying 'Kill, Kill.' This fierce and bloodthirsty campaign against our herds has been waged on the disputed assumption that tuberculosis in cattle is a menace to the public health." The *Gazette* charged that the "servile worshippers of asserted authority" had done millions of dollars in damage.[21]

The controversy intensified in December 1905 when Koch asserted that "bovine tuberculosis is not transmissible to man," in his Nobel laureate address. Prominent researchers challenged Koch's views. As an example, M. P. Ravenel, a Pennsylvania state veterinary official, isolated the bovine microorganism from a child with tuberculous meningitis in 1902 and found the microbe in a child's mesenteric lymph nodes in 1905. For most scientists, this was inconvertible proof. However, in spite of these and other findings, Koch adhered to his erroneous beliefs for more than a decade, thereby lending support to those groups and individuals opposed to regulating tuberculous cattle and infected milk. The controversy continued to echo in public debates about TB control long after the scientific arguments were settled.[22]

There remains considerable uncertainty about the incidence of bovine tuberculosis in humans and the number of deaths it caused before the introduction of livestock sanitation measures and milk pasteurization. A widely cited summary of studies conducted in the United States before 1939 found that *M. bovis* accounted for 11.7 percent of all TB infections.[23] However, the contemporary studies conducted both in the United States and Europe typically suffered from small sample sizes and selection biases. We suspect undercounts because many infants who died of intestinal disorders caused by *M. bovis* infections probably were never properly diagnosed. In addition, many studies cited as offering indicators of the problem in the preintervention age were in fact conducted after eradication programs and milk pasteurization campaigns had already reduced the rate of human infection.

In sharp contrast with those contemporary accounts, the recent medical literature commonly asserts that the bovine share of human deaths or infections was in the 20 to 30 percent range circa 1910. We review the contemporary and recent literatures in the appendix to this chapter. There has been a consensus that bovine-type infections were far more common in nonpulmonary cases and in children, especially infants, because of the consumption of untreated milk and their lower resistance to the disease. It is also evident that in the absence of the control programs, the rates would have risen as the disease spread among livestock.

Private Solutions

Both consumers and producers had strong motives to eliminate BTB from their everyday lives. However, in spite of growing awareness about BTB, private incentives did not yield a solution to the problem for the community at large—to the contrary, the disease was spreading. Health-conscious consumers should have been willing to pay a higher price for BTB-free meat and milk, but even if a few consumers possessed the expertise and equipment required to identify the tuberculosis bacteria in their food supplies, actually doing so would have been very expensive. Given this situation, one private market solution would have been for entrepreneurs to organize independent monitoring agencies to test and approve foods for the health-conscious market. In fact, private agencies did arise as part of the "certified dairy" movement, which was organized by public-spirited citizens. Initiated in 1893 by the New Jersey physician Henry L. Coit, the movement established local Medical Milk Commissions to enforce dairy hygienic standards, which included tuberculin testing the cows.[24] Approved dairies eventually opened across the country, and, operating under the aegis of local physicians, marketed their dairy products under the "Certified Label." The problem was that, in practice, inspections were infrequent and lax. Confidence in certified dairies took a big hit in 1916 when muckraking reporters exposed unsanitary conditions and tuberculous cattle at the movement's most prominent establishment, the Fairchild Dairy in Montclair, New Jersey.[25] Certified milk sold at a substantial premium over regular milk, and never captured more than 2 percent of the market.[26] Consumers could boil their milk on their own, but this was costly, time-consuming, and not foolproof unless done properly. Boiling also adversely affected the milk's taste. A consumer who contracted tuberculosis from milk could spread the disease to other humans (just as with *M. tuberculosis* cases), but the legal system provided few incentives for individual households to internalize the costs they might impose on others when taking precautions.[27]

Individual cattle owners also had strong private incentives to reduce the exposure of their herds to tuberculous animals, and many went to great lengths to do so. But several forces worked against achieving the socially optimal level of disease prevention. Owners had little incentive to prevent their animals from infecting others; the microscopic nature of the BTB organism, its long incubation period, and the innumerable channels of infection made it almost impossible to document in court when and how a sick animal (or person) contracted the disease. When an owner chose to cull his herd, he could reduce his losses by selling the infected or suspicious stock to other farmers or to meatpackers. As noted above, the tuberculin test made selling diseased stock easier.

A cattle owner could reduce the likelihood of exposure by maintaining a physically isolated, closed herd. Besides the out-of-pocket costs of maintaining protective barriers, this approach also denied farmers the advantages of specialization and raised the cost of replacing animals. It closed several of the main avenues for dairy improvement in the early twentieth century: engaging the services of a prize bull, competing in livestock contests at fairs, and participating in cooperative creameries (which returned the pooled skim milk to feed to calves). Moreover, it would be more efficient to build a fence around the entire country than to create barriers around each and every farm. The problems of achieving private solutions to the growing threat of BTB generated demands for governmental intervention. An analysis of the costs and benefits of government efforts requires that we have a better grasp of how policy options (such as eradication and quarantines) relate to the initial extent of infection and to the dynamics of its spread.

Options for Controlling BTB in Livestock

Although scientists had long discussed eradicating BTB, almost all European states chose to segregate infected animals and to try to block contaminated meat and milk from entering the food supply. The disease was so prevalent that killing all infected animals would have caused unacceptable food shortages. Reflecting this view, the acclaimed Danish veterinarian Bernhard Bang noted in 1896 that "in most European states a compulsory and quick butchering of all these animals is out of the question, the number of the reacting animals is so very large."[28] Impure food was preferable to insufficient food. Bang called for eliminating animals with advanced cases, periodically testing the entire herd, and isolating nonreactors into what became known as "Bang" herds. Germany followed an even less aggressive approach developed by Robert Ostertag, which did not employ the tuberculin test at all: only animals with open lesions were destroyed, and visibly infected animals were tracked. The Manchester plan, prevalent in England, called for periodic testing of milk for tubercle bacilli; when discovered, authorities traced the milk back to the dairy and tested the individual animals. The plan did not call for eradicating infected herds.[29] In all cases, the inadequate enforcement of these general plans left large gaps in coverage. In all countries, farmers contributed to the problem by denying and hiding the disease.

The BAI officials, who pursued the more aggressive goal of eradicating BTB, carefully considered how to gain the "hearty cooperation of the owners."[30] The program advocates argued that the government must pay indemnities to gain support, but they recognized that there were trade-offs because compensation payments could discourage farmers from protecting their herds. To ensure the disease was eliminated on a given farm, authorities conditioned participation and indemnity payments on testing the farmer's entire herd, removing the reactors for immediate slaughter, and disinfecting the premises before allowing the nonreactors to return. To reduce the spread across farms within a region, the officials expanded the geographic scale of the test-and-slaughter campaign under the so-called area plan. Authorities imposed quarantines to limit the spread of the disease across regions. To prevent "plugging," the BAI pushed to control the supply of tuberculin.

Of course, in designing the program it was not sufficient to consider the operation of individual incentives alone. As repeated experimental evidence reveals, many people are willing to contribute more to public good provision—here, suffer a loss of their own diseased cattle to reduce the aggregate level of infection—than pure self-interest would dictate.[31]

And again, for many people "equitable" treatment matters—they are willing to participate in a mutually beneficial venture if they receive a share of the benefits commensurate with the costs they bear. Cooperation with the program presumably would have been low if the losses from condemnation threatened to push farmers out of business. Apart from any sense of "fairness," farmers were more likely to be willing to participate if they knew their neighbors were also cooperating—otherwise, a participating farmer would take a loss, only to risk having his herd reinfected. These lessons on how to align incentives and manage the BTB program were informed by the real-world experiences of many states. As BAI program head J. A. Kiernan observed, the program designers could not simply "figure this out on paper."[32]

Laboratories of Reform

Within a few years of the introduction of tuberculin testing to the United States in 1892, many states and large municipalities had enacted regulatory measures to protect their citizens. State and local programs displayed enormous variety in keeping with Louis Brandeis's depiction of states as "laboratories of reform" in American federalism. The most vigorous early campaign began in Massachusetts. In 1894, the state enacted a strict, compulsory anti-BTB program that included quarantines, comprehensive testing, and partial compensation. In 1895, the state responded to farmer protests by offering full compensation. Farmers now jumped at the "opportunity to get rid of sick or unproductive cows at public expense," and expenditures soared—in 1896 and 1897 the program cost $550,000, mostly for compensation. This was an enormous sum— when Congress kicked off the national effort in 1917, it only allocated $75,000 (see Chapter 12). Fierce opposition continued, and in 1898 the state shifted to a voluntary program employing visual inspections instead of tuberculin testing. The Massachusetts experience provided other states with a striking object lesson, "showing how not to do it."[33]

Pennsylvania adopted a voluntary plan with free tuberculin testing in 1896. Visibly ill animals were destroyed, with the owner receiving the salvage value and a partial indemnity. This approach proved far more popular with dairymen than the 1894 Massachusetts program. Owners of reactors could choose either to slaughter reactors with partial compensation or to isolate reactors and heat their milk to kill the bacteria.

The latter choice essentially mirrored Bang's approach in Denmark. Given the complications of keeping segregated herds and the low price received for sterilized milk, most Pennsylvania cattle owners opted for the slaughter of their sick animals.

By 1900, many other states (and some cities) had initiated anti-BTB programs.[34] In Wisconsin, the state and the university designed programs to encourage widespread testing and remove reactors. Knowledge about how to use (and abuse) tuberculin was diffused broadly, even to undergraduate agricultural students and farmers attending university short courses. In Illinois, an experiment with aggressive measures provoked a backlash among powerful dairy interests, so the state shifted to providing voluntary testing of herds with no compensation for reactors. The New Jersey State Tuberculosis Commission offered testing of individual animals (rather than herds) and paid full compensation for reactors slaughtered. The State Board of Health bore the responsibility for BTB control in New York, providing partial compensation for condemned reactors. In Michigan, reactors were either isolated or slaughtered without state compensation. Delaware, Maine, Maryland, Minnesota, New Hampshire, Rhode Island, and Vermont also enacted legislation falling within this broad range of policy options.[35] Everywhere, some highly vocal farmers resisted the programs. In Massachusetts, Illinois, and Wisconsin, farmers forced the states to scale back their initiatives. At the municipal level, Chicago and Milwaukee led the way in 1908 with ordinances requiring testing of cows supplying milk to their citizens. Farmers responded with milk strikes and lawsuits. These varied experiments taught public health officials that they needed widespread farmer support to succeed.

BTB control measures stifled interstate and international trade. In 1891, Maine quarantined cattle from Massachusetts to prevent the spread of BTB; New Hampshire followed suit the next year. In 1900, seventeen states required tuberculin testing of cattle imported from other states for breeding and dairy purposes. The number increased to thirty-four states one decade later, and by 1917 such restrictions were virtually universal.[36] In addition, the USDA had required tuberculin testing for animals imported into the United States after 1900. Most state programs dictated that reactors be permanently marked by branding, tattooing, or tagging the animal's cheeks or ears. The myriad state and local attempts to control BTB before 1917 failed to yield permanent results and were particularly ineffective in controlling the interstate shipment of infected animals. On the contrary, state and local controls often encouraged farmers to ship reactors to neighboring states. As with CBPP, Texas fever, and other diseases, the states turned to the federal government for a centralized and coordinated policy.

The drive for mandatory milk pasteurization took a different course, primarily because of differences between the political economies of milk regulation and of those livestock disease control and meat-safety regulation. Powerful urban public health movements driven by consumer interests focused on milk safety. As we saw in Chapter 9, many public choice advocates have ignored or downplayed the importance of consumer interests in explaining the origins of meat inspection. But the evidence for milk is too overwhelming to obfuscate. Urban reformers, backed by both the conservative and liberal media, could control the local distribution of milk and thus impose their policies on outlying farmers. Milk did cross state lines, but local milk regulations could not be easily evaded. Dairymen tried, but as we detail in the next section, the courts eventually sided with urban consumers. Once within the city, the milk could be tested and destroyed if farmers had failed to cooperate. The products from outlying dairies that did not pass inspections could be banned. As a result, the pasteurization movement was largely a set of local movements. The federal government provided strategic support by generating research and other valuable public goods.

The Milk Problem

At the dawn to the twentieth century, health authorities were facing the "Milk Problem." Far from being "nature's perfect food," the fluid was so dangerous that it was sometimes called "white poison."[37] Under prevailing conditions, milk was an excellent medium for the multiplication and transmission to humans of the bacteria that cause typhoid fever, paratyphoid fever, diphtheria, streptococcal (septic) sore throat, scarlet fever, milk fever, undulant fever (brucellosis), dysentery, and other gastrointestinal infections (including many caused by *Escherichia coli* due to fecal contamination), tuberculosis, and many other diseases. As of 1908, epidemiologists had positively linked about 500 U.S. epidemics of typhoid fever, diphtheria, and scarlet fever to the milk supply. There were undoubtedly many more not enumerated.[38]

Contemporaries often asserted that about one-half of all infant deaths circa 1900 resulted from gastrointestinal complications and that a large fraction of these were due to milk-borne infections. Many historians have repeated these assertions. However, Samuel Preston and Michael Haines suggest that these early claims were exaggerated and that a better-grounded estimate was closer to one-quarter of all infant deaths were due to gastrointestinal diseases. Nonetheless, the toll was staggering, and contemporaries had good reason to associate many of these deaths with cow's milk. In the summer months, when it was harder keep milk cool, diarrhea deaths soared. Moreover, studies comparing the death rates of breastfed and bottle-fed babies reveal stark differences. For example, a study by the U.S. Children's Bureau covering eight cities between 1911 and 1915 found that the mortality rates for breastfed babies was one-quarter to one-third of the rates for artificially fed babies.[39]

Health reformers sought to improve the milk supply through two related efforts. The first concentrated on cleaning up and regulating the sanitation of dairies and milk handlers, with the goal of preventing disease-causing organisms from entering into the milk supply and multiplying. The second effort, focused on pasteurizing milk, aimed at destroying those harmful bacteria, molds, and viruses that escaped the cleanup efforts.

Over the late nineteenth and early twentieth centuries, most cities established milk regulations with commissioners (often physicians) to improve the sanitary conditions.[40] The USDA and state agricultural colleges got on board, publishing educational materials to instruct farmers on the newly understood dangers and on how to clean up their premises and procedures. Much of the advice would now seem obvious: use pure water supplies, wash the cow's udder and the milkers' hands, test milk workers to ensure that they were free from communicable diseases, control insects and rodents, and take precautions against introducing foreign matter into the milk (in particular, the use of covered pails designed to keep out cow droppings). Municipalities intensified the regulation of milk distribution within cities, inspecting holding plants, milk wagons, and stores; imposing standards for bacteria counts; and educating mothers about proper care of milk in their homes. In many large cities, private charities, such as those run by Nathan Straus, as well as local health departments established milk depots to provide clean milk to the poor, especially in the summer months.

The second major thrust of urban authorities to clean up milk supplies was more controversial: mandating pasteurization of all milk (with exceptions for certified raw milk) and requiring animals supplying milk to have passed a tuberculin test.[41] Pasteurization, a procedure known since the 1860s, involved heating the milk to kill disease-causing microorganisms. Much had to be learned before the practice could gain wide scientific and consumer appeal. Early techniques killed the bacteria that spoiled the milk but not those that spread disease to humans. This represented a bane to health because it allowed bad milk to remain in the market longer. As a consequence, many cities in the 1880s and 1890s actually banned the practice. Over time, as bacteriologists gained more knowledge, it was possible to kill the harmful bacteria and produce a safer product.

Pasteurization advocates debated whether it was preferable to heat milk to a high temperature for a short period (the so-called flash method) or to heat it to a somewhat lower temperature for a longer period (the so-called holding method). In 1906, Milton J. Rosenau, a public health physician working at the U.S. Marine Hospital, showed that the low and slow method (60°C for 20 minutes) killed the pathogens without imparting the "cooked" taste that had inhibited consumer acceptance. The consensus opinion over the early twentieth century shifted in favor of the holding method, and many cities enacted milk codes requiring use of this technique. The debates over the legislation were typically highly contentious, even long after Rosenau and others had demonstrated the extraordinary benefits of pasteurization. Noted physicians held that pasteurization destroyed some as yet undiscovered vital nutrients, and many consumers raised on raw milk preferred its taste and texture.[42]

In 1900, commercially pasteurized milk was a rarity in the United States. Over the next three decades, the supply of pasteurized milk increased rapidly. Based on data compiled from a number of surveys, Figure 10.2 charts the diffusion of pasteurized milk in cities of different size classes from 1902 to 1936. As early as 1915, most milk in major U.S. cities was pasteurized. In 1912, New York City imposed stringent requirements permitting only pasteurized or certified raw milk. Most large cities, including Boston, Philadelphia, and Baltimore, soon followed. By 1915, even in places without prohibitions on uncertified raw milk, consumers could purchase pasteurized milk if they desired. Commercially pasteur-

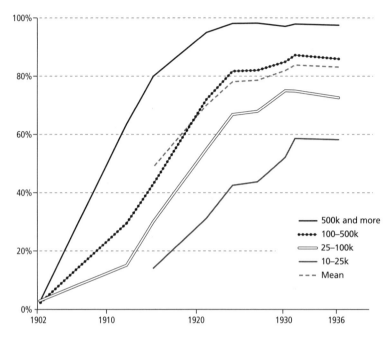

Figure 10.2. Extent of milk pasteurization by city size, 1902–1936. *Source:*
Compiled from Henry E. Alvord and Raymond A. Pearson, "The Milk
Supply of Two Hundred Cities and Towns," *BAI Bulletin,* no. 46 (Washing-
ton, DC: U.S. Government Printing Office, 1903); Edwin O. Jordan,
"Municipal Regulation of the Milk Supply," *Journal of the American Medical
Association* 61 (1913): 2281–91; S. Henry Ayers, "The Present Status of the
Pasteurization of Milk." *USDA Bulletin,* no. 342 (Washington, DC: U.S.
Government Printing Office, 1916), *USDA Bulletin,* no. 342, revised
(Washington, DC: U.S. Government Printing Office, 1922), *USDA Bulletin,*
no. 342, revised (Washington, DC: U.S. Government Printing Office,
1926); S. Henry Ayers, R. P. Hotis, and C. J. Babcock, "The Present Status
of the Pasteurization of Milk," *USDA Bulletin,* no. 342, 1932 revised
(Washington, DC: U.S. Government Printing Office, 1932); Ira V. Hiscock
and Robert Jordan, "The Extent of Milk Pasteurization in Cities of the
United States," in *Thirteenth Annual Report of the International Association of
Dairy and Milk Inspectors* (Washington, DC: Ivan C. Weld, 1924), pp. 89–97;
Leslie C. Frank and Frederic J. Moss, *The Extent of Pasteurization and Tuberculin
Testing in American Cities of 10,000 Population and Over in 1927 and 1931* (Public
Health Service, mimeo, 1932), pp. 2–7; A. W. Fuchs and L. C. Frank, "Milk
Supplies and Their Control in American Urban Communities of Over 1,000
Population in 1936," *Public Health Bulletin,* no. 245 (Washington, DC: U.S.
Government Printing Office, 1939), pp. 25, 29.

ized milk composed about 98 percent of the milk supply in major cities by 1936.[43]

Conflicts over Municipal Tuberculin-Testing Requirements

As part of this broader pure milk movement, Chicago, Milwaukee, and most other major cities issued regulations requiring tuberculin testing of cows supplying urban markets. The reach of the laws ranged beyond the city's limits to cover its entire milkshed, sometimes even extending into other states. Such regulations ignited a maelstrom of protest from dairy operators and milk dealers that lasted for years. In response to a 1908 Chicago ordinance, dairy organizations turned to the Illinois legislature. Edward Shurteff, the Speaker of the House and attorney for the "downstate" (non-Chicago) dairy interests, convened a special investigating committee. In 1911, the joint committee issued a 2,000 page report opposing tuberculin testing and pasteurization. Repeating Koch's long-discredited theories and liberally twisting the evidence, this document became a mainstay for the opposition for many years. In 1911, the legislature overturned existing municipal pure-milk ordinances throughout the state and prohibited cities from enacting future regulations. This rollback remained in effect until a new governor, Chicago-based reformer Edward Dunne, took office in 1913.[44]

These early disputes between the metropolitan interests and dairies often turned violent, with farmers repeatedly blockading milk shipments. Dairymen saw the health regulations as unilateral mandates that raised production costs without providing adequate compensation. The *Breeder's Gazette* sided with the opponents: "Strange as it may seem there is still suggestion of the 'kill all' policy—to kill all reacting cows. It would be a sad day if any legislature should so far forego sanity as to enact such a statute. It would mean a shot-gun reception to the . . . inspectors— a state of real anarchy. There must be more of fact and less of hypothesis before such a policy can be adopted in the name of public health."[45]

Both sides turned to the courts. The dairy interests prevailed in some lower courts, but the higher courts, beginning with the Minnesota Supreme Court in 1896 and including the U.S. Supreme Court's *Adams v. Milwaukee* decision (228 U.S. 572, decided 12 May 1913), almost universally upheld the constitutionality of the public health measures. We count at least eighteen other state supreme court cases adjudicated in

nine states dealing with the testing and destruction of tuberculous cattle.[46] As Figure 10.3 depicts, pure-milk crusaders saw these decisions as
a victory of good over evil.

Conflicts between municipal governments and organized dairy suppliers over tuberculin testing and pasteurization continued into the
1930s in America's major milksheds. One might think that producers of
high-quality milk would support reforms to reduce competition from
lower-quality producers, but we found little evidence of such divisions
rapidly creating competitive pressures to improve quality. To the contrary, as we show here, dairymen throughout Illinois rallied to support
other dairymen who were clearly involved in corrupt practices. Not until late 1926 did a group of Chicago-area dairy producers break away
from the disease deniers to form the Pure Milk Association. This association's members adopted a stance friendly to the city's revised tuberculin testing regulations. But many, probably most, dairy farmers in the
Chicago milkshed continued to fight the city's ordinances for years.[47]
Metropolitan governments were gradually winning the battle to improve milk safety, but the link between urban legislation and BTB control ruptured when it came to limiting the trade in infected animals.

Regulatory Arbitrage

State and local health regulations of goods and capital that could be
easily traded across state boundaries led to predictable problems, which
eventually increased the demand for interstate cooperation and federal
intervention. In 1914 the *Breeder's Gazette* prophesied that, in response to
the stricter enforcement of Milwaukee's tuberculin testing law, Wisconsin farmers would ship suspect cows to Illinois.[48] In fact, farmers and
cattle dealers had been arbitraging between the state regulatory regimes
for years.

On 25 May 1910, S. H. Ward, the State Veterinarian of Minnesota,
informed A. D. Melvin, Chief of the BAI, that Illinois residents were buying reactors in Wisconsin for re-export to other states. Ward singled out
James Dorsey of Gilberts, Illinois, as the principal offender. Gilberts (near
Dundee in Figure 10.4) was in the Elgin district, which bordered Chicago
and extended to Wisconsin. Melvin responded on 6 June 1910 that "immediate steps will be taken to investigate this matter." However, Dorsey
proved to be a slippery foe, and it would take the BAI several years to

THE COURTS SUSTAIN THE PASTEURIZATION ORDER.

Figure 10.3. Justice prevails. *Source:* Lina G. Straus, *Disease in Milk: The Remedy Pasteurization, The Life Work of Nathan Straus,* 2nd ed. (New York: E. P. Dutton, 1917), p. 108.

shut him down. Indeed, Dorsey would continue selling cattle up to the day he was finally indicted in 1915.[49]

In August 1914, the federal government and the state of Illinois began to crack down on a criminal conspiracy known as the "Tuberculous

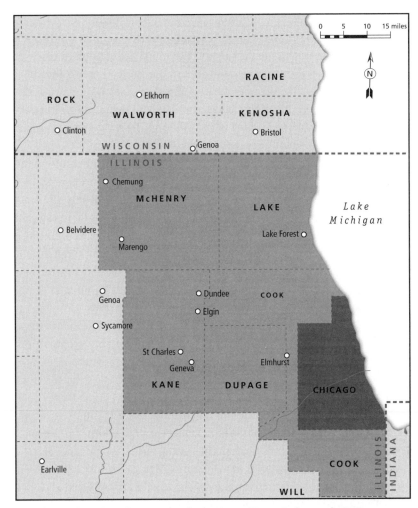

Figure 10.4. The Elgin district: Cook, DuPage, Kane, Lake, and McHenry counties. The distance between Dundee, Illinois, and Genoa, Wisconsin, is about 30 miles. *Source:* George Whitaker, "The Milk Supply of Chicago and Washington," *BAI Bulletin*, No. 138 (Washington, DC: U.S. Government Printing Office, 1911), p. 15.

Cattle Trust," imposing a five-county quarantine. The press had a field day, writing front-page headlines proclaiming that the "Entire West Has Been Flooded with Diseased Dairy Cattle for Last Ten Years" and that "Prosecutions Are Expected." The government charged that a group of Elgin cattle dealers had defrauded farmers and endangered the public by knowingly selling diseased animals, often with falsified bills of health. The editor of a major veterinary journal asserted that in addition to Dorsey "about ten other dealers in the Elgin district" traded in diseased animals and that they all operated under the protection "of the dairy interests of Illinois, the most powerful political organization in the state." By 1914, the tubercular dairy cows were widely dispersed among the "herds supplying Western cities with milk and have sown the 'seeds of death' in thousands of homes using this milk."[50]

Although many Elgin area dealers were trading in tuberculous cattle, the federal charges singled out Dorsey, the largest broker. In fact, USDA officials asserted that he "was for many years probably the leading dealer in dairy cows in the United States," shipping cattle to Canada, Mexico, and to nearly every state in the Union. At the height of his business, Dorsey was purportedly buying and selling annually some 20,000 animals, of which about one-half were tuberculous. Beginning as a small-scale dealer in 1904, Dorsey came to operate a number of large, modern farms and advertised in the leading farm journals. He achieved this rapid ascent by trading in "animals that had reacted to the tuberculin test or that the dairyman had reason to believe were tuberculous and wished to dispose of before the test was applied to his herd."[51]

Thousands of dairymen who knowingly supplied the diseased stock were complicit in the conspiracy. According to the St. Louis Republic, "It was clearly understood among many cattlemen that if tuberculosis developed in a herd that all that was necessary was to communicate with the 'clearing-house' at or near Elgin and a buyer would appear who would take over the cattle at a reduction of but $5 to $10 on the head below the market price." This made it very costly for farmers to "do the right thing" and slaughter their reactors. Farmers in Wisconsin (where the state provided partial compensation) could cut their losses by roughly one-half by selling to an Elgin broker; farmers in Illinois (which paid no compensation) could cut reduce their losses by about 80 percent.[52]

Importing animals from Minnesota, Wisconsin, Michigan, Pennsylvania, and several other states, Dorsey then paid unscrupulous Illinois veterinarians to sign certificates of health that fraudulently claimed that the cattle had passed a tuberculin test; in this manner, he falsified the standard approval mechanisms previously trusted in the marketplace. He also had veterinarians perform tests and issue certificates of health for sound animals in his home herd, which included cattle of a variety of ages and descriptions. Dorsey then used these valid certificates to ship diseased animals of similar appearance.[53] In many cases, he created phony paper trails and used surrogates to market the cattle to unsuspecting buyers. According to the BAI's "conservative" estimate, "Dorsey established at least 10,000 foci of tuberculosis among the dairy herds of this country."[54] This likely led to thousands, perhaps tens of thousands, of humans contracting the disease. In comparison with Dorsey, the infamous Typhoid Mary, who was once dubbed "the most dangerous woman in America," was a mere piker, responsible for forty-seven confirmed cases of typhoid fever and three deaths.[55]

The trail leading to Dorsey's arrest was littered with failed private and state attempts to stop his trade. In the early 1910s, state officials, individual farmers, their lawyers, and BAI inspectors from across the country barraged BAI administrators in Washington, D.C., with complaints about Dorsey and other Elgin cattle dealers. Major farm journals also joined the anti-Dorsey effort. As an example, in June 1913, *Hoard's Dairyman* published an announcement that warned farmers about Dorsey's dealings and noted that for several years the magazine had refused to accept his advertisements. After mid-1914, *Orange-Judd Farmer, Prairie Farmer, Twentieth Century Farmer,* and *Breeder's Gazette* all stopped carrying Dorsey's ads. Attacking Dorsey by name carried the risk of a libel suit.[56]

It was fairly easy for Dorsey to counter these private sanctions. As his notoriety increased, he took steps to hide his involvement in cattle transactions. He found accomplices to place ads in their names, and when other states quarantined his cattle and eventually the entire state of Illinois, he drove his animals overland and shipped them out of Wisconsin under an alias. Dorsey's complex laundering schemes made it very difficult for regulators to track animals. By 1913, the interstate trade in cattle was in disarray, and by 1914 at least a dozen states were quarantining cattle from Illinois.[57]

Railroads had long resisted state and federal requests—and later demands—to help control the movement of tuberculous animals, just as they had resisted government effort to take precautions against CBPP, Texas fever, and other diseases. During the early twentieth century, federal courts had strengthened the states' authority, opening the way for more effective controls (see Chapters 4 and 5). As one example, Missouri's regulations as posted in January 1914 required railroad companies to do much of the state's enforcement and held them liable if they failed to comply. Before shipping dairy and breeding cattle into the state, the railroads had to forward copies of health certificates to the state veterinarian. Furthermore, Missouri and numerous other states would not accept health certificates unless they were signed by *the* Illinois State Veterinarian or by federal agents. Animals accompanied by certificates signed by rank-and-file Illinois veterinarians would be subject to 90-day quarantines and then had to be retested at the owner's expense. South Dakota officials went further, requiring railroads to obtain a BAI inspector's signature on a health certificate to import "all live stock of any class" from Illinois. Without this paperwork, the animals would be subject to a state quarantine and tests at the owners' expense. Many other states pursued similar policies, with some mandating that payments be withheld until after the animals passed a sixty-day retest.[58]

Railroads began to feel the heat from the regulations and legal claims and sought policies to absolve themselves from liability claims. At the same time, they began to shut out the trade by refusing to accept shipments from Dorsey or other tarnished dealers. Meatpackers, hammered by BTB losses, urged states to enact tougher laws. The packers and livestock commission dealers in Chicago also began blacklisting individual shippers whose animals had proven to be tuberculous in the past, and beseeched various state veterinary officials to inspect the offenders' stock.[59] The various uncoordinated state and private initiatives were not working well.

With the widespread fraud and the costly loss of trade, state veterinarians united in petitioning the USDA to quarantine the entire state of Illinois.[60] The decisive blow came when the USDA announced that on 1 October 1914 it would quarantine Lake, McHenry, Kane, DuPage, and Cook Counties, thereby prohibiting the movement of cattle into or out of the area (except for those cattle destined for immediate slaughter).[61] These and subsequent state and federal actions against the Elgin area dealers put a major dent in the trade in tuberculous cattle, but the problem persisted. The Montana state veterinary surgeon determined that 9 percent of the purebred cattle brought into the state in 1916 were infected with BTB; as late as 1919, dairy farmers across the country were complaining that they had unknowingly bought infected cattle.

Many states were still imposing quarantines on breeding and dairy stock. Others were insisting on federal certificates for cattle imports because they did not trust officials and procedures in "tabooed" states. For example, Minnesota would not accept state certificates from Kansas or Iowa, Maryland would not accept New York state certificates, and so on. In 1919, Howard R. Smith (who represented Chicago stockyard interests) confirmed that state health certifications were of little value because many U.S. states and Canada only recognized tests conducted by federal inspectors.[62]

As a postscript to the Dorsey affair, justice was slow and convoluted. A federal grand jury indicted Dorsey in September 1915. After lengthy delays, the trial began on 23 January 1919 in the court of the famed jurist Kenesaw Mountain Landis (the first commissioner of baseball). The jury convicted Dorsey on January 31, and two weeks later Landis sentenced him to eight years in Leavenworth Penitentiary. The irony is that Dorsey was convicted of mail fraud, not of violating laws prohibiting the shipment of diseased animals. In 1920, President Woodrow Wilson commuted the sentence to four years because of Dorsey's poor health (which outraged Landis, who publicly lambasted both Dorsey and Wilson).[63]

The Dorsey case highlighted the failures of both the tort-based system and reputational solutions. The case demonstrated the futility of relying on the tort system to collect damages. The records of the BAI contain letters from state officials and attorneys from across the country noting suits or intents to sue Dorsey. All of the sixty-two cows that Max Freed of Washington State received from Dorsey (see Figure 10.1) had supposedly passed a tuberculin test in Illinois on 14 November 1913. When they arrived in Washington, many showed signs of BTB, so they were retested by a state livestock commissioner: thirty reacted and five were "suspicious." Fifteen of the reactors had such advanced cases that the carcasses were condemned. Freed initiated a suit in 1915, but he dropped the action when Dorsey settled out of court for one-half of the claimed loss. But this partial success was an exception to the general rule. W. H. Lytle, the Oregon State Veterinarian, noted in November 1913 that he saw little hope that the numerous "swindled" dairymen in his state would receive any redress unless Dorsey entered the state.[64] The handful of injured parties who won verdicts against Dorsey received little, as the trial had consumed much of his wealth. Given the enormity of the total losses, it was inevitable that most victims would not be compensated.

Second-party reputation mechanisms were also ineffective.[65] Dorsey's example reveals how reputation (and its recognized association with large scale and with advertising) could be manipulated. He attained high standing in the Elgin community, and both prominent local farmers and large-scale outside buyers reported to be "absolutely satisfied" with their repeated transactions with Dorsey. Thus, he created a concentrated local body of goodwill. He exploited this to engage in a form of informational market discrimination. His fraud was committed primarily against a diffuse and distant collection of small-scale, one-time purchasers, who found pursuing their complaints through the courts costly.[66] Dorsey's deceptive practices employed fraudulent third-party certifications. He contracted for tuberculin tests by supposedly independent veterinarians who, in fact, he paid to produce falsified papers. As part of the fallout from the widespread fraud, the representatives of five states met in Columbus, Ohio, in the fall of 1914 to draft common guidelines including rules for designating approved veterinarians. This was one of the many attempts to restore the interstate cattle trade. By that time, the practice of "plugging the test"—by preexposure of animals to tuberculin—was such a widespread problem that the test material became a controlled substance in most jurisdictions by the early 1920s.[67]

The Dorsey case had long-lasting repercussions, galvanizing demands for federal intervention. In fact, policy makers were still referring to problems Dorsey had caused for the livestock trade and the dairy industry twenty years after his conviction. A growing consensus held that only federal measures could remedy the interstate conflicts.[68] Stockyard interests, meatpackers, and Western cattlemen led the push for federal regulations. The standard public choice reaction to calls for increased regulations is to emphasize that the desires of special interests will limit competition. In this instance, there were serious market failures and serious health threats to livestock and humans, and federal intervention was sought to restore trade and improve market efficiency. In the case of Western cattlemen, it is hard to see how they would have benefited from cutting off their access to breeding stock. As we showed in Chapter 9, the Chicago interests were well positioned to see the increased flow of tuberculous stock into their yards and packing plants, and they were keenly aware of the failures of state policies and of the tort system to address the problem.

Conclusion

By the onset of World War I, much had been learned about BTB. Scientists had discovered the tubercle bacilli, demonstrated that tuberculosis was a contagious disease, developed a diagnostic test, identified a separate bovine strain, found this strain in infected children, and derived a rough sense of the prevalence of BTB in livestock and humans. The USDA had developed a post-mortem meat inspection system (in 1906; see Chapter 9) that provided quantitative evidence on the spread of the disease in livestock and protected the public from diseased meat. Authorities had begun testing dairy herds for the disease, and had figured out the parameters of effective pasteurization techniques. Armed with this knowledge of the disease and of the terrible cost it imposed on the farm sector and on human health, reformers campaigned to clean up the milk supply. Some states took steps to curtail the trade in tuberculous cattle, require testing of milk cows and breeding stock, and eradicate the disease within their jurisdictions. At the same time, municipalities increasingly attempted to protect their citizens by regulating the urban milk supply. The campaigns took two related tracks. One was to remove the source of contamination by shutting down swill dairies, cleaning dairies to remove feces and other foreign matter from milk, and requiring dairies and distributors to properly wash their equipment. This was no small task, but the bigger challenge required by this path was to identify and destroy sick animals. The second track was to clean contaminants from the milk itself via pasteurization.

Many dairymen and prominent dairy organizations fought legislative reform and publicly attempted to obstruct it when reforms were passed. But behind the scenes there was another form of insidious opposition: thousands of dairymen simply sold their sick animals to others. Market makers emerged to increase the size and scope of this nefarious trade. James Dorsey was the largest and most infamous of these dealers in tuberculous cattle. He and others took advantage of the very invention that made it possible to detect the disease before slaughter. By injecting tuberculin into diseased animals, they suppressed reactions for over six weeks, making it possible to resell the animals to unsuspecting buyers. The Dorsey case exposed the predictable flaw in the hodgepodge of uncoordinated private, state, and local initiatives to control BTB. Regulatory arbitrage was relatively easy and widely practiced. To counter state regulatory failures, many states imposed strict and costly quarantines on livestock traffic. Large segments of the farm community—the press, meatpackers, and many farmers—along with urban health advocates pleaded for the federal government to act. We address the development and operation of the federal eradication campaign in Chapter 12.

APPENDIX: Estimated Incidence and Impact of *M. Bovis* in Humans

Incidence

There is much uncertainty about the incidence of *M. bovis* in humans before BTB control policies, milk sanitation, and other measures dramatically reduced the risk. In recent years, *M. bovis* accounted for less than 2 percent of all human TB cases in the United States.[69] *M. bovis* was a far more serious problem in the past, but pinning down precise estimates of the incidence and the resulting deaths remains challenging. As an example of the wide range of estimates, the Centers for Disease Control and Prevention note that between 1900 and 1930 "*M. bovis* was isolated from 6%–30% of human tuberculosis patients in the United States and the United Kingdom."[70]

The historian Thomas Dormandy speculated that bovine tuberculosis accounted for about 15 percent of all TB deaths around 1900.[71] The recent medical literature commonly places the *M. bovis* share of all U.S. TB cases (and in some studies the share of all TB deaths) in the 20 to 25 percent range before 1917.[72] The veterinary epidemiologist Calvin Schwabe asserted that in the United States around 1900 "the form of the disease that then accounted for up to 10 percent of human pulmonary tuberculosis, and almost all human tuberculosis of other organs, was contracted from cattle rather than from other people."[73]

The paucity of early U.S. data has led many to refer to the European experience for guidance. Wayne Dankner et al., based on an analysis of case studies dealing with the interwar years in England, concluded that "bovine tuberculosis accounted for up to 25% of all human tuberculosis and 2 to 5% of pulmonary tuberculosis."[74] Myers and Steele report a number of higher incidence estimates: for example, Dr. Franklin Top, who served in Germany during the Allied occupation, "estimated that 30% or more of human tuberculosis in southern Germany, in the late 1940s and early 1950s was of the bovine type." Reports from U.S., French, and British scientists in occupied Germany lend credence to the severity of the problem.[75]

The conventional wisdom associates *M. tuberculosis* with pulmonary infections and *M. bovis* with nonpulmonary infections, although both forms can reside inside and outside the lungs. In adults, pulmonary infections were more common and more deadly. Both recent and historical studies suggest that roughly 50 percent of adult *M. bovis* sufferers exhibit nonpulmonary infections whereas about 10 to 15 percent of *M. tuberculosis* cases show nonpulmonary manifestations. In young children, about 90 percent of bovine infections are nonpulmonary.[76] So establishing the incidence of *M. bovis* in humans does not directly translate into establishing the death rate.

Case studies conducted in the United States and Europe before pasteurization became widespread suggest that roughly 1 to 20 percent of pulmonary infections and 20 to 60 percent of the nonpulmonary cases (infecting the skin, genitourinary system, bones, joints, intestines, eyes, lymph nodes, brain, and other locations) were of the bovine type. All of these forms were more prevalent in children than in adults, and all could be fatal; tubercular meningitis was nearly always fatal, and was a major killer of youngsters.[77]

In a survey of studies conducted up to 1927, B. Möllers reported that the bovine type accounted for 22.2 percent of cases of tuberculosis infections in children up to age 16, for 2.2 percent of adult cases (over 16 years of age), and 11.1 percent of total cases.[78] The greater prevalence of the bovine type in children was a general finding. R. M. Price's 1939 summary of scores of independent investigations, involving about 18,000 tests conducted around the world, suggested that the total incidence of bovine tubercle bacilli in human tuberculosis infections was approximately 10 percent.[79] The percentage of all tuberculosis cases in humans (as opposed to deaths) that were *M. bovis* varied widely across countries; the estimate for the United States was 11.7 percent. The estimates of Möllers and Price, which have been widely cited, were averages of the disparate case studies.

There are both upward and downward biases in the literature that Möllers and Price analyzed. In some cases, the tests for the bovine form were conducted because of a suspicion that it was present. In other cases, especially for young children with intestinal problems, physicians just did not bother to look. *M. bovis* infections were most lethal for infants, and according to the Cambridge pathologist Louis Cobbett there were an "enormous number of deaths from tuberculosis among children which never get recorded as such."[80] In addition, many of the investigations underpinning Price's result covered the period well after significant advances in milk sanitation and the introduction of measures to control TB in cattle, and thus likely understated what the infection rate was in the early twentieth century.[81]

Another reason to suspect that BTB was more serious than the older literature suggests is that most studies were conducted at large urban hospitals and underrepresented rural residents who had had frequent contact with cattle. Several studies conducted in England and Wales concluded that *M. bovis* was a negligible problem in adults and was a minor factor in pulmonary cases. This view led to an understatement of the dangers of *M. bovis*.[82] The development of a simpler test for type determination in Denmark in 1932 facilitated larger-scale studies. This, and a greater focus on rural populations, led to the realization that "bovine infection plays a much greater role in tuberculosis in man than assumed previously." Studies conducted in the 1930s and 1940s in Scotland and on the European continent discovered high rates of pulmonary tuberculosis infections of the bovine type in populations that lived near or worked with infected cattle.[83] The most thorough research was conducted in Denmark, where about 60 percent of all tuberculosis of the lungs in the farm population who had been in contact with heavily infected cattle was of the bovine type. Nationally, the study found that 5.3 percent of pulmonary TB and 23.4 percent of meningeal TB was of the bovine type.[84] These results suggest that, circa 1910, the bovine type accounted for many more cases of pulmonary TB among U.S. farmers and their families than had been supposed.

The upshot is that there is a wide gap between the relatively recent medical literature and most studies conducted in the early twentieth century as to the incidence and impact of *M. bovis* on humans. There is little basis for accepting the recent claims that about 25 percent of all TB deaths were due to *M. bovis,* but there are many reasons to suspect that *M. bovis* infection and death rates were higher than the older studies suggested. Both *M. bovis* infections and death rates appear to have varied widely among nations and regions.

Children were the principal victims. Among infants in particular, there is good reason to suspect far higher death rates than recorded by early observers. Infants with intestinal tuberculosis would have exhibited symptoms indistinguishable from other common diarrhea-inducing diseases. Pulmonary infections of the *M. bovis* type were far more common in rural areas than in cities. Such pulmonary infections were contracted by association with infected cattle—likely by inhalation of aerosols or infected dust particles—and from other humans.[85] Most studies investigating this issue looked at adults, but there is no reason to suspect that young farm children could not have contracted the disease in this manner.

Lives Saved

We now can estimate the savings in human lives resulting from eliminating BTB in cattle and milk. Three sets of estimates are presented, based on the assumptions that the bovine form initially accounted for 5, 10, or 20 percent of TB deaths. We consider the 10 percent figure the best benchmark. All the calculations assume that the eradication and pasteurization efforts reduced the actual *M. bovis* death rate to virtually zero by 1940. The measured death rate due to TB was 194.4 per 100,000 people in the United States in 1900.[86] The assumption that that *M. bovis* accounted for 10 percent of TB deaths yields a death rate of 19.4 per 100,000. The U.S. population was 131.7 million in 1940. Extrapolating the 1900 rate to 1940 (0.000194 times 131.7 million), implies that the elimination of the bovine form saved 25,600 lives in 1940. If the initial relative incidence of the bovine form was 20 percent, as much of the recent medical literature asserts, it implies that 51,200 lives were being saved in the year 1940. If the relative incidence of all TB deaths was 5 percent, the savings would be 12,800 lives. These estimates are admittedly crude because they ignore other forces working to increase or decrease the BTB death rate.

There were two potentially offsetting forces: the possible decline of the *M. bovis* death rate in line with what was occurring with the nonbovine form *M. tuberculosis,* and the likely increase due to the continued spread of the disease among animals in the absence of the eradication efforts. We know the total TB rate fell from 194.4 deaths per 100,000 in 1900 to 45.9 in 1940. However, it was unlikely that the bovine rate would have fallen in line with the nonbovine rate because BTB largely attacked a different population (the young), and it typically had an entirely different means of transmission. In fact, between 1900 and 1915, while the death rate from pulmonary TB (which was most associated with *M. tuberculosis*) declined by 32 percent, the death rate from nonpulmonary TB (highly associated with *M. bovis*) actually rose by 4 percent.[87] Given this evidence, we assume that the bovine rate would have remained constant in the absence of public intervention. On the other hand, without the eradication effort, BTB would have spread further among the cattle and swine populations, likely leading to a more than doubling of the livestock infection rate by 1940. This would have pushed the human disease and death rates higher.

11 The Eradication of Texas Fever

Conflict and Cooperation

CATTLE TICKS existed in Europe, Africa, Asia, the Americas, and Australia, but until 1906 nobody had seriously embraced eradication on a continental scale. The scientific and political obstacles were simply too imposing. To overcome private coordination failures, clearing cattle ticks from the United States required the massive application of government police power that affected the day-to-day activities of millions of farmers and extensively regulated intrastate and interstate trade. The Bureau of Animal Industry (BAI) launched a coordinated national vector-eradication campaign on 1 July 1906. The Bureau's tick program extended to fifteen states, segregating much of the South and a large part of California. This heavy-handed campaign fostered dramatic productivity increases but also ignited raw sectional and class conflicts. The cattle tick eradication campaign was part of a much larger effort; at the same time that the BAI ramped up this work, it was also immersed in parallel campaigns to eradicate sheep and cattle scab. In 1906, roughly three-fourths of the United States was under federal quarantine to stamp out parasitic livestock diseases. The lessons learned in fighting other diseases helped, but many of the institutional changes needed to eradicate pests had to be created *de novo*—and often in a hostile setting.

Creating the State-Federal Cattle Tick Eradication Campaign

With the breakthroughs of Theobald Smith, Cooper Curtice, and Frederick Kilborne, a few visionaries perceived that it might be possible to eradicate Texas fever. In 1896, Curtice floated the idea of cleansing large areas of the United States of ticks. By the early 1900s, North

251

Carolina and Virginia had set precedents by eradicating cattle ticks in counties near the quarantine line. These state campaigns involved outreach and education, along with coercion—including fencing laws and restrictions on moving cattle. Virginia, for example, imposed heavy fines on cattle owners who allowed tick-infested animals onto highways or commons. In these early experiments, many farmers were still cleaning ticks by picking them off by hand.[1]

As with most technological advances, the discovery of the cattle tick's role in the transmission of Texas fever required a succession of secondary discoveries to make eradication truly feasible. Curtice's studies of the tick's life cycle added to the understanding of the disease's transmission. His finding that ticks could not mature without attaching to a host suggested that if pastures were free of cattle for a sufficient period—about eight months, depending on the weather and the season—the ticks would starve to death, and the field could be cleansed. These life-cycle studies led Curtice to the novel conclusion that Texas fever could be controlled by killing the cattle tick. Veterinarian Calvin Schwabe considered this research so important that he acclaimed Curtice the "father of vector control." Curtice's revelations encouraged research across the South to establish various cattle rotation regimes to cleanse both fields and animals by starving the ticks. One scheme called for moving the animals every two weeks. Within about two months, the animals would be tick free, but the cattle had to be kept out of infested fields much longer to cleanse the land.[2] These rotation plans all required fenced pastures and entailed the additional cost of leaving land idle or devoting it to other uses. Before embarking on a more ambitious campaign, scientists also had to determine whether other animals, such as horses and deer, could serve as alternative hosts of the vector ticks.[3]

The discovery that Texas fever could be fought by attacking the cattle ticks led to a quest to discover cheaper and more rapid techniques to kill ticks. The search for effective poisons and application methods took nearly two decades.[4] Circa 1893, R. J. Kleberg, the secretary of the Texas Livestock Sanitary Commission, constructed a concrete dipping vat on the Santa Gertrudis Ranch in Nueces County, Texas. He placed the vat at the disposal of the BAI in 1894. Over the next five years, federal and state researchers tested myriad chemicals on more than 25,000 cattle, seeking a poison that would kill ticks without seriously harming the

stock. High-grade crude petroleum was the USDA's recommended product until around 1910.

However, the application methods were not standardized. As of
1906, some BAI agents were still recommending the "Oklahoma system," which required roping the cattle, throwing them to the ground,
and greasing them completely with crude oil.[5] In 1906, BAI veterinarian
Joseph Parker began to develop arsenic solutions. This research benefited from experiments with arsenic conducted in South Africa, Australia, and Cuba. In a sign of increasing federal-state cooperation, the
BAI had assigned Parker to work with the Texas Livestock Sanitary
Commission.

In November 1911, an arsenic-soda-pine-tar mixture called "boiled-
dip" became the officially approved dip for the interstate movement of
cattle out of the quarantine zone. Arsenic-based dips represented a key
discovery in tick eradication—they were cheap and effective.[6] The standard dipping protocol eventually called for treating the cattle every two
weeks. A first dipping killed the female ticks before they could fall to
the ground and lay eggs. Next, the cattle were repeatedly sent back into
the pasture to act as bait for the remaining ticks. After eight to ten dippings, all the ticks would be eradicated, if everything went well.[7] Figure
11.1 shows a dipping operation in Florida. Because the ticks also at-
tached to horses, they too had to be dipped regularly.

In addition to better technologies, the BAI officials needed stronger
support within the South before they could proceed. To this end, state
and federal agents conducted experiments across the South to demonstrate that the ticks could be killed. In 1905, the BAI's new chief, A. D.
Melvin, began corresponding with Southern officials to assess their interest in joining a federal campaign to eliminate the tick and to accu-
mulate information on the state laws and existing eradication efforts. In
the summer and fall of 1905, several national and regional associations
petitioned the federal government to initiate a cattle tick extermination
campaign. Momentum for an orchestrated campaign was building.

In November 1905, the Southern States Association of the Commissioners of Agriculture met in Richmond Virginia. Several state and federal officials addressed the group on cattle tick eradication. Based on
their optimistic reports, the association's members petitioned Congress
to appropriate $500,000 for the USDA to begin cattle tick education and

Figure 11.1. Cattle dipping: "Canals to Progress." *Source:* Florida Department of State, Division of Library and Information Services, "Florida Memories," www.floridamemory.com/fpc/memory/PhotographicCollection/photo _exhibits/Ranching/Images/_pr01396.jpg.

eradication. The U.S. Live Stock Sanitary Association, the national organization of state livestock regulatory officials, joined the campaign, calling for more aggressive action. Many Southern congressmen now supported this initiative in the hope of freeing the South from the costly federal embargo.[8] Congress responded with an initial appropriation of $82,500 to the USDA for tick eradication. It is notable that the start of this program to combat a livestock disease in the South predated any efforts by the federal government or large national philanthropies to fight maladies such as hookworm and malaria afflicting the people in the region.[9]

Building the Institutions for Effective Policy

With the new congressional mandate and funding, the BAI's leaders began their epic cattle tick eradication campaign on 1 July 1906. In December 1906, federal and state officials met in Nashville, Tennessee, to plot future directions. A key concern was the adequacy of the laws and institutions in the tick-infested states. Georgia, Kentucky, Oklahoma Territory, Tennessee, and Virginia all had legislation in place for effective joint state and federal action. The other infected states either had very weak animal health infrastructures or no germane legislation whatsoever.[10] This had to change if eradication was going to succeed.

The BAI generally concentrated its efforts in the territory near the national quarantine line.[11] To help guard against reinfestation, the Bureau encouraged states to target relatively large areas for eradication. The state would then draw its own quarantine line to prevent the movement of uninspected cattle in and out of the eradication area. In addition, counties and farmers had to pay a large part of the cost. Once a county signed up, participation was mandatory for all cattle owners, and the movement of cattle from neighboring counties even inside the quarantine area was prohibited. The expenses were shared. The federal government would provide funds only when the lower branches of government also anted up hard cash and formalized plans for cooperation. In general, dipping vats were built by local farmers and were either privately financed or paid for out of local and state coffers.

When eradication began in 1906, most Southern states had local-option regimes, which gave each county the choice of whether to participate. The political infighting was intense. In Simpson County, Mississippi, the "local government had opposed the program, but in 1913 a local veterinary inspector presented a petition signed by seven hundred citizens" supporting eradication. However, after opponents presented a petition with 1,500 signatures, the supervisors held fast in their refusal to cooperate. Struggles of this nature occurred across the South, with impassioned meetings, injunctions, court proceedings, and local elections on eradication.[12] The failure of some counties to support eradication eventually led Southern state governments to mandate participation.

Figure 11.2 highlights the progress of the tick eradication campaign. It presents for selected dates between 1906 and 1937 the status of tick eradication across the South and Southwest. Every state had a different story, and we will touch on only a few. In general, the border states approached high levels of eradication fairly rapidly. This was in part because colder weather made the task easier and in part because many counties in these states had begun eradication before 1906. Tennessee, which started eradication work in 1896, led the way.[13] It took about four years to convince many farmers in Tennessee that the regulations that prohibited letting cattle "run at large" meant precisely what they said. "At one time in a single county, forty-two people were indicted for violating the regulation."[14] The state supreme court settled the issue in favor of the state in 1909. In 1911, the new Republican governor, Ben Hooper, appointed a tough-minded State Veterinarian George R. White. When some counties refused to cooperate, White locked down all their shipping points and enlisted circuit court judges to warn that violators would be fined and incarcerated. These measures led to general compliance; by the close of 1913, the quarantines could be lifted in most of the state.[15]

A key element in the BAI's strategy was to prod local leaders into funding pilot programs so that farmers could see that tick eradication was actually feasible. The hope was that once a program got under way, opposition would wane. This tactic worked in Hinds County, Mississippi, where BAI agents persuaded the dubious county supervisors to fund the construction of twenty-five concrete dipping vats in 1912. The changes in Hinds County were representative of a larger picture; in 1913, Mississippi officials supervised roughly 3 million dippings in the state. During the first decade of eradication, Mississippi was a local-option state, which meant that supporters had to win a local election before proceeding. In 1916, Mississippi adopted a statewide law requiring dipping. This change led to near eradication by 1918, but ticks soon reinfested large areas. Extensive internal quarantines had to be reinstated in the early 1920s, and Mississippi would not be cleared of ticks until 1930.[16]

The problem of ticks making a comeback was common to many other states. Figure 11.3 summarizes the Louisiana story. Between about 1915 and 1918, the state made significant progress in freeing land. In 1918, the state's farmers employed nearly 4,500 vats to dip almost 15 million head—2.5 times the number dipped in Oklahoma, the second most active state. However, after this surge, Louisiana fell on hard times: the ticks made a comeback after cuts in the eradication budget. Louisiana (with parts of Florida and Texas) had a special problem because the state harbored the more aggressive *Boophilus microplus* tick, which proved harder to eradicate. A 1932 report noted that although Louisiana had been "losing ground and for the last five or six years, a new start has been made." To regain the initiative, the Pelican State imposed a special 1¼ percent tax on milk and meat products to finance the program.[17] The revitalized program managed to clear the state by 1936.

Texas, with its large cattle population and long-standing history of opposition to the BAI, warrants special attention. In 1906, owing to the lack of funding, the state did not employ any additional men for tick work, but it did allow its regular inspectors to cooperate with BAI agents if they had free time. The BAI sent eleven agents to seventeen counties located at northern edge of the quarantined area in Texas. Given that the line bisected much of the state, this meant that federal agents were working in the heart of Texas, albeit with no independent authority to enter property or order dipping. Texas had a constitutional provision that explicitly prohibited granting powers to federal agents to act as officers of the state. They could work only on an informal basis with local officials and ranchers, many of whom were anxious to get their lands released from quarantine. One manager of a large ranch offered to contribute "$50,000 on condition that the work be undertaken in his county and with the understanding that his cattle might be given an unrestricted northern market." Between August and the end of October, 1906, BAI agents inspected 410 herds with 185,857 head of cattle.[18]

Despite this promising start, state laws and widespread opposition slowed progress. Under the local-option rules of Texas, eradication opponents could force a countywide vote with a petition signed by seventy-five landowners, and circa 1915 the opponents almost always won these contests. To speed progress, the Texas state government passed legislation to make eradication mandatory in 1917, but the law did not take effect until 1919, and then only in the northern part of the state. The legislation called for shifting the legal boundary in stages over the following

A. February 1906

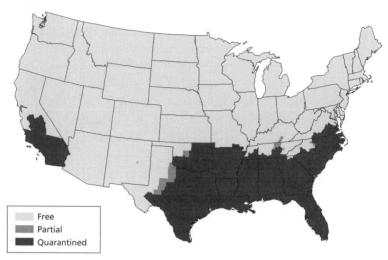

B. December 1917

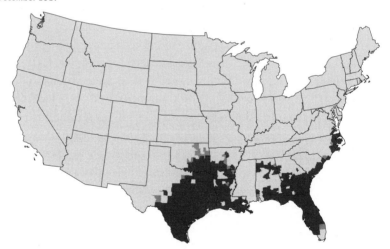

Figure 11.2. Area quarantined for Texas fever, 1906–1937. *Source:* U.S. Bureau of Animal Industry, *Report for 1906,* pp. 339–46; *Orders,* no. 255, 308, 363.

C. December 1927

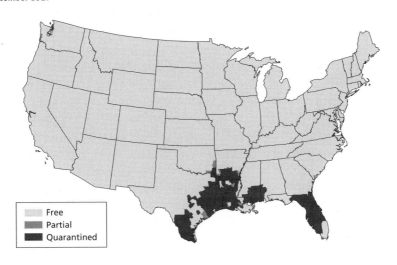

D. December 1937

decade. As in other parts of the South, there was often considerable ten-
sion between state officials, who pushed for eradication policies, and
many local officials, who were more responsive to constituents who
were hostile to the program.[19]

By 1920, many veterinarians were disdainful of the failure of Texas to
enact stronger measures. "In view of the fact that all of the Southern
states, with the exception of Florida and Texas, have worked conscien-
tiously and at great expense to obtain results now experienced, it is hardly
fair or just that the interstate shipment of ticky cattle from these two states
should jeopardize the live stock industry of eight other states that are suc-
ceeding in cleaning up." However, focusing on the official stance of Texas
masks the state's considerable progress. By the end of 1916, over 37,000
square miles of once infested land had been released from quarantine—
only California surpassed this achievement. Work in Texas accelerated

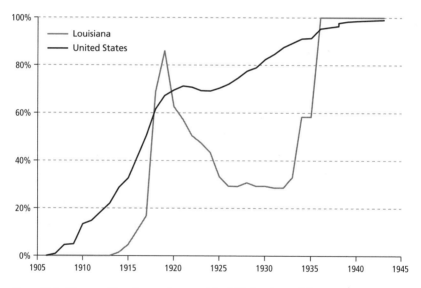

Figure 11.3. Share of land area (covered in 1906) released from quarantine,
Louisiana and United States, 1906–1943. *Source:* Compiled from U.S.
Bureau of Animal Industry (BAI), *Report for 1906*, pp. 339–46; U.S. BAI,
Orders, no. 141, 151, 158, 168, 194, 207, 341, 255, 262, 269, 271, 275, 279,
285, 290, 296, 300, 309, 312, 321, 328, 332, 339, 343, 349, 358, 360, 363,
369, 372, and 374.

after the state government more fully came on board. By 1 December 1918, "Texas operated 1,800 dipping vats and dipped during the season 4,929,013 cattle." Only Oklahoma and Louisiana dipped more cattle in that year.[20]

By 1929, roughly 80 percent of the original national quarantine area had been cleared, and by 30 June 1940, about 99 percent of the original territory was tick free. Pesky pockets remained in eight Texas counties, which were subject to reinfection from Mexico, and four Florida counties where white-tailed deer served as hosts. In a highly controversial move, after years of wrangling, officials culled the deer population in large areas of the state. In 1944, Florida appeared to be free of ticks, but subsequently the state experienced several outbreaks due to either the survival of ticks on wild animals or reintroductions from the Caribbean. Cattle ticks also continued to be a problem in a buffer zone in Texas that stretches roughly 500 miles along the Rio Grande, an area that remains under quarantine today.[21]

Removing the Texas Fever Exemption

In early 1914, the USDA Secretary requested that Congress remove the exemption for Texas fever that had been written into the BAI's organic legislation. This would have placed Texas fever on the same basis as other communicable diseases. The change was endorsed by the U.S. Live Stock Sanitary Association and the Southern Cattlemen's Association. Nothing came of this effort. In 1926, Congress again considered removing the Texas fever exemption at the behest of the states of Georgia, South Carolina, North Carolina, Florida, Alabama, and Arkansas. This change would allow the BAI to prohibit the interstate movement of infested cattle even for immediate slaughter. Southerners who had invested to free their lands of ticks sought to stimulate eradication in areas "where it had been lagging."[22] Texas representatives obtained an amendment allowing a two-year grace period ending on 1 May 1928. During this interregnum, cattle from infested areas could still be shipped in interstate commerce for immediate slaughter if they had been dipped once. When the grace period ended, the secretary could issue such regulations as he deemed necessary.

The opinion of USDA officials in 1926 was that Secretary Rusk had overstepped his authority when he declared Texas fever "a contagious and infectious disease" in 1889—the BAI had been working in a legal gray area for almost four decades. Arguing in favor of the 1926 measure, Representative Charles Crisp of Georgia repeatedly noted that the USDA had no authority to make rules and regulations governing Texas fever. USDA Secretary William Jardine and BAI Chief John R. Mohler shared this view even though they were at that very moment enforcing such rules. Under the existing transport regulations, the disease frequently re-infected cleansed areas. As a result, many state veterinarians prohibited cattle shipped from infected areas from unloading.[23] Despite the growing power of the federal government and the establishment of uniform national policies, the courts still recognized that the states had considerable leeway to control trade on health grounds.

The bill passed the House overwhelmingly, with 307 in favor and 26 opposed. The voting patterns and floor debate reveal the divisions that had arisen within the South as tick eradication progressed. Some representatives from Texas, Florida, and Louisiana, which remained tick-infested states, opposed the bill even with the favorable amendment. The vote divided Southern Democrats, who accounted for all 26 nays votes and 74 of the yea votes. The debate in the Senate was short, and the vote was positive but not recorded. President Coolidge signed the Act on 28 June 1926.[24]

Educational Initiatives

Education campaigns and community meetings were a standard component of most of the BAI's disease-fighting programs. The tick work in the South presented special problems because of the low literacy rate and the challenge of explaining the complicated parasite-disease relationship. However, the impact of the South's distinctive conditions probably has been overemphasized because it was also difficult to convince farmers in other regions of the causes and effects with other diseases. During the bovine tuberculosis campaign, for example, reluctant farmers needed to be persuaded that injecting their animals with tuberculin was safe.

In any case, BAI and state officials devoted considerable resources to educating farmers, along with business and community leaders, about the damage ticks inflicted and the process and benefits of eradication. Promoters had to convince disbelieving farmers that dipping cattle in toxic solutions was safe and that ridding areas of ticks was even possible. This was, after all, government intervention on a grand scale. The BAI and state agents held countless public and private meetings with farmers, and distributed thousands of letters, posters, and circulars, including literature in Spanish. As early as 1912, the USDA produced and released motion pictures that were even shown in the backwoods using a "portable outfit." Special literature targeted Southern youth, encouraging them to persuade their parents to pursue eradication. In 1915, the Georgia State Agricultural College promoted a special "livestock train" to hype the benefits of herd improvement that would be possible after eradication. The press closely monitored the train's schedule, and at least one estimate suggested that roughly 175,000 people visited the traveling exhibition.[25]

It is difficult to assess the impact of these educational efforts. Historian Claire Strom is decidedly skeptical, asserting that these initiatives often "had little effect on the yeoman farmer."[26] But even if the effect was primarily on the more educated, market-oriented Southerners, they would have helped sway local political support for eradication, set in motion pilot projects, and eventually influenced some of their more skeptical neighbors.

The lessons gleaned from outreach programs in developing countries suggest that the BAI's educational campaigns should earn high marks. The BAI involved outside experts as well as local citizens who were known and trusted in the communities; it built local alliances, allowed opponents a say in public meetings, tailored its literature and other programs for rural residents, and presented clear objectives.[27] The use of photographs on its posters and mailings and the distribution of motion pictures represented state-of-the-art communications at the time. These visual media were especially important for reaching illiterate farmers. Although the BAI noted that tick eradication would help modernize the South, this was not the primary message. Rather than appealing to lofty ideological goals, advocates touted the concrete benefits to individual farmers—more milk production, larger animals, the prospect of herd improvement, greater access to markets, and so on. This practical emphasis is in keeping with current public relations and educational practices.

Opposition to Tick Eradication

Opposition to the tick eradication campaign was to be expected because the program was invasive, coercive, and costly. Collective action problems were ever present. Unless all their neighbors cooperated, any farmers who invested in cleansing their property bore the high risk of reinfection, putting their cattle in mortal danger. The more a farmer distrusted the government and its ability to succeed, the more sense resistance made. Given that most Southern cattle had developed some immunity to Texas fever (to babesiosis, see the appendix to Chapter 5), many farmers preferred to coexist with the disease. However, this choice to maintain what scientists now call "endemic stability" often came at a high cost. Even if a farmer's cattle had immunity to babesiosis (and there are questions as to the extent of such immunity), the cattle still would carry a tick load that independently lowered their productivity. Farmers also opposed eradication because of the stress and harm to the animals from dipping cattle—even if done properly, dipping shocked the animals. Later research would show that cattle dipped in arsenic mixtures suffered a weight loss of as much as five pounds, and dairy cows typically ceased milk production for about a day.[28] Dipping opponents rightly complained that the treatment was often bungled, causing even more severe problems.

Compulsory dipping policies and tight controls on the movement of cattle were sure to incite opposition. According to Strom, economic self-interest as well as the political and cultural traditions of Southern "yeoman" made them particularly prone to resist government policies.[29] By her reckoning, yeoman farmers bore a high cost relative to any benefits that they might reap because they had no intention of selling cattle in distant markets, so they had little to gain from eradication. The unit cost of driving and dipping a small herd was greater than for a large herd. Strom asserts that yeomen also were more likely to let their cattle run free in rough terrain, which made rounding them up particularly difficult. "Counties dominated by yeomen, especially those without a stock law, chose not to participate. Areas run by large commercial-farmers embraced eradication as a potential salve to the incursions of the boll weevil."[30]

This emphasis on the role of Southern yeoman in the opposition movement reflects a larger historiographical tradition. Central to this interpretation is the purported opposition of small farmers to laws requiring the fencing of livestock ("stock law" counties) rather than of crops ("open range," "free range," or "fence law" counties). However, Shawn Kantor's analysis of the political economy of fencing laws in

Georgia raises serious doubts about the statistical association of small-scale operators with opposition to changing fencing laws.[31] Open-range environments made tick eradication more difficult, though hardly impossible. Early eradication efforts were tied to changing stock laws.[32] In 1905, the BAI's Mohler argued that "every county in all the infected States should have stock or 'no fence' laws to prevent stock owners from allowing ticky cattle on commons, uninclosed [sic] lands, or highways." But by the early 1920s, pro-dipping forces in Georgia sought to highlight successful eradication campaigns in open-range counties.[33] Our analysis of the records for Alabama, Georgia, Mississippi, and South Carolina shows that those counties with "stock laws" dating back to the early 1880s (the period of the most intense fence law debate) did initially accomplish tick eradication earlier than those without, but that the average difference was modest—less than two years. The gap is narrow in part because, even in many stock-law counties, cattle were turned loose to forage after the harvest was gathered. Overall, tick eradication preceded the eventual closure of the Southern range by several decades.[34] Thus, fencing laws that made livestock owners liable for damages aided eradication, but they were hardly a necessary condition.

Strom may be correct that most eradication opponents came from the lower echelons of Southern society, but the government policies also incurred the ire of more influential citizens who had a vested interest in the status quo. In Texas, leading breeders had developed a profitable trade exporting improved fever-resistant stock to other tick-plagued parts of the world. For example, Argentine interests ordered at least 900 registered immune bulls in 1913. These breeders and middlemen rightly feared that eradication would destroy this business.[35]

Across the South, conflicts between supporters and resisters tore communities apart. Irate farmers intimidated and attacked inspectors, and dynamited vats and other equipment. Our search of dozens of newspapers turned up hundreds of cases of vats being dynamited across eight states. We have uncovered many more cases involving additional states not recorded in these news accounts. The earliest in our sample was in Leake County, Mississippi, where three vats were destroyed in August 1912.[36] In the summer of 1915, six vats were dynamited in McIntosh County, Oklahoma. The latter case resulted in a rapid conviction—of the wrong man! The violence in Oklahoma continued: in December, arsonists destroyed the barns of two Pontiac county commissioners and the house of a third, and in January 1916, a county official narrowly escaped an assassination attempt. After a spate of violence in May 1916 in Cherokee and Adair Counties, the counties' commissioners temporarily suspended eradication. In 1920, "the dynamiting of cattle dipping vats has become of such frequent and general occurrence" in some areas that a beleaguered Oklahoma state agricultural official "appealed to governor to declare martial law."[37] He declined the request.

In North Carolina, "there was some lawlessness in dynamiting vats and intimidating those disposed to observe the law" in April 1918. Resistance continued in 1919 when anti-dipping forces dynamited forty vats. Opponents in Pitt County also fired on two federal inspectors.[38] Gunplay became common: in 1922, two inspectors in Arkansas were ambushed and shot, one of whom died. Dipping foes also burned down the barns of two other inspectors. In December 1924, a mob in the piney woods area of Calhoun County, Texas—led by a state senator no less—threatened deathly violence against the area's tick inspectors and range riders.

Resistance became especially violent in Georgia. May 1916 witnessed a wave of bombings in Brooks, Colquitt, Grady, and Thomas counties. Populist leader Thomas E. Watson railed against compulsory dipping in his influential paper the *Jeffersonian*. Watson may have been a spokesman for yeoman farmers, but he was hardly poor.[39] Watson's vocal opposition to the program has largely escaped attention, perhaps because it has been overshadowed by his active role promoting racial and religious hatred and violence—most visibly, the lynching of Leo Frank—during the same period. Editors of the *Macon Telegraph* and *Augusta Chronicle* denounced Watson for encouraging the mob spirit in opposition to the dipping campaign. The populists were not unified, however; Watson's ally, John J. Brown, supported the tick eradication program while he served as Georgia Agricultural Commissioner (1917–1927).[40]

In June 1922, a clandestine group dubbed the "Red Devils" reportedly was blowing up dipping vats in Echols and Lowndes counties as fast as they could be built. In mid-July, the *Atlanta Constitution* reported that "wreckers" had dynamited sixteen vats in Lowndes County in one night.[41] In February 1923, Mann Carter, a leader of the Red Devils, shot two federal inspectors, killing one.[42] The local grand jury, packed with Carter's neighbors and relatives, refused to indict. In a precursor to the Civil Rights cases of the 1960s, the federal government prosecuted in the federal courts, under provisions of the Cattle Contagious Disease Act of 3 March 1905, and won a conviction of Carter and his son on charge of " 'deterring and preventing' " BAI agents from " 'discharging their duties.' "[43] The case (*Thornton et al. v. United States,* 271 U.S. 414, decided 1 June 1926) went to the Supreme Court, where Chief Justice William Taft showed no patience for the resisters. Taft's decision had even broader implications for livestock disease control because the Court held that the USDA regulations did not require a state's acceptance to be valid, that Congress had the power "to provide measures for quarantining and disinfecting cattle in a state to prevent spread of disease to other states," and that the "ranging of cattle across a state line is interstate commerce." Mann Carter had unwittingly started a chain of events that significantly strengthened the federal government's powers.

In general, federal officials responded forcefully to the violence. Heavily armed state and federal agents manned military-style camps, complete with machine guns, in problem areas. The U.S. Bureau of Mines also got into the act. Under the provisions of the Explosives Act of 6 October 1917, the Bureau of Mines began licensing the sale of explosives and prosecuting their misuse. As of 1921, its agents had investigated 120 cases of dipping vat explosions and had tracked down the source of the explosives used in the wave of Arkansas vat bombings in the spring of 1919.[44]

Tensions ran high, and violence was rampant in many communities, but no Southern governor declared martial law as did Governor Dan Turner of Iowa in 1931 in the face of armed rioters who were blocking bovine tuberculosis testing (see Chapter 12).[45] The BAI and local livestock sanitation agents had also faced violent resistance outside the South during its CBPP and other eradication campaigns long before the tick eradication work got under way. As a small sampling, in the BAI *Report* for 1899, Salmon complained about agents being assaulted. In June of the following year, dairymen "launched paving-stones, brickbats and other missiles" upon BAI agents in a series of encounters in the New York City area. There were hand-to-hand fights and "in some instances pistols were drawn." These types of assaults led to legislation in 1905 to make it a federal crime to interfere, threaten, or injure BAI agents.[46]

Strom argues that the BAI seriously miscalculated by initially allowing considerable local volition, expecting farmers and communities to embrace eradication. She further asserts that when some did not, and after many of those who did unexpectedly suffered reinfection from neighboring areas, the authorities were caught off guard and had to resort to statewide dipping mandates and stricter internal quarantines.[47] It is extremely unlikely that BAI leaders, many of whom had worked in the South and had been fighting Southern cattle interests for over twenty years, had many illusions about the potential for opposition in the South. Except in the case of eruptions of highly infectious diseases such as foot-and-mouth disease, the BAI started every new disease-fighting initiative on a voluntary basis with considerable local autonomy. The general plan was to impose more regulations as political support from the owners of cleared lands and herds mounted. Cooper Curtice made this exact point a year before federal cattle tick eradication began when he noted that "Cattle owners who live along the [quarantine] line and have learend [sic] thoroughly the lessons of fever tick infection make the best guards, for they cannot afford reinfection of the stock."[48] The scientists-cum-policy makers who designed the program also thoroughly understood that, without collective action backed by laws and police, free-riders would move cattle willy-nilly.

A comparison with many other Northern disease-control programs helps explain the opposition to tick eradication. The BAI agents clearing ticks often had to work in one locale for much longer than they had to during other campaigns. In some areas, tick quarantines and dipping dragged on for years. State and federal officials also often imposed large unfunded mandates on county governments. As an example, in the early 1920s, the supervisors of Camden County, Georgia, repeatedly refused to heed the orders of State Veterinarian Peter F. Bahnsen to build and supervise more vats. The supervisors claimed that the county could not afford the expense. The State Supreme Court came down hard on the supervisors, ruling that they had to fund the program.[49] In the cases of Northern outbreaks of foot-and-mouth disease, contagious bovine pleuropneumonia, and later bovine tuberculosis, counties had to incur costs, but the federal and state governments bore a larger share of the expenses and often offered substantial compensation to farmers to encourage their cooperation. All these differences between tick eradication and the other stamping-out campaigns contributed to the opposition in the South.

With no past history of these more virulent diseases, many Southern states originally lacked the legal and administrative infrastructure to deal with Texas fever. It took time to create these institutions, and the same skirmishes over the power of the state versus the sanctity of property rights that had already occurred in the North had to be fought from scratch in the South. The rhetoric was similar in both regions.

The violent opposition increased the cost of tick eradication, threatened the safety of eradication personnel, and delayed the participation of some state and local governments. However, work did progress throughout the South. For all the attention devoted to law breakers, it should be emphasized that resolute supporters of the program fought back. States enacted dipping laws, local judges refused to issue injunctions to stop the program, and, as time went on, local sheriffs rounded up more dynamiters. Supporters, like the opponents of tick eradication, attended mass rallies and demanded stronger action.[50] Many private citizens built their own dipping tanks, and countless farmers dutifully drove their cattle week after week for treatment. The dominant story became that of the widespread cooperation among farmers to rid their property of the parasites.

Interpreting the Texas Fever Campaign in Light of Scab Eradication

The Texas fever campaign was one of many operations to control livestock diseases. All areas of the country were affected; the federal government was not just ganging up on the Southern yeomanry. The campaigns to fight cattle and sheep scab most closely paralleled the Texas fever programs. All three programs commenced at about the same time, were empowered by the same legislation, were led nationally by the same individuals, and involved many of the same methods (quarantines, inspections, and dippings). Figure 11.4 shows that the areas quarantined for sheep scab (1903) and cattle scab (1905) covered most of the Western United States.

Sheep and cattle scab are highly infectious diseases caused by mites. The diseases (also known as scabies, mange, or itch) damage the animals' fleece or hides, weaken its victims, and can result in death. Despite individual efforts, scab caused heavy losses and deterred "many ranchers from raising sheep." As with Texas fever, the failures of private and state efforts strengthened the drive for federal action. Between 1895 and 1900, the USDA issued a series of orders that progressively toughened regulations governing the shipment of scabby sheep. A major impetus for stronger action came in 1896 after Britain, which was engaged in its own scab eradication campaign, banned the importation of U.S. sheep.[51] In 1900,

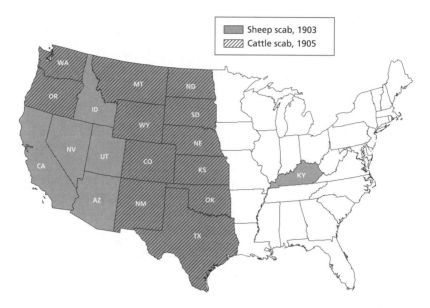

Figure 11.4. Sheep and cattle scab quarantine areas. *Source:* U.S. Department of Agriculture, *Yearbook of Agriculture, 1915,* plate 18 (between pp. 160 and 161); *Yearbook of Agriculture, 1942,* p. 910.

six years before it would begin the national tick eradication campaign, the BAI moved many of its 1,000 special sheep inspectors west to work with state officials. Effective 1 July 1905, the USDA placed the Western states under even stricter quarantine. In fiscal year 1905, federal agents supervised the inspection of roughly 54 million sheep and supervised 17 million dippings. In 1906, the federal expenditure on sheep and cattle scab eradication was about four times the allocation for tick eradication.[52]

The history of scab sheds light on the motivation for Texas fever controls. As with Texas fever, the issue of federal agents working on scab within a state's boundaries needed to be resolved. And, as with Texas fever, ranchers in sheep-exporting states came to prefer dealing with one federal agency and one set of rules rather than with a plethora of state regulations. Of course, there was controversy, court cases challenged the limits of state and federal authority, and farmers protested, hid the disease, and otherwise attempted to circumvent scab regulations. Sheriffs had to be assigned to assist and protect inspectors. However, by 1920, federal and state policies had significantly reduced the incidence and costs of scab. In 1913, R. A. Ramsay, chief of the BAI's Field Inspection Division who had worked in both the scab and Texas fever campaigns, noted that Southerners behaved pretty much like Northerners, and that "human nature is human nature in all the states, whether it is in the East, West, North, or South."[53]

Costs and Benefits

Researchers have generated a wide range of estimates of the benefits of the tick control program, but there has been much less discussion of the program's costs, and little of the costs borne by farmers. Comprehensive eradication cost numbers, including those borne by farmers, are hard to come by and thus are simply ignored in most treatments. Contemporaries estimated that in the early twentieth century ticks caused losses in the South worth between $40 and $200 million a year; $100 million was frequently cited.[54] These estimates are taken as proxies for the benefits of eradication. The calculations include such items as the effect of ticks and babesiosis on cattle weight gain, hide values, the deaths of nonimmune Southern stock and of breeding animals imported from outside the region, lower milk output, fatalities due to other diseases and to cold weather because of the weakened condition of ticky cattle, and the like. The differences between the lower and upper bound estimates are in part due to some observers double counting and comingling stocks and flows.[55]

Contemporary discussions of tick eradication deal with what we term "static costs"—the costs associated with ticks lowering the value and productivity of Southern cattle; and "dynamic costs"—the losses resulting from the inability of Southern farmers to adopt better breeds and practices over the longer run. The gaps between the lower and upper bound estimates are in large part due to the different accounting of counterfactual dynamic losses.[56] The treatment of milk production illuminates the venture into counterfactual worlds. In 1907, B. H. Rawl estimated that Southern dairymen could rapidly double the output per cow by introducing and breeding higher grade animals. By his accounting (implicitly assuming perfectly elastic demand), annual dairy income would rise by over $175 million if cattle ticks were eradicated and babesiosis was no longer a threat.

Ticks inhibited progress.[57] Experiments conducted in the South showed that "cows lightly infested with ticks produced 18.6 per cent less milk than cows kept free from ticks; and cows heavily infested produced 42.4 per cent less milk than cows that carried no ticks." Based on the 1920 U.S. census of agriculture, U. G. Houck noted that "the average milk production of dairy cows in the tick-free counties of eight Southern States was 47 per cent more than in the tick-infested counties of the same States." Indicative of a more progressive industry, farmers in recently cleansed areas began forming cow-testing associations, bull associations, creameries, and dairies. These were the type of collective institutions that were spurring the growth of yields in the North and in progressive regions of Western Europe.[58]

Southern cattle from infested areas fetched a lower price per hundredweight in Northern markets than cattle of a similar grade from tick-free areas. When areas in the South were cleared, their relative cattle prices went up. In 1916, Mohler placed "the difference between the prices realized for cattle from the tick-infested region and the prices of cattle of similar grades from above the quarantine line ranges from $2.25 to $5 a head at the principal northern live-stock markets, without taking into account the improvement in quality and weight of the cattle because of the eradication of the ticks."[59] Our detailed examination of the prices in the St. Louis cattle market between 1886 and 1914 suggests even larger price gaps than Mohler stated.

Of all the estimates of the damage inflicted by ticks (and thus the benefits from eradication), those offered by the BAI's John Mohler in 1906 stand apart.[60] Mohler reckoned that the static cost of ticks was roughly $40 million a year. This represents a reasonable cost approximation that is at the low end of the available estimates and does not incorporate any dynamic elements. However, neither Mohler nor anyone else has compared the real discounted annual flows of benefits and costs with a common base date that would allow an estimate of the benefit-cost ratio of tick eradication. We now venture upon this task, recognizing the perils of doing so. The counterfactual in our analysis is a continuation of the policy of quarantining and segregating Southern cattle rather than attempting to eradicate ticks. It does not incorporate the prospect of delaying until superior techniques became available.[61] The steps of the calculations are detailed in the appendix to this chapter.

To calculate the benefits of the program, we start with Mohler's 1906 static estimate and phase in the benefits—the reduced damaged—between 1906 and 1943 by estimating the percentage of Southern cattle in the previously infected counties freed from the quarantine at each date. After 1943, our calculations assume that the United States was free of tick damage. Using a 3 percent rate of interest, the discounted real sum of benefits from 1906 to 1943 is $475.4 million, and for the span from 1944 to 2010 is $385.0 million, both in 1906 dollars. In 2010 purchasing power, the combined sum for 1906 to 2010 is $21.5 billion.

Estimates of program costs require summing the real discounted government expenditures and estimated farmer costs. Most statements of the costs of eradication deal only with the expenditures of various government agencies and omit the considerable opportunity costs borne by farmers who had to drive their cattle to the dipping vats, leave pastures idle, suffer temporary reductions in milk production, and the like. As detailed in the appendix, we derive a high-end estimate of farmer costs. For a given fiscal year, we divide the sum of all costs by the consumer price index (CPI) to convert to real 1906 prices. Again assuming a 3 percent rate of interest, the discounted real sum of the cost is $50.4 million in 1906 dollars (or about $1.26 billion in 2010 purchasing power). Stated as a ratio of benefits to costs, the multiple for the period 1906–1943 was on the order of 9.4 to 1; and for the period 1906–2010, it was 17.0 to 1.

These favorable benefit-cost estimates reflect a lower bound, probably an extreme lower bound, of the returns on the investment in stamping out ticks. Without eradication, the South would have been forever denied access to the innovations that were increasing the productivity of Northern herds. Recently cleared areas offered a sense of what was possible. "More cattle were being raised, and a better grade of breeding stock is being introduced; calves grow faster and cattle put on flesh more rapidly during the grazing season and go into the winter in better condition because of the absence of the ticks; they can be marketed without quarantine restrictions, and higher prices are being obtained; dairy cows give a larger yield of milk; and values of farm lands are enhanced." Such changes gave Southerners an incentive to invest the livestock industry. Numerous observers testified to the rapid adoption of better breeds and practices in recently cleared areas.[62]

Eradication helped integrate the South into the national economy. For all the controversy and conflict associated with the spread of federally imposed tick policies, these efforts sped the adoption of laws, bureaucracies, and a spirit of cooperation in the Southern states that would be essential in fighting other livestock diseases. Tick eradication in the South also affected the dynamics of the *Northern* cattle industry, which made a conversion to higher-blooded Herefords and other productive European breeds, which were highly susceptible to Texas fever. If ticky cattle had continued to trail north, this transition would likely have been slower. The Northern states and cleansed areas in the South reap the benefits of this past work in perpetuity. Accounting for these dynamic benefits would significantly increase the benefits relative to the costs of eradication.

Conclusion

Recent events put the torturous campaign to control Texas fever into perspective. In 2009, Texas ranchers along the buffer zone on the Texas-Mexico border and their political representatives were in an uproar. Since 2003, the number of confirmed cases of Texas fever jumped from 19 to 149. In response, the federal government increased mandatory dipping requirements and enlarged the buffer zone from about 800 square miles to about 2,400 square miles. One estimate put the cost at $250 per year per head of cattle. The area's congressman sought more federal money for the fight. A Texas A&M study estimated that an outbreak of Texas fever in 2008 would cost the local cattle industry $1.3 billion. South Texas ranchers feared that their cattle might be banned from moving north.[63] These events occurred after the disease and its control methods were well understood, and after jurisdictional disputes between the federal government and Texas had been largely settled. There was no longer any question of *if* farmers should fight ticks—that difficult decision had been made long ago. This fight to defend a 2,400 square mile area provides a microcosm of the thousands of earlier skirmishes in a territory over 300 times as large, during an era when many citizens had little understanding of the disease, let alone any faith that it could be defeated. What had been a Herculean undertaking with an uncertain ending was now a manageable task.[64]

The success of the campaign against Texas fever required new science, new laws, and new constitutional interpretations. As great as the

BAI's scientific advances were, its public policy achievements were the major story. The principal challenges were to build cooperative arrangements with the states, to educate and secure the cooperation of the public, and, when necessary, to deploy federal and state police to control the destructive behavior of resisters. The program swept the cattle ticks and the disease-causing protozoa they carried from the nation by methodically quarantining areas, dipping livestock repeatedly, and then protecting cleansed areas from reinfection. In the process, this campaign created a public good—a vector-eradication model that would be used in the global fights against parasites and the diseases they carry.[65]

For all the short-run benefits of tick eradication to the cattle industry, the long-run effects on the development of the Southern dairy industry and the improvement of Southern cattle breeds helped transform the American South. These improved opportunities came when the South was still reeling from the destruction caused by the boll weevil.[66] It is ironic that the spread of one arthropod—the weevil—increased support for the extermination of another—the cattle tick. The boll weevil invasion stimulated individual farmers to diversify and encouraged Southern leaders to seek USDA support for research and control policies.

The boll weevil did not represent the only change. Around the same time, the final vestiges of Reconstruction had been replaced by Northern acceptance of Southern Jim Crow policies to suppress local African Americans, Southern Democrats were regaining seniority in both houses of Congress, and a new generation of politicians was taking the reins of power from the veterans of the Civil War. Opening the door for state-federal cooperation on livestock disease-control policies no longer posed much threat to Southern racial or party policies. In the new environment, many cattle raisers and their representatives began arguing that the South was not getting its fair share of the federal pie.

The Texas fever story comes into sharper focus when viewed in light of the fights against other diseases. The area eradication concept grew out of the CBPP campaign. The lockdown of cattle and sheep in the Western half of the United States due to scab along with the actions taken to control other diseases discredits the notion that quarantines were primarily anticompetitive schemes. Rather, the common denominator was the development of a federal bureaucracy armed with new knowledge and assisted by a more accepting legal environment—an environment that the BAI's own policies helped create. Increasingly, citizens in all areas of the country came to rely on the federal regulators to address what hitherto had been intractable collective action problems. These regulators who both spurred the major scientific advances and built the complicated institutions of eradication were among the quintessential entrepreneurs of the era.

APPENDIX: Benefits and Costs of Tick Eradication

We calculate the benefits of the program using Mohler's 1906 static estimate of $40 million as the annual damage caused by the Texas fever to the South.[67] We phase in the benefits—the reduced damages—between 1906 and 1943 by estimating the percentage of cattle in the counties freed from the quarantine. We do this by first compiling the quarantine status of each county in each year from the BAI orders. We then take the distributions of total cattle reported by county in the various volumes of the agricultural censuses from 1900 to 1935. For each distribution, we calculate the number of cattle in counties under quarantine in 1906 and each year thereafter. We calculate the percentage freed by year for each distribution and then take the average. This average percentage is multiplied by $40 million and applied for each year from 1907 to 1942. After 1943, we treat the entire continental United States as free of tick damage. We convert the annual benefits into 1906 net present value dollars assuming a 3 percent rate of interest. The discounted real sum from 1906 to 1943 is $475.4 million in 1906 dollars. The discounted real sum from 1944 to 2010 (a number that does not depend on assumptions of how the benefits were phased in) is $385.0 million.

To calculate the cost of the program, we sum the real discounted government expenditures and estimated farmer costs. Federal expenditures by the BAI (and in the mid-1930s by the Civilian Works Administration) can be pieced together from various congressional documents, such as the "Statement of Expenditures of the Department of Agriculture" and the "Agriculture Department Appropriations Bills." Expenditures by state and local governments are available on a reasonably consistent basis up to 1925. Thereafter, we estimate state and local government expenditures as 2.8 times the BAI expenditures, in line with the average ratio for 1916–1925. This ratio likely exaggerated the local expenditures in the 1930s, when county funding dropped off sharply.

Calculating the cost borne by farmers is more difficult. Our search of the literature reveals a range of estimates, mostly centered between $0.20 and $0.50 per head for a complete dipping regimen in the mid-1910s. To incorporate potential missing costs, we adopt the higher figure of $1.00 per head (in 1917).[68] We allow this estimate of farmer cost to vary over time with the Southern farm wage rate (monthly without board) as reported by the USDA Bureau of Agricultural Economics. We convert the number into cost per dipping (by assuming ten dippings per year), and multiply by the total number of inspections/dippings recorded in the BAI chief's *Annual Reports*.[69] For a given fiscal year, we add the expenditures by the federal, state, and local governments to the estimated farmers' costs, and divide by the CPI to convert to real 1906 purchasing power. We then discount the results into 1906 net present value dollars, assuming the same 3 percent rate of interest used previously. The discounted real sum of cost is $50.4 million 1906 dollars (or about $1.26 billion in 2010 purchasing power).

12 An Impossible Undertaking

Eradicating Bovine Tuberculosis

JUDGE KENESAW MOUNTAIN LANDIS emboldened livestock sanitation officials when he dropped the gavel on James Dorsey in February 1919 (see Chapter 10). The Dorsey affair exposed the glaring weaknesses of private initiatives, the torts system, and uncoordinated state and local bovine tuberculosis (BTB) regulations. It took nine years after officials first discovered Dorsey's maleficence in 1910 to gain a conviction for postal fraud—proving that he had knowingly shipped sick animals was too high of a barrier. By 1919, much had changed. The Bureau of Animal Industry (BAI) had stamped out BTB in the Washington D.C. area, and it had embarked on a national eradication campaign in 1917. The large meatpacking and stockyard interests had been won over, and they actively supported the effort. Rather than the often-told story of an industry capturing the regulators, in this case the regulators had captured the industry. By this time, the BAI had eradicated contagious bovine pleuropneumonia (CBPP), and had made enormous strides in pushing back the frontiers of Texas fever, and sheep and cattle scab. It had developed a vaccine for hog cholera and had stamped out a foot-and-mouth-disease epizootic that had contaminated twenty-two states. However, BTB eradication would be the BAI's most ambitious endeavor.

The BTB program would require a nationwide test-and-slaughter campaign to combat an established enzootic disease. In every county, trained agents would have to inspect every farm with cattle, conduct tuberculin tests, and condemn all of the reactors. By 1940, accredited veterinarians would administer roughly 232 million tuberculin tests and order the destruction of about 3.8 million cattle. BTB eradication would demand a massive agricultural education effort, cooperative agreements with every state, and the building of alliances in a rapidly shifting environment. Minds would have to be changed. Social capital would have to be built to earn the trust of most farmers. Officials knew there would be opposition and that they would have to marginalize fanatical adversaries. Entering private property and destroying animals on such a massive scale, with or without the owner's permission, was controversial. Explosive confrontations would erupt, leading to a hitherto unprecedented peacetime exercise of police power in the United States. The eradication of BTB would demand devising incentive-compatible compensation schemes. The federal government not only had to convey the "right" incentives to farmers, but also to state and local governments. Success would be complicated because the program would be carried out during the dark days of the farm crisis of 1920s and 1930s.

Exactly 100 years after the United States began its first BTB eradication effort in Washington, D.C., a student of BTB policy in Italy lamented that "non-technical" problems stymied progress in his country.[1] The Italian experience was the rule rather than the exception. The designers of the American program had no template, and they had no precedent except the uncoordinated and largely bungled state initiatives and their own experience in the nation's capital. The lessons with CBPP and other diseases helped, but a great deal would have to be figured out on the fly. There would be mistakes, and there would be adjustments. At the outset of the campaign in 1917, one of America's leading agricultural authorities, Henry C. Wallace, questioned whether the proposed campaign was not " 'an impossible undertaking.' "[2] Even to progressive agriculturalists like Wallace, BTB eradication seemed a bridge too far.

In Chapter 10, we saw how scientists isolated and defined the extent and risks of BTB in humans and livestock. Robert Koch's discovery of the tubercle bacillus *(Mycobacterium tuberculosis)* and creation of tuberculin, Theobald Smith's isolation of a distinct *M. bovis* bacillus, and M. P. Ravenel's isolation of the *M. bovis* in a child all contributed to the understanding of tuberculosis in humans and animals, and to knowledge of the modes of transfer between species. Regulatory and legal institutions strained to convert these findings into effective public policy. In this chapter, we deal with the political economy of BTB eradication—how the national program was organized, how it worked, and how it succeeded.

Contrasting the American experience with what transpired in Europe adds to our understanding of the development of successful policies to diffuse public health technologies and in particular to overcome resistance. Scientifically advanced countries all had access to the same technical information available in the United States. With the exception of Canada and Finland, all opted to coexist with BTB. This decision contributed to hundreds of thousands of avoidable human deaths. BTB remained enzootic in much of Europe, with cattle infection rates in some regions as high as 80 percent. Only after 1945 did most European nations explicitly adopt the American model and impose compulsory BTB test-and-slaughter programs along with the mandatory pasteurization of urban milk supplies.[3]

The State-Federal Program

The federal government took its first small step toward BTB eradication in 1906 with a campaign to improve milk safety in Washington, D.C. As with almost all its disease eradication drives, the BAI started with a voluntary program that emphasized educating the public and gathering evidence on the extent of the problem. The Bureau started by providing tuberculin tests at the request of area farmers. The initial results were disturbing—18 percent of the local dairy cows reacted. This finding set the stage for more compulsory policies. In line with the actions of many municipalities, in 1909 the commissioners of the District of Columbia made tuberculin testing mandatory for all of the roughly 2,000 cattle in the District and for any animals intended for importation. This led to tests of about 6,000 cattle in Maryland and Virginia each year. The commissioners also established a relatively generous compensation scheme to reimburse owners of slaughtered reactors. These efforts yielded quick results, with rapid declines in the reaction rate in 1910 and 1911. By 1919, only 0.63 percent of the cattle in the District reacted to the test. This early success, along with an about-face in the views of major Chicago packers and stockyard interests, convinced BAI officials that it might be possible to eradicate the disease nationally.[4]

The mounting evidence that tuberculosis was spreading rapidly in livestock, coupled with the failure of state and private initiatives to deal with the situation, created a new sense of urgency among industry and government leaders. In addition to protecting the public directly, federal meat inspection helped identify the prevalence and sources of livestock diseases. Between 1907 and 1917, the percentage of cattle and swine retained for BTB at federally inspected plants increased significantly. In the vast majority of cases, visual ante-mortem inspections could not detect whether an animal was infected with BTB. Given prevailing market compensation practices, packers were stuck with the losses for carcasses later condemned during post-mortem inspection. In anticipation of losses, the packers bid less for all animals. This pushed some costs to stock-raisers as a group, but it did not provide much incentive to individuals to take extra precautions. Meatpackers interpreted these trends in BTB rates as reflecting actual changes in the livestock supply chain, not just as artifacts of changing inspection standards. Faced with escalating losses, in 1916 the Chicago packers joined with the leaders of the Union Stock Yards and of the Livestock Exchange to form the Sanitary Committee of the Chicago Livestock Exchange. The guiding light and president the Exchange was Thomas E. Wilson.[5]

This was the same Thomas Wilson who in 1906 had represented the Chicago packers during the House hearings to counter the Neill-Reynolds findings and to gut the Beveridge bill pushed by President Theodore Roosevelt (Chapter 9). Promoting the BTB eradication campaign offered this rising leader of the industry an opportunity to turn over a new leaf and offset some of the negative public sentiment about the packers' past conduct. The Sanitary Committee hired a full-time professional to work with the USDA to promote the eradication of BTB; the new job of "Livestock Commissioner" went to Howard R. Smith, a former professor of animal science. Smith tracked bills in several states and advised legislators to enact tough control measures.

The turnabout in the packer and stockyard position on inspection was striking. In contrast with their history of denialism and mudslinging, they were now freely admitting that they had a BTB problem and were in the vanguard of promoting stronger federal intervention. In 1919, the president of the Chicago Live Stock Exchange testified that nearly every segment of the livestock business held the BAI and its meat inspectors in the highest possible esteem; at the same time, he voiced little confidence in state inspectors.[6]

The cooperative state-federal program got off to a modest start in March 1917 when Congress appropriated $75,000 for BTB eradication. In December 1917, the BAI approved a national plan advanced by the U.S. Live Stock Sanitary Association, the Sanitary Committee of the Chicago Live Stock Exchange, and various purebred cattle-breeder associations to provide voluntary testing for cattle herds.[7] This was an audacious move in light of the fact that the more efficient intradermic testing process would not become available for another three years. At this time, to test even a small herd required that a veterinarian be on site for roughly thirty-six hours (see Chapter 10). The plan's designers sought farmer cooperation and early successes, so they chose to focus initially on purebred animals. Purebred owners as a group were among the country's most educated and progressive farmers, they had been hit hard by the disease, and they depended on access to interstate markets. Additionally, their animals composed the foundation of the industry's breeding stock, which would help provide the replacements for cattle subsequently culled.

J. A. Kiernan, who was the first head of the BAI's Tuberculosis Eradication Division, emphasized that it was essential to educate farmers, to hold local meetings, and to spell out the precise details of the process and goals. If farmers did not want to participate, " 'it is best to leave them alone, until such time as they can see their way clear to cooperate.' " This was the time to use carrots and build alliances; the time for sticks would come later. The authorities assembled lists of targeted purebred herds to be tested, culled of reactors, and then retested. Those herds that passed were certified as "Tuberculosis-Free Accredited Herds," which allowed owners to ship their animals across state boundaries for one year without further testing.[8] The 1917 regulations also envisioned "tuberculosis-free areas" where all of the herds in a given zone were free of reactors, and "modified accredited areas," which met the less restrictive requirement that reactors made up less than 0.5 percent of cattle population.

The Chicago packing interests pushed hard for this legislation. In late 1917, Smith testified on behalf of a bill that would have appropriated $1 million to the USDA for BTB eradication. He fielded tough questions such as why Congress should allocate money to compensate farmers for sick animals. He maintained that this was needed because of the spillovers to human health and the need to create incentives for farmers to participate. Smith also proposed a state-federal indemnity-sharing plan that resembled what would eventually pass. As the legislation moved forward, he orchestrated a national lobbying effort. Both Houses passed a bill increasing the anti-BTB budget to $500,000, and authorizing indemnities; President Woodrow Wilson signed the legislation in October 1918.[9]

Beginning in fiscal year 1919, the federal government matched state indemnities, paying up to one-third of the difference between the animal's appraised value and salvage value. The federal payments were initially capped at $50 per head for registered purebreds and $25 per head for grade cattle. Legislation passed in 1919 tripled federal funding to $1.5 million, with $1 million earmarked for indemnities. Sharing the burden was a shrewd maneuver, because it both gave a state an incentive to participate (otherwise it would "lose" the federal appropriation), and also provided an incentive to mind the efficiency of local management.

In response to the federal overtures, states began increasing their appropriations, with New York and Illinois leading the way. Most of the states in the North Central region soon followed. The voluntary programs with indemnities proved highly popular, and by 1922, all but six states were participating. Over 16,000 herds (364,000 animals) had achieved accredited herd status, and 162,000 herds (1.5 million animals) had passed one test. As of August 1922, almost 65,000 farmers, who owned a total of 500,000 cattle, were on the waiting list for testing.[10] In this period, the program focused on cleaning up the breeding stock.

State spending increased from about $2 million in 1918 to $13 million by 1927. Intense debates raged in state legislatures across the country over the precise details of the state programs. Except during a brief period in the mid-1930s, the states and counties carried the main financial burden. In the late 1920s and early 1930s, state and local governments were spending more than twice the federal appropriation of about $6 million. By the mid-1930s, the state expenditures decreased, and emergency federal funds came online, causing the contribution ratio to reverse. At the peak in fiscal year 1935, the federal government contributed about $18 million compared to $9 million from the states. When the program entered the maintenance phase in the 1940s (involving total spending of about \$5–6 million per year), the ratio returned to roughly two state dollars for every one federal dollar.[11]

In the spring of 1922, the BAI and state livestock sanitary officials began to shift their clean-up efforts from individual herds to entire areas (such as counties). Under the "area plan," all the cattle in a region were tested during a relatively short period of time. The systematic eradication of the disease in an entire area reduced the chances of reinfection and was much more economical than testing individual herds. In many states, a simple majority of the cattle owners could initiate a local eradication campaign. However, New York and California at first required 90 percent approval for action, slowing the program's start-up.[12]

Throughout the 1920s, the program enjoyed broad-based political support. Among its powerful backers was President Calvin Coolidge. In his 1926 State of the Union address, Coolidge labeled the eradication campaign a "preventive measure of great economic and sanitary importance" and touted the success of "substantial expenditures" of the federal government in helping cut the infection rate nearly in half. His accompanying budget message called for raising federal outlays by over 25 percent, asserting that there was "no excuse . . . to withhold the funds necessary to effectively carry on this important campaign." In 1928, he further requested a supplemental appropriation to fund fully paying the increased indemnities. Congress obliged.[13] In general, enthusiasm for the program transcended traditional political boundaries, thriving under Republican and Democratic administrations at both the federal and state levels.

Federal legislation left the states considerable flexibility in fine-tuning their eradication policies and indemnity plans. Most states adopted schedules paralleling the federal plan, with similar payment shares and maximum limits. In Eastern states, where livestock prices were higher, state indemnity limits tended to be higher. States also differed over whether, and how much money, counties had to contribute. Among the more interesting modifications was one adopted by Montana; the state reimbursed a farmer for the full appraised value if the condemned animal proved to be free of BTB lesions in a post-mortem examination. This essentially insured the farmers against false-positive test results.

By 1928, every state except Alabama, Arkansas, and California participated. Our formal statistical analysis, reported elsewhere, indicates that
progress was faster in jurisdictions where farmers were wealthier, where
farmers' losses were lower, and where the farm population was more
homogeneous in terms of ethnicity and the size of operations. Farmer
losses depended on both the initial reaction rates and the generosity of
the indemnity schedule. Where the infection rates were higher, farmers
were less likely to sign on to the program, and progress was slower once
it started. All else being equal, the smaller the gap between the animal's
market price and its indemnity/slaughter value, the faster eradication
advanced. Clearly, incentives mattered. In addition, areas with heterogeneity in farm size and ethnic identity were more likely to have distributional conflicts, which slowed the establishment of effective eradication programs.[14]

The payment structure of the program took a crucial turn under the
Jones-Connally Cattle Act of 1934. This legislation dropped the requirement that states provide matching funds and released emergency federal money "to extend the work to sections of the country where no local funds are available."[15] This change occurred after Depression era
fiscal constraints led many states to cut back. In addition (and perhaps
to prevent the laggards from reaping all the rewards), the Act initiated a
state-federal brucellosis test-and-slaughter campaign modeled on the
BTB initiative.[16] Unprecedented sums of federal money ($25–30 million
per year) flowed into these campaigns. Low cattle prices, due to poor
business conditions and ongoing droughts, made the clean-up effort
economically and politically attractive.

Figure 12.1 charts the number and percentage of all cattle tuberculin-
tested annually between 1917 and 1953. The program grew rapidly
during the late 1910s and throughout the 1920s; between fiscal years
1919 and 1929, the number of tests increased by over 35 percent per
year. The Jones-Connally Act boosted the effort. At the campaign's
peak in fiscal year 1936, the BAI hired an additional 900 veterinarians
and 500 temporary employees to help test nearly 25 million cattle,
equivalent to roughly one-third of the nation's cattle stock. After this
"big push," tuberculin testing slowed to 8–12 million examinations
per year.[17]

A fuller sense of the geographical patterns of adoption of the eradication program can be gained from Figure 12.2, which maps county-level data on the extent of the disease in March 1922, July 1931, and November 1937. These maps show that progress in reducing the disease was highly uneven across the country. In 1922, the disease was widespread in the dairy regions of the Northeast and the Lake states, exceeding 15 percent in some areas; it was far less common in the South. Significant progress toward eradication was made by 1931. Entire states, including North Carolina (1928), Maine (1929), and Michigan (1930), had achieved the status of "modified accredited areas," but parts of the Northeast remained heavily infected. The contagion actually worsened in California

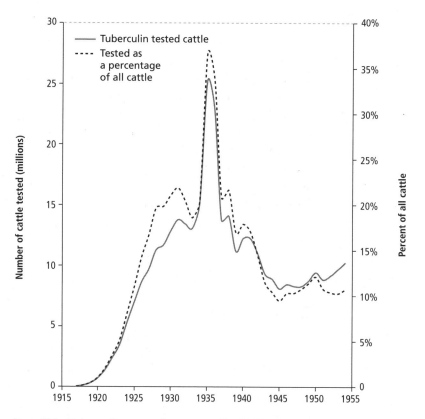

Figure 12.1. Tuberculin tests given annually, 1917–1953. *Source:* U.S. Bureau of Animal Industry, *Reports for 1918–54.*

between 1922 and 1931.[18] By late 1937, California and South Dakota were the only remaining hot spots.

The program's progress in one area created market pressures for its adoption elsewhere. As an example, after a large fraction of their stock proved to be reactors, Eastern dairymen needed replacements from the Western states. State and federal regulations aimed at preventing the reintroduction of BTB led to premiums for dairy cows from accredited counties.

This geographic diffusion pattern is exceptional in U.S. history. By almost every measure (including literacy, living standards, and rates of adoption of new technologies), California and New York were among the most progressive regions of the country during the first half of the twentieth century; North Carolina, with its impoverished tobacco road farmers, was among the most backward. The control of BTB progressed in an order opposite from the general pattern. This is in part because BTB was uncommon in the Southern states where improved dairy stock was rare. But the regional differences should not be exaggerated: there was only a 12-year gap between the date when the first state (North Carolina in 1928) was declared disease free and the date when the last (California in 1940) achieved control.

Indeed, the entire campaign required only twenty-four years. At the start of the federal-state program in 1917, the BAI estimated that about one in twenty cattle in the United States were tuberculous. Beginning in 1922, the BAI took biennial (and after 1934 annual) surveys of the extent of BTB infection in the United States. Figure 12.3 graphs the estimated infection rate of all cattle and the reaction rate for tested animals, providing a sense of the rate of progress achieved nationally. In 1922, about 4 percent of all U.S. cattle were infected with the disease. By 1928, the infection rate had been cut in half. The sharpest proportional rate of reduction occurred during the 1934–1937 period under the Jones-Connally program. By the late 1930s, the national rate had fallen below 0.5 percent.[19]

BTB was not truly eradicated in the United States. Given the imprecision of the tests, pushing the reaction rate below 0.5 percent would have been prohibitively expensive (note that the proportion of positive results that were false rose as the actual prevalence of the disease fell). Enforcement efforts flagged after the beginning of World War II, and localized

A. March 1922

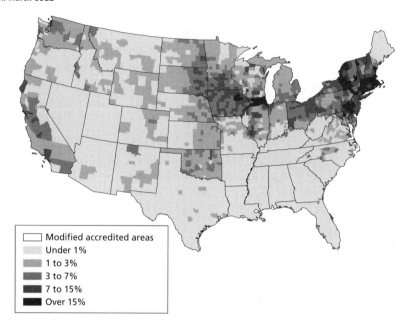

B. July 1931

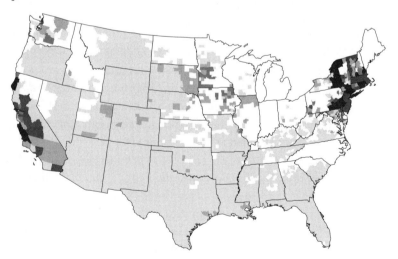

C. November 1937

Figure 12.2. Extent of bovine tuberculosis by county, 1922–1937. *Source:* U.S. Bureau of Animal Industry, *Status of Bovine Tuberculosis Eradication on Area Basis,* March 1922, July 1931, November 1937 (Washington, DC: U.S. Government Printing Office).

outbreaks of the disease cropped up periodically over the postwar years. The most notable example occurred in Michigan in the early 1950s. By the early 1960s, BTB was sufficiently controlled that the USDA suspended the continuous tuberculin testing of cattle to rely on a more targeted approach. During the testing era, the USDA perfected a tracking system that allowed it to identify the shippers of all cattle and swine processed at federally inspected slaughterhouses. When an inspector found an infected carcass, a veterinarian was dispatched to control the infection on the originating farm. As of 1965, the tracing system triggered by surveillance at packinghouses became the sole line of defense against BTB.[20]

The eradication campaign reversed the upward trend in the proportion of infected animals condemned at the slaughterhouse. Between 1908 and 1917, the percentage of all cattle carcasses retained for the disease rose from less than 1 percent to over 2.5 percent. The percentage of cattle carcasses condemned and tanked rose from 0.34 percent to 0.50

over this period. The rise in the share of swine retained for tuberculosis was even greater. In the mid-1920s, one out of seven hogs slaughtered at federally inspected packinghouses were retained due to tuberculous lesions. The share of bovine carcasses retained steadily declined after 1922, and the share for swine declined after 1925. For all its complexity, the eradication program was showing measurable results within a few years after it went into general operation.

Resistance

The BTB eradication program was highly controversial. In Chapter 10, we showed how the early municipal efforts to impose tuberculin testing met with farmer protests and milk strikes. Agitation against city ordinances continued into the 1920s. As an example, in January 1927, Illinois dairy farmers across nine counties threatened to strike unless they received a higher price for milk to cover the added cost imposed by tubercu-

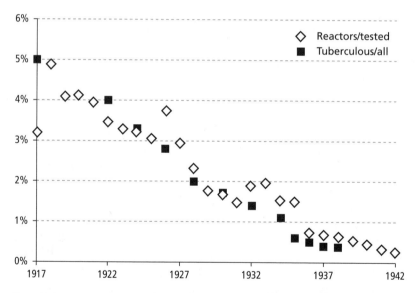

Figure 12.3. Extent of bovine tuberculosis infection among cattle, 1917–1942. *Source:* U.S. Agricultural Research Service, *Cooperative State-Federal Tuberculosis Eradication Program: Statistical Tables for Fiscal Year 1960* (Washington, DC: USDA, 1961); U.S. Department of Agriculture, *Yearbook of Agriculture, 1942*, p. 237; J. Arthur Myers, *Man's Greatest Victory over Tuberculosis* (Springfield, IL: Charles C. Thomas, 1940), pp. 314, 324–28.

lin testing.[21] Opponents disputed both the scientific underpinnings and the efficacy of tuberculin testing. The theoretical foundation for tuberculin testing was new, controversial, and, for many, counterintuitive. Eradication proponents espoused five principal scientific claims: apparently healthy cows could be diseased; this disease of cattle could pass to humans; a serum (that contained disease organisms) would produce a fever or swelling in an infected animal when injected; the same serum would not cause a reaction in a healthy animal; and the serum would not harm the animal or endanger humans who consumed its milk or meat. Disbelieving farmers and their political allies held that tuberculin was "filth" that would infect healthy animals with tuberculosis or activate the disease in animals with latent (and supposedly harmless) cases. Critics further asserted that the injections induced abortion, reduced milk output, and had other deleterious effects. In addition, opponents charged that the test was capricious because veterinarians could make any cow "react," and that many reactors showed no visible lesions in post-mortem inspections. Schisms within the scientific community combined with these concerns over the test inspired more resistance.

Many who accepted the underlying science opposed eradication as well, because they thought it was too ambitious and doomed to failure. In addition, opponents fumed over the distribution of the costs and benefits. The benefits were spread across a large and dispersed population, including consumers, meatpackers, and many farmers. The costs, on the other hand, were more concentrated, with some farmers facing financial ruin. Eradication proponents countered these objections with institutional mechanisms to partially compensate the losers. There were also widespread complaints about due process; many farmers were appalled that so-called experts could meddle in their day-to-day operations. To make matters worse, opponents bitterly complained that they had little or no recourse for appeals if their animals were condemned. Objectors often advanced an individualistic or libertarian theme deriding the heavy-handed actions of government bureaucrats who threatened individual liberty, property, and (if the science was wrong) even lives. The resistance to the test-and-slaughter program was most vigorous when existing organizations and communities took up the "anti" campaign as part of their broader agenda. In a world stacked against them, the program appeared as a wealth-destroying conspiracy of meatpackers looking for cheap stock, job-hungry veterinarians, and rent-seeking politicians. As the program progressed, and as its scientific foundations became more accepted, the emphases of the protesters shifted from disputing its underlying scientific merits to challenging the actual implementation and the distribution of the costs.

The campaign to eradicate BTB generally had support from the veterinary community, meatpackers, university agricultural colleges, and an assortment of public health officials. The country's farm journals and agricultural organizations were split on the issue. *Hoard's Dairyman* was a strong and early advocate, whereas *Breeder's Gazette* and the *Rural New Yorker* adopted hostile stances. The Farm Bureau and the National Grange endorsed the program, while the American Farmers' Union and the American Medical Liberty League (AMLL) mounted stiff opposition that delayed acceptance in several states.

The AMLL, a small but vocal group established in Chicago in 1918, remained a committed foe. Opposing the tuberculin testing of cattle was part of the League's broader agenda to "refuse and resist" compulsory vaccination and to confront organized medicine—especially the American Medical Association. The AMLL's followers generally rejected the germ theory of disease, characterizing vaccines, serums, and other biological products as poisons. Lora C. Little, one of the organization's chief advocates, was driven in part by the death of her son after he received a smallpox vaccination.[22] There was legitimate reason for concern, with many documented cases of tainted vaccines. One of the worse livestock epizootics in U.S. history—the 1914 foot-and-mouth disease outbreak—was exacerbated by impure hog cholera serums. Even more sensational was the 1930 tragedy in Lübeck, Germany, where over 200 infants died from tainted tuberculosis vaccine. In the early 1920s, the League flooded Midwestern counties likely to mandate testing with anti-tuberculin pamphlets. By the mid-1920s, the organization was assisting the newly formed Farmers' Protective Associations to rally farmers and to mount legal challenges against compulsory testing.[23]

The most prominent eradication critic was Senator Carter Glass of Virginia. In January 1922, a Commonwealth of Virginia veterinarian tested Glass's prized herd of Jerseys and concluded that two heifers had reacted and had to be destroyed. Glass asked for a retest. When the Virginia State Veterinarian, Dr. James Ferneyhough, refused, the senator embarked on a crusade against the program. In 1922, Glass distributed a long tirade, and in 1928 he issued a thirty-one-page U.S. Senate document entitled "Tale of Two Heifers." A few of the headings offer a hint of the his fury: "Unprofessional Conduct Charged," "Menace to Property Rights," "The Conspiracy Broadens," "Arbitrary Bureaucracy Rebuked," "An End to Official Terrorism," and "Deception and Despotism." Glass hit a nerve: farmers from across the country requested copies while registering their own complaints of arrogance and abuse by officials. His Senate office became a clearinghouse for the "anti" forces that distributed the "Tale of Two Heifers" at supervisor meetings and local elections where the testing program was under consideration.[24]

Rebellion in the Heartland

The clash between the pro-testing and anti-testing forces helped unleash one of the most serious civil disturbances in the history of American agriculture. The opening salvo in the conflict—the Iowa Cow War—was primarily a response to the BTB campaign. Voluntary tuberculin testing began in Iowa in 1919. A 1923 state law allowed counties to begin compulsory testing if three-quarters of the cattle owners petitioned to implement the program; the threshold was subsequently lowered. In 1929, the Iowa legislature made testing mandatory. The movement from voluntary to compulsory programs followed a general pattern in other states, reflecting the changing self-interest of many farmers. As more herds became TB free, their owners had an incentive to urge their political representatives to force all farmers to participate in order to prevent reinfection. As the scientific evidence became firmer, health officials, consumers, and pro-testing farmers became more emboldened to press for a general cleanup.[25]

The Cow War erupted in Tipton in eastern Iowa on 8 March 1931, when about 1,000 farmers confronted the state veterinarians and twenty sheriffs sent to test herds on the W. C. Butterbrodt and E. C. Mitchell farms. On March 19, some 1,500 protesters, egged on by Milo Reno of the Iowa Farmers' Union and Jacob W. Lenker of the Iowa Farmers' Protective Association, marched on the state capitol in Des Moines. Speakers from the group were allowed into the Iowa House chambers to address members on their demands to end compulsory testing. Besides criticizing the expense, mismanagement, and coercive nature of the program, speakers recited a litany of complaints challenging its scientific integrity. They asserted that tuberculosis could not be transmitted from cows to humans, denounced the tuberculin test as "unreliable," and charged that it caused the "cows to abort, become barren, and give unsaleable milk." They

denounced public health rhetoric as a mere ruse to cloak the real motives of creating graft opportunities for politicians and health officials as
well as cheap sources of meat for large-scale packers. A bill introduced
by Representative Lawrence Davis that would have made testing op-
tional failed to pass a few weeks after the marchers returned home.
Given the rural makeup of the legislature, it is unlikely that its members
would have defeated this bill unless many of the state's dairymen supported the mandate. In other incidents that spring, objectors stampeded
their cattle to avoid testing and roughed up officials and reporters.[26]

A second series of conflicts broke out when testing resumed in Cedar
County in September 1931. On September 21, several dozen state agents
descended on Lenker's farm in a high-profile effort to enforce the testing
mandate. Several hundred farmers confronted the veterinarians and
their phalanx of sheriff's deputies, violently driving the outsiders away.
In response, Governor Daniel Turner imposed martial law in the area,
calling out 1,700 national guardsmen to protect the testers (see Figure
12.4). Two protest leaders, Jacob Lenker and Paul Moore, were arrested
and charged with conspiring to interfere with the testing. During October
and November, hostilities spilled over into Des Moines, Henry, Jefferson,
Lee, and Muscatine counties. The troops remained in southeast Iowa for
two months (at a fiscal cost of over $100,000). The situation began to
quiet down in late 1931 after the state assured farmers that they could
use their own accredited veterinarians to administer the tests. But the
Iowa riots did bolster resistors in California, South Dakota, and Pennsylvania. The agitation also induced eradication activists such as Howard
R. Smith of the National Live Stock Exchange to redouble their efforts.[27]

Historians often treat the Cow War as the opening salvo in Milo
Reno's Farmers' Holiday Movement. During a series of violent strikes in
August 1932, armed Midwestern farmers blockaded roads to prevent the
shipment of dairy products. They also halted farm foreclosures and intimidated court officials, going so far as to kidnap Judge C. Bradley in
April 1933.[28] The literature stresses that the agricultural distress was a
major cause of the 1931 Cow War. The *Iowa Stater* argued that "farmers,
hard pressed by the Great Depression, found the testing and subsequent
condemnation of their cattle increasingly alarming." Historian John
Stover notes that "compulsory tuberculin testing was salt that stung the
wound of economic discontent."[29] This argument does not recognize the

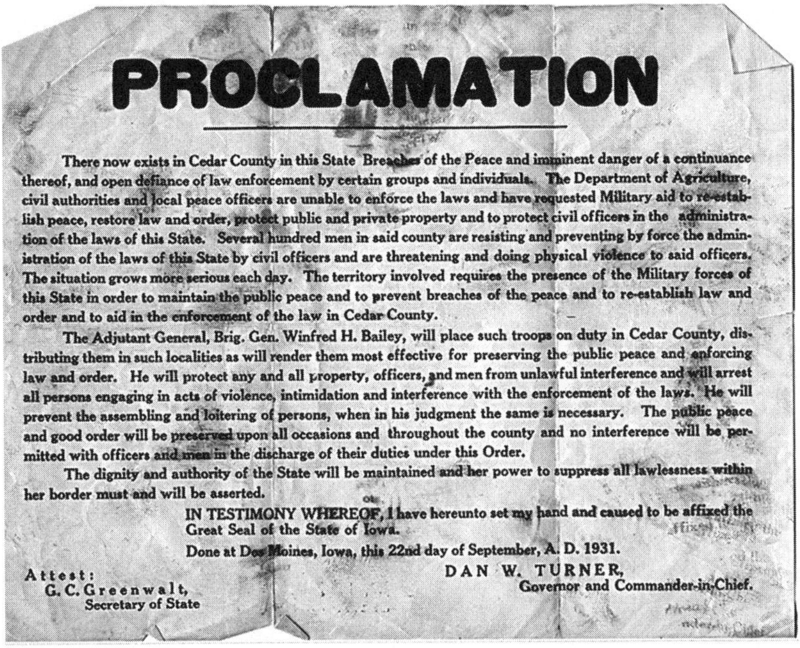

PROCLAMATION

There now exists in Cedar County in this State Breaches of the Peace and imminent danger of a continuance thereof, and open defiance of law enforcement by certain groups and individuals. The Department of Agriculture, civil authorities and local peace officers are unable to enforce the laws and have requested Military aid to re-establish peace, restore law and order, protect public and private property and to protect civil officers in the administration of the laws of this State. Several hundred men in said county are resisting and preventing by force the administration of the laws of this State by civil officers and are threatening and doing physical violence to said officers. The situation grows more serious each day. The territory involved requires the presence of the Military forces of this State in order to maintain the public peace and to prevent breaches of the peace and to re-establish law and order and to aid in the enforcement of the law in Cedar County.

The Adjutant General, Brig. Gen. Winfred H. Bailey, will place such troops on duty in Cedar County, distributing them in such localities as will render them most effective for preserving the public peace and enforcing law and order. He will protect any and all property, officers, and men from unlawful interference and will arrest all persons engaging in acts of violence, intimidation and interference with the enforcement of the laws. He will prevent the assembling and loitering of persons, when in his judgment the same is necessary. The public peace and good order will be preserved upon all occasions and throughout the county and no interference will be permitted with officers and men in the discharge of their duties under this Order.

The dignity and authority of the State will be maintained and her power to suppress all lawlessness within her border must and will be asserted.

IN TESTIMONY WHEREOF, I have hereunto set my hand and caused to be affixed the Great Seal of the State of Iowa.

Done at Des Moines, Iowa, this 22nd day of September, A. D. 1931.

Attest:
G. C. Greenwalt,
Secretary of State

DAN W. TURNER,
Governor and Commander-in-Chief.

Figure 12.4. Declaration of martial law in Iowa, 1931. *Source:* Cedar County Historical Society.

generosity of the eradication program in the early 1930s. In 1931, the losses from condemnation in Iowa were low by historic standards, and were comparable to those in Illinois, Missouri, and Kansas. These nearby states all faced similar Depression era problems but did not experience such disturbances.[30] The appraised values were typically above market value because appraisers were sympathetic to beleaguered dairymen. Indeed, allowing reactors to be condemned proved to be a better deal than holding onto them. In the early 1930s, the prospect of gaining cash indemnities from the government became attractive to many dairymen across the country. On 23 March 1933, BAI Chief John R. Mohler wrote to his agents: "During a period such as the present when the value of cattle are low, there seems to be more of a tendency on the part of unscrupulous persons to get possession of cattle, usually of a low grade, at very low prices, and then present them for the tuberculin test with the idea that State and Federal indemnity will be obtained."[31] Reports from several states purport that farmers in the early 1930s went so far as to tamper with the test by applying irritants to create a swelling at the injection site, thereby simulating a reaction in healthy animals.[32] The traditional historical accounts claiming that the anti-BTB riots were sparked by unbearable financial losses appear to be at odds with the evidence.

The Last Stand in California

Although many have written about the Iowa Cow War, the California story has gone largely untold. Contrary to its well-cultivated image as a pacesetter, the Golden State was a laggard in BTB eradication. Its slow progress highlights the interplay of poor leadership, funding pressures, constitutional limitations, and vigorous opposition. The effect of incentives and the social heterogeneity of dairy owners also played roles.

As of 1921, the state's constitution prohibited paying indemnities. Without state indemnities, there were no federal matching funds. Absent compensation, few cattle owners volunteered for the test-and-slaughter program. By the late 1920s, while BTB infection rates were falling elsewhere, they were rising in California. Indeed, the state had become a dumping ground for diseased animals. These trends created pressure for change. In 1929, California passed its first BTB law allowing state indemnity payments, and in November 1930 voters overwhelmingly passed a constitutional amendment explicitly allowing indemnities. That year, James "Sunny Jim" Rolph Jr. was elected governor. He replaced the respected head of the Division of Animal Industry with a crony. In 1931, the legislature appropriated $450,000 for indemnities, making California the forty-sixth state to join the national program. However, legalizing indemnities did not provide a quick fix. Depressed economic conditions undercut state revenues, and scandals eroded the program's support. In 1933, the state slashed eradication funding by over one-half and prevented new areas from entering the indemnity program.[33]

In 1934, the Jones-Connally Act allowed federal payments without state matching funds. At the behest of the Farm Bureau, several California counties imposed compulsory testing without state money. The available federal indemnities were low—covering only about one-third the average value of dairy cattle in the state. Nevertheless, there was a growing pressure to clean up; by the mid-1930s, most of the state's large cities were prohibiting dairy products from untested cows, and cattle buyers were rejecting animals from nonaccredited areas. It was clear that California dairymen would have to purge their reactors—the only question was at whose expense.[34]

In California, much of the resistance to testing came from a well-organized group of farmers of Portuguese descent. As early as 1929, a BAI inspector observed that this "antagonistic" ethnic group created serious problems for the eradication program. The resisters asserted that the testing program would discriminate against political outsiders such as the Portuguese and that the admittedly high reaction rates in their herds would drive many to bankruptcy. Violence erupted, including a riot in May 1937 when an angry mob of 500 protesters prevented testing at a Stanislaus County dairy. There were other confrontations, but the California opponents' primary challenge to testing came through the courts, where they repeatedly obtained injunctions to halt testing.[35]

The anti-testing forces in California emphasized a different message than earlier opponents (such as Senator Glass). By the mid-1930s, few lawsuits challenged the underlying science of BTB testing or argued that tuberculin poisoned cattle and humans. Rather, objectors in California emphasized distributional and procedural issues, and focused on the inadequacy of state indemnities—they wanted a better deal. Opponents everywhere complained of high-handed treatment by testing officials who were at once "accusers, prosecutors, judges, and executioners."[36] In July 1937, the California legislature redressed past grievances by extending indemnities to all the state's counties and allocating $1.5 million for the payments. By 1939, the state legislature had approved special appropriations to pay a number of past contested indemnity claims.[37] This buy-off effectively ended the last pockets of resistance in the United States.

Costs and Benefits

At the onset of the federal eradication program, the USDA estimated that the annual cost of BTB to the livestock sector was at least $40 million.[38] This estimate, which reckoned only the losses to animal production, failed to capture the effects on human health and the dynamic implication of the contagion. As J. A. Kiernan and L. B. Ernest observed in 1919, "Had the spread of [bovine] tuberculosis been allowed to continue at the same rate that it progressed from 1907 to 1917, the disease would undoubtedly have exacted an annual toll from the live-stock producers of this Nation of one hundred million dollars."[39]

Although there have been a number of similar attempts to compare the costs and benefits of the program, none meets conventional standards of economic analysis. Typically, the costs of the programs are measured as the cumulative undiscounted sum of nominal government expenditures. For the 1917–1962 period, this sum totals about $420 million. Besides ignoring interest rates and inflation, this approach completely overlooks the substantial costs that farmers bore through uncompensated losses for slaughtered reactors.

We can get closer to the mark if we estimate the net losses to farmers, adjust for changes in the price level, and discount using a constant 3 percent real interest rate to express the total in a specific reference year—we selected 1918, when the program got under way.[40] According to our calculations, the discounted cost of the program over the 1917–1962 period was $258 million in real 1918 dollars (adjusting for inflation, this would amount to about $3.74 billion in 2010 dollars). Of this, the federal government contributed about 31 percent, the state and local governments 54 percent, and farmers 15 percent. At the assumed 3 percent real interest rate, the $258 million investment in the program was equivalent to borrowing with the promise to repay $7.7 million in 1918 dollars ($111 million in 2010 dollars) each year in perpetuity.

Employing a similar procedure and assuming an annual BTB diffusion rate of 5 percent in cattle in the absence of the program suggests that the BTB eradication campaign saved roughly $3.2 billion over the 1918–1962 period, or the equivalent of a perpetuity paying $98.7 million per year (in 1918 dollars). Thus, for the livestock sector alone the annual benefits were approximately twelve times the annual costs.

Although the net benefits of eradication in the livestock sector were impressive, they represent only part of the story because the most important benefits came from alleviating human suffering and saving lives. To evaluate the effects of the eradication campaign on human health, we include the effects of milk pasteurization.[41] Tuberculin testing and pasteurization were twin approaches to reducing human infection by BTB through milk. Tuberculin testing attempted to prevent the entry of tubercle bacteria into the milk supply, whereas pasteurization sought to destroy those harmful bacteria that did enter before the milk was consumed. It is difficult to evaluate their effects separately, but we know that jointly they led to "almost eliminating human disease due to *M. bovis* by the 1940s."[42] By 1942, there had been such a marked decline in the incidence of "the bovine type infection in man that medical experts have stated it is practically impossible to find such cases for the clinical instruction of medical students."[43]

Finally, we estimate of the value of the human lives saved. In the appendix to Chapter 10, we develop estimates of the reduction of deaths in the United States in 1940 due to the campaign against BTB. Eradication and pasteurization prevented roughly 25,600 deaths from BTB a year circa 1940. Taking the value that Irving Fisher attributed to each tuberculosis death implies an annual savings of $327 million in 1918 purchasing power. This was several times larger than the annual savings to the livestock industry.[44] We realize that such estimates are inherently problematic, but it is clear that the benefits of the clean milk campaign were huge and primarily outside the agricultural sector.

International Comparisons

BTB policies in other countries highlight the significance of international spillovers and the importance of outside intervention in gaining success. The United States was not completely alone in its campaign against BTB because Canada took a parallel course, initiating voluntary testing in 1897, a countrywide anti-BTB campaign in 1919, and a mandatory area plan beginning in 1923. By 1961, a first round of testing succeeded in reducing the reaction rates from about 4 percent to 0.1 percent. The program continued, eventually leading to the administration of 100 million tests and the slaughter of 800,000 cattle.[45] Great Britain lagged well behind its North American offshoots. British farmers and butchers who blocked meat inspection also scuttled BTB control. Pre–World War II policies proved ineffective, in part because of the misuse of tuberculin. In 1946, the estimated incidence of bovine tuberculosis in the national herd was still 18 percent. In October 1950, Britain finally began a national compulsory eradication program and was largely free of the disease by 1960. This required the slaughter of 2.2 million cattle.[46]

The experience varied on the Continent. The Scandinavian countries were most aggressive, with Finland gaining an informal status roughly on par with that of the United States by 1940. Circa 1935, when Denmark adopted compulsory eradication, about 80 percent of the country's herds were infected. In 1952, Denmark was declared BTB free, and Sweden had it under control by the mid-1950s. Germany adopted a minimalist approach, which segregated obviously infected cattle but did not employ the tuberculin test. The French model was based on employing a vaccine developed by Albert Calmette and Jean-Marie Camille Guérin (the BCG vaccine). Nowhere in Europe was there much success with voluntary schemes. The hope that the BCG vaccine might provide a cheap solution to BTB delayed eradication in some countries. France did not bow to outside pressures and commence a compulsory test-and-slaughter regime until 1965. Europe's southern fringe had an even poorer record. As examples, neither Italy nor Spain embarked on comprehensive compulsory eradication programs until the late 1970s.[47]

Outside forces—first the United States and then European Economic Community (EEC) and its successor, the European Union (EU)—played an important part in BTB eradication in post-war Europe. European officials learned much from the American experiences. In most Western European countries, the United States directly kick-started the first truly compulsory area-wide programs with dedicated Marshall Plan aid and via the active involvement of U.S. Army veterinarians. In a sense, American involvement in Europe paralleled the role of the U.S. federal government vis-à-vis the several states.

Conclusion

The BTB program in the United States was built on several principles that remain central to livestock disease-control efforts. Federal officials laid the groundwork by meeting with and listening to a number of powerful farm, meatpacking, transportation, and veterinary interests. Not everyone was on board—far from it. But the program had the appearance of responding to citizen initiatives—even if those overtures were in part orchestrated by federal officials. Many state leaders, who had earlier resisted federal involvement, were anxious to cooperate by 1917. The Dorsey fiasco and the catastrophic failure of divided jurisdictions to deal with regulatory arbitrage helped ensure this turn of events. The BAI designed the program with shared financial and operational responsibility to help ensure active state participation. Previous successes against other diseases had built considerable moral and institutional capital—many states had the legal foundations needed for eradication partly in place, and state-federal agreements were no longer seen as unacceptable intrusions into state legal preserves.

The BAI started with a limited voluntary program, which targeted relatively sophisticated cattlemen who owned valuable breeding and dairy cattle. Officials recognized that there would be a political dynamic: farmers with clean herds would support stronger policies to force farmers with infected herds to participate in order to prevent reinfection. Officials also knew that they needed the carrot of indemnity payments, and they adjusted parameters, including indemnity levels and state-federal payment ratios, to meet changing conditions. Urban consumers became a potent force demanding clean milk. Urban milk legislation pushed the boundary of city regulatory power into the countryside. This ignited intense legal battles, which farmers eventually lost. Most livestock disease control efforts required that regulators deal with conflicting interests within the agricultural sector, but with BTB, meat inspection, and other cases that directly involved human health, the conflicts were far more complicated. The difficult issues were political, economic, and social in nature rather than scientific.

In 1941, *Hoard's Dairyman* boasted: "That bovine tuberculosis is well nigh exterminated from its cattle should be a source of great satisfaction to the people of this nation. It shows the strength of a democracy when an important work for the benefit of all people is to be done. No other nation in the world has accomplished such a gigantic undertaking."[48] As an early leader in the anti-BTB campaign, *Hoard's* editors had reason to gloat. However, it is paradoxical that the United States was so much more aggressive than most countries in Europe. The American philosophical bent toward pragmatism and compromise was at variance with the idealistic goal of the complete eradication of the disease. The compulsory nature of the area plan concept also ran against the American tradition of voluntarism. Moreover, one might expect that the European states, with their less democratic political systems, established bureaucracies, and centralized research establishments might have responded more rapidly to the evolving state of scientific knowledge. The greater severity of the problem in Europe surely was an important reason for inaction. In both the United States and Europe, it helped immensely to have a super state—the federal government and the European Union (and its predecessors)—to push eradication policies. Success in the United States required the unflinching use of police power and great expense, but the net benefits were enormous.

13 Getting Off the Fix

Hog Cholera Eradication

THE DECISION to eradicate hog cholera would be a long time coming. Daniel Salmon had naively proposed its elimination in 1878, well before any understanding of the disease's etiology and before a federal livestock bureaucracy existed. In 1915, Bureau of Animal Industry (BAI) Chief A. D. Melvin raised and rejected the notion, and in 1921 Secretary of Agriculture Henry C. Wallace floated the idea. Scientists had made great progress in understanding hog cholera, but eradication still seemed too daunting a task. The highly contagious disease was deeply entrenched, there were not enough enforcement agents, and there was little support among swine farmers and state officials. Without a simultaneous national effort, cleared areas would be constantly reinfected. The availability of vaccines, as imperfect as they were, made it easier to live with the disease, and ensured that most farmers would not be willing to make the sacrifices required to stamp it out.[1]

The history of hog cholera eradication is part of a broader story of progress. Beginning in the late eighteenth century, scientists created a succession of vaccines and sera to prevent the spread of diseases or to ameliorate their symptoms. Edward Jenner's achievement with using the relatively safe material extracted from cowpox blisters to control smallpox was a seminal advance. Robert Koch's pursuit of a vaccine for tuberculosis failed but led to the development of a diagnostic technology (Chapter 10). French scientists, led by Albert Calmette and Jean-Marie Camille Guérin, were in the forefront of the search for tuberculosis vaccines. Louis Pasteur's and Emile Roux's development of the rabies vaccine, Paul Ehrlich's hunt for magic bullets, and work in Europe, Africa, and North America on rinderpest vaccines were all part of this grand quest. As indicated in Chapter 7, the discovery of the hog cholera virus and the development of vaccines to combat the disease contributed to this larger scientific endeavor.

The early work on vaccines had enormous importance well beyond the particulars of any one disease because the search for specific cures both led to and was eventually guided by a new appreciation of the basic principles of disease causality and transmission. This work also created a new understanding of the immunological involvement of host response in disease control. Many new vaccines, sera, and antitoxins were indeed magic bullets in that they successfully triggered immunity to specific threats with minimal side effects to the recipients or costs to the broader community. In these cases, the agent that triggered the immune response was sufficiently attenuated (or perhaps killed or from a related, less virulent pathogen, as with the smallpox vaccine). But for other diseases, of which hog cholera was a prominent example, scientists were unable to create effective vaccines that did not contain live virus. This was not for want of trying. From the time of the development of the first hog cholera vaccines in Iowa, researchers sought safer processes. So long as veterinarians were seeding farms with active virus, eradication would be impossible.

There were significant public policy implications associated with the choice of disease-control methods. Across a wide spectrum of diseases there was a trade-off between employing vaccination policies and more draconian quarantine and eradication-by-culling policies. For human diseases, radical culling policies were not an option as they were for livestock diseases. In addition, for many diseases such as smallpox vaccination was essential to eradication, and as scientific technologies improved, the set of diseases for which the two policy options reinforced each other increased. Critics of the high cost of eradication often implored policy makers to wait—a cheap cure might be just over the horizon (paradoxically, many of these same critics opposed funding for research to find such cures). But to delay in addressing a contagion amplified the risks that the problem would multiply.

In the United States, contagious bovine pleuropneumonia (CBPP) was spreading, but it had not reached the open range. With no magic bullet in sight, policy makers chose to act decisively. This campaign would define the area-eradication model and create new state-federal agreements that set the stage for future disease control programs. The trade-off between vaccination and eradication by culling extended to other diseases. While much of the world opted for vaccines to control bovine tuberculosis and foot-and-mouth disease (FMD), other countries, including the United States, opted to cull diseased and exposed stock. Each disease and each country have a different story, but as a rule vaccination was more appealing where a disease was more entrenched. In addition, where human and social capital were lacking—that is, where farmers were poorly informed, where scientific personnel were few, and where the institutions needed for collective action were weak and not trusted—vaccination was apt to be the best available option.

Once taken, the path of deploying live-virus vaccines had a dynamic effect on government spending and industry organization. Individual farmers made the decision to employ (and pay for) the vaccines and live virus. This contrasted with the collective decisions to control and then eradicate CBPP, bovine tuberculosis, Texas fever, sheep and cattle scab, and other diseases. These coercive programs all strove to limit the free-rider problem. As a result, cattlemen and stockyard owners had to organize and pressure the state and federal governments for legislation and money. In part for this reason, the organizational efforts and government funding to control diseases afflicting cattle far exceeded those afflicting hogs. Rather than mobilizing the federal government to enforce collective action, hog farmers (and meatpackers) generally pressed the government to make the individualist—vaccine—approach work better. The BAI responded by playing a key role in improving vaccine technologies. In spite of important scientific advances, serious problems with the vaccine regime continued. These problems, along with the fear of other diseases, eventually altered the calculation for many hog farmers and meatpackers, making living with hog cholera less attractive.

Hope Springs Eternal

The post-1907 hog-cholera research enterprise aimed at perfecting the vaccine technologies. Important goals included the development of more efficient hyperimmune procedures, purer and more stable sera, more finely calibrated dosage guidelines, and more reliable transportation and storage procedures. Researchers also experimented with pasteurization and sundry chemical treatments to create modified sera so that they would pose less risk of transmitting diseases. The work on serum safety intensified after contaminated hog cholera serum caused the catastrophic 1914–16 FMD epizootic. In 1916, researchers hit on a several-step chemical and centrifuge procedure (dubbed the bean-salt process) to create a clear serum that could then be pasteurized. This new process gradually spread; in 1935, the BAI mandated that all hog cholera serum be heat-treated (effectively requiring the bean-salt process). This ensured that, barring protocol failures, sera were free of the FMD virus and the bacilli that caused tuberculosis and other diseases, but there was still no protection against contamination from most viruses. In another milestone, Paul Lewis and R. E. Shope of the Rockefeller Institute for Medical Research developed an improved diagnostic test for hog cholera.[2]

A major research thrust was directed at reducing or eliminating the use of active virus. The problem was to make the virus inactive (so that it would not transmit full-blown cases of hog cholera) while keeping it potent enough to trigger the immune process to provide long-lasting immunity. Many procedures showed promise, but in the mid-1930s attention focused on a method employing crystal violet as an attenuating agent to detoxify several viruses and bacilli.[3]

This research, begun by Marion Dorset in 1934 and continued by other BAI scientists, discovered that the crystal violet vaccine imparted immunity, but only after two to three weeks. This meant that the new vaccine was not suitable for farms where hog cholera already existed or was an immediate threat. Moreover, other disease-causing agents continued to contaminate these vaccines. In the mid-1940s, the BAI patented and licensed a violet-glycerin formula that proved relatively sterile.[4]

In the late 1940s and early 1950s, scientific advances fundamentally changed the course of hog cholera control policy. In 1946, James A. Baker of the Rockefeller Institute for Medical Research used state-of-the art techniques to develop an effective modified live-virus (MLV) vaccine.[5] The new MLV vaccines could be used alone or in conjunction with hyper-immune serum to provide immediate protection. As early as 1951, the USDA began to commercially license the production of MLV vaccines. At the same time, a series of "breaks," (that is, unexplained outbreaks) appeared in herds that had been immunized using the older generation of sera. These failures pushed hog growers to switch rapidly to the new vaccines. With the advent of this safer alternative, a number of states, starting with Alabama in 1954, phased out the usage of the fully virulent virus. As with other disease-control initiatives, acting alone had problems; farmers could easily import the banned vaccines across state lines. Nevertheless, by 1962, forty-four states had followed Alabama's lead.[6]

The newer MLV vaccines were far from perfect. Individual swine varied significantly in their natural susceptibility and/or resistance to the hog cholera virus and in their reaction to injections of serum and virus. Violent and fatal reactions to the treatments were all too frequent, especially with young pigs. In addition, the MLV vaccines continued to be plagued by breaks, often attributed to contaminated products or to improper application. Some products were not effective against all strains of hog cholera, and attenuated vaccines differed in their potency. As late as 1966, one-third of hog cholera outbreaks were traced to faulty vaccines.[7]

Disease Interactions and Public Policy

A nationwide outbreak of vesicular exanthema (VE) in swine created a new and powerful impetus for change. Vesicular exanthema is an acute, highly infectious disease that is clinically indistinguishable from several other serious diseases, most notably FMD. When VE first appeared in California in 1932, it caused a FMD panic. VE remained confined to California for 20 years, but in June 1952 it was discovered in a factory manufacturing biologicals in Grand Island, Nebraska. The disease was soon traced back to a herd in Cheyenne, Wyoming, which had been fed contaminated garbage from an east-bound transcontinental train. Within 15 months, the contagion had engulfed forty-two states and the District of Columbia.[8] Every occurrence of VE in swine had to be initially investigated and treated as if it was FMD. As a result, the political dynamics of swine disease policy rapidly changed. The federal government responded with an emergency campaign to eradicate VE. This involved a quarantine and slaughter program, along with new state and federal prohibitions on feeding raw garbage to swine. Success was declared in 1959.

The spread of VE helped galvanize support for policies that had a direct impact on controlling hog cholera, trichinosis, and other diseases. The campaign to stamp out VE represented the first time that the commercial swine industry was involved in a rigorous national eradication effort. The campaign induced a wave of regulations. By July 1952, Clinton Anderson, the Secretary of Agriculture, had placed eighteen states under quarantine; on August 1, he declared a state of emergency. In addition to the USDA, the U.S. Public Health Service issued rules that prohibited the interstate commerce in pork from swine that had ever been fed raw garbage. States also began adopting regulations to require heating garbage to sterilize it before it was fed to swine. Twenty-two states prohibited feeding raw garbage in 1953; this number rose to forty-six in 1956. The share of garbage-consuming swine fed raw garbage fell from 68 percent in December 1953 to 12 percent in November 1955 and to 1.5 percent in May 1961.[9]

Hog farmers and packers had staunchly resisted such reforms to control trichinosis, which affected humans but did little damage to swine. In the early 1950s these same interests came to view VE as a serious threat to their livelihood and began to clamor for forceful government action. The campaign against VE had important consequences. The combination of this new regulatory regime and the newly formed cooperative relationship between leaders of the swine industry and the animal health community created an environment more conducive to pursuing the eradication of hog cholera—a disease far more serious and costly than VE. The new MLV vaccines, as imperfect as they were, gave the USDA the technology to depart from the policies it had followed over the past seven decades. The prevalence of hog cholera could now be reduced to a low enough level that a concerted campaign to eradicate via depopulation became politically and economically feasible.

A Different Path

American policy makers did not have to look far for a successful hog cholera eradication model. Canada represented a constant reminder of the path not followed. It had started a policy of stamping out hog cholera in 1900 with the slaughter of infected herds and the payment of indemnities. In 1913, Canada prohibited the importation and manufacture of hog cholera vaccines, closing off the U.S. path. In 1916, it prohibited feeding raw garbage and heavily regulated feeding cooked garbage to swine. Such steps would not be taken in the United States for roughly a half century. Hog cholera had not invaded Canada until 1885. The fact that the government acted before the disease had gained a secure foothold undoubtedly made control much less costly. Although Canada did not officially eradicate hog cholera until 1964, its policies kept the prevalence of the disease at far lower levels than in the United States. The cost of control was a small fraction of what American swine producers were paying under the serum-virus technologies of the pre-1960 period.[10]

U.S. authorities had long sought treatments that would allow farmers to live with the disease. The USDA played a continuing role in advancing the basic science and applied technologies associated with hog cholera, and many states played an important role in producing hog cholera sera immediately following Dorset's breakthrough. But, as a matter of conscious policy, the USDA stepped back to encourage private pharmaceutical firms to capture the production and distribution of sera and vaccines. The federal government continued to set standards, license processes, inspect manufacturers, test vaccine potency and purity, and investigate when things went wrong. The federal and state governments also regulated the shipment of both biological products and live animals, especially breeding stock, that potentially could spread hog cholera. The serum-virus and vaccination technologies essentially gave individual farmers the means to protect their herds from catastrophic losses but at considerable private and social costs.

The continued problems and expenses associated with hog cholera vaccines sparked renewed interest in full-scale eradication. American farmers and packers were also jealous of the cost advantage and preferential access to world markets that Canadians enjoyed. The fear that a hog cholera strain resistant to vaccines might emerge gave added impetus to a change in policy. In fact, a "variant virus" apparently led to the death of thousands of pigs in 1949. The National Research Council studied the possibility of eradication in 1946, and it was proposed by an American Veterinary Medical Association committee in 1947. At the urging of the American Veterinary Medical Association, in 1951 the U.S. Livestock Sanitary Association (now the U.S. Animal Health Association) appointed a Committee on the Nationwide Eradication of Hog Cholera. Over the next decade, a number of private organizations, such as Livestock Conservation, Inc., intensified the push for eradication.[11]

In 1961, Congress debated legislation to eradicate hog cholera. During the hearings, Secretary of Agriculture Orville Freeman estimated that the disease was costing swine producers $60 million annually (due to direct losses, the cost of treatments, and trade losses). Producers spent roughly $25 million a year for control measures. Eleven nations were then restricting U.S. pork imports, and there was little likelihood of opening these markets until the United States dealt with hog cholera. In 1961, Congress passed legislation calling for the complete eradication of hog cholera from the United States. This legislation had broad-based bipartisan support—in the House it passed (on August 28) by a vote of 339 to 3. The days of unified Southern opposition to intrusive federal livestock policies were long gone. President John Kennedy signed the eradication law (S 1908) on 6 September 1961.[12]

During many previous eradication campaigns, the USDA had coaxed or even forced many state and local governments to participate. However, by 1961 there was little organized resistance to stamping out hog cholera. The leaders of America's major farm groups and meatpackers were on board; even the representatives of the National Farmers Union—an organization that had often opposed other campaigns—were strong supporters. More remarkably, Charles S. Greene, who represented approximately 20 hog-cholera pharmaceutical producers, testified in favor of eradication. Anti-hog cholera products were a big business for many of these companies, and Greene emphasized that eradication was not in their "own self interest." Nevertheless, "we are compelled by our own objectives to support a national hog cholera eradication program." Despite this extraordinary consensus, there would still be many controversies. The devil was in the details, and issues such as determining the level of compensation to be paid to farmers whose animals were culled remained contentious. Although the major veterinary associations led the eradication charge, many individual veterinarians were not so enthusiastic because hog cholera vaccination represented a major source of income.[13]

In the two decades after 1957, a new threat emerged that heightened the need to press forward with eradication. In 1957, African swine fever (ASF) jumped from Africa to Portugal. It appeared in France in 1964, in Italy in 1967, in Cuba in 1971, and in Brazil in 1978. This disease is highly contagious, incurable, and nearly always fatal, so stamping it out was the only acceptable policy. Because ASF is clinically indistinguishable from hog cholera, it would be easy to misdiagnose an ASF outbreak as just another hog cholera episode, critically delaying an aggressive response.

Thus, coexisting with hog cholera would have increased the risk of ASF, much like coexisting with VE would have increased the risk of FMD.[14]

The Eradication Campaign

Eradication would be a major undertaking. At the time, 1.5 million farms reported raising swine, with an annual production of about 80 million hogs. The USDA formally initiated eradication in 1962, and the following year it banned the interstate shipment of products containing the hog cholera virus. Actual condemnations began in 1965. The program followed the model set by earlier federal-state eradication efforts with the establishment of state and county eradication committees, investigations of suspected outbreaks, restrictions on movement, and depopulation of infected herds accompanied by the payment of indemnities, disposal of carcasses, and disinfection of infected premises. As the program moved forward, vaccines were progressively more tightly regulated within any given state. In rough accord with other programs, the federal government began funding indemnities of up to one-half of the net loss in value of the swine condemned; as in the past, the USDA adjusted its formula in response to heightened threats and political pressure. Most states supplied additional compensation.

By the end of 1964, every state except Texas had entered the program, and Vermont had achieved "hog cholera free" status. Eradication got a boost in 1965 with the development of improved laboratory diagnostic methods. But in spite of this and other advances, the program was not on schedule. Eradication proved far more difficult than anticipated, and states freed of the disease were often reinfected. Moreover, delays attributed to inadequate funding and complacency prevented the realization of the goal of eradicating the disease within ten years. A milestone was reached in 1969, when Wisconsin became the first of the top-ten hog-producing states to eradicate the disease.[15] The years 1969 and 1970 represented the peak period of the federal indemnity program, with nearly 430,000 animals condemned—this represented over half of all condemnations during the life of the eradication drive from 1965 to 1977.

Although most farmer organizations and nearly all members of Congress endorsed eradication, for many individual hog farmers the program was a "risky and radical" experiment. They were particularly concerned with the bans on biologic materials. Livestock dealers serving the feeder pig market doubted the efficacy of the newer vaccines and complained about the elimination of the tried-and-true serum-virus technology. Many hog shippers and garbage feeders objected to the costs of the new regulations. Compliance was often spotty.[16] To add to the problems, many modified and killed virus vaccines authorized during the transition period failed to provide adequate protection, others caused severe reactions in pigs, and a growing number of hog cholera cases were being attributed to vaccines previously thought to be incapable of spreading the disease. There was also increasing concern that vaccines were being misused.

In response to the criticisms and problems, USDA established a special study group in 1967 to investigate vaccine safety. In June 1967, the USDA recommended phasing out all vaccines by 1 January 1971. Heated confrontations erupted between supporters and opponents at a series of public forums. On 24 May 1969, the USDA signaled the end of the debate by prohibiting the interstate movement of modified live-virus vaccines after July 1, restricting the use of inactivated vaccines, and announcing its intention to eliminate the use of all vaccines by 1 January 1970—a year ahead of the previously announced date. The path was set. The USDA was unilaterally burning its bridges and committing the nation to stamping out hog cholera without the aid of vaccines. Even the American Veterinary Medical Association, which supported the USDA's plan, expressed concern about the wisdom of the "drastic restrictions on vaccines" in the absence of stronger state and federal quarantine and slaughter policies.[17]

A hog cholera outbreak in 1969–1970 raised further questions about the vaccine ban and further demonstrated the difficulties in gaining the cooperation of shippers and garbage feeders. As program officials responded with stronger enforcement, joint federal-state quarantines were becoming commonplace. As one example, the federal government placed portions of Delaware, Maryland, and Virginia under a strict hog cholera quarantine in 1969.[18] In 1970, officials mobilized an emergency task force to wipe out a lingering pocket of the contagion in the Dismal Swamp area, a vast wooded wetlands in Southeastern Virginia and Northeastern North Carolina.

The "heroic treatment" employed in the area-plan eradication campaign against CBPP was back in vogue. On 8 September 1970, an eleven-county area straddling the state borders was placed under tight quarantine. A USDA veterinarian with long experience in eradication work abroad assumed the "one man power" of coordinating the joint operation and exercising both federal and state authority. The operation established a local headquarters, set up field diagnostic laboratories, and assembled a task force of 170 specialists drawn from across the country. These officials fanned out to inspect (and reinspect) all local herds, record histories, collect samples, slaughter and safely dispose of infected and exposed animals, and disinfect contaminated premises and equipment. Movement of swine within the area required official permission. To secure local cooperation and overcome resistance, program officials engaged in an education campaign and provided generous indemnities. By November 20, the effort was complete. Over the three-month period, 12,000 swine were condemned and killed. In this rapid large-scale push, the Great Dismal Swamp area, which had been a major source of outbreaks of the hog cholera nationwide, was finally purged of the disease.[19]

During the last stages of the program, the USDA repeatedly assembled agents from around the country to deploy hard-hitting task forces to hot spots. Serious eruptions occurred in Ohio, Indiana, Pennsylvania, New Jersey, and several Southern states in August 1972. In response, Secretary of Agriculture Earl Butz declared a national state of emergency so that he could allocate more resources to the fight. The USDA took the extreme steps of banning all movement of swine in entire states, prohibiting hunting to reduce the likelihood of spreading the disease, and spraying large areas to kill flies that might transmit the virus. A joint federal-state task force destroyed 15,741 swine in New Jersey to stamp out the last flair up in 1976. Despite the delays, doubts, and dissent, success was at hand. On 31 January 1978, ninety-nine years after the USDA began its hog cholera research and seventeen years after the start of the eradication program, Secretary of Agriculture Bob Bergland triumphantly proclaimed the United States free of hog cholera.[20]

Eradication proved a wise policy. A comparison of the real discounted benefits of eradication from 1978 to 2010 to the real discounted program and indemnity expenditures from 1962 to 1977 yields a benefit-cost ratio exceeding 15 to 1.[21] This crude estimate probably significantly understates the true benefit-cost ratio. The cost data are fairly well defined and accounted for, but there were many additional benefits that we do not capture. As an example, hog cholera eradication provided insurance against the possibility that a potential outbreak of ASF might be misdiagnosed as hog cholera, thereby delaying the response. In addition, the calculations do not account for the greater access to foreign markets that came with eradication. Adding these and other benefits into the calculus would increase the benefit-cost ratio accordingly.

Conclusion

Until the 1960s, the USDA's hog cholera work was a far cry from the forceful policies employed against many other diseases. In other cases, federal agents (granted state emergency powers) declared and enforced widespread quarantines within a state's boundaries, entered onto individual farms—with or without the owner's permission—to confiscate and condemn livestock, and supervised intrusive cleaning operations. For hog cholera, policy makers and farmers chose to live with the disease.

Once the nation embarked on eradication, the task was finished in just seventeen years. Why did it take so long to begin to eradicate hog cholera? Some have asserted that swine farmers were less organized and somehow different from dairymen. A problem with this reasoning is that many farmers who raised swine also kept dairy cattle. A key distinction was that hog cholera had become deeply entrenched in the United States; given the state of scientific understanding in the late nineteenth century, it would have been nearly impossible to stamp out. Also, when the USDA finally turned to eradicating hog cholera, it already had many successes to its credit, which gave policy makers the confidence to undertake this next endeavor and generated the necessary public support. Besides the diseases detailed in this book, the BAI (or its successor organization) had made major advances in controlling scores of diseases of livestock, pets, and wild animals. Many of these, including anthrax and rabies, directly threatened humans.

As with the early scientific advances on hog cholera discussed in Chapter 7, government researchers played a key role in the search for improved vaccines, but scientists never were able to provide a cure or even an entirely safe treatment for hog cholera. The availability of treatments that suppressed the disease set the nation on a path where the ongoing search for better vaccines held out a hope—a new discovery might be forthcoming that would make biting the bullet and enduring the costs of eradication unnecessary. This hope of a scientific cure eroded the resolve for a costly public policy fix. Canada adopted an eradication strategy in 1900 and weaned itself of vaccines fairly early, but the disease was not as widely established there. Even so, Canada did not finally eradicate hog cholera until 1964. Australia eradicated hog cholera in 1963. Most of Europe also waited. The United Kingdom did not begin its successful eradication program until 1963 and declared success in 1967. Apart from the Scandinavian countries and Switzerland, most of continental Europe experienced repeated outbreaks. An epizootic struck much of Western Europe in 1997. The Netherlands was hardest hit; that one country destroyed almost 11 million pigs with losses exceeding $2.3 billion.[22] These international perspectives suggest that although the USDA might be faulted for not opting for eradication earlier, its leaders were not out of line with policy makers in most other scientifically advanced nations.

It is ironic that, when the Kennedy administration embarked on eradicating hog cholera in 1961, the BAI had already been disbanded—one of the key diseases at the time of the BAI's founding outlived the agency charged with fighting it. The most important killer of swine in the United States had remained beyond the BAI's reach. When Secretary of Agriculture Ezra Taft Benson transferred the BAI's many activities to the Agricultural Research Service in November 1953, the justification at the time emphasized that the reorganization would bring more synergy and efficiency. However, a primary cause was likely that the BAI had been too successful in building a strong constituency. This was essential for its early survival but a political liability by the 1950s.[23] The Bureau's demise is one reason why many of its exploits continue to go unheralded, and it is not as well known as other regulatory agencies created in the Gilded Age and Progressive Era.

The 1953 reorganization that cost the BAI its identity distributed its animal health functions to several units within the USDA's Agricultural Research Service. Further reorganizations occurred in the 1960s and 1970s. The most significant was the creation of the Animal and Plant Health Inspection Service (APHIS) in 1972. Later legislation broke off functions such as meat inspection (1977). In the wake of the 2001 terrorist attacks, Congress bolstered APHIS's powers.[24]

Animal health workers did not forget the Bureau of Animal Industry. As a 1978 APHIS publication declared, "The proud traditions of the BAI continued." Building on the Bureau's accomplishments, the Veterinary Service celebrated its eradication of VE of swine (1959), screwworms (1966), the horse sleeping-sickness, Venezuelan equine encephalitis (1971), sheep scabies (1973), and finally—after more than ninety years of struggle—hog cholera (1978).[25]

14 The Mirror of the Past

ON 19 APRIL 2012, the Animal and Food Safety Laboratory at the University of California–Davis notified the U.S. Animal and Plant Health Inspection Service (APHIS) of suspicious test results in a sample of the brain stem of a slaughtered dairy cow. A rendering operation, working with the bovine spongiform encephalopathy (BSE) surveillance system, had collected biological material from a suspect carcass; the animal was then traced back via an ear-tag identification number to a central California dairy. After further tests, the USDA confirmed on April 24 a fourth case of mad cow disease in the United States.[1]

BSE is a communicable disease that destroys the central nervous system of its victims. It is related to scrapie in sheep and to Creutzfeldt-Jakob Disease (CJD) in humans. BSE was first recognized in cattle in Britain in 1986; by 1993, over one-half of the country's dairy herds were implicated. In a reenactment of many past disease episodes, government authorities and farmers at first denied that the disease posed any risk to consumers, but many in the public remained wary. The leap of the disease to humans was first announced on 21 March 1996, when ten cases of variant CJD were reported in Britain. Panic ensued, consumers boycotted British beef, and other countries banned its importation. As of 2012, 226 people had died in the United Kingdom of variant CJD. British authorities discovered more than 180,000 infected cattle and slaughtered roughly 4.4 million. Stamping out the disease and restoring consumer confidence was a costly enterprise.[2]

The origin of the disease is mysterious. It is suspected to have jumped species as a result of adding scrapie-contaminated sheep meat and bone meal to protein supplements fed to cattle. Such feeding practices were not new, but small changes in the rendering process may have had un-

316

expected consequences. In the early 1980s, high petroleum prices led renderers to economize on the use of solvents in the tallow extraction process, which, it is thought, allowed the infectious agent to jump to cattle. The epizootic was possibly amplified by feeding calves supplements derived from infected cattle.[3] If so, seemingly trivial modifications in production practices had large unintended consequences.

The spread of many other diseases has been linked to feeding practices. Mad cow disease is a recent example of new (or variants of) diseases jumping species to infect humans. Mad cow, AIDS, avian influenza, severe acute respiratory syndrome (SARS), Middle Eastern respiratory syndrome (MERS), and other threats remind us of how vulnerable we are to diseases in a constantly evolving biological environment. Although imperfect, institutions that research, monitor, and control these problems are in place.

Arresting Contagion chronicles the origins and development of the infrastructure of animal disease control and food safety in the United States. Animal contagions represented grave threats to livestock and human health, generating negative externalities and serious collective action problems. Attempts at private market solutions to deal with many of these threats repeatedly failed and sometimes made the problems worse. Government regulations such as meat inspection and quarantines were chiefly efficiency-enhancing health measures rather than rent-seeking ruses for protectionism as claimed in the much of the prior literature. The disease-control policies paid for themselves many fold, and they pushed the economy to a new and better equilibrium. The spillovers for improved human health were enormous.

Addressing these problems effectively involved moving to a higher scale of governance—shifting the locus of authority from the state and local governments to the federal government and devising innovative means of intergovernmental cooperation. The New Deal of the 1930s did not mark the beginning of sustained federal involvement in health issues, certainly not from the One Health viewpoint. The federal role grew over the preceding fifty years, in a process of fits and starts, constrained by prevailing political and legal norms limiting the power of the centralized state, and at the same time pushed forward by scientific advances, new crises, and policy successes.

The instrument of change was the Bureau of Animal Industry (BAI). Founded in 1884, the BAI would reshape the American political and economic landscape. It built novel state-federal partnerships, it extended the scope of federal police power, it advanced the rise of regulatory bureaucracy, it engaged in pioneering extension and outreach work, and it helped establish a national market by gradually superseding a hodge-podge of state laws. The BAI was also a leader in the creation and dissemination of scientific knowledge. It launched the first significant biological research laboratory in the United States. Its researchers would make fundamental scientific discoveries, with far-reaching benefits for animal and human health.

The developments described in these pages were made possible by leaders who perceived the seriousness of the disease threats and designed bold and pragmatic policies to promote effective collective action. These scientifically trained policy makers initiated far-reaching campaigns that successfully eliminated numerous major diseases from the United States and created eradication models later used worldwide. Indeed, without the aid of modern pharmaceutical products, they eradicated contagious bovine pleuropneumonia (1892), fowl plague (1929), foot-and-mouth disease (1929), glanders (1934), bovine tuberculosis (1940), dourine fever (1942), and Texas fever (1943). Many more successes followed. These leaders sometimes confronted and overcame what appeared to be hopelessly difficult challenges. They built *de novo* institutions and protocols to deal with many issues that still confound scientists and policy makers today. Many lessons were learned:

Successful large-scale government interventions were possible.

- The cost of competing policy options had to be weighed against the expected benefits.
- Root-cause solutions such as eradication and stringent border control were often the most cost-effective policies for contagions.[4]
- Particularly dangerous contagions called for draconian measures that required the aggressive deployment of police power at many levels.
- Over-reach had to be avoided; measures had to be calibrated to match scientific knowledge, program capacity, and public support.
- There would be many errors and lapses, especially in the early phases.

Preparation was crucial.

- Early detection and rapid response were keys to success.
- Laws and procedures needed to be in place before a crisis hit. Although a crisis unleashed demands for action, it was hard to draft effective policies in the midst of an emergency.
- Developing the underlying science paved the way to long-run success. The scientific process involved many missteps and conflicts, but knowledge did advance.

Leadership mattered, especially in working within the constraints of a democracy.

- Policies had to survive in the court of public opinion—policy makers had to be able to clearly explain a given threat and justify their actions. This often required years of investment in education and extension services.
- It was a given that many would deny the existence of a problem, and some would oppose the solutions. Effective control strategies had to anticipate opposition and adjust to changing conditions.
- Public-private partnerships were valuable to secure support and cooperation.

Finding the appropriate level and means of governance was vitally important.

- Local authorities and industry insiders often were too closely tied to affected parties or lacked sufficient expertise to act effectively.
- The alternative to federal intervention was not laissez-faire; states could and did shut down both intrastate and interstate trade.
- Federal programs provided coordination, expertise, economies of scale, and greater funding.

Incentives mattered.

- Without measures to secure buy-in, stock owners often tried to conceal problems.
- Compensation policies had to be tailored to the threat and designed to limit moral hazard. This involved a trial-and-error process, subject to adjustment as conditions changed.

- The tort system failed to provide efficient signals; regulation aimed at prevention was more efficient than imposing fines or collecting damages *ex post*.
- The threat of losing market access created incentives to clean up and stay clean.

Success begat success.

- The problems associated with many diseases were interrelated, as were their solutions. Institutions built to address one threat could be adapted to deal with others.
- Successful pilot programs had important learning and demonstration effects.
- It proved desirable to start control programs (for all but the most dangerous diseases) in areas where the probability of success was high.
- Once an area was cleansed, its producers frequently began to push for mandatory programs elsewhere to help prevent reinfection.
- Opponents often shifted to become supporters as scientific knowledge advanced, as program capacity and trust grew, and as incentives changed.
- Success was never complete; continued vigilance was necessary to ward off new and re-emerging threats.

Our account is both specific and historical, but the nature of the problems and of the lessons learned has a general contemporary relevance. *Arresting Contagion* describes a dangerous and untidy world. Problems that emerged in one locale could affect an entire nation and the world. In addition to these negative spillovers, there were also large positive externalities associated with actions to arrest contagions. New knowledge often emerged from public institutions and was made available to all. Subsequent scientific research and technological development could draw from this body of knowledge. Methodologies and technologies developed for one purpose often had wide-ranging implications. Although scientific knowledge and technologies tended to spread rapidly, political and social innovations spread much more slowly.

In this world, scientists and policy makers identified problems that would have led to bad (less efficient) outcomes if left unchecked. The scientists specified the underlying causal mechanisms of diseases, developed new methods of discovery, and proposed novel root-cause solutions that included preventive methods and cures. Lives were often in the balance. The proposed solutions generally demanded collective action and required the creation of new centralized political institutions. There were no road maps for the large-scale interventions and no guarantees of success. Such solutions mandated preemptive regulation, transcended established judicial norms and jurisdictional boundaries, and required outside enforcement and verification. Continuous monitoring and the empowerment of experts were essential. The costs imposed were immediate, targeted, and concrete; the promised benefits were often far off, diffused, and uncertain. Many of those harmed by the policies fought change. Others, who feared of the growth of Big Government on ideological grounds, also opposed change; these ideological adversaries often switched sides when their interests were threatened by a serious disease. And sometimes the most aggressive resistance came from outside the normal political arena. Many opponents asserted the problems did not exist; or if they did exist, they were not important; or if the problems were important, they were beyond cure; or if cures were possible, they were worse than the afflictions.

The scientific process was filled with controversies, which initially provided grounds for the opposition to change. With further advances in knowledge, the justification for opposition diminished, yet many opponents clung to their increasingly discredited claims and even tried to block further research. The press often failed to distinguish between the views of quacks and those of eminent scientists. Recurrent crises demonstrated the growing threats, mobilizing support for change. Distributional questions often dominated public discussions.

Implementing pragmatic solutions required a trial-and-error process to ascertain appropriate combinations of carrots and sticks. Under some circumstances, planners compensated those suffering losses. This bought more support but also encouraged strategic resistance, as many held out for a better deal. There was also concern that power, once bestowed, would be misused for unintended purposes; the centralization of power was indeed a slippery slope. Many opponents of change advocated going slow, letting scientific and technological knowledge progress, and waiting to address problems until easier solutions became available. This made sense in many cases, and advances in knowledge did point to more efficient solutions. However, there was a balancing act because delay allowed problems to grow worse; the risk of overreach had to be weighed against the risks of paralysis and inaction.

Education programs targeted key audiences, success bred success, and social capital was built. Coalitions dissolved, breaking political log jams and helping to overcome the inertia that inhibited action. The first step was often the hardest. Once seemingly intolerable violations of the Constitution became a part of the new social contract, in time only a few (mostly those who had forgotten the past) wanted to return to the old ways. The enduring and familiar nature of these issues makes the achievements of the past even more remarkable and all the more relevant for the twenty-first century.

Abbreviations

AMA	American Medical Association
AMLL	American Medical Liberty League
APHIS	Animal and Plant Health Inspection Service
ASF	African swine fever
BAI	U.S. Bureau of Animal Industry
BCG	Bacillus Calmette and Guérin tuberculosis vaccine
BNPA	Butchers' National Protective Association
BSE	Bovine spongiform encephalopathy
BTB	Bovine tuberculosis
CBPP	Contagious bovine pleuropneumonia
CDC	Center(s) for Disease Control and Prevention
CJD	Creutzfeldt-Jakob disease
CPI	Consumer price index
DEFRA	Department of Environment, Food and Rural Affairs (United Kingdom)
EEC	European Economic Community
EU	European Union
FMD	Foot-and-mouth disease
FMS	Federal Meat-Inspection Service
HACCP	Hazard Analysis and Critical Control Points
ICA	Interstate Commerce Act
ICC	Interstate Commerce Commission
MHS	Marine Hospital Service
MLV	Modified live-virus
NBH	National Board of Health

NIH	National Institute(s) of Health
OIE	Office International des Epizooties
SARS	Severe acute respiratory syndrome
U.S. BAI	U.S. Bureau of Animal Industry
USDA	United States Department of Agriculture
VE	Vesicular exanthema
VS	Vesicular stomatitis
WSGA	Wyoming Stock Growers Association

Notes

CHAPTER 1   *An Enduring Struggle*

1. World Organization for Animal Health (OIE), "Rinderpest Eradication," *Bulletin,* no. 2011-2 (2011), pp. 1–10, www.oie.int/fileadmin/Home/eng/ Publications_&_Documentation/docs/pdf/bulletin/Bull_2011-2-ENG.pdf; Donald G. McNeil Jr., "Rinderpest, Scourge of Cattle, Is Vanquished," *New York Times,* 28 June 2011, p. D1.
2. Alan L. Olmstead, "The First Line of Defense: Inventing the Infrastructure to Combat Animal Diseases," *Journal of Economic History* 69, no. 2 (2009): 329–30; and Clive A. Spinage, *Cattle Plague: A History* (New York: Kluwer Academic, 2003).
3. Rinderpest could and did jump oceans. It entered Brazil in 1920 and Australia in 1923, but in both instances it was caught early and stamped out.
4. U.S. Senate, Committee on Agriculture, *Letter of the Commissioner of Agriculture, Communicating, In Compliance with a Resolution of the Senate of the 13th Instant, Information in Relation to the Rinderpest or Cattle Plague, Apr. 17, 1866,* Misc. Doc. No. 98, 39th Cong., 1st Sess. (Washington, DC: U.S. Government Printing Office, 1866), p. 21; "The Cattle Plague. The Natural History of the Rinderpest—Its Reappearance in Prussia and Ireland—Its Reported Appearance in United States Territory—Its True Character and Means of Its Prevention," *New York Times,* 15 July 1866, p. 4; Ulysses Grant Houck, *The Bureau of Animal Industry of the United States Department of Agriculture: Its Establishment, Achievements and Current Activities* (Washington, DC: [Hayworth Printing Company], 1924), p. 125.
5. An infectious disease is a class of clinical illnesses resulting from a pathogen residing in a host. Infectious pathogens include bacteria, viruses, fungi, protozoa, multicellular parasites, and aberrant proteins dubbed prions. These pathogens are the source of disease epidemics (in humans) and epizootics (in other animals). Transmission of these pathogens can occur in many ways, including direct contact, ingesting contaminated products, contact with contaminated body fluids, contact with contaminated inanimate objects, inhalation, or by the bite of an infected vector. Today, infectious diseases are synonymous with transmissible diseases and communicable diseases. Contagious diseases are a subset of infectious diseases that are highly infective or easily transmitted from one host to another by contact

with the sick host, with its secretions, or by inhalation. Diseases transmitted by vectors such as mosquitos are infectious but not contagious. Our usage of these terms may, in places, stray from strict conformity with these definitions.

6. This story builds on and extends our previous account of investments by American farmers and agricultural researchers to learn about and adapt to their dynamic and unstable biological environment. Alan L. Olmstead and Paul W. Rhode, *Creating Abundance: Biological Innovation and American Agricultural Development* (New York: Cambridge Univ. Press, 2008). These efforts began long before the "biological revolution" of the post-1940 period, here reflected in the introduction of sulfa drugs and antibiotics. U.S. Department of Agriculture, *Yearbook of Agriculture, 1956* (Washington, DC: U.S. Government Printing Office, 1956), pp. 94–97.

7. When other states and foreign nations conditioned market access on meeting sanitary standards, they added to the incentives to combat diseases, offsetting in part the underinvestment in measures to prevent the spread of contagions. Another consequence was to increase incentives to conceal and deny disease problems.

8. Centers for Disease Control and Prevention, National Center for Emerging and Zoonotic Infectious Diseases, www.cdc.gov/ncezid/, accessed 27 May 2013; Calvin W. Schwabe, *Veterinary Medicine and Human Health*, 3rd ed. (Baltimore: Williams & Wilkins, 1984), pp. 16, 194–251; James H. Steele, ed., *CRC Handbook Series in Zoonoses, Section A–D* (Boca Raton, FL: CRC Press, 1979).

9. Control of livestock diseases was more difficult because owners could sell sick or suspect animals, but people cannot sell sick family members.

10. Frank Fenner, Donald A. Henderson, Isao Arita, Zdeněk Ježek, and Ivan D. Ladnyi, *Small Pox and Its Eradication* (Geneva: World Health Organization, 1988), p. 372.

11. A. Hunter Dupree, *Science in the Federal Government: A History of Policies and Activities to 1940* (Cambridge, MA: Harvard Univ. Press, 1957), pp. 158–66, esp. 164.

12. Schwabe, *Veterinary Medicine*, p. 188.

13. Compensation was very controversial and at first not permitted in many states because it was interpreted as an illegal gift of public funds. Under the common law, nuisances could be destroyed without payment. Partial, as opposed to full, compensation has appeal on both efficiency and equity grounds because livestock owners stood to benefit more directly than the general taxpayer from the cleanup and thus should bear more of its costs.

14. Peter K. Olitsky, Jacob Traum, and Harry W. Schoening, "Report of the Foot-and-Mouth-Disease Commission," USDA, *Technical Bulletin*, no. 76 (Washington, DC: U.S. Government Printing Office, 1928), pp. 15–16, 30; United Kingdom, Minister of Agriculture, Fisheries, and Food, *Animal*

Health, A Centenary, 1865–1965: A Century of Endeavor to Control Diseases of Animals (London: Her Majesty's Stationery Office, 1965), pp. 125–263.

15. Kym Anderson, Gordon Rausser, and Johan Swinnen, "Political Economy of Public Policies: Insights from Distortions to Agricultural and Food Markets," *Journal of Economic Literature* 51, no. 2 (2013): 423–77; Gordon Rausser, Johan Swinnen, and Pinhas Zusman, *Political Power and Economic Policy: Theory, Analysis, and Empirical Applications* (New York: Cambridge Univ. Press, 2011), esp. pp. 3–29, 113–22, 209–23.

16. For a sampling of a rich literature on government involvement in the economy, see William J. Novak, "The Myth of the 'Weak' American State," *American Historical Review* 113, no. 3 (2008): 752–72; Jerry L. Mashaw, *Creating the Administrative Constitution: The Lost One Hundred Years of American Administrative Law* (New Haven, CT: Yale Univ. Press, 2012), esp. pp. 12–13, 187–208; Katharine Coman, *Economic Beginnings of the Far West: How We Won the Land Beyond the Mississippi*, vol. 1, *Explorers and Colonizers* (New York: MacMillan, 1912), pp. 298–99; Richard R. John, *Spreading the News: The American Postal System from Franklin to Morse* (Cambridge, MA: Harvard Univ. Press, 1995); Herbert Hovenkamp, *Enterprise and American Law, 1836–1937* (Cambridge, MA: Harvard Univ. Press, 1991); Scott C. James, *Presidents, Parties, and the State: A Party System Perspective on Democratic Regulatory Choice, 1884–1936* (New York: Cambridge Univ. Press, 2000); Thomas K. McGraw, *Prophets of Regulation: Charles Francis Adams, Louis D. Brandeis, James M. Landis, and Alfred E. Kahn* (Cambridge, MA: Harvard Univ. Press, 1984).

17. Brian Balogh, *A Government Out of Sight: The Mystery of National Authority in Nineteenth-Century America* (New York: Cambridge Univ. Press, 2009), pp. 1–17.

18. Price V. Fishback, Robert Higgs, Gary D. Libecap, et al., *Government and the American Economy: A New History* (Chicago: Univ. of Chicago Press, 2007).

19. Robert E. Gallman, "The U.S. Capital Stock in the Nineteenth Century: Estimates and Estimating Procedures," Current Value Estimates, tables B-4, B-9, H-6, Robert E. Gallman Papers No. 5000, Southern Historical Collection, Wilson Library, Univ. of North Carolina at Chapel Hill.

20. Edward L. Glaeser and Andrei Shleifer, "The Rise of the Regulatory State," *Journal of Economic Literature* 41, no. 2 (2003), pp. 401–2; Gary D. Libecap, "The Rise of the Chicago Packers and the Origins of Meat Inspection and Antitrust," *Economic Inquiry* 30, no. 2 (1992): 242–62.

21. Elaine Scallan, Robert M. Hoekstra, Frederick J. Angulo, Robert V. Tauxe, Marc-Alain Widdowson, Sharon L. Roy, Jeffery L. Jones, and Patricia M. Griffin, "Foodborne Illness Acquired in the United States—Major Pathogens," *Emerging Infectious Disease* 17, no. 1 (2011): 7–15; Elaine Scallan, Patricia Griffin, Frederick J. Anulo, Robert V. Tauxe, and Robert M. Hoekstra, "Foodborne Illness Acquired in the United States—Unspecified Agents," *Emerging Infectious Disease* 17, no. 1 (2011): 16–22.

22. Andrew C. Voetsch, Thomas J. Van Gilder, Frederick J. Angulo, Monica M. Farley, Sue Shallow, Ruthanne Marcus, Paul R. Cieslak, Valerie C. Deneen, and Robert V. Tauxe, for the Emerging Infections Program FoodNet Working Group, "FoodNet Estimate of the Burden of Illness Caused by Nontyphoidal *Salmonella* Infections in the United States," *Clinical Infectious Diseases* 38, Supplement 3 (2004): S127–34; European Food Safety Authority, "EFSA Assesses Risk of *Salmonella* from Pig Meat," EFSA Press Release, 19 Apr. 2010, www.efsa.europa.eu/en/press/news/biohaz100419.htm.

23. Andrei Shleifer, "The Enforcement Theory of Regulation," in *The Failure of Judges and the Rise of Regulators,* ed. Andrei Shleifer (Cambridge, MA: MIT Press, 2011), p. 4.

24. Information problems associated with contagious diseases make a Coasian solution infeasible.

25. William Schieffelin, "Work of the Committee of One Hundred on National Health," *Annals of the American Academy of Political and Social Science* 37, no. 2 (1911): 77–86; Irving Fisher, "Report on National Vitality: Its Waste and Conservation," American Associations for the Advancement of Science, Committee of One Hundred on National Health, *Bulletin,* no. 30 (Washington, DC: U.S. Government Printing Office, 1909), 126. While admiring the USDA's achievements, public health reformers also were jealous of its funding and repeatedly lamented that the federal government invested more in reducing the mortality of young livestock than in that of human babies. *New York Times,* 4 Apr. 1909, p. SM10; *Washington Post,* 17 Apr. 1914, p. 4.

26. Our estimate of human deaths rests on the growth in the population and the spread of BTB in cattle. See Chapter 12.

27. This discussion draws inspiration from William Cronon, "Two Cheers for the Whig Interpretation of History," *Perspectives on History,* Sept. 2012, www .historians.org/publications-and-directories/perspectives-on-history/ september-2012/two-cheers-for-the-whig-interpretation-of-history.

CHAPTER 2   *Livestock Disease Environment*
                       and Industry Dynamics

1. Schwabe, *Veterinary Medicine,* pp. 181–93, 352–53.

2. Ibid., p. 165; Bert W. Bierer, *A Short History of Veterinary Medicine in America* (East Lansing: Michigan State Univ. Press, 1955), pp. 62–65. Salmon also studied bacteriology at Alfort. The names of both schools would be changed.

3. U.S. Senate, *Information in Relation to the Disease Prevailing among Swine and Other Domestic Animals,* Ex. Doc. No. 35, 45th Cong., 2nd Sess. (Washington, DC: U.S. Government Printing Office, 1878), pp. 142–46.

4. USDA, "Contagious Diseases of Domesticated Animals," Special Report No. 22 (Washington, DC: U.S. Government Printing Office, 1880), pp. 202–8; U.S. BAI, *Special Report on Diseases of Horses, 1903 ed.* (Washington, DC: U.S.

Government Printing Office, 1903), pp. 532–54; G. Terry Sharrer, "The Great Glanders Epizootic, 1861–1866: A Civil War Legacy," *Agricultural History* 69, no. 1 (1995), pp. 79–97.

5. USDA, *Report of the Commissioner for 1872* (Washington, DC: U.S. Government Printing Office, 1873), pp. 209–48; Ann Norton Greene, *Horses at Work: Harnessing Power in Industrial America* (Cambridge, MA: Harvard Univ. Press, 2008), pp. 167–69.

6. *Raleigh Register,* 31 July 1858, p. 1; *American Farmer,* Sept. 1858, p. 82; *Charleston Mercury,* 11 Aug. 1858, p. 1; *Baltimore Sun,* 7 Sept. 1858, p. 1.

7. In the early 1860s, some informed observers conflated the two diseases. *Prairie Farmer,* 23 Aug. 1860, p. 116.

8. Claire Strom, *Making Catfish Bait Out of Government Boys: The Fight against Cattle Ticks and the Transformation of the Yeoman South* (Athens: Univ. of Georgia Press, 2009), pp. 7–42; Tamara Miner Haygood, "Cows, Ticks, and Disease: A Medical Interpretation of the Southern Cattle Industry," *Journal of Southern History* 52, no. 4 (1986): 551–64; U.S. BAI, *Special Report on Diseases of Cattle, 1916 ed.* (Washington, DC: U.S. Government Printing Office, 1916), pp. 473–77; U.S. Animal and Plant Health Inspection Service (APHIS) "Controlling Cattle Fever Ticks, August 2010," www.aphis.usda.gov /publications/animal_health/content/printable_version/cattle_fever_ticks .pdf; "Another Animal Disease," *Lancet,* 13 June 1868, p. 771.

9. Haygood, "Cows, Ticks, and Disease," pp. 557–58; Lewis C. Gray, *History of Agriculture in the Southern United States to 1860,* vol. 1 (New York: Peter Smith, 1941), p. 147; Houck, *Bureau of Animal Industry,* pp. 15–17.; J. F. Smithcors, "James Mease, M.D., on the Diseases of Domestic Animals," *Bulletin of the History of Medicine* 31, no. 2 (1957): 122–31. Mease's 1814 lecture and his subsequent 1826 publication are generally regarded as the first scientific accounts on Texas fever. James Mease, "An Account of a Contagious Disease Propagated by a Drove of Southern Cattle in Perfect Health," *Memoirs of the Philadelphia Society for Promoting Agriculture* 5 (1826), pp. 280–83; USDA, *Yearbook of Agriculture, 1942,* pp. 572–78.

10. *Prairie Farmer,* 26 Sept. 1868, p. 98; Missouri State Board of Agriculture, *Annual Report for 1866* (Jefferson City, MO: Emery S. Foster, 1867), p. 18; Claire Strom, "Texas Fever and the Dispossession of the Southern Yeoman Farmer," *Journal of Southern History* 66, no. 1 (2000), pp. 52–53. For an opposing view of shotgun quarantines and regulations more generally, see Joseph G. McCoy, *Historic Sketches of the Cattle Trade of the West and Southwest* (Kansas City, MO: Ramsey, Millett & Hudson, 1874), chapter 2.

11. The Springfield convention followed an earlier gathering on Texas fever held in Rochester, New York in September. J. R. Dodge, "Report of J. R. Dodge on Statistical and Historical Investigations of the Progress and Results of the Texas Cattle Disease," in USDA, *Report of the Commissioner of Agriculture on the Diseases of Cattle in the United States* (Washington, DC: U.S.

Government Printing Office, 1871), pp. 175–202; Missouri State Board of Agriculture, *Annual Report for 1868* (Jefferson City, MO: Ellwood Kirby, 1869), pp. 345–420.

12. Dodge, "Report of J. R. Dodge," pp. 175–202. Kansas loosened the enforcement of its 1865 quarantine after Joseph McCoy established a profitable trade shipping Texas cattle out of Abilene in 1867. Robert R. Dykstra, *The Cattle Towns* (New York: Alfred A. Knopf, 1968), pp. 16–21.

13. The *Husen* decision is sometimes dated 1877. The case arose because the St. Joseph and Missouri railroad contested Husen's claim of civil liability for damage to his animals caused by Texas cattle carried on the line. Regarding the *Husen* and related decisions, see Richard F. Bensel, *The Political Economy of American Industrialization, 1877–1900* (New York: Cambridge Univ. Press, 2000), pp. 9–10, 321–54, esp. 331–32.

14. U.S. BAI, *Report for 1884*, p. 326. Protective measures such as inoculations were relatively ineffective and kept the disease alive within the population.

15. U.S. House of Representatives, *Pleuro-Pneumonia*, 15 June 1860, Misc. Doc. No. 93, 30th Cong., 1st Sess. (Washington, DC: U.S. Government Printing Office, 1860); U.S. BAI, *Report for 1884*, pp. 52–54, 297–309; For examples of voluntary slaughter, see Justin Kastner, "Sanitary Related International Trade Disputes: A Multiple-Factor Analysis Based on Nineteenth-Century Precedents," Ph.D. diss. (Univ. of Guelph, 2003), p. 32.

16. U.S. Commissioner of Patents, *Annual Report for 1860* (Washington, DC: U.S. Government Printing Office, 1861), pp. 239–67; Houck, *Bureau of Animal Industry*, pp. 3–4, 38; U.S. Animal Health Association, Committee on Foreign and Emerging Diseases, *Foreign Animal Diseases*, 7th ed. (Boca Raton, FL: Boca Publishing, 2008), pp. 213–18; U.S. BAI, *Diseases of Cattle, 1916*, pp. 364–77.

17. *Massachusetts Ploughman* 12 Jan. 1878, p. 1; U.S. Senate, *Report of Dr. Charles P. Lyman on the Subject of Pleuro-pneumonia or Lung Plague among Cattle*, 21 Apr. 1880, Misc. Doc. No. 74, 46th Cong., 2nd Sess. (Washington, DC: U.S. Government Printing Office, 1880), pp. 1–17; U.S. BAI, *Report for 1884*, pp. 297–307.

18. *New York Times*, 10 Feb. 1879, p. 5; 14 Feb. 1879. p. 8; 2 Apr. 1879, p. 1; 17 Jan. 1880, p. 8; *Philadelphia Inquirer*, 6 Mar. 1879, p. 2; *Brooklyn Eagle*, 13 Feb. 1879, p. 2; 14 Feb. 1879, p. 2; 23 Feb 1879, p. 2; *New York Herald*, 15 Feb. 1879, p. 8; *New York Tribune*, 24 May 1879, p. 10; *Trenton (NJ) State Gazette*, 28 Jan. 1880, p. 3; U.S. BAI, *Report for 1884*, pp. 468–70. At this time, about 80,000 cattle and nearly 100,000 hogs were fed at registered distilleries. U.S. Treasury Department, *Report of the Secretary for 1881* (Washington, DC: U.S. Government Printing Office, 1881), pp. 112–14.

19. *New York Times*, 31 Jan. 1879, p. 3; 5 Feb. 1879, p. 8; 12 Feb. 1879, p. 8; 27 Feb. 1879, p. 5; *Chicago Tribune*, 16 Feb. 1879, p. 6; 27 Feb. 1879, p. 7; 1 Mar.

1879, p. 15; 2 Mar. 1879, p. 3; *Manchester Guardian,* 2 Apr. 1879, p. 7; 11 Aug. 1880, p. 7. In the eyes of the Chicago stockyard men, the USDA investigation was tied to the subsequent closure of the British market, even though (as noted herein) that decision was made on 10 February 1879, roughly a week before Detmers began his work. *Prairie Farmer,* 22 Mar. 1879, p. 92; 26 July 1879, p. 237; *Drovers Journal,* 13 Mar. 1884, p. 8; 2 Oct. 1884, p. 7.

20. New Jersey Board of Agriculture, *Annual Report for 1880* (Camden, NJ: Sinnickson Chew, 1881), p. 69; U.S. BAI, *Report for 1884,* p. 302; *Trenton (NJ) State Gazette,* 4 Mar. 1880, p. 2; 5 Mar. 1880, p. 2; 9 Mar. 1880, p. 2.

21. *New York Times,* 22 June 1882, p. 2; *Drovers Journal,* 27 Oct. 1883, p. 2; *Breeder's Gazette,* 6 Mar. 1884, p. 343; 15 Feb. 1888, p. 161. Even those who advocated control measures often downplayed the extent of the disease problems. In his 1880 Annual Message, President Rutherford B. Hayes claimed that the CBPP afflicting the country was of "a mild type." *New York Times,* 7 Dec. 1880, p. 3. This statement invoked an immediate retort from Philadelphia veterinarian John W. Gadsden, who observed that based on his long experience with the local variant of the disease, "there is *no* mildness" about it [emphasis in original]. John W. Gadsden to U.S. House Committee on Agriculture, 14 Dec. 1880, Drawer HR 46 A E1 to F2.1, U.S. House of Representatives Records, RG 233, Center for Legislative Archives, Washington, DC [hereafter U.S. House Records].

22. Houck, *Bureau of Animal Industry,* p. 2.

23. Dodge, "Report of J. R. Dodge," p. 197.

24. U.S. Senate, *Information on the Subject of Pleuro-pneumonia among Cattle,* 15 Feb. 1879, Misc. Doc. No. 71, 46th Cong., 2nd Sess. (Washington, DC: U.S. Government Printing Office, 1879); U.S. Senate, *Report of Dr. Charles P. Lyman,* pp. 1–17.

25. U.S. House of Representatives, *Pleuro-pneumonia in Neat Cattle: Letter from the Secretary of the Treasury,* 28 Feb. 1880, Ex. Doc. No. 53, 46th Cong., 2nd Sess. (Washington, DC: U.S. Government Printing Office, 1880), pp. 13–14; Houck, *Bureau of Animal Industry,* p. 2.

26. U.S. Senate, *Disease Prevailing among Swine,* pp. 142–46.

27. James Law to H. F. French, 29 Apr. 1879, Drawer HR 46 A E1 to F2.1, U.S. House Records. Law criticized a bill authored by William Hatch (HR 1378, 46th Cong., 1st Sess., 30 Apr. 1879) as counterproductive. The bill would have made it a misdemeanor for transportation companies to engage in the interstate shipment of animals affected with any contagious or infectious disease, especially pleuropneumonia. The bill also called for the Commissioner of Agriculture to establish inspection stations along the railroad lines and for the Secretary of the Treasury to establish port inspection stations for the export trade. Law opined that the bill, if passed, would create a "false sense of security" and "hinder the adoption of measures that would prove really useful and efficient."

28. U.S. Senate, *Imports and Exports Part I: Imports from 1867 to 1893, Inclusive,* Senate Report No. 259, Part 1, 53nd Cong., 2nd Sess. (Washington, DC: U.S. Government Printing Office, 1894), pp. 4–8.

29. The aggregate U.S. number comes from Susan Carter, Scott Gartner, Michael Haines, et al., *Historical Statistics of the United States, Millennial Edition,* vol. 4 (New York: Cambridge Univ. Press, 2006), series Da968, Da970, Da972. The state numbers come from Joseph Nimmo Jr., *Report in Regard to the Range and Ranch Cattle Business of the United States* (Washington, DC: U.S. Government Printing Office, 1885), pp. 28, 54–55; The European numbers from B. R. Mitchell, *International Historical Statistics, Europe, 1750–1988* (New York: Stockton Press, 1992), pp. 325–70.

30. Joseph Nimmo Jr., *The Production of Swine in the United States* (Washington, DC: U.S. Government Printing Office, 1884), p. 23; Mitchell, *International Historical Statistics,* pp. 325–70; Olmstead and Rhode, *Creating Abundance,* p. 270.

31. *Poor's Manual of Railroads* (New York: Poor's Publishing, various dates).

32. *Chicago Commerce, Manufacturing, Banking, and Transportation Facilities* (Chicago: S. Ferd. Howe, 1884), pp. 78–79; "Packing Houses [and] Union Stock Yards," Back of the Yards Collection, Box 1, folder 7, Special Collections, Chicago Public Library, Harold Washington Library Center, Chicago, IL.

33. U.S. BAI, *Report for 1886,* pp. 277–82, statistics from p. 278.

34. U.S. Treasury Department, Bureau of Statistics, *Monthly Summary of Commerce and Finance of the United States,* Feb. 1900, p. 2309; Carter et al., *Historical Statistics,* vol. 5, series Ee446.

35. The British policy was not targeted just at the United States. Privy Council orders enacted in 1878 and 1879 effectively partitioned trading partners into three classes. This prohibited animal imports from countries where diseases were enzootic. Stock from countries where diseases were less widespread had to be slaughtered at special wharves. Animals from a third set of countries where diseases were uncommon were allowed unrestricted access. Justin Kastner, "Food and Agriculture Security: An Historical Illustration of Contemporary Challenges," in *Food and Agricultural Security: An Historical, Multidisciplinary Approach,* ed. Justin Kastner (Santa Barbara, CA: Praeger, 2011), pp. 5–32, esp. 13–14.

36. *New York Times,* 1 Feb. 1879, p. 5; 5 Feb. 1879, p. 2; 16 Feb. 1879, p. 5; Houck, *Bureau of Animal Industry,* pp. 10–12, 58; Kastner, "Sanitary Related," pp. 25–50.

37. A. M. Farrington, "Quarantine Laws and Practices," in *Cyclopedia of American Agriculture,* vol. 4, ed. Liberty Hide Bailey (London: Macmillan, 1909), p. 486. Congress passed "An Act to prevent the spread of foreign diseases among the cattle of the United States" on 18 December 1865 and granted the Secretary of the Treasury authority in this area on 6 March 1866. There was a total ban on cattle imports until 1874, when restrictions

were temporally relaxed. However, the threat of foot-and-mouth disease led the Treasury to prohibit imports of cattle and hides from Spain on 31 July 1875 and from Britain on 3 November 1875.

38. The BAI performed port inspections but with the approval of the Treasury. The initial regulations covered only cattle; but by the 1890s, they were extended to all animals. As an extra precaution, the BAI stationed veterinarians in the United Kingdom to check cattle before they were shipped. Elsewhere, beginning in 1884, American consular agents issued export-import documents for animals from disease-free zones. The BAI also inspected the ships carrying American cattle exports to ensure safety and cleanliness. By 1890, the BAI already had a tagging system in place so that if a sick American animal arrived in the United Kingdom (and perhaps elsewhere), the BAI could trace its travel and origins. U.S. BAI, *Report for 1885*, pp. 290–92, 451, 458–59; *Reports for 1889 and 1890*, pp. 71–76.

39. Marshall noted (22 U.S. 1) that "in making these provisions, the opinion is unequivocally manifested, that Congress may control the State laws, so far as it may be necessary to control them, for the regulation of commerce." See James A. Tobey, *National Government and Public Health* (Baltimore: Johns Hopkins Univ. Press, 1926), pp. 48–60; William J. Novak, *People's Welfare: Law and Regulation in Nineteenth-Century America* (Chapel Hill: Univ. of North Carolina Press, 1996), pp. 149–90.

40. Tobey, *National Government*, pp. 48–60, 77–81. In the landmark case *Jacobson v. Massachusetts* (197 U.S. 11, decided 20 Feb. 1905), the Supreme Court ruled that private citizens did not have the right to refuse vaccinations. Writing for the majority, John M. Harlan wrote, "There are manifold restraints to which every person is necessarily subject for the common good" (p. 26). Harlan then cited the *Husen* and other livestock quarantine cases to demonstrate the Court's recognition that "persons and property were subject to all kinds of restraints and burdens in order to secure the general comfort, health, and prosperity of the state." The Court further held that the states, not the federal government, had primary jurisdiction for the regulation of public health: "The safety and the health of the people of Massachusetts are, in the first instance, for that Commonwealth to guard and protect. They are matters that do not ordinarily concern the National Government" (p. 28).

41. *Annals of Congress*, 12 May 1796, p. 1356.

42. John Duffy, *The Sanitarians: A History of American Public Health* (Urbana: Univ. of Illinois Press, 1992), pp. 157–64; Lawrence O. Gostin, *Public Health Law: Power, Duty, Restraint* (Berkeley: Univ. of California Press, 2000), pp. 205–6.

43. William H. Allen, "The Rise of the National Board of Health," *Annals of the American Academy of Political and Social Science* 15 (1900): 55–60.

44. *Congressional Globe,* 8 May 1866, p. 2445; Michael Les Benedict, "Contagion and the Constitution: Quarantine Agitation from 1859 to 1866," *Journal of the History of Medicine* 25, no. 2 (1970): 177–93.

45. Peter W. Bruton, "The National Board of Health," Ph.D. diss. (Univ. of Maryland, 1974), pp. 59–114.

46. Margaret Warner, "Local Control versus National Interest: The Debate over Southern Public Health, 1878–1884," *Journal of Southern History* 50, no. 3 (1984): 407–28; Edwin Maxey, "Federal Quarantine Laws," *Political Science Quarterly* 23, no. 4 (1908), p. 625; *New York Times,* 28 May 1879, pp. 1, 4; Bruton, "National Board of Health," pp. 50–164.

47. *Congressional Record,* 27 May 1879, pp. 1641–44; Bruton, "National Board of Health," pp. 50–164; Allen, "Rise of the National Board," pp. 51–68.

48. The final vote in the House on 3 March 1879 registered 170 yeas to 65 nays. There were no decided divisions by either regions or parties. Northern and Western Democrats voted 43 yeas to 21 nays; Southern Democrats 48 to 13; Republicans 77 to 29. Two Independent Democrats made up the remaining positive vote. *Congressional Record,* 3 Mar. 1879, pp. 240–2; 22 May 1879, pp. 1507–20; 23 May 1879, pp. 1539–52; 27 May 1879, pp. 1637–50; Allen, "Rise of the National Board," p. 64.

49. Bruton, "National Board of Health," pp. 50–164; Duffy, *Sanitarians,* pp. 157–174, esp. 172; Allen, "Rise of the National Board," p. 64; Dupree, *Science in the Federal Government,* pp. 259–62. The MHS became the Public Health and Marine Hospital Service, which later became the National Institute (and then Institutes) of Health.

50. *Chicago Tribune,* 7 Oct. 1873, p. 1. For contemporary charges that crowding on long railroad trips badly harmed cattle and made their meat unhealthy and unwholesome to consume, see John W. Street, *Cattle Shipping by Railway in the United States* (Des Moines, IA: Mills, 1870), pp. 8–13.

51. *New York Times,* 27 Jan. 1875, p. 10; 4 May 1878, p. 1; 5 June 1878, p. 1; 23 May 1879, p. 3; 27 May 1879, p. 6; 28 May 1879, p. 1; *Chicago Tribune,* 25 Jan. 1878, p. 1; 8 Feb. 1878, p. 2; 22 Mar. 1878, p. 2; 21 May 1878, p. 1; 28 May 1879, p. 1; 4 Apr. 1879, p. 12.

52. *Congressional Record* 27 May 1879, pp. 1610–20, 1625–34; also see 21 Feb. 1879, pp. 1704–7.

53. *Congressional Record,* 27 May 1879, pp. 1638–39; *Chicago Tribune,* 14 Apr. 1879, p. 4.

54. Warner, "Local Control," pp. 407–28.

CHAPTER 3   *The Battle to Create the Bureau of Animal Industry*

1. *Washington Post,* 12 Jan. 1884, p. 1; *Detroit Free Press,* 13 Jan. 1884, p. 9; USDA, *Report of the Commissioner for 1884* (Washington, DC: U.S. Government Printing Office, 1884), pp. 182–84; USDA, *Contagious Diseases of Domesticated*

Animals: Investigations by Department of Agriculture, 1883–1884 (Washington, DC: U.S. Government Printing Office, 1884), pp. 8, 16–21.

2. Gary W. Cox and Mathew D. McCubbins, *Setting the Agenda: Responsible Party Government in the U.S. House of Representatives* (New York: Oxford Univ. Press, 2005).

3. *Congressional Record,* 25 Feb. 1884, pp. 1362–63; *Chicago Tribune,* 29 Feb. 1884, p. 1.

4. *Congressional Record,* 6 Feb. 1884, p. 929; 12 Mar. 1884, pp. 1794–95; 25 Apr. 1884, p. 3392.

5. *Congressional Record,* 26 May 1879, pp. 1618–19. Many Americans disputed the British findings of CBPP, claiming the cattle had bronchitis.

6. The American veterinarians were influenced by the aggressive campaigns conducted in Britain, Scandinavia, and Switzerland to stamp out livestock diseases. O. H. V. Stalheim and W. M. Moulton, "Veterinary Medicine in the United States Department of Agriculture," in *100 Years of Animal Health, 1884–1984,* ed. Vivian Wiser, Larry Mark, and H. Graham Purchase (Beltsville, MD: Associates of the National Agricultural Library, 1987), pp. 24–25; U.S. BAI, *Report for 1884,* pp. 35–50; *Breeder's Gazette,* 31 Jan. 1884, pp. 146–47.

7. *New York Times,* 9 July 1860, p. 2; U.S. BAI, *Report for 1884,* pp. 51–54, 297–309.

8. In 1881, Congress received a flurry of printed petitions bearing individuals' signatures in favor of strong measures to control CBPP. At least twelve states were represented. See Drawer HR 46A H 1.1 to HR 46A H 2.2, U.S. House Records.

9. *Congressional Record,* 14 Jan. 1881, p. 620; 27 Jan. 1881, pp. 987–88; 18 Feb. 1881, pp. 1664–65; 19 Feb. 1881, pp. 1796–97; 21 Feb. 1881, pp. 1829–38; *New York Times,* 29 Jan. 1881, p. 2.

10. *Congressional Record,* 19 Feb. 1881, pp. 1830–36. In 1882, Ingalls spoke against and voted to kill a similar bill (HR 896). *Congressional Record,* 3 Aug. 1882, pp. 6827–32. Despite vigorously supporting federal anti-CBPP measures, the *National Live-Stock Journal* (Mar. 1881), p. 91 labeled Senate bill 2097 "crude, ill-digested, and impracticable."

11. *Congressional Record,* 19 Feb. 1881, pp. 1831, 1835–36. Livestock owners stood to benefit more directly than the general taxpayer from the cleanup; many argued on both efficiency and equity grounds that they should bear more of its costs.

12. *New York Times,* 17 July 1881, p. 1; 6 Jan. 1883, p. 2; 10 Jan. 1884, p. 2; *Breeder's Gazette,* 31 Jan. 1884, pp. 146–47.

13. Thomas Sturgis Correspondence, 15 Apr. 1881, entry ah00014_004903; 27 Apr. 1881, entry ah00014_004899, Wyoming Stock Growers Association (WSGA) papers, digitalcollections.uwyo.edu:8180/luna/servlet, accessed 6 Feb. 2013. The internal correspondence gives every indication that the health concerns were genuine.

14. *Congressional Record,* 16 Dec. 1881, p. 158; 19 June 1882, pp. 5113–14.

15. *Congressional Record,* 19 June 1882, pp. 5115–16; 3 Aug. 1882, p. 6830.

16. *Drovers Journal,* 15 Oct. 1883, p. 4; *Prairie Farmer,* 20 Oct. 1883, p. 8.

17. *New York Times,* 16 Nov. 1883, p. 5.

18. *Washington Post,* 4 Dec. 1883, p. 2.

19. Carl V. Harris, "Right Fork or Left Fork? The Section-Party Alignments of the Southern Democrats in Congress," *Journal of Southern History* 42, no. 4 (1976), p. 474. After considerable turmoil, John G. Carlisle was elected speaker of the new House. Jeffery A. Jenkins and Charles Stewart III, *Fighting for the Speakership: The House and the Rise of Party Government* (Princeton, NJ: Princeton Univ. Press, 2012), pp. 265–66. Carlisle's position on animal disease control can be gauged from a floor speech on 12 April 1879. Carlisle supported federal efforts to exclude contagious diseases but asserted that federal authority extended only to preventing the interstate and foreign shipment of diseased animals. It did not include operating within states to exercise police powers such as seizing and slaughtering diseased animals. *Congressional Record,* 12 Apr. 1879, pp. 401–2; *New York Times,* 13 Apr. 1879, p. 10.

20. *Congressional Record,* 26 Jan. 1884, p. 682; 30 Jan. 1882, p. 754; 5 Feb. 1884, p. 899; U.S. House of Representatives, Committee on Agriculture, *Bureau of Animal Industry,* 26 Jan. 1884, House Report No. 119, 48th Cong., 1st Sess. (Washington, DC: U.S. Government Printing Office, 1884).

21. *Congressional Record,* 5 Feb. 1884, p. 899. Unlike Hatch's HR 896 of 1882, his 1884 bill included no role for the NBH.

22. For examples of the numerous petitions regarding the Bureau of Animal Industry bill, see Box No. 9, files HR 48A F 1.1 to F 2.11, U.S. House Records. Most were in favor the bill; file 2.5 contains the signed original of the 19 February 1884 petition from the Union Stock Yards dealers opposed to the bill.

23. *Congressional Record,* 25 Feb. 1884, p. 1364; 26 Feb. 1884, p. 1406.

24. *New York Tribune,* 18 Feb. 1884, p. 4; *Breeder's Gazette,* 3 Apr. 1884, p. 503.

25. *Congressional Record,* 5 Feb. 1884, pp. 901–2.

26. *Congressional Record,* 3 Aug. 1882, p. 6828.

27. *Congressional Record,* 5 Feb. 1884, pp. 902–3; 23 Feb. 1884, p. 1333; 25 Feb. 1884, p. 1365; *Breeder's Gazette,* 31 Jan. 1884, pp. 146–47. For a treatment of the cost of many livestock diseases in Britain, see J. R. Fisher, "The Economic Effects of Cattle Disease in Britain and Its Containment, 1850–1900," *Agricultural History* 54, no. 2 (1980): 278–94.

28. In a January 1884 report, the Treasury Cattle Commission recommended that the federal government prevent the shipment northward of cattle from the area infected with Texas fever, except during the winter months. *New York Times,* 10 Jan. 1884, p. 2.

29. *Congressional Record,* 6 Feb. 1884, pp. 926–29; 23 Feb. 1884, p. 1333; 26 Feb. 1884, p. 1401; 24 Apr. 1884, p. 3343.

30. Keith T. Poole and Howard Rosenthal, "Congress and Railroad Regulation: 1874–1887," in *The Regulated Economy: A Historical Approach to Political Economy,* ed. Claudia Goldin and Gary D. Libecap (Chicago: Univ. of Chicago Press, 1994), pp. 81–120, quotation from p. 99; Ben H. Proctor, *Not Without Honor: The Life of John H. Reagan* (Austin: Univ. of Texas Press, 1962), pp. 218–60.

31. Keith T. Poole and Howard Rosenthal, "The Enduring Nineteenth-Century Battle for Economic Regulation: The Interstate Commerce Act Revisited," *Journal of Law and Economics* 36, no. 2 (1993), p. 837. For an alternative interpretation emphasizing constituents' interests, see Thomas W. Gilligan, William J. Marshall, and Barry R. Weingast, "Regulation and the Theory of Legislative Choice: The Interstate Commerce Act of 1887," *Journal of Law and Economics* 32, no. 1 (1989): 35–61.

32. This was three years before the ICA's passage, but Reagan's views were known from his earlier efforts. *Congressional Record,* 6 Feb. 1884, p. 936.

33. *Congressional Record,* 23 Feb. 1884, pp. 1327–28, 1331–32; 25 Feb. 1884, pp. 1360, 1364; 26 Feb. 1884, p. 1401; 25 Apr. 1884, p. 3395; 28 Apr. 1884, pp. 3464–65; Maxey, "Federal Quarantine," p. 625.

34. *Congressional Record,* 6 Feb. 1884, p. 930.

35. *Congressional Record,* 6 Feb. 1884, pp. 933–94; 23 Feb. 1884, p. 1327; 25 Feb. 1884, p. 1364.

36. *Congressional Record,* 25 Feb. 1884, p. 1365; 26 Feb. 1884, pp. 1401–2.

37. *Congressional Record,* 27 Feb. 1884, pp. 1436–41.

38. *Congressional Record,* 28 Feb. 1884, pp. 1465–67. Under the rules in effect, the House did not record the roll calls of the earlier votes.

39. *Chicago Tribune,* 29 Feb. 1884, p. 1; *New York Times,* 28 Feb. 1884, p. 1. Party solidarity broke down at other times during that session. Carlisle had won the speaker's office in December 1883 after a bitter contest with Samuel Randall (D-Pa.), the party's previous speaker. The two continued to feud. On 6 May 1884, "Randall and his 40 Thieves" (protectionist Democrats) joined all the voting Republicans to defeat tariff reform, which was the main item on the majority's agenda. On 10 May 1884, Theodore Lyman (R-Mass.) noted in his personal correspondence that " 'there is something wrong with the Democratic side. There are some able and very many honest men over there, but they have no unity of action, nor ruling ideas.' " H. Wayne Morgan, *From Hayes to McKinley: National Party Politics, 1877–1896* (Syracuse, NY: Syracuse Univ. Press, 1969), pp. 182–85.

40. *Congressional Record,* 28 Feb. 1884, pp. 1466.

41. Elizabeth Sanders, *Roots of Reform: Farmers, Workers, and American State, 1877–1917* (Chicago: Univ. of Chicago Press, 1999), pp. 101–47. James Moore also concluded that "in the decisive economic clashes of the Gilded

Age" Southern Democrats "consistently joined forces" with those in West. James Tice Moore, "Redeemers Reconsidered: Change and Continuity in the Democratic South, 1870–1900," *Journal of Southern History* 44, no. 3 (1978), p. 378; see also Harris, "Right Fork." Political attitudes and behavior regarding federal intervention in the economy were more complicated than such findings indicate. Among House members in the 48th Congress, voting in favor of the BAI bill on 28 February 1884 was negatively correlated (−0.16) with voting on Reagan's Interstate Commerce bill on 8 January 1885. Democrats were more likely to have divergent views than Republicans. One source of the difference in support may be that the BAI bill created a new regulatory agency whereas the Reagan bill imposed judicial remedies, relying on laws and courts.

42. At this time, roughly 30 percent of the cattle destined for the Chicago yards were from Texas. *Boston Daily Advertiser,* 29 Apr. 1884, p. 8.

43. *Chicago Tribune,* 13 Feb. 1884, p. 7; 1 May 1884, p. 4; *Drovers Journal,* 11 Feb. 1884, p. 4; 16 Feb. 1884, p. 1; 19 Feb. 1884, p. 2; 18 Mar. 1884, p. 2; *Congressional Record,* 23 Feb. 1884, p. 1326; Louise C. Wade, *Chicago's Pride: The Stockyards, Packingtown, and Environs in the Nineteen Century* (Urbana: Univ. of Illinois Press, 1987), pp. 191–92.

44. *Rocky Mountain News,* 24 Feb. 1884, p. 8; 28 Feb. 1884, p. 5; 24 Mar. 1884, p. 1; *Chicago Tribune,* 14 Feb. 1884, p. 1; 19 Feb. 1884, p. 9; 21 Feb 1884, p. 8; 23 Feb. 1884, p. 7; 24 Feb. 1884, p. 4; 29 Feb., 1884, p. 4; 1 Mar. 1884, p. 10; Ernest Staples Osgood, *The Day of the Cattleman* (Minneapolis: Univ. of Minnesota Press, 1929), pp. 169–75; John Clay, *My Life on the Range* (Chicago: author, 1924), pp. 116–20, 245–49.

45. *Drovers Journal,* 18 Mar. 1884, p. 4; 31 Mar. 1884, p. 2; 1 Apr. 1884, p. 4.

46. *Congressional Record,* 12 Mar. 1884, pp. 1791–95.

47. On March 13, Trumbower began to have doubts. Salmon arrived in Kansas on March 15 and concluded that the cattle suffered from ergot poisoning, which mimicked FMD but was not contagious. Salmon's tests of suspect herds in Missouri and Illinois led to the same finding. But the threat of state and foreign quarantines persisted. Only after Salmon returned to Kansas and Illinois in late April and again declared the cattle free of FMD did the scare subside. *Congressional Record,* 23 Apr. 1884, p. 3286; U.S. BAI, *Report for 1884,* pp. 175–85, 310–20.

48. *Congressional Record,* 14 Mar. 1884, pp. 1886–1903; 17 Mar. 1884, pp. 1961–74; *Washington Post,* 24 Mar. 1884, p. 1; *Rocky Mountain News,* 27 Mar. 1884, p. 2.

49. *Congressional Record,* 14 Mar. 1884, pp. 1898–1901.

50. *Congressional Record,* 17 Mar. 1884, p. 1963.

51. *Drovers Journal,* 31 Mar. 1884, p. 2; 1 Apr. 1884, p. 4; *Chicago Tribune,* 24 Mar. 1884, p. 6; Emery Storrs, *The Animal Industry Bill: Further Suggestions against the Passage of the Bill* (Chicago: Chicago Live Stock Exchange, 1884), Rutherford B. Hayes Presidential Center.

52. *Congressional Record,* 23 Apr. 1884, pp. 3287–88, 3292; 24 Apr. 1884, pp. 3336–37; U.S. BAI, *Report for 1884,* pp. 299, 302.

53. *Congressional Record,* 23 Apr. 1884, pp. 3291–92; 29 Apr. 1884, pp. 3523–25.

54. *Congressional Record,* 24 May 1884, p. 4477; 28 Apr. 1884, pp. 3461–62.

55. G. W Simpson to Thomas Sturgis, 10 May 1884, entry ah00014_004449-50, Wyoming Stock Growers Association Records.

56. *Chicago Tribune,* 23 May 1884, p. 8; *Drovers Journal,* 23 May 1884, p. 4. As drafted, the Texas fever exemption specifically protected the trade of the Chicago stockyard and packing interests. This history is difficult to square with accounts treating the animal disease control measures of the period as subterfuges pushed by Northern stock owners to limit competition from Texas long horns. The BAI bill passed only after the provisions affecting Texas cattle were effectively neutered. Conflicts over Texas livestock likely delayed rather than hastened passage.

57. In a letter that circulated widely among public officials, Law wrote the bill's language had "been carefully manipulated" to render the BAI ineffective: if "the Bill is intended to provide for the extinction of any one contagious disease it must prove a complete failure." James Law to H. F. French, 31 May 1884, Box No. 9, U.S. House Records. Law singled out the lobbying efforts of Emery Storrs for weakening the BAI. *National Live-Stock Journal,* Dec. 1884, p. 561.

58. *Chicago Tribune,* 13 May 1884, p. 1; *Congressional Record,* 28 Apr. 1884, pp. 3471–73; 29 Apr. 1884, pp. 3530–31; 7 May 1884, p. 3944; 24 May 1884, p. 4477.

59. Supporters formed the "National Cattle Growers Association" in Chicago in mid-November 1884. At roughly the same time, a large assembly of stock growers met in St. Louis. Southwest interests dominated the contentious proceedings. An organizational outgrowth was the "National Cattle and Horse Growers Association," which was initially more critical of the BAI. *Breeder's Gazette,* 20 Oct. 1884, pp. 635–36; 27 Nov. 1884, pp. 778–79.

60. *Chicago Tribune,* 25 May 1884, p. 2; 1 May 1884, p. 4.

CHAPTER 4 *The BAI in Action*

1. *Washington Post,* 26 Sept. 1892, p. 5.

2. Fenner et al., *Smallpox,* p. 372.

3. U.S. House of Representatives, Committee of Agriculture, "Hearings Regarding HR 7208, 30 Jan. 1886," unpublished hearings, 49th Cong., 1st Sess., p. 5.

4. U.S. BAI, *Diseases of Cattle, 1916,* pp. 356–509.

5. *Breeder's Gazette,* 28 Aug. 1884, pp. 290–92; U.S. BAI, *Report for 1884,* pp. 16–24, 62–63; *National Live-Stock Journal* 15, no. 9 (Sept. 1884), pp. 393–94.

6. *Chicago Tribune,* 28 Aug. 1884, p. 3.

7. U.S. BAI, *Report for 1884*, pp. 22–24; Houck, *Bureau of Animal Industry*, p. 40.

8. *Drovers Journal*, 18 Sept. 1884, p. 4; 25 Sept. 1884, pp. 2, 4; 2 Oct. 1884, pp. 4, 7; *Chicago Tribune*, 27 Sept. 1884, p. 3. To demonstrate that the cattle disease was in fact contagious, BAI personnel did conduct experiments on Barren Island (near Brooklyn, New York) from late September 1884 to January 1885. U.S. BAI, *Report for 1884*, pp. 170–71.

9. *Farmers' Review*, 14 May 1885, p. 352.

10. USDA, *Report of the Commissioner for 1885*, p. 433; U.S. BAI, *Report for 1884*, p. 27; *Report for 1885*, p. 13.

11. USDA, *Report of the Commissioner for 1885*, p. 436; U.S. BAI, *Report for 1885*, pp. 10–11. Salmon misdates Knott's proclamation as being issued in 1885.

12. USDA, *Report of the Commissioner for 1885*, p. 448; U.S. BAI, *Report for 1884*, pp. 27–30; *Report for 1885*, pp. 11–24.

13. Kentucky General Assembly, *Journal of the House of Representatives, 1885–86* (Frankford, KY: John Woods, 1886), pp. 661–70; U.S. BAI, *Report for 1886*, pp. 9–10; *Chicago Tribune*, 25 Sept. 1885, p. 7.

14. Colman became a proponent of eradication only after an outbreak hit in his home state of Missouri in the spring 1885. His attempt to spend BAI funds to purchase and destroy affected animals was blocked by the U.S. Attorney General. *St. Louis Globe-Democrat*, 24 Apr. 1885, p. 4; 25 Apr. 1885, p. 8; *Atchison Globe*, 27 Apr. 1885, p. 1; George F. Lemmer, *Norman J. Colman and Colman's Rural World: A Study in Agricultural Leadership*, Univ. of Missouri Studies 25, no. 3 (Columbia: Curators of the Univ. Missouri, 1953), pp. 90–93.

15. The 1884 organic legislation called for a budget of $150,000, but in light of considerable unspent funds on the books in the spring of 1885, the 1885 Appropriations Act passed 3 March 1885 allocated $100,000 of new funds. In the spring of 1886 the "new" appropriation was again set at $100,000 given another large carryover. USDA, *Report of the Secretary for 1910* (Washington, DC: U.S. Government Printing Office, 1911), pp. 591–619. Cleveland signed the 1886–87 Agricultural Appropriations Act (49 HR 7481, 24 Stat. 100, Ch. 575) into law on 30 June 1886. *Congressional Record*, 10 June 1886, p. 5501; 29 June 1886, pp. 6280, 6304; 1 July 1886, p. 6417. The pace of the changes did not satisfy advocates of stronger federal powers. *Breeder's Gazette*, 22 Apr. 1886, p. 414; 10 June 1886, p. 834; 17 June 1886, p. 866.

16. U.S. BAI, *Report for 1885*, pp. 150–56.

17. Illinois State Board of Live Stock Commissioners, *Annual Report for 1887* (Springfield, IL: State Printers, 1887), p. 4.

18. *Chicago Tribune*, 15 Sept. 1886, p. 8; 18 Sept. 1886, p. 6; 19 Sept. 1886, p. 1; 20 Sept. 1886, p. 1.

19. *Chicago Tribune,* 21 Sept. 1886, p. 1; 1 Oct. 1886, p. 6; *New York Times,* 20 Sept. 1886, p. 1; 21 Sept. 1886, p. 5.

20. *Chicago Tribune,* 22 Sept. 1886, p. 1; 23 Sept. 1886, p. 2; 24 Sept. 1886, p. 1; 25 Sept. 1886, p. 6; 29 Sept. 1886, p. 3; *Chicago Daily News,* 22 Sept. 1886, p. 1; 23 Sept. 1886, p. 1; *Chicago Herald,* 22 Sept. 1886, p. 1; 23 Sept. 1886, p. 1; 24 Sept. 1886, p. 1.

21. U.S. BAI, *Reports for 1887 and 1888,* pp. 9–10. Illinois General Assembly, *Journal of the House of Representatives for Thirty-Third General Assembly* (Springfield, IL: H. W. Rokker, 1883), pp. 961, 1090; *Laws of the State of Illinois Enacted by the Thirty-Fourth General Assembly* (Springfield, IL: H. W. Rokker, 1885), pp. 1–3, quotation from p. 3.

22. *Chicago Daily News,* 24 Sept. 1886, p. 1; *Chicago Herald,* 24 Sept. 1886, p. 1; 25 Sept. 1886, p. 1.

23. *Chicago Tribune,* 22 Sept. 1886, p. 1.

24. *Chicago Tribune,* 24 Sept. 1886, p. 1; 25 Sept. 1886, p. 4; *Breeder's Gazette,* 30 Sept. 1886, pp. 483–84.

25. *Detroit Free Press,* 28 Sept. 1886, p. 14; *Chicago Tribune,* 26 Sept. 1886, p. 9; 27 Sept. 1886, p. 4; 28 Sept. 1886, p. 4. The concerns of the large packers were justified. The *Butchers' Advocate,* an organ of the Eastern meat trade, took advantage of the Chicago outbreak in its attacks against the unhealthy and unwholesome qualities of dressed beef. *Farmers' Review,* 18 Oct. 1886, p. 228. During the crisis, Commissioner McChesney noted that "'if the Stock Yards people were to come forward and offer to pay for the cattle and rely for their remuneration on the generosity of the Legislature, I, for one, would receive them.'" *Chicago Herald,* 29 Sept. 1886, p. 1. But this Coasian solution was not pursued.

26. *New York Times,* 27 Sept. 1886, p. 5; 28 Sept. 1886, p. 4; *Chicago Tribune,* 29 Sept. 1886, p. 2; 3 Oct. 1886, p. 3.

27. *Chicago Tribune,* 30 Sept. 1886, p. 2; Illinois State Board of Live Stock Commissioners, *Annual Report for 1887,* pp. 8–17.

28. *Chicago Tribune,* 5 Oct. 1886, p. 4; 6 Oct. 1886, p. 3; 12 Oct. 1886, pp. 1, 4; *New York Times,* 9 Oct. 1886, p. 1.

29. *Chicago Tribune,* 13 Oct. 1886, p. 1; 14 Oct. 1886, p. 8; 15 Oct. 1886, p. 2; 16 Oct. 1886, pp. 4, 9, 10; 19 Oct. 1886, p. 3; 31 Oct. 1886, p. 7; *Chicago Inter Ocean,* 2 Oct. 1886, p. 1; 10 Oct. 1886, p. 10; 21 Oct. 1886, p. 7.

30. *Chicago Tribune,* 15 Sept. 1886, p. 8; 18 Sept. 1886, p. 6.

31. Given the lax state of the inspection system in most regions of the country, butchering CBPP-infected cattle was probably the norm. *New York Times,* 7 Jan. 1887, p. 8.

32. U.S. BAI, *Report for 1886,* pp. 16–19; *Chicago Herald,* 23 Sept 1886, p. 1; *Detroit Free Press,* 28 Sept. 1886, p. 14; *Farmers' Review* 17 Nov. 1886, p. 306. For Morris's earlier denials, see *Drovers Journal,* 13 Mar. 1884, p. 8.

33. *Scotsman,* 27 Dec. 1886, p. 2.

34. *Chicago Tribune*, 28 Sept. 1886, p. 4; 17 Nov. 1886, p. 2. Washburn played a leadership role in the Consolidated Cattle Growers Association, which was formed in an 1886 merger of the Chicago- and St. Louis-based stock-growers organizations. The Chicago group was home to the original supporters of the BAI; the St. Louis group contained its opponents. The Consolidated Association favored strong measures to eradicated CBPP exercised by a temporary body granted emergency powers.

35. Illinois State Board of Live Stock Commissioners, *Annual Report for 1887*, pp. 7–8, 98–117; U.S. BAI, *Reports for 1887 and 1888*, pp. 15–19; *Chicago Tribune*, 25 Jan. 1887, p. 4; 28 Dec. 1886, p. 4; 27 Jan. 1887, p. 4; 4 May 1887, p. 4; 27 May 1887, p. 4; *New York Times*, 1 Jan. 1887, p. 1; 3 Jan. 1887, p. 2.

36. Illinois General Assembly, *Journal of the Senate of the Thirty-fourth General Assembly, 1885* (Springfield, IL: State Printers, 1885), p. 171.

37. *Breeder's Gazette*, 30 Dec. 1886, p. 97; 13 Feb. 1887, p. 160; *New York Times*, 7 Dec. 1886, pp. 3–4.

38. USDA, *Report of the Secretary for 1910*, pp. 596–98; *New York Times*, 1 Mar. 1887, p. 2; *Congressional Record*, 25 Feb. 1887, pp. 2182–98; 25 Feb. 1887, pp. 2242–57; 28 Feb. 1887, pp. 2379–86; 2 Mar. 1887, pp. 2575–79. Petitions in favor and opposed to the Miller bill and its successor, the Palmer bill, flooded Congress in 1887 and 1888; see Box 15, file HR49AH 2.5 and Box 120, file HR50A H 1.15, U.S. House Records.

39. USDA, *Report of Commissioner for 1887*, pp. 458–59.

40. U.S. BAI, *Reports for 1887 and 1888*, pp. 9–13.

41. Ibid., p. 13.

42. U.S. BAI, *Report for 1886*, pp. 15–19; *Reports for 1887 and 1888*, pp. 9–14.

43. U.S. BAI, *Report for 1885*, p. 39; *Reports for 1887 and 1888*, pp. 10–16; Houck, *Bureau of Animal Industry*, p. 44.

44. U.S. BAI, *Reports for 1887 and 1888*, pp. 13–16. The first letters with the proposed legislation were sent 7 April 1887. *New York Times*, 10 Apr. 1887, p. 2.

45. Compiled from C. J. Marshall, "Presidential Address," *American Journal of Veterinary Medicine* 48 (1915): 84–87.

46. U.S. BAI, *Reports for 1887 and 1888*, pp. 10.

47. Illinois General Assembly, *Laws of the State of Illinois Enacted by the Thirty-Fifth General Assembly* (Springfield, IL: H. W. Rokker, 1887), pp. 8–13. This Act amended the Act that took effect 1 July 1885. *Chicago Tribune*, 4 May 1887, p. 4.

48. *New York Times*, 28 May 1887, pp. 2, 4; *Chicago Tribune*, 29 Sept. 1886, p. 3; 1 Oct. 1886, p. 6.

49. Illinois General Assembly, *Laws of the State of Illinois Enacted by the Thirty-Fifth General Assembly*, pp. 13–17; *Farmers' Review*, 22 June 1887, p. 8; *Farm, Field, and Stockman*, 25 June 1887, p. 4; *Chicago Tribune*, 25 June 1887, p. 2; 12 July 1887, p. 4.

50. James Bryce, *American Commonwealth* (London: MacMillan, 1888), vol. 1, pp. 314, 330–31. Historian Max Edling in summarizing Brian Balogh's work, emphasized that in all but a few proscribed areas, such as conducting the nation's foreign affairs, the federal government tiptoed cautiously. In "the more contested zones of federal government activity, direct rule was not the norm." Elding is one of a long list of observers who have emphasized the limits on federal power. Max M. Edling, Review of *"A Government Out of Sight: the Mystery of National Authority in Nineteenth-Century America,* by Brian Balogh, *Journal of Policy History* 21, no 4 (2009): 462–68, esp. 468. See also Balogh, *Government Out of Sight,* pp. 1–17, 309–51.

51. *Chicago Tribune,* 23 Apr. 1887, p. 1; 4 May 1887, p. 4; 27 May 1887, p. 4; Houck, *Bureau of Animal Industry,* p. 43; U.S. BAI, *Reports for 1887 and 1888,* pp. 5, 9–10, 17–22; Illinois State Board of Live Stock Commissioners, *Annual Report for 1887,* pp. 14–15, 95.

52. Daniel Salmon, "The Outbreak of Pleuro-Pneumonia at Chicago, and the Lessons Which It Teaches," *National Live-Stock Journal* 18, no. 11 (1887): 392–94.

53. In late 1887, Senator Thomas Palmer (R-Mich.) introduced legislation (S 2083) that would have replaced the BAI with an emergency commission empowered to eradicate CBPP without state cooperation. The Texas Livestock Association and Senator Coke opposed the bill, which died in the Senate. *Washington Post,* 29 Feb. 1888, p. 6; 4 May 1888, p. 4; *Congressional Record,* 3 May 1888, pp. 3681–85; 7 May 1888, pp. 3780–83.

54. U.S. BAI, *Report for 1886,* pp. 16–19; *Reports for 1887 and 1888,* pp. 6–38; *Operations for 1890,* pp. 3–7; Houck, *Bureau of Animal Industry,* p. 45.

55. U.S. BAI, *Reports for 1887 and 1888,* pp. 9–38; *Operations for 1890,* pp. 3–7; Houck, *Bureau of Animal Industry,* p. 45; *New York Times,* 16 May 1888, pp. 3–4; *Brooklyn Eagle,* 15 May 1888, p. 6; 1 June 1888, p. 1; 17 July 1888, p. 2; 21 July 1888, p. 2; 4 Aug. 1888, p. 1; *Washington Post,* 12 June 1890, p. 1.

56. With an eye to reopening the British market, Rusk had intended to announce the limitation of CBPP in the late 1891, but the discovery of the disease in a few New Jersey herds scuttled his plans. J. Rusk to J.H. Sanders, 9 Sept. 1891; J. Rusk to George A. Halsey, 5 Oct. 1891, Box 10, Jeremiah Rusk Papers, Wisconsin Historical Society [hereafter Rusk Papers].

57. The leaders of the USDA had hoped the CBPP eradication would convince the British government to end the requirement that U.S. cattle be slaughtered at the docks shortly after arrival. This did not happen.

58. Carter et al., *Historical Statistics,* vol. 4, series Da 968, 969; U.S. BAI, *Diseases of Cattle, 1916 ed.,* p. 371.

59. Houck, *Bureau of Animal Industry,* pp. 44–47; U.S. BAI, *Reports for 1891 and 1892,* pp. 23, and 71–74.

60. U.S. BAI, *Reports for 1887 and 1888*, pp. 22–79.
61. *Dundee Courier & Argus*, 8 July 1890, p. 3; James Law, *Textbook on Veterinary Medicine*, vol. 4 (Ithaca, NY: author, 1902), pp. 618–19.
62. United Kingdom, Minister of Agriculture, Fisheries, and Food, *Animal Health*, pp. 157–62; John R. Fisher, "To Kill or Not to Kill: The Eradication of Contagious Bovine Pleuro-Pneumonia in Western Europe," *Medical History* 47 (2003): 314–31; British Board of Agriculture, *Extracts Relating to Pleuro-pneumonia in the United States of America, from the First Report of the Secretary of Agriculture, Washington* (London: Her Majesty's Stationary Office, 1890).
63. L.G. Newton and R. Norris, *Clearing a Continent: The Eradication of Bovine Pleuropneumonia from Australia*, SCARM Report No. 74 (Collingwood, Victoria: CSIRO, 2000), p. 2. For a sense of the turmoil associated with CBPP in Africa, see J.B. Peires, *Dead Will Arise: Nongqawuse and the Great Xhosa Cattle-Killing Movement of 1856–57* (Bloomington: Indiana Univ. Press, 1989), pp. 70–73, 87, 97, 124–28, 166–69.
64. Harry N. Scheiber, "Federalism and the American Economic Order, 1789–1910," *Law and Society Review* 57 (1975–76): 57–118, esp. 107–8; James, *Presidents, Parties, and the State*, pp. 36–122. See Mashaw, *Creating the Administrative Constitution*, pp. 12–15, 91, for a critique of the primacy assigned to the ICC in the formation of the administrative state. As we emphasize in Chapter 1, the federal government was involved in many economic activities such as running the post office and providing land grants for railroads before the ICC, but few if any of these activities involved the day-to-day intrusion into private affairs on a scale comparable to that of the ICC or the BAI.
65. *Los Angeles Times*, 25 Mar. 1887, p. 5; 2 Apr. 1887, p. 4; U.S. Interstate Commerce Commission, *First Annual Report* (Washington, DC: U.S. Government Printing Office, 1887), p. 86; Gabriel Kolko, *Railroads and Regulation, 1877–1916* (Princeton, NJ: Princeton Univ. Press, 1965), pp. 45–65.
66. Jane P. Clark, *The Rise of a New Federalism: Federal-State Cooperation in the United States* (New York: Columbia Univ. Press, 1938). Zimmerman and Lawrence list the BAI Act (1884) with the ICA (1887) and Sherman Anti-Trust Act (1890) as among a handful of examples of nineteenth century federal preemptions of state regulation of commerce. Joseph F. Zimmerman and Sharon Lawrence, *Federal Statutory Preemption of State and Local Authority: History, Inventory, and Issues*, U.S. Advisory Commission on Intergovernmental Relations Report A-121 (Washington, DC: ACIR, 1992), p. 53.
67. Balogh, *Government Out of Sight*, pp. 309–51.
68. Scheiber, "Federalism," pp. 57–118.
69. Kimberly S. Johnson, *Governing the American State: Congress and the New Federalism, 1877–1929* (Princeton, NJ: Princeton Univ. Press, 2007), p. 11.

Johnson also maintains that Congress, not the executive branch, "was responsible for the ebb and flow of intergovernmental policy." Clearly, Congress initiated legislation and controlled the purse strings, but the history of the BAI shows how an aggressive bureaucracy drove policy. Through the Secretary of Agriculture, the Bureau's chiefs set rules and regulations, conducted eradication operations, and prosecuted violators.

70. Daniel P. Carpenter, *The Forging of Bureaucratic Autonomy: Reputations, Networks, and Policy Innovation in Executive Agencies, 1862–1928* (Princeton, NJ: Princeton Univ. Press, 2001), pp. 179–367.

71. Stephen Skowronek, *Building a New American State: The Expansion of National Administrative Capacities, 1877–1920* (New York: Cambridge Univ. Press, 1982), pp. 45–46, 165.

72. Richard L. McCormick, *The Party Period and Public Policy* (New York: Oxford Univ. Press, 1986), pp. 176–77, 185.

73. Robert Higgs, *Crisis and Leviathan: Critical Episodes in the Growth of American Government* (New York: Oxford Univ. Press, 1987), pp. 82–83. In the broader literature, the regulation of oleomargarine and Cleveland's veto of a relatively minor seed bill have received far more attention than the activities of the BAI occurring under his watch. Peter Zavodnyic, *The Rise of the Federal Colossus: The Growth of Federal Power from Lincoln to F.D.R.* (Santa Barbara, CA: Praeger, 2011), pp. 145–46, 161–63.

CHAPTER 5 *Bad Blood*

1. Franklin L. Riley, "Diary of a Mississippi Planter, January 1, 1840 to April, 1863," *Publications of the Mississippi Historical Society* 10 (1909), pp. 312, 323, 326–27; M. Philips, *Cultivator* (Sept. 1843), p. 139.

2. Haygood, "Cows, Ticks, and Disease," p. 551.

3. There is considerable disagreement today among the researchers whom we consulted as to whether animals born and raised in tick-infested areas suffered productivity losses due to the infectious diseases, as opposed to just the stress of blood loss due to the ticks. See the chapter appendix.

4. Texas fever is not a zoonotic disease. Humans do acquire babesiosis, but from a different tick.

5. Haygood, "Cows, Ticks, and Disease," pp. 551–64; U.S. BAI, *Diseases of Cattle, 1916*, pp. 473–77.

6. Terry L. Anderson and Peter J. Hill, *The Not So Wild, Wild West: Property Rights on the Frontier* (Stanford, CA: Stanford Univ. Press, 2004); David Galenson, "The End of the Chisholm Trail," *Journal of Economic History* 34, no. 2 (1974): 350–64.

7. Strom, *Catfish Bait;* Strom, "Texas Fever," pp. 49–74.

8. Haygood, "Cows, Ticks, and Disease," pp. 551–64; USDA, *Yearbook of Agriculture, 1942*, p. 573; U.S. BAI, *Diseases of Cattle, 1916*, p. 480.

9. Gray, *History of Agriculture,* p. 14; Houck, *Bureau of Animal Industry,* pp. 15–17; John S. Andrews, "Animal Parasitology in the United States Department of Agriculture, 1886–1984," in *100 Years of Animal Health, 1884–1984,* ed. Vivian Wiser, Larry Mark, and H. Graham Purchase (Beltsville, MD: Associates of the National Agricultural Library, 1987), p. 124; U.S. BAI, *Report for 1885,* p. 461.

10. USDA, *Report of the Commissioner for 1868,* pp. 38–41; John Gamgee, "Report of Professor Gamgee on Splenic and Periodic Fever of Cattle" in USDA, *Report of the Commissioner of Agriculture on the Diseases of Cattle in the United States* (Washington, DC: U.S. Government Printing Office, 1871), pp. 82–155, especially p. 118; O. H. V. Stalheim, *The Winning of Animal Health* (Ames: Iowa State Univ. Press, 1994), p. 15; Stalheim and Moulton, "Veterinary Medicine," p. 24; Houck, *Bureau of Animal Industry,* pp. 318–41; *Ohio Farmer,* 5 Apr. 1879, p. 212; 2 Sept. 1882, p. 132; *Prairie Farmer,* 22 Sept. 1877, p. 301; *Medical and Surgical Reporter,* 4 Mar. 1871, p. 181; *Breeder's Gazette,* 31 May 1883, p. 689.

11. Dupree, *Science in the Federal Government,* p. 154.

12. Strom, *Catfish Bait,* p. 31.

13. James W. Whitaker, *Feedlot Empire: Beef Cattle Feeding in Illinois and Iowa, 1840–1900* (Ames: Iowa State Univ. Press, 1975), pp. 59–62.

14. For Anderson and Hill, this trivial indemnity program made McCoy the "quintessential institutional entrepreneur" for increasing trade by internalizing "both the costs and benefits" of his activities. However, by McCoy's own story, he conned the local farmers (McCoy, *Historic Sketches,* chapters 4 and 9; Anderson and Hill, *Not So Wild,* pp. 146–47). Dykstra suggests that a clique "of wealthy and important enterprises" wrangled favorable provisions in the 1867 Kansas livestock protection act that "paved the way for McCoy's project" (*Cattle Towns,* p. 17). Edward Dale, *The Range Cattle Industry: Ranching on the Great Plains from 1865 to 1925* (Norman: Univ. of Oklahoma Press, 1960/1930), pp. 43–44, is also critical of McCoy, noting that he likely used fraudulent certificates to gain market access.

15. Galenson, "Chisholm Trail," pp. 362, 364. Galenson quotes from Nimmo, *Range and Ranch.*

16. In 1888, Supreme Court justices Morrison Waite, John Marshall Harlan, and Horace Gray offered an insight into the court's reasoning in the *Husen* case. They asserted that "it was only because the Missouri statues embraced cattle that were free from the disease that it was declared unconstitutional." *Bowman v. Chicago and Northwestern Railway Co.* (125 U.S. 465, 492, decided 19 Mar. 1888), p. 5213.

17. Kansas, *House Journal, Special Session 1884, Proceeding of the House of Representatives* (Topeka: Kansas Publishing House, 1885), pp. 3, 27, 48, 62–70, 84. Dale argues, that the 1884 Kansas quarantine after Texas fever "seriously checked the northern drive" (*Cattle Industry,* pp. 52, 54–55). This statement

is in line with the contentions of Galenson critic R. Taylor Dennen, "Cattle Trailing in the Nineteenth Century," *Journal of Economic History* 35, no. 2 (1975): 458–60.

18. Kansas, *Senate Journal, Special Session 1886, Proceeding of the Senate* (Topeka: Kansas Publishing House, 1886), pp. 228–33, quotation from pp. 229, 231; Strom, "Texas Fever," pp. 52–53; Houck, *Bureau of Animal Industry*, pp. 15–17; U.S. BAI, *Report for 1885*, pp. 471–552; *Report for 1886*, pp. 303–73.

19. *Statist*, 13 Feb. 1886, p. 177. Nimmo made similar assertions (*Range and Ranch*, pp. 35–39).

20. Anderson and Hill, *Not So Wild*, pp. 1–33, 145–48; Galenson, "Chisholm Trail," pp. 362, 364.

21. Osgood, *Day of the Cattleman*, p. 173. Also see Dale, *Cattle Industry*, p. 92; *Chicago Tribune*, 27 May 1884, p. 4.

22. Osgood, *Day of the Cattleman*, pp. 164–66. For details of the losses in Colorado and Nebraska in 1884 and the role of railroads, see U.S. BAI, *Report for 1885*, pp. 303–8.

23. *Washington Post*, 21 Nov. 1884, p. 1; *Chicago Tribune*, 4 Oct. 1884, p. 10; 15 Dec. 1884, p. 9; 20 Jan. 1885, p. 3; 18 Feb. 1885, p. 10; U.S. BAI, *Report for 1885*, p. 297–98; Frank Wilkerson, "Cattle-Raising on the Plains," *Harper's Monthly* 72, no. 431 (1886), p. 792; *Congressional Record*, 19 Mar. 1886, pp. 2521–22; 28 Apr. 1886, pp. 3935–36; U.S. House of Representatives, *National Live-Stock Highway*, 23 Mar. 1886, Report No. 1228, 49th Cong., 1st Sess. (Washington, DC: U.S. Government Printing Office, 1886), p. 5.

24. *Galveston Daily News*, 10 May 1884, p. 4.

25. As quoted in the *Breeder's Gazette*, 22 Feb. 1888, p. 182; 29 Feb. 1888, p. 206; U.S. BAI, *Report for 1885*, p. 80.

26. *Congressional Record*, 6 Feb. 1884, p. 936.

27. U.S. BAI, *Report for 1884*, pp. 214–17; *Report for 1885*, pp. 247–74 (see map between pp. 274 and 275); Stalheim, *Winning of Animal Health*, p. 15; Stalheim and Moulton, "Veterinary Medicine," p. 24; Houck, *Bureau of Animal Industry*, pp. 318–41.

28. "Recent Outbreaks of Texas Fever," *National Live-Stock Journal* 8, no. 11 (1877): 470–71; U.S. BAI, *Report for 1885*, pp. 301–2; U.S. House of Representatives, Committee on Agriculture, *Letter from the Commissioner of Agriculture, Transmitting a List of Persons Employed and Statement of Expenditures and of Means Adopted for the Suppression of Contagious and Infectious Diseases among Domestic Animals*, 17 Dec. 1884, Ex. Doc. No. 46, 48th Cong., 2nd Sess. (Washington, DC: U.S. Government Printing Office, 1885), p. 5.

29. *Galveston Daily News*, 14 Feb. 1885, p. 1; *Dallas Weekly Herald*, 19 Feb. 1885, p. 2; *St. Louis Globe-Democrat*, 13 Feb. 1885, p. 12.

30. U.S. BAI, *Report for 1885*, pp. 549–50.

31. U.S. BAI, *Report for 1886*, pp. 359–61; *Chicago Tribune*, 23 Aug. 1888, p. 1; 8 Aug. 1889, p. 9.

32. *Breeder's Gazette,* 18 July 1888, pp. 51–52; 1 Aug. 1888, p. 160; 7 Aug. 1889, p. 122; 15 Aug. 1888, p. 147; 29 Aug. 1888, p. 194; *Chicago Tribune* 11 Aug. 1888, p. 3; 13 Oct. 1888, p. 1.

33. U.S. BAI, *Reports for 1889 and 1890,* pp. 13–14.

34. *Dallas Morning News,* 31 July 1889, p. 6; U.S. BAI, *Reports for 1889 and 1890,* pp. 13–14; *Breeder's Gazette,* 21 Aug. 1889, p. 107.

35. U.S. BAI, *Reports for 1889 and 1890,* pp. 13–14; *Congressional Record,* 24 May 1884, p. 4477; 28 Apr. 1884, pp. 3461–62.

36. *Congressional Record,* 26 Feb. 1884, p. 1406; U.S. BAI, *Reports for 1889 and 1890,* pp. 13–15, 67–70; *Reports for 1891 and 1892,* pp. 25–28, 74–78; Houck, *Bureau of Animal Industry,* p. 318; *Congressional Record,* 3 Feb. 1887, p. 1332.

37. U.S. BAI, *Reports for 1891 and 1892,* p. 27. "The Department was compelled in a measure to rely upon the railroad companies for an observance of this part of the regulations and for the thoroughness of the work." Some complied cheerfully and carefully; others were careless.

38. Nelson Morris to J. Rusk 4 Sept. 1890, Reel 28, Benjamin Harrison Presidential Papers, Library of Congress Microfilm. See also E. W. Halford to J. Rusk, 13 Sept. 1890, relating that President Harrison had read the letter from Morris "with great interest and satisfaction" (Box 2, Rusk Papers).

39. On 28 February 1893, H. P. Child of the Kansas City Stock Yard wrote to incoming USDA Secretary J. Sterling Morton that Rusk's Texas fever inspection "has proven one of the greatest benefits that has ever come to the cattle business"; Reel 19, J. Sterling Morton Papers, Nebraska Historical Society [hereafter Morton papers]. In a 10 March 1893 letter to Morton, C. W. Baker, secretary of the Chicago Live Stock Exchange wrote, "The Live Stock Interest has been greatly benefited by the system of sanitary and inspection measures promulgated and enforced by" Secretary Rusk and "we recommend his successor to adopt and continue his policy" (Reel 18, Morton Papers).

40. U.S. BAI, *Operations for 1890,* p. 9; U.S. Treasury, Bureau of Statistics, *Monthly Summary of Commerce and Finance of the United States,* Feb. 1900, p. 2334; U.S. BAI, *Reports for 1891 and 1892,* p. 78.

41. As quoted in the *Breeder's Gazette,* 9 Mar. 1892, p. 188.

42. *Breeder's Gazette,* 7 Mar. 1894, p. 151.

43. James C. Olson, *J. Sterling Morton* (Lincoln: Univ. of Nebraska Press, 1942), pp. 356–62; U.S. Senate, *Letter from the Secretary of Agriculture, Transmitting, in Response to a Resolution, of the Senate dated Feb. 12, 1896, Copies of the Regulations Establishing the Quarantine Line in the Southwestern States for the Years 1895 and 1896,* 13 Feb. 1896, Senate Doc. No. 121, 54th Cong., 1st Sess. (Washington, DC: U.S. Government Printing Office, 1896). State court decisions, such as *Fort Worth & Denver City Railway Company v. R. B. Masterson, et al.,* 66 S.W. Rep. 833 (6 Mar. 1902), also eroded the ability of federal officials to operate within states.

44. *Congressional Record*, 17 Feb. 1896, pp. 1784–85.

45. William H. Cowles, "State Quarantine Laws and the Federal Constitution," *American Law Review* 25 (1891), p. 45. See also James W. Ely Jr., *The Chief Justiceship of Melville W. Fuller, 1888–1910* (Columbia: Univ. of South Carolina Press, 1995), pp. 142–43.

46. *Missouri, Kansas & Texas Railroad Co. v. Haber*, 169 U.S. 623.

47. *Rasmussen v. Idaho*, 181 U.S. 200, 202.

48. On the same day as its *Rasmussen* decision, the U.S. Supreme Court confirmed in *Smith v. St. Louis & Southwestern Ry. Co.* (181 U.S. 248, decided 22 Apr. 1901) the constitutionality of "reasonable" state quarantines. This case arose when Texas embargoed all cattle from Louisiana, which was suffering an anthrax outbreak.

49. States had long accepted the lower standard of proof. In *H. P. Croff v. C. M. Cresse* (7 Okla. 408, decided June 1898), the Oklahoma Supreme Court affirmed a law holding those who drove cattle from a district known to be infected across the state and federal quarantine line liable for damages, regardless of whether they knew the animals were diseased. In *Grayson v. Lynch* (163 U.S. 468, decided 25 May 1896), the U.S. Supreme Court also upheld a New Mexico case dealing with similar issues.

50. The Supreme Court ruled in the same way at the same time in the related case *Illinois Central Railroad Co. v. T. C. Edwards* (203 U.S. 531, decided 17 Dec. 1906).

51. M. P. Buel to James Wilson, 19 Dec. 1906, Entry 1, Box 2, RG17, Bureau of Animal Industry Records, National Archives, College Park, MD [hereafter U.S. BAI Records]; *Washington Post*, 23 Dec. 1906, p. 12.

52. This was one of several occasions when Salmon directed his staff to conduct research that might contradict his previous published findings. See Schwabe, *Veterinary Medicine*, pp. 188, 343–44, 516; Claude E. Dolman and Richard J. Wolfe, *Suppressing the Diseases of Animals and Man: Theobald Smith, Microbiologist* (Boston: Boston Medical Library in the Countway Library of Medicine, 2003), pp. 103–7.

53. Theobald Smith and F. L. Kilborne, "Investigations into the Nature, Causation, and Prevention of Texas or Southern Cattle Fever," *BAI Bulletin*, no. 1 (Washington, DC: U.S. Government Printing Office, 1893). Preliminary reports possibly linking the disease to protozoa had appeared two years earlier in U.S. BAI, *Reports for 1889 and 1890*, pp. 80–81, 93–98.

54. Dolman speculated that "Salmon's vengeful act possibly cost Smith a Nobel Prize." See Claude E. Dolman, "Theobald Smith, 1859–1934: A Fiftieth Anniversary Tribute," *ASM News* [American Society Microbiology] 50, no. 12 (1984), p. 578; Schwabe, *Veterinary Medicine*, pp. 262–64. Curtice, in turn, felt Smith did not fully appreciate his contributions. Such conflicts highlight the difficulties in assigning individual credit in a collaborative research environment. Jeanne N. Logue, *Beyond the Germ Theory: The Story*

of Dr. Cooper Curtice (College Station: Texas A&M Univ. Press, 1995), pp. 25–28, 30–36. Myron Schultz also emphasized the collaborative nature of the research. Myron Schultz, "Theobald Smith," *Emerging Infectious Diseases* 14, no. 12 (2008): 1940–42.

55. Schwabe, *Veterinary Medicine*, pp. 343–45; Strom, "Texas Fever," pp. 55–56; Houck, *Bureau of Animal Industry*, pp. 318–22. Smith likely would have been aware of C. L. A. Laveran's discovery in 1880 that malaria was caused by a protozoon in the victim's blood and of work investigating the possible link to mosquitos. Andrew Spielman and Michael D'Antonio, *Mosquito: A Natural History of Our Most Persistent and Deadly Foe* (New York: Hyperion, 2001), pp. 85–87.

56. Victoria A. Harden, *Inventing the NIH: Federal Biomedical Research Policy, 1887–1937* (Baltimore: Johns Hopkins Univ. Press, 1986), pp. 1–26; David M. Morens et al., *The Indispensable Forgotten Man: Joseph James Kinyoun and the Founding of the National Institutes of Health* (Washington, DC: National Institute of Allergy and Infection Diseases, 2012), pp. 12–22; Duffy, *Sanitarians*, pp. 239–41, quotations from pp. 9–10, 14; Dupree, *Science in the Federal Government*, pp. 267–68.

57. Houck, *Bureau of Animal Industry*, p. 55.

58. Charles E. Rosenberg, *No Other Gods: On Science and American Social Thought*, expanded ed. (Baltimore: Johns Hopkins Univ. Press, 1997), pp. 135–99.

59. Neal Black, *Animal Health: A Century of Progress* (Richmond, VA: U.S. Animal Health Association, 1996), pp. 1–2, 27–29; Illinois State Board of Live Stock Commissioners, *Annual Report for the Fiscal Year Ending Oct. 31, 1897* (Springfield, IL: Phillips Bros., State Printers, 1897), pp. 200–21.

60. U.S. BAI, *Reports for 1891 and 1892*, p. 226.

61. Conversations and correspondence from 23 January to 2 February 2013 with several tick and tick-borne disease scientists including Robert Lane, Patricia Conrad, Nicholas Jonsson, and John E. George. USDA, *Yearbook of Agriculture, 1956*, pp. 268–73; Dee Whittier, Nancy Currin, and John F. Currin, "Anaplasmosis in Beef Cattle," Virginia Cooperative Extension Publication 400-465 (Blacksburg: College of Agriculture and Life Sciences, Virginia Polytechnic Institute and State University, 2009), http://pubs.ext .vt.edu/400/400-465/400-465_pdf.pdf.

62. Tick-borne blood diseases are a world-wide problem, because some species of the family *Ixodidae* (hard ticks, which comprise about 80 percent of all tick species) can carry diseases similar to Texas fever. See Heinz Mehlhorn, *Encyclopedia of Parasitology*, 3rd ed., vol. 1 (New York: Springer, 2008), p. 1379.

63. USDA, *Yearbook of Agriculture, 1956*, pp. 268–73; U.S. BAI, *Reports for 1891 and 1892*, pp. 58–63; 96–98; 281–85; *Diseases of Cattle, 1916*, pp. 473–505; Houck, *Bureau of Animal Industry*, pp. 318–21; Dolman and Wolfe, *Suppressing the Diseases*.

CHAPTER 6   *Contagions and Crises*

1. Department of Environment, Food and Rural Affairs (DEFRA), Great Britain, "Origin of the UK Foot and Mouth Disease Epidemic in 2001," June 2002, http://archive.defra.gov.uk/foodfarm/farmanimal/diseases/atoz/fmd /documents/fmdorigins1.pdf; DEFRA, "Animal Health and Welfare: FMD Data Archive," http://footandmouth.csl.gov.uk/; Abigail Woods, "'Flames and Fear on the Farms': Controlling Foot and Mouth Disease in Britain, 1892–2001," *Historical Research* 77, no. 198 (2004): 520–42. There were 2,030 confirmed cases of FMD, implying that 1,980 animals were culled for every confirmed case. Abigail Woods, "Why Slaughter? The Cultural Dimensions of Britain's Foot and Mouth Disease Control Policy," *Journal of Agricultural and Environmental Ethics* 17, no. 4–5 (2004), p. 342.

2. J. M. Scudamore and D. M. Harris, "Control of Foot and Mouth Disease: Lessons from the Experience of the Outbreak in the United Kingdom in 2001," *Revue Scientifique et Technique* (OIE) 21, no. 3 (2002), p. 700.

3. Abigail Woods, *A Manufactured Plague: The History of Foot-and-Mouth Disease in Britain* (London: Earthscan, 2004).

4. Philippe Mesmer, "South Korea Hit by Fast-Spreading Outbreak of Foot-and-Mouth Disease," *Guardian Weekly,* 18 Jan. 2011, www.theguardian.com /world/2011/jan/18/south-korea-foot-and-mouth; Alistair Driver, "FMD Wipes Out One-Third of South Korea's Pigs," *Farmers Guardian,* 11 Mar. 2011; APHIS, "Notes on Foot and Mouth Disease (FMD) in South Korea," www.aphis.usda.gov/animal_health/acah/downloads/documents/korea _fmd_update_sacah.pdf.

5. Murphy, *Foundations of Virology.*

6. R. P. Kitching, A. M. Hutber, and M. V. Thrusfield, "A Review of Foot-and-Mouth Disease with Special Consideration for the Clinical and Epidemiological Factors Relevant to Predictive Modelling of the Disease," *Veterinary Journal* 169, no. 2 (2005): 197–209; John R. Mohler and Milton J. Rosenau, "The Origin of the Recent Outbreak of Foot-and-Mouth Disease in the United States," *BAI Circular,* no. 147 (Washington, DC: U.S. Government Printing Office, 1909), pp. 7–15.

7. T. E. Carpenter and A. Thieme, "A Simulation Approach to Measuring the Economic Effects of Foot-and-Mouth Disease in Beef and Dairy Cattle," in *Proceedings of the Second International Symposium of Veterinary Epidemiology and Economics,* ed. W. A. Geering, R. T. Roe, and L. A. Chapman (Canberra: Australian Government Publishing Service, 1980), p. 512; USDA, *Yearbook of Agriculture, 1942,* pp. 263–75.

8. There may have been an even earlier occurrence. A letter dated July 1825 in the *American Farmer* noted that a contagious hoof disease plagued cattle. *American Farmer,* 5 Aug. 1825, p. 157.

9. *Chicago Tribune,* 24 Feb. 1871, p. 2; *Pittsfield Sun,* 27 Apr. 1871, p. 3; *National Live-Stock Journal,* Jan. 1871, pp. 147, 149; Feb. 1871, pp. 182–83; Mar. 1871, p. 215; May 1871, pp. 297–96; Houck, *Bureau of Animal Industry,* pp. 31–32; U.S. BAI, *Diseases of Cattle, 1916,* p. 382.

10. Houck, *Bureau of Animal Industry,* pp. 125–28, 280–81; U.S. BAI, *Diseases of Cattle, 1916,* pp. 383–85; *New York Times,* 23 Jan. 1881, p. 5; 22 Feb. 1884, p. 1; *Chicago Tribune,* 20 Feb. 1884, p. 5.

11. Mohler and Rosenau, "Origin of the Recent Outbreak," pp. 10–12. Some sources attribute the outbreak to infected hay, straw, ropes, halters, and the like imported into Massachusetts. U.S. BAI, *Report for 1902,* p. 393.

12. The inoculation tests involved injecting calves and perhaps other animals known to be free of the disease with contaminated matter to see if they developed FMD symptoms. John R. Mohler, "Foot-and-Mouth Disease, with Special Reference to the Outbreaks in California, 1924, and Texas, 1924 and 1925," USDA, *Department Circular,* no. 400 (Washington, DC: U.S. Government Printing Office, 1926), pp. 2–3.

13. U.S. BAI, *Report for 1902,* pp. 392–93, 406–410; Houck, *Bureau of Animal Industry,* pp. 282–83; Willard Lee Hoing, "James Wilson as Secretary of Agriculture, 1897–1913," Ph.D. diss. (Univ. of Wisconsin, 1964), pp. 42–43.

14. U.S. House of Representatives, Committee on Agriculture, *Contagious and Infectious Disease of Live Stock,* 11 Dec. 1902, Report No. 2819, 57th Cong., 2nd Sess. (Washington, DC: U.S. Government Printing Office, 1902), pp. 1–2; *Quarantine Districts for Live Stock,* 3 Feb. 1905, Report No. 4200, 58th Cong., 3rd Sess. (Washington, DC: U.S. Government Printing Office, 1905), pp. 1–5.

15. 32 Stat. 791, 21 U.S.C. §§ 111, 120–122.

16. U.S. BAI, *Report for 1904,* p. 564; Farrington, "Quarantine Laws," p. 487; Fred W. Powell, *Bureau of Animal Industry: Its History, Organization, and Activities* (Baltimore: Johns Hopkins Univ. Press, 1927), p. 16.

17. U.S. House of Representatives, *Quarantine Districts,* pp. 1–5.

18. Italics added, 32 Stat. 791, 21 U.S.C. §§ 111, 120–122.

19. U.S. House of Representatives, *Message from the President of the United States,* 1 Mar. 1905, Doc. No. 375, 58th Cong., 3rd Sess. (Washington, DC: U.S. Government Printing Office, 1905), pp. 1–2; *Washington Post,* 2 May 1905, p. 4; U.S. BAI, *Report for 1905,* pp. 348–49; U.S. Senate, Committee on Agriculture, *Quarantine Districts for Live Stock,* 25 Feb. 1905, Report No. 4352, 58th Cong., 3rd Sess. (Washington, DC: U.S. Government Printing Office, 1905), p. 4.

20. Pearson was a leading veterinarian of the era. U.S. BAI, *Report for 1908,* pp. 379–80. Pennsylvania Department of Agriculture, *Annual Report for 1909* (Harrisburg, PA: C. E. Aughinbaugh, 1910), pp. 181–247; Mohler and Rosenau, "Origin of the Recent Outbreak," p. 10; *Breeder's Gazette,* 18 Nov. 1908, p. 970.

21. Pennsylvania Department of Agriculture, *Annual Report for 1909*, pp. 181–89.

22. *Breeder's Gazette*, 25 Nov. 1908, pp. 1024, 1026; 30 Dec. 1908, p. 1350; U.S. BAI, *Report for 1908*, pp. 379–92.

23. U.S. BAI, *Report for 1908*, pp. 379–92. The testing requirements for human vaccines applied only to products imported or intended for interstate traffic.

24. John R. Mohler, "Foot-and-Mouth Disease with Special Reference to the Outbreak of 1914," USDA, *Department Circular*, no. 325 (Washington, DC: U.S. Government Printing Office, 1924), pp. 1–5. Although standard practice called for inoculation tests to identify FMD, this was not done until early October. The BAI's excuse was that Schaffter failed to diagnose FMD because the cases were unusually mild and the cattle did not exhibit the characteristic vesicles. Houck, *Bureau of Animal Industry*, pp. 286–87.

25. Mohler, "Outbreak of 1914," pp. 1–5; U.S. Live Stock Sanitary Association, *Report of Annual Meeting for 1914*, pp. 56–57.

26. Mohler, "Outbreak of 1914," pp. 4–5; *Drovers Journal*, 31 Oct. 1914, p. 1; 2 Nov. 1914, p. 1; 3 Nov. 1914, p. 3; 11 Nov. 1914, p. 1; 16 Nov. 1914, p. 1.

27. Over the entire month of November, the Union Stock Yard made virtually no shipments out of cattle, calves, hogs, or sheep and from November 6 to 14 received no new stock. Union Stock Yard and Transit Company of Chicago, *Receipts and Shipments of Live Stock at Union Stock Yard, Chicago, for the Year 1914* (Chicago: Union Stock Yard and Transit, 1915), p. 50.

28. *Drovers Journal*, 31 Oct. 1914, p. 1; 2 Nov. 1914, p. 1; 4 Nov. 1914, p. 1; 5 Nov. 1914, p. 1; 7 Nov. 1914, p. 1; 9 Nov. 1914, p. 1; 10 Nov. 1914, p. 1; 11 Nov. 1914, p. 1; 16 Nov. 1914, p. 1; 27 Nov. 1914, p. 1; Illinois General Assembly, *Foot and Mouth Disease in Illinois: Its Cause, Character, Cost and Eradication* (Springfield, IL: Illinois State Journal, 1915), pp. 39, 46–50. The BAI took considerable heat from farm interests for not discovering the disease sooner. *Breeder's Gazette*, 29 Oct. 1914, p. 742; 19 Nov. 1914, pp. 877, 880; *Chicago Tribune*, 11 Nov. 1914, p. 13; 12 Nov. 1914, p. 13; U.S. Senate, Committee on Agriculture and Forestry, *Arrest and Eradication of Foot-and-Mouth Disease, Hearings of Dec. 9, 18, 1914, May 17, 18, 1915*, 63rd Cong., 3rd Sess. (Washington, DC: U.S. Government Printing Office, 1916); *Arrest and Eradication of Foot-and-Mouth Disease, Hearings of Dec. 28, 29, 1915*, 64th Cong., 1st Sess. (Washington, DC: U.S. Government Printing Office, 1916).

29. *Drovers Journal*, 23 Oct. 1914, p. 1; 26 Oct. 1914, p. 5; 3 Nov. 1914, p. 3; 9 Nov. 1914, p. 3; 13 Nov. 1914, pp. 1, 3; 14 Nov. 1914, p. 1; 21 Nov. 1914, p. 1; Illinois General Assembly, *Foot and Mouth Disease*, pp. 45–46.

30. Mohler, "Outbreak of 1914," pp. 5, 8, 27; Houck, *Bureau of Animal Industry*, pp. 166, 289. The Great Western Serum Company evidently had used material extracted from contaminated hogs at the Chicago stockyards during the early phase of the epizootic. *Breeder's Gazette*, 12 Nov. 1914, p. 837, 19 Nov. 1914, p. 880. Clearly, the impurity of medicines remained a major problem.

31. U.S. Live Stock Sanitary Association, *Report of Annual Meeting for 1914,* p. 57; Mohler, "Outbreak of 1914," pp. 16–27; Houck, *Bureau of Animal Industry,* p. 289; *Breeder's Gazette,* 19 Nov. 1914, p. 880; 3 Dec. 1914, p. 965; 10 Dec. 1914, p. 100. For samples of opposition, see *Chicago Tribune,* 13 Jan. 1915, p. 10; 14 Jan. 1915, p. 5.

32. *Chicago Tribune,* 13 Sept. 1915, p. 1; 19 Sept. 1915, p. 8; 3 Oct. 1915, p. 10; 5 Oct. 1915, p. 7; 7 Nov. 1915, p. 9; 10 Nov. 1915, p. 5, 30 Dec. 1915, p. 13; *New York Times,* 7 Nov. 1915, p. 15; 10 Nov. 1915, p. 7; U.S. Senate, *Arrest and Eradication, . . . 1915,* pp. 164–71, offers the Durand testimony.

33. Houck, *Bureau of Animal Industry,* p. 288; Mohler, "Outbreak of 1914," pp. 5–8; U.S. Senate, *Arrest and Eradication, . . . 1915,* pp. 156–58.

34. U.S. Live Stock Sanitary Association, *Report of Annual Meeting for 1914,* pp. 34–35, 52–54. U.S. House of Representatives, Agricultural Committee, *Quarantine of Cattle: Hearings on H.R. 21443, a Bill to Reimburse Owners of Cattle Exhibited at the National Dairy Show,* 63rd Cong., 3rd Sess. (Washington, DC: U.S. Government Printing Office, 1915), pp. 3–56, attests to the political influence of the owners of the show cattle.

35. U.S. House of Representatives, *Agricultural Department Appropriation Bill for 1934,* 72nd Cong., 2nd Sess. (Washington, DC: U.S. Government Printing Office, 1932), p. 143; USDA, *Proceedings of a Conference to Consider Means for Combating Foot-and-Mouth Disease, Held at Chicago, Ill. Nov. 29 and 30, 1915* (Washington, DC: U.S. Government Printing Office, 1916).

36. Mohler, "Outbreaks in California, 1924," pp. 65–66.

37. Ibid., pp. 65–70.

38. Ibid.

39. Ibid., pp. 68–78.

40. Ibid., pp. 1–9; University of California Agricultural Experiment Station, "Foot-and-Mouth Disease Notice No. 1, Feb. 25, 1924," in Box No. 29, folder 5, John Randolph Haynes Papers, No. 1241, Special Collections, Charles E. Young Library, UCLA.

41. Mohler, "Outbreaks in California, 1924," pp. 6–8.

42. Donald P. Spear, "California Besieged: the Foot-and-Mouth Epidemic of 1924," *Agricultural History* 56, no. 3 (1982): 533–37; Mohler, "Outbreaks in California, 1924," pp. 10–11, 18–22, 32, 59.

43. Spear, "California Besieged," pp. 533–37; Charles Keane, "The Epizootic of Foot and Mouth Disease in California," California Department of Agriculture, Special Publication No. 65 (Sacramento: State Printing Office, 1926); *Los Angeles Times,* 25 Feb. 1924, p. 1; 17 Mar. 1924, p. 12; 26 Mar. 1924, p. A2; 27 Mar. 1924, p. A1; 3 Apr. 1924, pp. 1, 2; 5 Apr. 1924, p. 1; 9 Apr. 1924, pp. A1, A8; 12 Apr. 1924, p. 2; 13 Apr. 1924, p. 1; 16 Apr. 1924, p. 1; 17 Apr. 1924, p. 10; 19 Apr. 1924, p. 3; 23 Apr. 1924, pp. 1, 3; 24 June 1924, p. 4.

44. Spear, "California Besieged," pp. 533–37; Mohler, "Outbreaks in California, 1924," pp. 10–11, 18–22, 32, 59; *Los Angeles Times,* 2 Apr. 1924, p. 2; 19 Apr. 1924, p. 2.

45. Mohler, "Outbreaks in California, 1924," pp. 10–12. As of July 23, the bankers had delivered only about $500,000; by this time, the state was seeking $2 million. *Los Angeles Times,* 11 Apr. 1924, p. 1; 24 July 1924, p. 5.

46. *Los Angeles Times,* 19 Jan. 1929, p. A2; *Chicago Tribune,* 10 Feb. 1929, p. B2; USDA, *Yearbook of Agriculture, 1930,* p. 76; John R. Mohler and Rudolph Snyder, "The 1929 Outbreak of Foot-and-Mouth Disease in Southern California," USDA, *Miscellaneous Publication,* no. 68 (Washington, DC: U.S. Government Printing Office, 1930), pp. 1–15; John R. Mohler, "The 1929 Outbreak of Foot-and-Mouth Disease in California," *Journal of American Veterinary Medical Association* 75 (1929), p. 309. The state and the federal governments each expended $92,274 to suppress the outbreak (*Los Angeles Times,* 6 June 1929, p. 9).

47. In April 1932, swine in several herds in Buena Park, California, came down with a vesicular disease that was soon diagnosed as FMD. The epizootic led to the quarantining of sections of Los Angeles, Orange, and San Bernardino countries. State and Federal forces conquered the outbreak in sixteen days, after the slaughter and burial of 118,817 hogs, 46 cattle, and 24 goats. See *Los Angeles Times,* 30 Apr. 1932, p. A2; 1 May 1932, p. A2; 9 May 1932, p. A2; 7 June 1932, p. A4; 14 June 1932, p. A2; 15 June 1932, p. A4; John R. Mohler and Rudolph Snyder, "The 1932 Outbreak of Foot-and-Mouth Disease in Southern California," USDA, *Miscellaneous Publication,* no. 163 (Washington, DC: U.S. Government Printing Office, 1933), pp. 1–10.

   At the time, observers noted that the contagion did not spread through the livestock populations with the speed typical of FMD, but they attributed this to the efficiency of the control efforts. A similar disease appeared among San Diego swine in 1933. In this case, investigators determined that the causal agent was a new disease, vesicular exanthema of swine. This had symptoms that mimicked FMD and vesicular stomatitis. The vesicular exanthema discovery led to a consensus that 1929 was the last outbreak of FMD in the United States. B. W. J. Mahy, "Introduction and History of the Foot-and-Mouth Disease Virus," *Current Topics in Microbiology and Immunology* 288 (2006), p. 7.

48. Manuel A. Machado Jr., *Aftosa: A Historical Survey of Foot-and-Mouth Disease and Inter-American Relations* (Albany: State Univ. of New York Press, 1969), pp. 49–59; William Dusenberry, "Foot and Mouth Disease in Mexico, 1946–1951," *Agricultural History* 29, no. 2 (1955): 82–90; Manuel A. Machado Jr., *An Industry in Crisis: Mexican-United States Cooperation in the Control of Foot-and-Mouth Disease* (Berkeley: Univ. of California Press, 1968), pp. 1–62.

49. U.S. BAI, *Special Report on Diseases of Cattle, 1908 ed.* (Washington, DC: U.S. Government Printing Office, 1908), p. 381; Houck, *Bureau of Animal Industry*, p. 283; Alejandro E. Segarra and Sean M. Rawson, "Foot and Mouth Disease: A Threat to U.S. Agriculture," CRS Report for Congress, Congressional Research Service, Library of Congress, Apr. 16, 2001, www .nationalaglawcenter.org/wp-content/uploads/assets/crs/RS20890.pdf, quote on p. 4.

50. U.S. BAI, *Diseases in Cattle, 1916*, pp. 383–84; U.S. Live Stock Sanitary Association, *Report of Annual Meeting for 1914*, p. 21.

51. Data on the stock of animals are from DEFRA, *Agriculture in the United Kingdom 2001* (London: Stationery Office, 2002), p. 46. The cattle population in 2000 was below normal because of previous cullings aimed at mad cow disease.

52. Dustin L. Pendell, John Leatherman, Ted C. Schroeder, and Gregory S. Alward, "The Economic Impacts of a Foot-and-Mouth Disease Outbreak: A Regional Analysis," *Journal of Agricultural and Applied Economics* 39 (2007), pp. 19–33; Javier M. Elboir, *Potential Impact of Foot-and-Mouth Disease in California* (Davis, CA: Agricultural Issues Center, 1999); E. Hunt McCauley et al., *A Study of the Potential Economic Impact of Foot-and-Mouth Disease in the United States* (Washington, DC: U.S. Government Printing Office, 1979), p. 102; Philip L. Paarlberg, John G. Lee, and Ann H. Seitzinger, "Measuring the Welfare Effects of an FMD Outbreak in the United States," *Journal of Agricultural and Applied Economics* 35 (2003): 53–65.

53. Elboir, *Potential Impact*, pp. 66–67.

54. A summary of physical losses in twenty-eight studies of FMD outbreaks in other counties yields a wide range of estimates reflecting the differing virulence and animal management practices. McCauley et al., *Potential Economic Impact*, pp. 26–32.

55. Ibid., p. 89.

56. U.S. House of Representatives, *Agricultural Department Appropriation Bill for 1934*, pp. 143–44.

57. U.S. Bureau of the Census, *Fifteenth Census of the United States: 1930, Agriculture*, vol. 4, *General Report, Statistics by Subjects* (Washington, DC: U.S. Government Printing Office, 1932), p. 559; N. St. G. Hyslop, "The Epizootiology and Epidemiology of Foot and Mouth Disease," *Advances in Veterinary Science and Comparative Medicine* 14 (1970), p. 262; Schwabe, *Veterinary Medicine*, p. 31.

58. In 1903, the BAI noted that if the disease was left unattended that practically all cattle would contract it. The BAI's assessments coincide with those in the text—5 percent of cattle would die, and the survivors would decline in value by 25 percent. U.S. BAI, *Report for 1903*, p. 168.

59. McCauley et al., *Potential Economic Impact*, pp. 25–26, 82; U.S. Bureau of the Census, *Fifteenth Census*, pp. 573, 587, 595. We use 1925 for this exercise

because the census reported the livestock distribution by age in a more convenient manner than for 1930.

CHAPTER 7   *The Hog Cholera Puzzle*

1. Paul De Kruif, *Hunger Fighters* (New York: Harcourt, Brace, 1928), p. 70; Marion Dorset Papers, MS 32, Special Collections, Iowa State University. www.lib.iastate.edu/spcl/manuscripts/MS032.html; Hoing, "James Wilson," pp. 43–44.
2. In Europe, the disease is usually termed "swine fever" or "classical swine fever" to differentiate it from "African swine fever," which is a different disease. In 1889, the BAI presumed that hog cholera had been imported from Europe. U.S. BAI, *Reports for 1887 and 1888,* p. 189.
3. *Prairie Farmer,* Apr. 1853, p. 163; Ohio State Board of Agriculture, *Annual Report for 1856* (Columbus, OH: Richard Nevins, 1857), pp. 370–74. The *Cincinnati Times* article is quoted in *Philadelphia North American and United States Gazette,* 22 Dec. 1856, p. 1.
4. U.S. Senate, *Disease Prevailing among Swine;* U.S. BAI, *Reports for 1887 and 1888,* pp. 187–305; USDA, *Hog Cholera: Its History, Nature, and Treatment* (Washington, DC: U.S. Government Printing Office, 1889); U.S. BAI, *Reports for 1887 and 1888,* pp. 218, 274. An alternative source dates the first outbreak to 1810 near Franklin, Tennessee; see R. P. Hanson, "Origin of Hog Cholera," *Journal of American Veterinary Medical Association* 131 (1957): 211–18.
5. Stalheim, *Winning of Animal Health,* p. 5. We saw no mention of such outbreaks in the Indiana State Board of Agriculture *Annual Report* (various years) or the Ohio State Board of Agriculture *Annual Report* (various years).
6. *Zanesville Ohio Republican,* 1833 and early 1834; *Zanesville Gazette,* 1833; *Chillicothe (OH) Scioto Gazette,* summer of 1833. There were scattered reports of disease among Ohio swine in the early 1830s, but the descriptions do not match hog cholera; see *Genesee Farmer,* 19 Apr. 1834, p. 122; 3 May 1834, p. 141.
7. Marion Dorset and O. B. Hess, "Hog Cholera: Prevention and Treatment," USDA, *Farmers' Bulletin,* no. 834 (Washington, DC: U.S. Government Printing Office, 1917), p. 2; U.S. BAI, *Reports for 1887 and 1888,* p. 190.
8. *Prairie Farmer,* 22 July 1858, p. 9; *New York Times,* 12 Sept. 1886, p. 3.
9. G. T. Brown, "Report on Swine-Fever in Great Britain," in *Annual Report of the Agricultural Department of the Privy Council Office of the Contagious Diseases, Inspection and Transit of Animals; for the Year 1885. . . .* (London: Eyre and Spottiswoode, 1886), pp. 4–5, 9–13; William Budd, "Observations on Typhoid (Intestinal) Fever in the Pig," *British Medical Journal,* 29 July 1865, pp. 81–87; "Dr. William Budd," *British Medical Journal* 1, no. 994 (1880): 102–3; Robert Moorhead, "William Budd and Typhoid Fever," *Journal of the Royal Society of Medicine* 95, no. 11 (2002): 561–64; Otto M. Radostits, Clive C. Gay,

Douglas C. Blood, and Kenneth W. Hinchcliff, *Veterinary Medicine,* 9th ed. (London: Saunders, 2005), pp. 1019–20.

10. O.H.V. Stalheim, "The Hog Cholera Battle and Veterinary Professionalism," *Agricultural History* 62, no. 2 (1988), p. 116; *New York Times,* 22 Sept. 1885, p. 2; 21 Sept. 1889, p. 2; 3 Nov. 1895, p. 23; 11 Aug. 1912, p. 1.

11. For coverage of this controversy, see *London Times,* 19 Feb. 1881, p. 5; *New York Times,* 2 Mar. 1881, p. 5; 3 Mar. 1881, p. 5; 6 Mar. 1881, p. 2; 18 Mar. 1881, p. 2; 28 Dec. 1883, p. 3; Kastner, "Sanitary Related," pp. 68–70; U.S. House of Representatives, *Message of President on Restrictions Imposed by French Government on Pork Exported from United States,* 26 May 1882, Ex. Doc. No. 209, 47th Cong., 1st Sess. (Washington, DC: U.S. Government Printing Office, 1882), pp. 20, 102–3, 112, 127, 129, 135–44, 161, and 207.

12. Stan Deming, "Nineteenth Century Hog Cholera: Some of Its History and Social Effects," master's thesis, Northern Illinois Univ., 1965, pp. 62–65.

13. Ohio State Board of Agriculture, *Annual Report for 1857* (Columbus: Richard Nevins, 1858), p. 371; USDA, *Hog Cholera, 1889,* pp. 12–32; George Sutton, "Observations on the Supposed Relations between Epizootics and Epidemics. . . . ," *North American Medico-Chirurgical Review* (1858): 495–99.

14. Joseph H. Galloway, *Farm Animal Health and Disease Control* (Philadelphia: Lea & Febiger, 1972), pp. 128–29; USDA, *Hog Cholera, 1889,* p. 52; Dorsey W. Bruner and James H. Gillespie, *Hagan's Infectious Diseases of Domestic Animals,* 6th ed. (Ithaca, NY: Comstock, 1973), pp. 1266–68; Marie-Frédérique Le Potier, Alain, Mesplède, Philippe Vannier, "Classical Swine Fever and Other Pestiviruses," in *Diseases of Swine,* 9th ed., ed. Barbara E. Straw et al. (Ames, IA: Blackwell, 2006), pp. 309–22.

15. USDA, *Yearbook of Agriculture, 1942,* pp. 686, 695, 726. Among the diseases now recognized to be caused by secondary infections are *necrotic enteritis,* an inflammation of the intestines that greatly hastens mortality in combination with the hog cholera infection, *hemorrhagic septicemia,* a form of pneumonia that became identified as swine plague, and swine influenza.

16. C.G. Cole, R.R. Henley, C.N. Dale, L.O. Mott, J.P. Torrey, and M.R. Zinober, *History of Hog Cholera Research in the U.S. Department of Agriculture, 1884–1960, Agricultural Information Bulletin,* no. 241 (Washington, DC: USDA, 1962), pp. 3–5; Ho Yin Tang, "The Enigma of Hog Cholera: Controversies, Cause, and Control, 1833–1917," Ph.D. diss., Univ. of Minnesota, 1986, pp. 16–38.

17. Telegrams exchanged between Morton and Frelinghuysen, 29 Dec. 1883, in U.S. Senate, Committee on Foreign Relations, *Swine Products of United States: Production, Healthfulness, and Restrictions on Importation by Germany and France, with Minority Report,* 19 Mar. 1884, Senate Report No. 345, 48th Cong., 1st Sess. (Washington, DC: U.S. Government Printing Office, 1884), pp. 88–89.

18. Detmers asserted that European protectionists had willfully distorted his findings. *Prairie Farmer*, 5 Jan. 1884, p. 42.

19. E. W. Blatchford, "Hog Raising and the Pork Packing Industry in America," Steward survey, p. 6, Crerar Ms 207, Special Collections Research Center, Univ. of Chicago Library.

20. National Swine Breeders' Association, *Proceedings, 1885* (Springfield, IL: Springfield Printing, 1886), pp. 10–12.

21. USDA, *Yearbook of Agriculture, 1922*, pp. 215–16; *Yearbook of Agriculture, 1942*, p. 674; Sutton, "Observations," p. 492.

22. *New York Times*, 18 Dec. 1884; p. 3; USDA, *Hog Cholera, 1889*, p. 13.

23. U.S. BAI, *Report for 1884*, pp. 221–32; *Report for 1885*, pp. 184–246; USDA, *Hog Cholera, 1889*, p. 109; Cole et al., *History of Hog Cholera Research*, p. 6; Dolman and Wolfe, *Suppressing the Diseases*, pp. 74–98; Tang, "Enigma of Hog Cholera," pp. 64–65; Stalheim, *Winning of Animal Health*, pp. 65–66.

24. Susan L. Plotkin and Stanley A. Plotkin, "A Short History of Vaccination," in *Vaccines*, 4th ed., ed. Stanley A. Plotkin and Walter A. Orenstein (Philadelphia: Elsevier, 2004), p. 3; Cole et al., *History of Hog Cholera Research*, p. 6; Stalheim, *Winning of Animal Health*, p. 66. In light of the later criticism of Salmon for usurping credit for this research (see Dolman and Wolfe, *Suppressing the Diseases*, pp. 53–58, 77–80, 88–90, 94, 98), it is noteworthy that in his letter of transmittal for the (USDA, *Hog Cholera, 1889*, pp. 7–8) Salmon stated that "the greater part of the detailed study of the disease, the planning of experiments, and the bacteriological investigations have been carried out by Dr. Theobald Smith, while the conduction of the experiments, and . . . the general management of the experiment station have been under the direction of Dr. F. L. Kilborne." Important terminology changed over time. As one example, in the late nineteenth century, the term "virus" was used to refer to a toxin or poison. The terms "serum" and "vaccine" appear to have been used interchangeably. By the 1930s, the term vaccine was increasingly reserved for medicines in which the dangerous virus or bacteria had been rendered inactive and incapable of spreading the disease in question, but when administered was still capable of triggering an animal's immune system to create antibodies to fight off the invader.

25. Stalheim, *Winning of Animal Health*, p. 66; U.S. BAI, *Report for 1885*, pp. 184–246, esp. 221; *Report for 1886*, pp. 20–75; USDA, *Hog Cholera, 1889*, 107–8. Salmon and Smith's research built on ideas emerging from laboratories across Europe. Schwabe, *Veterinary Medicine*, pp. 186–89.

26. U.S. BAI, *Report for 1886*, pp. 6–7, 20–75.

27. Dolman and Wolfe, *Suppressing the Diseases*, pp. 78–81.

28. Stalheim, *Winning of Animal Health*, pp. 67–68; Cole et al., *History of Hog Cholera Research*, p. 7.

29. Richard Compton, *A Legacy for Tomorrow, 1885–1985: The 100 Year History of the College of Veterinary Medicine* (Columbus: Ohio State Univ. Press, 1984),

pp. 7–8; Dolman and Wolfe, *Suppressing the Diseases,* p. 74; USDA, "Investigation of Diseases of Swine and Infectious and Contagious Diseases Incident
to Other Classes of Domesticated Animals," *Special Report,* no. 12 (Washington, DC: U.S. Government Printing Office, 1879), pp. 19–52; USDA,
"Contagious Diseases of Domesticated Animals: Continuation of Investigation," *Special Report,* no. 34 (Washington, DC: U.S. Government Printing
Office, 1881), pp. 153–96.

30. Salmon also entered into an intense scientific conflict with Detmers, who
had been researching swine diseases since at least the mid-1870s. He had
identified a candidate bacterial cause in 1879, well before Salmon's work
with Smith. Paul Fischer, "H. J. Detmers," *Veterinary Alumni Quarterly* 6,
no. 4 (1919): 217–19.

31. Frank S. Billings, *Swine Plague* (Lincoln, NE: Journal Company, 1888);
Richard A. Overfield, "Hog Cholera, Texas Fever, and Frank S. Billings: An
Episode in Nebraska Veterinary Science," *Nebraska History* 57, no. 1 (1976),
pp. 102–3. Salmon was clearly sensitive to Billings's attacks and filled two
large scrapbooks with articles on Billings. See "Nebraska Hog Cholera
Controversy Scrapbook, Vol. 1 and 2," Daniel E. Salmon Papers, Collection
No. 6585, Division of Rare and Manuscript Collections, Cornell University
Library.

32. Part of the confusion was due to interaction effects between hog cholera
and other diseases. See Richard F. Ross, "*Pasteurella multocida* and Its Role
in Porcine Pneumonia," *Animal Health Research Reviews* 7, no. 1–2 (2006),
pp. 13–29.

33. Stalheim, *Winning of Animal Health,* p. 67; Dolman and Wolfe, *Suppressing the
Diseases,* pp. 86–88; Frank S. Billings, *Inoculation: Prevention of Swine Plague*
(Lincoln, NE: Journal Company, 1892). See also *Farmers' Review,* 14 Aug.
1889, p. 9; 11 Sept. 1889, p. 4.

34. William H. Welch, "Preliminary Report of Investigations Concerning the
Causation of Hog Cholera," *Johns Hopkins Hospital Bulletin* 1, no. 1 (1889):
9–10.

35. Daniel E. Salmon, "Results of Experiments with Inoculation for the
Prevention of Hog Cholera," USDA, *Farmers' Bulletin,* no. 8 (Washington,
DC: U.S. Government Printing Office, 1892), p. 5.

36. Cole et al., *History of Hog Cholera Research,* pp. 9–10.

37. Ibid., pp. 10–11.

38. Stalheim, *Winning of Animal Health,* p. 69–71; Stalheim, "Hog Cholera
Battle," pp. 117–18; Cole et al., *History of Hog Cholera Research,* pp. 10–11,
quotation from p. 10. In 1892, Dmitry Ivanovsky working in Russia
discovered that a "filterable" virus (and later just a virus) caused tobacco
mosaic disease, and in 1898 the Germans Paul Frosch and Friedrich
Loeffler discovered that a virus caused foot-and-mouth disease. Frosch and
Loeffler were the first to grasp the significance that viruses were funda-

mentally different from bacteria. By the end of 1903, only twelve filterable virus agents of disease had been identified. Murphy, "Foundations of Medical"; M.H.V. van Regenmortel, "Nature of Viruses," in *Desk Encyclopedia of General Virology*, ed. Brian W.J. Mahy and Marc H.V. van Regenmortel (Oxford: Elsevier, 2010), pp. 19–23; Schwabe, *Veterinary Medicine*, 1984, p. 188; H.P. Schmiedebach, "The Prussian State and Microbiological Research—Friedrich Loeffler and His Approach to the 'Invisible' Virus," *Archives of Virology, Supplementum* 15 (1999): 9–23.

39. USDA, *Yearbook of Agriculture, 1942*, pp. 680–84; Stalheim, "Hog Cholera Battle," p. 118.

40. Daniel Gilfoyle, "Veterinary Research and the African Rinderpest Epizootic: The Cape Colony, 1896–1898," *Journal of Southern African History* 29, no. 1 (2003): 133–54; Roy Mack, "The Great African Cattle Plague Epidemic of the 1890s," *Tropical Animal Health and Production* 2 (1970), p. 216.

41. M. Lombard, P.P. Pastoret, and A.M. Moulin, "A Brief History of Vaccines and Vaccination," *Revue Scientifique et Technique* (OIE) 26, no. 1 (2007): 29–48.

42. Marion Dorset, C.N. McBryde, and W.B. Niles, "Further Experiments Concerning the Production of Immunity from Hog Cholera," *BAI Bulletin*, no. 102 (Washington, DC: U.S. Government Printing Office, 1908), pp. 91–93, 95–96; Stalheim, *Winning of Animal Health*, pp. 70–71; Cole et al., *History of Hog Cholera Research*, pp. 13–15, quotation from p. 13.

43. U.S. BAI, *Report for 1908*, pp. 177–217; Cole et al., *History of Hog Cholera Research*, pp. 15–19, 24–25.

44. Deming, "Nineteenth Century Hog Cholera," pp. 21–28. Serums and sera are both accepted plural forms of serum and are used here interchangeably (typically in line with usage in the specific context).

45. Parke, Davis & Co. to James McMillan, 3 Jan. 1899, Entry 1, Box 1, U.S. BAI Records.

46. James McMillan to James Wilson, 6 Jan. 1899; Wilson to McMillan, 11 Jan. 1899, Entry 1, Box 1, U.S. BAI Records.

47. The original blackleg vaccine was developed in France and improved upon in Germany. This product proved costly and risky. Victor Norgaard of the BAI further perfected a vaccine, and the BAI began free distributions in 1897. John R. Mohler, "Blackleg: Its Nature, Cause, and Prevention," USDA, *Farmers' Bulletin*, no. 1355 (Washington, DC: U.S. Government Printing Office, 1923), pp. 1–2, 8–10; U.S. BAI, *Report for 1898*, pp. 27–81; Stalheim, *Winning of Animal Health*, pp. 22–34; Houck, *Bureau of Animal Industry*, pp. 74, 342–48.

48. Alfred Lucking to James Wilson, 3 May 1904; Wilson to Lucking, 1 June 1904, Entry 1, Box 1, U.S. BAI Records.

49. Alfred Lucking to James Wilson, 25 May 1904, Entry 1, Box 1, U.S. BAI Records.

50. "Free Medicine," *The Conservative* 2, no. 43 (3 May 1900), p. 5.
51. James Wilson to Alfred Lucking, 1 June 1904, Entry 1, Box 1, U.S. BAI Records.
52. Hoing, "James Wilson," p. 44. Congress received many petitions from stock growers in favor of free distribution of vaccines and from wholesale druggists opposed to the practice. See Box No. 147, file SEN 56A J1.2 Blackleg Vaccine, U.S. Senate Records, RG 46, Center for Legislative Archives, National Archives, Washington, DC.
53. Mohler, "Blackleg," p. 10.
54. U.S. BAI, *Report for 1909,* pp. 53–54. Melvin reckoned that twenty states were producing serum.
55. Cole et al., *History of Hog Cholera Research,* pp. 16–19; Stalheim, *Winning of Animal Health,* pp. 72–73.
56. Jim Monke, "The Virus-Serum-Toxin Act: A Brief Historical Analysis," CRS Report for Congress, RS22014 (3 Jan. 2005).
57. U.S. Senate, *Remedies for Hog Cholera,* Senate Doc. No. 489, 63rd Cong., 2nd Sess. (Washington, DC: U.S. Government Printing Office, 1914), p. 12; U.S. House of Representatives, *Report to Accompany S. 3439,* 11 Feb. 1914, Report No. 246, 63rd Cong., 2nd Sess. (Washington, DC: U.S. Government Printing Office, 1914), p. 2. The $75,000 appropriation was passed in March 1913 for the fiscal year ending 30 June 1914; U.S. House of Representatives, *Conference Report on Agriculture Department Appropriation Bill, 1914,* 1 Mar. 1913, House Report No. 1628, 62nd Cong., 3rd Sess. (Washington, DC: U.S. Government Printing Office, 1913).
58. U.S. House of Representatives, Committee of Agriculture, *Hearings of Agriculture Appropriations Bill,* 8–12, 14–15, 18–21, 24–28, 31 Jan.; 5, 7–12, 14, 16, 29 Feb. 1916, 64th Cong., 1st Sess. (Washington, DC: U.S. Government Printing Office, 1916), p. 262; Houck, *Bureau of Animal Industry,* pp. 185, 304–17.
59. A.D. Melvin and M. Dorset, "The Control of Hog Cholera," *USDA Bulletin,* no. 584 (Washington, DC: U.S. Government Printing Office, 1917), pp. 5–9.
60. G.H. Wise, *Hog Cholera and Its Eradication: A Review of U.S. Experience,* APHIS 91–55 (Washington, DC: U.S. Government Printing Office, 1981), pp. 5, 31–32.
61. Houck, *Bureau of Animal Industry,* pp. 304–17.

CHAPTER 8   *Trichinosis, Trade, and Food Safety*

1. *Chicago Tribune,* 23 June 1891, p. 9; U.S. BAI, *Report for 1891,* p. 33. The BAI initially hired both men and women as assistant microscopists. Officials soon judged the females "more careful, apter to learn," and quicker than the males, and restricted employment to women. Men still filled the less

numerous but higher-paid positions of chief microscopists. *Chicago Tribune,* 25 Sept. 1891, p. 7; *Washington Post,* 25 Sept. 1891, p. 1; 22 Jan. 1898, p. 7; *Atlanta Constitution,* 17 June 1900, p. A5.

2. Between 1997 and 2001, there averaged only twelve reported cases a year with no deaths. Lynne S. Garcia, *Diagnostic Medical Parasitology,* 5th ed. (Washington, DC: ASM Press, 2007), pp. 283–89; Berton Roueché, "A Pig from Jersey," *New Yorker,* 18 Nov. 1950, pp. 157–66.

3. Willard H. Wright, K. B. Kerr, and Leon Jacobs, "Studies on Trichinosis XV: Summary of the Findings of *Trichinella Spiralis* in a Random Sampling and Other Samplings of the Population of the United States," *Public Health Reports* 58, no. 35 (1943), p. 1311.

4. Olmstead, "First Line of Defense," p. 342.

5. Suellen Hoy and Walter Nugent, "Public Health or Protectionism? The German-American Pork War, 1880–1891," *Bulletin of the History of Medicine* 63 no. 2 (1989): 198–224; Charles Wardell Stiles, "Trichinosis in Germany," *BAI Bulletin,* no. 30 (Washington, DC: U.S. Government Printing Office, 1901), pp. 9–34; William C. Campbell, "Historical Introduction," in *Trichinella and Trichinosis,* ed. William C. Campbell (New York: Plenum Press, 1983), pp. 18–20; James H. Cassedy, "Applied Microscopy and American Pork Diplomacy: Charles Wardell Stiles in Germany 1898–1899," *Isis* 62, no. 1 (1971), p. 6; W. C. W. Glazier, *Report on Trichinae and Trichinosis,* Ex. Doc. No. 9, 40th Cong., 3rd Sess. (Washington, DC: U.S. Government Printing Office, 1881), pp. 199–201; Glazier offers a contemporary discussion of the efficacy of various measures to kill trichinae (pp. 144–45).

6. Patrick Zylberman, "Making Food Safety an Issue: Internationalized Food Politics and French Public Health from the 1870s to the Present," *Medical History* 48, no. 1 (2004), pp. 6–7; Alessandro Stanzianni, "Food Safety and Expertise: The Trichinosis Epidemic in France, 1878–1891," *Food and Foodways* 10, no. 4 (2003): 215–18.

7. Janet W. Crouse, "The Decline of German-American Friendship: Beef, Pork, and Politics, 1890–1906," Ph.D. diss. (Univ. of Delaware, 1980), pp. 58–63; Uwe Spiekermann, "Dangerous Meat? German-American Quarrels over Pork and Beef, 1870–1900," *Bulletin of the GHI* [German Historical Institute] 46 (2010), pp. 98–99; Glazier, *Report on Trichinae,* pp. 183–205; U.S. House of Representatives, *Restrictions upon the Exportation of Pork from the United States by the French Government,* Ex. Doc. No. 207, 47th Cong., 1st Sess. (Washington, DC: U.S. Government Printing Office, 1882); Stanzianni, "Food Safety," pp. 209–37.

8. *London Times,* 19 Feb. 1881, p. 5; Crouse, "Decline of German-American," p. 67; John L. Gignilliat, "Politics, and Protection: the European Boycott of American Pork, 1879–1891," *Agricultural History* 35, no. 1 (1961): 3–8; Justin Kastner, "Managing Human and Animal-Health Threats: Additional Lessons from the 19th-Century Trading World," in *Food and Agricultural Security:*

An Historical, Multidisciplinary Approach, ed. Justin Kastner (Santa Barbara, CA: Praeger, 2011), pp. 108–9.

9. Animals and animal products accounted for nearly 20 percent of all U.S. merchandise exports over the fiscal years 1877 through 1879. Trade data compiled from U.S. Treasury Department, *Monthly Summary,* Feb. 1900, p. 2309; Carter et al., *Historical Statistics,* vol. 5, series Ee446; U.S. Senate, *Swine Products,* pp. 344, 360; U.S. Treasury Department, Bureau of Statistics, *Annual Report of the Chief,* various years.

10. Stiles, "Trichinosis in Germany," p. 15; Louis L. Snyder, "The American-German Pork Dispute, 1879–1881," *Journal of Modern History* 17, no. 1 (1945): 18–22; U.S. Senate, *Swine Products,* pp. 110–11, 113–16, 128–29.

11. Hoy and Nugent, "Public Health," pp. 206–8; James L. Erlenborn, "The American Meat and Livestock Industry and American Foreign Policy, 1880–1896," master's thesis (Univ. of Wisconsin, 1966), pp. 30–34.

12. Stanzianni, "Food Safety," pp. 230–31, noted that the chambers of commerce of Paris and Bordeaux favored abolishing the embargo. Opponents of the trade could point to the findings of Frank Billings that many American hogs were indeed infected (Hoy and Nugent, "Public Health," pp. 205–6).

13. Economists have long recognized that regulatory barriers ostensibly motivated by health and safety can provide protection for domestic industries. Real-world examples are easy to find. Daniel A. Sumner and Hyunok Lee, "Sanitary and Phytosanitary Trade Barriers and Empirical Trade Modeling," in *Understanding Technical Barriers to Trade,* ed. David Orden and Donna Roberts (Minneapolis: International Agricultural Trade Research Consortium, 1997), pp. 273–85; Daniel A. Sumner and Stefan Tangermann, "International Trade Policy and Negotiations," in *Handbook of Agricultural Economics,* vol. 4, ed. Bruce Gardner and Gordon Rausser (Amsterdam: North Holland/Elsevier, 2002), pp. 1999–2055.

14. One sign that sanitary motives are genuine is that the same rules were imposed on both local and imported goods, but uniform rules are not conclusive evidence because they could disproportionally raise the cost of the rival imported goods. A significant fraction of sanitary trade restrictions are, in the eyes of outside observers, based on fraudulent or overblown claims. Limiting market access based on sanitary conditions can lead in the short run to the concealment of disease outbreaks and the use of hidden (and presumably less effective) remedies and in the long run to the outright denial of real health problems and the adoption of policies that allow these unacknowledged problems to grow worse. Alternatively, limiting market access based on sanitary conditions can spur nations to recognize and invest resources to address their health problems.

15. *Lancet,* 30 Dec. 1882, p. 1141; Hoy and Nugent, "Public Health," pp. 200–1; and Stiles, "Trichinosis in Germany," pp. 19–21, 29–33.

16. Stiles estimated that all of Germany had upwards to 100,000 microscopists. Stiles, "Trichinosis in Germany," pp. 9–34; Hoy and Nugent, "Public Health," pp. 198–224; Campbell, "Historical Introduction," pp. 18–24; Cassedy, "Applied Microscopy," p. 6.

17. Bert also created problems for Americans when his research refuted the widely held belief that the salting methods in use killed all trichinae. U.S. Senate, *Swine Products,* p. 86; Stanzianni, "Food Safety," pp. 222–23.

18. U.S. BAI, *Report for 1884,* pp. 475–78.

19. *Washington Post,* 4 Dec. 1883, p. 2; U.S. Senate, *Swine Products,* pp. 195, 206, 307–10.

20. U.S. House of Representatives, *Restrictions upon the Exportation,* pp. 51–52; Hoy and Nugent, "Public Health," pp. 211–12.

21. Erlenborn, "American Meat," pp. 49–50; U.S. House of Representatives, *Report from the Secretary of State Relative to the Importation of the Swine Products of the United States,* 1 Mar. 1884, Ex. Doc. No. 106, 48th Cong., 1st Sess. (Washington, DC: U.S. Government Printing Office, 1884), p. 136; U.S. House of Representatives, Committee of Commerce, "Importation of American Hog Products into Germany and France," 25 Mar. 1884, 48th Cong., 1st Sess., unpublished hearings, pp. 1–20; Bessie Louise Pierce, *History of Chicago,* vol. 3, *The Rise of the Modern City, 1871–1893* (Chicago: Alfred. A. Knopf, 1957), pp. 182–84.

22. *Congressional Record,* 17 June 1886, p. 5818; 21 Mar. 1888, p. 2227.

23. U.S. House of Representatives, *Inspection of Meats for Exportation, Etc.,* 28 Apr. 1890, House Report No. 1792, 51st Cong., 1st Sess. (Washington, DC: U.S. Government Printing Office, 1890).

24. *New York Times,* 6 Dec. 1891, p. 5; Gignilliat, "Politics," p. 11; Stanzianni, "Food Safety," p. 230; Bingham Duncan, "Protectionism and Pork: Whitelaw Reid as Diplomat: 1889–1891," *Agricultural History* 33, no. 4 (1959): 190–95; U.S. BAI *Reports for 1891 and 1892,* pp. 39–40; Snyder, "American-German Pork Dispute," pp. 27–28.

25. Stiles, "Trichinosis in Germany," pp. 16–21; Crouse, "Decline of German-American," pp. 104–16, 283.

26. Crouse, "Decline of German-American," pp. 205–55.

27. Stiles, "Trichinosis in Germany," pp. 19–20, 37–39; Crouse, "Decline of German-American," pp. 158–60; Sylvester E. Gould, *Trichinosis* (Springfield, IL: Charles C. Thomas, 1945), p. 285. Stiles would become a scientific luminary. Among his many credits, he identified a new species of hookworm *(Nector americanus)* that accounted for about 95 percent of the human hookworm cases in the United States. He was instrumental in the creation of the Rockefeller Sanitary Commission for the Eradication of Hookworm Disease. Willard H. Wright, "Charles Wardell Stiles, 1867–1941," *Journal of Parasitology* 27, no. 3 (1941): 195–201.

28. U.S. Senate, *Estimate of Appropriation for Microscopic Meat Inspection*, 16 Apr.
    1912, Doc. No. 569, 62nd Cong., 2nd Sess. (Washington, DC: U.S. Govern-
    ment Printing Office, 1912), pp. 1–2.
29. Hoy and Nugent, "Public Health," pp. 200–1; and Stiles, "Trichinosis in
    Germany," pp. 19–21, 29–33.
30. Spiekermann, "Dangerous Meat?" pp. 99–110.
31. William J. Zimmermann, J. H. Steele, and I. G. Kagan, "Trichiniasis in the
    U.S. Population, 1966–1970," *Health Services Reports* 88, no. 7 (1973): 611–13;
    Willard H. Wright, K. B. Kerr, and Leon Jacobs, "Trichinosis XV," pp. 1302–3;
    Olmstead, "First Line of Defense," pp. 345–53; Willard H. Wright, Leon
    Jacobs, and Arthur C. Walton, "Studies on Trichinosis XVI: Epidemiological
    Considerations Based on the Examination for Trichinae of 5,313 Diaphragms
    from 189 Hospitals in 37 States and the District of Columbia," *Public Health
    Reports* 59, no. 21 (1944): 669–82. Wright followed Maurice C. Hall as chief
    of the Division of Zoology at the NIH.
32. Maurice C. Hall, "Studies on Trichinosis VII: The Past and Present Status
    of Trichinosis in the United States, and the Indicated Control Measures,"
    Public Health Reports 53, no. 33 (1938): 1473–74.
33. Roueché, "A Pig from Jersey," pp. 157–66.
34. Ibid.
35. Fred W. Tanner and Louise P. Tanner, *Food-borne Infections and Intoxications*
    (Champaign, IL: Garrard Press, 1953), pp. 8–9.
36. Scallan et al., "Major Pathogens," pp. 7–15; Scallan et al., "Unspecified
    Agents," pp. 16–22; and Andrew C. Voetsch et al., "FoodNet Estimate,"
    pp. S127–34.
37. There is no strict correlation between the intensity of infection and the
    clinical symptoms, because immunological responses vary considerably.
    If even a few larvae migrated to the brain, heart, or central nervous
    system, the outcome could be fatal. Ernest C. Faust, Paul F. Russell, and
    Rodney C. Jung, *Craig and Faust's Clinical Parasitology*, 8th ed. (Philadel-
    phia: Lea & Febiger, 1970), p. 265.
38. Wright et al., "Trichinosis XV," pp. 1302–3; Olmstead, "First Line of
    Defense," pp. 343–53; Maurice C. Hall, "Studies on Trichinosis I: The
    Incidence of Trichinosis as Indicated by Post-Mortem Examination of 300
    Diaphragms," *Public Health Reports* 52, no. 16 (1937), pp. 477–78, 487, 489;
    Schwabe, *Veterinary Medicine*, p. 549; New York State, *Meat for Millions: Report
    of the New York State Trichinosis Commission*, 2nd ed. (Albany, NY: Fort
    Orange Press, 1941), pp. 13–15.
39. Hall, "Trichinosis I," pp. 477–78. Before going to the NIH, Hall had been
    head of the BAI's Zoological Division. While at the BAI, he made the
    momentous discovery in 1921 that carbon tetrachloride had effective
    anthelmintic properties. This greatly facilitated the eradication of hook-
    worm in humans around the world. Eloise Cram Papers, Special Collec-

tions, National Agricultural Library, Beltsville, MD, http://specialcollections
.nal.usda.gov/guide-collections/eloise-cram-papers; P.D. Lamso, A.S.
Minot, and B.H. Robbins, "The Prevention and Treatment of Carbon
Tetrachloride Intoxication," *Journal of the American Medical Association* 90,
no. 5 (1928): 345–49.

40. Hall, "Trichinosis VII," pp. 1473–74.

41. William J. Zimmermann, "Salt Cure and Drying-Time and Temperature
Effects on Viability of Trichinella Spiralis in Dry-Cured Hams," *Journal of
Food Science* 36, no. 1 (1971): 58–62; B.H. Ransom, B. Schwartz, and H.B.
Raffensperger, "Effects of Pork-Curing Processes on Trichinae," *USDA
Bulletin,* no. 880 (Washington, DC: U.S. Government Printing Office,
1920), pp. 1–2, 36–37.

42. Zimmermann et al., "Trichiniasis," pp. 611–13.

43. Benjamin Schwartz, "The Trichinosis Situation in the United States,"
Scientific Monthly 51, no. 3 (1940), p. 246. Earlier USDA guidelines for
curing most likely overstated the efficacy of the recommended processes
(Olmstead, "First Line of Defense," pp. 347–48).

44. Olmstead, "First Line of Defense," p. 347.

45. F.G. Ashbrook and J.D. Bebout, "Disposal of City Garbage by Feeding to
Hogs," *USDA Circular,* no. 80 (Washington, DC: U.S. Government Printing
Office, 1917), pp. 3–8; Irwin S. Osborn, "Effect of the War on the Produc-
tion of Garbage and Methods of Disposal," *American Journal of Public Health*
8, no. 5 (1918): 368–72; M.P. Horowitz, "Feeding Garbage to Hogs,"
American Journal of Public Health 8, no. 5 (1918), p. 392; U.S. Food Adminis-
tration, *Garbage Utilization with Particular Reference to Utilization by Feeding*
(Washington, DC: U.S. Government Printing Office, 1918).

46. Charles V. Chapin, "Garbage as Food for Swine," *American City* 17, no. 2
(1917): 177–83; James H. Cassedy, *Charles V. Chapin and the Public Health
Movement* (Cambridge, MA: Harvard Univ. Press, 1962), pp. 52, 184; Daniel
J. Zarin, "Searching for Pennies in Piles of Trash: Municipal Refuse Utilization in the United States, 1870–1930," *Environmental Review* 11, no. 3
(1987), pp. 214–16.

47. Canadian Commission of Conservation, *Garbage as Feed for Hogs* (Ottawa,
1918); Brock Chisholm, "Quotations from an Address," *American Journal of
Public Health* 43, no. 3 (1953), p. 340.

48. Wise, *Hog Cholera,* p. 9; W.A. Hagan, "The Control and Eradication of
Animal Diseases in the United States," *Annual Review of Microbiology* 12
(1958), p. 141; U.S. Agricultural Research Service, Animal Disease Eradication Branch, "National Status on Control of Garbage-Feeding," various
years; Martin V. Melosi, *Garbage in the Cities: Refuse, Reform, and the Environment,* rev. ed. (Pittsburgh: Univ. of Pittsburgh Press, 2005), pp. 187–88;
Olmstead, "First Line of Defense," p. 348.

49. A notable exception is Spiekermann, "Dangerous Meat?" pp. 107–8.

CHAPTER 9   *The Benevolence of the Butcher*

1. *New York Times,* 28 May 1906, p. 2. Upton Sinclair, *The Jungle* (New York: Doubleday, Jabber, 1906).
2. "USDA Celebrates 100 Years of Food Safety," News release, 28 June 2006, www.usda.gov/wps/portal/usda/usdahome?contentidonly=true&contentid=2006/06/0226.xml.
3. Libecap, "Rise of the Chicago Packers," pp. 242–62; Marc T. Law and Gary D. Libecap, "The Determinants of Progressive Era Reform: The Pure Food and Drug Act of 1906," in *Corruption and Reform: Lessons from America's Economic History,* ed. Edward L. Glaeser and Claudia Goldin (Chicago: Univ. of Chicago Press, 2006), p. 324.
4. Gabriel Kolko, *The Triumph of Conservatism: A Reinterpretation of American History, 1900–1916* (Chicago: Quadrangle, 1967), pp. 98–108.
5. For example, Libecap, "Rise of the Chicago Packers," pp. 242–62.
6. Ibid., p. 254n27. Claims denying disease problems have entered the popular history literature; see Jim Powell, *Bully Boy: The Truth about Theodore Roosevelt's Legacy* (New York: Crown Forum, 2006), pp. 164–65.
7. Law and Libecap, "Determinants of Progressive Era Reform," pp. 322–23; William A. Niskanen, *Bureaucracy and Representative Government* (Chicago: Aldine-Atherton, 1971). The economics literature also wrestles to explain why as history unfolded Progressive Era leaders opted for regulation rather than relying on the tort system to safeguard consumer interests. Glaeser and Shleifer, "Rise," pp. 401–25, esp. 418.
8. Shleifer, "Enforcement Theory," p. 4; Libecap, "Rise of the Chicago Packers," p. 242.
9. Poultry and eggs were not subject to federal inspection until 1957 and 1970, respectively, but inspecting meat was a logical and perhaps necessary first step to toward broader inspection.
10. Standard economic models of reputation mechanisms hold that cheating will be deterred if the probability of getting caught times the long-run financial losses outweighs the short-run gains from dishonest behavior. By this reasoning, large established concerns stand to lose larger sums and are therefore less likely to cheat. See Benjamin Klein and Keith B. Leffler, "The Role of Market Forces in Assuring Contractual Performance," *Journal of Political Economy* 89, no. 4 (1981): 615–41. The problems facing consumers in detecting unsanitary meats are discussed in Roger W. Weiss, "The Case for Federal Meat Inspection Examined," *Journal of Law and Economics* 7 (Oct. 1964), pp. 108–12.
11. Robert Ostertag, *Handbook of Meat Inspection,* trans. Earley Wilcox (New York: William R. Jenkins, 1904), pp. 389–664, 867–84.
12. USDA, *Yearbook of Agriculture, 1894,* pp. 67–80. Salmon noted that federal inspection has "a duty to protect the consumer from meat which was

offensive and repugnant to him, as well as from that which was actually dangerous to his health" (p. 70). See also Susan D. Jones, *Valuing Animal: Veterinarians and Their Patients in Modern America* (Baltimore: Johns Hopkins Univ. Press, 2003), p. 88. Even if an animal's most obvious infection is not communicable to humans, banning its flesh and milk may be a wise policy because sick animals often suffer from multiple illnesses, some of which could be zoonotic. The presence of nonzoonotic diseases, use of biological waste as feed, confined high-density populations, unsanitary production conditions, and reliance on chemical preservatives may all be correlates of actual threats to human health.

13. Helen Tangires, *Public Markets and Civic Culture in Nineteenth-Century America* (Baltimore: Johns Hopkins Univ. Press, 2003), pp. 151–72. The *Slaughter-house Cases* (83 U.S. 36, decided 14 Apr. 1873), which offered the U.S. Supreme Court's first interpretation of the Fourteen Amendment, affirmed the police power of Louisiana to restrict the butchers of New Orleans to operate in a publicly chartered centralized abattoir (downstream from the city).

14. U.S. Senate, *Report of the Select Committee on the Transportation and Sale of Meat Products*, Senate Report No. 829, 51st Cong., 1st Sess. (Washington, DC: U.S. Government Printing Office, 1890), pp. 23, 26. In the final report, Vest advocated establishing voluntary national inspection of beef for export as a means of opening foreign markets and raising U.S. cattle prices. *Chicago Tribune*, 30 Apr. 1890, p. 5.

15. *Chicago Tribune*, 14 Oct. 1886, p. 8; 11 Sept. 1888, p. 6; 1 Oct. 1886, p. 6; *New York Times*, 24 Dec. 1888, p. 5; *Chicago Inter Ocean*, 13 Sept. 1888, p. 6; U.S. BAI, *Report for 1884*, pp. 267–68; U.S. BAI, *Report for 1885*, pp. 282–84.

16. *Chicago Inter Ocean*, 13 Sept. 1888, p. 6; U.S. Senate, *Swine Products*, pp. 284–85; Wade, *Chicago's Pride*, pp. 191–92; Chicago, *Report of the Department of Health*, various years. The post-mortem inspections appear cursory at best. On one occasion, Lamb stated, "I can tell a cholera hog or a diseased beef or sheep as soon as the hide is removed, and so can any one [sic] who has had a month's experience in the business." *Chicago Tribune*, 1 Dec. 1885, p. 8. On another occasion, he said, "I inspect all the meat in the various slaughter-houses every night, and I find it in pretty good condition." *Chicago Tribune*, 28 Aug. 1886, p. 8.

17. Their mutual animosity is revealed in a stunning blowup concerning a shipment of lumpy-jaw cattle to a Chicago rendering plant in December 1888. In the ensuing battle, the State Board of Live Stock Commissioners and the Chicago Department of Health each accused the other of dumping diseased meat into the local market. The resulting bad publicity did not please the large packers. *Chicago Tribune*, 31 Dec. 1889, p. 3; 1 Jan. 1890, p. 4; 5 Jan. 1890, p. 6; 8 Jan. 1890, p. 3; 16 Jan. 1890, p. 3; *Chicago Inter Ocean*, 10 Jan. 1890, p. 4.

18. Chicago Board of Trade, *Annual Report of the Trade and Commerce of Chicago for 1892* (Chicago: J. M. W. Jones, 1893), p. 41; Chicago Department of Health, *Report of the Department of Health for 1888* (Chicago: Powers, Crichfield, 1889), p. 88; *Report of the Department of Health for 1889* (Chicago: Barnard and Gunthrorp, 1891), p. 128; *Report of the Department of Health for 1890* (Chicago: Pettibone, 1891), p. 139. Critics of Matthew Lamb accused him of corruption, of taking bribes to allow meat and animals to pass inspection, and of holding city office due to political influence. *Chicago Inter Ocean*, 19 Feb. 1894, p. 3.

19. *Chicago Tribune*, 11 Sept. 1888, p. 6. See also Chicago, *Department of Health for 1888*, p. 13.

20. *Chicago Inter Ocean*, 7 Oct. 1889, p. 10; *Chicago Tribune*, 10 Jan. 1890, p. 8.

21. *Chicago Inter Ocean*, 13 Sept. 1888, p. 6; Wade, *Chicago's Pride*, pp. 183–84, 371–72.

22. Rudolf A. Clemen, *American Livestock and Meat Industry* (New York: Roland Press, 1923), p. 319, discusses the inspection regime at Chicago before 1891 (reproducing almost verbatim text from Edward Perry's article in U.S. BAI, *Report for 1884*, pp. 267–68.) After a bout of bad publicity in September 1882, the "principal packers and shippers of beef at once exerted themselves to assist the city health authorities of Chicago. . . . An inspector was stationed at each slaughter house, and one was constantly on duty at the stockyards during the hours when the gates of the yards were open for the passage of stock. The officers scrutinized the animals offered for sale, especially those destined to be slaughtered in Chicago." See also *Chicago Tribune*, 21 Oct. 1882, p. 7; 2 Nov. 1882, p. 4. In 1890, the city had a staff of six official meat inspectors (including those assigned to the large wholesale markets) in addition to the twelve "special inspectors" hired by the large packers. Chicago, *Department of Health for 1890*, pp. 2, 7–10. This staff was too far small to have one inspector stationed at each of the fifty-six slaughtering establishments (including forty-one with meatpacking plants) operating in Chicago in that year. U.S. Bureau of the Census, *Eleventh Census: 1890*, vol. 6, *Report on Manufacturing Industries in the United States*, pt. 2, *Statistics of Cities* (Washington, DC: U.S. Government Printing Office, 1895), pp. 41–42.

23. *Drovers Journal*, 6 Aug. 1884, p. 4; *Chicago Tribune*, 19 Aug. 1884, p. 8; 21 Aug. 1884, p. 8; 31 Aug. 1884, p. 16.

24. *Drovers Journal*, 10 Mar. 1884, p. 4. According to laudatory accounts of Morris's career, he got his start in the livestock business trading in diseased and dead cattle; *Chicago Tribune*, 13 Apr. 1890, p. 10. See also Bartham Fowler, *Men, Meat, and Miracles* (New York: Messner, 1952), pp. 19–20.

25. *Drovers Journal*, 18 Mar. 1886, p. 2; 17 Apr. 1886, p. 2.

26. *Chicago Inter Ocean*, 5 Oct. 1886, p. 5.

27. U.S. Senate, *Testimony Taken by the Select Committee on the Transportation and Sale of Meat Products to Accompany Senate Report No. 829*, 51st Cong., 1st Sess.

(Washington, DC: U.S. Government Printing Office, 1890), pp. 474–76. "Expertise" was in the eye of the beholder, and Armour obviously excluded Law, Salmon, and other leading scientists from his implied list of "best experts."

28. U.S. BAI, *Operations for 1895*, pp. 33–34, 41–49.

29. *New York Times,* 9 Mar. 1886, p. 3: *Chicago Inter Ocean,* 17 Mar. 1887, p. 4: *Galveston Daily News,* 22 Mar. 1887, p. 4.

30. *Chicago Tribune,* 26 Oct. 1888, p. 9; 20 Nov. 1888, p. 2; 22 Nov. 1888, p. 4; 23 Nov. 1888, p. 4; 24 Nov. 1888, p. 10; 22 May 1889, p. 4; *New York Times,* 18 Nov. 1888, p. 6; 20 Nov. 1888, p. 2; 21 Nov. 1888, p. 4; 22 Nov. 1888, p. 5; Mar. 16, 1889, p. 4. A group of participants seceded from the main conference in St. Louis and passed a resolution supporting national meat inspection; *Chicago Tribune,* 23 Nov. 1888, p. 1. In early 1889, the Chicago Live Stock Exchange petitioned Congress in favor of federal inspection; *Congressional Record,* 6 Feb. 1889, p. 1544; Box No. 121, file HR 50 AH 1.8, U.S. House Records.

31. *Chicago Tribune,* 14 Mar. 1889, p. 6; *New York Times,* 6 Apr. 1889, p. 5; 9 May 1889, p. 4; *Chicago Inter Ocean,* 22 Mar. 1889, p. 1; Clemen, *American Livestock,* pp. 242–43, 245–51; Donald J. Boudreaux and Thomas J. DiLorenzo, "The Protectionist Roots of Antitrust," *Review of Austrian Economics* 6, no. 2 (1993): 81–96.

32. *New York Times,* 12 May 1889, p. 1; 14 Aug. 1889, p. 1; 24 Sept. 1889, p. 8; 30 Nov. 1889, p. 1.

33. Mary Yeager, *Competition and Regulation: The Development of Oligopoly in the Meat Packing Industry* (Greenwich, CT: JAI Press, 1981), p. 177, quotes extensively the Senate testimony of Detroit butcher John Duff, who not only favored state over federal inspection but considered it sufficient to control the big packers. U.S. Senate, *Testimony Taken by the Select Committee,* p. 156. See also Charles W. McCurdy, "American Law and the Marketing Structure of the Large Corporation, 1875–1890," *Journal of Economic History* 37, no. 3 (1978): 644–48.

34. *Chicago Tribune,* 2 Feb. 1889, p. 4. See also John Clay, "American Cattle Markets and the Dressed Beef Trade, with Some Statistics of the Live-Stock Trade in the United States," *Journal of the Royal Agricultural Society of England* 25 (1889), pp. 149–50.

35. *Chicago Tribune,* 17 Jan. 1890, p. 4; 19 Nov. 1888, p. 17.

36. U.S. Senate, *Transportation and Sale,* p. 24; *Congressional Record,* 29 May 1890, p. 5428; The scientific debates about the dangers of actinomycosis came to a head in the celebrated Peoria, Illinois, lumpy-jaw trial of November 1891. R. W. Hickman, "Actinomycosis, Lumpy Jaw," *Journal of Comparative Medicine and Veterinary Archives* 13, no. 2 (1892): 110–16. In early 1891, the Illinois Live Stock Commissioners destroyed 125 head of infected cattle at the Peoria distillery of Joseph B. Greenhut. Greenhut was the president of

the Whiskey Trust and a business associate of packer Nelson Morris. Greenhut, Morris, and four others sued Illinois for damages. A who's who of the American veterinary profession, including Frank S. Billings for the plaintiffs and James Law for the defense, testified at the trial. The experts conflicted sharply: "The majority of the scientists and veterinary surgeons maintain that the disease is contagious and the meat of an animal infected with it unhealthful . . . cattle-raisers and shippers testify that the reverse is true..., [and a] few of the scientists agree with the cattlemen" (*Portland Morning Oregonian*, 27 Nov. 1891, p. 4). The jury was unable to reach a verdict, and the case was settled out of court several years later. See *Chicago Inter Ocean*, 20 Jan. 1894, p. 1; *Chicago Tribune*, 13 Nov. 1891, p. 1; 14 Nov. 1891, p. 1; 17 Nov. 1891, p. 1; 18 Nov. 1891, p. 1; 19 Nov. 1891, p. 1; 20 Nov. 1891, p. 1; 26 Nov. 1891, p. 1; 29 Dec. 1891, p. 7; *New York Times*, 22 Nov. 1891, p. 20; 26 Nov. 1891, p. 4; 29 Nov. 1891, p. 4; *Chicago Inter Ocean*, 15 Nov. 1891, p. 5; 19 Nov. 1891, p. 1; 25 Nov. 1891, p. 5; 26 Nov. 1891, p. 10; Illinois State Board of Live Stock Commissioners, *Annual Report for the Fiscal Year ending October 31, 1892*, pp. 15–34.

37. L. H. Anderson, *Natural Way in Diet; or, the Proper Food of Man* (Chicago: National Institute of Science, 1898), pp. 110–13; *Chicago Inter Ocean*, 5 Oct. 1888, p. 10. In the same period, Chicago and Pittsburgh officials sparred about shipments of lumpy-jaw cattle. *Chicago Tribune*, 11 Sept. 1888, p. 6; 23 Sept. 1888, p. 13.

38. *Chicago Tribune*, 10 Oct. 1888, p. 9; 23 Nov. 1888, p. 4; Illinois State Board of Live Stock Commissioners, *Annual Report for 1888*, pp. 24–26. The Illinois State Board of Live Stock Commissioners later entered into a fight with the BAI over lumpy jaw. The federal meat inspectors asserted, based on European practices, that removal of the infected parts was sufficient to render the remaining meat safe for human consumption.

39. USDA, *Report of the Secretary for 1889*, pp. 39–40.

40. Undated Memorandum, Box 4, file 4, Rusk Papers.

41. *Milwaukee Sentinel*, 20 Apr. 1890, p. 14.

42. Thomas B. Reed, "Rules of the House of Representatives," *Century* 37 (1889), p. 795.

43. *Congressional Record*, 26 Feb. 1890, p. 1716; 5 Mar. 1890, p. 1930; 10 Mar. 1890, pp. 2070–73; 17 Mar. 1890, p. 2327; 5 Apr. 1890, pp. 3056–58.

44. *Congressional Record*, 20 Mar. 1890, p. 2426; *Chicago Tribune*, 12 Mar. 1890, p. 3; *Drovers Journal*, 12 Mar. 1890, p. 4; 13 Mar. 1890, p. 4; 15 Mar. 1890, p. 2; 20 Mar. 1890, p. 2; *Milwaukee Journal*, 26 Mar. 1890, p. 1.

45. *Congressional Record*, 5 Apr. 1890, p. 3058.

46. *Congressional Record*, 9 Apr. 1890, p. 3224; 28 Apr. 1890, p. 3955.

47. *Chicago Tribune*, 21 Aug. 1890, p. 5; *Congressional Record*, 20 Aug. 1890, pp. 8874, 8892–94, 9838.

48. U.S. BAI, *Reports for 1891 and 1892*, p. 36.

49. *Congressional Record,* 1 May 1890, p. 4067; *Washington Post,* 2 May 1890, p. 2. In a parallel decision, *Leisy v. Hardin* (135 U.S. 100, decided 28 Apr. 1890), the U.S. Supreme Court overruled an Iowa ban on out-of-state alcohol imports. Congress immediately responded to the Court's decision by passing legislation authorizing the states to regulate the interstate commerce of intoxicating beverages. On 29 May 1890, Vest attempted to amend the bill (S 396) to cover meat inspection as well. His amendment attracted only five positive votes, indicating little or no support in the Senate for permitting state on-the-hoof meat inspection. See *Congressional Record,* 29 May 1890, pp. 5425–29, esp. 5429.

50. *Congressional Record,* 23 May 1890, p. 4516; 11 June 1890, pp. 5928–29.

51. *Congressional Record,* 11 June 1890, pp. 5928–31; 13 June 1890, p. 6075, 19 Aug. 1890, p. 8840.

52. *Congressional Record,* 24 June 1890, p. 6415; 18 Sept. 1890, p. 10191; 9 Dec. 1890, p. 274.

53. U.S. House of Representatives, *Inspection of Live Cattle, Hogs, Etc.,* 9 Dec. 1890, House Report No. 3262, 51st Cong., 2nd Sess. (Washington, DC: U.S. Government Printing Office, 1890), pp. 1–2; Olof Schwartzkopff, "National and International Meat Inspection," *Journal of Comparative Medicine and Veterinary Archives* 11, no. 11 (1890): 599–608.

54. *Congressional Record,* 13 Dec. 1890, pp. 423–26.

55. *Congressional Record,* 11 Feb. 1891, p. 2533; 2 Mar. 1891, p. 3712.

56. *Congressional Record,* 2 Mar. 1891, pp. 3713–16.

57. *Congressional Record,* 2 Mar. 1891, p. 3680.

58. Had Congress not acted in the final days of the lame duck session is likely that meat inspection would have met as same fate as Paddock's 1892 pure food bill (S 1). This passed the Republican-led Senate in March 1892 but died in the heavily Democratic House.

59. John R. Mohler, "History and Present Status of Meat Inspection in the United States," in Robert Ostertag, *Handbook of Meat Inspection,* 3rd ed., trans. Earley Wilcox (New York: William R. Jenkins, 1907), p. xvii.

60. Armour & Co. to J. Rusk, 27 Mar. 1891; Nelson Morris to J. Rusk, 30 Mar. 1891; G. F. Swift to J. M. Rusk, 14 Sept. 1891; Philip Armour to J. Rusk, 23 Mar. 1892; Box 3, Rusk Papers. See also *Chicago Tribune,* 22 Mar. 1891, p. 3, which asserts that the Chicago packers, who were initially anxious for a national law to "escape vexatious State and municipal inspections," soon perceived its value "in widening the foreign market."

61. Houck, *Bureau of Animal Industry,* p. 258; *Chicago Inter Ocean,* 17 July 1891, p. 8; 28 July 1892, p. 1; Henry Casson, *"Uncle Jerry:" Life of General Jeremiah M. Rusk* (Madison, WI: Junius W. Hill, 1895), pp. 286–91, 295–96.

62. U.S. Senate, *Report of the Commission Appointed by the President to Investigate the Conduct of the War Department in the War with Spain,* vol. 7, Senate Doc. No. 221, 56th Cong., 1st Sess. (Washington, DC: U.S. Government Printing

Office, 1900), pp. 3488–91; Charles S. Plumb, "Marketing Live Stock," USDA, *Farmers' Bulletin*, no. 184 (Washington, DC: U.S. Government Printing Office, 1903), pp. 15–17.

63. Jones, *Valuing Animals*, pp. 82–84, 88; Daniel E. Salmon, "Report Upon Investigations Relating to the Treatment of Lumpy-jaw, Or Actinomycosis, in Cattle," *BAI Bulletin*, no. 2 (Washington, DC: U.S. Government Printing Office, 1893), pp. 7–8, 22–28; *Chicago Inter Ocean*, 10 Feb. 1894, p. 5; 19 Feb. 1894, p. 1; 20 Feb. 1894, p. 1; 21 Feb. 1894, p. 1; 21 Feb. 1894, p. 6; 22 Feb. 1892, p. 1; 24 Feb. 1892, p. 1.

64. Olson, *J. Sterling Morton*, pp. 356–62. To reduce political job-seeking and increase professionalism, the Meat Inspection Division was placed in the Civil Service on 1 July 1894.

65. W. R. Goodwin Jr. to James A. Canfield, 27 Feb. 1893, Reel 21, Morton Papers.

66. *Chicago Inter Ocean*, 5 July 1893, p. 6; 9 July 1893, p. 20; 24 July 1893, p. 6; *Chicago Tribune*, 4 July 1893, p. 9; 14 July 1893, p. 7; *New York Times*, 14 July 1893, p. 7; USDA, *Report of the Secretary for 1895*, p. 6.

67. *Washington Post*, 18 Sept. 1893, p. 7; 30 Sept. 1893, p. 4. The later reported that Eastern packers were displeased with Morton's expansion of inspection.

68. Quoted in *Galveston Daily News*, 2 Oct. 1893, p. 2.

69. Joy Morton to J. S. Morton, 17 Apr. 1894, Box 13, folder 5, Morton Family Papers, Chicago Historical Society.

70. *Chicago Tribune*, 17 May 1894, p. 3. Morton asked his son to assure any "packing-house people with whom you come into contact, that the investigation will be conducted carefully and conclusions arrived at after great deliberation and upon the best testimony obtainable. There will be no publicity given to any doubtful evidence against any packing concern." J. S. Morton to Joy Morton, 21 May 1894, Reel 4, USDA, Records of the Office of the Secretary of Agriculture, RG 16, Microfilm M 440, National Archives, College Park, MD [hereafter USDA Secretary Records].

71. See the BAI document dated 3 Sept. 1894 included in James Wilson to George B. Davis, 15 Mar. 1899, Reel 182, USDA Secretary Records.

72. J. S. Morton to John F. Hopkins, 7 June 1894, Reel 51, Morton Papers; *Chicago Tribune*, 8 July 1894, p. 11.

73. *Chicago Tribune*, 17 May 1894, p. 3; 18 May 1894, p. 8.

74. *Chicago Tribune*, 28 Mar. 1895, p. 7.

75. *Chicago Tribune*, 12 Mar. 1899, p. 1; 14 Mar. 1899, p. 2; 5 Apr. 1899, p. 5; *Washington Post*, 5 Apr. 1899, p. 5.

76. J. S. Morton to Nelson Morris, 21 July 1894, Reel 176, USDA Secretary Records. Four days later, Morton wrote to Joy Morton's main informant to explain why he was not pursuing legal action: "It is doubtful if a conviction could be obtained under our laws with the evidence which the agents of this Department have been able to secure. This being the case, there is every

reason for not taking the matter into the courts, as further publicity would undoubtedly damage the domestic meat trade, and be ruinous to the foreign trade without a prospect of accomplishing anything by such proceeding." J.S. Morton to James McGregor, 25 July 1894, Reel 176, USDA Secretary Records.

77. J.S. Morton to Swift & Co., 6 Mar. 1895 and 14 Mar. 1895, Reel 176; J.S. Morton to Secretary of State, 8 Mar. 1895, Reel 176; and J.S. Morton to Joy Morton, 5 Mar. 1895, Reel 176, USDA Secretary Records.

78. For a sample of Morton's correspondence on selling condemned meat, see J.S. Morton to A.D. Melvin, 16 June 1894, Reel 4; J.S. Morton to Chicago Packing and Provision Co., 21 Apr. 1894, Reel 176; for the fraudulent labeling cans, see J.S. Morton to Richard Olney, 31 Jan. 1895, Reel 176. For the creation of secret supply-chains for diseased hogs, see J.S. Morton to A.D. Melvin, 16 June 1894, Reel 4, J.S. Morton to Edward Shelden, 8 June 1894, Reel 4, and J.S. Morton to Evan Pritchard, of Kingan & Co., 21 July 1894, Reel 176, USDA Secretary Records. On this latter issue, Morton accused Kingan & Co., a large Indianapolis packer, of receiving the shipments of diseased swine from Chicago dealer who specialized in the trade.

79. J.S. Morton to Joy Morton, 21 May 1894, Reel 4. Also see J.S. Morton to Joy Morton, 5 Mar. 1895, Reel 176, USDA Secretary Records.

80. J.S. Morton to Harry Botsford, 8 Feb. 1895, Reel 176; J.S. Morton to Armour & Co., 22 Apr. 1895, Reel 176; J.S. Morton to W.J. Dee, 8 Mar. and 16 Apr. 1895, Reel 176, USDA Secretary Records. To reduce losses, Morton advised packers to cook the pork to kill the trichinae and then can the suitable portions.

81. *Chicago Tribune,* 20 June 1895, p. 12.

82. U.S. BAI, *Report for 1906,* p. 440, notes that "this practice does not have the sanction of law." The excess demand for inspection services did generate complaints of discrimination in favor of large as opposed to small packers.

83. Mohler, "History and Present Status," pp. xix–xx, and U.S. BAI, *Report for 1897,* p. 37, stressed the importance of developing proper expertise and procedures, as well as gaining authority to dispose of the carcasses of condemned animals. U.S. BAI, *Report for 1906,* p. 10.

84. Higgs, *Crisis and Leviathan,* p. 83; Zavodnyik, *Rise of the Federal Colossus,* pp. 145, 202–3.

85. Libecap, "Rise of the Chicago Packers," p. 253n25; U.S. BAI, *Report for 1885,* pp. 382–83; *Chicago Commerce, Manufacturing,* p. 83. *Detroit Free Press,* 28 Sept. 1886, p. 14; *Chicago Tribune,* 11 Sept. 1888, p. 6; 1 Oct. 1888, p. 6; 12 Jan. 1889, p. 9.

86. "Live Stock Exchange Inspection of Animals Is a Success," *Chicago Live Stock World,* 25 Mar. 1908, pp. 1–2. For an extensive exposé of the trade in lumpy jaw cattle, see *Chicago Inter Ocean,* 19 Feb. 1894, pp. 1–2. See also *Chicago Tribune,* 7 Mar. 1894, p. 7; 24 Mar. 1894, p. 4; 7 Aug. 1894, p. 4; 12 Mar. 1895, p. 7.

87. Houck, *Bureau of Animal Industry*, p. 258.

88. *New York Times,* 1 Mar. 1898, p. 5; *Chicago Tribune,* 1 Mar. 1898, p. 6.

89. *Butcher's Advocate,* 9 Mar. 1898, pp. 1, 12.

90. James Wilson to John Greggs, 24 Feb. 1898; John Walker to John Greggs, 15 Nov. 1897 and 1 Feb. 1898, Entry 1, Box 1, U.S. BAI Records.

91. *Chicago Tribune,* 2 Mar. 1898, p. 9; *Butcher's Advocate,* 9 Mar. 1898, pp. 1, 12.

92. *Butcher's Advocate,* 9 Mar. 1898, p. 1.

93. Ibid., pp. 1, 12; *Chicago Tribune,* 2 Mar. 1898, p. 9.

94. *Drovers Journal,* 4 Mar. 1898, p. 2.

95. *Ohio Farmer,* 10 Mar. 1898, p. 198.

96. David Gordon, "Swift & Co. v. United States: The Beef Trust and the Stream of Commerce Doctrine," *American Journal of Legal History* 28, no. 3 (1984): 244–79.

97. *New York Times,* 8 Apr. 1899, p. 4. In September 1905, Daniel Salmon was ousted from the BAI because of his business relationship with a USDA contractor and because of Theodore Roosevelt's dissatisfaction with the meat inspection service. *Washington Post,* 5 Aug. 1905, p. 2; 14 Aug. 1905, p. 4; 31 Aug. 1905, p. 2; 7 Sept. 1905, p. 3. *New York Times,* 7 Sept. 1905, p. 4. Jones, *Valuing Animals,* pp. 84–85.

98. Graham A. Cosmas, *An Army for Empire: The United States Army in the Spanish-American War* (Columbia: Univ. of Missouri Press, 1971), pp. 286–96; Vincent J. Cirillo, *Bullets and Bacilli: The Spanish-American War and American Medicine* (New Brunswick, NJ: Rutgers Univ. Press, 1999), pp. 106–10.

99. *Chicago Tribune,* 10 Mar. 1899, p. 1; 11 Mar. 1899, p. 1.

100. Edward F. Keuchel, "Chemicals and Meat: the Embalmed Beef Scandal of the Spanish-American War," *Bulletin of the History of Medicine* 48, no. 2 (1974): 249–64; *New York Times,* 8 Apr. 1899, p. 4.

101. Carl Sandburg, *Always the Young Strangers* (New York: Harcourt, Brace, 1952), p. 417.

102. James Wilson to W. W. Wilson, 23 Jan. 1899, James Wilson Papers, Iowa State University [hereafter Wilson Papers]; Hoing, "James Wilson," pp. 59–60. Later, Wilson shared with his brother a draft USDA report of its chemical investigation for the Board of Inquiry to "look over and hand over to your packer friends," adding, "You may depend upon it I shall leave no stone unturned here in this beef business." James Wilson to W. W. Wilson, 16 Feb. 1899, Wilson Papers.

103. James Wilson to W. W. Wilson, 23 Jan. 1899, Wilson Papers. Later in 1899, Wilson wrote privately to the Secretary of War about "the unscrupulous character of some of the packers" who "do not hesitate to . . . put the meat of diseased animals upon the market." Wilson's animus was directed not just at smaller packing companies: in October, he had threatened to withdraw his inspectors from the Armour plant in Kansas City, Missouri,

because the firm had repeatedly processed uninspected carcasses in violation of its agreements with the USDA. James Wilson to Secretary of War, 22 Nov. 1899; James Wilson to Armour & Co., 4 Oct. 1899, Reel 183, USDA Secretary Records.

104. *Chicago Tribune*, 29 Mar. 1899, p. 5; 3 Apr. 1899, p. 7; 4 Apr. 1899, p. 3; James Wilson to George B. Davis, 15 Mar. 1899 and 28 Mar. 1899, Reel 182, USDA Secretary Records.

105. Everett B. Miller, "Veterinary Medical Service of the Army in the Spanish-American War, 1898 (with Notes on the 'Embalmed Beef' Scandal)," *Veterinary Heritage* 11, no. 1 (1988): 14–38, esp. 30. When asked by the former Secretary of War for their 1901 assessment of the scandal, officials at Armour & Co. reported "being quite content to let the subject rest upon the reports of the Commission and Court of Inquiry." Armour & Co. to R. A. Alger, 18 Jan 1901; Russell A. Alger Papers, William L. Clements Library, University of Michigan, Ann Arbor, MI.

106. *Lancet*, 7 Jan. 1905, pp. 49–52; 14 Jan. 1905, pp. 120–23; 21 Jan. 1905, pp. 183–85; 28 Jan. 1905, pp. 258–60; Kolko, *Triumph of Conservatism*, p. 101.

107. U.S. House of Representatives, Agricultural Committee, *Hearings on the So-Called "Beveridge Amendment" to the Agricultural Appropriation Bill (H. R. 18537) as Passed by the Senate May 25 1906—To Which Are Added Various Documents Bearing upon "Beveridge Amendment."* 6–9, 11 June 1906, 59th Cong., 1st Sess. (Washington, DC: U.S. Government Printing Office, 1906), pp. 241–43, 251–52. In early 1906, USDA Secretary Wilson was lobbying Congress to expand inspection services and to shift the cost to the packers. *Southern Planter*, Feb. 1906, p. 144.

108. J. Ogden Armour, *The Packers, the Private Car Lines, and the People* (Philadelphia: Henry Altemus, 1906), pp. 62–63; Yeager, *Competition and Regulation*, pp. 199, 202; Kolko, *Triumph of Conservatism*, p. 102; Jones, *Valuing Animals*, p. 86.

109. The *World's Work* was edited by the highly regarded journalist, publisher, and diplomat, Walter Hines Page. Mark Sullivan, *Our Times: The United States 1900–1925*, vol. 2, *America Finding Herself* (New York: Charles Scribner, 1927), p. 536; John Braeman, "The Square Deal in Action: A Case Study in the Growth of the 'National Police Power,'" pp. 35–80 in *Change and Continuity in Twentieth-Century America*, ed. John Braeman, Robert H. Bremmer, and Everett Walters (Columbus: Ohio State Univ. Press, 1964), pp. 47–49.

110. U.S. House of Representatives, *"Beveridge Amendment,"* pp. 271–320, 333–50.

111. Ibid., pp. 325–29, 242–43.

112. Neill and Reynolds briefed Theodore Roosevelt in early May and delivered a final report on 2 June 1906. For the text of the report and Roosevelt's cover letter, see U.S. House of Representatives, *"Beveridge Amendment,"*

pp. 263–73; *Chicago Tribune*, 25 May 1906, p. 3; C. C. Reiger, "The Struggle for Federal Food and Drugs Legislation," *Law and Contemporary Problems* 1, no. 1 (1933): 3–15; Braeman, "Square Deal," p. 54; Yeager, *Competition and Regulation*, pp. 201–2.

113. Joel A. Tarr, *A Study of Boss Politics: William Lorimer of Chicago* (Urbana: Univ. of Illinois Press, 1971), pp. 152–63, esp. 157, 162.

114. Roosevelt to Wadsworth, 26 May 1906, in Elting E. Morison, ed., *The Letters of Theodore Roosevelt*, vol. 5 (Cambridge, MA: Harvard Univ. Press, 1952), pp. 282–83; William H. Harbaugh, *The Life and Time of Theodore Roosevelt*, rev. ed. (New York: Collier, 1963), pp. 248–50; George W. Mowry, *The Era of Theodore Roosevelt* (New York: Harper-Row, 1958), pp. 207–8; Braeman, "Square Deal," pp. 58–60.

115. "Packing Houses," pp. 3–4, in Charles P. Neill Correspondence, Collection 2001M-0078, Houghton Library, Harvard University.

116. Roosevelt to Wadsworth, 29 May 1906 and 15 June 1906, in Morison, *Letters of Theodore Roosevelt*, vol. 5, pp. 291–92, 298–99; Reiger, "Struggle for Federal Food and Drugs," p. 13; Yeager, *Competition and Regulation*, pp. 201–6; *Chicago Tribune*, 28 May 1906, p. 1.

117. U.S. House of Representatives, *"Beveridge Amendment,"* pp. 272–73. The text that Theodore Roosevelt quoted was in a private letter (1 June 1906) from McDowell to her friend James Reynolds. *New York Times*, 10 June 1906, p. 2; *Washington Post*, 12 June 1906, p. 4; "Government Inspection of Products of Packing Plants," 24 Jan. 1923 MSS, Part 1, file 1, Mary McDowell Settlement records, Chicago Historical Society; Allen F. Davis, *Spearheads for Reform: The Social Settlements and the Progressive Movement, 1890–1914* (New York: Oxford Univ. Press, 1967), pp. 120–22; Braeman, "Square Deal," pp. 51–52; Sullivan, *Our Times*, pp. 541–42.

118. U.S. House of Representatives, *"Beveridge Amendment,"* pp. 5, 205.

119. Wilson J. Warren, *Tied to the Great Packing Machine: The Midwest and Meatpacking* (Iowa City: Univ. of Iowa Press, 2007), p. 126; Nelson Morris, Wilson's boss, complained that Theodore Roosevelt's investigations would cause the U.S. meat trade to vanish. *New York Times*, 11 July 1906, p. 1.

120. Yeager, *Competition and Regulation*, p. 210.

121. James Wilson was aggrieved by Sinclair's charges against federal meat inspection and regretted the "mischief" they were causing at home and abroad. But the USDA secretary had long advocated enhanced inspection and used the crisis to secure greater powers and funding. James Wilson to Sen. Redfield Proctor, 27 May 1906; James Wilson to W. W. Wilson, 28 May 1906, Wilson Papers.

122. USDA, *Regulations Governing the Meat Inspection of the United States Department of Agriculture*, BAI Order 211, Issued 30 July 1914 (Washington, DC: U.S. Government Printing Office, 1914); *Chicago Tribune*, 10 Apr. 1906, pp. 1, 4.

123. Houck, *Bureau of Animal Industry,* pp. 260, 272–78.

124. Pennsylvania agricultural officials detailed many unhygienic conditions of non-federally inspected abattoirs and their own efforts to improve the situation. Pennsylvania Department of Agriculture, *Annual Report for 1915* (Harrisburg, PA: Wm. Stanley Ray, 1916), p. 93.

125. Both Secretaries Rusk and Morton spent considerable time dealing with patronage requests to fill meat inspection positions. But both secretaries had an eye on efficiency, noting that failures and incompetence would entail unacceptable political costs. J. Rusk to A. M. Jones, 6 Jan. 1892, Box 10, Rusk Papers; J. S. Morton to J. R. Stoller, 13 Feb. 1895, Reel 51, Morton Papers.

126. U.S. BAI, *Report for 1908,* pp. 83–107; *Reports for 1893 and 1894,* p. 30; John Roberts, "State and Municipal Meat Inspection," *American Journal of Public Health* 10, no. 9 (1920): 697–703; *Chicago Tribune,* 23 Apr. 1895, p. 8; Bert W. Bierer, "Survey of Municipal & State Meat Inspection," typed ms., 1942, p. 17; "Supplement to 'A Survey of Municipal & State Meat Inspection,' 1942," p. 28.

127. Jones, *Valuing Animals,* pp. 74–77, 88–89; Caroline B. Crane, "U.S. Inspected and Passed," *Pearson's Magazine* 29 (Mar. 1913), pp. 257–68; (Apr. 1913), pp. 436–46; (May 1913), pp. 524–34; (June 1913), pp. 738–48; *Washington Post,* 21 Oct. 1909, p. 1; 9 May 1912, p. 5; 10 May 1912, p. 4; 11 May 1912, p. 4; 12 May 1912, p. W1; Albert Leffingwell, *American Meat and Its Influence upon the Public Health* (London: George Bell, 1910).

128. *Congressional Record,* 20 Mar. 1890, p. 2426; *Milwaukee Journal,* 26 Mar. 1890, p. 1. The *Chicago Tribune* (14 Dec. 1890, p. 9) observed that the main opposition to the "Inter-State Meat Inspection" bill came from "State-Rights Democrats."

129. *Chicago Tribune,* 4 Mar. 1891, p. 2. Under the headline "All Believe It an Excellent Idea; Packers Look on the Meat Inspection Bill with High Favor," the *Chicago Tribune* (31 Mar. 1891, p. 9) noted the packers moved quickly to take advantage of inspection "with a view to foreign trade." In late 1889, P. D. Armour deplored that "the various cattle quarantine regulations and continued domestic agitation as to the unhealthful character of American beef cattle have had a decidedly harmful effect abroad" (*Chicago Tribune,* 1 Dec. 1889, p. 8).

130. Kolko, *Triumph of Conservatism,* pp. 98–108, esp. 100, 105.

131. Harper Leech and John C. Carroll, *Armour and His Times* (New York: Appleton-Century, 1938), pp. 175–76, 188. See also Clement, *American Livestock,* pp. 225–29, 242–51, 317–30; Louis F. Swift and Arthur Van Vlissingen Jr., *Yankee of the Yards: The Biography of Gustavus Franklin Swift* (Chicago: A. W. Shaw, 1927), p. 7, 48–49. According to Louis Swift, G. F. Swift's expressed genuine concerns for sanitation and sought to make improvements. The biography further asserts that Swift's scientifically

derived methods "formed a basis for the inspection and control exercised by the Bureau of Animal Industry" (p. 7). Given that the principal inspection manuals used in the U.S. in the 1890s and early 1900s were translations from German texts, this claim is hard to credit. G. F. Swift did criticize the operation of the inspection regime before the advent of federal regulation in 1891. This is one of many packer reminiscences critical of conditions before 1891. U.S. Senate, *Report of the Commission,* p. 3489.

132. *National Provisioner,* 26 May 1906, pp. 1, 14, 21.

133. *National Provisioner,* 2 June 1906, pp. 1, 14, 15, 16, 21, 26, 30.

134. *National Provisioner,* 9 June 1906, pp. 1, 14–18, 21–23, 25–26.

135. C. P. Neill to Carroll D. Wright, 13 June 1906; C. P. Neill to John P. Frey, 13 June 1906; C. P. Neill to James J. Neill, 30 June 1906. Charles Patrick Neill Papers, American Catholic Research Center and University Archives, Collection ACUA 012, Apr.–July 1906. Also see Sullivan, *Our Times,* pp. 544–50, for an account of the packers' brass-knuckled defense.

136. *National Provisioner,* 9 June 1906, p. 26; 7 July 1906, p. 1.

137. Nelson Morris to J. Rusk, 5 Nov. 1891, Box 3, Rusk Papers.

138. Llewellyn E. James to J. S. Morton, 11 Apr. 1893, Reel 21, Morton Papers.

139. Howard R. Smith, *The Conquest of Bovine Tuberculosis in the United States* (Somerset, MI: author, 1958), pp. 2–7.

140. Libecap, "Rise of the Chicago Packers," p. 259.

141. Ibid., pp. 245–46.

142. In 1916, New York City officials discovered that for roughly forty years a group of Williamsburg butchers had been bribing city meat inspectors to pass cattle with advanced cases of tuberculosis. For several decades "diseased meat was being put on the market in defiance of law and with a total disregard of the health of millions of the poor of New York." *New York Times,* 27 May 1916, p. 4.

143. U.S. BAI, *Report for 1905,* p. 25.

144. U.S. House of Representatives, *"Beveridge Amendment,"* p. 5; *National Provisioner,* 2 June 1906, p. 30.

145. U.S. BAI, *Report for 1905,* pp. 9–10, 24–35, quotations on pp. 9–10, 30–31.

146. John R. Mohler, "Federal Meat Inspection as a Safeguard to Public Health," *American Journal of Public Health* 10, no. 5 (1920): 441–46.

147. Houck, *Bureau of Animal Industry,* p. 266.

148. Ch. Wardell Stiles, "The Inspection of Meats for Animal Parasites," USDA *Bulletin,* no. 19 (Washington, DC: U.S. Government Printing Office, 1898); *Butcher's Advocate,* 16 Feb. 1898, p. 1. Stiles reported that about 50 percent of human sufferers typically died within five years after becoming infected with the hydatid parasite (p. 124).

149. P. J. Atkins, "The Glasgow Case: Meat, Disease, and Regulation, 1889–1924," *Agricultural History Review* 52, no. 2 (2004), p. 168; J. Brian Derbyshire, "Early History of the Canadian Federal Meat Inspection Service," *Canadian Veterinarian Journal* 47, no. 6 (2006), pp. 542–43, 545–49; U.S. BAI, *Report for 1899*, p. 535.

150. Ostertag, *Handbook*, 3rd ed., pp. 8–9, 26–121, 523–34, 717–41; Melvin, "Federal Meat Inspection," pp. 97–100; Emilia Kanthack, "Utility of the German 'Freibank' as a Factor in Social Economy," *Public Health* (1908): 119–21.

151. Derrick Rixson, *History of Meat Trading* (Nottingham, United Kingdom: Nottingham Univ. Press, 2000), pp. 368–69; Atkins, "Glasgow Case," pp. 163–64; F. V. Collins, *Meat Inspection* (Adelaide, South Australia: Rigby, 1966), p. 9, dates the earliest "modern" Act to 1835.

152. John Gamgee, *Diseased Meat Sold in Edinburgh and Meat Inspection, in Connection with the Public Health, and with the Interests of Agriculture: A Letter to the Right Hon. the Lord Provost of Edinburgh* (Edinburgh: Sutherland and Knox, 1857), pp. 3–9, 15–19; Keir Waddington, "To Stamp Out 'So Terrible a Malady': Bovine Tuberculosis and Tuberculin Testing in Britain, 1890–1939," *Medical History* 48 (2004): 29–48; Rixson, *Meat Trading*, p. 367; Atkins, "Glasgow Case," pp. 169, 173–75.

153. United Kingdom, Minister of Agriculture, Fisheries, and Food, *Animal Health*, p. 283–87; Collins, *Meat Inspection*, p. 10.

154. Michael Ollinger, "Structural Change in the Meat and Poultry Industry and Food Safety Regulations," *Agribusiness* 27, no. 2 (2011): 244–57; John M. Antle, "No Such Thing as a Free Safe Lunch: The Cost of Food Safety Regulation in the Meat Industry," *American Journal of Agricultural Economics* 82, no. 2 (2000): 310–22.

CHAPTER 10   *Bovine Tuberculosis and the Milk Problem*

1. *Woman Citizen*, 13 Mar. 1920, pp. 984–85.

2. Fisher, "National Vitality," p. 126.

3. U.S. Bureau of the Census, "Tuberculosis in the United States," in *Mortality Statistics 1907* (Washington, DC: U.S. Government Printing Office, 1909), table 17, p. 516, and *Mortality Rates 1910–1920 with Population of the Federal Censuses of 1910 and 1920 and Intercensal Estimates of Population* (Washington, DC: U.S. Government Printing Office, 1923), pp. 16, 27.

4. Irving Fisher, "The Cost of Tuberculosis in the United States and Its Reduction," in *Transactions of the Sixth International Congress on Tuberculosis*, vol. 3, *Proceedings of Section V: Hygienic, Social, Industrial, and Economic Aspects of Tuberculosis* (Philadelphia: William F. Fell, 1908), p. 34. Fisher's estimates assign zero value to the pain and suffering of the victims, their friends, and families.

5. To clarify the basic terminology, the formal name of the bovine strain of tuberculosis is *Mycobacterium bovis,* which is often summarized as *M. bovis.* The corresponding terminology for the human strain of tuberculosis is *Mycobacterium tuberculosis* and *M. tuberculosis.* The bovine strain can be passed from cattle to humans and vice versa (as well as to a number of other animals). There are other strains of tuberculosis, but they were of relatively minor significance to human health.

6. A. W. Fuchs and L. C. Frank, "Milk Supplies and Their Control in American Urban Communities of Over 1,000 Population in 1936," *Public Health Bulletin,* no. 245 (Washington, DC: U.S. Government Printing Office, 1939), p. 29.

7. U.S. National Research Council, Committee on Bovine Tuberculosis, *Livestock Disease Eradication: Evaluation of the Cooperative State-Federal Bovine Tuberculosis Eradication Program* (Washington, DC: National Academy Press, 1994), p. 13.

8. The estimates on productivity losses vary significantly. U.S. BAI, *Report for 1908,* p. 103; U.S. National Research Council, *Livestock,* p. 56; E. T. Faulder, "Bovine Tuberculosis: Its History, Control and Eradication," *New York State Department of Agriculture and Markets Bulletin,* no. 218 (1928), p. 14.

9. J. Arthur Myers, *Man's Greatest Victory over Tuberculosis* (Springfield, IL: Charles C. Thomas, 1940), pp. 264, 267–68, 309, 323.

10. Koch evidently did not foresee its diagnostic potential. Bernhard Bang of Denmark and W. Gutmann of Russia usually receive the credit for this breakthrough. Myers, *Man's Greatest Victory,* pp. 114–15; U.S. BAI, *Diseases of Cattle, 1916,* pp. 416–17.

11. Thomas Dormandy, *The White Death: A History of Tuberculosis* (London: Hambledon, 1999), pp. 330–31; René Dubos and Jean Dubos, *The White Plague: Tuberculosis, Man, and Society* (Boston: Little, Brown, 1952), p. 260.

12. *In Memoriam: Leonard Pearson* ([Philadelphia: Univ. of Pennsylvania, 1910]), https://archive.org/details/inmemoriamleonar00np__, pp. 5–9 and 66–70. Beginning in 1893, the BAI produced and distributed freely to state livestock sanitary officials diagnostic materials including tuberculin for testing bovines for BTB and mallein (discovered in 1890) for testing equines for glanders. USDA, *Yearbook of Agriculture, 1906,* pp. 347–54.

13. Myers, *Man's Greatest Victory,* p. 115; J. Arthur Myers and James H. Steele, *Bovine Tuberculosis Control in Man and Animals* (St. Louis: W. H. Green, 1969), pp. 44–45.

14. Jens Madsen to A. D. Melvin, 30 Jan. 1914, Entry 3, Box 337, U.S. BAI Records.

15. William W. Wright to J. R. Mohler, 20 Jan. 1920, Entry 3, Box 340, U.S. BAI Records; Everett B. Miller, "Tuberculous Cattle Problem in the United States to 1917," *Historia Medicinae Veterinariae* 14, no. 1–2 (1989), pp. 15–16; U.S. BAI, *Diseases of Cattle, 1916,* pp. 416–18; Houck, *Bureau of Animal Industry,* pp. 364–66; Myers, *Man's Greatest Victory,* pp. 115, 125.

16. U.S. BAI, *Diseases of Cattle, 1916*, pp. 417–18; Smith, *Conquest of Bovine Tuberculosis*, pp. 7–9; Houck, *Bureau of Animal Industry*, pp. 364–66; Myers, *Man's Greatest Victory*, p. 125. The U.S. National Research Council (*Livestock*, pp. 17–19) noted the probability that an uninfected animal would test positive was less than 2 percent. The probability of an uninfected animal having a positive test depends on the prevalence of the disease. As the disease becomes less common, a positive result under a given test procedure is more likely to be incorrect.

17. Smith, *Conquest of Bovine Tuberculosis*, pp. 18–20; Alan L. Olmstead and Paul W. Rhode, "The 'Tuberculous Cattle Trust': Disease Contagion in an Era of Regulatory Uncertainty," *Journal of Economic History* 64, no. 4 (2005): 929–63.

18. USDA, *Yearbook of Agriculture, 1915*, p. 168; U.S. BAI, *Diseases of Cattle, 1916*, p. 409. According to U.S. BAI, *Report for 1922*, p. 142, "probably 90 per cent of all tuberculosis in swine is from cattle sources."

19. John A. Kiernan and Alexander E. Wight, "Tuberculosis in Livestock, Detection, Control, and Eradication," USDA, *Farmers' Bulletin*, no. 1069, 1929 revised (Washington, DC: U.S. Government Printing Office, 1929), p. 5; U.S. BAI, *Special Report on Diseases of Cattle, 1912 ed.* (Washington, DC: U.S. Government Printing Office, 1912), p. 417; Myers, *Man's Greatest Victory*, p. 222.

20. Alexander E. Wight, "Tuberculosis in Livestock, Detection, Control, and Eradication," USDA, *Farmers' Bulletin*, no. 1069, 1936 revised (Washington, DC: U.S. Government Printing Office, 1936), p. 5; U.S. BAI, *Report for 1908*, pp. 101–2; Myers and Steele, *Bovine Tuberculosis Control*, pp. 256–57, 280–81.

21. *Breeder's Gazette*, 2 Oct. 1901, p. 507; Myers, *Man's Greatest Victory*, pp. 345–46.

22. Miller, "Tuberculous Cattle," p. 35; *New York Times*, 1 June 1904, p. 1; Myers, *Man's Greatest Victory*, pp. 106–9, 200, 211–19, 226; Myers and Steele, *Bovine Tuberculosis Control*, pp. 57–59; Wayne M. Dankner, Norman J. Waecker, Mitchell A. Essey, Kathleen Moser, Muriel Thompson, and Charles E. Davis, "*Mycobacterium bovis* Infections in San Diego: A Clinico-epidemiologic Study of 73 Patients and a Historical Review of a Forgotten Pathogen," *Medicine* 72, no. 1 (1993): 20–24.

23. R. M. Price, "The Bovine Tubercle Bacillus in Human Tuberculosis," *American Journal of the Medical Sciences*, 2nd Ser., 197 (1939), p. 421.

24. Henry L. Coit, "The Origin, General Plan, and Scope of the Medical Milk Commission," in *Proceedings of the First Conference of the Medical Milk Commissions in the United States* (Cincinnati, OH: American Association of Medical Milk Commissions, 1908), pp. 10–17; Manfred J. Waserman, "Henry L. Coit and the Certified Milk Movement in the Development of Modern Pediatrics," *Bulletin of the History of Medicine* 46, no. 4 (1972): 359–90.

25. Fairfield Dairy File, 1914, Entry 3, Box 337, U.S. BAI Records. The Fairfield Dairy in New Jersey was discovered shipping tuberculous cattle to butchers, who were later caught bribing New York City meat inspectors to pass the carcasses. *New York Times,* 27 May 1916, p. 4.

26. In 1920, the premium averaged about 67 percent. Calculated from *Creamery and Milk Plant Monthly,* Feb. 1920, pp. 25–29; Sept. 1920, pp. 27–32.

27. Richard A. Epstein, "Let the Shoemaker Stick to His Last: A Defense of the 'Old' Public Health," *Perspectives in Biology and Medicine* 46 Supplement (2003), pp. S143–44; Andrei Shleifer, "Efficient Regulation," in *Regulation vs. Litigation: Perspectives from Economics and Law,* ed. Daniel P. Kessler (Chicago: Univ. of Chicago Press, 2011), pp. 27–43.

28. Cited in Myers, *Man's Greatest Victory,* pp. 245–46.

29. Ibid., p. 265.

30. USDA, *Yearbook of Agriculture, 1919,* p. 282.

31. Robyn M. Dawes and Richard H. Thaler, "Cooperation," *Journal of Economic Perspectives* 2, no. 3 (1988): 188–90; and Ernst Fehr and Klaus M. Schmidt, "A Theory of Fairness, Competition and Cooperation," *Quarterly Journal of Economics* 114, no. 3 (1999), pp. 838–39.

32. U.S. House of Representatives, *Tuberculosis in Livestock, Hearings on H.R. 6188, a Bill Making Appropriation for the Control and Eradication of Tuberculosis in Live Stock,* 65th Cong., 2nd Sess. (Washington, DC: U.S. Government Printing Office, 1918), p. 10.

33. Austin Peters, "Bovine Tuberculosis in Massachusetts: A History of the Earlier Agitation Concerning It, and Efforts of the State for Its Eradication and Control," in *Tuberculosis in Massachusetts,* ed. Edwin A Locke (Boston: Wright and Potter, 1908), pp. 37–64; C. E. Thorne, "Bovine Tuberculosis," *Bulletin of the Ohio Agricultural Experiment Station,* no. 108 (1899), p. 369.

34. Leonard Pearson and M. P. Ravenel, "Tuberculosis of Cattle," *Pennsylvania Department of Agriculture Bulletin,* no. 75 (1901), pp. 167–200; M. H. Reynolds, "The Problem of Bovine Tuberculosis Control," *American Veterinary Review* 33 (1909), pp. 451–58; Michael E. Teller, *The Tuberculosis Movement: A Public Health Campaign in the Progressive Era* (New York: Greenwood Press, 1988), p. 20; Eric E. Lampard, *The Rise of the Dairy Industry in Wisconsin* (Madison: State Historical Society of Wisconsin, 1963), pp. 188–89; Myers, *Man's Greatest Victory,* pp. 272–79, 283; Daniel E. Salmon "Legislation with Reference to Bovine Tuberculosis," *BAI Bulletin,* no. 28 (Washington, DC: U.S. Government Printing Office, 1901).

35. Myers, *Man's Greatest Victory,* pp. 278–79; Salmon, *Legislation.*

36. Myers, *Man's Greatest Victory,* p. 267; USDA, *Yearbook of Agriculture, 1910,* p. 231.

37. E. M. DuPuis, *Nature's Perfect Food: How Milk Became America's Drink* (New York: New York Univ. Press, 2002), pp. 77–78, 82–83, 254–55, 274–75.

38. John W. Kerr, "Certified Milk and Infants' Milk Depots," in *Milk and Its Relation to the Public Health Public Health,* Marine-Hospital Service of the

United States, Treasury Department, Hygienic Laboratory, *Bulletin,* no. 41 (Washington, DC: U.S. Government Printing Office, 1908), pp. 565–88.

39. Samuel Preston and Michael Haines, *Fatal Years: Child Mortality in Late Nineteenth-Century America* (Princeton, NJ: Princeton Univ. Press, 1991), p. 4; Robert M. Woodbury, "Causal Factors in Infant Mortality: A Statistical Study Based on Investigations in Eight Cities," *U.S. Children's Bureau Bulletin,* no. 142 (Washington, DC: U.S. Government Printing Office, 1925), pp. 88–94, esp. 89; J. M. Eager, "Morbidity and Mortality Statistics as Influenced by Milk," in *Milk and Its Relation to the Public Health Public Health,* Marine-Hospital Service of the United States, Treasury Department, Hygienic Laboratory, *Bulletin,* no. 41 (Washington, DC: U.S. Government Printing Office, 1908), pp. 229–42. Factors other than milk might have played a role in determining these results, but all contemporaries laid most of the blame on the impurities in commercial milk.

40. For the situation the early 1900s, see Charles V. Chapin, *Municipal Sanitation in the United States* (Providence, RI: Snow & Farnham, 1901), pp. 385–420; New York Milk Committee files, Charles E. North papers, Special Collections, National Agricultural Library, Beltsville, MD.

41. U.S. Live Stock Sanitary Association, *Report of Annual Meeting for 1931,* pp. 370–75.

42. Milton J. Rosenau, "Pasteurization," in *Milk and Its Relation to the Public Health,* Marine-Hospital Service of the United States, Treasury Department, Hygienic Laboratory, *Bulletin,* no. 41 (Washington, DC: U.S. Government Printing Office, 1908), pp. 591–628. Later discoveries in fact showed that pasteurization destroyed about 15 to 30 percent of the of the milk's vitamin C and thiamine, but milk is not an important source of these vitamins. Martina Newell-McGloughlin and Edward Re, *The Evolution of Biotechnology: From Natufians to Nanotechnology* (Dordrecht, The Netherlands: Springer, 2006), p. 18.

43. Fuchs and Frank, "Milk Supplies," p. 29.

44. Olmstead and Rhode, "Cattle Trust," pp. 940–42, 954; Thomas R. Pegram, "Public Health and Progressive Dairying in Illinois," *Agricultural History* 65, no. 1 (1991): 36–50; *Chicago Tribune,* 20 Sept. 1914, pp. 1, 3; Illinois General Assembly, *Report of the Joint Committee of Tuberculin Test, 1911* (Springfield, IL: Illinois State Journal Co., 1911); *Evidence Taken Before the Joint Committee on Tuberculin Test, 1911,* vols. 1 and 2 (Springfield, IL: Illinois State Journal Co., 1912).

45. *Breeder's Gazette,* 16 June 1909, p. 1362; Olmstead and Rhode, "Cattle Trust," p. 941.

46. James A. Tobey, *Legal Aspects of Milk Sanitation,* 2nd ed. (Washington, DC: Milk Industry Foundation, 1947), pp. 76–81.

47. *Chicago Tribune,* 19 Feb. 1926, p. 2. The opponents were emboldened in 1926 when the noted French scientist Albert Calmette claimed that BTB represented a minor threat to humans. *Chicago Tribune,* 7 Jan. 1926, p. 7.

48. *Breeder's Gazette,* 27 Aug. 1914, p. 317.

49. S.H. Ward to A.D. Melvin, 25 May 1910; Chief of the Bureau to S. H. Ward, 6 June 1910, Entry 3, Box 337, U.S. BAI Records. The *Elgin Daily News* (1 Oct. 1915, p. 1) noted that although indicted, "Mr. Dorsey continues to do business."

50. *St. Louis Republic,* 1 Sept. 1914, p. 1–2; 20 Sept. 1914, p. 1.

51. J.R. Mohler to Fitts, 9 July 1920, Entry 3, Box 340, U.S. BAI Records; *Elgin Daily News,* 29 Sept. 1915, p. 1.

52. *St. Louis Republic,* 1 Sept. 1914, p. 1; Olmstead and Rhode, "Cattle Trust," p. 944.

53. *St. Louis Republic,* 1 Sept. 1914, p. 1; "Imprisonment for Dealing in Tuberculous Cattle," *American Journal of Veterinary Medicine* 13, no. 5 (1918): 236–37.

54. J.R. Mohler to Fitts, 9 July 1920, Entry 3, Box 340, U.S. BAI Records. A common practice of illicit dealers was to sell the cattle to the buyer and then have the buyer ship them across state lines to himself.

55. Judith Leavitt, *Typhoid Mary: Captive to the Public's Health* (Boston: Beacon Press, 1996), pp. xvii–xviii.

56. *St. Louis Republic,* 20 Sept. 1914, p. 2; *Prairie Farmer,* 15 Jan. 1913, p. 26; 1 Apr. 1914, p. 14; 15 Jan. 1916, p. 14; *Hoard's Dairyman,* 20 June 1913; *Elgin Daily News,* 20 Nov. 1914, p. 4; correspondence in Dorsey files, Entry 3, Boxes 337 and 340, U.S. BAI Records.

57. Olmstead and Rhode, "Cattle Trust," pp. 942–46.

58. Ibid., pp. 947–48

59. Ibid., pp. 947–48; Smith, *Conquest of Bovine Tuberculosis,* pp. 10–11.

60. *Chicago Tribune,* 20 Sept. 1914, p. A11; *Drovers Journal,* 29 Sept. 1915, p. 1. Federal legislation in 1905 made any shipment of diseased cattle across quarantine lines for purposes other than immediate slaughter illegal, but this change did not apply to shipments across state lines in the absence of quarantines. John A. Kiernan, "Tuberculosis Eradication," *American Journal of Veterinary Medicine* 14, no. 3 (1919), p. 104.

61. *Chicago Tribune,* 20 Sept. 1914, part 2, p. 3; USDA, *Weekly News Letter,* 7 May 1919, p. 3; 25 June 1919, p. 2; 30 July 1919, p. 4.

62. U.S. House of Representatives, Agricultural Committee, *Hearings on the Agricultural Appropriation Bill for Fiscal Year 1921,* 66th Cong., 2nd Sess. (Washington, DC: U.S. Government Printing Office, 1920), pp. 179–97, esp. 181–82.

63. Olmstead and Rhode, "Cattle Trust," pp. 950–51; U.S. Department of Justice, *Annual Report of the Attorney General for 1920* (Washington, DC: U.S. Government Printing Office, 1920), p. 778.

64. Jens Madsen to A.D. Melvin, 30 Jan. 1914; 13 Mar. 1915; 31 Mar. 1915; W.H. Lytle to W.D. Hoard, 28 Nov. 1913, Entry 3, Box 340, U.S. BAI Records.

65. Klein and Leffler, "Role of Market Forces."

66. The *Prairie Farmer* (17 May 1919, p. 22) noted that Dorsey had a rule of never cheating a man who lived within twenty miles of Elgin, Illinois. See also *Prairie Farmer,* 5 Apr. 1919, p. 12.

67. U.S. House of Representatives, *Agricultural Appropriation Bill . . . 1921,* pp. 181, 183. *Breeder's Gazette,* 29 Oct. 1914, p. 743; Jason Waterman and William Fowler, "State Laws and Regulations Pertaining to Public Health," years 1917–1922, *U.S. Public Health Report, Supplement,* nos. 37, 38, 42, 43, 45, 47 (1920–1925).

68. C. N. McArthur to W. D. Hoard, 2 Dec. 1913, Entry 3, Box 340, U.S. BAI Records.

69. Centers for Disease Control and Prevention, "*Mycobacterium bovis* (Bovine Tuberculosis) in Humans," Aug. 2011, www.cdc.gov/tb/publications /factsheets/general/mbovis.pdf.

70. Centers for Disease Control and Prevention, "Bovine Tuberculosis— Pennsylvania," *Mortality and Morbidity Weekly Report* 39, no. 12 (1990): 201–13; USDA, *Yearbook of Agriculture, 1942,* pp. 237–49, esp. 242.

71. Dormandy, *White Death,* p. 329.

72. D. G. Pritchard, "A Century of Bovine Tuberculosis 1888–1988: Conquest and Controversy," *Journal of Comparative Pathology* 99 (1988), p. 371. According to Herbert M. Sommers, "In 1917 it was estimated . . . that approximately 25 percent of the deaths from tuberculosis in adult human beings was caused by *M. bovis*" in the United States; from "Disease Due to Mycobacteria Other Than *Mycobacterium tuberculosis,*" in *Tuberculosis,* ed. Guy P. Youmans (Philadelphia: W. B. Saunders, 1979), p. 388. Also see Lewis S. Forbes, "The Programme for the Eradication of Tuberculosis in the United States of America and Some Possible Applications in Africa," *Bulletin of Epizootic Diseases of Africa* 12 (1964): 429–35; Lewis noted that "in the early days, 20% of cases were due to the bovine bacillus" (p. 431).

73. Calvin W. Schwabe, *Cattle, Priests, and Progress in Medicine* (Minneapolis: Univ. of Minnesota Press, 1978), p. 190; Schwabe, *Veterinary Medicine,* p. 48. Case studies show very high infection rates among populations known to have consumed milk from tuberculous cows. Ingela Sjogren and Ian Sutherland, "Studies of Tuberculosis in Man in Relation to Infection in Cattle," *Tubercle* 56 (1974), pp. 113–27.

74. Dankner et al., "*Mycobacterium,*" pp. 21–22.

75. Myers and Steele, *Bovine Tuberculosis Control,* p. 264, and telephone interview with James Steele, 1 Aug. 2002. Franklin Top later served as head of the Department of Preventive Medicine and Environmental Health at the University of Iowa. Phillip R. Carter, "Bovine Tuberculosis in Germany," *Medical Bulletin* 1 (1946): 65–70; M. Daniels and P. D'Arcy, "Tuberculosis in the British Zone in Germany," *Medical Bulletin* 5 (1948): 29–54.

76. Dankner et al., *"Mycobacterium,"* pp. 11–37; and telephone interview with Wayne Dankner, 9 Aug. 2002.

77. J. Arthur Myers, *Tuberculosis: A Half Century of Study and Conquest* (St. Louis, MO: W. H. Green, 1970), p. 235; J. M. Grange and C. H. Collins, "Bovine Tubercle Bacilli and Disease," *Epidemiology and Infection* 99, no. 2 (1987), p. 227; William C. Harvey and Harry Hill, *Milk: Production and Control* (London: H. K. Lewis, 1936), p. 26; Chester L. Roadhouse and James L. Henderson, *Milk Market,* 2nd ed. (New York: McGraw-Hill, 1950), pp. 65–66; Myers, *Man's Greatest Victory,* 219–29; U.S. Live Stock Sanitary Association, *Report of Annual Meeting for 1942,* pp. 75–78.

78. Arnold R. Rich, *The Pathogenesis of Tuberculosis* (Springfield, IL: Charles C. Thomas, 1944), p. 58.

79. Price, "Bovine Tubercle," pp. 411–27.

80. Louis Cobbett, *The Causes of Tuberculosis* (Cambridge: Cambridge Univ. Press, 1917), p. 11. Cobbett then disregarded his own intuition and evidence and accepted official sources for his published estimates (pp. 657–58).

81. R. J. Anderson, "The Public Health Importance of Animal Tuberculosis," *Annals of the New York Academy of Sciences* 70 (1958), pp. 632–35.

82. DEFRA, *Animal Health 2004: The Report of the Chief Veterinary Officer* (London: DEFRA, May 2005), p. 49.

83. A. Stanley Griffth and J. Smith, "Types of Tubercule Bacilli in Pulmonary Tuberculosis in North-East Scotland," *Lancet* 236, no. 6106 (1940), pp. 291–94; "Bovine Tuberculosis in the Lungs," *Lancet* 249, no. 6457 (1947): 756–57. Quotation from Jón Sigurdsson, *Studies on the Risk of Infection with Bovine Tuberculosis to the Rural Population* (London: Oxford Univ. Press, 1945), p. 98.

84. There was a similar rural-urban disparity in the rate of *M. bovis* among adult pulmonary TB suffers in the Netherlands. Price, "Bovine Tubercle," p. 421; "Bovine Tuberculosis in the Lungs"; "Distribution of Bovine Tuberculosis in Man," *Lancet* 224, no. 5789 (1934): 317–18; Sigurdsson, *Studies on the Risk of Infection,* pp. 73–75, 93–102, 207.

85. Sigurdsson, *Studies on the Risk of Infection,* pp. 32–33, 43–59.

86. Smith, *Conquest of Bovine Tuberculosis,* p. 33; Grove and Hetzel, *Vital Statistics,* pp. 559–603; U.S. Bureau of the Census, *Mortality,* pp. 16, 27.

87. Smith, *Conquest of Bovine Tuberculosis,* p. 33; Grove and Hetzel, *Vital Statistics,* pp. 559–603.

CHAPTER 11   *The Eradication of Texas Fever*

1. USDA, *Yearbook of Agriculture, 1942,* p. 574; Houck, *Bureau of Animal Industry,* pp. 326–31; Cooper Curtice, "On the Extermination of the Cattle-Tick and the Disease Spread by It," *Journal of Comparative Medicine and Veterinary Archives* 17, no. 9 (1896): 46–55.

2. H. A. Morgan of Tennessee and other scientists working for state agencies also made important advances in understanding the tick's life-cycle. Tait Butler to James Wilson, 1 Jan. 1906, Entry 1, Box 2, U.S. BAI Records; U.S. BAI, *Diseases of Cattle, 1916*, pp. 485–94; U.S. BAI, *Report for 1910*, pp. 255–65; Schwabe, *Veterinary Medicine*, p. 516.

3. Although many give Curtice the credit for these developments, he maintained that the North Carolina Commissioner of Agriculture, S. L. Patterson, initiated the momentum within the USDA to consider eradication in 1899. Strom, "Texas Fever," p. 61; U.S. BAI, *Diseases of Cattle, 1916*, pp. 485–94; Houck, *Bureau of Animal Industry*, pp. 326–31; O. H. Graham and J. L. Hourrigan, "Eradication Programs for Arthropod Parasites of Livestock," *Journal of Medical Entomology* 13, no. 6 (1977), p. 632.

4. Scientists also experimented with inoculating imported animals with varying success to induce a mild case of the disease. Inoculation made little sense in the long run because it did not destroy the ticks, which independent of the infections their carried could severely burden cattle productivity. Strom, "Texas Fever," p. 56; Houck, *Bureau of Animal Industry*, pp. 322–24; U.S. BAI, *Diseases of Cattle, 1916*, p. 483. Inoculation was of great interest to practical cattlemen: *Breeder's Gazette*, 24 May 1899, pp. 623–24; 21 June 1899, p. 744; 19 July 1899, pp. 60–62; 15 Nov. 1898, pp. 596–98; 15 Aug. 1890, p. 177.

5. U.S. BAI, *Reports for 1893 and 1894*, p. 12; *Reports for 1895 and 1896*, pp. 11, 109–18; *Report for 1904*, p. 19; USDA, *Yearbook of Agriculture, 1898*, pp. 453–72; *Breeder's Gazette*, 2 June 1897, p. 417; Strom, "Texas Fever," pp. 55–56, 63; *Hoard's Dairyman*, 8 May 1896, p. 227; 24 July 1896, p. 449.

6. Arsenic indiscriminately dumped near dipping vats still contaminates the landscape. In addition, cattle ticks eventually developed resistance to many poisons, prompting a search for more sustainable control methods. BAI, *Operations for 1900*, p. 200; Stalheim, *Winning of Animal Health*, pp. 140–43; Houck, *Bureau of Animal Industry*, pp. 95, 324–26, 333–35; Strom, "Texas Fever," p. 63.

7. William P. Ellenberger and Robert M. Chapin, "Cattle-Fever Ticks and Methods of Eradication," USDA, *Farmers' Bulletin*, no. 1057 (Washington, DC: USDA, 1919, revised 1932); Houck, *Bureau of Animal Industry*, pp. 330–35; U.S. BAI, "Proceedings of a Conference of Federal and State Representatives to Consider Plans for the Eradication of the Cattle Tick, Held at Nashville, Tenn. December 5 and 6, 1906," *BAI Bulletin*, no. 97 (Washington, DC: U.S. Government Printing Office, 1907), pp. 20–27; Strom, "Texas Fever," pp. 57, 63–70; USDA, *Yearbook of Agriculture, 1942*, pp. 572–78; Louis A. Klein, "Methods of Eradicating Cattle Ticks," *BAI Circular*, no. 110 (Washington, DC: U.S. Government Printing Office, 1907), pp. 5–16.

8. Strom, *Catfish Bait*, p. 140; B. W. Kilgore, ed., *Proceedings of the Seventh Annual Convention of the Southern States Association of the Commissioners of Agriculture,*

held at Richmond, Virginia, 23–25 Nov. 1905 (Raleigh, NC: Edwards & Broughton, 1906), pp. 23–34, 95–96, 102–8; Black, *Animal Health*, pp. 16–17; *Atlanta Constitution*, 14 Feb. 1906, p. 11; 15 Feb. 1906, p. 6; 21 Feb. 1906, p. 4; *Washington Post*, 16 Feb. 1906, p. 4. For others associations petitioning for federal intervention, see documents accompanying Tait Butler to James Wilson, 1 Jan. 1906, Entry 1, Box 2, U.S. BAI Records.

9. John Ettling, *The Germ of Laziness: Rockefeller Philanthropy and Public Health in the New South* (Cambridge, MA: Harvard Univ. Press, 1981); Garland L. Brinkley, "The Economic Impact of Disease in the American South, 1860–1940," Ph.D. diss. (Univ. of California at Davis, 1994); Hoyt Bleakley, "Disease and Development: Evidence from Hookworm Eradication in the American South," *Quarterly Journal of Economics* 122, no. 1 (2007): 73–117; Daniel Sledge, "War, Tropical Disease, and the Emergence of National Public Health Capacity in the United States," *Studies in American Political Development* 26 , no. 2 (2012): 125–62.

10. USDA, *Yearbook of Agriculture, 1942*, p. 574; Houck, *Bureau of Animal Industry*, pp. 326–31; Curtice, "Extermination," pp. 46–55; U.S. BAI, "Proceedings . . . Cattle Tick," pp. 10–20, 28–35; Harry Goding, "State Laws and Court Decisions Relating to Cattle-Tick Eradication," USDA, *Department Circular*, no. 184 (Washington, DC: U.S. Government Printing Office, 1921); U.S. BAI, *Report for 1906*, pp. 101–12; *Report for 1910*, p. 256. Strom offers a slightly different accounting of the states with adequate and insufficient legal structures in *Catfish Bait*, pp. 76–81, 141–42.

11. For political reasons, eradication also began in some pockets well south of the quarantine line, particularly in Georgia, Alabama, and Mississippi. U.S. BAI, *Report for 1910*, map, p. 258.

12. Strom, *Catfish Bait*, pp. 82–83, 76–104, 139–64.

13. U.S. Live Stock Sanitary Association, *Report of Annual Meeting for 1920*, p. 137.

14. John A. Kiernan, "The Most Successful Methods of Tick Eradication," in *Report of the Seventeenth Annual Meeting of the United States Live Stock Sanitary Association*, held in Chicago, IL, 2–4 Dec. 1913 (Chicago: 1914), p. 166.

15. Work also progressed rapidly in California. The passage of stronger state legislation in 1907 aided eradication, and by 1916 the entire state was released from quarantine. U.S. Live Stock Sanitary Association, *Report of Annual Meeting for 1913*, pp. 166–67; "Veterinary Profession Receives Official Recognition in Tennessee," *American Veterinary Review* 39 (1911): 381–82; U.S. BAI, "Proceedings . . . Cattle Tick," pp. 12–20; Houck, *Bureau of Animal Industry*, pp. 330–31.

16. U.S. Live Stock Sanitary Association, *Report of Annual Meeting for 1913*, pp. 163–84; *Report of Annual Meeting for 1930*; A. D. Melvin, "Some Results of Cattle-Tick Eradication," *BAI Circular*, no. 196 (Washington, DC: U.S. Government Printing Office, 1912), p. 4. The work in Hinds County had its

hiccups. In early 1914, the Mississippi State Legislature passed legislation empowering the Hinds County supervisors to pay H.E. McIntosh for seven cattle killed as a result of "drinking a poisonous solution that flowed from a dipping vat." This and other cases reflected the normal workings of an orderly grievance process. Mississippi, *Laws of the State of Mississippi Passed at a Regular Session of the Mississippi Legislature,* January 6, 1914 to March 28, 1914, and an *Extraordinary Session* held in June 1913, Chapter 351, House Bill No. 653 (Memphis, TN: E.R. Clarke & Bros., 1914), pp.431–32, Strom, *Catfish Bait,* pp.52, 82; USDA, *Report of the Secretary for 1919,* p.114.

17. U.S. Live Stock Sanitary Association, *Report of Annual Meeting for 1918,* pp.26–28, and *Report of Annual Meeting for 1933,* pp.524–25.

18. U.S. BAI, "Proceedings . . . Cattle Tick," pp.15–17.

19. Georgia passed a statewide mandatory eradication bill in 1918. U.S. Live Stock Sanitary Association, *Report of Annual Meeting for 1914,* pp.67–77. Strom, "Texas Fever," p.70; *Catfish Bait,* pp.129–40.

20. U.S. Live Stock Sanitary Association, *Report of Annual Meeting for 1920,* p.136; *Report of Annual Meeting for 1913,* p.220; *Report of Annual Meeting for 1918,* pp.26–28.

21. Graham and Hourrigan, "Eradication Programs," pp.635–36; Julian Aguilar, "South Texas Fever Tick Infestation Grows," *Texas Tribune,* 1 Feb. 2010, www.texastribune.org/2010/02/01/south-texas-fever-tick-infestation -grows/.

22. U.S. House of Representatives, Committee on Agriculture, *Hearing on Agricultural Appropriations Bill, HR 13679,* 63th Cong., 2nd Sess. (Washington, DC: U.S. Government Printing Office, 1914), pp.38–40; "Congress Asked to Prohibit Movement of Ticky Cattle Beyond the Quarantine Area," *American Journal of Veterinary Medicine* 9, no. 2 (Feb. 1914): 130–31; USDA, *Weekly News Letter,* 14 Jan. 1914, pp.1–2; USDA, *Yearbook of Agriculture, 1942,* p.210; *Congressional Record,* 14 Apr. 1926, p.7452.

23. *Congressional Record,* 14 Apr. 1926, pp.7452–53.

24. *Congressional Record,* 14 Apr. 1926, p.7455; USDA, *Yearbook of Agriculture, 1926,* p.80.

25. U.S. Live Stock Sanitary Association, *Report of Annual Meeting for 1913,* pp.163–84; Strom, *Catfish Bait,* pp.50–54; USDA, *A Tick-Free South* (Washington, DC: USDA, 1917); USDA, *The Story of the Cattle Tick: What Every Southern Child Should Know about Cattle Ticks* (Washington, DC: U.S. Government Printing Office, 1922). The latter source also appeared in Spanish.

26. Strom, *Catfish Bait,* p.50; Strom, "Texas Fever," p.65.

27. The BAI's multipronged educational approach captured many of the ideas recommended today. Gershon Feder and Sara Savastano, "The Role of Opinion Leaders in the Diffusion of New Knowledge: The Case of Integrated Pest Management," World Bank Policy Research Working Paper No. 3916 (May 2006); D. Sunding and David Zilberman, "The Agricultural

Innovation Process: Research and Technology Adoption in Changing Agriculture Sector," in *Handbook of Agricultural Economics,* vol. 1A, in *Agricultural Production,* ed. Bruce Gardner and Gordon Rausser (Amsterdam: North Holland/Elsevier, 2001), pp. 207–26.

28. George F. Gee, *The Economic Importance of Cattle Tick in Australia* (Canberra, Australia: Bureau of Agricultural Economics, 1959), p. 22.

29. Strom, *Catfish Bait,* pp. 2–3.

30. As North Carolina State Veterinarian Tait Butler noted in 1905, a farmer did not have to be an exporter to benefit from eradication. All farmers would have received higher prices in local markets for tick-free cattle, and all would have benefited from more productive animals whether or not they sold them or their products. Other factors may have made small-scale farmers more inclined to oppose eradication. Coordination costs would have been higher in areas with many small farms, and investing in eradication would have been less advantageous to farmers with less access to credit, who thus faced higher implicit interest rates. Kilgore, *Proceedings,* p. 31; Strom, *Catfish Bait,* p. 83.

31. Strom, *Catfish Bait,* pp. 3–4, 62–63; Strom, "Texas Fever," pp. 68–71; Shawn Everett Kantor, "Razorbacks, Ticky Cows, and the Closing of the Georgia Open Range: The Dynamics of Institutional Change Uncovered," *Journal of Economic History* 51, no. 4 (1991): 861–86.

32. In the first few years in Alabama, resources were devoted exclusively to stock-law counties, but coverage soon expanded to counties without such laws. Alabama State Veterinarian, *Annual Report, 1907* (Montgomery, AL: 1908), pp. 3–5.

33. John R. Mohler, "Texas Fever (Otherwise Known as Tick Fever, Splenetic Fever or Southern Cattle Fever), with Methods for Its Prevention," *BAI Bulletin,* no. 78 (Washington, DC: U.S. Government Printing Office, 1905), p. 45; Georgia Department of Agriculture, "Annual Report for 1921," Serial No. 88, *Quarterly Bulletin* (Jan.–Mar. 1922), p. 47.

34. J. Crawford King Jr., "The Closure of the Southern Range: An Exploratory Study," *Journal of Southern History* 48, no. 1 (1982), pp. 54, 60; U.S. BAI, *Report for 1910,* pp. 259–60.

35. U.S. Live Stock Sanitary Association, *Report of Annual Meeting for 1914,* pp. 177–80.

36. *New Orleans Times-Picayune,* 17 Aug. 1912, p. 15.

37. J. Stanley Clark, "Texas Fever in Oklahoma," *Chronicles of Oklahoma* 29 (1951–1952): 433–36; *Atlanta Constitution,* 31 May 1920, p. 4.

38. North Carolina Department of Agriculture, *Biennial Report from Dec. 1, 1916 to Nov. 30, 1918* (Raleigh, NC: Edwards & Broughton, 1918), p. 13; *Biennial Report from Dec. 1, 1918 to Dec. 30, 1920* (Raleigh, NC: Edwards & Broughton, 1920), p. 59.

39. *Jeffersonian*, 8 June 1916, p. 6; 15 June 1916, pp. 9, 11. Watson "owned several splendid farms, totaling 9000 acres of the best land in McDuffie County." William W. Brewton, *Life of Thomas E. Watson* (Binghamton, AL: Wall-Ballou, 1926), p. 359.

40. *Macon Telegraph*, 4 June 1917, p. 4; *Augusta Chronicle*, 12 July 1916, p. 6; 2 Dec. 1916, p. 4; Walter J. Brown, *J. J. Brown and Thomas E. Watson: Georgia Politics, 1912–1928* (Macon, GA: Mercer Univ. Press, 1988), pp. 60–61; C. Vann Woodward, *Tom Watson: Agrarian Rebel* (Savannah, GA: Beehive Press, 1938), pp. 373–89.

41. *Atlanta Constitution*, 24 Apr. 1919, p. 6; 24 Mar. 1922, p. 16; 26 Mar. 1992; 22 June 1922, pp. 5–6; 23 June 1922, p. 6; 27 June 1922, p. 3; 15 July 1922, p. 1; Georgia Department of Agriculture, "Annual Report for 1921," pp. 47–49.

42. Mann Carter's economic stature and activities hardly fit the conventional uses of the term "yeoman." He owned 4,000 acres of land, 200 head of cattle, about 50 hogs, hired a sizable workforce, leased land to tenants, ran a lumber business, and lent money to other farmers. Strom, *Catfish Bait*, pp. 61, 74ff.

43. Strom, *Catfish Bait*, pp. 1, 63–75, 89, 93–95, 162, 177, quotation from p. 95; Holly Hope, *Dip That Tick: Texas Tick Fever Eradication in Arkansas, 1907–1943* (Little Rock: Arkansas Historic Preservation Program, 2005), p. 11; Houck, *Bureau of Animal Industry*, p. 339. In the Carter case, twenty others were charged for conspiracy.

44. Charles E. Munroe, "Regulation of Explosives in the United States with Especial Reference to the Administration of the Explosives Act of Oct. 6, 1917," U.S. Bureau of Mines *Bulletin*, no. 198 (Washington, DC: U.S. Government Printing Office, 1921), pp. 22–25.

45. USDA, Office of Solicitor, *Laws Applicable to the United States Department of Agriculture, 1908* (Washington, DC: U.S. Government Printing Office, 1908), pp. 111–13.

46. *Washington Post*, 12 June 1890, p. 1; U.S. BAI, *Report for 1905*, pp. 348–49. There were several prosecutions outside the South under this law. As examples, in 1907 a Wyoming rancher, Daniel Donoahue, was convicted of bludgeoning a BAI scab inspector, and several packinghouse employees were convicted of assaulting BAI meat inspectors circa 1907 and 1908. USDA, *Annual Report for 1908*, pp. 804–5.

47. Strom, *Catfish Bait*, pp. 2–3.

48. *Breeder's Gazette*, 30 Aug. 1905, p. 365.

49. *Atlanta Constitution*, 19 Oct. 1923, p. 18; 11 Feb. 1923, p. A4.

50. As an example of the legal strife, from January to October 1913, Mississippi prosecuted 190 quarantine violators, winning 118 convictions. USDA, *Report of the Secretary for 1919*, p. 114; *Atlanta Constitution*, 22 July 1922, p. 1; Clark, "Texas Fever," pp. 434–35.

51. U.S. BAI, *Report for 1897*, pp. 98–165; *Report for 1899*, pp. 102–25; *Report for 1902*, pp. 45–61; A. C. Kirkwood, "History, Biology and Control of Sheep Scab," *Parasitology Today* 2, no. 11 (1986): 302–7; USDA, *Yearbook of Agriculture, 1942*, p. 904; *Idaho Daily Statesman*, 11 Aug. 1905, p. 3.

52. U.S. BAI, *Report for 1900*, pp. 69–86; *Report for 1903*, pp. 41–53; *Report for 1904*, pp. 447–60; *Report for 1905*, pp. 19, 322–27, 334; *Report for 1906*, pp. 24–25; Graham and Hourrigan, "Eradication Programs," p. 640; USDA, *Yearbook of Agriculture, 1915*, pp. 159–72, esp. maps between pp. 180 and 181.

53. *San Antonio (TX) Daily Express*, 30 June 1904. *Aberdeen (SD) Daily News*, 6 July 1905, p. 4; 1 Aug. 1905, p. 6. *Fort Worth Telegram*, 5 Aug. 1905, p. 2; 15 Aug. 1905, p. 6. *Dallas Morning News*, 22 June 1905, p. 4. U.S. Live Stock Sanitary Association, *Report of Annual Meeting for 1913*, p. 173.

54. August Mayer, "The Cattle Tick in Relation to Southern Agriculture," USDA, *Farmers' Bulletin*, no. 261 (Washington, DC: U.S. Government Printing Office, 1906), pp. 17–22; Wilmon Newell and M. S. Dougherty, "The Cattle Tick," The State Crop Pest Commission of Louisiana *Circular*, no. 10, 1906; John R. Mohler, "Texas or Tick Fever and Its Prevention," USDA, *Farmers' Bulletin*, no. 258 (Washington, DC: U.S. Government Printing Office, 1906), pp. 21–23; U.S. BAI, *Report for 1910*, p. 255; U.S. Live Stock Sanitary Association, *Report of Annual Meeting for 1914*, pp. 67–77; *New York Times*, 4 Dec. 1912, p. 1. A decade later Mohler changed the details of his calculations, but the totals remained roughly the same. U.S. BAI, *Diseases of Cattle, 1916*, pp. 481–84, 505–6.

55. Houck, *Bureau of Animal Industry*, p. 333; USDA, *Yearbook of Agriculture, 1942*, p. 576; Mayer, "Cattle Tick," pp. 17–22. August Mayer's 1906 estimate (cited previously) that ticks cost the South from $100 to $200 million annually is an example of muddled accounting that has been uncritically reproduced.

56. The loss of Northern cattle was minor in most years after nearly two decades of segregating Southern animals in transit. The hypothetical losses were potentially large.

57. U.S. BAI, *Report for 1907*, p. 333.

58. USDA, *Yearbook of Agriculture, 1922*, pp. 342–43; Houck, *Bureau of Animal Industry*, pp. 333, 338–39. The increase noted by Houck would have been due to both static effects and dynamic effects. In addition, some of the areas cleared early probably had climates more conducive to milk production.

59. U.S. BAI, *Diseases of Cattle, 1916*, p. 505. As an indication of the conservative nature of Mohler's estimates, both Melvin and Houck reckoned much greater price difference. U.S. BAI, *Report for 1909*, pp. 14–16; Houck, *Bureau of Animal Industry*, p. 333.

60. Mohler, "Texas or Tick Fever," pp. 21–23.

61. New ideas were on the horizon. In the late 1930s, Edward Knipling and Raymond Bushland, entomologists at the USDA's Menard, Texas, labora-

tory, envisioned controlling another cattle parasite, the screwworm, through the sterile insect technique (SIT). The concept was to generate and release massive populations of infertile males to disrupt the pest's reproductive cycle. According to the *New York Times*, 11 Jan. 1970, p. 220, many scientists considered SIT " 'the single most original thought in the 20th century.' " It required refinement to become practical. In a campaign initiated in 1957, the USDA employed SIT to eradicate screwworms from the United States by 1966. It has been successfully applied to control other pests, but not cattle ticks. Screwworm Eradication Program Records, Special Collections, National Agricultural Library (Beltsville, MD), last modified 19 May 2014, http://specialcollections.nal.usda.gov/guide-collections/screwworm-eradication-program-records.

62. U.S. BAI, *Diseases of Cattle, 1916*, p. 505; Melvin, "Some Results," pp. 3–4; USDA, *Yearbook of Agriculture, 1922*, pp. 321–22.

63. Aguilar, "South Texas Fever Tick."

64. Graham and Hourrigan, "Eradication Programs," pp. 634–36; Raymond A. Dietrich and L. Gary Adams, *Potential Animal Health Concerns Relative to Cattle Fever Ticks, Classical Swine Fever, and Bovine Brucellosis—With Special Emphasis on Texas* (College Station: Texas Agricultural Experiment Station, 2000), pp. 2–3; A. Flores, "The Continuing Fight against Cattle Ticks," *Agricultural Research* 54 (2006): 8–9; Roberta Duhaime, "Surveillance Requirements of Cattle Fever Tick Outbreak," *NAHSS Outlook*, Dec. 2009, pp. 1–7, http://naldc.nal.usda.gov/download/40159/PDF; Aguilar, "South Texas Fever Tick."

65. Schwabe, *Veterinary Medicine*, pp. 420–21; Alan R. Walker, "Eradication and Control of Livestock Ticks: Biological, Economic and Social Perspectives," *Parasitology* 138, no. 8 (2011): 945–59; Graham and Hourrigan, "Eradication Programs," pp. 629–58; Morton D. Winsberg, *Modern Breeds of Cattle in Argentina* (Lawrence, KS: Center of Latin American Studies, 1968), p. 22.

66. Southern leaders connected tick eradication with the spread of the weevil in their early overtures to Congress for federal funding. Kilgore, *Proceedings*, pp. 95–96, 103.

67. Mohler, "Texas Fever;" "Texas or Tick Fever."

68. *New Orleans Times-Picayune*, 18 June 1917, p. 1.

69. We do not know the ratio of inspections to dippings, but our procedure overstates farmer costs because inspections were cheaper than dippings.

CHAPTER 12   *An Impossible Undertaking*

1. Giuliana Moda, "Non-technical Constraints to Eradication: The Italian Experience," *Veterinary Microbiology* 112 (2006): 253–58.

2. Smith, *Conquest of Bovine Tuberculosis*, p. 12.

3. Myers and Steele, *Bovine Tuberculosis Control*, pp. 256–60. The BAI's model for BTB eradication was also adapted for other campaigns such as the fight against brucellosis in the United States and around the world.

4. USDA, *Yearbook of Agriculture, 1910*, pp. 231–42.

5. Fowler, *Men, Meat, and Miracles*, pp. 113–18; Thomas E. Wilson, "The Economic Importance of Eradicating Tuberculosis," *Journal of the American Veterinary Medical Association* 61, no. 14 (1922): 55–62.

6. U.S. House of Representatives, *Agricultural Appropriation Bill . . . 1921*, p. 215.

7. Alan L. Olmstead and Paul W. Rhode, "An Impossible Undertaking: The Eradication of Bovine Tuberculosis in the United States," *Journal of Economic History* 64, no. 3 (2004): 751.

8. USDA, *Yearbook of Agriculture, 1918*, pp. 215–20; Myers and Steele, *Bovine Tuberculosis Control*, p. 75.

9. U.S. House of Representatives, *Tuberculosis in Livestock*, pp. 17–24; Smith, *Conquest of Bovine Tuberculosis*, pp. 13–15; Myers, *Man's Greatest Victory*, p. 295. The economics literature has emphasized the capture of regulators by industry; here, the regulators reversed the process, inducing the industry to adopt their agenda.

10. Olmstead and Rhode, "Impossible Undertaking," pp. 751–52.

11. Ibid., p. 752.

12. Smith, *Conquest of Bovine Tuberculosis*, p. 28; USDA, *Yearbook of Agriculture, 1926*, p. 182.

13. U.S. House of Representatives, *Message of the President to Congress, Dec. 7, 1926*, House Doc. No. 483, 69th Cong., 2nd Sess. (Washington, DC: U.S. Government Printing Office, 1926), p. 7; *Congressional Record*, 8 Dec. 1926, p. 78; U.S. House of Representatives, *Communication from the President of the United States Transmitting Supplemental Estimate of Appropriation for the Department of Agriculture Amounting to $500,000 for the Fiscal Year 1930 for an Additional Amount for the Eradication of Tuberculosis in Animals*, House Doc. No. 476, 70th Cong., 2nd Sess. (Washington, DC: U.S. Government Printing Office, 1928).

14. Olmstead and Rhode, "Impossible Undertaking," pp. 752–56.

15. U.S. House of Representatives, *Agricultural Department Appropriation Bill for 1939*, 75th Cong., 3rd Sess. (Washington, DC: U.S. Government Printing Office, 1938), pp. 242–45.

16. Brucellosis is a bacterial disease that reduces milk production, induces abortions in cattle, and causes undulant fever in humans. In 1934, roughly one in ten U.S. bovines were infected; by 2009, the contagion had been eliminated from the U.S. cattle population. USDA, *Yearbook of Agriculture, 1942*, p. 505; U.S. Animal and Plant Health Inspection Service (APHIS), *National Bovine Brucellosis Surveillance Plan* (Washington, DC: USDA, 2012), p. 3.

17. Olmstead and Rhode, "Impossible Undertaking," pp. 756–58.

18. Smith, *Conquest of Bovine Tuberculosis,* p. 29; U.S. BAI, *Status of Bovine Tuberculosis Eradication on Area Basis* (Washington, DC: U.S. Government Printing Office), various issues.

19. Olmstead and Rhode, "Impossible Undertaking," pp. 758–60.

20. U.S Agricultural Research Service, "Why Tuberculosis in Livestock is Increasing," *ARS,* no. 91-21 (Washington, DC: USDA, 1960), pp. 1–3; Smith, *Conquest of Bovine Tuberculosis,* p. 48; U.S. National Research Council, *Livestock,* pp. 36–39. In recent years, when meat inspectors discover tuberculous animals, the authorities "depopulate" the entire herd.

21. Urban milk wagon drivers also resorted to violence. As an example, in 1925 at least eleven people were indicted for fifty urban dynamite attacks. *Chicago Tribune,* 4 Jan. 1924, p. 3; 20 Jan. 1924, p. A7; 21 Jan. 1925, p. 15; 29 Nov. 1925, p. 3; 2 Dec. 1925, p. 4; 10 Dec. 1925, p. 24; 5 Nov. 1926, p. 3; 13 Jan. 1927, p. 15; 25 Dec. 1927, p. 4.

22. Robert D. Johnston, *The Radical Middle Class: Populist Democracy and the Question of Capitalism in Progressive Era Portland, Oregon* (Princeton, NJ: Princeton Univ. Press, 2002), pp. 197–213. The loss of loved ones or valued colleagues to infectious diseases similarly drove many proponents of BTB control measures. John A. Kiernan himself suffered from tuberculosis, making his professional mission personal.

23. Dormandy, *White Death,* pp. 344–45. American Medical Liberty League materials in file 15, Box 49 and files 1–4, Box 50, in Historical Health Fraud and Alternative Medicine Collection, American Medical Association Archives. James Colgrove, *State of Immunity: The Politics of Vaccination in Twentieth-Century America* (Berkeley: Univ. of California Press, 2006), pp. 52–61.

24. Alan L. Olmstead and Paul W. Rhode, "Not on My Farm! Farmer Resistance to the Tuberculin-Testing Program to Eradicate Bovine Tuberculosis in the United States, 1893–1941," *Journal of Economic History* 67, no. 3 (2007): 768–809, esp. 784–85; U.S. Senate, *Tubercular Infection in Animals: Methods of Treatment of Breeders and Dairymen in the Enforcement of Regulations for the Elimination of Bovine Tuberculosis,* Senate Doc. No. 85, 70th Cong., 1st Sess. (Washington, DC: U.S. Government Printing Office, 1928); various documents in Box 11, file B, and Box 88, files 1–3, Carter Glass Papers, University of Virginia Special Collections.

25. Iowa Department of Agriculture, *Laws Relating to Bovine Tuberculosis Eradication, Including Amendments by the Forty-Third General Assembly, Effective July 4, 1929* (Des Moines, IA, 1929), pp. 2–14; Myers, *Man's Greatest Victory,* pp. 363–64.

26. Jan Choate, *Disputed Ground: Farm Groups That Opposed the New Deal Agricultural Program* (Jefferson, NC: McFarland, 2002), p. 44; Roland A. White, *Milo Reno: Farmers Union Pioneer, The Story of a Man and a Movement* (New York: Arno Press, 1975/1941), pp. 53–55; Olmstead and Rhode, "Not

on My Farm!" pp. 786–87; George J. Ormsby Papers, Iowa State University Special Collections, Box 2, file E.

27. Olmstead and Rhode, "Not on My Farm!" pp. 784–85; Howard R. Smith to J. A. Barger, 3 Nov. 1931, Entry 3, Box 373, U.S. BAI Records; Howard R. Smith, *Ridding the Nation of Tuberculosis in Livestock* (Chicago: National Live Stock Exchange, 1931); various documents in Box 1, files 1–5, Howard R. Smith papers, Michigan State Univ. Archives and Historical Collections.

28. Joseph F. Wall, "The Iowa Farmer in Crisis, 1920–1936," *Annals of Iowa*, 3rd series, 47, no. 2 (1983), p. 124. For examples of the opposition of the Farmers Holiday movements to the BTB program, see *Farm Holiday News*, 16 Apr. 1934, p. 2; 1 May 1934, p. 2.

29. John L. Shover, *Cornbelt Rebellion: The Farmers' Holiday Association* (Urbana: Univ. of Illinois Press, 1965), p. 29; Frank D. DiLeva, "Frantic Farmers Fight Law," *Annals of Iowa* 32 (1953): 81–109.

30. For a fuller treatment of the Iowa Cow War, including the role of Norman Baker's inflammatory radio broadcasts, see Olmstead and Rhode, "Not on My Farm!" pp. 785–94.

31. John R. Mohler (Chief of BAI) to his agents, 23 Mar. 1933, Entry 3, Box 375, U.S. BAI Records.

32. Munce, "Tampering," 29 Mar. 1932, Entry 3, Box 375, U.S. BAI Records. In addition to tampering with test to produce reactions, others assembled large herds of infected cattle to capture the generous payments. Olmstead and Rhode, "Not on My Farm!" pp. 796–97.

33. Olmstead and Rhode, "Not on My Farm!" p. 787.

34. *Fresno Bee*, 13 Dec. 1934, p. A4; 20 Dec. 1934, pp. B1–B2; 30 Dec. 1934, p. B2; 10 Jan. 1935, p. A2.

35. Olmstead and Rhode, "Not on My Farm!" pp. 794–800; Smith, *Conquest of Bovine Tuberculosis*, pp. 31, 48; Foster to John R. Mohler, 21 Jan. 1929, Entry 3, Box 356, U.S. BAI Records.

36. *Panther v. Dept. of Ag. Iowa*, 211 Iowa 868 (20 Jan. 1931).

37. Olmstead and Rhode, "Not on My Farm!" pp. 798–802.

38. Kiernan and Wight, "Tuberculosis," p. 2. This estimate is likely a lower-bound figure.

39. USDA, *Yearbook of Agriculture, 1919*, pp. 280–81.

40. To estimate the net losses to farmers, we use the difference between the appraised value and the sum of the salvage value and the government indemnities.

41. We do not include the cost of pasteurization because it was more than offset by the resulting value of the increased shelf life of milk.

42. U.S. National Research Council, *Livestock*, p. 9.

43. U.S. BAI, *Diseases of Cattle, 1942*, p. 376.

44. Fisher, "Cost of Tuberculosis," p. 34. See Chapter 10 and its appendix.

45. Myers and Steele, *Bovine Tuberculosis Control*, p. 241; N. G. Willis, "Canada," in Charles Thoen and James H. Steele, *Mycobacterium bovis Infection in Animals and Humans* (Ames: Iowa State Univ. Press, 1995), pp. 195–98.

46. Alan L. Olmstead and Paul W. Rhode, "The Eradication of Bovine Tuberculosis in the United States in a Comparative Perspective," in *Human and Animal Agriculture in Developing Countries,* ed. David Zilberman et al. (New York: Springer-FAO, 2012), pp. 7–30.

47. Olmstead and Rhode, "Eradication," pp. 23–26.

48. *Hoard's Dairyman,* 25 June 1941, p. 1. Successes kept coming. Based on a test-and-slaughter program, dourine was eliminated from the United States in 1942. A French stallion had carried this sexually transmitted disease to the United States in 1886. Control proved difficult until a diagnostic test was developed in 1912. The federal government assisted eradication by providing test facilities and funding indemnities (to be matched by states) to compensate owners of condemned animals. USDA, *Yearbook of Agriculture, 1942,* pp. 413–16. Another major disease of horses, glanders, had disappeared by 1934. Improved diagnostic technologies and compulsory testing played a role, but perhaps more important was the elimination of large concentrations of work horses (Hagan, "Control and Eradication," p. 131).

CHAPTER 13   *Getting Off the Fix*

1. Stalheim, *Winning of Animal Health,* pp. 82–84, 99; U.S. BAI, *Report of the Chief for 1915* (Washington, DC: U.S. Government Printing Office, 1915), p. 55.

2. Cole et al., *History of Hog Cholera Research,* pp. 20–30; Stalheim, *Winning of Animal Health,* p. 74. In 1914, John D. Rockefeller gave $1,000,000 to create a department at the Rockefeller Center for the study of animal diseases. At that time, James J. Hill donated as well and added $50,000 explicitly for the study of hog cholera. In announcing the gifts, the *New York Times* (1 Apr. 1914, p. 1) reported that hog cholera had killed swine valued at $60 million in the Northwest in the past year.

3. Cole et al., *History of Hog Cholera Research,* pp. 47–53; Stalheim, *Winning of Animal Health,* pp. 77–82.

4. Cole et al., *History of Hog Cholera Research,* pp. 47–67; Wise, *Hog Cholera,* p. 7.

5. James A. Baker, "Serial Passage of Hog Cholera Virus in Rabbits," *Proceedings of the Society for Experimental Biology and Medicine* 63 (1946): 183–87. A team headed by Hilary Koprowski at the Lederle Laboratories of the American Cyanamid Company, and William H. Boynton of the University of California also made important advances.

6. Wise, *Hog Cholera,* pp. 7–8, 31; Cole et al., *History of Hog Cholera Research,* pp. 74–75; Stalheim, *Winning of Animal Health,* pp. 79–80.

7. Stalheim, *Winning of Animal Health*, pp. 80–81.

8. Wise, *Hog Cholera*, p. 9; USDA, *Yearbook of Agriculture, 1956*, pp. 369–73.

9. USDA, *Yearbook of Agriculture, 1956*, pp. 369–73; Hagan, "Control and Eradication," p. 141; U.S. Agricultural Research Service, "Control of Garbage-Feeding," various years.

10. Hagan, "Control and Eradication," p. 142; U.S. Livestock Sanitary Association, *Report of Annual Meetings for 1952*, pp. 209–13. Canadian Commission of Conservation, *Garbage as Feed;* U.S. Food Administration, *Garbage Utilization;* Wise, *Hog Cholera*, p. 4.

11. "Hog Cholera Problem," *Journal of the American Veterinary Medical Association* 118, no. 889 (1951): 261–62; Black, *Animal Health*, p. 21; Stallheim, *Winning*, pp. 93–94, 100–3; Wise, *Hog Cholera*, p. 4; A. H. Quin, "Past and Future of Hog Cholera Control," *Journal of the American Veterinary Medical Association* 116, no. 879 (1950): 411–16.

12. "Hog Cholera Eradication Bills Introduced," *Journal of the American Veterinary Medical Association*, 138, no. 12 (1961): 667; Wise, *Hog Cholera*, pp. 9–10; U.S. Senate, Committee on Agriculture and Forestry, *Eradication of Hog Cholera, Hearings on S. Bill 1908*, 26 July 1961, 87th Cong., 1st Sess. (Washington, DC: U.S. Government Printing Office, 1961), pp. 2–3.

13. U.S. Senate, *Eradication*, pp. 1–41, quotation from p. 33.

14. José Manuel Sánchez-Vizcaíno, "African Swine Fever," in *Diseases of Swine*, 9th ed., ed. Barbara E. Straw et al. (Ames, IA: Blackwell, 2006), pp. 291–98; Wise, *Hog Cholera*, p. 62.

15. Stalheim, *Winning of Animal Health*, p. 104; Wise, *Hog Cholera*, pp. 16–20, 34; "Wisconsin Is Hog Cholera Free," *Journal of the American Veterinary Medical Association* 154, no. 7 (1969): 859–60.

16. Wise, *Hog Cholera*, pp. 36–37, 43–44.

17. Black, *Animal Health*, pp. 39–40; Stalheim, *Winning of Animal Health*, pp. 80–81; Wise, *Hog Cholera*, pp. 39–42; "Public Hearing on Halting Shipments of Hog Cholera Vaccines," *Journal of the American Veterinary Medical Association* 154, no. 10 (1969): 1148–49; "AVMA Reiterates Stand on Hog Cholera," *Journal of the American Veterinary Medical Association* 154, no. 10 (1969): 1157–58.

18. Wise, *Hog Cholera*, pp. 44–45; Black, *Animal Health*, p. 40; W. F. Althoff, "The 1976 Outbreak of Hog Cholera in New Jersey: An Application of Geology to a Biological Emergency," *Environmental Management* 1, no. 6 (1977): 505–13.

19. R. E. Omohundro, "The Dismal Swamp Operation," *Journal of the American Veterinary Medical Association* 159, no. 11 (1971): 1564–66; "Intensive Hog Cholera Eradication Effort Successful," *Journal of the American Veterinary Medical Association* 158, no. 3 (1971): 318–19; Wise, *Hog Cholera*, pp. 46–48.

20. Wise, *Hog Cholera*, pp. 49–52; USDA, "History of Research at the U.S. Department of Agriculture and Agricultural Research Service: Hog

Cholera," Agricultural Research Service, first published in *Agricultural Research*, Mar. 1978, www.ars.usda.gov/IS/timeline/cholera.htm; Black, *Animal Health*, pp. 40–41.

21. E. H. McCauley and W. B. Sundquist, "Potential Economic Consequences of African Swine Fever and Its Control in the United States," Department of Agricultural and Applied Economics, Staff Paper P79-11 (St. Paul: Univ. of Minnesota, Apr. 1979, http://ageconsearch.umn.edu/bitstream/13530/1/21502.pdf). They reported on annual damages of $90 million in 1960–62 (p. 15) and annual expenditures from 1962 to 1976 (p. 17). Following the examples herein in Chapter 11 and Chapter 12, we convert to real purchasing power using the consumer price index (CPI) and discount at 3 percent to calculate the real discounted sum.

22. Of the 11 million swine slaughtered in the Netherlands, about 700,000 were actually infected. A. A. Dijkhuizen, "The 1997–1998 Outbreak of Classical Swine Fever in the Netherlands," *Preventive Veterinary Medicine* 42 (1999): 135–37.

23. L. Z. Saunders, "A History of the Pathological Division of the Bureau of Animal Industry, United States Department of Agriculture, between 1891 and 1921," *Veterinary Pathology* 26 (1989): 531–32.

24. U.S. Animal and Plant Health Inspection Service (APHIS), "About APHIS," updated 19 May 2014, www.aphis.usda.gov/about_aphis/history.shtml.

25. U.S. APHIS, *Protecting America's Animal Health*, rev. ed. (Washington, DC: U.S. Government Printing Office, 1978), pp. 3, 5.

CHAPTER 14   *The Mirror of the Past*

1. The USDA was reorganized many times. APHIS now performs many of the BAI's former functions. Animal and Plant Health Inspection Service (APHIS), "Summary Report: California Bovine Spongiform Encephalopathy Case Investigation," July 2012, www.aphis.usda.gov/animal_health/animal_diseases/bse/downloads/BSE_Summary_Report.pdf.

2. United Kingdom Department for Environment, Food & Rural Affairs, "Summary of Passive Surveillance Reports in Great Britain," data valid to 31 Mar. 2014, www.defra.gov.uk/ahvla-en/files/pub-tse-stats-gboverview.pdf; James Meikle, "Mad Cow Disease—A Very British Response to an International Crisis," *Guardian*, 25 Apr. 2012, www.theguardian.com/uk/2012/apr/25/mad-cow-disease-british-crisis; Sean Henahan, "Mad Cow Disease, the BSE Epidemic in Great Britain: An Interview with Dr. Frederick A. Murphy," National Health Museum: *Access Excellence* [1996], www.accessexcellence.org/WN/NM/madcow96.php; David Brown, "The 'Recipe for Disaster' That Killed 80 and Left a £5bn Bill," *Telegraph*, 27 Oct. 2000, www.telegraph.co.uk/news/uknews/1371964/The-recipe-for-disaster-that-killed-80-and-left-a-5bn-bill.html.

3. U.S. Animal Health Association, Committee on Foreign and Emerging Diseases, *Foreign Animal Diseases,* 6th ed. (Richmond, VA: U.S. Animal Health Association, 1998), pp. 120–23; *Foreign Animal Diseases,* 7th ed. (Boca Publishing: Boca Raton, FL, 2008), pp. 185–88; Henahan, "Mad Cow Disease."

4. The feasibility of eradication depended on eliminating the disease from reservoirs including nondomesticated animals.

Bibliography

Books, Articles, and Government Documents

Aguilar, Julian. "South Texas Fever Tick Infestation Grows." *Texas Tribune,* 1 Feb. 2010. www.texastribune.org/2010/02/01/south-texas-fever-tick -infestation-grows/.

Alabama State Veterinarian. *Annual Report, 1907.* Montgomery, AL: Live Stock Sanitary Board, 1908.

Allen, William H. "The Rise of the National Board of Health." *Annals of the American Academy of Political and Social Science* 15 (1900): 51–68.

Althoff, W. F. "The 1976 Outbreak of Hog Cholera in New Jersey: An Applica- tion of Geology to a Biological Emergency." *Environmental Management* 1, no. 6 (1977): 505–13.

Alvord, Henry E., and Raymond A. Pearson. "The Milk Supply of Two Hun- dred Cities and Towns." *BAI Bulletin,* no. 46. Washington, DC: U.S. Govern- ment Printing Office, 1903.

Anderson, Kym, Gordon Rausser, and Johan Swinnen. "Political Economy of Public Policies: Insights from Distortions to Agricultural and Food Mar- kets." *Journal of Economic Literature* 51, no. 2 (2013): 423–77.

Anderson, L. H. *Natural Way in Diet; or, the Proper Food of Man.* Chicago: National Institute of Science, 1898.

Anderson, R. J. "The Public Health Importance of Animal Tuberculosis." *Annals of the New York Academy of Sciences* 70 (1958): 632–35.

Anderson, Terry L., and Peter J. Hill. *The Not So Wild, Wild West: Property Rights on the Frontier.* Stanford, CA: Stanford Univ. Press, 2004.

Andrews, John S. "Animal Parasitology in the United States Department of Agriculture, 1886–1984." In *100 Years of Animal Health, 1884–1984,* edited by Vivian Wiser, Larry Mark, and H. Graham Purchase, 113–66. Beltsville, MD: Associates of the National Agricultural Library, 1987.

Annals of Congress. Various dates.

Antle, John M. "No Such Thing as a Free Safe Lunch: The Cost of Food Safety Regulation in the Meat Industry." *American Journal of Agricultural Economics* 82, no. 2 (2000): 310–22.

Armour, J. Ogden. *The Packers, the Private Car Lines, and the People.* Philadelphia: Henry Altemus, 1906.

Ashbrook, F. G., and J. D. Bebout. "Disposal of City Garbage by Feeding to Hogs." *USDA Circular,* no. 80. Washington, DC: U.S. Government Printing Office, 1917.

Atkins, P. J. "The Glasgow Case: Meat, Disease, and Regulation, 1889–1924." *Agricultural History Review* 52, no. 2 (2004): 161–82.

"AVMA Reiterates Stand on Hog Cholera." *Journal of the American Veterinary Medical Association* 154, no. 10 (1969): 1157–58.

Ayers, S. Henry. "The Present Status of the Pasteurization of Milk." *USDA Bulletin,* no. 342. Washington, DC: U.S. Government Printing Office, 1916.

———. "The Present Status of the Pasteurization of Milk." *USDA Bulletin,* no. 342, revised. Washington, DC: U.S. Government Printing Office, 1922.

———. "The Present Status of the Pasteurization of Milk." *USDA Bulletin,* no. 342, revised. Washington, DC: U.S. Government Printing Office, 1926.

Ayers, S. Henry, R. P. Hotis, and C. J. Babcock. "The Present Status of the Pasteurization of Milk." *USDA Bulletin,* no. 342, 1932 revised. Washington, DC: U.S. Government Printing Office, 1932.

Baker, James A. "Serial Passage of Hog Cholera Virus in Rabbits." *Proceedings of the Society for Experimental Biology and Medicine* 63 (1946): 183–87.

Balogh, Brian. *A Government Out of Sight: The Mystery of National Authority in Nineteenth Century America.* New York: Cambridge Univ. Press, 2009.

Benedict, Michael Les. "Contagion and the Constitution: Quarantine Agitation from 1859 to 1866." *Journal of the History of Medicine* 25, no. 2 (1970): 177–93.

Bensel, Richard F. *The Political Economy of American Industrialization, 1877–1900.* New York: Cambridge Univ. Press, 2000.

Bierer, Bert W. *A Short History of Veterinary Medicine in America.* East Lansing: Michigan State Univ. Press, 1955.

———. "Survey of Municipal & State Meat Inspection." Unpublished, typed ms., 1942. Available at the National Agricultural Library, Beltsville, MD.

Billings, Frank S. *Inoculation: Prevention of Swine Plague.* Lincoln, NE: Journal Co., 1892.

———. *Swine Plague.* Lincoln, NE: Journal Co., 1888.

Black, Neal. *Animal Health: A Century of Progress.* Richmond, VA: U.S. Animal Health Association, 1996.

Bleakley, Hoyt. "Disease and Development: Evidence from Hookworm Eradication in the American South." *Quarterly Journal of Economics* 122, no. 1 (2007): 73–117.

Boudreaux, Donald J., and Thomas J. DiLorenzo. "The Protectionist Roots of Antitrust." *Review of Austrian Economics* 6, no. 2 (1993): 81–96.

"Bovine Tuberculosis in the Lungs." *Lancet* 249, issue 6457 (1947): 756–57.

Braeman, John. "The Square Deal in Action: A Case Study in the Growth of the 'National Police Power.'" In *Change and Continuity in Twentieth-Century America,* edited by John Braeman, Robert H. Bremmer, and Everett Walters, 35–80. Columbus: Ohio State Univ. Press, 1964.

Brewton, William W. *Life of Thomas E. Watson.* Binghamton, AL: Wall-Ballou, 1926.

Brinkley, Garland L. "The Economic Impact of Disease in the American South, 1860–1940." Ph.D. diss., Univ. of California at Davis, 1994.

British Board of Agriculture. *Extracts relating to Pleuro-pneumonia in the United States of America, from the First Report of the Secretary of Agriculture, Washington.* London: Her Majesty's Stationary Office, 1890.

Brown, David. "The 'Recipe for Disaster' That Killed 80 and Left a £5bn Bill." *Telegraph,* 27 Oct. 2000. www.telegraph.co.uk/news/uknews/1371964/The-recipe-for-disaster-that-killed-80-and-left-a-5bn-bill.html.

Brown, G. T. "Report on Swine-Fever in Great Britain." In *Annual Report of the Agricultural Department of the Privy Council Office of the Contagious Diseases, Inspection and Transit of Animals; for the Year 1885. . . .* London: Eyre and Spottiswoode, 1886.

Brown, Walter, J. *J. J. Brown and Thomas E. Watson: Georgia Politics, 1912–1928.* Macon, GA: Mercer Univ. Press, 1988.

Bruner, Dorsey W., and James H. Gillespie. *Hagan's Infectious Diseases of Domestic Animals.* 6th ed. Ithaca, NY: Comstock, 1973.

Bruton, Peter W. "The National Board of Health." Ph.D. diss., Univ. of Maryland, 1974.

Bryce, James. *American Commonwealth.* London: MacMillan, 1888.

Budd, William. "Observations on Typhoid (Intestinal) Fever in the Pig." *British Medical Journal* (29 July 1865): 81–87.

Campbell, William C. "Historical Introduction." *Trichinella and Trichinosis,* edited by William C. Campbell, 1–30. New York: Plenum Press, 1983.

Canadian Commission of Conservation. *Garbage as Feed for Hogs.* Ottawa, 1918.

Carpenter, Daniel P. *The Forging of Bureaucratic Autonomy: Reputations, Networks, and Policy Innovation in Executive Agencies, 1862–1928.* Princeton, NJ: Princeton Univ. Press, 2001.

Carpenter, T. E., and A. Thieme. "A Simulation Approach to Measuring the Economic Effects of Foot-and-Mouth Disease in Beef and Dairy Cattle." In *Proceedings of the Second International Symposium of Veterinary Epidemiology and*

Economics, edited by W. A. Geering, R. T. Roe, and L. A. Chapman, 511–16. Canberra: Australian Government Publishing Service, 1980.

Carter, Phillip R. "Bovine Tuberculosis in Germany." *Medical Bulletin* 1 (1946): 65–70.

Carter, Susan, Scott Gartner, Michael Haines, et al. *Historical Statistics of the United States, Millennial Edition.* New York: Cambridge Univ. Press, 2006.

Cassedy, James H. "Applied Microscopy and American Pork Diplomacy: Charles Wardell Stiles in Germany 1898–1899." *Isis* 62, no. 1 (1971): 5–20.

———. *Charles V. Chapin and the Public Health Movement.* Cambridge, MA: Harvard Univ. Press, 1962.

Casson, Henry. *"Uncle Jerry:" Life of General Jeremiah M. Rusk.* Madison, WI: Junius W. Hill, 1895.

"The Cattle Plague. The Natural History of the Rinderpest—Its Reappearance in Prussia and Ireland—Its Reported Appearance in United States Territory—Its True Character and Means of Its Prevention." *New York Times,* 15 July 1866, 4.

Centers for Disease Control and Prevention. "Bovine Tuberculosis— Pennsylvania." *Mortality and Morbidity Weekly Report* 39, no. 12 (1990): 201–13.

———. *"Mycobacterium bovis* (Bovine Tuberculosis) in Humans." Aug. 2011. www.cdc.gov/tb/publications/factsheets/general/mbovis.pdf.

———. National Center for Emerging and Zoonotic Infectious Diseases. www .cdc.gov/ncezid/.

Chapin, Charles V. "Garbage as Food for Swine." *American City* 17, no. 2 (1917): 177–83.

———. *Municipal Sanitation in the United States.* Providence, RI: Snow & Farn- ham, 1901.

Chicago Board of Trade. *Annual Report of the Trade and Commerce of Chicago for 1892.* Chicago: J. M. W. Jones, 1893.

Chicago Commerce, Manufacturing, Banking, and Transportation Facilities. Chicago: S. Ferd. Howe, 1884.

Chicago Department of Health. *Report of the Department of Health for 1888.* Chicago: Powers, Crichfield, 1889.

———. *Report of the Department of Health for 1889.* Chicago: Barnard and Gunthrorp, 1891.

———. *Report of the Department of Health for 1890.* Chicago: Pettibone, 1891.

Chisholm, Brock. "Quotations from an Address." *American Journal of Public Health* 43, no. 3 (1953): 340.

Choate, Jan. *Disputed Ground: Farm Groups That Opposed the New Deal Agricultural Program.* Jefferson, NC: McFarland, 2002.

Cirillo, Vincent J. *Bullets and Bacilli: The Spanish-American War and American Medicine.* New Brunswick, NJ: Rutgers Univ. Press, 1999.

Clark, J. Stanley. "Texas Fever in Oklahoma." *Chronicles of Oklahoma* 29 (1951–1952): 433–36.

Clark, Jane P. *The Rise of a New Federalism: Federal-State Cooperation in the United States.* New York: Columbia Univ. Press, 1938.

Clay, John. "American Cattle Markets and the Dressed Beef Trade, with Some Statistics of the Live-Stock Trade in the United States." *Journal of the Royal Agricultural Society of England* 25 (1889): 124–56.

———. *My Life on the Range.* Chicago: author, 1924.

Clemen, Rudolf A. *American Livestock and Meat Industry.* New York: Roland Press, 1923.

Cobbett, Louis. *The Causes of Tuberculosis.* Cambridge: Cambridge Univ. Press, 1917.

Coit, Henry L. "The Origin, General Plan, and Scope of the Medical Milk Commission." In *Proceedings of the First Conference of the Medical Milk Commissions in the United States,* 10–17. Cincinnati, OH: American Association of Medical Milk Commissions, 1908.

Cole, C. G., R. R. Henley, C. N. Dale, L. O. Mott, J. P. Torrey, and M. R. Zinober. *History of Hog Cholera Research in the U.S. Department of Agriculture, 1884–1960. Agricultural Information Bulletin,* no. 241. Washington, DC: USDA, 1962.

Colgrove, James. *State of Immunity: The Politics of Vaccination in Twentieth-Century America.* Berkeley: Univ. of California Press, 2006.

Collins, F. V. *Meat Inspection.* Adelaide, South Australia: Rigby, 1966.

Coman, Katharine. *Economic Beginnings of the Far West: How We Won the Land Beyond the Mississippi.* Vol. 1, *Explorers and Colonizers.* New York: MacMillan, 1912.

Compton, Richard. *A Legacy for Tomorrow, 1885–1985: The 100 Year History of the College of Veterinary Medicine.* Columbus: Ohio State Univ. Press, 1984.

"Congress Asked to Prohibit Movement of Ticky Cattle Beyond the Quarantine Area." *American Journal of Veterinary Medicine* 9, no. 2 (1914): 130–31.

Congressional Globe. Various dates.

Congressional Record. Various dates.

Cosmas, Graham A. *An Army for Empire: The United States Army in the Spanish-American War.* Columbia: Univ. of Missouri Press, 1971.

Cowles, William H. "State Quarantine Laws and the Federal Constitution." *American Law Review* 25 (1891): 45–73.

Cox, Gary W., and Mathew D. McCubbins. *Setting the Agenda: Responsible Party Government in the U.S. House of Representatives.* New York: Oxford Univ. Press, 2005.

Crane, Caroline B. "U.S. Inspected and Passed." *Pearson's Magazine* 29 (Mar. 1913): 257–68; (Apr. 1913): 436–46; (May 1913): 524–34; (June 1913): 738–48.

Cronon, William. "Two Cheers for the Whig Interpretation of History." *Perspectives on History,* Sept. 2012. www.historians.org/publications-and -directories/perspectives-on-history/september-2012/two-cheers-for-the -whig-interpretation-of-history.

Crouse, Janet W. "The Decline of German-American Friendship: Beef, Pork, and Politics, 1890–1906." Ph.D. diss., Univ. of Delaware, 1980.

Curtice, Cooper. "On the Extermination of the Cattle-Tick and the Disease Spread by It." *Journal of Comparative Medicine and Veterinary Archives* 17, no. 9 (1896): 46–55.

Dale, Edward. *The Range Cattle Industry: Ranching on the Great Plains from 1865 to 1925.* Norman: Univ. of Oklahoma Press, 1960. First published in 1930.

Daniels, M., and P. D'Arcy. "Tuberculosis in the British Zone in Germany." *Medical Bulletin* 5 (1948): 29–54.

Dankner, Wayne M., Norman J. Waecker, Mitchell A. Essey, Kathleen Moser, Muriel Thompson, and Charles E. Davis. "*Mycobacterium bovis* Infections in San Diego: A Clinicoepidemiologic Study of 73 Patients and a Historical Review of a Forgotten Pathogen." *Medicine* 72, no. 1 (1993): 11–37.

Davis, Allen F. *Spearheads for Reform: The Social Settlements and the Progressive Movement, 1890–1914.* New York: Oxford Univ. Press, 1967.

Dawes, Robyn M., and Richard H. Thaler. "Cooperation." *Journal of Economic Perspectives* 2, no. 3 (1988): 187–97.

De Kruif, Paul. *Hunger Fighters.* New York: Harcourt, Brace, 1928.

Deming, Stan. "Nineteenth Century Hog Cholera: Some of Its History and Social Effects." Master's thesis, Northern Illinois Univ., 1965.

Dennen, R. Taylor. "Cattle Trailing in the Nineteenth Century." *Journal of Economic History* 35, no. 2 (1975): 458–60.

Department for Environment, Food & Rural Affairs, Great Britain (DEFRA). *Agriculture in the United Kingdom 2001.* London: Stationery Office, 2002.

———. *Animal Health 2004: The Report of the Chief Veterinary Officer.* London: DEFRA, May 2005.

———. "Animal Health and Welfare: FMD Data Archive." Last modified 19 Mar. 2004. http://footandmouth.csl.gov.uk/.

———. "Origin of the UK Foot and Mouth Disease Epidemic in 2001." June 2002. http://archive.defra.gov.uk/foodfarm/farmanimal/diseases/atoz/fmd /documents/fmdorigins1.pdf, accessed 16 May 2013.

———. "Summary of Passive Surveillance Reports in Great Britain." Data valid to 31 Mar. 2014. www.defra.gov.uk/ahvla-en/files/pub-tse-stats-gboverview .pdf.

Derbyshire, J. Brian. "Early History of the Canadian Federal Meat Inspection Service." *Canadian Veterinarian Journal* 47, no. 6 (2006): 542–49.

Dietrich, Raymond A., and L. Gary Adams. *Potential Animal Health Concerns Relative to Cattle Fever Ticks, Classical Swine Fever, and Bovine Brucellosis—With Special Emphasis on Texas.* College Station: Texas Agricultural Experiment Station, 2000.

Dijkhuizen, A. A. "The 1997–1998 Outbreak of Classical Swine Fever in the Netherlands." *Preventive Veterinary Medicine* 42 (1999): 135–37.

DiLeva, Frank D. "Frantic Farmers Fight Law." *Annals of Iowa* 32 (1953): 81–109.

"Distribution of Bovine Tuberculosis in Man." *Lancet* 224, no. 5789 (1934): 317–18.

Dodge, J. R. "Report of J. R. Dodge on Statistical and Historical Investigations of the Progress and Results of the Texas Cattle Disease." In USDA, *Report of the Commissioner of Agriculture on the Diseases of Cattle in the United States.* 175–202. Washington, DC: U.S. Government Printing Office, 1871.

Dolman, Claude. E. "Theobald Smith, 1859–1934: A Fiftieth Anniversary Tribute." *ASM News* [American Society Microbiology] 50, no. 12 (1984): 577–80.

Dolman, Claude E., and Richard J. Wolfe. *Suppressing the Diseases of Animals and Man: Theobald Smith, Microbiologist.* Boston: Boston Medical Library in the Countway Library of Medicine, 2003.

Dormandy, Thomas. *The White Death: A History of Tuberculosis.* London: Hambledon, 1999.

Dorset, Marion, and O. B. Hess. "Hog Cholera: Prevention and Treatment." USDA, *Farmers' Bulletin,* no. 834. Washington, DC: U.S. Government Printing Office, 1917.

Dorset, Marion, C. N. McBryde, and W. B. Niles. "Further Experiments Concerning the Production of Immunity from Hog Cholera." *BAI Bulletin,* no. 102. Washington, DC: U.S. Government Printing Office, 1908.

Driver, Alistair. "FMD Wipes Out One-Third of South Korea's Pigs." *Farmers Guardian,* 11 Mar. 2011.

"Dr. William Budd." *British Medical Journal* 1, no. 994 (1880): 102–3.

Dubos, René, and Jean Dubos. *The White Plague: Tuberculosis, Man, and Society.* Boston: Little, Brown, 1952.

Duffy, John. *The Sanitarians: A History of American Public Health.* Urbana: Univ. of Illinois Press, 1992.

Duhaime, Roberta. "Surveillance Requirements of Cattle Fever Tick Outbreak." National Animal Health Surveillance System. *NAHSS Outlook,* Dec. 2009, 1–7. http://naldc.nal.usda.gov/download/40159/PDF.

Duncan, Bingham. "Protectionism and Pork: Whitelaw Reid as Diplomat: 1889–1891." *Agricultural History* 33, no. 4 (1959): 190–95.

Dupree, A. Hunter. *Science in the Federal Government: A History of Policies and Activities to 1940.* Cambridge, MA: Harvard Univ. Press, 1957.

DuPuis, E. M. *Nature's Perfect Food: How Milk Became America's Drink.* New York: New York Univ. Press, 2002.

Dusenberry, William. "Foot and Mouth Disease in Mexico, 1946–1951." *Agricultural History* 29, no. 2 (1955): 82–90.

Dykstra, Robert R. *The Cattle Towns.* New York: Alfred A. Knopf, 1968.

Eager, J. M. "Morbidity and Mortality Statistics as Influenced by Milk." In *Milk and Its Relation to the Public Health Public Health.* Marine-Hospital Service of the United States, Treasury Department, Hygienic Laboratory. *Bulletin,* no. 41, 229–42. Washington, DC: U.S. Government Printing Office, 1908.

Edling, Max M. Review of *A Government Out of Sight: the Mystery of National Authority in Nineteenth-Century America,* by Brian Balogh. *Journal of Policy History* 21, no. 4 (2009): 462–68.

Elboir, Javier M. *Potential Impact of Foot-and-Mouth Disease in California.* Davis, CA: Agricultural Issues Center, 1999.

Ellenberger, William P., and Robert M. Chapin. "Cattle-Fever Ticks and Methods of Eradication." USDA, *Farmers' Bulletin,* no. 1057. Washington, DC: USDA, 1919, revised 1932.

Ely, James W., Jr. *The Chief Justiceship of Melville W. Fuller, 1888–1910.* Columbia: Univ. of South Carolina Press, 1995.

Epstein, Richard A. "Let the Shoemaker Stick to His Last: A Defense of the 'Old' Public Health." *Perspectives in Biology and Medicine* 46, Supplement (2003): S138–59.

Erlenborn, James L. "The American Meat and Livestock Industry and American Foreign Policy, 1880–1896." Master's thesis, Univ. of Wisconsin, 1966.

Ettling, John. *The Germ of Laziness: Rockefeller Philanthropy and Public Health in the New South.* Cambridge, MA: Harvard Univ. Press, 1981.

European Food Safety Authority. "EFSA Assesses Risk of *Salmonella* from Pig Meat." EFSA Press Release, 19 Apr. 2010. www.efsa.europa.eu/en/press/news/biohaz100419.htm.

Farrington, A. M. "Quarantine Laws and Practices." In *Cyclopedia of American Agriculture,* vol. 4, edited by Liberty Hide Bailey, 485–89. London: Macmillan, 1909.

Faulder, E. T. "Bovine Tuberculosis: Its History, Control and Eradication." *New York State Department of Agriculture and Markets Bulletin,* no. 218 (1928).

Faust, Ernest C., Paul F. Russell, and Rodney C. Jung. *Craig and Faust's Clinical Parasitology.* 8th ed. Philadelphia: Lea & Febiger, 1970.

Feder, Gershon, and Sara Savastano. "The Role of Opinion Leaders in the Diffusion of New Knowledge: The Case of Integrated Pest Management." World Bank Policy Research Working Paper No. 3916, May 2006. http://dx.doi.org/10.1596/1813-9450-3916.

Fehr, Ernst, and Klaus M. Schmidt. "A Theory of Fairness, Competition and Cooperation." *Quarterly Journal of Economics* 114, no. 3 (1999): 817–68.

Fenner, Frank, Donald A. Henderson, Isao Arita, Zdeněk Ježek, and Ivan D. Ladnyi. *Smallpox and Its Eradication.* Geneva: World Health Organization, 1988.

Fischer, Paul. "H. J. Detmers." *Veterinary Alumni Quarterly* 6, no. 4 (1919): 217–19.

Fishback, Price V., Robert Higgs, Gary D. Libecap, et al. *Government and the American Economy: A New History.* Chicago: Univ. of Chicago Press, 2007.

Fisher, Irving. "The Cost of Tuberculosis in the United States and Its Reduction." In *Transactions of the Sixth International Congress on Tuberculosis,* vol. 3, *Proceedings of Section V: Hygienic, Social, Industrial, and Economic Aspects of Tuberculosis,* 5–36. Philadelphia, PA: William F. Fell, 1908.

———. "Report on National Vitality: Its Waste and Conservation." American Associations for the Advancement of Science, Committee of One Hundred on National Health. *Bulletin,* no. 30. Washington, DC: U.S. Government Printing Office, 1909.

Fisher, John R. "The Economic Effects of Cattle Disease in Britain and Its Containment, 1850–1900." *Agricultural History* 54, no. 2 (1980): 278–94.

———. "To Kill or Not to Kill: The Eradication of Contagious Bovine Pleuro-Pneumonia in Western Europe." *Medical History* 47 (2003): 314–31.

Flores, A. "The Continuing Fight against Cattle Ticks." *Agricultural Research* 54 (2006): 8–9.

Florida Department of State, Division of Library and Information Services. "Florida Memories." www.floridamemory.com/fpc/memory/Photographic-Collection/photo_exhibits/Ranching/Images/_pr01396.jpg, accessed 18 May 2013.

Forbes, Lewis S. "The Programme for the Eradication of Tuberculosis in the United States of America and Some Possible Applications in Africa." *Bulletin of Epizootic Diseases of Africa* 12 (1964): 429–35.

Fowler, Bartham. *Men, Meat, and Miracles.* New York: Messner, 1952.

Frank, Leslie C., and Frederic J. Moss. *The Extent of Pasteurization and Tuberculin Testing in American Cities of 10,000 Population and Over in 1927 and 1931.* Public Health Service, mimeo, 1932.

"Free Medicine." *The Conservative* 2, no. 43 (1900): 5.

Fuchs, A. W., and L. C. Frank. "Milk Supplies and Their Control in American Urban Communities of Over 1,000 Population in 1936." *Public Health Bulletin,* no. 245. Washington, DC: U.S. Government Printing Office, 1939.

Galenson, David. "The End of the Chisholm Trail." *Journal of Economic History* 34, no. 2 (1974): 350–64.

Galloway, Joseph H. *Farm Animal Health and Disease Control.* Philadelphia: Lea & Febiger, 1972.

Gamgee, John. *Diseased Meat Sold in Edinburgh and Meat Inspection, in Connection with the Public Health, and with the Interests of Agriculture: A Letter to the Right Hon. the Lord Provost of Edinburgh.* Edinburgh: Sutherland and Knox, 1857.

———. "Report of Professor Gamgee on Splenic and Periodic Fever of Cattle." In USDA, *Report of the Commissioner of Agriculture on the Diseases of Cattle in the United States,* 82–155. Washington, DC: U.S. Government Printing Office, 1871.

Garcia, Lynne S. *Diagnostic Medical Parasitology.* 5th ed. Washington, DC: ASM Press, 2007.

Gaynes, Robert P. *Germ Theory: Medical Pioneers in Infectious Diseases.* Washington, DC: ASM Press, 2011.

Gee, George F. *The Economic Importance of Cattle Tick in Australia.* Canberra, Australia: Bureau of Agricultural Economics, 1959.

Georgia Department of Agriculture. "Annual Report for 1921." Serial No. 88, *Quarterly Bulletin* (Jan.–Mar. 1922).

Gignilliat, John L. "Politics and Protection: The European Boycott of American Pork, 1879–1891." *Agricultural History* 35, no. 1 (1961): 3–12.

Gilfoyle, Daniel. "Veterinary Research and the African Rinderpest Epizootic: The Cape Colony, 1896–1898." *Journal of Southern African History* 29, no. 1 (2003): 133–54.

Gilligan, Thomas W., William J. Marshall, and Barry R. Weingast. "Regulation and the Theory of Legislative Choice: The Interstate Commerce Act of 1887." *Journal of Law and Economics* 32, no. 1 (1989): 35–61.

Glaeser, Edward L., and Andrei Shleifer. "The Rise of the Regulatory State." *Journal of Economic Literature* 41, no. 2 (2003): 401–25.

Glazier, W. C. W. *Report on Trichinae and Trichinosis*. Ex. Doc. No. 9, 40th Cong., 3rd Sess. Washington, DC: U.S. Government Printing Office, 1881.

Goding, Harry. "State Laws and Court Decisions Relating to Cattle-Tick Eradication." USDA, *Department Circular,* no. 184. Washington, DC: U.S. Government Printing Office, 1921.

Gordon, David. *"Swift & Co. v. United States:* The Beef Trust and the Stream of Commerce Doctrine." *American Journal of Legal History* 28, no. 3 (1984): 244–79.

Gostin, Lawrence O. *Public Health Law: Power, Duty, Restraint*. Berkeley: Univ. of California Press, 2000.

Gould, Sylvester E. *Trichinosis*. Springfield, IL: Charles C. Thomas, 1945.

Graham, O. H., and J. L. Hourrigan. "Eradication Programs for Arthropod Parasites of Livestock." *Journal of Medical Entomology* 13, no. 6 (1977): 629–58.

Grange, J. M., and C. H. Collins. "Bovine Tubercle Bacilli and Disease." *Epidemiology and Infection* 99, no. 2 (1987): 221–34.

Gray, Lewis C. *History of Agriculture in the Southern United States to 1860*. 2 vols. New York: Peter Smith, 1941.

Greene, Ann Norton. *Horses at Work: Harnessing Power in Industrial America*. Cambridge, MA: Harvard Univ. Press, 2008.

Griffth, A. Stanley, and J. Smith. "Types of Tubercule Bacilli in Pulmonary Tuberculosis in North-East Scotland." *Lancet* 236, no. 6106 (1940): 291–94.

Hagan, W. A. "The Control and Eradication of Animal Diseases in the United States." *Annual Review of Microbiology* 12 (1958): 127–44.

Hall, Maurice C. "Studies on Trichinosis I: The Incidence of Trichinosis as Indicated by Post-Mortem Examination of 300 Diaphragms." *Public Health Reports* 52, no. 16 (1937): 468–90.

———. "Studies on Trichinosis VII: The Past and Present Status of Trichinosis in the United States, and the Indicated Control Measures." *Public Health Reports* 53, no. 33 (1938): 1472–86.

Hanson, R. P. "Origin of Hog Cholera." *Journal of American Veterinary Medical Association* 131 (1957): 211–18.

Harbaugh, William H. *The Life and Time of Theodore Roosevelt*. Rev. ed. New York: Collier, 1963.

Harden, Victoria A. *Inventing the NIH: Federal Biomedical Research Policy, 1887–1937*. Baltimore: Johns Hopkins Univ. Press, 1986.

Harris, Carl V. "Right Fork or Left Fork? The Section-Party Alignments of the Southern Democrats in Congress." *Journal of Southern History* 42, no. 4 (1976): 471–506.

Harvey, William C., and Harry Hill. *Milk: Production and Control.* London: H. K. Lewis, 1936.

Haygood, Tamara Miner. "Cows, Ticks, and Disease: A Medical Interpretation of the Southern Cattle Industry." *Journal of Southern History* 52, no. 4 (1986): 551–64.

Henahan, Sean. "Mad Cow Disease, the BSE Epidemic in Great Britain: An Interview with Dr. Frederick A. Murphy." National Health Museum: *Access Excellence* [1996]. www.accessexcellence.org/WN/NM/madcow96.php.

Hickman, R. W. "Actinomycosis, Lumpy Jaw." *Journal of Comparative Medicine and Veterinary Archives* 13, no. 2 (1892): 110–16.

Higgs, Robert. *Crisis and Leviathan: Critical Episodes in the Growth of American Government.* New York: Oxford Univ. Press, 1987.

Hiscock, Ira V., and Robert Jordan. "The Extent of Milk Pasteurization in Cities of the United States." In *Thirteenth Annual Report of the International Association of Dairy and Milk Inspectors,* 89–97. Washington, DC: Ivan C. Weld, 1924.

"Hog Cholera Eradication Bills Introduced." *Journal of the American Veterinary Medical Association* 138, no. 12 (1961): 667.

"Hog Cholera Problem." *Journal of the American Veterinary Medical Association* 118, no. 889 (1951): 261–62.

Hoing, Willard L. "James Wilson as Secretary of Agriculture." Ph.D. diss., Univ. of Wisconsin, 1964.

Hope, Holly. *Dip That Tick: Texas Tick Fever Eradication in Arkansas, 1907–1943.* Little Rock: Arkansas Historic Preservation Program, 2005.

Horowitz, M. P. "Feeding Garbage to Hogs." *American Journal of Public Health* 8, no. 5 (1918): 392.

Houck, Ulysses Grant. *The Bureau of Animal Industry of the United States Department of Agriculture: Its Establishment, Achievements and Current Activities.* Washington, DC: [Hayworth Printing Company], 1924.

Hovenkamp, Herbert. *Enterprise and American Law, 1836–1937.* Cambridge, MA: Harvard Univ. Press, 1991.

Hoy, Suellen, and Walter Nugent. "Public Health or Protectionism? The German-American Pork War, 1880–1891." *Bulletin of the History of Medicine* 63, no. 2 (1989): 198–224.

Hyslop, N. St. G. "The Epizootiology and Epidemiology of Foot and Mouth Disease." *Advances in Veterinary Science and Comparative Medicine* 14 (1970): 261–307.

Illinois General Assembly. *Evidence Taken Before the Joint Committee on Tuberculin Test, 1911*. Vols. 1 and 2. Springfield, IL: Illinois State Journal, 1912.

———. *Foot and Mouth Disease in Illinois: Its Cause, Character, Cost and Eradication*. Springfield, IL: Illinois State Journal, 1915.

———. *Journal of the House of Representatives for Thirty-Third General Assembly*. Springfield, IL: H. W. Rokker, 1883.

———. *Journal of the Senate of the Thirty-Fourth General Assembly, 1885*. Springfield, IL: State Printers, 1885.

———. *Laws of the State of Illinois Enacted by the Thirty-Fourth General Assembly*. Springfield, IL: H. W. Rokker, 1885.

———. *Laws of the State of Illinois Enacted by the Thirty-Fifth General Assembly*. Springfield, IL: H. W. Rokker, 1887.

———. *Report of the Joint Committee of Tuberculin Test, 1911*. Springfield, IL: Illinois State Journal, 1911.

Illinois State Board of Live Stock Commissioners. *Annual Report*. Various years.

"Imprisonment for Dealing in Tuberculous Cattle." *American Journal of Veterinary Medicine* 13, no. 5 (1918): 236–37.

In Memoriam: Leonard Pearson. [Philadelphia: Univ. of Pennsylvania, 1910]. https://archive.org/details/inmemoriamleonar00np__.

Indiana State Board of Agriculture. *Annual Report*. Various years.

"Intensive Hog Cholera Eradication Effort Successful." *Journal of the American Veterinary Medical Association* 158, no. 3 (1971): 318–19.

Iowa Department of Agriculture. *Laws Relating to Bovine Tuberculosis Eradication, Including Amendments by the Forty-Third General Assembly, Effective July 4, 1929*. Des Moines, IA, 1929.

James, Scott C. *Presidents, Parties, and the State: A Party System Perspective on Democratic Regulatory Choice, 1884–1936*. New York: Cambridge Univ. Press, 2000.

Jenkins, Jeffery A., and Charles Stewart III. *Fighting for the Speakership: The House and the Rise of Party Government*. Princeton, NJ: Princeton Univ. Press, 2012.

John, Richard R. *Spreading the News: The American Postal System from Franklin to Morse*. Cambridge, MA: Harvard Univ. Press, 1995.

Johnson, Kimberly S. *Governing the American State: Congress and the New Federalism, 1877–1929*. Princeton, NJ: Princeton Univ. Press, 2007.

Johnston, Robert D. *The Radical Middle Class: Populist Democracy and the Question of Capitalism in Progressive Era Portland, Oregon*. Princeton, NJ: Princeton Univ. Press, 2002.

Jones, Susan D. *Valuing Animals: Veterinarians and Their Patients in Modern America.* Baltimore: Johns Hopkins Univ. Press, 2003.

Jordan, Edwin O. "Municipal Regulation of the Milk Supply." *Journal of the American Medical Association* 61 (1913): 2281–91.

Kansas, State of. *House Journal, Special Session 1884, Proceeding of the House of Representatives.* Topeka: Kansas Publishing House, 1885.

———. *Senate Journal, Special Session 1886, Proceeding of the Senate.* Topeka: Kansas Publishing House, 1886.

Kanthack, Emilia. "Utility of the German 'Freibank' as a Factor in Social Economy." *Public Health* (1908): 119–21.

Kantor, Shawn Everett. "Razorbacks, Ticky Cows, and the Closing of the Georgia Open Range: The Dynamics of Institutional Change Uncovered." *Journal of Economic History* 51, no. 4 (1991): 861–86.

Kastner, Justin. "Food and Agriculture Security: An Historical Illustration of Contemporary Challenges." In *Food and Agricultural Security: An Historical, Multidisciplinary Approach,* edited by Justin Kastner, 5–32. Santa Barbara, CA: Praeger, 2011.

———. "Managing Human and Animal-Health Threats: Additional Lessons from the 19th-Century Trading World." In *Food and Agricultural Security: An Historical, Multidisciplinary Approach,* edited by Justin Kastner, 105–28. Santa Barbara, CA: Praeger, 2011.

———. "Sanitary Related International Trade Disputes: A Multiple-Factor Analysis Based on Nineteenth-Century Precedents." Ph.D. diss., Univ. of Guelph, 2003.

Kastner, Justin, Douglas Powell, Terry Crowley, and Karen Huff. "Scientific Conviction amidst Scientific Controversy in the Transatlantic Livestock and Meat Trade." *Endeavour* 29, no. 2 (2005): 78–83.

Keane, Charles. "The Epizootic of Foot and Mouth Disease in California." California Department of Agriculture, Special Publication No. 65. Sacramento, CA: State Printing Office, 1926.

Kentucky General Assembly. *Journal of the House of Representatives, 1885–86.* Frankford, KY: John Woods, 1886.

Kerr, John W. "Certified Milk and Infants' Milk Depots." In *Milk and Its Relation to the Public Health Public Health.* Marine-Hospital Service of the United States, Treasury Department, Hygienic Laboratory. *Bulletin,* no. 41, 565–88. Washington, DC: U.S. Government Printing Office, 1908.

Keuchel, Edward F. "Chemicals and Meat: the Embalmed Beef Scandal of the Spanish-American War." *Bulletin of the History of Medicine* 48, no. 2 (1974): 249–64.

Kiernan, John A. "The Most Successful Methods of Tick Eradication." In *Report of the Seventeenth Annual Meeting of the United States Live Stock Sanitary Association,* held in Chicago, IL, 2–4 Dec. 1913, 163–184. Chicago: 1914.

———. "Tuberculosis Eradication." *American Journal of Veterinary Medicine* 14, no. 3 (1919): 103–11.

Kiernan, John A., and Alexander E. Wight. "Tuberculosis in Livestock: Detection, Control, and Eradication." USDA, *Farmers' Bulletin,* no. 1069. Washington, DC: U.S. Government Printing Office, 1919.

———. "Tuberculosis in Livestock, Detection, Control, and Eradication." USDA, *Farmers' Bulletin,* no. 1069, revised. Washington, DC: U.S. Government Printing Office, 1929.

Kilgore, B. W., ed. *Proceedings of the Seventh Annual Convention of the Southern States Association of the Commissioners of Agriculture, held at Richmond, Virginia, 23–25 Nov. 1905.* Raleigh, NC: Edwards & Broughton, 1906.

King, J. Crawford, Jr. "The Closure of the Southern Range: An Exploratory Study." *Journal of Southern History* 48, no. 1 (1982): 53–70.

Kirkwood, A. C. "History, Biology and Control of Sheep Scab." *Parasitology Today* 2, no. 11 (1986): 302–7.

Kitching, R. P., A. M. Hutber, and M. V. Thrusfield. "A Review of Foot-and-Mouth Disease with Special Consideration for the Clinical and Epidemiological Factors Relevant to Predictive Modelling of the Disease." *Veterinary Journal* 169, no. 2 (2005): 197–209.

Klein, Benjamin, and Keith B. Leffler. "The Role of Market Forces in Assuring Contractual Performance." *Journal of Political Economy* 89, no. 4 (1981): 615–41.

Klein, Louis A. "Methods of Eradicating Cattle Ticks." *BAI Circular,* no. 110. Washington, DC: U.S. Government Printing Office, 1907.

Kolko, Gabriel. *Railroads and Regulation, 1877–1916.* Princeton, NJ: Princeton Univ. Press, 1965.

———. *The Triumph of Conservatism: A Reinterpretation of American History, 1900–1916.* Chicago: Quadrangle, 1967.

Lampard, Eric E. *The Rise of the Dairy Industry in Wisconsin.* Madison: State Historical Society of Wisconsin, 1963.

Lamso, P. D., A. S. Minot, and B. H. Robbins. "The Prevention and Treatment of Carbon Tetrachloride Intoxication." *Journal of the American Medical Association* 90, no. 5 (1928): 345–49.

Law, James. *Textbook on Veterinary Medicine.* Ithaca, NY: author, 1902.

Law, Marc T., and Gary D. Libecap. "The Determinants of Progressive Era Reform: The Pure Food and Drug Act of 1906." In *Corruption and Reform: Lessons from America's Economic History,* edited by Edward L. Glaeser and Claudia Goldin, 319–42. Chicago: Univ. of Chicago Press, 2006.

Le Potier, Marie-Frédérique, Alain, Mesplède, and Philippe Vannier. "Classical Swine Fever and Other Pestiviruses." In *Diseases of Swine,* 9th ed., edited by Barbara E. Straw, Jeffery J. Zimmerman, Sylvie D'Allaire, and David J. Taylor, 309–22. Ames, IA: Blackwell, 2006.

Leavitt, Judith. *Typhoid Mary: Captive to the Public's Health.* Boston: Beacon Press, 1996.

Leech, Harper, and John C. Carroll. *Armour and His Times.* New York: Appleton-Century, 1938.

Leffingwell, Albert. *American Meat and Its Influence upon the Public Health.* London: George Bell, 1910.

Lemmer, George F. *Norman J. Colman and Colman's Rural World: A Study in Agricultural Leadership.* Univ. of Missouri Studies 25, no. 3. Columbia: Curators of the Univ. Missouri, 1953.

Libecap, Gary D. "The Rise of the Chicago Packers and the Origins of Meat Inspection and Antitrust." *Economic Inquiry* 30, no. 2 (1992): 242–62.

"Live Stock Exchange Inspection of Animals Is a Success." *Chicago Live Stock World,* 25 Mar. 1908, 1–2.

Logue, Jeanne N. *Beyond the Germ Theory: The Story of Dr. Cooper Curtice.* College Station: Texas A&M Univ. Press, 1995.

Lombard, M., P. P. Pastoret, and A. M. Moulin. "A Brief History of Vaccines and Vaccination." *Revue Scientifique et Technique* (OIE) 26, no. 1 (2007): 29–48.

Machado, Manuel A., Jr. *Aftosa: A Historical Survey of Foot-and-Mouth Disease and Inter-American Relations.* Albany: State Univ. of New York Press, 1969.

———. *An Industry in Crisis: Mexican-United States Cooperation in the Control of Foot-and-Mouth Disease.* Berkeley: Univ. of California Press, 1968.

Mack, Roy. "The Great African Cattle Plague Epidemic of the 1890s." *Tropical Animal Health and Production* 2 (1970): 210–19.

Mahy, B. W. J. "Introduction and History of the Foot-and-Mouth Disease Virus." *Current Topics in Microbiology and Immunology* 288 (2006): 1–8.

Marshall, C. J. "Presidential Address." *American Journal of Veterinary Medicine* 48 (1915): 80–87.

Mashaw, Jerry L. *Creating the Administrative Constitution: The Lost One Hundred Years of American Administrative Law.* New Haven, CT: Yale Univ. Press, 2012.

Maxey, Edwin. "Federal Quarantine Laws." *Political Science Quarterly* 23, no. 4 (1908): 617–36.

Mayer, August. "The Cattle Tick in Relation to Southern Agriculture." USDA, *Farmers' Bulletin*, no. 261. Washington, DC: U.S. Government Printing Office, 1906.

McCauley, E. H., and W. B. Sundquist. "Potential Economic Consequences of African Swine Fever and Its Control in the United States." Department of Agricultural and Applied Economics, Staff Paper P79-11. St. Paul: Univ. of Minnesota, Apr. 1979. http://ageconsearch.umn.edu/bitstream/13530/1 /21502.pdf.

McCauley, E. Hunt, John C. New Jr., Nasser A. Aulaqi, et al. *A Study of the Potential Economic Impact of Foot-and-Mouth Disease in the United States.* Washington, DC: U.S. Government Printing Office, 1979.

McCormick, Richard L. *The Party Period and Public Policy.* New York: Oxford Univ. Press, 1986.

McCoy, Joseph G. *Historic Sketches of the Cattle Trade of the West and Southwest.* Kansas City, MO: Ramsey, Millett & Hudson, 1874.

McCurdy, Charles W. "American Law and the Marketing Structure of the Large Corporation, 1875–1890." *Journal of Economic History* 37, no. 3 (1978): 631–49.

McGraw, Thomas K. *Prophets of Regulation: Charles Francis Adams, Louis D. Brandeis, James M. Landis, and Alfred E. Kahn.* Cambridge, MA: Harvard Univ. Press, 1984.

McNeil, Donald G., Jr. "Rinderpest, Scourge of Cattle, Is Vanquished." *New York Times,* 28 June 2011, D1. www.nytimes.com/2011/06/28/health /28rinderpest.html.

Mease, James. "An Account of a Contagious Disease Propagated by a Drove of Southern Cattle in Perfect Health." *Memoirs of the Philadelphia Society for Promoting Agriculture* 5 (1826): 280–83.

Mehlhorn, Heinz. *Encyclopedia of Parasitology.* 3rd ed. 2 vols. New York: Springer, 2008.

Meikle, James. "Mad Cow Disease—A Very British Response to an International Crisis." *Guardian,* 25 Apr. 2012. www.theguardian.com/uk/2012/apr/25/mad -cow-disease-british-crisis.

Melosi, Martin V. *Garbage in the Cities: Refuse, Reform, and the Environment.* Rev. ed. Pittsburgh: Univ. of Pittsburgh Press, 2005.

Melvin, A. D. "Some Results of Cattle-Tick Eradication." *BAI Circular,* no. 196. Washington, DC: U.S. Government Printing Office, 1912.

Melvin, A. D., and M. Dorset. "The Control of Hog Cholera." USDA *Bulletin,* no. 584. Washington, DC: U.S. Government Printing Office, 1917.

Mesmer, Philippe. "South Korea Hit by Fast-Spreading Outbreak of Foot-and-Mouth Disease." *Guardian Weekly,* 18 Jan. 2011. www.theguardian.com /world/2011/jan/18/south-korea-foot-and-mouth.

Miller, Everett B. "Tuberculous Cattle Problem in the United States to 1917." *Historia Medicinae Veterinariae* 14, no. 1–2 (1989): 1–64.

———. "Veterinary Medical Service of the Army in the Spanish-American War, 1898 (with Notes on the 'Embalmed Beef' Scandal)." *Veterinary Heritage* 11, no. 1 (1988): 14–38.

Mississippi, State of. *Laws of the State of Mississippi Passed at a Regular Session of the Mississippi Legislature,* January 6, 1914 to March 28, 1914, and an *Extraordinary Session* held in June 1913, Chapter 351, House Bill No. 653. Memphis, TN: E. R. Clarke & Bros., 1914.

Missouri State Board of Agriculture. *Annual Report for 1866.* Jefferson City, MO: Emery S. Foster, 1867.

———. *Annual Report for 1868.* Jefferson City, MO: Ellwood Kirby, 1869.

Mitchell, B. R. *International Historical Statistics, Europe, 1750–1988.* New York: Stockton Press, 1992.

Moda, Giuliana. "Non-technical Constraints to Eradication: the Italian Experience." *Veterinary Microbiology* 112 (2006): 253–58.

Mohler, John R. "Blackleg: Its Nature, Cause, and Prevention." USDA, *Farmers' Bulletin,* no. 1355. Washington, DC: U.S. Government Printing Office, 1923.

———. "Federal Meat Inspection as a Safeguard to Public Health." *American Journal of Public Health* 10, no. 5 (1920): 441–46.

———. "Foot-and-Mouth Disease with Special Reference to the Outbreak of 1914." USDA, *Department Circular,* no. 325. Washington, DC: U.S. Government Printing Office, 1924.

———. "Foot-and-Mouth Disease, with Special Reference to the Outbreaks in California, 1924, and Texas, 1924 and 1925." USDA, *Department Circular,* no. 400. Washington, DC: U.S. Government Printing Office, 1926.

———. "History and Present Status of Meat Inspection in the United States." In Robert Ostertag, *Handbook of Meat Inspection.* 3rd ed., xv–xxxv. Translated by Earley Wilcox. New York: William R. Jenkins, 1907.

———. "The 1929 Outbreak of Foot-and-Mouth Disease in California." *Journal of American Veterinary Medical Association* 75 (1929): 309–18.

———. "Texas Fever (Otherwise Known as Tick Fever, Splenetic Fever or Southern Cattle Fever), with Methods for its Prevention." *BAI Bulletin,* no. 78. Washington, DC: U.S. Government Printing Office, 1905.

———. "Texas or Tick Fever and Its Prevention." USDA, *Farmers' Bulletin,* no. 258. Washington, DC: U.S. Government Printing Office, 1906.

Mohler, John R., and Milton J. Rosenau. "The Origin of the Recent Outbreak of Foot-and-Mouth Disease in the United States." *BAI Circular,* no 147. Washington, DC: U.S. Government Printing Office, 1909.

Mohler, John R., and Rudolph Snyder. "The 1929 Outbreak of Foot-and-Mouth Disease in Southern California." USDA, *Miscellaneous Publication,* no. 68. Washington, DC: U.S. Government Printing Office, 1930.

———. "The 1932 Outbreak of Foot-and-Mouth Disease in Southern California." USDA, *Miscellaneous Publication,* no. 163. Washington, DC: U.S. Government Printing Office, 1933.

Monke, Jim. "The Virus-Serum-Toxin Act: A Brief Historical Analysis." CRS Report for Congress, RS22014 (3 Jan. 2005).

Moore, James Tice. "Redeemers Reconsidered: Change and Continuity in the Democratic South, 1870–1900." *Journal of Southern History* 44, no. 3 (1978): 357–78.

Moorhead, Robert. "William Budd and Typhoid Fever." *Journal of the Royal Society of Medicine* 95, no. 11 (2002): 561–64.

Morens, David M., Victoria A. Harden, Joseph Kinyoun Houts Jr., and Anthony S. Fauci. *The Indispensable Forgotten Man: Joseph James Kinyoun and the Founding of the National Institutes of Health.* Washington, DC: National Institute of Allergy and Infection Diseases, 2012.

Morgan, H. Wayne. *From Hayes to McKinley: National Party Politics, 1877–1896.* Syracuse, NY: Syracuse Univ. Press, 1969.

Morison, Elting E., ed. *The Letters of Theodore Roosevelt.* 8 vols. Cambridge, MA: Harvard Univ. Press, 1952.

Mowry, George W. *The Era of Theodore Roosevelt.* New York: Harper-Row, 1958.

Munroe, Charles E. "Regulation of Explosives in the United States with Especial Reference to the Administration of the Explosives Act of October 6, 1917." U.S. Bureau of Mines *Bulletin,* no. 198. Washington, DC: U.S. Government Printing Office, 1921.

Murphy, Frederick A. *The Foundations of Virology: Discoverers and Discoveries, Inventors and Inventions, Developers and Technologies.* Rev. ed. West Conshohocken, PA: Infinity, 2014. www.utmb.edu/virusimages/.

Myers, J. Arthur. *Man's Greatest Victory over Tuberculosis.* Springfield, IL: Charles C. Thomas, 1940.

———. *Tuberculosis: A Half Century of Study and Conquest.* St. Louis: W. H. Green, 1970.

Myers, J. Arthur, and James H. Steele. *Bovine Tuberculosis Control in Man and Animals.* St. Louis: W. H. Green, 1969.

National Swine Breeders' Association. *Proceedings, 1885.* Springfield, IL: Springfield Printing, 1886.

New Jersey Board of Agriculture. *Annual Report for 1880.* Camden, NJ: Sinnickson Chew, 1881.

New York State. *Meat for Millions: Report of the New York State Trichinosis Commission.* 2nd ed. Albany, NY: Fort Orange Press, 1941.

Newell, Wilmon, and M. S. Dougherty. "The Cattle Tick." State Crop Pest Commission of Louisiana *Circular,* no. 10. 1906.

Newell-McGloughlin, Martina, and Edward Re. *The Evolution of Biotechnology: From Natufians to Nanotechnology.* Dordrecht, The Netherlands: Springer, 2006.

Newton, L. G., and R. Norris. *Clearing a Continent: The Eradication of Bovine Pleuropneumonia from Australia.* SCARM Report No. 74. Collingwood, Victoria: CSIRO, 2000.

Nimmo, Joseph, Jr. *The Production of Swine in the United States.* Washington, DC: U.S. Government Printing Office, 1884.

———. *Report in Regard to the Range and Ranch Cattle Business of the United States.* Washington, DC: U.S. Government Printing Office, 1885.

Niskanen, William A. *Bureaucracy and Representative Government.* Chicago: Aldine-Atherton, 1971.

North Carolina Department of Agriculture. *Biennial Report from December 1, 1916 to November 30, 1918.* Raleigh, NC: Edwards & Broughton, 1918.

———. *Biennial Report from December 1, 1918 to December 30, 1920.* Raleigh, NC: Edwards & Broughton, 1920.

Novak, William J. "The Myth of the 'Weak' American State." *American Historical Review* 113, no. 3 (2008): 752–72.

———. *People's Welfare: Law and Regulation in Nineteenth-Century America.* Chapel Hill: Univ. of North Carolina Press, 1996.

Ohio State Board of Agriculture. *Annual Report.* Various years.

Olitsky, Peter K., Jacob Traum, and Harry W. Schoening. "Report of the Foot-and-Mouth-Disease Commission." USDA, *Technical Bulletin,* no. 76. Washington, DC: U.S. Government Printing Office, 1928.

Ollinger, Michael. "Structural Change in Meat and Poultry Industry and Food Safety Regulations." *Agribusiness* 27, no. 2 (2011): 244–57.

Olmstead, Alan L. "The First Line of Defense: Inventing the Infrastructure to Combat Animal Diseases." *Journal of Economic History* 69, no. 2 (2009): 327–57.

Olmstead, Alan L., and Paul W. Rhode. *Creating Abundance: Biological Innovation and American Agricultural Development.* New York: Cambridge Univ. Press, 2008.

———. "The Eradication of Bovine Tuberculosis in the United States in a Comparative Perspective." In *Human and Animal Agriculture in Developing Countries,* edited by David Zilberman, Joachim Otte, David Roland Holst, and Dirk Pfeiffer, 7–30. New York: Springer-FAO, 2012.

———. "An Impossible Undertaking: The Eradication of Bovine Tuberculosis in the United States." *Journal of Economic History* 64, no. 3 (2004): 734–72.

———. "Not on My Farm! Farmer Resistance to the Tuberculin-Testing Program to Eradicate Bovine Tuberculosis in the United States, 1893–1941." *Journal of Economic History* 67, no. 3 (2007): 768–809.

———. "The 'Tuberculous Cattle Trust': Disease Contagion in an Era of Regulatory Uncertainty." *Journal of Economic History* 64, no. 4 (2005): 929–63.

Olson, James C. *J. Sterling Morton.* Lincoln: Univ. of Nebraska Press, 1942.

Omohundro, R. E. "The Dismal Swamp Operation." *Journal of the American Veterinary Medical Association* 159, no. 11 (1971): 1564–66.

Osborn, Irwin S. "Effect of the War on the Production of Garbage and Methods of Disposal." *American Journal of Public Health* 8, no. 5 (1918): 368–72.

Osgood, Ernest Staples. *The Day of the Cattleman.* Minneapolis: Univ. of Minnesota Press, 1929.

Ostertag, Robert. *Handbook of Meat Inspection.* Translated by Earley Wilcox. New York: William R. Jenkins, 1904.

———. *Handbook of Meat Inspection,* 3rd ed. Translated by Earley Wilcox. New York: William R. Jenkins, 1907.

Overfield, Richard A. "Hog Cholera, Texas Fever, and Frank S. Billings: An Episode in Nebraska Veterinary Science." *Nebraska History* 57, no. 1 (1976): 99–128.

Paarlberg, Philip L., John G. Lee, and Ann H. Seitzinger. "Measuring the Welfare Effects of an FMD Outbreak in the United States." *Journal of Agricultural and Applied Economics* 35 (2003): 53–65.

Pearson, Leonard, and M. P. Ravenel. "Tuberculosis of Cattle." *Pennsylvania Department of Agriculture Bulletin,* no. 75 (1901).

Pegram, Thomas R. "Public Health and Progressive Dairying in Illinois." *Agricultural History* 65, no. 1 (1991): 36–50.

Peires, J. B. *Dead Will Arise: Nongqawuse and the Great Xhosa Cattle-Killing Movement of 1856–57.* Bloomington: Indiana Univ. Press, 1989.

Pendell, Dustin L., John Leatherman, Ted C. Schroeder, and Gregory S. Alward. "The Economic Impacts of a Foot-and-Mouth Disease Outbreak: A Regional Analysis." *Journal of Agricultural and Applied Economics* 39 (2007): 19–33.

Pennsylvania Department of Agriculture. *Annual Report for 1909.* Harrisburg, PA: C. E. Aughinbaugh, 1910.

———. *Annual Report for 1915.* Harrisburg, PA: Wm. Stanley Ray, 1916.

Perren, Richard. "The North American Beef and Cattle Trade with Great Britain, 1870–1914." *Economic History Review* 24, no. 3 (1971): 430–44.

Peters, Austin. "Bovine Tuberculosis in Massachusetts: A History of the Earlier Agitation Concerning It, and Efforts of the State for Its Eradication and Control." In *Tuberculosis in Massachusetts,* edited by Edwin A Locke, 37–64. Boston, MA: Wright and Potter, 1908.

Pierce, Bessie Louise. *History of Chicago.* Vol. 3, *The Rise of the Modern City, 1871–1893.* Chicago: Alfred A. Knopf, 1957.

Plotkin, Susan L., and Stanley A. Plotkin. "A Short History of Vaccination." In *Vaccines,* 4th ed., edited by Stanley A. Plotkin and Walter A. Orenstein, 1–15. Philadelphia: Elsevier, 2004.

Plumb, Charles S. "Marketing Live Stock." USDA *Farmers' Bulletin,* no. 184. Washington, DC: U.S. Government Printing Office, 1903.

Poole, Keith T., and Howard Rosenthal. "Congress and Railroad Regulation: 1874–1887." In *The Regulated Economy: A Historical Approach to Political Economy,* edited by Claudia Goldin and Gary D. Libecap, 81–120. Chicago: Univ. of Chicago Press, 1994.

———. "The Enduring Nineteenth-Century Battle for Economic Regulation: The Interstate Commerce Act Revisited." *Journal of Law and Economics* 36, no. 2 (1993): 837–60.

Poor's Manual of Railroads. New York: Poor's Publishing, various dates.

Powell, Fred W. *Bureau of Animal Industry: Its History, Organization, and Activities.* Baltimore: Johns Hopkins Univ. Press, 1927.

Powell, Jim. *Bully Boy: The Truth about Theodore Roosevelt's Legacy.* New York: Crown Forum, 2006.

Preston, Samuel, and Michael Haines. *Fatal Years: Child Mortality in Late Nineteenth-Century America.* Princeton, NJ: Princeton Univ. Press, 1991.

Price, R. M. "The Bovine Tubercle Bacillus in Human Tuberculosis." *American Journal of the Medical Sciences* 197, Series 2 (1939): 411–27.

Pritchard, D. G. "A Century of Bovine Tuberculosis 1888–1988: Conquest and Controversy." *Journal of Comparative Pathology* 99 (1988): 357–99.

Proctor, Ben H. *Not Without Honor: The Life of John H. Reagan.* Austin: Univ. of Texas Press, 1962.

"Public Hearing on Halting Shipments of Hog Cholera Vaccines." *Journal of the American Veterinary Medical Association* 154, no. 10 (1969): 1148–49.

Quin, A. H. "Past and Future of Hog Cholera Control." *Journal of the American Veterinary Medical Association* 116, no. 879 (1950): 411–16.

Radostits, Otto M., Clive C. Gay, Douglas C. Blood, and Kenneth W. Hinchcliff. *Veterinary Medicine.* 9th ed. London: Saunders, 2005.

Ransom, B. H., B. Schwartz, and H. B. Raffensperger. "Effects of Pork-Curing Processes on Trichinae." *USDA Bulletin,* no. 880. Washington, DC: U.S. Government Printing Office, 1920.

Rausser, Gordon, Johan Swinnen, and Pinhas Zusman. *Political Power and Economic Policy: Theory, Analysis, and Empirical Applications.* New York: Cambridge Univ. Press, 2011.

"Recent Outbreaks of Texas Fever." *National Live-Stock Journal* 8, no. 11 (1877): 470–71.

Reed, Thomas B. "Rules of the House of Representatives." *Century* 37 (1889): 792–95.

Reiger, C. C. "The Struggle for Federal Food and Drugs Legislation." *Law and Contemporary Problems* 1, no. 1 (1933): 3–15.

Reynolds, M. H. "The Problem of Bovine Tuberculosis Control." *American Veterinary Review* 33 (1909): 449–81.

Rich, Arnold R. *The Pathogenesis of Tuberculosis.* Springfield, IL: Charles C. Thomas, 1944.

Riley, Franklin L. "Diary of a Mississippi Planter, January 1, 1840 to April, 1863." *Publications of the Mississippi Historical Society* 10 (1909): 305–482.

Rixson, Derrick. *History of Meat Trading.* Nottingham, United Kingdom: Nottingham Univ. Press, 2000.

Roadhouse, Chester L., and James L. Henderson. *Milk Market.* 2nd ed. New York: McGraw-Hill, 1950.

Roberts, John. "State and Municipal Meat Inspection." *American Journal of Public Health* 10, no. 9 (1920): 697–703.

Rosenau, Milton J. "Pasteurization." In *Milk and Its Relation to the Public Health.* Marine-Hospital Service of the United States, Treasury Department, Hygienic Laboratory. *Bulletin,* no. 41, 591–628. Washington, DC: U.S. Government Printing Office, 1908.

Rosenberg, Charles E. *No Other Gods: On Science and American Social Thought.* Expanded ed. Baltimore: Johns Hopkins Univ. Press, 1997.

Ross, Richard F. "*Pasteurella multocida* and Its Role in Porcine Pneumonia." *Animal Health Research Reviews* 7, no. 1–2 (2006): 13–29.

Roueché, Berton. "A Pig from Jersey." *New Yorker,* 18 Nov. 1950, 157–66.

Salmon, Daniel. "The Outbreak of Pleuro-Pneumonia at Chicago, and the Lessons Which It Teaches." *National Live-Stock Journal* 18, no. 11 (1887): 392–94.

Salmon, Daniel E. "Legislation with Reference to Bovine Tuberculosis." *BAI Bulletin,* no. 28. Washington, DC: U.S. Government Printing Office, 1901.

———. "Report Upon Investigations Relating to the Treatment of Lumpy-jaw, Or Actinomycosis, in Cattle." *BAI Bulletin,* no. 2. Washington, DC: U.S. Government Printing Office, 1893.

———. "Results of Experiments with Inoculation for the Prevention of Hog Cholera." USDA, *Farmers' Bulletin,* no. 8. Washington, DC: U.S. Government Printing Office, 1892.

Sánchez-Vizcaíno, José Manuel. "African Swine Fever." In *Diseases of Swine,* 9th ed., edited by Barbara E. Straw, Jeffery J. Zimmerman, Sylvie D'Allaire, and David J. Taylor, 291–98. Ames, IA: Blackwell, 2006.

Sandburg, Carl. *Always the Young Strangers.* New York: Harcourt, Brace, 1952.

Sanders, Elizabeth. *Roots of Reform: Farmers, Workers, and American State, 1877–1917.* Chicago: Univ. of Chicago Press, 1999.

Saunders, L. Z. "A History of the Pathological Division of the Bureau of Animal Industry, United States Department of Agriculture, between 1891 and 1921." *Veterinary Pathology* 26 (1989): 531–50.

Scallan, Elaine, Patricia M. Griffin, Frederick J. Anulo, Robert V. Tauxe, and Robert M. Hoekstra. "Foodborne Illness Acquired in the United States— Unspecified Agents." *Emerging Infectious Disease* 17, no. 1 (2011): 16–22.

Scallan, Elaine, Robert M. Hoekstra, Frederick J. Angulo, Robert V. Tauxe, Marc-Alain Widdowson, Sharon L. Roy, Jeffery L. Jones, and Patricia M. Griffin. "Foodborne Illness Acquired in the United States—Major Pathogens." *Emerging Infectious Disease* 17, no. 1 (2011): 7–15.

Scheiber, Harry N. "Federalism and the American Economic Order, 1789– 1910." *Law and Society Review* 57 (1975–76): 57–118.

Schieffelin, William. "Work of the Committee of One Hundred on National Health." *Annals of the American Academy of Political and Social Science* 37, no. 2 (1911): 77–86.

Schmiedebach, H. P. "The Prussian State and Microbiological Research— Friedrich Loeffler and His Approach to the 'Invisible' Virus." *Archives of Virology, Supplementum* 15 (1999): 9–23.

Schultz, Myron. "Theobald Smith." *Emerging Infectious Diseases* 14, no. 12 (2008): 1940–42.

Schwabe, Calvin W. *Cattle, Priests, and Progress in Medicine.* Minneapolis: Univ. of Minnesota Press, 1978.

————. *Veterinary Medicine and Human Health*. 3rd ed. Baltimore: Williams & Wilkins, 1984.

Schwartz, Benjamin. "The Trichinosis Situation in the United States." *Scientific Monthly* 51, no. 3 (1940): 241–47.

Schwartzkopff, Olof. "National and International Meat Inspection." *Journal of Comparative Medicine and Veterinary Archives* 11, no. 11 (1890): 599–608.

Scudamore, J. M., and D. M. Harris. "Control of Foot and Mouth Disease: Lessons from the Experience of the Outbreak in the United Kingdom in 2001." *Revue Scientifique et Technique* (OIE) 21, no. 3 (2002): 699–710.

Segarra, Alejandro E., and Sean M. Rawson. "Foot and Mouth Disease: A Threat to U.S. Agriculture." CRS Report for Congress, Congressional Research Service, Library of Congress, Apr. 16, 2001. www.nationalaglawcenter.org/wp-content/uploads/assets/crs/RS20890.pdf.

Sharrer, G. Terry. "The Great Glanders Epizootic, 1861–1866: A Civil War Legacy." *Agricultural History* 69, no. 1 (1995): 79–97.

Shleifer, Andrei. "Efficient Regulation." In *Regulation vs. Litigation: Perspectives from Economics and Law*, edited by Daniel P. Kessler, 27–43. Chicago: Univ. of Chicago Press, 2011.

————. "The Enforcement Theory of Regulation." In *The Failure of Judges and the Rise of Regulators*, edited by Andrei Shleifer, 1–21. Cambridge, MA: MIT Press, 2011.

Shover, John L. *Cornbelt Rebellion: The Farmers' Holiday Association*. Urbana: Univ. of Illinois Press, 1965.

Sigurdsson, Jón. *Studies on the Risk of Infection with Bovine Tuberculosis to the Rural Population*. London: Oxford Univ. Press, 1945.

Sinclair, Upton. *The Jungle*. New York: Doubleday, Jabber, 1906.

Sjogren, Ingela, and Ian Sutherland. "Studies of Tuberculosis in Man in Relation to Infection in Cattle." *Tubercle* 56 (1974): 113–27.

Skowronek, Stephen. *Building a New American State: The Expansion of National Administrative Capacities, 1877–1920*. New York: Cambridge Univ. Press, 1982.

Sledge, Daniel. "War, Tropical Disease, and the Emergence of National Public Health Capacity in the United States." *Studies in American Political Development* 26, no. 2 (2012):125–62.

Smith, Howard R. *The Conquest of Bovine Tuberculosis in the United States*. Somerset, MI: the author, 1958.

————. *Ridding the Nation of Tuberculosis in Livestock*. Chicago: National Live Stock Exchange, 1931.

Smith, Theobald, and F. L. Kilborne. "Investigations into the Nature, Causation, and Prevention of Texas or Southern Cattle Fever." *BAI Bulletin,* no. 1. Washington, DC: U.S. Government Printing Office, 1893.

Smithcors, J. F. "James Mease, M.D., on the Diseases of Domestic Animals." *Bulletin of the History of Medicine* 31, no. 2 (1957): 122–31.

Snyder, Louis L. "The American-German Pork Dispute, 1879–1881." *Journal of Modern History* 17, no. 1 (1945): 16–28.

Sommers, Herbert M. "Disease Due to Mycobacteria Other Than *Mycobacterium tuberculosis.*" In *Tuberculosis,* edited by Guy P. Youmans, 386–403. Philadelphia: W. B. Saunders, 1979.

Spear, Donald P. "California Besieged: The Foot-and-Mouth Epidemic of 1924." *Agricultural History* 56, no. 3 (1982): 533–37.

Spiekermann, Uwe. "Dangerous Meat? German-American Quarrels over Pork and Beef, 1870–1900." *Bulletin of the GHI* [German Historical Institute] 46 (2010): 93–110.

Spielman, Andrew, and Michael D'Antonio. *Mosquito: A Natural History of Our Most Persistent and Deadly Foe.* New York: Hyperion, 2001.

Spinage, Clive A. *Cattle Plague: A History.* Kluwer Academic: New York, 2003.

Stalheim, O. H. V. "The Hog Cholera Battle and Veterinary Professionalism." *Agricultural History* 62, no. 2 (1988): 116–21.

———. *The Winning of Animal Health.* Ames: Iowa State Univ. Press, 1994.

Stalheim, O. H. V., and W. M. Moulton. "Veterinary Medicine in the United States Department of Agriculture." In *100 Years of Animal Health, 1884–1984,* edited by Vivian Wiser, Larry Mark, and H. Graham Purchase, 19–62. Beltsville, MD: Associates of the National Agricultural Library, 1987.

Stanzianni, Alessandro. "Food Safety and Expertise: The Trichinosis Epidemic in France, 1878–1891." *Food and Foodways* 10, no. 4 (2003): 209–37.

Steele, James H., ed. *CRC Handbook Series in Zoonoses, Section A–D.* Boca Raton, FL: CRC Press, 1979.

Stiles, Charles Wardell. "The Inspection of Meats for Animal Parasites." USDA *Bulletin,* no. 19. Washington, DC: U.S. Government Printing Office, 1898.

———. "Trichinosis in Germany." *BAI Bulletin,* no. 30. Washington, DC: U.S. Government Printing Office, 1901.

Storrs, Emery. *The Animal Industry Bill: Further Suggestions against the Passage of the Bill.* [Chicago]: Chicago Live Stock Exchange, 1884.

Straus, Lina G. *Disease in Milk: The Remedy Pasteurization, The Life Work of Nathan Straus.* 2nd ed. New York: E. P. Dutton, 1917.

Strauss, Frederick, and Louis H. Bean. "Gross Farm Income and Indices of Farm Production and Prices in the United States, 1869–1937." USDA, *Technical Bulletin,* no. 703. Washington, DC: U.S. Government Printing Office, 1940.

Street, John W. *Cattle Shipping by Railway in the United States.* Des Moines, IA: Mills, 1870.

Strom, Claire. *Making Catfish Bait Out of Government Boys: The Fight against Cattle Ticks and the Transformation of the Yeoman South.* Athens: Univ. of Georgia Press, 2009.

———. "Texas Fever and the Dispossession of the Southern Yeoman Farmer." *Journal of Southern History* 66, no. 1 (2000): 49–74.

Sullivan, Mark. *Our Times: The United States 1900–1925.* Vol. 2, *America Finding Herself.* New York: Charles Scribner, 1927.

Sumner, Daniel A., and Hyunok Lee. "Sanitary and Phytosanitary Trade Barriers and Empirical Trade Modeling." In *Understanding Technical Barriers to Trade,* edited by David Orden and Donna Roberts, 273–85. Minneapolis: International Agricultural Trade Research Consortium, 1997.

Sumner, Daniel A., and Stefan Tangermann. "International Trade Policy and Negotiations." In *Handbook of Agricultural Economics,* vol. 4, edited by Bruce Gardner and Gordon Rausser, 1999–2055. Amsterdam: North Holland/ Elsevier, 2002.

Sunding, D., and David Zilberman. "The Agricultural Innovation Process: Research and Technology Adoption in Changing Agriculture Sector." *Handbook of Agricultural Economics,* vol. 1A, *Agricultural Production,* edited by Bruce Gardner and Gordon Rausser, 207–26. Amsterdam: North Holland/ Elsevier, 2001.

Sutton, George. "Observations on the Supposed Relations between Epizootics and Epidemics. . . ." *North American Medico-Chirurgical Review* (1858): 483–504.

Swift, Louis F., and Arthur Van Vlissingen Jr. *The Yankee of the Yards: The Biography of Gustavus Franklin Swift.* Chicago: A. W. Shaw, 1927.

Tang, Ho Yin. "The Enigma of Hog Cholera: Controversies, Cause, and Control, 1833–1917." Ph.D. diss., Univ. of Minnesota, 1986.

Tangires, Helen. *Public Markets and Civic Culture in Nineteenth-Century America.* Baltimore: Johns Hopkins Univ. Press, 2003.

Tanner, Fred W., and Louise P. Tanner. *Food-Borne Infections and Intoxications.* Champaign, IL: Garrard Press, 1953.

Tarr, Joel A. *A Study of Boss Politics: William Lorimer of Chicago.* Urbana: Univ. of Illinois Press, 1971.

Teller, Michael E. *The Tuberculosis Movement: A Public Health Campaign in the Progressive Era.* New York: Greenwood Press, 1988.

Thorne, C. E. "Bovine Tuberculosis." *Bulletin of the Ohio Agricultural Experiment Station,* no. 108 (1899).

Tobey, James A. *Legal Aspects of Milk Sanitation.* 2nd ed. Washington, DC: Milk Industry Foundation, 1947.

———. *The National Government and Public Health.* Baltimore: Johns Hopkins Univ. Press, 1926.

U.S. Agricultural Research Service. *Cooperative State-Federal Tuberculosis Eradication Program: Statistical Tables for Fiscal Year 1960.* Washington, DC: USDA, 1961.

———. "Why Tuberculosis in Livestock Is Increasing." *ARS,* no. 91-21. Washington, DC: USDA, 1960.

U.S. Agricultural Research Service, Animal Disease Eradication Branch. "National Status on Control of Garbage-Feeding." Washington, DC: USDA, various years.

U.S. Animal and Plant Health Inspection Service (APHIS). "About APHIS." Updated 19 May 2014. www.aphis.usda.gov/about_aphis/history.shtml.

———. "Controlling Cattle Fever Ticks, August 2010." www.aphis.usda.gov /publications/animal_health/content/printable_version/cattle_fever_ticks .pdf.

———. *National Bovine Brucellosis Surveillance Plan.* Washington, DC: USDA, 2012.

———. "Notes on Foot and Mouth Disease (FMD) in South Korea." [2010.] www.aphis.usda.gov/animal_health/acah/downloads/documents/korea _fmd_update_sacah.pdf.

———. *Protecting America's Animal Health.* Rev. ed. Washington, DC: U.S. Government Printing Office, 1978.

———. "Summary Report: California Bovine Spongiform Encephalopathy Case Investigation." July 2012. www.aphis.usda.gov/animal_health/animal _diseases/bse/downloads/BSE_Summary_Report.pdf.

U.S. Animal Health Association, Committee on Foreign and Emerging Diseases. *Foreign Animal Diseases.* 6th ed. Richmond, VA: U.S. Animal Health Association, 1998.

———. *Foreign Animal Diseases.* 7th ed. Boca Raton, FL: Boca Publishing, 2008.

U.S. Bureau of Animal Industry (BAI). *Operations.* Washington, DC: U.S. Government Printing Office, various years.

———. *Orders.* Washington, DC: U.S. Government Printing Office, various dates.

———. "Proceedings of a Conference of Federal and State Representatives to Consider Plans for the Eradication of the Cattle Tick, Held at Nashville, Tenn. December 5 and 6, 1906." *BAI Bulletin,* no. 97. Washington, DC: U.S. Government Printing Office, 1907.

———. *Report.* Washington, DC: U.S. Government Printing Office, various years.

———. *Report of the Chief.* Washington, DC: U.S. Government Printing Office, various years.

———. *Special Report on Diseases of Cattle, 1908 ed.* Washington, DC: U.S. Government Printing Office, 1908.

———. *Special Report on Diseases of Cattle, 1912 ed.* Washington, DC: U.S. Government Printing Office, 1912.

———. *Special Report on Diseases of Cattle, 1916 ed.* Washington, DC: U.S. Government Printing Office, 1916.

———. *Special Report on Diseases of Horses, 1903 ed.* Washington, DC: U.S. Government Printing Office, 1903.

———. *Status of Bovine Tuberculosis Eradication on Area Basis.* Washington, DC: U.S. Government Printing Office, various issues.

U.S. Bureau of the Census. *Eleventh Census: 1890.* Vol. 6, *Report on Manufacturing Industries in the United States.* Pt. 2, *Statistics of Cities.* Washington, DC: U.S. Government Printing Office, 1895.

———. *Fifteenth Census of the United States: 1930. Agriculture.* Vol. 2, *Reports by States.* Washington, DC: U.S. Government Printing Office, 1932.

———. *Fifteenth Census of the United States: 1930. Agriculture.* Vol. 4, *General Report, Statistics by Subjects.* Washington, DC: U.S. Government Printing Office, 1932.

———. *Fourteenth Census of the United States: 1920.* Vol. 5, *Agriculture, General Report and Analysis.* Washington, DC: U.S. Government Printing Office, 1922.

———. *Mortality Rates 1910–1920 with Population of the Federal Censuses of 1910 and 1920 and Intercensal Estimates of Population.* Washington, DC: U.S. Government Printing Office, 1923.

———. *Mortality Statistics 1907.* Washington, DC: U.S. Government Printing Office, 1909.

———. *Sixteenth Census of the United States: 1940. Agriculture.* Vol. 3, *General Report, Statistics by Subjects.* Washington, DC: U.S. Government Printing Office, 1943.

———. *Thirteenth Census of the United States: 1910.* Vol. 5, *Agriculture, 1909 and 1910, General Report and Analytical Tables.* Washington, DC: U.S. Government Printing Office, 1914.

———. *Twelfth Census of the United States: 1900. Agriculture.* Pt. 1, *Farms, Live Stock, and Animal Products.* Washington, DC: U.S. Government Printing Office, 1902.

———. *United States Census of Agriculture: 1935.* Vol. 3, *General Report, Statistics by Subjects.* Washington, DC: U.S. Government Printing Office, 1937.

U.S. Commissioner of Patents. *Annual Report for 1860.* Washington, DC: U.S. Government Printing Office, 1861.

U.S. Department of Agriculture (USDA). "Contagious Diseases of Domesticated Animals." Special Report No. 22. Washington, DC: U.S. Government Printing Office, 1880.

———. "Contagious Diseases of Domesticated Animals: Continuation of Investigation." Special Report No. 34. Washington, DC: U.S. Government Printing Office, 1881.

———. *Contagious Diseases of Domesticated Animals: Investigations by Department of Agriculture, 1883–1884.* Washington, DC: U.S. Government Printing Office, 1884.

———. "History of Research at the U.S. Department of Agriculture and Agricultural Research Service: Hog Cholera." Agricultural Research Service. First published in *Agricultural Research,* Mar. 1978. www.ars.usda.gov/IS/timeline/cholera.htm.

———. *Hog Cholera: Its History, Nature, and Treatment.* Washington, DC: U.S. Government Printing Office, 1889.

———. "Investigation of Diseases of Swine and Infectious and Contagious Diseases Incident to Other Classes of Domesticated Animals." *Special Report* No. 12. Washington, DC: U.S. Government Printing Office, 1879.

———. *Livestock, Meats, and Wool Market Statistics and Related Data, 1942.* Washington, DC: USDA, 1943.

———. *Proceedings of a Conference to Consider Means for Combating Foot-and-Mouth Disease, Held at Chicago, Ill. November 29 and 30, 1915.* Washington, DC: U.S. Government Printing Office, 1916.

———. *Regulations Governing the Meat Inspection of the United States Department of Agriculture.* Washington, DC: U.S. Government Printing Office, 1914.

———. *Report of the Commissioner.* Washington, DC: U.S. Government Printing Office, various years.

———. *Report of the Secretary.* Washington, DC: U.S. Government Printing Office, various years.

———. *The Story of the Cattle Tick: What Every Southern Child Should Know about Cattle Ticks.* Washington, DC: U.S. Government Printing Office, 1922.

———. *A Tick-Free South.* Washington, DC: USDA, 1917.

———. *The Twenty-Eight Hour Law and the Animal Quarantine Laws Annotated.* Washington, DC: U.S. Government Printing Office, 1915.

———. "USDA Celebrates 100 Years of Food Safety." News release, 28 June 2006. www.usda.gov/wps/portal/usda/usdahome?contentidonly=true&contentid=2006/06/0226.xml.

———. *Weekly News Letter.* Washington, DC: USDA, various dates.

———. *Yearbook of Agriculture.* Washington, DC: U.S. Government Printing Office, various years.

U.S. Department of Agriculture (USDA), Office of Solicitor. *Laws Applicable to the United States Department of Agriculture, 1908.* Washington, DC: U.S. Government Printing Office, 1908.

U.S. Department of Justice. *Annual Report of the Attorney General for 1920.* Washington, DC: U.S. Government Printing Office, 1920.

U.S. Food Administration. *Garbage Utilization with Particular Reference to Utilization by Feeding.* Washington, DC: U.S. Government Printing Office, 1918.

U.S. House of Representatives. *Agricultural Department Appropriation Bill for 1934.* 72nd Cong., 2nd Sess. Washington, DC: U.S. Government Printing Office, 1932.

———. *Agricultural Department Appropriation Bill for 1939.* 75th Cong., 3rd Sess. Washington, DC: U.S. Government Printing Office, 1938.

———. *Communication from the President of the United States Transmitting Supplemental Estimate of Appropriation for the Department of Agriculture Amounting to $500,000 for the Fiscal Year 1930 for an Additional Amount for the Eradication of Tuberculosis in Animals.* House Doc. No. 476, 70th Cong., 2nd Sess. Washington, DC: U.S. Government Printing Office, 1928.

———. *Conference Report on Agriculture Department Appropriation Bill, 1914.* 1 Mar. 1913, 6334 H.rp. 1628, 62nd Cong., 3rd Sess. Washington, DC: U.S. Government Printing Office, 1913.

———. *Inspection of Live Cattle, Hogs, Etc.* 9 Dec. 1890, House Report No. 3262, 51st Cong., 2nd Sess. Washington, DC: U.S. Government Printing Office, 1890.

———. *Inspection of Meats for Exportation, Etc.* 28 Apr. 1890, House Report No. 1792, 51st Cong., 1st Sess. Washington, DC: U.S. Government Printing Office, 1890.

———. *Message from the President of the United States.* 1 Mar. 1905, Doc. No. 375, 58th Cong., 3rd Sess. Washington, DC: U.S. Government Printing Office, 1905.

———. *Message of President on Restrictions Imposed by French Government on Pork Exported from United States.* 26 May 1882, Ex. Doc. No. 209, 47th Cong., 1st Sess. Washington, DC: U.S. Government Printing Office, 1882.

———. *Message of the President to Congress, December 7, 1926.* House Doc. No. 483, 69th Cong., 2nd Sess. Washington, DC: U.S. Government Printing Office, 1926.

———. *National Live-Stock Highway.* 23 Mar. 1886, Report No. 1228, 49th Cong., 1st Sess. Washington, DC: U.S. Government Printing Office, 1886.

———. *Pleuro-Pneumonia.* 15 June 1860, Misc. Doc. No. 93, 30th Cong., 1st Sess. Washington, DC: U.S. Government Printing Office, 1860.

———. *Pleuro-pneumonia in Neat Cattle: Letter from the Secretary of the Treasury.* 28 Feb. 1880, Ex. Doc. No. 53, 46th Cong., 2nd Sess. Washington, DC: U.S. Government Printing Office, 1880.

———. *Report from the Secretary of State Relative to the Importation of the Swine Products of the United States.* 1 Mar. 1884, Ex. Doc. No. 106, 48th Cong., 1st Sess. Washington, DC: U.S. Government Printing Office, 1884.

———. *Report to Accompany S. 3439.* 11 Feb. 1914, Report No. 246, 63rd Cong., 2nd Sess. Washington, DC: U.S. Government Printing Office, 1914.

———. *Restrictions upon the Exportation of Pork from the United States by the French Government.* Ex. Doc. No. 207, 47th Cong., 1st Sess. Washington, DC: U.S. Government Printing Office, 1882.

———. *Tuberculosis in Livestock, Hearings on H.R. 6188, A Bill Making Appropriation for the Control and Eradication of Tuberculosis in Live Stock.* 65th Cong., 2nd Sess. Washington, DC: U.S. Government Printing Office, 1918.

U.S. House of Representatives, Agricultural Committee. *Bureau of Animal Industry.* 26 Jan. 1884, House Report No. 119, 48th Cong., 1st Sess. Washington, DC: U.S. Government Printing Office, 1884.

———. *Contagious and Infectious Disease of Live Stock.* 11 Dec. 1902, Report No. 2819, 57th Cong., 2nd Sess. Washington, DC: U.S. Government Printing Office, 1902.

———. *Hearing on Agricultural Appropriations Bill, HR 13679.* 63th Cong., 2nd Sess. Washington, DC: U.S. Government Printing Office, 1914.

———. *Hearings of Agriculture Appropriations Bill.* 8–12, 14–15, 18–21, 24–28, 31 Jan.; 5, 7–12, 14, 16, 29 Feb. 1916, 64th Cong., 1st Sess. Washington, DC: U.S. Government Printing Office, 1916.

———. *Hearings on the Agricultural Appropriation Bill for Fiscal Year 1921.* 66th Cong., 2nd Sess. Washington, DC: U.S. Government Printing Office, 1920.

———. *Hearings on the So-Called "Beveridge Amendment" to the Agricultural Appropriation Bill (H. R. 18537) as Passed by the Senate May 25 1906—To Which Are Added Various Documents Bearing upon "Beveridge Amendment."* 6–9, 11 June 1906, 59th Cong., 1st Sess. Washington, DC: U.S. Government Printing Office, 1906.

———. "Hearings Regarding H. R. 7208, 30 Jan. 1886." 49th Cong., 1st Sess. Unpublished hearings.

———. "Importation of American Hog Products into Germany and France." 25 Mar. 1884, 48th Cong., 1st Sess. Unpublished hearings.

———. *Letter from the Commissioner of Agriculture, Transmitting a List of Persons Employed and Statement of Expenditures and of Means Adopted for the Suppression of Contagious and Infectious Diseases among Domestic Animals.* 17 Dec. 1884, Ex. Doc. No. 46, 48th Cong., 2nd Sess. Washington, DC: U.S. Government Printing Office, 1885.

———. *Quarantine Districts for Live Stock.* 3 Feb. 1905, Report No. 4200, 58th Cong., 3rd Sess. Washington, DC: U.S. Government Printing Office, 1905.

———. *Quarantine of Cattle: Hearings on H.R. 21443, a Bill to Reimburse Owners of Cattle Exhibited at the National Dairy Show.* 63rd Cong., 3rd Sess. Washington, DC: U.S. Government Printing Office, 1915.

U.S. Interstate Commerce Commission. *First Annual Report.* Washington, DC: U.S. Government Printing Office, 1887.

U.S. Live Stock Sanitary Association. *Report of Annual Meeting.* Various years.

U.S. National Research Council. Committee on Bovine Tuberculosis, *Livestock Disease Eradication: Evaluation of the Cooperative State-Federal Bovine Tuberculosis Eradication Program.* Washington, DC: National Academy Press, 1994.

U.S. Senate. *Estimate of Appropriation for Microscopic Meat Inspection.* 16 Apr. 1912, Doc. No. 569, 62nd Cong., 2nd Sess. Washington, DC: U.S. Government Printing Office, 1912.

———. *Imports and Exports Part I: Imports from 1867 to 1893, Inclusive.* Senate Report No. 259, Part 1, 53nd Cong., 2nd Sess. Washington, DC: U.S. Government Printing Office, 1894.

———. *Information in Relation to the Disease Prevailing among Swine and Other Domestic Animals.* Ex. Doc. No. 35, 45th Cong., 2nd Sess. Washington, DC: U.S. Government Printing Office, 1878.

———. *Information on the Subject of Pleuro-pneumonia among Cattle.* 15 Feb. 1879, Misc. Doc. No. 71, 46th Cong., 2nd Sess. Washington, DC: U.S. Government Printing Office, 1879.

———. *Letter from the Secretary of Agriculture, Transmitting, in Response to a Resolution, of the Senate dated February 12, 1896, Copies of the Regulations Establishing the Quarantine Line in the Southwestern States for the Years 1895 and 1896.* 13 Feb. 1896, Senate Doc. No. 121, 54th Cong., 1st Sess. Washington, DC: U.S. Government Printing Office, 1896.

———. *Remedies for Hog Cholera.* Senate Doc. 489, 63rd Cong., 2nd Sess. Washington, DC: U.S. Government Printing Office, 1914.

———. *Report of Dr. Charles P. Lyman on the Subject of Pleuro-pneumonia or Lung Plague among Cattle.* 21 Apr. 1880, Misc. Doc. No. 74, 46th Cong., 2nd Sess. Washington, DC: U.S. Government Printing Office, 1880.

———. *Report of the Commission Appointed by the President to Investigate the Conduct of the War Department in the War with Spain.* Vol. 7, Senate Doc. No. 221, 56th Cong., 1st Sess. Washington, DC: U.S. Government Printing Office, 1900.

———. *Report of the Select Committee on the Transportation and Sale of Meat Products.* Senate Report No. 829, 51st Cong., 1st Sess. Washington, DC: U.S. Government Printing Office, 1890.

———. *Testimony Taken by the Select Committee on the Transportation and Sale of Meat Products to Accompany Senate Report No. 829.* 51st Cong., 1st Sess. Washington, DC: U.S. Government Printing Office, 1890.

———. *Tubercular Infection in Animals: Methods of Treatment of Breeders and Dairymen in the Enforcement of Regulations for the Elimination of Bovine Tuberculosis.* Senate Doc. No. 85, 70th Cong., 1st Sess. Washington, DC: U.S. Government Printing Office, 1928.

U.S. Senate, Committee on Agriculture and Forestry. *Arrest and Eradication of Foot-and-Mouth Disease, Hearings of Dec. 9, 18, 1914, May 17, 18, 1915.* 63rd Cong., 3rd Sess. Washington, DC: U.S. Government Printing Office, 1916.

———. *Arrest and Eradication of Foot-and-Mouth Disease, Hearings of Dec. 28, 29, 1915.* 64th Cong., 1st Sess. Washington, DC: U.S. Government Printing Office, 1916.

———. *Eradication of Hog Cholera, Hearings on S. bill 1908.* 26 July 1961, 87th Cong., 1st Sess. Washington, DC: U.S. Government Printing Office, 1961.

———. *Letter of the Commissioner of Agriculture, Communicating, In Compliance with a Resolution of the Senate of the 13th Instant, Information in Relation to the Rinderpest or Cattle Plague, April 17, 1866.* Misc. Doc. No. 98, 39th Cong., 1st Sess. Washington, DC: U.S. Government Printing Office, 1866.

———. *Quarantine Districts for Live Stock.* 25 Feb. 1905, Report No. 4352, 58th Cong., 3rd Sess. Washington, DC: U.S. Government Printing Office, 1905.

U.S. Senate, Committee on Foreign Relations. *Swine Products of United States: Production, Healthfulness, and Restrictions on Importation by Germany and France, with Minority Report.* 19 Mar. 1884, Senate Report No. 345, 48th Cong., 1st Sess. Washington, DC: U.S. Government Printing Office, 1884.

U.S. Treasury Department. *Report of the Secretary for 1881.* Washington, DC: U.S. Government Printing Office, 1881.

U.S. Treasury Department, Bureau of Statistics. *Annual Report of the Chief.* Washington, DC: U.S. Government Printing Office, various years.

———. *Monthly Summary of Commerce and Finance of the United States.* Washington, DC: U.S. Government Printing Office, various issues.

Union Stock Yard and Transit Company of Chicago. *Receipts and Shipments of Live Stock at Union Stock Yard, Chicago, for the Year 1914.* Chicago: Union Stock Yard and Transit, 1915.

United Kingdom, Minister of Agriculture, Fisheries, and Food. *Animal Health, A Centenary, 1865–1965: A Century of Endeavor to Control Diseases of Animals.* London: Her Majesty's Stationery Office, 1965.

Van Regenmortel, M. H. V. "Nature of Viruses." In *Desk Encyclopedia of General Virology,* edited by Brian W. J. Mahy and Marc H. V. van Regenmortel, 19–23. Oxford: Elsevier, 2010.

"Veterinary Profession Receives Official Recognition in Tennessee." *American Veterinary Review* 39 (1911): 381–82.

Voetsch, Andrew C., Thomas J. Van Gilder, Frederick J. Angulo, Monica M. Farley, Sue Shallow, Ruthanne Marcus, Paul R. Cieslak, Valerie C. Deneen, and Robert V. Tauxe, for the Emerging Infections Program FoodNet Working Group. "FoodNet Estimate of the Burden of Illness Caused by Nontyphoidal *Salmonella* Infections in the United States." *Clinical Infectious Diseases* 38, Supplement 3 (2004): S127–34.

Waddington, Keir. "To Stamp Out 'So Terrible a Malady': Bovine Tuberculosis and Tuberculin Testing in Britain, 1890–1939." *Medical History* 48 (2004): 29–48.

Wade, Louise C. *Chicago's Pride: The Stockyards, Packingtown, and Environs in the Nineteen Century.* Urbana: Univ. of Illinois Press, 1987.

Walker, Alan R. "Eradication and Control of Livestock Ticks: Biological, Economic and Social Perspectives." *Parasitology* 138, no. 8 (2011): 945–59.

Wall, Joseph F. "The Iowa Farmer in Crisis, 1920–1936." *Annals of Iowa,* 3rd series, 47, no. 2 (1983): 116–27.

Warner, Margaret. "Local Control versus National Interest: The Debate over Southern Public Health, 1878–1884." *Journal of Southern History* 50, no. 3 (1984): 407–28.

Warren, Wilson J. *Tied to the Great Packing Machine: The Midwest and Meatpacking.* Iowa City: Univ. of Iowa Press, 2007.

Waserman, Manfred J. "Henry L. Coit and the Certified Milk Movement in the Development of Modern Pediatrics." *Bulletin of the History of Medicine* 46, no. 4 (1972): 359–90.

Waterman, Jason, and William Fowler. "State Laws and Regulations Pertaining to Public Health." *U.S. Public Health Report, Supplement.* Washington, DC: U.S. Government Printing Office, various years.

Weiss, Roger W. "The Case for Federal Meat Inspection Examined." *Journal of Law and Economics* 7 (1964): 107–20.

Welch, William H. "Preliminary Report of Investigations Concerning the Causation of Hog Cholera." *Johns Hopkins Hospital Bulletin* 1, no. 1 (1889): 9–10.

Whitaker, George. "The Milk Supply of Chicago and Washington." *BAI Bulletin*, no. 138. Washington, DC: U.S. Government Printing Office, 1911.

Whitaker, James W. *Feedlot Empire: Beef Cattle Feeding in Illinois and Iowa, 1840–1900.* Ames: Iowa State Univ. Press, 1975.

White, Roland A. *Milo Reno: Farmers Union Pioneer, The Story of a Man and a Movement.* New York: Arno Press, 1975. First published in 1941.

Whittier, Dee, Nancy Currin, and John F. Currin. "Anaplasmosis in Beef Cattle." Virginia Cooperative Extension Publication 400-465. Blacksburg: College of Agriculture and Life Sciences, Virginia Polytechnic Institute and State University, 2009. http://pubs.ext.vt.edu/400/400-465/400-465_pdf.pdf.

Wight, Alexander E. "Tuberculosis in Livestock, Detection, Control, and Eradication." USDA *Farmers' Bulletin*, no. 1069, 1936 revised. Washington, DC: U.S. Government Printing Office, 1936.

Wilkerson, Frank. "Cattle-Raising on the Plains." *Harper's Monthly* 72, no. 431 (1886): 788–94.

Willis, N. G. "Canada." In *Mycobacterium bovis Infection in Animals and Humans*, edited by Charles Thoen and James H. Steele, 195–98. Ames: Iowa State Univ. Press, 1995.

Wilson, Thomas E. "The Economic Importance of Eradicating Tuberculosis." *Journal of the American Veterinary Medical Association* 61, no. 14 (1922): 55–62.

Winsberg, Morton D. *Modern Breeds of Cattle in Argentina.* Lawrence, KS: Center of Latin American Studies, 1968.

"Wisconsin Is Hog Cholera Free." *Journal of the American Veterinary Medical Association* 154, no. 7 (1969): 859–60.

Wise, G. H. *Hog Cholera and Its Eradication: A Review of U.S. Experience.* APHIS 91-55. Washington, DC: U.S. Government Printing Office, 1981.

Woodbury, Robert M. "Causal Factors in Infant Mortality: A Statistical Study Based on Investigations in Eight Cities." *U.S. Children's Bureau Bulletin*, no. 142. Washington, DC: U.S. Government Printing Office, 1925.

Woods, Abigail. "'Flames and Fear on the Farms': Controlling Foot and Mouth Disease in Britain, 1892–2001." *Historical Research* 77, no. 198 (2004): 520–42.

———. *A Manufactured Plague: The History of Foot-and-Mouth Disease in Britain.* London: Earthscan, 2004.

———. "Why Slaughter? The Cultural Dimensions of Britain's Foot and Mouth Disease Control Policy." *Journal of Agricultural and Environmental Ethics* 17, no. 4–5 (2004): 341–6.

Woodward, C. Vann, *Tom Watson: Agrarian Rebel.* Savannah, GA: Beehive Press, 1938.

World Organization for Animal Health (OIE). "Rinderpest Eradication." *Bulletin,* no. 2011-2 (2011), pp. 1–10. www.oie.int/fileadmin/Home/eng/Publications_&_Documentation/docs/pdf/bulletin/Bull_2011-2-ENG.pdf.

Wright, Willard H. "Charles Wardell Stiles, 1867–1941." *Journal of Parasitology* 27, no. 3 (1941): 195–201.

Wright, Willard H., K. B. Kerr, and Leon Jacobs. "Studies on Trichinosis XV: Summary of the Findings of *Trichinella Spiralis* in a Random Sampling and Other Samplings of the Population of the United States." *Public Health Reports* 58, no. 35 (1943): 1293–313.

Wright, Willard H., Leon Jacobs, and Arthur C. Walton. "Studies on Trichinosis XVI: Epidemiological Considerations Based on the Examination for Trichinae of 5,313 Diaphragms from 189 Hospitals in 37 States and the District of Columbia." *Public Health Reports* 59, no. 21 (1944): 669–82.

Yeager, Mary. *Competition and Regulation: The Development of Oligopoly in the Meat Packing Industry.* Greenwich, CT: JAI Press, 1981.

Zarin, Daniel J. "Searching for Pennies in Piles of Trash: Municipal Refuse Utilization in the United States, 1870–1930." *Environmental Review* 11, no. 3 (1987): 207–22.

Zavodnyic, Peter. *The Rise of the Federal Colossus: The Growth of Federal Power from Lincoln to F.D.R.* Santa Barbara, CA: Praeger, 2011.

Zimmerman, Joseph F., and Sharon Lawrence. *Federal Statutory Preemption of State and Local Authority: History, Inventory, and Issues.* U.S. Advisory Commission on Intergovernmental Relations Report A-121. Washington, DC: ACIR, 1992.

Zimmerman, William David. "Live Cattle Export Trade between United States and Great Britain, 1868–1885." *Agricultural History* 36, no. 1 (1962): 46–52.

Zimmermann, William J. "Salt Cure and Drying-Time and Temperature Effects on Viability of *Trichinella spiralis* in Dry-Cured Hams." *Journal of Food Science* 36, no. 1 (1971): 58–62.

Zimmermann, William J., J. H. Steele, and I. G. Kagan. "Trichiniasis in the U.S. Population, 1966–1970." *Health Services Reports* 88, no. 7 (1973): 611–13.

Zylberman, Patrick. "Making Food Safety an Issue: Internationalized Food Politics and French Public Health from the 1870s to the Present." *Medical History* 48, no. 1 (2004): 1–28.

Newspapers and Periodicals

Aberdeen (SD) Daily News

American Farmer

Atchison Globe

Atlanta Constitution

Augusta Chronicle

Baltimore Sun

Boston Daily Advertiser

Breeder's Gazette

Brooklyn Eagle

Butcher's Advocate

Charleston Mercury

Chicago Daily News

Chicago Herald

Chicago Inter Ocean

Chicago Record

Chicago Tribune

Chillicothe (OH) Scioto Gazette

Creamery and Milk Plant Monthly

Cultivator

Dallas Morning News

Dallas Weekly Herald

Detroit Free Press

Drovers Journal

Dundee Courier & Argus

Elgin Daily News

Farm Holiday News

Farm, Field, and Stockman

Farmers' Review

Fort Worth Telegram

Fresno Bee

Galveston Daily News

Genesee Farmer

Hoard's Dairyman

Idaho Daily Statesman

Jeffersonian

Lancet

London Times

Los Angeles Times

Macon Telegraph

Manchester Guardian

Massachusetts Ploughman

Medical and Surgical Reporter

Milwaukee Journal

Milwaukee Sentinel

National Live-Stock Journal

National Provisioner

New Orleans Times-Picayune

New York Herald

New York Times

New York Tribune

Ohio Farmer

Philadelphia Inquirer

Philadelphia North American and United States Gazette

Pittsfield Sun

Portland Morning Oregonian

Prairie Farmer

Raleigh Register

Rocky Mountain News

San Antonio (TX) Daily Express

Scotsman

Southern Planter

St. Louis Globe-Democrat

St. Louis Republic

Statist

Texas Tribune

Trenton (NJ) State Gazette

Washington Post
Weekly Eastern Argus
Woman Citizen
World's Work
Zanesville Gazette
Zanesville Ohio Republican

Archival Material

Russell A. Alger Papers. William L. Clements Library. Univ. of Michigan, Ann Arbor.

American Medical Association Archives. Chicago, IL.

Back of the Yards Collection, Special Collections. Chicago Public Library, Harold Washington Library Center, Chicago, IL.

E. W. Blatchford Papers. "Hog Raising and the Pork Packing Industry in America." Crerar Ms 207, Special Collections Research Center. Univ. of Chicago Library, Chicago, IL.

Cedar County Historical Society, Tipton, IA.

Marion Dorset Papers. MS 32. Special Collections, Iowa State Univ., Ames. www .lib.iastate.edu/spcl/manuscripts/MS032.html, accessed 17 Mar. 2011.

Eloise Cram Papers. Special Collections. National Agricultural Library, Beltsville, MD. http://specialcollections.nal.usda.gov/guide-collections /eloise-cram-papers, accessed 24 Apr. 2013.

Robert E. Gallman Papers., No. 5000, Southern Historical Collection. Wilson Library, Univ. of North Carolina at Chapel Hill.

Carter Glass Papers. Special Collections. Univ. of Virginia, Charlottesville.

Benjamin Harrison Presidential Papers. Microfilm. Manuscript Division. Library of Congress, Washington, DC.

John Randolph Haynes Papers, No. 1241, Special Collections. Charles E. Young Library, Univ. of California–Los Angeles.

Library of Congress, Washington, DC.

Mary McDowell Settlement Records. Chicago Historical Society, Chicago, IL.

Morton Family Papers. Chicago Historical Society, Chicago, IL.

J. Sterling Morton Papers. Nebraska Historical Society, Lincoln.

Charles P. Neill Correspondence. Collection 2001M-0078. Houghton Library, Harvard Univ., Cambridge, MA.

Charles Patrick Neill Papers. Collection ACUA 012. American Catholic Research Center and Univ. Archives, Catholic Univ., Washington, DC.

Charles E. North Papers. Special Collections. National Agricultural Library, Beltsville, MD.

George J. Ormsby Papers. Special Collections. Iowa State Univ., Ames.

Jeremiah Rusk Papers. Wisconsin Historical Society, Madison.

Daniel E. Salmon Papers. Collection No. 6585. Division of Rare and Manuscript Collections. Cornell Univ. Library, Ithaca, NY.

Screwworm Eradication Program Records. Special Collections. National Agricultural Library, Beltsville, MD. http://specialcollections.nal.usda.gov/guide-collections/screwworm-eradication-program-records, accessed 8 May 2013.

Howard R. Smith Papers. Collection No. 46. Michigan State Univ. Archives and Historical Collections, East Lansing, MI.

U.S. Bureau of Animal Industry (BAI). Bureau of Animal Industry Records. Records, RG17. National Archives, College Park, MD.

USDA. Records of the Office of the Secretary of Agriculture. RG 16. Microfilm M 440. National Archives, College Park, MD.

U.S. House of Representatives Records. RG 233. Center for Legislative Archives. National Archives, Washington, DC.

U.S. Senate Records. RG 46. Center for Legislative Archives. National Archives, Washington, DC.

James Wilson Papers. Special Collections. Iowa State Univ., Ames.

Wyoming Stock Growers Association (WSGA) Records. Univ. of Wyoming, Laramie. digitalcollections.uwyo.edu:8180/luna/servlet, accessed 6 Feb. 2013.

Court Cases

Adams v. Milwaukee. 228 U.S. 572, decided 12 May 1913.

Bowman v. Chicago and Northwestern Railway Co. 125 U.S. 465, 492, decided 19 Mar. 1888.

Brimmer v. Rebman. 138 U.S. 78, decided 19 Jan. 1891.

Coe v. Errol. 116 U.S. 517, decided 25 Jan. 1886.

Fort Worth & Denver City Railway Company v. R. B. Masterson, et al. 66 S.W. Rep. 833, decided 6 Mar. 1902.

Gibbons v. Odgen. 22 U.S. 1, decided 1824.

Grayson v. Lynch. 163 U.S. 468, decided 25 May 1896.

H. P. Croff v. C. M. Cresse. 7 Okla. 408, decided June 1898.

Hannibal and St. Joseph Railroad Co. v. Husen. 95 U.S. 465, published 1878.

Idaho v. Rasmussen. 7 Idaho 1, 59 Pac 733, decided 23 Jan. 1900.

Illinois Central Railroad Co. v. McKendree. 203 U.S. 514, decided 17 Dec. 1906.

Illinois Central Railroad Co. v. T. C. Edwards. 203 U.S. 531, decided 17 Dec. 1906.

Jacobson v. Massachusetts. 197 U.S. 11, decided 20 Feb. 1905.

Lawton v. Steele. 152 U.S. 136, decided 6 Mar. 1894.

Leisy v. Hardin. 135 U.S. 100, decided 28 Apr. 1890.

Minnesota v. Barber. 36 U.S. 313, decided 19 May 1890.

Missouri, Kansas & Texas Railroad Co. v. Haber. 169 U.S. 623, decided 14 Mar. 1898.

Munn v. Illinois. 94 U.S. 113, decided 1 Mar. 1877.

Panther v. Dept. of Ag. Iowa. 211 Iowa 868, decided 20 Jan. 1931.

P. C. Kimmish v. John J. Ball. 129 U.S. 217, decided 28 Jan. 1889.

Rasmussen v. Idaho. 181 U.S. 200, decided 22 Apr. 1901.

Slaughterhouse Cases. 83 U.S. 36, decided 14 Apr. 1873.

Smith v. St. Louis & Southwestern Ry. Co. 181 U.S. 248, decided 22 Apr. 1901.

Swift & Co. v. United States. 196 U.S. 375, decided 30 Jan. 1905.

Thornton et al. v. United States. 271 U.S. 414, decided 1 June 1926.

U.S. v. E. C. Knight. 156 U.S. 1, decided 21 Jan. 1895.

United States v. Harry Boyer. 85 Fed. 425, decided 28 Feb. 1898.

Correspondence

Telephone interview with Dr. James Steele, Professor Emeritus of Veterinary Medicine, Univ. of Texas, Austin, 1 Aug. 2002.

Telephone interview with Dr. Wayne Dankner, Pediatric Infectious Disease Medicine, Durham, NC, 9 Aug. 2002.

Telephone interview with Dr. Patricia Conrad, Professor of Pathology, Microbiology, and Immunology, Univ. of California–Davis, 23 Jan. 2013.

Telephone interviews and correspondence with Dr. Robert Lane, Professor of the Graduate School, Univ. of California–Berkeley, 24 Jan. 2013 to 2 Feb. 2013.

Telephone interview with Dr. John E. George, Livestock Insects Research Laboratory, Kerrville, Texas, 29 Jan. 2013.

Correspondence with Dr. Nicholas Jonsson, Professor of Animal Production and Public Health, School of Veterinary Medicine, Univ. of Glasgow, Scotland, United Kingdom, 30 Jan. 2013.

Acknowledgments

WE HAVE INCURRED enormous debts in writing this book. Julian Alston encouraged us to embark on this project and has been a frequent sounding board for our ideas. Many other colleagues and friends have offered support and challenged us to focus our thoughts. We would like to thank Jeremy Atack, Martha Bailey, Hoyt Bleakley, John Brown, Karen Clay, Richard Easterlin, Price Fishback, Victor Goldberg, Barbara Hahn, Naomi Lamoreaux, Gary Libecap, Peter Lindert, Dean Lueck, Thomas A. Mroz, Roger Noll, Barbara Orland, Ariel Ron, Jean-Laurent Rosenthal, Clive Spinage, Mark Stegeman, Claire Strom, Koleman Strumpf, Daniel Sumner, Richard Sutch, Werner Troesken, Gavin Wright, and David Zilberman. Harvard University Press's anonymous reviewers provided helpful guidance and directed us to valuable sources.

We are economists, not veterinary or medical scientists. This book would not have been possible without the insights gained from experts who have made pioneering research contributions in these areas. Among those scientists who have been generous with their time and knowledge are William Campbell, Tim Carpenter, Patricia Conrad, Wayne Dankner, Janet Foley, John George, Linda Harris, Nicholas Jonsson, Don Klingborg, Robert Lane, Jonna Mazet, Frederick Murphy, Bennie Osburn, Edward Rhode, Peter Schantz, Myron Schultz, Calvin Schwabe, and James Steele. We hope that we have done justice to the histories of their disciplines.

We have profited greatly from the comments received in seminars at the California Institute of Technology, Carlos III University, European University Institute, Stanford University, Swiss Federal Institute of Technology, U.C. Davis, University of Arizona, University of Chicago Booth School, University of Guelph, University of Malaya, University of Michigan, University of North Carolina, University of Virginia, University of Zaragoza, and Virginia Polytechnic Institute and State University. Our work has been enriched by the discussants and participants at the meetings of the Agricultural History Society, All U.C. Group in Economic History, Allied Social Science Association, American Economic Association, Australian Agricultural and Resource

Society, Economic History Association, International Conference on Economics and Human Biology, International Consortium on Applied Bioeconomy Research, Latin-American and Caribbean Economic Association, NBER Development of the American Economy program, the Policy History Conference, U.C. Berkeley Bio-economy Conference, and the Western Economics Association International.

We have benefited from the exceptional assistance of Janis Carey, Helen Goldstein, Phyllis Goodnow, Jeffrey Graham, Susan Iranzo, Shelagh Mackay, Daniel Marcin, Hope Mitchell, Philip Perry, Sigrid Perry, Gregory Smith, and Janine L. F. Wilson.

We also would like to acknowledge the staffs at American Medical Association Library, Chicago History Society, Chicago Public Library, Library of Congress, National Archives, and the National Agricultural Library, along with the special collections librarians at the Catholic University of America, Cornell University, University of California at Davis, Iowa State University, University of Michigan, University of North Carolina, University of Pennsylvania, and University of Virginia. We would like to extend special thanks to Rodney Ross at the Center for Legislative Affairs at the National Archives, and Susan Fugate and Sara Lee at Special Collections at the National Agricultural Library. Only those who attempt original research can appreciate the enormous contributions of professional librarians.

Olmstead gratefully acknowledges the support from the International Centre for Economic Research (ICER) in Turin, Italy, and its director, Enrico Colomatto; the Giannini Foundation of Agricultural Research and its director, Colin Carter; the Farm Foundation and its president, Neilson Conklin; and the Department of Economics at the University of Malaya. Rhode would like to acknowledge the support from the National Science Foundation, Collaborative Research Grant, SES- 0921732.

It has been a pleasure to work with Michael Aronson and Kathleen Drummy at Harvard University Press. We thank Isabelle Lewis for constructing our illustrations, Brian Ostrander for editorial assistance, and Christine Hoskin for building our index. All showed professionalism and patience.

Index

449